Women Officeholders
in Early Christianity
Epigraphical and Literary Studies

Ute E. Eisen

Preface by
Gary Macy

Translated by
Linda M. Maloney

A Michael Glazier Book
✠ THE LITURGICAL PRESS
Collegeville, Minnesota

A Michael Glazier Book published by The Liturgical Press

Cover design by David Manahan, O.S.B. Illustration: "The Church of the Gentiles," mosaic detail, 5th cent., Santa Sabina, Rome.

Originally published as *Amtsträgerinnen im frühen Christentum. Epigraphische und literarische Studien* (Göttingen: Vandenhoeck & Ruprecht, 1996).

Library of Congress Cataloging-in-Publication Data

Eisen, Ute E.
    [Amtsträgerinnen im frühen Christentum. English]
    Women officeholders in early Christianity : epigraphical and literary studies /
Ute E. Eisen ; preface by Gary Macy ; translated by Linda M. Maloney.
       p.   cm.
    Includes bibliographical references and index.
    ISBN 0-8146-5950-0 (alk. paper)
    1. Women in Christianity—History—Early church, ca. 30–600. 2. Women in church work—History. 3. Inscriptions. I. Title.

BR195.W6 E5713 2000
262'.1'08209015—dc21   99-055857

Foreword

The inspiration for my work was Bernadette Brooten's 1982 book, *Women Leaders in the Ancient Synagogue: Inscriptional Evidence and Background Issues.* Even when I was still a student I recognized the importance and necessity of such a study for early Christianity. This book is the result.

I was also motivated by my fascination with feminist questions and the increasing emergence of feminist hermeneutics within theological scholarship as well as elsewhere. Feminist theories constructively thematize women's thought and at the same time critique the many attempts to marginalize women in religion and society, to render them inferior or invisible. With the aid of feminist theories I was able to give expression to my dissatisfaction and, in cooperation with others, to develop a different interpretation and a different praxis.

Thus I entered on the search for early Christian women as officeholders in the Church, and I found them. However, I found not only Christian women, but Jewish women and pagan women as well, who had lived differently from the way they are frequently portrayed in men's versions of history. I found religious officeholders, but also politicians and managers, philosophers and theologians, mathematicians and poets, and many others. I realized that from before the Christian era until the present time there has been a struggle going on over the question of women's participation in the most varied spheres of life, in religion and society. At all times there were people and groups who attempted to fix women in a role subordinate to men and to portray them as visualized by "male projections," but there were always women and men as well who recognized women as responsible, independent, and self-determined people. Unfortunately the former group was very often victorious. Nevertheless, "patriarchy is at an end. It happened—and not by accident," in the words of the famous and challenging "Sottosopra rosso" of the women of the Libreria delle donne di Milano.

An important aspect of my work was and is the fabric of relationships in which I live. The women of the Libreria delle donne di Milano call it the praxis of relationships and lived conflicts. I was fortunate enough to grow up within such a praxis and to continue living in it. My parents, Karen and Wolfgang Eisen, provided an atmosphere of relationships and conversations that was and is vital and challenging. I cultivated that same kind of atmosphere during my studies and in recent years as a University instructor, especially with my friends Silke Petersen and Vivian Wendt, with whom I founded the first feminist-exegetical *societas* at the University of Hamburg. I am indebted to them, and to so many others, for their challenging and ultimately encouraging companionship on the way.

Ute E. Eisen
February 2000

Contents

Preface

In the introduction to her important new study, Ute Eisen refers to a "different way of seeing" church history that allows women to "appear as independent, active subjects in history." What Dr. Eisen provides, in fact, is far more. First, in an exhaustive review of previous literature on women officeholders in the early Church, she provides a skilled diagnosis of the centuries-old myopia by which a patriarchal interpretation of the past has blinded historians and church leaders alike. Historians have often misunderstood past narrative and law as descriptions of historical reality, missing, to use Dr. Eisen's own words, "that these texts are not appropriate for reception as 'reflections' of the reality of early Christian life. They must be interpreted as refractions of desire and reality." Second, the epigraphic evidence so carefully retrieved in this study provides a firm corrective to politically motivated misreadings to which texts have too frequently been subjected. Third, Dr. Eisen provides a complete bibliographical guide not only to the growing literature on the history of women leaders in the Church, but also to the extensive discussions of the present role (or lack thereof) of women in modern Christianity.

The most delightful experience of reading this very enjoyable book, however, is the way real women, not the stylized objects of male authors, really do emerge from the monuments left to their honor. Who could not be moved by Flavia Theophila's dedication to "the sweetest of mothers," on the tomb of the widow Flavia Arcas? What respect appears in the dedication by her students on the tomb of the teacher Theodora, "divine gift, teacher of chastity, possessing the blessing of the Lord, mother of the pious virgins!" The words of a grateful congregation grace the tomb of Maria the deacon, who "raised children, sheltered guests, washed the feet of the saints, and shared her bread with the needy." The way that women leaders were lovingly commemorated by their communities, families, and friends belies the longstanding conviction that such women either did not exist or played no significant role in Church governance.

From every corner of Christianity, East and West, monuments emerge that give witness to the women who organized and guided early Christian communities as apostles, prophets, teachers, presbyters, widows, deacons, stewards, and even bishops. Dr. Eisen skillfully couples this new evidence with the existing narrative texts to provide an exhilarating new view of the early Church, one that includes within its horizon both men and women. Dr. Eisen draws no theological or ecclesial conclusions from her study, as indeed is fitting. Theological conclusions do not flow directly from historical conclusions. Those historical conclusions, however, are powerful in themselves and challenge the present male-dominated structures of many Christian communities. To quote Dr. Eisen, "In short, to the question whether there were women officeholders in the Church's first centuries our study returns a resounding answer . . . yes!"

Gary Macy
University of San Diego

I. Introduction

A. The Subject and the Method

The focus of this book is on Christian women in the ancient Church and the early Middle Ages who were active in theology and Church politics, either as holders of official positions in the Church or as persons acting independently of the institution itself. The starting point is the fund of epigraphical and, in individual cases, papyrological evidence that identifies women through functional titles and thus shows them to have been officeholders or persons exercising official functions. Particular attention will be devoted to the great variety of attestations that women bore specific titles. In this way a hasty reduction of the field of view to offices traditionally acknowledged by scholars as having been exercised by women, such as those of "deaconess" and "widow," will be avoided. The findings from the inscriptions and papyri will be discussed in the context of the literary evidence that attests to the existence of other Christian women with similar titles or exercising comparable functions.

This set of questions exists within the context of feminist exegesis,[1] feminist Church history,[2] and women's history.[3] Common to these different and variegated fields of research is the attempt at a revision of previous exegetical and historical scholarship. "The common aim is the correction of an image of the world and of history that gives the impression that women made no contributions to culture and only in exceptional cases had anything to do with historical events. This impression is the result of a male-dominated account of history as well as a male-dominated reception of philosophical concepts, with the result that women's contribution to culture and history was trivialized or ignored."[4]

A Shift in Perspective: A "Different Way of Seeing"

Historical scholarship until recently has been marked by an androcentric perspective that regards women as "the second sex" (Simone de Beauvoir) and to a great extent "reduces the existence of women to their biological functions."[5] Women are regarded primarily as mothers, sisters, daughters, wives, or hetaerae. This list in itself marks a further characteristic of the view of the his-

1

torical existence of women: they are dependent on men and are often considered subordinate to them. They are projected as men's students, girlfriends, and spouses.

Within the study of Church history such a view is nourished particularly by patristic constructions of femininity, the ideological character of which has previously received little attention or appropriate critical analysis.[6] Instead, texts from the ancient Church that describe the "nature" and "purpose" of women are for the most part interpreted in real-historical terms and read as images of historical reality.

In this study, in contrast, I will begin with the premise that women appear as independent, active subjects in history[7] and as such can be historically perceived even in texts written by men about women. Women, like men, live in complex, individually developing social, economic, and religious relationships that they themselves participate in shaping.

Consequently, the focus of this study will be on texts and traditions by and about individual women—not texts about the genus "woman." These traditions will be decoded outside the androcentric paradigm described above—an endeavor that proves difficult in light of the "fact that women have no image or memory of what a woman was or could be before, or apart from, a history conceived and transmitted by males; that is how much her own history is bound up with the masculine subject."[8]

Exegetical and church-historical scholarship especially in recent years has shown, however, that through an altered perspective women can be made visible in their political, economic, and cultural activities. For the New Testament and the traditions of the ancient Church it has been shown that a great many women were demonstrably active in important religious positions—women who are frequently characterized by social and economic independence and not defined by a father, husband, or brother (for example, Chloe, Phoebe, Lydia, Evodia, Syntyche, Triphaena, Tryphosa, Mary Magdalene, Salome, Thecla, Philomena, the Desert Mothers, and many others). These and other women were active, just as men were, in the religious life of the Christian communities in all its different forms. Phoebe, for example, was a preacher of the gospel and at the same time a businesswoman who was not defined by a male. Prisca was an artisan whose religious reputation exceeded that of her husband.[9] Thecla was the model for the unmarried Christian woman who devoted herself entirely to the proclamation of the word of God.

Selection and Evaluation of the Sources

In the context of feminist exegesis and feminist Church history there has been a growing awareness of the problem of selection and evaluation of sources for reconstructing the history of women.[10] The necessity and thus the problem of distinguishing "gender ideology" and "the reality of women's lives" is increasingly obvious, as I have indicated above. A primary concentration on texts by men about "women as a species" leads to a reconstruction of male images of women and only very indirectly sheds light on the many-faceted reality of women's lives.[11] In some ancient texts, especially philosophical writings, there is a concept of gender that assigns women to the household sphere and thus to the field of reproduction in the broadest sense. In the context of such a worldview there is frequently an effort to forbid women to take an active role in economic, cultural, and religious life. Such texts and traditions are found in Christian as well as in Jewish and pagan literature. Concentration on a tradition that reflects the determination of the sexes in such a fashion and thus attempts to regulate it can shed only the dimmest light on the actual lives of women.

Orientation to such restrictive texts, which are then interpreted as real-historical witnesses, has until now been characteristic of research on "offices held by women." By preference the author starts with regulatory texts such as 1 Cor 14:33b-36 and 1 Tim 2:11-12, the Church orders of the third to sixth centuries, synodal canons, or the repressive utterances of individual Church fathers about women, such as Tertullian, Ambrosiaster, Jerome, and John Chrysostom. That such statements and normative regulations are often reactions to a different praxis is scarcely ever noted.[12] It must be shown that these texts are not appropriate for reception as "reflections" of the reality of early Christian life. They must be interpreted as refractions of desire and reality.

The inclusion of sources previously accorded little attention has shown that it is by no means adequate to develop a history of Christian women that is primarily oriented to prohibitory traditions from the ancient Church. Arlette Farge rightly points out that in the early stages of the writing of women's history "the descriptive aspect outweighed the consideration of the problems involved, which itself created problems later when we realized that the emergence of the feminine event was based almost exclusively on the axis of domination and oppression."[13]

In recent years some necessary distinctions have been developed in order that the reality of women's lives may be viewed in more appropriate fashion. Instead of focusing on normative texts about women, scholars have concentrated more deliberately on the traditions of individual women or groups of women, with the result that women appear as varied personalities and independent agents. The work, for example, of Bernadette Brooten on Junia,[14] of Monika Fander on the women in Mark,[15] of Ivoni Richter Reimer on Prisca and other women in Acts,[16] of Ruth Albrecht on Macrina and Thecla,[17] of Elizabeth Clark on Melania the Younger,[18] of Anne Jensen on the women martyrs, the "new prophets," and Philomena[19] have shown how women have shaped Christian traditions and theology.[20] Besides the study of texts and traditions about women, in recent years some texts by women of the ancient Church have been rescued from oblivion and increasingly discussed in the context of the theological-literary activity of women.[21]

The contribution of the present study to the development of a history of women consists in bringing to the discussion women whose historical memory as persons who exercised Church offices and functions has been preserved in inscriptions. These Christian women officeholders, previously acknowledged only on the margins of scholarship or ignored altogether, can be appropriately understood in regard to their importance for the beginnings and development of the Church only in connection with the many women attested in literature. Against that background the prohibitory traditions from the ancient Church can also appear in a new light.

This initiative requires a comprehensive view of the most varied types of sources, and a re-reading of Christian tradition. Elizabeth Clark forcefully pointed out in 1990 that only a narrow segment of patristic literature refers to "real women." Much richer information, in contrast, is offered by the so-called "lower genres" of literature, such as letters, hagiography, apocryphal acts of apostles, and others that are regarded as marginal by a scholarship oriented primarily to dogmatic texts.[22] Something similar may be said of non-literary sources such as inscriptions and papyrus letters, plastic images, and archaeological sources. In analyzing the individual types of historical sources we should keep in mind that "pictures, texts, archaeological documents, each of these types of source has a language of its own, and none allows an immediate reading of reality, but each is to one degree or another a transposition of reality. . . . We must not give preferential treatment to one type of source in order to draw up a reference model . . . . But we must be able to compare the messages that all these sources give without wishing at all cost to make them say the same thing."[23] The problem of the partial impossibility of disentangling fiction and reality remains inherent to the interpretation of every individual historical source.[24]

The Problem of Language

A special problem in the context of a reconstruction of the history of women, in this case of women who held office or exercised functions in the early Church, and at the same time a difficulty in describing them, is the character of Greek and Latin, as well as modern languages, with respect to gender distinctions.[25]

One central problem in this regard is that as a rule the masculine plural, functioning as "gender neutral," is chosen for describing groups of mixed gender. This has real consequences, however: "When the masculine form assumes the function of gender neutrality, the male half of humanity becomes the norm, and the female half is given a subordinate status. Through use of the generic masculine women and their achievements are rendered invisible."[26] This recognition demands that we bring to awareness, problematize, and revise linguistic structures and conventions that threaten to conceal the presence and identity of women.[27]

The problem of generic language and its implications for the history of women is especially virulent for the questions posed by this investigation in light of Christians' grammatically masculine self-descriptions and functional designations.[28] In the New Testament the words used for believers as well as those for persons who exercised specific functions are without exception grammatically masculine, e.g., ἅγιοι, ἐκλεκτοί, δίκαιοι, ἀπόστολοι, διδάσκαλοι, ἐπίσκοποι. It is significant that in exegetical literature non-functional designations such as "saints," "elect," "righteous" are interpreted inclusively—that is, both men and women are understood to be described by these terms. On the other hand, terms that mark leadership functions, such as ἀπόστολος, διδάσκαλος, ἐπίσκοπος are understood exclusively, that is, as applying only to men. This asymmetrical interpretation corresponds to the conscious or unconscious premise that women could not exercise any positions of leadership in the early Church.

However, women mentioned by name and described with terms denoting functions in early Christianity quite clearly illustrate the inclusive character of those terms—for example, the διάκονος Phoebe and the ἀπόστολος Junia. There have been different reactions to this situation in the history of interpretation. Phoebe the διάκονος, for example, was accommodated to the possibilities conceivable within the interpreters' mental horizon by being reduced to a "helper" or "deaconess," and not understood within the context of Pauline use of the word as a proclaimer of the word of God like Paul and other διάκονοι who were males.[29] Junia the ἀπόστολος underwent a temporary sex-change operation in that from the twelfth century onward her name was interpreted as the masculine "Junias"—a name that, as Bernadette Brooten has shown, is not attested in Greco-Roman antiquity.[30]

For the groups of ἐπίσκοποι and διδάσκαλοι the problem of the gender-abstract masculine plural is uniquely virulent. In the New Testament no Christian, male or female, is named as a teacher or bishop. Both these functional designations are found exclusively in the summary masculine plural. This fact—augmented by the opinion, nourished and generalized by 1 Cor 14:33b-36 and 1 Tim 2:11-12, that women could not act as teachers or leaders—has obliterated the historical memory of women as exercisers of corresponding functions.[31]

This linguistic convention, which makes no consistent generic distinction, leads, as Luce Irigaray has so sharply emphasized, to a situation in which women neither have an identity nor can discover one.[32] In light of this set of problems a consistent gender-differentiating rule of language has been applied throughout this study.[33]

B. Tendencies in Scholarship

> History is full of contradictions, of alternating currents, of overlapping events where consistency and inconsistency both have a place. Nothing lasts forever in history. . . . It would be an important achievement to establish finally a history of the tensions between masculine and feminine roles and to show how their conflicts and complementarities are a thread running through the whole account of history. There can be no question of constituting a closed field of knowledge . . . .
>
> Arlette Farge[34]

Friedrich Loofs wrote in 1890, in a critical reflection on research into the history of the constitution of Christianity: "this comment applies only to the current *status controversiae* and incidentally indicates that in this field we are dealing with obvious facts to a much lesser extent than Harnack's vivid version of things reveals: not only the Pastoral letters . . . but other sources for the history of [the Church's] constitution resemble a kaleidoscope that can be shaken this way or that."[35] This accurate observation indicates a problem that still exists a century after it was first so lucidly described. Early Christian literature gives only snapshots and occasional information about the organization of Christian communities,[36] and the documents that address explicit questions of community constitution, such as the Pastoral letters, 1 Clement, the letters of Ignatius, or the "Church orders," project their ideas of community against an existing and disparate reality. This is evident not least from the differences in the theology and tradition-history of these writings, which are articulated in divergent manner both regionally and in time.

It remains to observe that "those who write about practical questions of church constitution must always keep in mind what Firmilian wrote in a letter to Cyprian of Carthage, namely that not everything was true in Rome that was the rule in Jerusalem, and that in most of the other provinces as well a good many things diverged according to the differences of the locality and the people . . . . One must guard against the temptation to make a universal Church institution of the special custom of an individual community. In the ancient Church there was no written law and no universally valid norm . . . ."[37] The question of the participation of women in the offices and services of the Church also lies within the horizon of this problem of reconstructing the constitutional history of Christian communities.[38]

Women's History Beyond "General History"

The question of the participation of women in community organization and divine worship is traditionally not investigated in the context of the general question of offices in the community. This arrangement implies the premise behind the history of research: that women were not, as a matter of course, participants in mission and community services in their manifold expression. This premise corresponds to the hypothesis of a special "service of women" distinct from the "normal" Church offices.[39] In "general" research on Church offices, accordingly, the question of participation of women in those offices either does not arise at all or appears only as a subordinate special problem.[40]

The Debate Over Women's Ordination

It is scarcely possible or logical to discuss these findings independently of the lively and thoroughly controversial discussion within the churches over the "ordination" and "priesthood" of women.[41] The exclusion of all women from "priesthood" and "diaconate" is still the rule in the Roman Catholic and Orthodox churches, and it is accompanied by an exegetical, historical, canonical, and systematic-theological apologetics that has shaped and continues to shape even the scholarly discussions in Roman Catholic, Orthodox, and Protestant circles.

Since the public protests in connection with Vatican Council II (1962–1965) against the exclusion of women from offices in the Roman Catholic Church the question has been more or less constantly discussed, in Catholic contexts as well as others.[42] There have been numerous publications on the subject since the 1960s. We should mention especially the works of Haye van der Meer and Ida Raming, both of which have been translated into English and have given impetus to the movement for women's ordination. Haye van der Meer's study of the theological history of the question, *Priestertum der Frau?* was completed in 1962 but not published until 1969; it engages critical exegetical and dogmatic arguments against the ordination of women.[43] It comes to the conclusion that these arguments are not persuasive, and in particular that they are not adequate for the Church's future; however, the author does not speak decisively in favor of an immediate ordination of women.[44]

Ida Raming's study *The Exclusion of Women from the Priesthood: Divine Law or Sex Discrimination?* concentrates—as a supplement to van der Meer's work—especially on sources from the history of law such as Gratian's 1140 textbook on canon law, *Concordia discordantium canonum*.[45] On the basis of her analyses of legal history and dogmatics she comes to the conclusion "that the exclusion of woman from ecclesiastical offices is ultimately based on the idea of her biological-ontic and moral inferiority, and that as a consequence access to ordination and office should be opened to woman for the sake of her human dignity and on the basis of the equality of man and woman established by Gal 3:28."[46]

A central work touching the question of the history of "women's offices" in the ancient Church is Roger Gryson's book, *Le Ministère des Femmes dans l'Eglise Ancienne,* published in 1972 and translated into English in 1976.[47] This book attempts a historical review of the topic and is the work most often cited in connection with women officeholders in the early Church. Gryson subjects a great many literary sources from the first to the sixth centuries[48]—especially texts of the Church fathers, Church orders, and synodal acts—to a renewed testing.[49] He comes to the following conclusion:

> From the beginnings of Christianity, women assumed an important role and enjoyed a place of choice in the Christian community. Paul praised several women who assisted him in his apostolic works. Women also possessed the charism of prophecy. There is no evidence, however, that they exercised leadership roles in the community. Even though several women followed Jesus from the onset of his ministry in Galilee and figured among the privileged witnesses of his resurrection, no women appeared among the Twelve or even among the other apostles. As Epiphanius of Salamis pointed out, the successors of the Apostles were all men, and in the Catholic Church there have never been women presbyters. The only duty with which women have been invested is the diaconate, but two centuries had to pass before the female diaconate took a distinct shape.

A few pages later he continues:

> Analogously, the priesthood, since it was a ministry of salvation, in their opinion implied mental superiority in the one exercising the ministry over those for whom it is exercised, and for this reason they felt it right, as the *Ecclesiastical Canons of the Apostles* says, that "the weak should be saved by the strong," i.e., woman by man, and not the reverse. Underlying this line of argument, and more than once explicitly affirmed, is the idea of the natural superiority or primacy of man over woman, which appears frequently and approvingly in the quoted biblical verses, such as Genesis: "Your desire shall be for your husband, and he shall rule over you," and St. Paul: "The head of a woman is her husband," whose meaning was probably forced to make it, as in the *Apostolic Constitutions,* the decisive slogan in this matter. To this background one should add—details no doubt, but relevant details nonetheless—unkind references to the "female race" which present it as weak, fickle, lightheaded, of mediocre intelligence, a chosen instrument of the devil in his desire to establish his reign in the world.[50]

This excerpt from Roger Gryson's book is an exemplary summary of current paradigms in research on the theme of women as officeholders in the Church:

> (a) For the early period it is emphasized that women "assumed an important role," affected by their "unique" acceptance by Jesus, and took a corresponding part in

the mission of the Church. Qualitatively, in this view of things women's functions are described as "assisting," that is, they are regarded as subordinated to the functions of men.

(b) The initial premise from which the discussion proceeds is that women in the Great Church never held leadership roles, and exercised sacramental functions only in exceptional cases. The principal reason given is that Jesus called no women in the group of the Twelve.

(c) The only "real" office of women in the ancient Church is the "female diaconate," qualitatively different from the diaconate of men in the sense indicated above, and developing significantly only in later centuries.

Inter insigniores, the declaration of the Congregation for the Doctrine of the Faith on the question of the admission of women to the priesthood of October 15, 1976[51] (appearing in a new edition on May 22, 1994 under the title *Ordinatio sacerdotalis*)[52] provoked debate in the broad public arena and released a flood of reactions, especially in the United States.[53] The declaration officially confirms the exclusion in principle of all women from the priesthood of the Roman Catholic Church. One of its central arguments is again that Jesus called no women among the Twelve. In his critique of the declaration Karl Rahner correctly points to the lack of reflection on the problem of the transition from the concept of the apostles and the Twelve to that of the priest (and bishop). He poses the well-justified question "whether it is possible to deduce from Jesus' choice of men for the college of the Twelve any definite and unambiguous conclusions with regard to the question of an ordinary, simple leader of the community and president of the eucharistic celebration in a particular congregation of a later period."[54]

Another central argument of *Inter insigniores/Ordinatio sacerdotalis* is the so-called "fact of tradition." Here we read: "The Catholic Church has never felt that priestly or episcopal ordination can be validly conferred on women."[55] The conviction that women in the Great Church never were or could be valid priests (presbyters) or bishops can be found in large parts of confessionally-shaped research, not only Catholic, but Protestant and Orthodox as well.[56] This assumption is supported by implications drawn from what is taken to be a linear and unified development of the Church's constitution. This is true especially of the concept of the "priest," which remains quite unclear and is projected, in its particular confessional coloration, into the early period of Christianity, when in fact we cannot speak of a Christian "priestly office" in the sense of later developments at that period.[57] Rahner describes the problem, in the context of his critique of *Inter insigniores,* as follows: "Moreover, the declaration does not have a clear and comprehensive concept of the priesthood. Especially in points five and six it appears that the true task of the priest is more or less reduced to the sacramental power of consecration, so that one almost has the impression that the declaration would be prepared to concede practically all Church functions to women except for this one (and the 'official and public proclamation of the Good News,' which, however, is difficult to distinguish from Jesus' order to the women to proclaim the first Easter message even to the apostles . . .). But there can be no doubt that such a reduction in the idea of the priest would provoke the most serious dogmatic and especially pastoral concerns."[58] He thus touches an essential problem of this Church declaration, true also of other such declarations[59] and of parts of the scholarly research on the priesthood of women.[60]

Texts from the ancient Church are often very arbitrarily cited in support of the hypothesis that there have never been women presbyters/priests or bishops in the Great Church. Patristic topoi from polemic against heretics, misogynist traditions, prohibitions on women's teaching and the like are collected, but not always viewed in their literary and tradition-historical context[61] or tested with regard to their deviation from norm and reality.

It is especially consequential that this paradigm in large part obstructs, and must necessarily obstruct, the possibility of acknowledging those texts from the ancient Church and the early Middle Ages that point to a different praxis. One exception, for example, is the work of Giorgio Otranto, who on the basis of a critical reading of a letter of Pope Gelasius I as well as a study of inscriptions demonstrates the existence of women presbyters in the Church in southern Italy in the fifth century.[62]

The question whether the early Church had not only women presbyters/priests, but also women bishops or even popes is, with very few exceptions, not even discussed, since in the thought-horizon just described such leading offices for women are simply unimaginable.[63]

The degree to which this paradigm has shaped not only the scholarship and real existence of the Catholic, Orthodox, and Anglican churches, but also of the Protestant churches, and continues to shape them, is indicated by the fact that it is only since the 1960s that the ordination of women to equal pastoral service has been increasingly accepted,[64] and it is only since the end of the 1980s that women bishops have also been installed.[65]

The discussion of the admission of women to the priesthood has been rekindled since November 11, 1992, when the General Synod of the Church of England agreed to the ordination of women.[66] The Vatican reacted with a reissue of *Inter insigniores* under the title *Ordinatio sacerdotalis* on May 22, 1994. In his Foreword, Pope John Paul II calls on the Church's faithful to regard it as "definitive" that the Church has no authority to confer Holy Orders on women.[67]

*Christian Women as Equally Endowed with Office
in the First and Early Second Centuries*

Alongside the tendency in scholarship that fundamentally questions an independent and unrestricted ecclesiastical activity on the part of women, as represented by Gryson, there also exists the idea of an equal and independent missionary activity of women in the first and early second centuries. It is closely associated with the name of Adolf von Harnack and has continued in a variety of forms. Harnack wrote as early as 1902 in the first edition of his *Expansion of Christianity in the First Three Centuries:* "Anyone who reads the New Testament attentively, as well as those writings which immediately succeeded it, cannot fail to notice that in the apostolic and sub-apostolic ages women played an important rôle in the propagation of Christianity and throughout the Christian communities."[68]

In what follows he shows, on the basis of the numerous women mentioned in the New Testament and the Christian writings of the second century, that women worked as apostles, prophets, teachers, community leaders, widows, deacons, and martyrs. He summarizes: "Even after the middle of the second century women are still prominent, not only for their number and position as widows and deaconesses in the service of the church, but also as prophetesses and teachers."[69] Harnack thus takes as his starting point the active ecclesiastical engagement of women to the end of the second century. Only "by her very opposition offered to gnosticism and Montanism [was] the church . . . led to interdict women from any activity within the church—apart, of course, from such services as they rendered to those of their own sex."[70]

The paradigm of an early egalitarian period in which women were active just as men were in the constitution of the Christian communities has been hermeneutically considered and developed since the 1970s, especially by Elisabeth Schüssler Fiorenza and Luise Schottroff,[71] and has found considerable acceptance even in traditional scholarship.[72] It is accompanied by the assumption of an increasing "decline" in this egalitarian praxis since the second generation of Christianity. The inculturation of Christianity, which necessitated an accommodation to the patriarchal environment, is accepted as one of the principal reasons for this change.[73] This is said to have led to an ecclesiastical praxis that assigned women a role in the house and excluded them from general Church activity. This paradigm operates on the premise of a "thoroughly patriarchal society" that has been increasingly subjected to critical examination by research on the history of women:

(a) A "different way of seeing" has replaced the androcentrically oriented view of history with one oriented to women, and insists on a distinction between "gender ideology" and factual reality.

(b) The consideration of types of sources previously given little attention has opened new perspectives on the reality of women's lives in late antiquity.[74]

Against the background of this newer research we can no longer work with the image of a one-dimensional society designated as "patriarchal," treated as the negative image of a Christianity of egalitarian character in the early period and after the second century as the model for a Church "that subjugated women." Social history is proving to be as complex and multivalent as the history of Christianity, and neither is reducible to categories like "egalitarian" or "patriarchal."

This historical model of increasing "accommodation to the patriarchal environment" is accompanied by a complementary argument that equality for women was retained only in so-called "heretical groups." This assumption, which has scarcely been subjected to a thorough testing,[75] is employed within this historical model as a further argument for a rejection of women as officeholders.

The Offices of Widow and "Deaconess"

The question of the forms of ecclesiastical service for women in the "Great Church" after the end of the second century, that is, after their postulated "suppression" in equal service, is answered by scholars through the assertion of Church offices of widows and "deaconesses." The shape and ordering of these two "women's offices" is judged differently according to the selection, evaluation, and weighting of the sources.

The so-called unified hypothesis combines the different titles of women found in the sources, such as widow, presbytera, virgin, and deacon or deaconess as descriptions of the same office for women that was differently named at different times and in different regions of the Church.[76] No significance with regard to content is thus assigned to the existing terminological differences. Adolf Kalsbach describes this scholarly position as follows: "The fact that the communities . . . at first accepted only real widows, but then from the days of Ignatius of Antioch *(Smyrn.* 13.1) and Tertullian *(Virg. vel.* 9) and with the higher valuing of celibate life increasingly accepted virgins into this office as well accounts for the change in the name: in the first three centuries the sources speak almost exclusively of widows, but afterward almost solely of deaconesses. Everything that was said anywhere and at any time about the functions of widows and deaconesses was transferred to this office, with the result that a very full picture of women's official activity in the ancient Church was provided."[77]

Heinrich Schäfer was a vehement proponent of this hypothesis.[78] He emphasizes that in most of the sources the installed widows are not mentioned alongside deaconesses. From this he concludes: "Thus the old contested question about the identity or difference of the offices of widows and deacons can most probably be decided in favor of the Western (Roman Catholic) view, namely that both terms used at different periods described one and the same office . . . . If one were to assume on the basis of 1 Timothy or the *Testamentum Domini* that there were two different clerical offices for women in the first centuries one would stumble over many unsolvable riddles and difficulties . . . ."[79]

It is true that the hypothesis of a single office for women has been proposed even in the present era,[80] but as early as 1873 Theodor Zahn addressed the problem of the different terms for Christian women officeholders with his three-stage hypothesis:

> In a *first* stage there was a guild of old widows who were supported by the community, had certain pastoral duties toward the female sex, and received a corresponding position of honor; there were also younger deaconesses. In a *second* stage the female diaconate almost entirely disappeared, and from the guild of widows, which continued as a community of widows supported by the Church, a few widows or *presbytides* were selected to perform the services that previously had been the duty of all the ecclesiastically registered widows and deaconesses. In a *third* stage, which remained completely foreign to the West, the female diaconate was renewed; widows were also included in it or, where the official Church widows of the previous stage were not eliminated, they were added to the τάγμα τῶν διακονισσῶν.[81]

In 1902 Leopold Zscharnack developed this initiative into a two-office hypothesis. He writes that the sources "demand" that "the two offices of widows and deaconesses be strictly distinguished from one another," for "the services of the χήρα and the διάκονος were different both in personnel and in function."[82] This distinction has been largely accepted in scholarly study of the offices of women. The manifold exegetical problem fields of the offices of widows and deaconesses in the ancient Church are as a rule examined separately.

The "Office of Deaconess"

Previous research on the office of deaconess was to a large extent shaped by the attempt to describe the origins and development of that office in as linear and unified a fashion as possible.[83] The witness of the New Testament (Rom 16:1-2; 1 Tim 3:11)[84] and the subsequent centuries is frequently not considered in its uniqueness and its literary and cultural context, but compared in such a way that differences are primarily evaluated as "preliminary stages" or "intermediate phases." The thesis is frequently presented that an office of deaconesses existed in the Church only from the third century onward, with its first literary witness being the *Didascalia Apostolorum*.[85] This hypothesis collides with implicit and explicit attestation of women deacons in the first and second centuries.[86] The gender-specific designation διακόνισσα is not found in Christian literature before the fourth century, and even later διάκονος and διακόνισσα were used synonymously.[87]

The sphere of the deaconesses' duties was broadly defined and was not essentially different from that of the deacons. Deacons and deaconesses primarily performed duties that were proper to the bishops (male and female), such as assisting at baptism and at the eucharistic assembly. In addition they had sacramental functions: they took communion to the sick and to pregnant women. We also find that they had catechetical functions and activities in relation to care of the sick and provision for the poor.

The much-disputed ordination of deaconesses and thus their belonging to the higher clergy of the Church is founded primarily on the findings of Evangelos Theodorou.[88]

The Office of Widows

Central to the discussion of an office of widows is the problem of distinguishing between "official" widows and those simply in need of care.[89] The debate surrounding 1 Tim 5:3-16 exemplifies the spectrum of the discussion.[90] It is disputed whether this refers to a *status* as widow, so that the widows here mentioned are regarded entirely as recipients of support,[91] or whether the text refers to an *office* of widow.[92] Later sources also document a lack of sharp distinction between widows as recipients of care and "installed" widows. In particular, the Church orders undoubtedly indicate the existence of an office of widows in the early Church.

The duties of the installed widows were especially prayer and intercession, theological instruction, anointing the newly baptized, and care for the sick, but we can be sure that the sphere of the widows' duties was considerably larger than that. Hans Achelis shows, with regard to the *Didascalia Apostolorum,* that the activities of the widows were in competition with those of the bishops, which led in that writing to a shrinking of the widows' responsibilities.[93]

Christian Women in Their Social Context

The question of women officeholders in the Christian Church is closely associated in scholarship with implicit and explicit determinations of the social, political, economic, and religious situation of women in Greco-Roman antiquity.[94] Such classifications often serve as a backdrop against which the situation of Christian women is apologetically described, mainly in positive terms.

The opinion that Jesus shaped the situation of women "uniquely" in a "patriarchal world" is widely held. As early as Paul, it is said, we can observe an accommodation to "Jewish values" as regards the position of women, and in the third generation, as the Pastoral letters show most clearly, this led, through a further social accommodation on the part of Christians, to the surrender of the freer status of Christian women in the early period. This paradigm implies the social, political, economic, and partially also the religious inferiority of women in the Greco-Roman world.

However, research on the social, political, economic, and legal situation of women in Greco-Roman antiquity has become increasingly more sophisticated, and it shows that such hypotheses, which simplify the complex realities of life, are untenable; the question requires greater refinement.

Historical Research on Women in Greco-Roman Antiquity

In the field of historical research on the history of women in antiquity as well, the paradigm and the choice of sources are mutually conditioned.[95] While research on the history of ancient women has been marked to a signal degree by a concentration on "great women"[96]—analogously to the "great men" syndrome—in recent years especially the interest of scholars has been increasingly directed to women and men of all classes. This new point of view also made a revision of the basic sources necessary. There has been increased attention to epigraphical, papyrological, numismatic, archaeological, and iconographic sources in scholarly discussion. The interest of "historical research on women" lies primarily in a reconstruction of the history of women and can be described as follows:

> Research on women describes a direction in research and a conception of scholarship that is particularly critical of dominant scholarship for having "forgotten" women and having allowed the feminine perspective to be underrepresented. It sets itself the task of filling the holes in scholarship with regard to women and introducing the women's perspective, until a balance has been achieved. The ultimate goal is that scholarship will really make general statements about humanity and not only pretend to do so.[97]

This new "different view" of history, as well as the intensive introduction of non-literary sources, has opened new perspectives in the study of the history of women in antiquity and should also yield a fruitful harvest in the study of Church history.

For example, in studies of history, including Church history, we frequently encounter the hypothesis that Greek women lived exclusively in the "household" and were not active in the "public sphere." This opinion has been revealed as "an ideological construct" by newer research.[98] This has consequences for the study of women officeholders in the Church as well. Frequently, when the field of activity of women officeholders in the Church is discussed, we find the assertion that there was a "women's sphere." This is meant to explain why an official Church function exercised by women was necessary (namely because of the "women's sphere"), and why it remained restricted to that non-public, household realm.

The works of Susan Treggiari, Ramsay MacMullen, Natalie Kampen, Rosmarie Günther, and Monika Eichenauer have shown that women practiced the greatest variety of independent professions and callings, that they could have and indeed did have economic independence.[99] As early as 1983 Wayne Meeks wrote: "Inscriptions show that women were active in commerce and manufacture and, like their male counterparts, used some of the money they made in ways that would win them recognition in their cities."[100]

The question of women's participation in political offices has not been thoroughly investigated by researchers to date, and even today, as Otto Braunstein wrote in 1911, it is frequently "dismissed with a brief negative remark."[101] His thesis, that especially in Asia Minor it is possible to demonstrate from inscriptions, papyri, and coins that women were "active as citizens" in the liturgies and magistracies, has been confirmed, refined, and elaborated by more recent work on Asia Minor.[102] In the discussion of epigraphically confirmed official titles for women, such as the imperial priestesses[103] and *flaminicae,*[104] it appears that we encounter paradigms in the history of research and interpretation similar to those that have applied to epigraphically attested Jewish and Christian women officeholders. The following interpretations are common:

  (a) Women so titled are presumed to be the wives of supposed male officials.
  (b) The titles of the women are interpreted as honorary.
  (c) They are interpreted as officials, but having restricted competencies in comparison to corresponding male officials.

These points of view are increasingly being subjected to methodical reflection and revision.

Women's participation in the humanities and natural sciences, for example as philosophers, doctors, or mathematicians, is also being increasingly focused and cannot be regarded by far as exhaustively investigated.[105] The same is true for the related question of the opportunities women had for education in Greco-Roman society.[106]

Research into the participation of women in the religious life of Greco-Roman antiquity has been pursued in exemplary fashion during the last two decades by Ross S. Kraemer, who has devoted her work to the analysis not only of Christian, but also of Jewish and pagan women's religious self-understanding.[107] She explains the existing desiderata of research as follows:

. . . until the last two decades, women's history and women's religion were largely ignored by scholars of late antiquity, as they were by scholars of most disciplines. In retrospect the reasons seem painfully obvious: bastions of male scholars rarely even thought about the study of women. Behind their disinterest, which was largely shared by the small number of women scholars, lay the insidious, significant, and unarticulated assumption that human religions and human history were identical with men's religion and men's history.[108]

Kraemer attempts, in the context of her depiction of the different religious traditions, to illuminate the roots of the marked Jewish and Christian resistance to a "priesthood" for women—a resistance that cannot be found in such a decided form in paganism, although the Greco-Roman cults, Judaism, and Christianity were all located in the same androcentrically-oriented Greco-Roman society.[109]

Jewish Women

Very widespread in the context of defining Christianity as distinct from Judaism is the paradigm of the "misogyny" of the Jewish religion. This paradigm, frequently nourished by Christian antijudaism or resulting in it, has been subjected to critical inspection by Jewish and Christian theologians for some years now.[110] This research has shown that the selection and ordering of the sources and of the paradigm itself yield different results. Most recently Kraemer has shown how different Jewish tradition appears if it is not illustrated exclusively from rabbinic sources, but also by the use of epigraphic, papyrological, and non-rabbinic literary materials.[111] This observation is confirmed, for example, by a comparison of the works of Günter Mayer and Bernadette Brooten, which illustrates the mutual effect of paradigm and choice of source material. Mayer reconstructs "the life of the Jewish woman in antiquity" primarily on the basis of rabbinic texts as well as those of Philo and Josephus, and thus arrives at a striking reconstruction of the history of Jewish ideas on the subject of women.[112] Against this background epigraphic evidence that shows women as bearing titles of synagogal office becomes for him a *crux interpretum*.[113] Brooten and Kraemer, on the other hand, place epigraphic, papyrological, and archaeological sources at the center of their reconstruction and come to the conclusion that women in the Jewish Diaspora exercised synagogal offices just as men did, that the existence of a separate area for women is not demonstrable from archaeological excavations of ancient synagogues, and that Jewish women could and did have economic and religious independence.[114]

Studies of Jewish divorce law have shown similar results.[115] Monika Fander summarizes: "The new research work in Judaic studies and the study of the ancient Orient . . . confirms Brooten's theses; that is, there is a centuries-old legal tradition that can be shown to have existed at least from the fifteenth century B.C.E. to the eleventh century C.E. that acknowledged Jewish women's right to divorce."[116]

In summary we can say that historical research on women and theological research on Judaism have shown in the last several decades that no unified picture of the situation of Greco-Roman women can be garnered, be it social, political, economic, or religious. Every description and ordering of the social, political, economic, and religious status of women must, as in the case of men, be tested for individual differences. The reality of women's lives, such as those of Lydia, Phoebe, or Prisca, can be adequately understood only by an appreciation of the social, cultural, economic, and religious complexity in which these women lived, just as did men. An interpretation of the history of these and other women against the background of an ancient history of ideas about women shaped by a masculine perspective can scarcely lead to an adequate reconstruction of the reality of these women's lives.

C. The Sources

Inscriptions

In my inspection and selection of inscriptions I began with an initial collection of epigraphic and papyrological materials by G. H. R. Horsley, and with the inscriptions that have already been associated with official ecclesiastical activity on the part of women.[117] This material was expanded through a review of the most important bodies of inscriptions and of periodical literature.

Because of the great number of existing Christian inscriptions, a survey of the totality of epigraphic material of Christian provenience cannot be undertaken.[118] That would mean working from a basis of more than fifty thousand Christian inscriptions.[119] A comparison with the approximately two thousand surviving ancient Jewish inscriptions may illustrate how great this number is.[120] An additional problem is the distribution of the material throughout countless collections of inscriptions, periodicals, and individual publications, some of them very difficult of access.

The Greek Christian inscriptions I have studied[121] come primarily from Asia Minor, which offers a rich epigraphical tradition that has been and is being studied in model fashion.[122] The smaller group of Greek Christian inscriptions considered here comes primarily from Egypt,[123] Syria, and Palestine.[124] This corresponds to the overall epigraphic findings, because those countries contain a comparatively small number of surviving Christian tomb inscriptions. Emilian Popescu gives as one reason for this the Arab rule that penetrated those regions from the sixth century onward.[125] There are more numerous instances from Greece[126] and Macedonia;[127] for the Balkan peninsula much the same can be said as for Palestine, Syria, and Egypt.[128] The Latin Christian inscriptions studied come primarily from Italy.[129]

In general we find that the number of Byzantine inscriptions in comparison to those from the Greco-Roman period is markedly smaller. Emilian Popescu traces this fact on the one hand to the changes in political, economic, and social conditions in the cities, but he does not exclude the neglect of research in Byzantine documents as a cause.[130] Beginning in the seventh century the epigraphic tradition was strikingly in decline, which may be traced to the general crisis experienced by the Byzantine empire in all its aspects.[131]

In this study the focus is not on the completeness of materials in a given region. What is intended, rather, is a presentation of the multiplicity and variety of official titles held by Christian women in the Roman and Byzantine empires and not an inquiry focused on territorial history, which would necessarily have been restricted to a single region. In terms of time, the focus is on the period from the discernible beginnings of a Christian epigraphy at the end of the second century until the end of the Byzantine era.

The inscriptions collected are, as a rule, taken from tombs, which furnish the majority of surviving ancient inscriptions.[132] Most of them are prosaic and often contain little more than the name and title of the deceased. As a rule they follow a given formula varying according to time and place.[133] A lesser number of ancient inscriptions, and therefore also a minority of those documented in this study, belong to the genre of tomb poetry,[134] the topics of which follow certain stereotypes.[135]

As a rule scholarship has considered the historical source value of epigraphic material highly important, insofar as this question has been discussed at all alongside those of the technical interpretation and documentation of the material.[136] Carl Kaufmann wrote in 1917: "In its content ancient Christian epigraphy presents such an immediate and unfalsified insight into the conditions of life and belief in ancient Christianity that all other monuments pale beside it . . . . But it is also true of our texts, as an old master of epigraphical research, Theodor Mommsen, said of the pagans that 'the inscriptions are not monuments of literature, but of life!'"[137]

The significance of inscriptions for church-historical research is undisputed. Inscriptions have repeatedly forced a revision of historical knowledge.[138] Yet we must maintain that inscriptions are no more an immediate reflection of the reality of ancient life than are literary sources. If historical facts are derived from inscriptions we must proceed just as cautiously as we would in the analysis of literary sources. The epithets that are applied to the deceased are often formulaic and tributary to social and religious norms. The fictionality of such characterizations should thus not be lost sight of.[139] Nevertheless, the inscriptions, and with them the papyri, to the extent they can be stripped of their formulaic character, remain unique testimonies to daily life.

The majority of the inscriptional material is documented according to a structure derived from epigraphical principles:

(a) The localization, when possible, proceeds from the general to the specific and precedes the text, accompanied by a date if available.

(b) Each inscription is provided with as comprehensive a bibliography as possible, in chronological sequence beginning with the oldest editions.

(c) The text of the inscriptions is as a rule taken from the most recent publication, with the source note at the end of the inscriptional text. The prosaic inscriptions are printed according to the length of lines on the stone, and the tomb poetry according to its metric style.[140] In general the Leiden system of parentheses is followed.[141]

(d) The descriptions of the stones and the inscription—material, form, mass, state of preservation, and the style and size of the letters—are taken from the epigraphical literature, since it was not possible for me to make a personal inspection of the epigraphical materials,[142] and are in each case appended in a footnote.

(e) A text-critical apparatus adds variant readings, emendations, conjectures, parallel traditions, and remarks.

This documentation is followed by a commentary on the inscription, focusing on the official title here attested and its bearer. Further epigraphic and literary sources are cited insofar as they contribute to the interpretation of the inscriptional evidence. Sources from the same time and region are considered as of first importance, though we must remember that many epigraphical and literary sources can be dated and located only approximately.

Documentary Papyri

Christian documentary papyri (private letters, official documents, contracts, etc.)[143] are brought into the present discussion only in individual cases,[144] because the focus of this study is on an initial examination and documentation of the epigraphic material on women officeholders in the Church. In the presentation of the documentary papyri I will follow the same scheme as for the inscriptions.

The Christian documentary papyri, like the ancient Christian inscriptions, can scarcely be regarded as having been thoroughly researched by Church historians.[145] Their importance for research on women's history has been shown especially by the works of Susanna Elm for Christians and of Ross S. Kraemer for the Jewish sphere.[146]

D. Summary of Purpose and Procedure

The history of research has shown that inscriptions and papyri have scarcely been brought into the discussion as sources for the history of Christian women officeholders. Where they have received individual attention it has always been in the context of an androcentric paradigm that regards women primarily as servant virgins, heretics, or "exceptional women," when the designations of office are not interpreted as "honorary titles" for the wives of men holding the corresponding office.

This book will present the first extensive documentation of selected Greek and Latin inscriptions, plus a few documentary papyri, that witness to the existence of Christian women officeholders. The intent of the selection is to show the multiplicity of titles borne by women, and thus to illustrate the narrowness of previous research on this topic. A single chapter is devoted to each of the titles of office or functional designations found in the sources. The epigraphical, papyrological, and literary witnesses are accordingly grouped by function.[147]

Central to this book are the epigraphical witnesses, because to this point they have been only marginally incorporated in research on women officeholders in the Church and they are urgently in need of investigation.[148] In order to ensure an epigraphically correct interpretation the majority of the inscriptions discussed will be given an extensive epigraphical documentation, with the result that this study has, in part, the character of an edition of inscriptions. They will be organized geographically and chronologically, and besides the epigraphical documentation they will be commented on in the context of the existing literary sources. This placement in the literary context is subordinate to the presentation and interpretation of the inscriptions because there have already been a number of studies of the literary sources for women as officeholders in the Church.[149]

Notes

[1] For this cf. the two principal works of Elisabeth Schüssler Fiorenza, *In Memory of Her. A Feminist Theological Reconstruction of Christian Origins* (New York: Crossroad, 1983), and *Bread Not Stone. The Challenge of Feminist Biblical Interpretation* (Boston: Beacon, 1984). (On the former see, for example, Jacqueline Field-Bibb, *Women towards Priesthood. Ministerial Politics and Feminist Praxis* [Cambridge and New York: Cambridge University Press, 1991] 247–61.) See also Schüssler Fiorenza's numerous other essays on feminist exegesis (many of which are listed in the bibliography). There is a paraphrastic summary of Schüssler Fiorenza's hermeneutics by Nicole Zunhammer in "Feministische Hermeneutik" (in Christine Schaumberger and Monika Maasen, eds., *Handbuch Feministische*

Theologie [Münster: Morgana, 1986; 3d ed. 1989] 256–84); see also Luise Schottroff, "Women as Disciples of Jesus in New Testament Times," in Luise Schottroff, *Let the Oppressed Go Free. Feminist Perspectives on the New Testament.* Translated by Annemarie S. Kidder (Louisville: Westminster/John Knox, 1992) 80–130; eadem, "How Justified is the Feminist Critique of Paul?" in ibid., 35–59; eadem, "Die Frauen haben nicht geschwiegen. Über Prophetinnen, Apostelinnen und Bischöfinnen im frühen Christentum," in *". . . das Weib rede in der Gemeinde." Maria Jepsen: Erste lutherische Bischöfin. Dokumente und Stellungnahmen.* GTB 1118 (Gütersloh: Gerd Mohn, 1992) 41–48; Bernadette Brooten, "Feminist Perspectives on New Testament Exegesis," *Concilium* (Oct. 1980) 55–61; eadem, "Early Christian Women and their Cultural Context: Issues of Method in Historical Reconstruction," in Adela Yarbro Collins, ed., *Feminist Perspectives on Biblical Scholarship* (Chico: Scholars, 1985) 65–91; Monika Fander, "'Und ihnen kamen diese Worte vor wie leeres Geschwätz, und sie glaubten ihnen nicht' (Lk 24,11). Feministische Bibellektüre des Neuen Testaments. Eine Reflexion," in Schaumberger and Maassen, eds., *Handbuch Feministische Theologie,* 299–311; eadem, "Das Frauenbild im Neuen Testament. Methoden der Feministischen Bibellektüre," *Schlangenbrut* 23 (1988) 10–12. For a critique of feminist exegesis see especially Susanne Heine, *Women and Early Christianity: A Reappraisal.* Translated by John Bowden (1st U.S. ed. Minneapolis: Augsburg, 1988).

[2] On this see Ruth Albrecht, "Wir gedenken der Frauen, der bekannten wie der namenlosen. Feministische Kirchengeschichtsschreibung," in Schaumberger and Maassen, eds., *Handbuch Feministische Theologie* 312–22; Elisabeth Gössmann, "Philosophie- und theologiegeschichtliche Frauenforschung. Eine Einführung," in Elisabeth Gössmann and Dieter R. Bauer, eds., *Eva: Verführerin oder Gottes Meisterwerk? Philosophie- und theologiegeschichtliche Frauenforschung.* Hohenheimer Protokolle 21 (Stuttgart: Akademie der Diözese Rottenburg-Stuttgart, 1987) 19–35; eadem, *Wie könnte Frauenforschung im Rahmen der Katholischen Kirche aussehen?* EichHR 57 (Munich: 1987); eadem, "Geschichte – Philosophiegeschichte – feministische Theorie," *Die Philosophin* 4 (1993) 40–47; Elizabeth Clark, "Early Christian Women: Sources and Interpretation," in Lynda L. Coon, Katherine J. Haldane, and Elisabeth W. Sommer, eds., *That Gentle Strength: Historical Perspectives on Women in Christianity* (Charlottesville: University Press of Virginia, 1990) 19–35. See also the review of current scholarship by Kari Børresen, "Women's Studies of the Christian Tradition," *Contemporary philosophy* 6 (1990) 901–1001, especially on the history of the ancient Church and the Middle Ages.

[3] For this see, e.g., Joan Kelly, "The Social Relation of the Sexes. Methodological Implications of Women's History" (1976) in eadem, *Women, History & Theory. The Essays of Joan Kelly* (Chicago: University of Chicago Press, 1984) 1–18; Gisela Bock, "Historisches Fragen nach Frauen. Historische Frauenforschung: Fragestellungen und Perspektiven," in Karin Hausen, ed., *Frauen suchen ihre Geschichte. Historische Studien zum 19. und 20. Jahrhundert.* Beck'sche Schwarze Reihe 276 (Munich: Beck, 1983) 22–60; eadem, "Geschichte, Frauengeschichte, Geschlechtergeschichte," *GeGe* 14 (1988) 364–91; Karin Hausen, "Einleitung" in eadem, ed., *Frauen suchen ihre Geschichte* 7–20; Arlette Farge, "Method and Effects of Women's History," in Michelle Perrot, ed., *Writing Women's History.* Translated by Felicia Pheasant; from an original idea by Alain Paire (Oxford, UK; Cambridge, Mass.: Blackwell, 1992) 10–24; Claudia Opitz, "Der 'andere Blick' der Frauen in die Geschichte – Überlegungen zu Analyse- und Darstellungsmethoden feministischer

Geschichtsforschung," in *beiträge zur feministischen theorie und praxis. Frauenforschung oder feministische Forschung?* 7/11, 2 (Cologne: Eigenverlag des Vereins Beiträge zur Feministischen Theorie und Praxis [corrected ed. 1984]) 61–70; Ute Frevert, *Frauen-Geschichte. Zwischen Bürgerlicher Verbesserung und Neuer Weiblichkeit.* Neue Historische Bibliothek, edition suhrkamp n.s. 284 (Frankfurt: Suhrkamp, 1986); Judith Newton, "History as Usual? Feminism and the 'New Historicism,'" *Cultural Critique* 9 (1988) 87–121; Uta Lindgren, "Wege der historischen Frauenforschung," *HJ* 109 (1989) 211–19; Heide Wunder, "Historische Frauenforschung – Ein neuer Zugang zur Gesellschaftsgeschichte," in Werner Affeldt, ed., *Frauen in Spätantike und Frühmittelalter. Lebensbedingungen – Lebensnormen – Lebensformen. Beiträge zu einer internationalen Tagung am Fachbereich Geschichtswissenschaften der Freien Universität Berlin 18. bis 21. Februar 1987* (Sigmaringen: J. Thorbecke, 1990) 31–41; Herta Nagl-Docekal, "Feministische Geschichtswissenschaft – ein unverzichtbares Projekt," *L'Homme* 1 (1990) 7–18; eadem, "Für eine geschlechtergeschichtliche Perspektivierung der Historiographieforschung," in Wolfgang Küttler, Jörn Rüsen, and Ernst Schulin, eds., *Geschichtsdiskurs.* Vol. 1: *Grundlagen und Methoden der Historiographiegeschichte* (Frankfurt: Fischer Taschenbuch Verlag, 1993) 233–56; Katharina Fietze, "Interdisziplinäre Aspekte von historischer und philosophischer Frauenforschung," *Die Philosophin* 4 (1993) 33–39. See also the reviews of current scholarship by Ute Frevert, "Bewegung und Disziplin in der Frauengeschichte. Ein Forschungsbericht," *GeGe* 14 (1988) 240–62, on the nineteenth and twentieth centuries, and Hedwig Röckelein, "Historische Frauenforschung. Ein Literaturbericht zur Geschichte des Mittelalters," *HZ* 255/2 (1992) 377–409, on medieval history.

[4] Fietze, "Interdisziplinäre Aspekte," 34. For the increasing postulation of a model of historical writing as writing gender history cf. especially the works of Gisela Bock, "Historische Frauenforschung" (1983); eadem, "Der Platz der Frauen in der Geschichte" in Herta Nagl-Docekal and Franz Wimmer, eds., *Neue Ansätze in der Geschichtswissenschaft.* Conceptus-Studien 1 (Vienna: VWGO, 1984) 108–27; see the critique by Nagl-Docekal, "Frauengeschichte als Perspektive und Teilbereich der Geschichtswissenschaft. Bemerkungen zum Referat 'Der Platz der Frauen in der Geschichte' von Gisela Bock," in ibid., 128–32, and Hans-Jürgen Puhle, "Frauengeschichte und Gesellschaftsgeschichte. Kommentar zum Beitrag von Gisela Bock," in ibid., 133–36; Bock, "Geschlechtergeschichte" (1988); cf. also Wunder, "Historische Frauenforschung" (1990).

[5] Opitz, "Der 'andere Blick,'" 62.

[6] Exceptions are, for example, the work of Kari Børressen, *Subordination and Equivalence. The Nature and Role of Woman in Augustine and Thomas Aquinas.* Translated by Charles H. Talbot (Washington, D.C.: University Press of America, 1981); Elisabeth Gössmann, "The Construction of Women's Difference in the Christian Theological Tradition," *Concilium* (Dec. 1991) 50–59; Karen Jo Torjesen, "In Praise of Noble Women: Gender and Honor in Ascetic Texts," *Semeia* 56–58 (1992) 41–64. For an analysis and deconstruction of concepts of femininity see also the study by Christa Rohde-Dachser, *Expedition in den dunklen Kontinent. Weiblichkeit im Diskurs der Psychoanalyse* (2nd ed. Berlin and Heidelberg: 1992) which, although devoted to a different field of scholarship, namely psychoanalysis, is a model of analysis and offers an impetus for work in Church history as well. In her Foreword she writes: "More urgent than the reformulation of a psychoanalytic theory of femininity, my original project, appears to me now the fundamental ideology-critical reflection of

psychoanalytical discourse from the perspective of its latent gender specificity, with the goal of a systematic *de*construction through the laying bare of its 'structural principles,' namely the collective (conscious and unconscious) fantasies that support that discourse" (p. vii).

[7] For the problem of the concept of the "subject" cf. Waltraud Hummerich-Diezun, "'Unbeschreiblich weiblich.' Zum Subjekt feministischer Theologie," in Forschungsprojekt zur Geschichte der Theologinnen Göttingen, eds., *Querdenken. Beiträge zur feministisch-befreiungstheologischen Diskussion. FS für Hannelore Erhart zum 65. Geburtstag* (Pfaffenweiler: Centaurus, 1992) 103–28 at 117: "Postmodern thought also—cautioned by the devastating consequences of the postulation of the autonomous subject and its claims to dominance in the modern period—is undergirded by a fundamental skepticism toward the modern concept of the subject, and therefore foregoes a notion of the unified subject as well as the formulation of political values. Feminist critique, in contrast, formulates a critique of society that makes male rationality's mechanisms of domination responsible for racism and militarism. It cannot share the depoliticizing conclusions of postmodern thought, because it is connected to the women's movement, which for the accomplishment of its political demands and goals in the interest of women cannot utterly renounce the effort to achieve a concept of the unified subject in which women would also be represented. Such a renunciation would lead to the self-destruction of the project itself. Feminist theory and politics are therefore faced with a conflict: as a political movement feminism requires a determinable subject, while in theory this project is rendered problematic through the differentiation of various contexts of life and through the categories of the theoretical work itself."

[8] Sigrid Weigel, *Topographien der Geschlechter. Kulturgeschichtliche Studien zur Literatur* (Reinbek bei Hamburg: Rowohlt Taschenbuch Verlag, 1990) 262.

[9] For this see the extensive study by Ivoni Richter Reimer, *Women in the Acts of the Apostles* (Minneapolis: Fortress, 1995) 195–226.

[10] Cf. especially Bernadette Brooten, "Issues of Method" (1985); Elizabeth Clark, "Sources and Interpretation" (1990); Kari Børresen, "Women's Studies" (1990).

[11] The observations of Pauline Schmitt Pantel, "The Difference Between the Sexes: History, Anthropology and the Greek City," in Michelle Perrot, ed., *Writing Women's History*, 70–89, at 78, about the treatment of sources from the fourth century B.C.E. by historical scholarship applies very closely to the attitude of researchers in Church history to the patristic literature: "The starting-point is my observation that texts by Xenophon and Attic orators of the fourth century on the question of the division between the masculine and feminine have been wrongly used. Most modern authors consider these texts to be scrupulously accurate descriptions of the feminine condition and masculine activities and value them as concrete eyewitness reports. They are not treated in the same way as Plato and Aristotle's theories, and no one questions their status as privileged historical documents. But if we were to place these texts in the context of fourth-century writing as a whole, we would see that the different ways of looking at the division of the sexes constituted a coherent and articulate whole. If Xenophon's writings give the impression of real-life observations rather more than those of Plato or Aristotle, they are none the less attempts at ordering the world, and just as theoretical."

[12] For Jerome and John Chrysostom see the studies by Elizabeth Clark, *Jerome, Chrysostom, and Friends. Essays and Translations.* SWR 2 (New York and Toronto: Edwin Mellen, 1979; 2nd ed. 1982), which make this discrepancy especially evident.

[13] Farge, "Method and Effects of Women's History," 13.

[14] Bernadette Brooten, "Junia. . . . Outstanding among the Apostles," in Leonard Swidler and Arlene Swidler, eds., *Women Priests: A Catholic Commentary on the Vatican Declaration* (New York: Paulist, 1977) 141–44.

[15] Monika Fander, *Die Stellung der Frau im Markusevangelium. Unter besonderer Berücksichtigung kultur- und religionsgeschichtlicher Hintergründe.* MThA 8 (Altenberge: Oros-Verlag, 1989*)*; cf. also her summary of her own work in eadem, "Frauen in der Nachfolge Jesu. Die Rolle der Frau im Markusevangelium," *EvTh* 52 (1992) 413–32.

[16] Richter Reimer, *Women in Acts* (1995).

[17] Ruth Albrecht, *Das Leben der heiligen Makrina auf dem Hintergrund der Thekla-Traditionen. Studien zu den Ursprüngen des weiblichen Mönchtums im 4. Jahrhundert in Kleinasien.* FKDG 38 (Göttingen: Vandenhoeck & Ruprecht, 1986*)*.

[18] Elizabeth Clark, [Gerontius], *The Life of Melania the Younger.* Introduction, Translation, and Commentary. SWR 14 (New York and Toronto: Edwin Mellen, 1984); "Piety, Propaganda, and Politics in the Life of Melania the Younger," *StPatr* 18/2 (1989) 167–83.

[19] Anne Jensen, "Thekla. Vergessene Verkündigerin," in Karin Walter, ed., *Zwischen Ohnmacht und Befreiung. Biblische Frauengestalten* (Freiburg, Basel, and Vienna: Herder, 1988) 173–79; eadem, "Philumene oder Das Streben nach Vergeistigung," in Karin Walter, ed., *Sanft und rebellisch. Mütter der Christenheit – von Frauen neu entdeckt* (Freiburg, Basel, and Vienna: Herder, 1990) 221–43; eadem, "Maria von Magdala – Traditionen der frühen Christenheit," in Dietmar Bader, ed., *Maria Magdalena – Zu einem Bild der Frau in der christlichen Verkündigung.* Schriftenreihe der Katholischen Akademie Freiburg (Munich and Zürich: 1990) 33–50; eadem, "Die ersten Christinnen der Spätantike," in Veronika Straub, ed., *Auch wir sind die Kirche. Frauen in der Kirche zwischen Tradition und Aufbruch* (Munich: J. Pfeiffer, 1991) 35–58; but see especially her book, *God's Self-Confident Daughters. Early Christianity and the Liberation of Women.* Translated by O. C. Dean, Jr. (Louisville: Westminster/John Knox, 1996).

[20] For the "biographical initiative" cf. also Ruth Albrecht, "Feministische Kirchengeschichtsschreibung," 316–17.

[21] Cf., for example, the text editions by Helene Homeyer, *Dichterinnen des Altertums und des frühen Mittelalters. Zweisprachige Textausgabe* (Paderborn, Munich, Vienna, and Zürich: F. Schöningh, 1979); Patricia Wilson-Kastner, *A Lost Tradition. Women Writers of The Early Church* (Washington, D.C.: University Press of America, 1981); Elizabeth A. Clark and Diane F. Hatch, *The Golden Bough, the Oaken Cross. The Virgilian Cento of Faltonia Betitia Proba.* AAR.TTS 5 (Chico: Scholars, 1981). For the discussion of this question cf. Peter Dronke, *Women Writers of the Middle Ages. A Critical Study of Texts from Perpetua (✝ 203) to Marguerite Porete (✝ 1310)* (Cambridge and New York: Cambridge University Press, 1984); Ruth Albrecht, *Makrina* (1986) 233–38; Madeleine Scopello, "Jewish and Greek Heroines in the Nag Hammadi Library," in Karen L. King, ed., *Images of the Feminine in Gnosticism.* Studies in Antiquity and Christianity 4 (Philadelphia: Fortress, 1988) 71–90; Anne Jensen, "Christinnen" (1991); Ross S. Kraemer, "Women's Authorship of Jewish and Christian Literature in the Greco-Roman Period," in Amy-Jill Levine, ed., *"Women Like This." New Perspectives on Jewish Women in the Greco-Roman World.* SBL. Early Judaism and its Literature 1 (Atlanta: Scholars, 1991) 221–42; Mary R. Lefkowitz, "Did Ancient Women Write Novels?" in ibid., 199–219; Patricia Demers, *Women as Interpreters of the Bible* (New York and Mahwah, N.J.: Paulist, 1992).

[22] Cf. Clark, "Sources and Interpretation," 19.

[23] Schmitt Pantel, "Difference Between the Sexes," 76.

[24] For the problem of distinguishing text from reality cf. Roland Barthes, *Literatur oder Geschichte*. Translated from French by Helmut Scheffel. edition suhrkamp 303 (Frankfurt: Suhrkamp 1969) 11ff.; Elisabeth Schüssler Fiorenza, "Text as Reality – Reality as Text: The Problem of a Feminist Historical and Social Reconstruction Based on Texts," *StTh* 43 (1989) 19–34.

[25] For fundamental remarks on the problems of androcentric language see Senta Trömel-Plötz, *Frauensprache. Sprache der Veränderung* (Frankfurt: Fischer Taschenbuch Verlag, 1982); eadem, "Feminismus und Linguistik" in Luise F. Pusch, ed., *Feminismus. Inspektion der Herrenkultur. Ein Handbuch.* edition suhrkamp n.s. 192 (Frankfurt: Suhrkamp, 1983) 33–51; eadem, ed., *Gewalt durch Sprache. Die Vergewaltigung von Frauen in Gesprächen* (Frankfurt: Fischer Taschenbuch Verlag, 1984); eadem, *Vatersprache – Mutterland. Beobachtungen zu Sprache und Politik* (2nd rev. ed. Munich: 1993); Luise F. Pusch, *Das Deutsche als Männersprache. Aufsätze und Glossen zur feministischen Linguistik.* edition suhrkamp n.s. 217 (Frankfurt: Suhrkamp, 1984); eadem, *Alle Menschen werden Schwestern. Feministische Sprachkritik.* edition suhrkamp n.s. 565 (Frankfurt: Suhrkamp, 1990); Luce Irigaray, "How do we Become Civil Women?" in eadem, *Thinking the Difference: for a peaceful revolution.* Translated by Karin Montin (New York: Routledge, 1994) 37–64; Susanna Häberlin, Rachel Schmid, and Eva Lia Wyss, *Übung macht die Meisterin. Ratschläge für einen nichtsexistischen Sprachgebrauch* (Munich: Verlag Frauenoffensive, 1992). For the problem of androcentric language in theological and ecclesiastical contexts cf. Letty M. Russell's 1976 collection, *The Liberating Word. A Guide to Nonsexist Interpretation of the Bible* (Philadelphia: Westminster, 1976); Elisabeth Schüssler Fiorenza, *In Memory of Her* 43–53; Jacqueline Field-Bibb, "'By any other name': The Issue of Inclusive Language," *MCM* 31/2 (1989) 5–9.

[26] Häberlin, Schmid, and Wyss, *Meisterin* 16–17.

[27] Similarly Schüssler Fiorenza, "Text as Reality," 28: "Androcentric texts produce the marginality and absence of women from historical records because they are written in grammatically masculine language which functions as *generic* language. Such language generally subsumes women under masculine terms. How we read the silences of such unmarked grammatically masculine generic texts and how we fill in their blank spaces depends on their contextualization in historical and present experience. An historically adequate interpretation of such generic androcentric texts therefore must read grammatically masculine biblical language as inclusive of women and men unless a case can be made for an exclusive reading." Luce Irigaray, *This Sex Which Is Not One.* Translated by Catherine Porter with Carolyn Burke (Ithaca, N.Y.: Cornell University Press, 1985) 85, also makes pointed reference to this problem: "Women's social inferiority is reinforced and complicated by the fact that the woman does not have access to language, except through recourse to 'masculine' systems of representation which disappropriate her from her relation to herself and to other women. The 'feminine' is never to be identified except by and for the masculine . . . ."

[28] For what follows see also Schüssler Fiorenza, *In Memory of Her* 44–46.

[29] On this see ibid., 47–48, and ch. 7 below.

[30] On this see ch. 2 below; Hedwig Meyer-Wilmes, *Rebellion auf der Grenze. Ortsbestimmung feministischer Theologie* (Freiburg: Herder, 1990) 191: "But since in an androcentric horizon of thought a woman in a leading position, and not only that, but called to apostolic discipleship, is unthinkable, the woman who is here called an apostle cannot have been a woman."

[31] On this, see chs. 4 and 8 below.

[32] Cf. Irigaray, "How do we Become Civil Women?" (1991). On the feminist necessity for analysis and alteration of language, as well as Irigaray's linguistic theory, cf. also the introduction to her collection, *Thinking the Difference,* which includes that essay.

[33] Translator's note: At this point the author enunciates a set of principles she will follow in her use of German, including the use of the grammatically feminine form for women in the singular (e.g., Christin, Diakonin, Bischöfin), and the so-called "capital I form" in the plural (e.g., ChristInnen for a gender-mixed group of Christians). These principles cannot be univocally applied in English, especially since the use of the -ess ending to translate the German feminine ending -in would run contrary to the rules of inclusive language being shaped in the English-speaking world.

[34] Farge, "Method and Effects of Women's History," 21, 23.

[35] Friedrich Loofs, "Die urchristliche Gemeindeverfassung mit spezieller Beziehung auf Loening und Harnack," *ThStKr* 63 (1890) 619–58 at 637.

[36] This is a problem fundamental to the historiography of ancient Christianity. Martin Hengel, *Acts and the History of Earliest Christianity.* Translated by John Bowden (Philadelphia: Fortress, 1980) writes (p. 3): "The basic problem in writing a history of early Christianity lies in the fragmentariness of the sources and the haphazard way in which they have survived. However, this situation hampers not only research into the origins of our faith, but also the study of ancient history generally, in both the political and the cultural and religious spheres."

[37] Leopold Zscharnack, *Der Dienst der Frau in den ersten Jahrhunderten der christlichen Kirche* (Göttingen: Vandenhoeck & Ruprecht, 1902) 1, with reference to Cyprian, *Epistles* 75.

[38] For the problems of a historiography of early Christianity cf. the collected volume edited by Helmut Koester and James M. Robinson, *Trajectories through Early Christianity* (Philadelphia: Fortress, 1971), especially Robinson's "Introduction: The Dismantling and Reassembling of the Categories of New Testament Scholarship," 1–19, as well as Koester, "*GNOMOI DIAPHOROI:* The Origin and Nature of Diversification in the History of Early Christianity," 114–57, and idem, "Conclusion: The Intention and Scope of Trajectories," 269–79. For a critique of the volume, cf. Hahn, "Neuorientierung in der Erforschung des frühen Christentums?" *EvTh* 33 (1973) 537–44. Dieter Lührmann, "Erwägungen zur Geschichte des Urchristentums," *EvTh* 32 (1972) 452–67; Henning Paulsen, "Zur Wissenschaft vom Urchristentum und der alten Kirche – ein methodischer Versuch," in idem, *Zur Literatur und Geschichte des frühen Christentums,* ed. Ute E. Eisen. WUNT 99 (Tübingen: Mohr Siebeck, 1997); idem, "Auslegungsgeschichte und Geschichte des Urchristentums: die Überprüfung eines Paradigmas" (1989) in ibid., 412–25. Hengel, *Acts and the History* (1979) 3–68; Brooten, "Issues of Method" (1985); Schüssler Fiorenza, *In Memory of Her* 3–95.

[39] The most important studies, very different in their scope, are: Adolf von Harnack, *The Expansion of Christianity in the First Three Centuries.* Translated and edited by James Moffatt (New York: G. P. Putnam's Sons, 1904–05) 2:217–39; Zscharnack, *Dienst der Frau* (1902); Eduard von der Goltz, *Der Dienst der Frau in der christlichen Kirche. Geschichtlicher Überblick mit einer Sammlung von Urkunden.* 2 parts. 2nd. revised ed. (Potsdam: Stiftungsverlag, 1914); K. Heinrich Schäfer, *Die Kanonissenstifter im deutschen Mittelalter. Ihre Entwicklung und innere Einrichtung im Zusammenhang mit dem altchristlichen Sanktimonialentum.* KRA 43, 44 (Stuttgart: F. Enke, 1907); idem, "Kanonis-

sen und Diakonissen. Ergänzungen und Erläuterungen," *RQ* 24 (1910) II, 49–90; Lydia
Stöcker, *Die Frau in der alten Kirche* (Tübingen: Mohr, 1907); Hermann Jordan, *Das
Frauenideal des Neuen Testaments und der ältesten Christenheit* (Leipzig: A.
Deichert'sche Verlagsbuchhandlung Nachf. [G. Böhme], 1909); A. Ludwig, "Weibliche
Kleriker in der altchristlichen und frühmittelalterlichen Kirche," *Theologisch-praktische
Quartalschrift* 20 (1910) 548–57, 609–17; 21 (1911) 141–49; Thomas Bateson Allworthy,
*Women in the Apostolic Church. A Critical Study of the Evidence in the New Testament for
the Prominence of Women in Early Christianity* (Cambridge: W. Heffer & Sons, 1917);
Georg Fangauer, *Stilles Frauenheldentum oder Frauenapostolat in den ersten drei Jahrhun-
derten des Christentums* (Münster: 1922); Adolf Kalsbach, *Die altkirchliche Einrichtung
der Diakonissen bis zu ihrem Erlöschen.* RQ.S 22 (Freiburg: Herder, 1926); Albrecht Oepke,
"Der Dienst der Frau in der urchristlichen Gemeinde," *NAMZ* 16 (1939) 39–53, 81–86;
Franz J. Leenhardt and Fritz Blanke, *Die Stellung der Frau im Neuen Testament und in der
Alten Kirche.* KZF 24 (Zürich: 1949); Johannes Leipoldt, *Die Frau in der antiken Welt und
im Urchristentum* (Leipzig: Koehler & Amelang, 1954); Jean Daniélou, *The Ministry of
Women in the Early Church.* Translated by Glyn Simon (London: Faith Press; New York:
Morehouse-Barlow, 1961); Mary Lawrence McKenna, *Women of the Church. Role and Re-
newal* (New York: P. J. Kenedy, 1967); Otto Bangerter, *Frauen im Aufbruch. Die Geschichte
einer Frauenbewegung in der Alten Kirche. Ein Beitrag zur Frauenfrage* (Neukirchen-
Vluyn: Neukirchener Verlag, 1971); Roger Gryson, *The Ministry of Women in the Early
Church.* Translated by Jean Laporte and Mary Louise Hall (2nd ed. Collegeville: The Litur-
gical Press, 1980); Leonard Swidler and Arlene Swidler, eds., *Women Priests* (1977);
Friedrich Heiler, *Die Frau in den Religionen der Menschheit.* TBT 33 (Berlin and New
York: Walter de Gruyter, 1977) 87ff.; Karl Hermann Schelkle, *The Spirit and the Bride:
Woman in the Bible.* Translated by Matthew J. O'Connell (Collegeville: The Liturgical
Press, 1979) 143–75; Dorothy Irvin, "The Ministry of Women in the Early Church: The Ar-
chaeological Evidence," *DDSR* 45 (1980) 76–86; Arthur Frederick Ide, *Women in Early
Christianity and Christian Society* (Mesquite, Tex.: Ide House, 1980); idem, *God's Girls.
Ordination of Women in the Early Christian & Gnostic Churches* (Garland, Tex.: Tangel-
wüld, 1986); Elisabeth M. Tetlow, *Women and Ministry in the New Testament* (New York:
Paulist, 1980); Jean LaPorte, *The Role of Women in Early Christianity.* SWR 7 (New York
and Toronto: Edwin Mellen, 1982) 109ff.; E. Margaret Howe, *Women & Church Leadership*
(Grand Rapids: Zondervan, 1982); Aida Besançon-Spencer, *Beyond the Curse. Women
Called to Ministry* (Nashville: Thomas Nelson, 1985); Elisabeth Schüssler Fiorenza, "Die
Anfänge von Kirche, Amt und Priestertum in feministisch-theologischer Sicht," in Paul
Hoffmann, ed., *Priesterkirche.* TzZ 3 (Düsseldorf: Patmos, 1987) 62–95; eadem, *In Mem-
ory of Her;* Elisabeth Gössmann, "Äußerungen zum Frauenpriestertum in der christlichen
Tradition," in Elisabeth Gössmann and Dietmar Bader, eds., *Warum keine Ordination der
Frau? Unterschiedliche Einstellungen in den christlichen Kirchen* (Munich: Schnell &
Steiner, 1987) 9–25; Ben Witherington III, *Women in the Earliest Churches.* MSSNTS 59
(New York: Cambridge University Press, 1989); Lesly F. Massey, *Women and the New Tes-
tament. An Analysis of Scripture in Light of New Testament Era Culture* (Jefferson, N.C.:
McFarland & Co., 1989); Judith Lang, *Ministers of Grace. Women in the Early Church*
(Middlegreen, Slough: St. Paul's Publications, 1989); Schottroff, "Frauen haben nicht
geschwiegen" (1992). See also the source collections by Elfriede Gottlieb, *Die Frau in der
frühchristlichen Gemeinde.* Quellenhefte zum Frauenleben in der Geschichte 5 (Berlin:

1928); Josephine Mayer, *Monumenta de viduis diaconissis virginibusque tractantia.* Flor-Patr 42 (Bonn: P. Hanstein, 1938); Ross S. Kraemer, *Maenads, Martyrs, Matrons, Monastics. A Sourcebook on Women's Religions in the Greco-Roman World* (Philadelphia: Fortress, 1988).

[40] Cf. Edwin Hatch, *The Organization of the Early Christian Churches: eight lectures delivered before the University of Oxford, in the year 1880, on the foundation of the late Rev. John Bampton* (2nd revised ed. London: Rivingtons, 1882); Edgar Loening, *Die Gemeindeverfassung des Urchristenthums. Eine kirchenrechtliche Untersuchung* (Aalen: Scientia Verlag, 1966; reprint of the Halle ed. of 1888); Friedrich Loofs, "Die urchristliche Gemeindeverfassung mit spezieller Beziehung auf Loening und Harnack," *ThStKr* 63 (1890) 619–58; Adolf von Harnack, *The Constitution and Law of the Church in the First Two Centuries.* Translated by F.L. Pogson; edited by H.D.A. Major (London: Williams & Norgate; New York: G. P. Putnam's Sons, 1910); Hans Lietzmann, "Zur altchristlichen Verfassungsgeschichte," *ZWTh* n.s. 20 (1914) 97–153 (reprinted in idem, *Kleine Schriften I.* TU 67 [Berlin: Akademie-Verlag, 1958] 141–85); Karl Müller, *Beiträge zur Geschichte der Verfassung der alten Kirche.* APAW.PH 3 (Berlin: Verlag der Akademie der Wissenschaften in Kommission bei der Vereinigung wissenschaftlicher Verleger Walter de Gruyter u. Co., 1922); Joseph Brosch, *Charismen und Ämter in der Urkirche* (Bonn: P. Hanstein, 1951); Jean Colson, *Les Fonctions Ecclésiales: aux deux premiers siècles* (Paris: Desclée de Brouwer, 1956); Hans von Campenhausen, *Kirchliches Amt und geistliche Vollmacht in den ersten drei Jahrhunderten.* BHTh 14 (Tübingen: J.C.B. Mohr [Paul Siebeck], 1953; 2nd rev. ed. 1963) (to which cf. Wilhelm Maurer, "Von Ursprung und Wesen kirchlichen Rechts," *ZevKR* 5 [1956] 1–32); Eduard Schweizer, *Church Order in the New Testament.* Translated by Frank Clarke (Naperville, Ill.: A.R. Allenson, 1961); Ernst Käsemann, "Amt und Gemeinde im Neuen Testament" (1960) in idem, *Exegetische Versuche und Besinnungen* (6th ed. Göttingen: Vandenhoeck & Ruprecht, 1970) 1:109–34; Ulrich Brockhaus, *Charisma und Amt. Die paulinische Charismenlehre auf dem Hintergrund der frühchristlichen Gemeindefunktionen* (Wuppertal: Theologischer Verlag Brockhaus, 1972); Karl Kertelge, *Gemeinde und Amt im Neuen Testament.* BiH 10 (Munich: Kösel, 1972); idem, ed., *Das Kirchliche Amt im Neuen Testament.* WdF 439 (Darmstadt: Wissenschaftliche Buchgesellschaft, 1977); Heinrich Kraft, "Die Anfänge des geistlichen Amtes," *ThLZ* 100 (1975) 81–98; Joachim Rohde, *Urchristliche und frühkatholische Ämter. Eine Untersuchung zur frühchristlichen Amtsentwicklung im Neuen Testament und bei den apostolischen Vätern.* ThA 33 (Berlin: Evangelische Verlagsanstalt, 1976); Johannes Mühlsteiger, "Zum Verfassungsrecht der Frühkirche," *ZKTh* 99 (1977) 129–55, 257–85); Jürgen Roloff, "Amt / Ämter / Amtsverständnis. IV. Neues Testament," *TRE* 2 (1978) 509–33.; Richard P. Hanson, "Amt / Ämter / Amtsverständnis V. Alte Kirche," *TRE* 1 (1978) 533–52; Hahn, "Charisma und Amt. Die Diskussion über das kirchliche Amt im Lichte der neutestamentlichen Charismenlehre," *ZThK* 76 (1979) 419–49; Edward Schillebeeckx, *Ministry: Leadership in the Community of Jesus Christ.* Translated by John Bowden (New York: Crossroad, 1981). For the history of scholarship cf. Olof Linton, *Das Problem der Urkirche in der neueren Forschung. Eine kritische Darstellung.* Diss. theol. (Uppsala: Almqvist & Wiksells, 1932), as well as the bibliographic report on New Testament research by André Lemaire, "The Ministries in the New Testament. Recent Research," *BTB* 3 (1973) 133–66.

[41] For what follows, cf. also Ida Raming, "Priestertum der Frau," *WFT* (1991) 328–30.

[42] Cf. Gertrud Heinzelmann, ed., *Wir schweigen nicht länger! Frauen äussern sich zum II. Vatikanischen Konzil // We Won't Keep Silence Any Longer! Women Speak Out to Vatican*

Council II (Zürich: Interfeminas, 1964); eadem, *Die geheiligte Diskriminierung. Beiträge zum kirchlichen Feminismus* (Bonstetten: Interfeminas, 1986); and especially Ida Raming, *Frauenbewegung und Kirche. Bilanz eines 25jährigen Kampfes für die Gleichberechtigung und Befreiung der Frau seit dem 2. Vatikanischen Konzil* (Weinheim: Deutscher Studien, 1989). For the popular organizations such as "Maria von Magdala" or the Women's Ordination Conference, as well as others, see ibid., 117ff. passim.

[43] Haye van der Meer, *Priestertum der Frau? Eine theologiegeschichtliche Untersuchung.* QD 42 (Freiburg, Basel, and Vienna: Herder, 1969). This dissertation was completed in 1962 under the direction of Karl Rahner. English: *Women Priests in the Catholic Church? A theological-historical investigation.* Translated and with a foreword and afterword by Arlene and Leonard Swidler. Foreword by Cynthia C. Wedel (Philadelphia: Temple University Press, 1973).

[44] Cf. ibid. 99–105.

[45] Ida Raming, *The Exclusion of Women from the Priesthood: Divine Law or Sex Discrimination? A historical investigation of the juridical and doctrinal foundations of the code of canon law, canon 968, 1.* Translated by Norman R. Adams, with a preface by Arlene and Leonard Swidler (Metuchen, N.J.: Scarecrow Press, 1976).

[46] Raming, *Frauenbewegung und Kirche* (1989) 41; eadem, *Exclusion of Women* 130–34.

[47] Roger Gryson, *Le Ministère des Femmes dans l'Eglise Ancienne* (Gembloux, 1972) (cf. the completely uncritical review by Ingetraut Ludolphy in *ThLZ* 98 [1973] 595–97). The book was translated into English as *The Ministry of Women in the Early Church* by Jean Laporte and Mary Louise Hall (2nd ed. Collegeville: The Liturgical Press, 1980).

[48] Some inscriptional evidence of deaconesses is briefly mentioned, but not further evaluated (ibid. 90–91).

[49] Something similar had been done by Zscharnack, *Dienst der Frau;* Kalsbach, *Einrichtung.*

[50] Gryson, *Ministry* 109 and 113.

[51] *AAS* 69 (1977) 98–116.

[52] In reaction to the admission of women to the priesthood by the General Synod of the Church of England on November 11, 1992, *Inter insigniores* was issued in a new edition, augmented by a foreword from Pope John Paul II; since that date it is to be found under the title *Ordinatio sacerdotalis.*

[53] Examples of the immediate reaction are the volume edited by Leonard Swidler and Arlene Swidler, published in 1977: *Women Priests: A Catholic Commentary on the Vatican Declaration,* and another edited by Carroll Stuhlmueller, c.p.: *Women and Priesthood. Future Directions. A Call to Dialogue from the Catholic Theological Union at Chicago* (Collegeville: The Liturgical Press, 1978). Both volumes contain a wealth of exegetical, historical, systematic theological, canonical, and pastoral theological essays on the general question of women and priesthood. See on this subject also Karl Rahner, "Women and the Priesthood" in idem, *Concern for the Church.* Theological Investigations XX (New York: Crossroad, 1981) 35–47; John Kevin Coyle, "The Fathers on Women's Ordination," *EeT* 9 (1978) 51–101; also published in David M. Scholer, ed., *Women in Early Christianity.* Studies in Early Christianity 14 (New York: Garland, 1993) 117–67; Elisabeth Gössmann, "Frauen in der Kirche ohne Sitz und Stimme? Oder: Roma locuta – causa non finita sed disputanda," in Norbert Greinacher and Hans Küng, eds., *Katholische Kirche – wohin? Wider den Verrat am*

Konzil (Munich: Piper, 1986) 295–306; Hervé Legrand, "Die Frage der Frauenordination aus der Sicht katholischer Theologie. 'Inter Insigniores' nach zehn Jahren," in Elisabeth Göss-mann and Dietmar Bader, eds., *Warum keine Ordination der Frau?* 89–111; Johanna Schiessl, "Priestertum der Frau," *StZ* 211 (1993) 115–22. For the pre- and post-history of the declaration see especially Ida Raming, *Frauenbewegung und Kirche* 43ff.

[54] Rahner, "Women and the Priesthood," 40.

[55] *Inter insigniores* 6.

[56] For the standpoints of an Orthodox theology see the collection edited by Thomas Hopko, *Women and the Priesthood* (Crestwood, N.Y.: St. Vladimir's Seminary Press, 1983). For the Protestant sector cf. Ingetraut Ludolphy, "Frau. V. Alte Kirche und Mittelalter," *TRE* 11 (1983) 436–41 at 436.

[57] On this see Jochen Martin, *Der priesterliche Dienst III. Die Genese des Amts-priestertums in der frühen Kirche.* QD 48 (Freiburg, Basel, and Vienna: Herder, 1972); Robert Zollitsch, *Amt und Funktion des Priesters. Eine Untersuchung zum Ursprung und zur Gestalt des Presbyterats in den ersten zwei Jahrhunderten.* FThSt 96 (Freiburg, Basel, and Vienna: Herder, 1974); Paul Hoffmann, "Priestertum und Amt im Neuen Testament. Eine Bestandsaufnahme," in idem, ed., *Priesterkirche,* 12–61; Ernst Ludwig Grasmück, "Vom Presbyter zum Priester. Etappen der Entwicklung des neuzeitlichen katholischen Priesterbildes," in Hoffmann, ed., *Priesterkirche,* 96–131.

[58] Rahner, "Priestertum der Frau?" 214–15.

[59] Cf., besides *Inter insigniores/Ordinatio sacerdotalis,* especially the final report of the Inter-Orthodox Consultation from Oct. 30 to Nov. 7, 1988, held on Rhodes, with the theme: "The Position of Woman in the Orthodox Church and the Question of the Ordination of Women" (German translation in *Orthodoxes Forum* 3 [1989] 93–102. Cf., on this, Heinz Ohme, "Die orthodoxe Kirche und die Ordination von Frauen – Zur Konferenz von Rhodos vom 30. Oktober bis 7. November 1988," *ÖR* 42 (1993) 52–65.

[60] For monographs, essays, and collections on the question of a "priesthood of women" from historical, canonical, dogmatic, and pastoral perspectives cf. van der Meer, *Priester-tum* (1969); Raming, *Exclusion of Women* (1976); Swidler and Swidler, eds., *Women Priests* (1977); Stuhlmueller, ed., *Priesthood* (1978); Constance F. Parvey, ed., *The Ordination of Women in Ecumenical Perspective: Workbook for the Church's Future.* Faith and Order Paper 105 (Geneva: World Council of Churches, 1980); Manfred Hauke, *Women in the Priesthood? A Systematic Analysis in the Light of the Order of Creation and Redemption.* Translated by David Kipp (San Francisco: Ignatius Press, 1988); Howe, *Women and Church Leadership* (1982) 129ff. passim; Hopko, ed., *Priesthood* (1983); Gössmann and Bader, eds., *Ordination* (1987); Field-Bibb, *Priesthood* (1991). For further literature, Church dec-larations, conference reports, and cassettes on the theme with a short summary of contents see the bibliography in Patricia A. Kendall, *Women and the Priesthood: A Selected and An-notated Bibliography* ([Philadelphia]: Committee to Promote the Cause of and to Plan for the Ordination of Women to the Priesthood, The Episcopal Diocese of Pennsylvania, 1976).

[61] On this see the excellent contribution of John Kevin Coyle, "The Fathers on Women's Ordination," (n. 53 above), which subjects the texts cited in *Inter insigniores* (see nn. 7 and 8 of the commentary) to substantiate the thesis of the "eternal" prohibition on or-dination of women to a critical examination, and comes to the conclusion: "It *may* be that further serious research will lead to a final conclusion not substantially different from the conclusion already reached by the *Declaration.* But, if texts are ever found in the Fathers of

the Church that give unquestionable support to that conclusion, we should expect that the sources invoked by the *Declaration* will not be among them."

[62] Giorgio Otranto, "Note sul sacerdozio femminile nell'antichità in margine a una testimonianza di Gelasio I," *VetChr* 19 (1982) 341–60 (cf. also the English translation in Mary Ann Rossi, "Priesthood, Precedent and Prejudice. On Recovering the Women Priests of Early Christianity. Containing a translation from the Italian of 'Notes on the Female Priesthood in Antiquity,' by Giorgio Otranto," *JFSR* 7 [1991] 73–94).

[63] For women bishops cf. the works by Joan Morris, *The Lady was a Bishop. The Hidden History of Women with Clerical Ordination and the Jurisdiction of Bishops* (New York and London: Macmillan, 1973); Schottroff, "Frauen haben nicht geschwiegen" (1992) 45, and a note in Martin Leutzsch, *Die Wahrnehmung sozialer Wirklichkeit im "Hirten des Hermas."* FRLANT 150 (Göttingen: Vandenhoeck & Ruprecht, 1989) 161 n. 26. For a woman pope in the ninth century cf. Joan Morris, *Pope John VIII: an English Woman alias Pope Joan* (London: Vrai, 1985); Gössmann, "Die 'Päpstin Johanna.' Zur vor- und nachreformatorischen Rezeption ihrer Gestalt," in Gössmann and Bauer, eds., *Eva: Verführerin oder Gottes Meisterwerk?* 143–66; eadem, "Zur Rezeptionsgeschichte der Gestalt der Päpstin Johanna," in Elisabeth Moltmann-Wendel, ed., *Weiblichkeit in der Theologie. Verdrängung und Wiederkehr* (Gütersloh: Gerd Mohn, 1988) 93–111; eadem, *Mulier Papa. Der Skandal eines weiblichen Papstes. Zur Rezeptionsgeschichte der Gestalt der Päpstin Johanna.* APTGF 5 (Munich: Iudicium, 1994).

[64] On this cf., for example, Erika Reichle, "Frauenordination," in Claudia Pinl et al., eds., *Frauen auf neuen Wegen. Studien und Problemberichte zur Situation der Frauen in Gesellschaft und Kirche.* Kennzeichen 3 (Gelnhausen and Berlin: Burckhardthaus-Verlag; Stein/Mfr.: Laetare-Verlag, 1978) 103–80; J. Christine Janowsky, "Umstrittene Pfarrerin. Zu einer unvollendeten Reformation der Kirche," in Martin Greiffenhagen, ed., *Das evangelische Pfarrhaus. Eine Kultur- und Sozialgeschichte* (Stuttgart: Kreuz, 1984; 2nd ed. 1991) 83–107; and the "Forschungsprojekt zur Geschichte der Theologinnen Göttingen," begun in 1987, which in 1992 published a Festschrift for Hannelore Erhart's sixty-fifth birthday with essays on this topic: *Querdenken. Beiträge zur feministisch-befreiungstheologischen Diskussion. FS für Hannelore Erhart zum 65. Geburtstag* (Pfaffenweiler: Centaurus, 1992); cf. Rainer Hering, "Frauen auf der Kanzel? Die Auseinandersetzung um Frauenordination und Gleichberechtigung der Theologinnen in der Hamburger Landeskirche. Von der Pfarramtshelferin zur ersten evangelisch-lutherischen Bischöfin der Welt," *ZVHaG* 79 (1993) 163–209.

[65] In 1989 the first woman bishop was consecrated in the Anglican Church (Barbara Harris), and in 1992 the first Lutheran woman bishop (Maria Jepsen) was elected. For the election of the Lutheran bishop cf. the documents and position papers printed in ". . . *das Weib rede in der Gemeinde." Maria Jepsen: Erste lutherische Bischöfin. Dokumente und Stellungnahmen.* GTB 1118 (Gütersloh: Gerd Mohn, 1992); see also Hering, "Frauen auf der Kanzel?" 202ff., especially on the critical situation in Hamburg. Cf. also Field-Bibb, "From Deaconess to Bishop: The Vicissitudes of Women's Ministry in the Protestant Episcopal Church in the USA," *HeyJ* 33 (1992) 61–78.

[66] On this cf. Erich Geldbach, "Frauenordination: Dienst an der Ökumene?" *MdKI* 43 (1992) 103–107, and Martin Conway, "Frauen im Priestertum. Die kurzfristigen Konsequenzen der Entscheidung der Kirche von England für die Frauenordination," *MdKI* 45 (1994) 3–6. For the renewed discussion of the theme of women's ordination see also the third issue of the *Theologische Quartalschrift* for 1993.

[67] Apostolic Letter from Pope John Paul II on the reservation of the priesthood to men, May 22, 1994 *(Ordinatio sacerdotalis)* 6.

[68] Harnack, *Expansion of Christianity* 2:217.

[69] Ibid. 2:228.

[70] Ibid. 2:230.

[71] On this cf. Elisabeth Schüssler Fiorenza, "The Twelve" in Swidler and Swidler, eds., *Women Priests,* 114–22; eadem, "The Apostleship of Women in Early Christianity," in ibid., 135–40; eadem, "Women in the Pre-Pauline and Pauline Churches," *USQR* 33 (1978) 153–66; eadem, "Word, Spirit and Power: Women in Early Christian Communities," in Rosemary Ruether and Eleanor McLaughlin, eds., *Women of Spirit. Female Leadership in the Jewish and Christian Tradition* (New York: Simon & Schuster, 1979) 29–70; eadem, "Der Beitrag der Frau zur urchristlichen Bewegung. Kritische Überlegungen zur Rekonstruktion urchristlicher Geschichte," in Willy Schottroff and Wolfgang Stegemann, eds., *Traditionen der Befreiung. Sozialgeschichtliche Bibelauslegungen.* Vol. 2: *Frauen in der Bibel* (Munich: Kaiser, 1980) 60–90; eadem, *In Memory of Her* (1983); eadem, *Bread not Stone* (1984); eadem, "Anfänge von Kirche" (1987); Schottroff, "Women as Disciples" (1980); eadem, "'Leaders of the Faith' or 'Just Some Pious Womenfolk?'" in eadem, *Let the Oppressed Go Free,* 60–79; eadem, "BotschafterInnen an Christi Statt," in Frithard Scholz and Horst Dickel, eds., *Vernünftiger Gottesdienst. Kirche nach der Barmer Theologischen Erklärung. FS zum 60. Geburtstag von Hans-Gernot Jung* (Göttingen: Vandenhoeck & Ruprecht, 1990) 271–92; eadem, "Dienerinnen der Heiligen. Der Diakonat der Frauen im Neuen Testament," in Gerhard K. Schäfer and Theodor Strohm, eds., *Diakonie – biblische Grundlagen und Orientierungen. Ein Arbeitsbuch.* VDWI 2 (Heidelberg: Heidelberger Verlagsanstalt, 1990) 222–42; eadem, "Wanderprophetinnen. Eine feministische Analyse der Logienquelle," *EvTh* 51 (1991) 332–34; eadem, "Frauen haben nicht geschwiegen" (1992); eadem, "Frauenwiderstand im frühen Christentum," in Frauenforschungsprojekt zur Geschichte der Theologinnen Göttingen, eds., *Querdenken,* 129–59.

[72] Cf., for example, Alfons Weiser, "Die Rolle der Frau in der urchristlichen Mission," in Gerhard Dautzenberg, Helmut Merklein, and Karlheinz Müller, eds., *Die Frau im Urchristentum*. QD 95 (Freiburg, Basel, and Vienna: Herder, 1983) 158–81; Gerhard Dautzenberg, "Zur Stellung der Frauen in den paulinischen Gemeinden," in ibid., 182–224; Herbert Frohnhofen, "Die Stellung der Frau im frühen Christentum," *StZ* 203 (1985) 844–52.

[73] For other assumed causes cf. Witherington, *Women* 211ff.

[74] On this see below: "Christian Women in their Social Context."

[75] Initiatives toward a detailed investigation of the question of women schismatics are found in Zscharnack, *Dienst der Frau* 156ff., and Virginia Burrus, "The Heretical Woman as Symbol in Alexander, Athanasius, Epiphanius, and Jerome" *HThR* 84 (1991) 229–48.

[76] Kalsbach, *Einrichtung* 3.

[77] Ibid. 2.

[78] Cf. Schäfer, *Kanonissenstifter* (1907); idem, "Kanonissen und Diakonissen" (1910).

[79] Schäfer, *Kanonissenstifter* 65.

[80] Most recently by Wolfgang Karl Wischmeyer, *Von Golgatha zum Ponte Molle. Studien zur Sozialgeschichte der Kirche im dritten Jahrhundert.* FKDG 49 (Göttingen: Vandenhoeck & Ruprecht, 1992) 118: "The widows were a special group in the Christian community from New Testament times . . . . Their active participation in care for the community under the title of deaconesses developed differently from time to time and from

place to place within the framework of the development of episcopal organization of deacons. Genuine deaconesses can be found first in the East in the Syrian *Didascalia* (3.12) in the middle of the third century."

[81] Theodor Zahn, *Ignatius von Antiochien* (Gotha: Perthes, 1873) 585.

[82] Zscharnack, *Dienst der Frau* 124–25.

[83] On the office of deaconess in the ancient Church and the early Middle Ages cf. Theodor Schäfer, *Die weibliche Diakonie in ihrem ganzen Umfang dargestellt. I: Die Geschichte der weiblichen Diakonie. Vorträge* (Stuttgart: Verlag von D. Gundert, 1887–94) 1–58; Hans Achelis, "Diakonissen, altkirchliche," *RE³* 4 (1898) 616–20; Zscharnack, *Dienst der Frau* 99ff.; K. Heinrich Schäfer, *Kanonissenstifter* (1907); idem, "Kanonissen und Diakonissen" (1910); Adolf Kalsbach, *Einrichtung* (1926) and his summary: idem, "Diakonisse," *RAC* 3 (1957) 917–28; Evangelos Theodorou, "Η 'ΧΕΙΡΟΤΟΝΙΑ,' Η 'ΧΕΙΡΟΘΕΣΙΑ' ΤΩΝ ΔΙΑΚΟΝΙΣΣΩΝ," *Theologia* 25 (1954) 430–69, 576–601; 26 (1955) 57–76 (= "Die Weihe [Cheirotonia] oder Segnung [Cheirothesia] der Diakonissen," German translation by Anne Jensen); idem, "Das Diakonissenamt in der griechisch-orthodoxen Kirche," in World Council of Churches, *Die Diakonisse. Ein Dienst der Frau in der heutigen Welt.* English: *The Deaconess; a Service of Women in the World of Today.* (Geneva: World Council of Churches, 1966); idem, "Das Amt der Diakoninnen in der kirchlichen Tradition. Ein orthodoxer Beitrag zum Problem der Frauenordination." Translation from Greek, with notes, by Theodor Nikolaou. *US* 33 (1973) 162–72; idem, "Berühmte Diakonissen der byzantinischen Zeit" in *ΙΣΤΟΡΙΑ ΚΑΙ ΘΕΩΡΙΑ ΤΗΣ ΕΚΚΛΗΣΙΑΣΤΙΚΗΣ ΚΟΙΝΩΝΙΚΗΣ ΔΙΑΚΟΝΙΑΣ* (Athens: 1985) 147–64; J. G. Davies, "Deacons, Deaconesses and the Minor Orders in the Patristic Period" *JEH* 14 (1963) 1–15; Bangerter, *Frauen im Aufbruch* 111ff.; G. Ferrari, "La diaconesse nella Traditione Orientale," *OrCr(P)* 14 (1974) 28–50; Peter Hünermann, "Conclusions Regarding the Female Diaconate," *TS* 36 (1975) 325–33; Aimé Georges Martimort, *Deaconesses: An Historical Study.* Translated by K. D. Whitehead (San Francisco: Ignatius Press, 1985); K. K. Fitzgerald, "The Characteristics and Nature of the Order of the Deaconess," in Thomas Hopko, ed., *Women and the Priesthood,* 75–95; M.-J. Aubert, *Des Femmes Diacres. Un Nouveau chemin pour l'Eglise.* Préface de Régine Pernoud. PoTh 47 (Paris: Beauchesne, 1987); Dirk Ansorge, "Der Diakonat der Frau. Zum gegenwärtigen Forschungsstand," in Teresa Berger and Albert Gerhards, eds., *Liturgie und Frauenfrage. Ein Beitrag zur Frauenforschung aus liturgiewissenschaftlicher Sicht.* PiLi 7 (St. Ottilien: EOS Verlag, 1990) 31–65; Joseph Ysebaert, "The deaconesses in the Western Church of late Antiquity and their origin," in G.J.M. Bartelink, A. Hilhorst, and C.H. Kneepkens, eds., *Eulogia: mélanges offerts à Antoon A.R. Bastiaensen à l'occasion de son soixante-cinquième anniversaire.* Instrumenta patristica 24 (Steenbrugge: in Abbatia S. Petri; The Hague: Nijhoff, 1991) 421–36; Anne Jensen, "Diakonin" *WFT* 1991, 58–60; eadem, *God's Self-Confident Daughters* 59–71.

[84] For women as deacons in the New Testament cf. the analytic essay by Gerhard Lohfink, "Weibliche Diakone im Neuen Testament" in Gerhard Lohfink, Helmut Merklein, and Karlheinz Müller, eds., *Die Frau im Urchristentum.* QD 95 (4th ed. Freiburg, Basel, and Vienna: Herder, 1989) 320–38, with a look forward to the early Church; Herbert Frohnhofen, "Weibliche Diakone in der frühen Kirche," *StZ* 204 (1986) 269–78; Elisabeth Schüssler Fiorenza, "The 'Quilting' of Women's History: Phoebe of Cenchreae," in Paula M. Cooey, Sharon A. Farmer, and Mary Ellen Ross, eds., *Embodied Love. Sensuality and Relationship as Feminist Values* (San Francisco: Harper & Row, 1987) 35–49; eadem, "'Waiting at Table': A Critical Feminist Reflection on Diakonia," *Concilium* (Aug. 1988) 84–94; Luise

Schottroff, "BotschafterInnen an Christi Statt" (1990); eadem, "Dienerinnen der Heiligen. Der Diakonat der Frauen im Neuen Testament" (1990); Jennifer H. Stiefel, "Women Deacons in 1 Timothy: A Linguistic and Literary Look at 'Women likewise . . .' (1 Tim 3.11)," *NTS* 41 (1995) 442–57. In principle it must be said of the New Testament in particular that the terms διάκονος and διακονία as well as the verb διακονέω embrace a variety of meanings. On this, see the overviews by H. W. Beyer, "διακονέω κτλ.," *TDNT* 2:81–93, and Alfons Weiser, "διακονέω κτλ.," *EDNT* 1:302–304. On διακονία in Greco-Roman antiquity, early Judaism, and the New Testament cf. the volume of essays edited by G. K. Schäfer and Theodor Strohm, *Diakonie—biblische Grundlagen und Orientierungen. Ein Arbeitsbuch.* VDWI 2 (Heidelberg: Heidelberger Verlagsanstalt, 1990), as well as the extensive study by John N. Collins, *Diakonia. Re-interpreting the Ancient Sources* (New York and Oxford: Oxford University Press, 1990).

[85] Cf., as a representative of this thesis, Martimort, *Deaconesses* 32, 35ff.

[86] Implicit evidence for women deacons in the New Testament includes the διάκονοι in Phil 1:1, obviously present in the Pauline communities, who, in light of the explicit evidence of a διάκονος called Phoebe who is named by Paul (Rom 16:1-2) cannot have been restricted to men. This observation is confirmed for the sphere of Pauline tradition by the women deacons mentioned in 1 Tim 3:11: on this cf. Jürgen Roloff, *Der erste Brief an Timotheus.* EKK XV (Neukirchen-Vluyn: Neukirchener Verlag, 1988) 164ff., and most recently Stiefel, "Women Deacons in 1 Timothy" (1995). For the second century there is a further attestation (in addition to 1 Tim 3:11) in Pliny, *Ep.* X, 96.8.

[87] The first attestation is *Conc. Nic. can.* 19 from the year 325. For the synonymous usage cf. the witness of the inscriptions in ch. 7 below.

[88] For the ordination of deaconesses cf. especially Theodorou, "Die Weihe (Cheirotonia) oder Segnung (Cheirothesia) der Diakonissen" (1954/1955); but see also Adolf Kalsbach, "Die Diakonissenweihe im Kan. 19 des Konzils von Nicäa," *RQ* 32 (1924) 166–69; Friedrich Wiechert, "Die Geschichte der Diakonissenweihe," *EHK* 21 (1939) 57–79; Cipriano Vagaggini, "L'ordinazione delle diaconesse nella tradizione greca e bizantina," *OrChrP* 40 (1974) 145–89; Giorgio Orioli, "Il Testo dell'Ordinazione delle Diaconesse nella Chiesa di Antiochia dei Siri," *Apoll.* 62 (1989) 633–40; Kristin Arat, "Die Weihe der Diakonin in der armenisch-apostolischen Kirche," in Berger and Gerhards, eds., *Liturgie und Frauenfrage* 67–76.

[89] Cf. especially Zscharnack, *Dienst der Frau* (1902) 99ff.; Linus Bopp, *Das Witwentum als organische Gliedschaft im Gemeinschaftsleben der alten Kirche. Ein geschichtlicher Beitrag zur Grundlegung der Witwenseelsorge in der Gegenwart* (Mannheim: 1950); McKenna, *Women of the Church* (1967) 35ff.; Bangerter, *Frauen im Aufbruch* (1971) 65ff.; Bonnie Bowman Thurston, *The Widows. A Women's Ministry in the Early Church* (Minneapolis: Fortress, 1989).

[90] On this see, most recently, Ulrike Wagener, *Die Ordnung des "Hauses Gottes." Der Ort von Frauen in der Ekklesiologie und Ethik der Pastoralbriefe.* WUNT 65 (Tübingen: Mohr, 1994) 115ff.

[91] Thus, for example, Leenhardt and Blanke, *Stellung der Frau* 64; Alexander Sand, "Witwenstand und Ämterstrukturen in den urchristlichen Gemeinden," *BiLe* 12 (1971) 186–97.

[92] Thus, most recently, Wagener, *Ordnung des "Hauses Gottes,"* 115ff.; see also, for example, Johannes Müller-Bardorff, "Zur Exegese von I. Timotheus 5,3-16," in *Gott und*

die Götter. FS für Erich Fascher (Berlin: 1958) 113–33, and Hans-Werner Bartsch, *Die Anfänge urchristlicher Rechtsbildungen. Studien zu den Pastoralbriefen.* ThF 34 (Hamburg-
Bergstedt: H. Reich, 1965) 112, 114, 117ff.

[93] *Die ältesten Quellen des orientalischen Kirchenrechts II: Die syrische Didaskalia,
übers. und erkl. v. Hans Achelis und Johannes Flemming.* TU 25,2 (Leipzig: J. C. Hinrichs,
1904) 276.

[94] Explicit descriptions are given, for example, by Fangauer, *Frauenheldentum* (1922);
Leipoldt, *Frau* (1954); Klaus Thraede, "Frau," *RAC* 8 (1972) 197–269; idem, "Ärger mit der
Freiheit. Die Bedeutung von Frauen in Theorie und Praxis der alten Kirche," in Gerta Scharf-
fenorth and Klaus Thraede, eds., *"Freunde in Christus werden . . . ." Die Beziehung von
Mann und Frau als Frage an Theologie und Kirche.* Kennzeichen 1 (Gelnhausen and Berlin:
Burckhardthaus Verlag, 1977) 31–178; James Donaldson, *Woman; Her Position and Influ-
ence in Ancient Greece and Rome, and among Early Christians* (New York and London:
Longmans, Green, 1907; reprint New York: Gordon, 1973); Gryson, *Ministry* (1976) 112;
Heiler, *Frau* (1977); Tetlow, *Women and Ministry* (1980); Witherington, *Women* (1989).

[95] Important overviews of the history of women in antiquity are Thraede, "Frau"
(1972), Sarah B. Pomeroy, *Goddesses, Whores, Wives, and Slaves. Women in Classical Antiquity* (New York: Schocken, 1975; 9th ed. 1985); Wolfgang Schuller, *Frauen in der
griechischen Geschichte.* Konstanzer Bibliothek 3 (Konstanz: Universitätsverlag Konstanz,
1985); idem, *Frauen in der römischen Geschichte* (Konstanz: Universitätsverlag Konstanz,
1992; note the expanded bibliography on pp. 156–59). See also Jane F. Gardner, *Women in
Roman Law and Society* (London: Croom Helm; Bloomington: Indiana University Press,
1986). Noteworthy also are the text collections by Mary R. Lefkowitz and Maureen B. Fant,
Women's Life in Greece and Rome. A Source Book in Translation (London: Duckworth, and
Baltimore: Johns Hopkins University Press, 1982; 2nd ed. 1985), and Ross S. Kraemer,
Maenads (1988). For further literature see the bibliographies by Leanna Goodwater, *Women
in Antiquity. An Annotated Bibliography* (Metuchen, N. J.: Scarecrow Press, 1976); Marylin
B. Arthur, "Classics," *Signs* 2 (1976) 382–403; Pomeroy, "Women in Roman Egypt. A pre-
liminary study based on papyri," in Helene P. Foley, ed., *Reflections on Women in Antiquity*
(New York: Gordon and Breach Science Publishers, 1981; 2nd ed. 1984) 303–22.

[96] Cf. especially Ernst Kornemann, *Grosse Frauen des Altertums. Im Rahmen
zweitausendjährigen Weltgeschehens.* Sammlung Dietrich 86 (Wiesbaden: Dietrich, 1952).
In the same direction J.P.V.D. Balsdon, *Roman Women: Their History and Habits* (London:
Bodley Head, 1962; 5th ed. 1977); Schuller, *Frauen in der griechischen Geschichte*—so
also Sarah Pomeroy in her review in *Gnomon* 59 (1985) 277–78; Schuller, *Frauen in der
römischen Geschichte.*

[97] Gössmann, "Frauenforschung," 20, quoted from a lecture by Helga Bilden.

[98] On this see the extensive essay, with review of the state of research, by Schmitt Pantel, "Difference Between the Sexes." Similarly also Newton, "History as Usual?" 107ff.;
Lynda L. Coon, Katherine J. Haldane, and Elisabeth W. Sommer, "Introduction" to *That
Gentle Strength* 10: "Separation of the sexes remained the ideal, but in reality women
worked with men. Thus the separation was only theoretical . . . ."

[99] On this see Susan Treggiari,"Jobs for Women," *American Journal of Ancient History*
1 (1976) 76–104; Ramsay MacMullen, "Women in Public in the Roman Empire," *Hist* 29
(1980) 208–18; Natalie Kampen, *Image and Status: Roman Working Women in Ostia*
(Berlin: Mann, 1981; Rosmarie Günther, *Frauenarbeit– Frauenbindung. Untersuchungen*

zu unfreien und freigelassenen Frauen in den stadtrömischen Inschriften. Veröffentlichungen des Historischen Instituts der Universität Mannheim 9 (Munich: W. Fink, 1987); Monika Eichenauer, *Untersuchungen zur Arbeitswelt der Frau in der römischen Antike.* EHS.G. 360 (Frankfurt and New York: Peter Lang, 1988). On the businesswomen see also Gardner, *Women in Roman Law and Society* 233–55.

[100] Wayne A. Meeks, *The First Urban Christians. The Social World of the Apostle Paul* (New Haven: Yale University Press, 1983) 24.

[101] Otto Braunstein, *Die politische Wirksamkeit der griechischen Frau. Eine Nachwirkung griechischen Mutterrechtes* (Leipzig: Druck von A. Hoffmann, in kommission bei G. Fock, 1911) 9.

[102] Cf., for example, R. A. Kearsley, "Women in Public Life in the Roman East: Iunia Theodora, Claudia Metrodora and Phoibe, Benefactress of Paul," *Ancient Society* (Macquarie University) 15 (1985) 124–37, and Paul R. Trebilco, *Jewish Communities in Asia Minor.* MSSNTS 69 (New York: Cambridge University Press, 1991) 113–26.

[103] On this cf. Michael Wörrle, *Stadt und Fest im kaiserzeitlichen Kleinasien. Studien zu einer agonistischen Stiftung aus Oinoanda.* Vestigia 39 (Munich: C. H. Beck, 1988) 101–102.

[104] On this cf. S. L. Mohler, "Feminism in the Corpus Inscriptionum Latinarum," *CIW* 25 (1932) 113–17; Geza Alföldy, *Flamines provinciae hispaniae citerioris.* Anejos de Archivo Español de Arqueologia VI (Madrid: Consejo Superior de Investigaciones Científicas, Instituto Español de Arqueología, 1973) 49ff.

[105] Cf., for example, Georg Luck, "Die Dichterinnen der griechischen Anthologie" (1954) in Gerhard Pfohl, ed., *Das Epigramm. Zur Geschichte einer inschriftlichen und literarischen Gattung* (Darmstadt: Wissenschaftliche Buchgesellschaft, 1969) 85–109; Elfriede W. Tielsch, "Die Philosophin. Geschichte und Ungeschichte ihres Berufsstandes seit der Antike," in Halina Bendkowski and Brigitte Weisshaupt, eds., *Was Philosophinnen denken. Eine Dokumentation* (Zürich: Ammann, 1986), 309–28; Dronke, *Women Writers;* Marilyn Bailey Ogilvie, *Women in Science. Antiquity through the Nineteenth Century. A Biographical Dictionary with Annotated Bibliography* (Cambridge, Mass., and London: M.I.T. Press, 1986; 2nd ed. 1988); Margaret Alic, *Hypatia's Heritage: A History of Women in Science from Antiquity through the Nineteenth Century* (Boston: Beacon, 1986); the essays edited by Mary Ellen Waithe since 1987 under the series title *A History of Women Philosophers,* covering the period from 600 B.C.E. to the present (vol. 1, 600 B.C.E.–500 C.E. deals with ancient philosophers); see also the review of the first three volumes by Rose Staudt in *Die Philosophin* 4 (1993) 87–89. Staudt writes that Waithe "is aware that the *History* is not complete and hopes that it will be the starting point for further researches." See also vol. 1 of *Hypatia* (1989), with the special issue "The History of Women in Philosophy" edited by Linda Lopez McAlister and dedicated to Veda Cobb-Stevens (1948–1989), "founder of the Society for the Study of Women Philosophers." Jane McIntosh Snyder, *The Woman and the Lyre. Women Writers in Classical Greece and Rome* (Carbondale and Edwardsville, Ill.: Southern Illinois University Press, 1989) devotes ch. 4 (pp. 99–121) to ancient women philosophers; see also Ferrucio Bertini, ed., *Medioevo al femminile* (Rome: Laterza, 1989; German: *Heloise und ihre Schwestern. Acht Frauenporträts aus dem Mittelalter.* Translated by Ernst Voltmer [Munich: Beck, 1991]).

[106] For women's education in Rome see especially Ludwig Friedländer, *Darstellungen aus der Sittengeschichte Roms in der Zeit von Augustus bis zum Ausgang der Antonine.* 4

vols (10th ed. Leipzig: Hirzel, 1921–23) 1:269ff., and Anne E. Hickey, *Women of the Roman Aristocracy as Christian Monastics.* SR(AA) 1 (Ann Arbor: UMI Research Press, 1987) 61ff. For Greek-speaking women of the classical period see Edith Specht, *Schön zu sein und gut zu sein. Mädchenbildung und Frauensozialisation im antiken Griechenland.* Reihe Frauenforschung 9 (Vienna: Wiener Frauenverlag, 1989); for the classical and Hellenistic period see especially Susan G. Cole, "Could Greek Women Read and Write?" in Helene P. Foley, ed., *Reflections on Women in Antiquity* 219–45. For the history of education in antiquity in general see Henri-Irénée Marrou, *Histoire de l' éducation dans l' antiquité* (3rd ed. Paris: Editions du Seuil, 1955).

[107] Ross S. Kraemer, *Ecstatics and Ascetics: Studies in the Functions of Religious Activities for Women in the Greco-Roman World* (Ann Arbor: University Microfilms, 1978); eadem, "The Conversion of Women to Ascetic Forms of Christianity," *Signs* 6 (1980) 298–307; eadem, "Women in the Religions of the Greco-Roman World," *RSR* 9 (1983) 127–39 (with bibliography); eadem, "A New Inscription from Malta and the Question of Women Elders in the Diaspora Jewish Communities," *HThR* 78 (1985) 431–38; eadem, "Non-Literary Evidence for Jewish Women in Rome and Egypt," in M. B. Skinner, ed., *Rescuing Creusa: New Methodological Approaches to Women in Antiquity.* Special number of the periodical *Helios*, n.s. 13/2 (1986) 85–101; eadem, "Hellenistic Jewish Women: The Epigraphical Evidence," *SBL Seminar Papers* (1986) 183–200; eadem, "Monastic Jewish Women in Greco-Roman Egypt: Philo Judaeus on the Therapeutrides," *Signs* 14 (1989) 342–70; eadem, *Her Share of the Blessings. Women's Religions among Pagans, Jews, and Christians in the Greco-Roman World* (New York and Oxford: Oxford University Press, 1992).

[108] Kraemer, *Her Share of the Blessings* 4.

[109] On this see ibid., 191ff.

[110] On this see especially Judith Plaskow, "Blaming Jews for Inventing Patriarchy," *Lilith* 7 (1980) 11–12; eadem, "Christian Feminism and Anti-Judaism," *Cross Currents* 33 (1978) 306–309; Bernadette Brooten, "Jüdinnen zur Zeit Jesu. Ein Plädoyer für Differenzierung," in Bernadette J. Brooten and Norbert Greinacher, eds., *Frauen in der Männerkirche* (Munich: Kaiser, 1982) 141–48; eadem, "Jewish Women's History in the Roman Period: A Task for Christian Theology," *HThR* 79 (1986) 22–30; Monika Fander, "Frauen im Urchristentum am Beispiel Palästinas," *JBTh* 7 (1992) 165–85, at 180ff.; also the collected volumes, one edited by Christine Schaumberger, *Weil wir nicht vergessen wollen . . . zu einer Feministischen Theologie im deutschen Kontext.* AnFragen 1. Diskussionen Feministischer Theologie (Münster: Morgana, 1987) and the other edited by Leonore Siegele-Wenschkewitz, *Verdrängte Vergangenheit, die uns bedrängt. Feministische Theologie in der Verantwortung für die Geschichte* (Munich: Kaiser, 1988). For a development of the history of Judaism from a feminist point of view see the collected volumes *On Being a Jewish Feminist* (New York: Schocken, 1983), edited by Susannah Heschel, and *"Women Like This." New Perspectives on Jewish Women in the Greco-Roman World* (Atlanta: Scholars, 1991), edited by Amy-Jill Levine, as well as the Jewish-feminist theology in Judith Plaskow, *Standing Again at Sinai. Judaism from a Feminist Perspective* (San Francisco: Harper & Row, 1990).

[111] On this cf. the general overview of the state of research in Kraemer, *Her Share of the Blessings* 93–127. She writes: "Strikingly different portraits both of Jewish women and women's Judaism emerge from ancient rabbinic sources on the one hand, and inscriptional,

archaeological, and neglected Greek literary sources from the Greco-Roman period on the other. Rabbinic writings have led many scholars to conclude that Jewish women led restricted, secluded lives and were excluded from much of the rich ritual life of Jewish men, especially from the study of Torah. Evidence from the Greco-Roman Diaspora suggests, however, that at least some Jewish women played active religious, social, economic, and even political roles in the public lives of Jewish communities" (ibid., 93).

[112] Günter Mayer, *Die jüdische Frau in der hellenistisch-römischen Antike* (Stuttgart, Berlin, Cologne, and Mainz: Kohlhammer, 1987). He does include inscriptions and papyri as well. See especially his ch. 7: "Women in Public," 85–87, and ch. 8: "Women in the Cult," 88–91.

[113] Mayer, *Jüdische Frau* 90.

[114] Cf. Bernadette Brooten, *Women Leaders in the Ancient Synagogue. Inscriptional Evidence and Background Issues* (Chico: Scholars, 1982); eadem, "Jüdinnen zur Zeit Jesu" (1982); eadem, "Jewish Women's History" (1986); Ross S. Kraemer, "Non-Literary Evidence" (1986); eadem, "Jewish Women" (1986). But see also Luise Schottroff, "'Leaders of the Faith'" (1987). Brooten's findings were acknowledged and confirmed by Trebilco, *Jewish Communities* (1991) 104ff., and by Pieter W. van der Horst, *Ancient Jewish Epitaphs. An Introductory Survey of a Millennium of Jewish Funerary Epigraphy (300 BCE–700 CE)*. Contributions to Biblical Exegesis and Theology 2 (Kampen: Kok Pharos, 1991) 105ff. For the history of Jewish women in late antiquity and their recognition in scholarship see also Brooten, "The Gender of Ιαηλ in the Jewish Inscription from Aphrodisias," in Harold W. Attridge et al., eds., *Of Scribes and Scrolls: Essays in Honor of John Strugnell* (Lanham, Md.: University Press of America, 1990) 163–73; eadem, "Ιαελ προστάτης in the Jewish Donative Inscription of Aphrodisias," in Birger A. Pearson, ed., *The Future of Early Christianity. Essays in Honor of Helmut Koester* (Minneapolis: Fortress, 1991) 149–62.

[115] Cf. especially Brooten, "Konnten Frauen im alten Judentum die Scheidung betreiben? Überlegungen zu Mk 10,11-12 und 1 Kor 7,10-11," *EvTh* 42 (1982) 65–80; eadem, "Zur Debatte über das Scheidungsrecht der jüdischen Frau," *EvTh* 43 (1983) 466–78.

[116] Fander, "Feministische Bibellektüre," 305. On this see also eadem, *Frau im Markusevangelium* 200ff. and eadem, "Frauen im Urchristentum," 182ff.

[117] G. H. R. Horsley, *New Documents Illustrating Early Christianity*. 5 vols. Vol. 1: *A Review of the Greek Inscriptions and Papyri published in 1976* (North Ryde, N.S.W.: Macquarie Ancient History Association, 1981) 120 no. 79. Cf. also the initial work by Carl M. Kaufmann, *Handbuch der altchristlichen Epigraphik* (Freiburg: Herder, 1917) 282ff.; Gryson, *Ministry* 90–91; Morris, *The Lady Was a Bishop* 4–8; Irvin, "Ministry" (1980).

Collections of epigraphic witnesses to women officeholders that do not, however, publish the whole texts of the inscriptions or offer further commentary are Charles Pietri, "Appendice Prosopographique à la Roma Christiana (311–440)," *MEFRA* 89 (1977) 371–415 for Rome from 311–440, and Konstantina Mentzu-Meimare, "Ἡ παρουσία τῆς γυναίκας στίς Ἑλληνικές επιγραφές, από τόν Δ´ μέχρι τόν Γ´ μ.Χ. αιωνα (sic)," *JÖB* 32/2 (1982) 433–43. The studies by Wischmeyer, *Die archäologischen und literarischen Quellen zur Kirchengeschichte von Apulia et Calabria, Lucania et Bruttii bis zum Jahr 600. Sammlung und Auswertung von Materialien zur Geschichte zweier spätantiker Provinzen*. Dissertation in typescript (Essen, 1972), and Yiannis Meimaris, *Sacred Names, Saints, Martyrs and Church Officials in the Greek Inscriptions and Papyri pertaining to the Christian Church of Palestine*. ΜΕΛΕΤΗΜΑΤΑ 2 (Athens: National Hellenic Research Foundation, Centre for

Greek and Roman Antiquity, 1986) collected and evaluated inscriptions in connection with questions related to local history; however, epigraphic witnesses to officeholders, both women and men, are considered.

[118] For an introduction to Christian epigraphy cf. the handbooks by Orazio Marucchi, *Christian Epigraphy. An Elementary Treatise with a Collection of Ancient Christian Inscriptions Mainly of Roman Origin.* Translated by J. Armine Willis (Chicago: Ares Publishers, 1974; original publication 1910); Kaufmann, *Epigraphik*; Felice Grossi Gondi, *Trattato di epigrafia cristiana latina e greca del mondo romano occidentale. I. Monumenti Cristiani dei Primi sei Secoli I* (Rome: Università Gregoriana, 1968; reprint of the 1920 edition); Pasquale Testini, *Archeologia cristiana; nozioni generali dalle origini alla fine del sec. VI* (Rome: Desclée, 1958; 2nd ed. with analytic index and bibliographic appendix Bari: Edipuglia, 1980). But see also the essays by Gerhard Pfohl, "Grabinschrift I (griechische)," *RAC* 12 (1983) 467–514, at 495ff. (on Greek Christian inscriptions); Charles Pietri, "Grabinschrift II (lateinisch)," translated by Josef Engemann, *RAC* 12 (1983) 514–90, at 548ff. (on Latin Christian inscriptions); for Byzantine epigraphy cf. especially Ladislav Besevliev, "Probleme der byzantinischen Epigraphik," in Johannes Irmscher and Kurt Treu, eds., *Das Korpus der Griechischen Christlichen Schriftsteller. Historie, Gegenwart, Zukunft. Eine Aufsatzsammlung.* TU 120 (Berlin: Akademie Verlag, 1977) 179–82; Emilian Popescu, "Griechische Inschriften," in Friedhelm Winkelmann and Wolfram Brandes, eds., *Quellen zur Geschichte des frühen Byzanz (4.–9. Jahrhundert). Bestand und Probleme.* BBA 55 (Amsterdam: Gieben, 1990) 81–105; and for an introduction to the epigraphy of the Middle Ages and the early modern period cf. Rudolf M. Kloos, *Einführung in die Epigraphik des Mittelalters und der frühen Neuzeit* (Darmstadt: Wissenschaftliche Buchgesellschaft, 1980).

For a general introduction to Greek epigraphy cf. Wilhelm Larfeld, *Handbuch der griechischen Epigraphik.* 2 vols. (Leipzig: O. R. Reisland, 1898–1907); J. J. E. Hondius, *Saxa loquuntur. Inleiding tot de Grieksche Epigraphiek* (Leiden: A.W. Sijthoff, 1938); A. G. Woodhead, *The Study of Greek Inscriptions* (Cambridge: Cambridge University Press, 1959); and for an introduction to Latin epigraphy see especially Ernst Meyer, *Einführung in die lateinische Epigraphik* (2nd ed. Darmstadt: Wissenschaftliche Buchgesellschaft, 1983), and Knud P. Almar, *Inscriptiones Latinae. Eine illustrierte Einführung in die lateinische Epigraphik.* OUCS 14 (Odense: Odense University Press, 1990). An excellent and indispensable aid to epigraphic work is the bibliography edited by François Bérard et al., *Guide de l'Epigraphiste. Bibliographie choisie des épigraphies antiques et médiévales.* Bibliothèque de l'Ecole normale supérieure, Guides et Inventaires Bibliographiques II (Paris: Presses de l'Ecole normale supérieure, 1986).

[119] Wolfgang Wischmeyer, *Griechische und lateinische Inschriften zur Sozialgeschichte der Alten Kirche.* TKTG 28 (Gütersloh: Gerd Mohn, 1982) 21.

[120] Pieter W. van der Horst, "Das Neue Testament und die jüdischen Grabinschriften aus hellenistisch-römischer Zeit," *BZ* 36 (1992) 161–78, at 161. Women are mentioned in some forty percent of Jewish inscriptions; on this see also Kraemer, "Non-Literary Evidence," 85–87, and her tables on the percentage share of women and men in Jewish inscriptions, arranged by region. For Jewish inscriptions cf. the *Corpus Inscriptionum Iudaicarum. Recueil des Inscriptions juives qui vont du IIIᵉ siècle avant Jésus-Christ au VIIᵉ siècle de notre ère,* 2 vols. (Vatican City: Pontificio istituto di archeologia cristiana, 1936, 1952), edited by Jean-Baptiste Frey, as well as the *Jewish Inscriptions of Graeco-Roman Egypt* published by William Horbury and David Noy (Cambridge and New York: Cambridge University Press, 1992). For an introduction to ancient Jewish epigraphy cf. van der Horst, *Ancient Jewish Epitaphs.*

[121] For geographically comprehensive corpora of Greek and Latin inscriptions incorporating primarily Christian inscriptions, see especially:

• The *Inscriptiones Latinae Christianae Veteres (ILCV)*, 3 vols., edited by Ernst Diehl (1925–1931), with a new, revised edition (Dublin and Zürich: Weidmann, 1961) by Roland Gründel and Jacques Moreau and a supplement edited by Jacques Moreau and Henri Marrou (Zürich: Weidmann, 1967). Antonio Ferrua's corrections appeared in 1981 (*Nuove Correzioni alla Silloge del Diehl Inscriptiones Latinae Christianae Veteres*. SSAC 7. Vatican City: Pontificio Istituto di archeologia cristiana, 1981).

• The *Bulletin Epigraphique (BE)* edited by Jeanne and Louis Robert, appearing as part of the *Revue des Etudes Grecques (REG)* since 1938, offers an annual report by Denis Feissel on the "Inscriptions chrétiennes et byzantines." The *Bulletin Epigraphique* has been reprinted in 10 volumes (Paris: Les belles lettres, 1972–1982), and the Institut Fernand Courby from Lyons has published indexes: *I. Les mots grecs* (Paris: Les belles lettres, 1972); *II. Les publications* (Paris: Les belles lettres, 1974); *III: Les mots français* (Paris: Institut Fernand Courby, 1975). Jean Marcillet-Jaubert and Anne-Marie Verilhac edited in a single volume an *Index du Bulletin épigraphique 1966–1973. Mots grecs, Publications, Mots français* (Paris: Les belles lettres, 1971), and the same for *BE* 1974–1977 (Paris: Les belles lettres, 1983).

• Margherita Guarducci, *Epigrafia Greca IV. Epigrafi Sacre Pagane e Cristiane* (Rome: Istituto poligrafico dello Stato, Libreria dello Stato, 1978).

• The *New Documents Illustrating Early Christianity* edited by G. H. R. Horsley (North Ryde, N.S.W.: Macquarie Ancient History Association, 1981–1989) and continued after 1992 by S. R. Llewelyn, with the assistance of R. A. Kearsley (*New Documents Illustrating Early Christianity*. Vol. 6: *A Review of the Greek Inscriptions and Papyri published in 1980–81;* Vol. 7: *A Review of the Greek Inscriptions and Papyri published in 1982–8* [North Ryde, N.S.W.: Macquarie University, 1992, 1994]).

[122] For Greek Christian inscriptions in Asia Minor cf. especially Franz Cumont, "Les inscriptions chrétiennes de l'Asie Mineure," *MAH* 15 (1895) 245–99; Josef Keil and Anton von Premerstein, *Reisen in Lydien*. 3 vols. DAWW.PH 53/2; 54/2; 57/1 (Vienna: In Kommission bei A. Hölder, 1908–1914); John G. C. Anderson, Franz Cumont, and Henri Grégoire, *Studia Pontica III, Fasc. 1: Recueil des inscriptions grecques et latines du Pont et de l'Arménie* (Brussels: 1910); Henri Grégoire, *Recueil des inscriptions grecques chrétiennes d'Asie Mineure* I (Amsterdam: A. M. Hakkert, 1968 [reprint of the Paris edition of 1922]). The second volume never appeared. See also the "Lexique explicatif du Recueil des inscriptions grecques chrétiennes d'Asie Mineure," *Byz* 4 (1927/28) 53–136 prepared by E. Hanson; C. H. E. Haspels, *The Highlands of Phrygia. Sites and Monuments*. 2 vols. (Vol. 1: *The Text*; Vol. 2: *The Plates*. Princeton: Princeton University Press, 1971); Elsa Gibson, "Montanist Epitaphs at Uçak," *GRBS* 16 (1975) 433–42; eadem, *The "Christians for Christians" Inscriptions of Phrygia. Greek Texts, Translation and Commentary*. HThS 32 (Missoula: Scholars, 1978); Marc Waelkens, *Die kleinasiatischen Türsteine. Typologische und epigraphische Untersuchungen der kleinasiatischen Grabreliefs mit Scheintür* (Mainz: P. von Zabern, 1986); Gilbert Dagron and Denis Feissel, *Inscriptions de Cilicie*. TMCB. Collège de France, Monographies 4 (Paris: De Boccard, 1987), as well as numerous individual publications in various periodicals and festschrifts: see the bibliography at the end of this book. See also the study by William M. Ramsay, *The Cities and Bishoprics of Phrygia. Being an Essay of The Local History of Phrygia from the Earliest Times to the*

Turkish Conquest. 2 vols. (Oxford: Clarendon Press, 1895, 1897), rich in epigraphic sources, and Victor Schultze, *Altchristliche Städte und Landschaften. II. Kleinasien.* 2 vols. (Gütersloh: Gerd Mohn, 1922, 1926). Christian inscriptions from Asia Minor are also found in the major series of published inscriptions:

• *Tituli Asiae Minoris (TAM)*, edited by Ernst Kalinka et al., published since 1901 by the Österreichische Akademie der Wissenschaften: a regional corpus.

• *Monumenta Asiae Minoris Antiqua (MAMA)*, edited by William M. Calder et al., published 1928–1962 by Manchester University Press in 8 vols. in the series Publications of the American Society for Archaeological Research in Asia Minor.

• *Inschriften griechischer Städte aus Kleinasien (IK)*, appearing under the direction of Reinhold Merkelbach since 1972 under the auspices of the Kommission für die archäologische Erforschung Kleinasiens of the Österreichischen Akademie der Wissenschaften.

For names in Asia Minor see especially Ladislav Zgusta, *Kleinasiatische Personennamen* (Prague: Verlag der Tschechoslowakischen Akademie der Wissenschaften, 1964); idem, *Neue Beiträge zur kleinasiatischen Anthroponymie* (Prague: Academia, 1970). For the Greek inscriptions in Lycia see the special grammar by Karl Hauser, *Grammatik der griechischen Inschriften Lykiens* (Basel: Buchdruckerei E. Birkhäuser, 1916).

[123] For Greek Christian inscriptions in Egypt see the corpora edited by M. G. Lefebvre, *Recueil des inscriptions grecques-chrétiennes d'Egypte* (Cairo: Impr. de l'Institut français d'archéologie orientale, 1907), and Jadwiga Kubinska, *Faras IV. Inscriptions grecques chrétiennes* (Warsaw: 1974) (Christian inscriptions from the Sudan from the eighth to the twelfth centuries). S. Kent Brown,"Coptic and Greek Inscriptions from Christian Egypt: A Brief Review," in Birger A. Pearson and James E. Goehring, eds., *The Roots of Egyptian Christianity* (Philadelphia: Fortress, 1986) 26–41, at 26 rightly laments the difficulty of access to Egyptian Christian inscriptions because of the paucity of published inscriptional corpora. For the names cf. Friedrich Preisigke, *Namenbuch, enthaltend alle griechischen, lateinischen, ägyptischen usw. Menschennamen, soweit sie in griechischen Urkunden (Papyri, Ostraka, Inschriften, Mumienschildern usw.) Ägyptens sich vorfinden* (Heidelberg: by the author, 1922) and the supplement by Daniele Foraboschi, *Onomasticon alterum papyrologicum. Supplemento al Namenbuch di Friedrich Preisigke.* TDSA 16, Serie papirologica 2 (Milan: Istituto editoriale Cisalpino, 1967). Cf. also the instructive bibliography of Greek inscriptions in Egypt by Etienne Bernard, "Le Corpus des inscriptions grecques de l'Egypte," *ZPE* 26 (1977) 95–117.

[124] For Greek Christian inscriptions in Syria cf. especially Enno Littman, David Magie, and Duane Reed Stuart, eds., *Syria. Publications of the Princeton University Archaeological Expeditions to Syria in 1904–5 and 1909, Division III. Greek and Latin Inscriptions. A. Southern Syria* (Leiden: E. J. Brill, 1904–1921), abbreviated *Syria-Princeton III A.* Christian inscriptions are also to be found in the *Inscriptions grecques et latines de la Syrie (IGLS)* edited by Louis Jalabert, René Mouterde, and J.-P. Rey-Coquais (Paris: P. Geuthner, 1929–1982). See also the bibliography of Greek and Latin inscriptions in Syria by Wilfried van Rengen, "L'épigraphie grecque et latine de Syrie. Bilan d'un quart de siècle de recherches épigraphiques," *ANRW* II/8 (1977) 31–53.

For Greek Christian inscriptions in Palestine cf. especially Albrecht Alt, *Die griechischen Inschriften der Palaestina tertia westlich der ʾAraba* (Berlin and Leipzig: Walter de Gruyter, 1921); Peter Thomsen, *Die lateinischen und griechischen Inschriften der Stadt Jerusalem und ihrer nächsten Umgebung* (Leipzig: J. C. Hinrichs, 1922); D. Reginetta Canova, *Is-*

crizioni e monumenti protocristiani del paese di Moab. SSAC 4 (Vatican City: Pontificio Istituto di archeologia cristiana, 1954); Avraham Negev, *The Greek Inscriptions from the Negev.* SBF.CMi 25 (Jerusalem: Franciscan Printing Press, 1981); Yiannis E. Meimaris, *Sacred Names, Saints, Martyrs and Church Officials in the Greek Inscriptions and Papyri pertaining to the Christian Church of Palestine.* ΜΕΛΕΤΗΜΑΤΑ 2 (Athens: National Hellenic Research Foundation, Centre for Greek and Roman Antiquity, 1986); G. Mussies, "Christelijke Inscripties in Palestina," in Roelof van den Broek et al., eds., *Kerk en kerk en in Romeins-Byzantijns Palestina. Archeologie en geschiedenis.* Palestina Antiqua deel 6 (Kampen: Kok, 1988) 186–211. For Greek Christian inscriptions in Arabia cf. Charles B. Welles, "The Inscriptions of Gerasa," in Carl H. Kraeling, ed., *Gerasa. City of the Decapolis* (New Haven: American Schools of Oriental Research, 1938), 355–616. For Semitic names in Greek inscriptions and papyri of the Near East cf. Heinz Wuthnow, *Die semitischen Menschennamen in griechischen Inschriften und Papyri des Vorderen Orients* (Leipzig: Dietrich, 1930).

[125] Popescu, "Griechische Inschriften," 83.

[126] For Greek Christian inscriptions in Greece cf. especially Charles Bayet, *De titulis Atticae christianis antiquissimis. Commentatio historica et epigraphica* (Paris: 1878); Nikos A. Bees, *Corpus der griechisch christlichen Inschriften von Hellas. Inschriften von Peloponnes, 1. Isthmos – Korinthos* (Chicago: Ares, 1978; original publication 1941). The planned *Corpus der griechisch christlichen Inschriften von Hellas* in 9 volumes unfortunately never extended beyond this initial volume. See also J. S. Creaghan and A. E. Raubitschek, "Early Christian Epitaphs from Athens," *Hesp* 16 (1947) 1–54; and Anastasius C. Bandy, *The Greek Christian Inscriptions of Crete* (Athens: Christian Archaeological Society, 1970). For the Greek names in the Aegean islands see Peter M. Fraser and Elaine Matthews, *A Lexicon of Greek Personal Names. I: The Aegean Islands, Cyprus, Cyrenaica* (Oxford: Clarendon Press, 1987).

[127] For Greek Christian inscriptions in Macedonia cf. especially Denis Feissel, *Recueil des inscriptions chrétiennes de Macédoine du IIIe au VIe siècle.* BCH Supplément 8 (Paris: Dépositaire, Diffusion de Boccard, 1983). For Philippi in particular see Paul Lemerle, *Philippes et la Macédoine orientale à l'époque chrétienne et byzantine.* Recherches d'Histoire et d'Archéologie (Paris: E. de Boccard, 1945); Charalampos Bakirtzis, "Exposition des Antiquités Paléochrétiennes au Musée des Philippes," *Athens Annals of Archaeology* 13 (1980) 90–98.

[128] On this cf. Popescu, "Griechische Inschriften," 83.

[129] Latin Christian inscriptions from Italy outside of Rome are found in collections such as the *Corpus Inscriptionum Latinarum (CIL); Inscriptiones Latinae Christianae Veteres (ILCV);* and Carolus Wessel, *Inscriptiones graecae christianae veteres occidentis. Curaverunt Antonio Ferrua et Carolus Carletti* (Bari: Edipuglia, 1988).

For Rome see especially Giovanni Baptista de Rossi, ed., *Inscriptiones christianae urbis Romae septimo saeculo antiquiores (ICUR),* 3 vols. (Rome: Ex Officina Libraria Pontificia, 1857–1915), and the supplement to Vol. 1 provided by Joseph Gatti (Rome: Ex Officina Libraria aem Cuggiani, 1915), as well as the new series now including eleven volumes *(ICURns),* initiated by Angelus Silvagni in 1922 and continued since the 3d vol. (1956) by Antonio Ferrua et al (Rome: Ex Officina Libraria Doct. Befani, 1922–1985). For *ICURns* 1 cf. the expansions and corrections by Ferrua, *Corona di osservazioni alle iscrizioni cristine di Roma incertae originis.* MPARA 3 (Vatican City: Tipografia poliglotta vaticana, 1979). In addition see Carlo Carletti, *Iscrizioni cristiane inedite del cimitero di*

Bassilla "ad S. Hermetem." MPARA 2 (Vatican City: Tipografia poliglotta vaticana, 1976); idem, *Iscrizioni cristiane de Roma. Testimonianze di vita cristina (secoli III–VII).* BPat 7 (Florence: Nardini: Centro internazionale del libro, 1986).

For the Greek Christian inscriptions in Sicily cf. Vincentius Strazzula, *Mvsevm Epigraphicvm seu Inscriptionvm Christianarvm, quae in Siracusanis catacumbis repertae sunt. Corpusculum.* Documenti alla Storia di Sicilia III/3 (Panormi: 1897); Santi Luigi Agnello, *Silloge di Iscrizioni Paleocristiane della Sicilia* (Rome: "L'Erma" di Bretschneider, 1953); and idem, "Scoperte e studi di Epigrafia cristiana in Sicilia," *Atti del VI congresso internazionale di archeologia cristiana* (1962; 1965) 215–22, a bibliography of the Christian inscriptions in Sicily; also Maria Teresa Manni Piraino, *Iscrizioni greche lapidarie del Museo di Palermo.* ΣΙΚΕΛΙΚΑ VI (Palermo: S. F. Flaccovio, 1972).

For the Greek Christian inscriptions in Gaul cf. especially the works by Edmond le Blant, *Inscriptions Chrétiennes de la Gaule antérieures au VIIIe siècle.* 2 vols (Paris: l'Imprimerie impériale, 1856–1865); idem, *L'Epigraphie chrétienne en Gaule et dans l'Afrique Romaine* (Paris: Leroux, 1890); idem, *Nouveau Recueil des Inscriptions chrétiennes de la Gaule antérieures au VIIIe siècle* (Paris: l'Imprimerie nationale, 1892); idem, *Paléographie des Inscriptions latines du IIIe siècle à la fin du VIIe* (Paris: Leroux, 1898).

[130] Popescu, "Griechische Inschriften," 82. For the problem of Byzantine epigraphy cf. also Besevliev, "Probleme der byzantinischen Epigraphik."

[131] Cf. Popescu, "Griechische Inschriften," 83; Haralambie Mihaescu, "Lateinische Inschriften," in Winkelmann and Brandes, eds., *Quellen zur Geschichte des frühen Byzanz* 106–19, at 106.

[132] For the genres of ancient inscriptions cf. Wischmeyer, *Griechische und lateinische Inschriften* 21, as well as the handbooks on epigraphy mentioned above.

[133] For the formulae, besides the handbooks (above and in the bibliography) see especially the introductions and commentaries to the various series and inscription collections, as well as Gerhard Pfohl, "Grabinschrift I (griechische)," *RAC* 12 (1983) 467–514, at 495ff.; Charles Pietri, "Grabinschrift II (lateinisch)," translated by Josef Engemann, *RAC* 12 (1983) 514–90, at 554ff.; Popescu, "Griechische Inschriften," 84ff.

[134] Cf. the collection by Franz Buecheler, *Carmina Latina Epigraphica, conlegit, I–II* (Leipzig: Teubner, 1895–1897), with a supplement edited by Ernst Lommatzsch (Leipzig: Teubner, 1926); on this see the concordance by Antonio Ferrua, "I 'Carmina epigraphica' del Bücheler e la silloge del Diehl. Una concordanza," *VetChr* 112 (1975) 111–20.

[135] On this see Joachim Gensichen, *De Scripturae Sacrae vestigiis in inscriptionibus latinis christianis* (Greifswald: Julius Abel, 1910); Richmond Lattimore, *Themes in Greek and Latin Epitaphs.* Illinois Studies in Language and Literature 28/1-2 (Urbana: University of Illinois Press, 1942); Pietri, "Grabinschriften II" 580ff.

[136] See, for example, Hermann Bengtson, *Einführung in die Alte Geschichte* (7th rev. and expanded ed. Munich: Beck, 1975) 131ff.

[137] Kaufmann, *Epigraphik* 2.

[138] Popescu, "Griechische Inschriften," 84; Mihaescu, "Lateinische Inschriften" 118.

[139] On this see especially the work by Bärbel von Hesberg-Tonn, *Coniunx Carissima. Untersuchungen zum Normcharakter im Erscheinungsbild der römischen Frau* (Stuttgart: Historisches Institut der Universität Stuttgart, 1983).

[140] On this, cf. Woodhead, *The Study of Greek Inscriptions* 7.

[141] Ibid. 7ff.; Almar, *Inscriptiones Latinae* 8.

[142] Photographs do not enable a primary epigraphic examination.

[143] The importance of the papyri for historical research is emphasized by Bengtson, *Alte Geschichte* 137ff., and for women's history by Brooten, "Issues of Method." For a general introduction see Ludwig Mitteis and Ulrich Wilcken, *Grundzüge und Chrestomathie der Papyruskunde*. 2 vols. (Hildesheim: G. Olms, 1963; reprint of the B. Teubner edition of 1912); a good introduction to the Byzantine papyri is offered by Kurt Treu, "Byzantinische Papyri," in Winkelmann and Brandes, eds., *Quellen zur Geschichte des frühen Byzanz* 120–33, with references to the most important periodical literature (126 n. 2), as well as to more general introductions to papyrology (127–28 and the Postscript), and to the reports of current research (131 n. 2).

See the editions of Christian papyrus letters, especially those by Giuseppe Ghedini, *Lettere cristiane dai papiri greci del III e IV secolo*. Suppl. ad Aegyptus Ser. div. – Sez. gr.-rom. 3 (Milan: 1923); Maria Teresa Cavassini, "Lettere cristiane nei papiri greci d'Egitto," *Aeg* 34 (1954) 266–82; Mario Naldini, *Il Cristianesimo in Egitto. Lettere private nei papiri dei secoli II–IV*. STP 3 (Florence: Le Monnier, 1968) (for a critique of this last, see Ewa Wipszycka, "Remarques sur les Lettres Privées Chrétiennes des IIe-IVe Siècles (A Propos d'un Livre de M. Naldini)," *JJP* 18 (1974) 203–21; Giuseppe Tibiletti, *Le lettere private nei papiri greci dell III e IV secolo d. C. Tra paganesimo e cristianesimo*. Scienze filologiche e letteratura 15 (Milan: Vita e pensiero, 1979). Outstanding commentaries on recent text editions can be found in G. H. R. Horsley, *New Documents Illustrating Early Christianity* 1–5 (1981–1989), continued by S. R. Llewelyn, *New Documents Illustrating Early Christianity* 6–7 (1992, 1994).

[144] Cf. ch. IV A.

[145] Exceptions are, for example, Adolf Deissmann, *Light from the Ancient East; the New Testament illustrated by recently discovered texts of the Graeco-Roman world* (New York: Doran, 1927); E. A. Judge and S. R. Pickering, "Papyrus Documentation of Church and Community in Egypt to the Mid-Fourth Century," *JAC* 20 (1977) 47–71; and the works mentioned in the following notes.

[146] For Christians see Susanna K. Elm, *The Organization and Institutions of Female Asceticism in Fourth Century Cappadocia and Egypt*. Diss.Phil. Oxford (1986). Microfiche, 194ff.; eadem, "An Alleged Book-Theft in Fourth-Century Egypt: P. Lips. 43," *StPatr* 18/2 (1989) 209–15. See also Ewa Wipszycka, *Les ressources et les activités économiques des églises en Egypte du IVe au VIIIe siècle (Papy. Brux. 10)* (Brussels: Fondation Égyptologique Reine Élisabeth, 1972) passim; Alanna Emmett, "Female Ascetics in the Greek Papyri," *JÖB* 32 (1982) 507–15. For the Jewish field cf. Kraemer, "Non-Literary Evidence" 94ff. She estimates the total number of surviving Jewish papyri at 400.

[147] A special problem is presented by the so-called Church orders of the third to sixth centuries; the most important of these are the *Didache (Did)*, the *Traditio Apostolica (TA)*, the *Didascalia Apostolorum (Didasc.)*, the *Canones Hippolyti (CanHipp)*, the *Constitutiones Ecclesiasticae Apostolorum (CEA)*, the *Constitutiones Apostolorum (CA)*, and the *Testamentum Domini (TD)*. These writings have a complicated tradition-history and are to some extent literarily dependent on one another. Thus in particular the *Traditio Apostolica* influenced the *CEA, CanHipp, CA* VIII, and *TD*, the *Didache* influenced the *CEA* and *CA* VII, the *Didascalia Apostolorum* affected *CA* I–VI. In each case, at the first extended mention of a Church order the most important text editions and additional literature will be noted.

Since the Church orders are among the few witnesses to early Christian constitutional history they are an indispensable source. However, the fact that the desires and ideals of the individual compilers are reflected in the Church orders must be taken into account in a historical evaluation of them. As far as the value of these witnesses as sources is concerned, we must consider that they can by no means be read as faithful reflections of the congregational reality of their times and generalized as if they were such. They thus remain a shadowed witness to early Christian constitutional history. Paul Bradshaw, "Kirchenordnungen (I. Altkirchliche)," *TRE* 18 (1989) 662–70, at 662–63, has written of the character of these sources: "The old Church orders represent a genus of pseudo-apostolic literature that claims to give binding 'apostolic' commands regarding questions of moral behavior, liturgical usage, and Church discipline. The earliest example of this is the Didache, and for the majority of the writings in this literary group we must posit an origin in Syria and Egypt in the third and fourth centuries. They thus offer valuable source material for Church life in that time and place, but caution is required in evaluating them because it is possible that they contain more of the desires and ideals of the individual compilers than of the historical reality of their times." On this see, in general, Bradshaw, "Kirchenordnungen," and especially the study by Bruno Steimer, *Vertex Traditionis. Die Gattung der altchristlichen Kirchenordnungen.* BZNW 63 (Berlin and New York: Walter de Gruyter, 1992).

[148] Most recently Karen Jo Torjesen, "Reconstruction of Women's Early Christian History," in Elisabeth Schüssler Fiorenza, ed., *Searching the Scriptures I: A Feminist Introduction* (New York: Crossroad, 1993) 290–310, at 293, pointed to this desideratum in research.

[149] The most important of these are Zscharnack, *Dienst der Frau* (1902); Kalsbach, *Einrichtung* (1926); van der Meer, *Priestertum* (1969); Gryson, *Ministry* (1976; 1980); Martimort, *Deaconesses* (1982; 1985); for other studies cf. n. 39 above.

II. Apostles

A. Women Apostles in the New Testament

In 1977 Bernadette Brooten revived an ancient tradition by demonstrating that the accusative IOYNIAN attested in Rom 16:7 designates a woman named Junia, and therefore a woman apostle, and is not the name of a man called Junias as had been repeatedly posited since the twelfth century.[1] The following facts speak in favor of this interpretation:

(a) The masculine name Junias is not attested in antiquity, while the feminine Junia is frequently encountered in Greek and Latin literature and inscriptions.[2]

(b) The oldest and weightiest manuscript tradition for Rom 16:7 reads one of two feminine names: Junia or Julia. Peter Arzt has subjected the evidence of the most important biblical manuscripts of Rom 16:7 as well as the text editions since Erasmus to an exhaustive examination,[3] finding that the interpretation of the name as that of a man is a violent manipulation of the textual tradition that cannot be defended on text-critical grounds.[4] All the majuscules containing the verse, if they indicate an accent, as well as all the minuscules consulted,[5] read Ἰουνίαν, that is, the feminine name Junia. The same is true of the most important ancient biblical translations: the Old Latin and most of the Vulgate manuscripts, with the sole exception of Codex Reginensis, read *Juliam*, that is, the feminine name Julia. The Coptic translations, that is, the Sahidic and Bohairic versions, clearly read Junia, as does the Syriac translation. These findings are confirmed by the most important New Testament text editions since Erasmus. Only in Erwin Nestle's text-critical edition of the New Testament from 1927 onward is the clearly masculine form Ἰουνιᾶν used.[6] Since then this interpretation has stubbornly persisted, as the text editions appearing since the 1930s show.[7]

(c) In addition to the text tradition, the Greek and Latin commentaries on Romans from John Chrysostom (344/54–407) to Peter Abelard (1079–1142), as well as the liturgical traditions of the ancient Church and the early Middle Ages unquestioningly read the feminine names Junia or Julia (in the latter case Ambrosiaster and Atto of Vercelli).[8] Aegidius of Rome (1245–1316) was the first to assert that the name was masculine.[9]

A striking witness within the Greek tradition of interpretation to the fact that Junia was identified in the early Church as a woman is the work of John Chrysostom. He comments on Rom 16:7 with the words: "It is certainly a great thing to be an apostle; but to be outstanding among the apostles—think what praise that is! She was outstanding in her works, in her good deeds; oh, and how great is the philosophy (ἡ φιλοσοφία) of this woman, that she was regarded as worthy to be counted among the apostles!"[10]

In the *Liturgikon,* the missal of the Byzantine Church, Junia is honored to this day in the *Menologion* as an apostle, together with fifty-six male apostles and the two "like to the apostles," Mary Magdalene and Thecla.[11] For the Latin-speaking regions we should mention especially the commentaries on Romans by Ambrosiaster (4th c.) and Rufinus of Aquileia (ca. 345–410), who as a matter of course read the feminine names Junia[12] or Julia[13] and accounted this woman among the apostles.

With the rediscovery of the New Testament apostle Junia the centuries-old opinion (still emphatically maintained by the Roman Catholic Church) that in the apostolic period there were only male apostles has been finally disproved.[14]

Until 1865, when J. B. Lightfoot began the historical-critical examination of the concept of "apostles,"[15] it was taken for granted that the New Testament presents a unified concept of the apostolate: Jesus, during his earthly work, commissioned his twelve disciples as apostles (Luke 6:13). After the defection of Judas, then, the remaining eleven chose Matthias as the twelfth (Acts 1:15-26). Paul was the only other person called, outside Damascus, by the Risen Lord to be an apostle for the Gentiles. But historical-critical research has shown that this conception essentially reflects Luke's idea of apostles,[16] which is not representative for all of early Christian literature. Research in the history of traditions has shown that early Christianity had different understandings of the notion of apostolate.[17] We may distinguish, in essence, between a broader and a narrower conception of the apostle.

Jürgen Roloff has pointed to two "indispensable *methodological insights*" that have emerged from the previous discussion of the apostolate: first, we can no longer posit without further consideration a unified early Christian idea of the apostolate;[18] second, the Pauline understanding of what it means to be an apostle must constitute the "decisive fixed point" of every investigation of this theme.[19] The genuine Pauline letters offer not only the oldest witness to the early Christian understanding of the apostles[20] but also Paul's own personal understanding, proposed in dependence on and in contradiction to other interpretations of apostleship, and thus representing a "key to understanding the apostolate before and contemporary with Paul."[21]

Analysis of Paul's letters shows that at no point does Paul refer to a defined, generally applicable concept of apostleship. We may conclude from this that in Paul's time there was as yet no generally-held definition of apostleship with an established content.[22] Paul's own idea of apostleship is complicated.[23] Two points are especially important for the question before us:

(a) The group of apostles is not numerically limited in Paul's writings (cf. 1 Thess 2:7; 1 Cor 4:9; 9:5-7; 12:28; 15:5, 7; 2 Corinthians 11; Rom 16:7). It is true that Paul is aware of the "Twelve" (1 Cor 15:5), but he does not regard that group as identical with the apostles, whom he thinks of as much more numerous (1 Cor 15:7).

(b) Paul emphasizes, in connection with his own apostolate, the importance of the appearance of the Risen One and the apostle's personal call and sending by Christ (Gal 1:1, 11-12, 15-16; 1 Cor 9:1; 15:5-9; Rom 1:1, etc.). He sees himself as the apostle called last of all (1 Cor 15:8). Thus are criteria for the Pauline apostolate marked out that are not valid for all of early Christianity; this is evident especially from Paul's polemic against an apostolate understood charismatically (2 Corinthians 10–13), something that continued in the tradition represented by the *Didache* (*Did.* 11,3-6).

We may conclude, as regards the apostle Junia (Rom 16:7),[24] that she and her partner Andronicus[25] belonged to the earliest group of apostles in Jerusalem (Gal 1:17-19).[26] This is also indicated by Paul's statement that she was "in Christ" before him (καὶ πρὸ ἐμοῦ γέγοναν ἐν Χριστῷ). She was actively engaged in mission, which brought her—like Paul—into captivity. Paul, by recalling Junia's imprisonment, places her *expressis verbis* in the tradition of the apostolic discipleship of the cross, which he posits especially in 2 Corinthians in counterdistinction to the ψευδαπόστολοι (2 Cor 11:13; cf. 2 Cor 6:4-10; 12:9-13).

B. Women Apostles in the Tradition of the Ancient Church

In the ancient Church and the early Middle Ages the apostles were increasingly depicted as the bearers and guarantors of what was affirmed as authentic tradition.[27] It is all the more significant that women appear and are treated respectfully in a great many commentaries written in the ancient Church, as well as in novels, liturgical works, and hagiographical literature, as apostles, and therefore as proclaimers of the Christian message.

As we have already shown, Junia was acknowledged as an apostle in the ancient Church. The commentaries on Romans and liturgical traditions from the early centuries of the Church's life saw then, and in part still see no problem in the idea that a woman was an apostle. Moreover, Junia is not the only New Testament woman regarded as an apostle in early Church literature.

Others were the Samaritan woman, Mary Magdalene, and the other women at the tomb. This shows that in the ancient Church's interpretations of the gospels and during the early Middle Ages women were regarded as apostles even though they were not so entitled *expressis verbis* in the gospels themselves. This finding reveals that these interpreters maintained a broader concept of apostolicity, and it also shows that the title ἀπόστολος was closely associated with primary missionary activity. Such commentaries not only preserve the memory that women as well as men were disciples of Jesus and among the first to proclaim the gospel; they also underscore the fact and the legitimacy of such activity.[28] Also part of this tradition are the post-New Testament writings that describe women as apostles; these latter include especially Thecla and Nino.

Origen interprets the Samaritan woman who met Jesus at Jacob's well (John 4:5-30, especially vv. 28-29) as an apostle and evangelist: "Christ sends the woman as an apostle to the inhabitants of the city (οἱονεὶ δὲ καὶ ἀποστόλῳ πρὸς τοὺς ἐν τῇ πόλει χρῆται τῇ γυναικὶ ταύτῃ), because his words have enflamed this woman." A little later he continues: "Here a woman proclaims Christ to the Samaritans (γυνὴ εὐαγγελίζεται τὸν Χριστόν). At the end of the gospels a woman even reports to the apostles the resurrection of the Savior, which she was the first to behold."[29]

Seven centuries later the Samaritan woman was also called ἀπόστολος by Theophylact, the archbishop of Bulgaria (ca. 1050–1108). Theophylact expands on this title by describing her as "anointed with priesthood" (χειροτονηθεῖσα) and as teacher of the entire city (πόλιν ὁλόκληρον διδάσκει).[30]

Mary Magdalene and the other women

> (a) at Jesus' crucifixion (Mark 15:40-41; Matt 27:55-56; Luke 23:49; John 19:25) and burial (Mark 15:47; Matt 27:61; Luke 23:55-56);
> (b) at the discovery of the empty tomb and reception of the angel's message, and, with the exception of Mark 16:8, the women's handing on of the message (Mark 16:1-8; Matt 28:1-10; Luke 24:1-11);
> (c) and at the appearance of the Risen One (Mark 16:9-11) and Jesus' commission (Matt 28:9-10; John 20:11-18)

are not explicitly called apostles. But they are the first to receive the message of Jesus' resurrection, and they are commissioned by angels to hand on the news. According to Matt 28:10 the whole group of women, and according to John 20:16-17 Mary Magdalene alone receive(s) this commission directly from Jesus himself. Finally, John 20:18 relates Mary's first proclamation after her encounter with and commissioning by Jesus. According to these traditions, Mary and the other women can be interpreted as apostles, in line with the Pauline definition of an apostle (1 Cor 9:1). In what follows I will not undertake another analysis of the New Testament traditions about Mary Magdalene or test their historicity.[32] Apart from the clarification of the historical question, from a synchronic point of view her depiction as the first proclaimer of the resurrection is significant, as is her reception as such in the ancient Church and the Middle Ages. At the same time, a development of the history of the early Church's reception of the figures of Mary Magdalene and the other women at the tomb is not within the scope of this investigation; it would extend its boundaries far too broadly.[33] For what Elisabeth Gössmann writes about the history of reception of the figure of Mary Magdalene alone in the Middle Ages applies in similar fashion to the ancient Church as well: "An attempt to classify and evaluate the numerous and extremely varied expressions regarding the Mary Magdalene motif in the Middle Ages would not be possible without writing a monograph of some five hundred pages with a bibliography of at least fifty additional pages."[34]

In what follows I will use two examples from exegetical literature of the ancient Church to illustrate how Mary Magdalene was interpreted as an apostle: Hippolytus of Rome (✝ 235/36) explains the gospels' description of women having been the first witnesses of the resurrection by saying that Christ met the women on Easter morning "so that women, too, would be Christ's apostles."[35] Theologically, he proposes the events at the tomb and the women's acting as the first witnesses (Matt 28:8-10; Luke 24:10; John 20:16-18; Mark 16:9-11) as the antithesis of Eve's disobedience,[36] and he emphasizes Christ's empowerment of women as apostles: "When I [Christ] appeared to the women, sending [them] to you, I desired to send [them] as apostles."[37] Gregory of Nyssa (ca. 334–394) also interpreted the women's status as first witnesses as antithetical to the story of the Fall. He mentions Mary Magdalene as witness to the empty tomb, as recipient of the angel's message, as eyewitness to the Risen One, and finally as the bearer of the joyful news to the disciples.[38]

The problem some interpreters had with the fact that the Risen One, according to the evidence of the gospels, first appeared to women and commissioned women to proclaim his resurrection (a different tradition is found in 1 Cor 15:5) led, in the history of interpretation, to an Eve-Mary typology. This tradition did not question Mary's act of proclamation. On the contrary, she was fully recognized for it by being given the title of apostle.[39]

At the end of the second century the figure of Thecla in the *Acts of Paul and Thecla* is the type of the preaching, baptizing, and teaching Christian woman.[40] The *Acts of Thecla* were probably written some time between 185 and 195 in Asia Minor,[41] and by the beginning of the third century they were already known and "much read" in Egypt (Origen), Rome (Hippolytus), and Carthage (Tertullian).[42] In many areas they were regarded in these early centuries as canonical.[43]

While these late-second-century *Acts of Thecla* attest to Thecla's activity as preacher and teacher,[44] she is not entitled "apostle." That, however, is not surprising, especially in view of the fact that she is depicted in the *Acts* as a disciple of Paul. She is situated in Pauline contexts and not, like the Samaritan woman or Mary Magdalene, in association with Jesus. Only in a hagiographical writing from the fifth century is Thecla accorded the title of apostle.[45] In this work, entitled Πράξεις τῆς ἁγίας ἀποστόλου καὶ μάρτυρος τοῦ Χριστοῦ Θέκλας, she is repeatedly called ἀπόστολος.[46] In the fifth century Thecla was already a figure of identification for ascetic women; she was well known and her reputation was widespread. There was an extensive cult of Thecla; the pilgrim Egeria describes her visit to the centers where Thecla was venerated.[47] The context of the Thecla-traditions and her veneration explains why she was given the title of apostle. In addition, the unabashed use of the title ἀπόστολος in this case was certainly nourished also by the historical distance from the apostolic era; at the same time, however, it is significant that it was bestowed on a woman.

Nino was another woman of the ancient Church who was given the title of apostle. Ruth Albrecht has shown that the kernel of the hagiographical traditions about Nino[48] witnesses to her as "apostle and evangelist."[49] In the Georgian traditions Nino's missionary work is very pointedly interpreted as apostolic. The "Collection of Satberti," dated to the year 973,[50] but with origins in the seventh century, contains, among other things, two principal sections in which the missionary activity of Nino the apostle is described at length.[51]

(a) The "Conversion of Georgia"[52] is a cumulative chronicle of Georgian history beginning with the appearance of Alexander the Great and ending with the advent of Arab rule. Nino's activity is placed in the reign of Constantine. She came to the Eastern Empire as a prisoner of war. It is said that "in the fourth year" after she arrived in Georgia she began "to preach the God Christ and religion."[53] In what follows she is described as the country's missionary, beginning with the conversion of the Georgian royal house. It is said that she "preached," "converted," and "baptized." The interpretation and appreciation of her missionary activity culminates in her ultimately being entitled "apostle" and "evangelist."[54]

(b) The "Life of Nino"[55] consists primarily of accounts of Nino's life and work. The traditions it contains are represented in part as oral traditions of Nino written down by her disciples, female and male. Nino is portrayed as a woman who had converted "all to confess the Father and the Son and the Holy Spirit, [to faith in] the coming of Christ through baptism."[56] Two of the events described are important as preparation for her activity as a preacher. The first of these was her two years of study with a woman teacher of theology;[57] of her it is said that "there was and had been no one in Jerusalem who was her equal in knowledge, both of the old ways of religion and of the new."[58] Nino is thus depicted by the tradition as someone who had received the teaching of a spiritual mother who was regarded as the best theological teacher in Jerusalem. This teacher prepared Nino for her work. The transmission of Nino's teaching to her disciples can be seen as analogous to her own experience.[59]

Besides this theological education received from a woman teacher and spiritual mother, Nino was also ordained by the patriarch and spiritual father Juvenal of Jerusalem: "He placed me on the steps of the altar and laid his hands on my shoulders and sighed to heaven and said: 'Lord God of the fathers and the centuries, I commend this orphan, my sister's child, into your hands, and I send her to preach your divinity and that she may proclaim your resurrection wherever it is your pleasure that she may go. Christ, be Thou her way, her companion, her haven, her teacher in the knowledge of languages . . . like those who in days past have feared your name."

The patriarch sends her out with cross and blessing.[60] Thus Nino is shown to be an official officeholder and "her preaching activity is explicitly designated as not only in the sense of the Church, but by the Church's commissioning."[61] A general description of Nino's missionary activity follows, emphasizing her preaching, teaching, and baptizing.

The account of the Jewish priest Abiathar attests to Nino's knowledge of the Scriptures, as well as her teaching and baptizing. He writes: "She told me my Scriptures by heart and explained them to me."[62] Nino's teaching is repeatedly emphasized; in particular it is said that she "taught everyone day and night the true way of faith."[63] These traditions show no interest at all in depicting this woman's teaching as restricted to women. The tradition shows her as equally free in her baptizing; we read that the former Jewish priest Abiathar received "baptism from the hand of Nino."[64]

Nino's missionary and catechetical activity is considered in these traditions as all-encompassing. Besides being given the title of "apostle" she is also characterized as "teacher,"[65] "preacher,"[66] "proclaimer of the truth" or "of the Son of God,"[67] "leader,"[68] "mother,"[69] and "one sent by the Son of God."[70] All these titles are intended to document Nino's powerful missionary activity, authorized by God, and the tradition sees no problem in her preaching, teaching, and baptizing.[71]

Rufinus's church history, written about 403, is the oldest literary attestation of the conversion of Georgia by a prisoner of war *(captiva)*, who received the name of Nino in the Georgian tradition. Rufinus also portrays her as a preacher of the Christian message.[72] However, Rufinus's account is more restrained than the Georgian traditions in what it attributes to this woman. It attests to her preaching of Christ. She taught *"Christum(que) esse Deum, Dei summi Filium, qui salutem hanc contulerit."*[73] He also says that she gave instruction in the ritual of prayer and the form of divine service *(supplicandi ritum venerandique modum)*. This is followed, however, by the restriction: "insofar as a woman had the right to do so *(in quantum de his aperire feminae fas erat)*."[74] Accordingly, the king is then described as the apostle of Georgia and not, as in the later Georgian tradition, the prisoner of war herself.

Rufinus thus shows himself indebted to a tradition that regarded the ecclesiastical activity of women as restricted. Within this horizon of thought the actual work of this woman, who preached, taught, and apparently also celebrated divine worship, had to be described in such a way that it harmonized with that ideology. Utterances like those of Rufinus "reflect the Church's struggle over the pastoral engagement of Christian women,"[75] with the discrepancy between the supposed prohibition and the reality establishing the point of conflict.

In Georgia's hagiographical literature, by contrast, Nino's missionary activity was described quite freely. Eva Maria Synek summarizes in her study of literary traditions about holy women: "it is said of a great many saints that they taught and preached, did theology, gave counsel on ecclesiastical problems and made decisions, then founded and led ecclesiastical communities. As spiritual mothers they provided spiritual advice, they blessed and in some cases exercised liturgical functions, including the administration of baptism."[76]

In contrast we find other traditions subservient to the prohibitory texts in the New Testament, which endeavor to suppress preaching and, consequently, sacramental ministry by women. Thus Rufinus waters down Nino's work because he feels himself obligated to those prohibitory traditions,[77] and is at pains to depict Nino's teaching as restricted to women.[78]

In summary we can say that in the New Testament one woman is referred to by name as an apostle, and that in later centuries the title of apostle was also applied to other women. Paul commends the apostle Junia to the community at Rome (Rom 16:7), emphasizing that she is "prominent among the apostles." It is significant that Paul, whose letters are a vivid witness to the conflict over apostolic legitimacy, does not argue on the basis of gender: according to Paul a genuine apostleship is legitimated primarily by the commissioning of the Risen One.

It is only the later Lukan concept of apostleship, which restricted the group of apostles to the Twelve, that led to women apostles' disappearance from the picture. Throughout subsequent history the Lukan notion was frequently put to use in excluding women from the work of proclamation, with all its implications, such as preaching, teaching, baptizing, and celebrating the Eucharist. This interpretation, however, is inadequate to the Lukan idea of the "twelve apostles," whose intention was not to exclude women.[79]

While there are no other women besides Junia in the New Testament context who are accorded the title of apostle, several have central importance in the first proclamation of the Christian message, especially Mary Magdalene and the other women at the tomb. This explains why these women were regarded as apostles and evangelists in the traditions of the ancient Church and the early Middle Ages.

We find vivid witness to the fact that the work of women active in mission was also taken seriously and respected in later centuries especially in the ha-giographical traditions about Thecla and Nino, which describe and entitle these women as apostles. It is true that these witnesses stand in contrast to at-tempts to restrict the comprehensive missionary activity of women, as articu-lated, for example, in the deprecatory expressions of Rufinus. But these traditions also reveal a fragmenting that hints that the reality was different. Eva Maria Synek accurately describes this conflict: "Famed theologians such as John Chrysostom, for example . . . made an effort to interpret these awkward texts [the prohibitory traditions] so as to show the biblical admonitions to be compatible with their practical experience of the graced activity of saintly women teachers. We can also understand Rufinus in this way: He recognizes Nino in fact as an apostle and teacher, but attempts to harmonize her role with the prohibitions directed against women's teaching."[80]

Notes

[1] Cf. Bernadette Brooten, "Junia . . . Outstanding among the Apostles," in Leonard Swidler and Arlene Swidler, eds., *Women Priests: A Catholic Commentary on the Vatican Declaration* (New York: Paulist, 1977) 141–44. Thus also Elisabeth Schüssler Fiorenza ("Women Apostles: The Testament of Scripture," in Anne Marie Gardiner, ed., *Women and Catholic Priesthood. An Expanded Vision*. Proceedings of the Detroit Ordination Confer-ence [New York: Paulist, 1976] 94–102, at 96): "An unbiased reading of Rom. 16:7 provides us with one instance in the New Testament where a woman is called apostle. There is no rea-son to understand Junia as a short form of the male name Junianus, when Junia was a well-known name for women at the time. . . . Andronicus and Junia were a missionary couple like a Aquila and Prisca . . . ."

Adolf von Harnack (*The Expansion of Christianity in the First Three Centuries*. 2 vols. Translated and edited by James Moffatt [New York: G. P. Putnam's Sons, 1904–05] 2:220 n. 1) had already expressed his doubts, with reference to the fact that Chrysostom took the name to be feminine. Leopold Zscharnack (*Der Dienst der Frau in den ersten Jahrhun-derten der christlichen Kirche* [Göttingen: Vandenhoeck & Ruprecht, 1902] 102) reads "Junia" in his commentary on the text. Brooten refers to other exegetes in this century who identified Junia as a woman, writing: "In our century, the most notable protester against the *Junias* hypothesis has been M.-J. Lagrange [in his commentary on Romans (Paris, 1916; sixth ed. 1950, p. 366)]." For other examples see Brooten's article at p. 142. The newer German and English commentaries on Romans, e.g., those by Rudolf Pesch, *Römerbrief.* NEB 6 (Würzburg: Echter, 1983) 108, and Ulrich Wilckens, *Der Brief an die Römer*. 3 vols.

EKK VI/1–3 (2nd rev. ed. Neukirchen-Vluyn: Neukirchener Verlag, 1987–1989) 3:132–36, have adopted these results and understand Junia to be a woman and an apostle.

[2] For this see Brooten, "Junia," 142–43; Peter Arzt, "Junia oder Junias? Zum textkritischen Hintergrund von Röm 16,7," in Friedrich V. Reiterer and Petrus Eder, eds., *Liebe zum Wort. Beiträge zur klassischen und biblischen Philologie, P. Ludger Bernhard zum 80. Geburtstag* (Salzburg: Müller, 1993) 83–102, at 84–85, and the extensive discussion in Richard S. Cervin, "A Note Regarding the Name 'Junia(s)' in Romans 16.7," *NTS* 40 (1994) 464–70.

[3] For what follows see Arzt, "Junia oder Junias?" passim.

[4] Ibid. 98.

[5] Arzt gives a detailed listing of some seventy minuscules on pp. 89ff.

[6] Ibid. 95.

[7] See the citations in Arzt, "Junia oder Junias?" 97.

[8] For the history of interpretation see Brooten, "Junia," 141–42, and Arzt, "Junia oder Junias," 85–86, but especially the extensive discussion by Valentin Fabrega, "War Junia(s), der hervorragende Apostel (Röm 16,7), eine Frau?" *JAC* 27/28 (1984/85) 47–64, at 54ff. Fabrega has collected the most important interpretations.

[9] Brooten, "Junia," 141–42.

[10] John Chrysostom, *In epist. ad Rom. homil.* 31,2 (*MPG* 60.669–70). On this see, at length, Fabrega, "War Junia(s) eine Frau?" 54ff.

[11] *Liturgikon* for 17 May (Junia), 22 July (Mary Magdalene), 24 September (Thecla); in the list of saints "Junias" is identified as a "female apostle" (Neophytos Edelby, ed., *"Messbuch" der byzantinischen Kirche* [Recklinghausen: A. Bongers, 1967] 895–96; 955; 622; 1040). On this cf. Anne Jensen, "Maria von Magdala – Traditionen der frühen Christenheit," in Dietmar Bader, ed., *Maria Magdalena – Zu einem Bild der Frau in der christlichen Verkündigung.* Schriftenreihe der Katholischen Akademie Freiburg (Munich and Zürich: 1990) 33–50, at 42–43.

[12] Rufinus of Aquileia at Romans 16:7 (Heinrich Josef Vogels, ed., *Das Corpus Paulinum des Ambrosiaster.* BBB 13 [Bonn: P. Hanstein, 1957] 31). Rufinus's commentary on Romans is said to be a translation of the Greek commentary on Romans by Origen, but not much in the way of conclusions about Origen's exegesis can be drawn from the translation. Rufinus himself emphasizes that he has treated his copy of Origen very freely. Beyond that, scholars have expressed doubts especially about whether Origen commented on the greetings list at all. In the Greek fragments of Origen's commentary that have been preserved there is nothing on Rom 16:7: cf. A. Ramsbotham, "The Commentary of Origen on the Epistle to the Romans," *JThS* 13 (1912) 209–24, 357–68; 14 (1913) 10–22; Karl Staab, "Neue Fragmente aus dem Kommentar des Origenes zum Römerbrief," *BZ* 18 (1929) 72–82. For the value of the text fragments cf. *Origenes. Commentarii in epistulam ad Romanos: Liber Primus, Liber Secundus / Römerbriefkommentar: Erstes und zweites Buch,* translated and with an introduction by Theresia Heither. FC 2/1 (Freiburg and New York: Herder, 1990) 14–15.

On this whole question see Fabrega, "War Junia(s) eine Frau?" 58ff.; Heither, *Römerbriefkommentar* 11ff. passim. For the relationship between Ambrosiaster's commentary on Romans and that of Rufinus cf. Vogels, *Untersuchungen zum Text paulinischer Briefe bei Rufin und Ambrosiaster.* BBB 9 (Bonn: P. Hanstein, 1955).

[13] Ambrosiaster, *Ad Rom.* Recens. α β 16,7 (CSEL 81/I 480,7) reads "Junia (Julia);" Ambrosiaster, *Ad Rom.* Recens. γ (CSEL 81/I 481,7) reads "Julia."

[14] This assertion still constitutes an essential element in the Roman Catholic Church's argumentation against the ordination of women to all the functions and offices in the Church. Cf. *Inter insigniores/Ordinatio sacerdotalis* 3 (Wolfgang Beinert, *Frauenbefreiung und Kirche. Darstellung – Analyse – Dokumentation. Mit Beiträgen von Wolfgang Beinert, Herlinde Pissarek-Hudelist, Rudolf Zwank* (Regensburg: Pustet, 1987) 164–65). The same opinion is encountered in scholarly debate; thus, for example, K. H. Rengstorf emphasizes ("ἀπόστολος, κτλ.," *TDNT* 1:407–37, at 430–31) that **the apostles are witnesses of the resurrection,** though not all witnesses of the resurrection are apostles. The circle of apostles does not seem to have been particularly large. It still did not include any women, though women were the first to see the risen Lord and there were also women prophets." (Emphasis supplied.)

[15] J. B. Lightfoot, *Saint Paul's Epistle to the Galatians* (9th ed. London: Macmillan, 1887) 92–101, with his excursus: "The Name and Office of an Apostle." For the history of research see Günter Klein, *Die zwölf Apostel. Ursprung und Gehalt einer Idee.* FRLANT 77 (Göttingen: Vandenhoeck & Ruprecht, 1961) 20–65; Jürgen Roloff, *Apostolat – Verkündigung – Kirche. Ursprung, Inhalt und Funktion des kirchlichen Apostelamtes nach Paulus, Lukas und den Pastoralbriefen* (Gütersloh: Gerd Mohn, 1965) 9–37; idem, "Apostel / Apostolat / Apostolizität. I. Neues Testament," *TRE* 3 (1978) 430–45; Ferdinand Hahn, "Der Apostolat im Urchristentum. Seine Eigenart und seine Voraussetzungen," *KuD* 20 (1974) 54–77, at 54–56. On the early Christian apostolate as a whole see especially Adolf von Harnack, *Die Lehre der zwölf Apostel nebst Untersuchungen zur ältesten Geschichte der Kirchenverfassung und des Kirchenrechts.* TU II/1, 2 (Leipzig: Hinrichs, 1884; reprint Berlin: Akademie-Verlag, 1991) 93ff., 111ff.; Hans von Campenhausen, "Der urchristliche Apostelbegriff," *StTh* 1 (1947/48) 96–130; idem, *Kirchliches Amt und geistliche Vollmacht in den ersten drei Jahrhunderten.* BHTh 14 (Tübingen: J.C.B. Mohr [Paul Siebeck], 1953; 2nd rev. ed. 1963) 13ff.; Alfred Wikenhauser, "Apostel," *RAC* 1 (1950) 553–55; K. H. Rengstorf, "ἀπόστολος, κτλ.," *TDNT* 1:407–37; Walter Schmithals, *Das kirchliche Apostelamt. Eine historische Untersuchung.* FRLANT 79 (Göttingen: Vandenhoeck & Ruprecht, 1961); Günter Klein, *Die zwölf Apostel;* Dieter Georgi, *The Opponents of Paul in Second Corinthians: A Study of Religious Propaganda in Late Antiquity* (Philadelphia: Fortress, 1986) 32–39; Jürgen Roloff, *Apostolat – Verkündigung – Kirche;* idem, "Apostel;" Karl Kertelge, *Gemeinde und Amt im Neuen Testament.* BiH 10 (Munich: Kösel, 1972) 77ff.; Ferdinand Hahn, "Der Apostolat im Urchristentum;" Elisabeth Schüssler Fiorenza, "The Twelve," in Leonard Swidler and Arlene Swidler, eds., *Women Priests,* 114–22; eadem, "The Apostleship of Women in Early Christianity," in ibid., 135–40; Schuyler Brown, "Apostleship in the New Testament as an Historical and Theological Problem," *NTS* 30 (1984) 474–80; Jan-A. Bühner, "ἀπόστολος, ου, ὁ," *EDNT* 1:142–46.

[16] For the Lukan concept of apostles see especially Klein, *Die zwölf Apostel;* Schmithals, *Das kirchliche Apostelamt,* 233ff.; Roloff, *Apostolat – Verkündigung – Kirche,* 169ff.; idem, "Apostel," 442–43; Schüssler Fiorenza, "The Twelve;" eadem, "Apostleship of Women," 138; Bühner, "ἀπόστολος," 144–46.

In the context of the historical question of apostles in early Christianity it is important to recall that the Lukan idea of the apostolate, which concentrates on the Twelve as "the twelve apostles," is a theological and not a historical concept. There is certainly good reason to think that the pre-Easter group of the Twelve is historical (thus Roloff, "Apostel," 433), but in spite of this the exclusive identification of the Twelve with the apostles is a theologoumenon that, indeed, is found also outside the Lukan corpus (on this, cf. Bühner, "ἀπόστολος," and Schmithals, *Das kirchliche Apostelamt* 217ff.).

[17] On this see the compromised depiction by Roloff, "Apostel." See also the overview in Harnack, *Expansion* 1:398–408. He summarizes: "This survey of the primitive usage of the word 'apostle' shows that while two conceptions existed side by side, the narrower was successful in making headway against its rival" (p. 408).

[18] Roloff, "Apostel," 432.

[19] Ibid.; see idem, *Apostolat – Verkündigung – Kirche;* thus, for example, Schmithals, *Das kirchliche Apostelamt* 13; Hahn, "Der Apostolat im Urchristentum," 54.

[20] Kertelge, *Gemeinde und Amt* 79.

[21] Roloff, "Apostel," 432.

[22] Thus Georgi, *Opponents* 35. He adds: "The vehemence of the discussion also speaks for the unclear understanding of 'apostle' in Pauline times."

[23] On this see especially Schmithals, *Das kirchliche Apostelamt* 14ff.; Roloff, *Apostolat – Verkündigung – Kirche* 38ff.; idem, "Apostel," 436–40; Hahn, "Der Apostolat im Urchristentum," 56ff.

[24] On this see also Gerhard Lohfink, "Weibliche Diakone im Neuen Testament" (1980) in Gerhard Lohfink, Helmut Merklein, and Karlheinz Müller, eds., *Die Frau im Urchristentum.* QD 95 (4th ed. Freiburg, Basel, and Vienna: Herder, 1989) 320–38, at 327–32; Fabrega, "War Junia(s) eine Frau?"; Peter Lampe, "Iunia/Iunias: Sklavenherrschaft im Kreise der vorpaulinischen Apostel (Röm 16,7)," *ZNW* 76 (1985) 132–34.

Paul calls Junia συγγενής. She was therefore a Jew, or rather a Jewish Christian. Fabrega, "War Junia(s) eine Frau?" 49–50, however, doubts Junia's Jewish origin. Lampe, "Iunia/Iunias," 133, concludes on the basis of prosopographic considerations that Junia "should be regarded as a *liberta* of a patron named Junius—or at least her paternal family probably originated among the liberated slaves of the gens *Iunia.*"

[25] For missionary couples see Gottfried Schille, *Die urchristliche Kollegialmission.* AThANT 48 (Zürich: Zwingli Verlag, 1967) 89ff. passim; Mary Rose D'Angelo, "Women Partners in the New Testament," *JFSR* 6 (1990) 65–86.

[26] Thus also Hahn, "Der Apostolat im Urchristentum," 57; Roloff, "Apostel," 434.

[27] For the development of the apostolic tradition and the concept of apostolicity in the early Church cf. especially G. G. Blum, "Apostel /Apostolat / Apostolizität II. Alte Kirche," *TRE* 3 (1978) 445–66, at 457; Roloff, "Apostel," 434.

[28] For the missionary activity of women as witnesses to the gospel cf. especially Luise Schottroff, "Women as Disciples of Jesus in New Testament Times," in Luise Schottroff, *Let the Oppressed Go Free. Feminist Perspectives on the New Testament.* Translated by Annemarie S. Kidder (Louisville: Westminster/John Knox, 1992) 80–130; eadem, "Mary Magdalene and the Women at Jesus' Tomb," ibid. 168–203; eadem, "Wanderprophetinnen. Eine feministische Analyse der Logienquelle," *EvTh* 51 (1991) 332–34; Monika Fander, *Die Stellung der Frau im Markusevangelium. Unter besonderer Berücksichtigung kultur- und religionsgeschichtlicher Hintergründe.* MThA 8 (Altenberge: Oros-Verlag, 1989); eadem, "Frauen in der Nachfolge Jesu. Die Rolle der Frau im Markusevangelium," *EvTh* 52 (1992) 413–32; eadem, "Frauen im Urchristentum am Beispiel Palästinas," *JBTh* 7 (1992) 165–85.

[29] Origen, *Comm. S. Jean* 4,26-27 (SC 222, 126); 4,28 (SC 222, 132).

[30] Theophylact, *Joh.* 4,28ff. (*MPG* 123, 1241D).

[31] See also the summaries in Luke 23:49, 55, and Acts 1:14.

[32] On this cf. Martin Hengel, "Maria Magdalena und die Frauen als Zeugen," in Otto Betz, Martin Hengel, and Peter Schmidt, eds., *Abraham unser Vater. Juden und Christen im*

Gespräch über die Bibel. FS für Otto Michel zum 60. Geburtstag (Leiden: E. J. Brill, 1963) 243–56; Luise Schottroff, "Mary Magdalene and the Women at Jesus' Tomb;" eadem, "Maria Magdalena I. Neues Testament," *WFT* (1991) 275–77; Fander, *Die Stellung der Frau im Markusevangelium* 135–76; Susanne Heine, "Eine Person von Rang und Namen. Historische Konturen der Magdalenerin," in Dietrich-Alex Koch, Gerhard Sellin, and Andreas Lindemann, eds., *Jesu Rede von Gott und ihre Nachgeschichte im frühen Christentum. Beiträge zur Verkündigung Jesu und zum Kerygma der Kirche. FS für Willi Marxsen* (Gütersloh: Gerd Mohn, 1988) 179–94; Helen Schüngel-Straumann, "Maria von Magdala – Apostolin und erste Verkünderin der Osterbotschaft," in Dietmar Bader, ed., *Maria Magdalena – Zu einem Bild der Frau in der christlichen Verkündigung* (Munich and Zürich: Schnell and Steiner, 1990) 9–32; Richard Atwood, *Mary Magdalene in the New Testament Gospels and Early Tradition.* EHS.T 457 (Bern et al.: Peter Lang, 1993) 11ff. See also the summary of the discussion regarding the historicity of Mary Magdalene in Eva Maria Synek, *Heilige Frauen der frühen Christenheit: zu den Frauenbildern in hagiographischen Texten des christlichen Ostens* (Würzburg: Augustinus-Verlag, 1994) 16–28.

[33] On this cf. Urban Holzmeister, "Die Magdalenenfrage in der kirchlichen Überlieferung," *ZKTh* 46 (1922) 402–22, 556–84; Peter Ketter, *Die Magdalenenfrage* (Trier: Paulinus-Dr., 1929); Hans Hansel, *Die Maria-Magdalena-Legende. Eine Quellenuntersuchung.* Diss. phil. Greifswald, 1937; Victor Saxer, "Les Saintes Marie Madeleine et Marie de Béthanie dans la tradition liturgique et homilétique orientale," *RevScR* 32 (1958) 1–37; idem, "Maria Maddalena," *BSS* 8 (1966) 1078–1104, with extensive bibliography; Elisabeth Gössmann, *Die Frau und ihr Auftrag. Die Liebe zum Vergänglichen* (Freiburg, et al.: Herder, 1961); eadem, "Maria Magdalena als Typus der Kirche. Zur Aktualität mittelalterlicher Reflexionen," in Bader, ed., *Maria Magdalena* 51–71; Elisabeth Moltmann-Wendel, *The Women Around Jesus.* Translated by John Bowden (New York: Crossroad, 1982) 61–90; eadem, "Maria Magdalena II. In der Tradition," *WFT* (1991) 277–79; Anne Jensen, "Maria von Magdala—Traditionen der frühen Christenheit," in Bader, ed., *Maria Magdalena* 33–50; Renate Schmid, "Maria Magdalena in gnostischen Schriften." Material-Edition 29. Staats-Examensarbeit, Munich 1990; Synek, *Heilige Frauen* 16–84; Atwood, *Mary Magdalene* 147ff.

[34] Gössmann, "Maria Magdalena," 52. The so-called Magdalene motif is "a mixture of at least three New Testament women: the anointing woman (Mark 14:3-9, par. Matt 26:6-13), who according to John 12:1-8 was Mary of Bethany, the sister of Martha and Lazarus, the penitent woman in Luke 7, and Mary of Magdala, first named by Luke in 8:1-3 and appearing in all four gospels in the Passion and resurrection narratives. These three—if not four—New Testament figures the Middle Ages frequently melted together with the Samaritan woman at Jacob's well into the Magdalene motif, and Mary of Egypt was also added" (Gössmann, "Maria Magdalena," 51–52). The motif was dominant in the Western Church at least from the time of Pope Gregory the Great (✝ 604). On this see Holzmeister, "Magdalenenfrage"; Ketter, *Magdalenenfrage;* and especially Hansel, *Maria-Magdalena-Legende* and Jensen, "Maria von Magdala," 33–35.

[35] Hippolytus, *Kommentar zum Hohenlied* XV 3,1-4 (GCS 1, 350–55).

[36] GCS 1, 354: ". . . so that women, too, would be Christ's apostles and the fault of the first Eve's disobedience would be revealed through the present corrective obedience. O marvelous counselor, Eve becomes an apostle!" On this see Monika Leisch-Kiesl, *Eva als Andere: eine exemplarische Untersuchung zu Frühchristentum und Mittelalter* (Cologne, Weimar, and Vienna: Bohlau, 1992) 49. For the Eve-Magdalene parallels see the same work, passim, and Gössmann, "Maria Magdalena," 58.

[37] GCS 1, 355.

[38] Gregory of Nyssa, *Or.* II (*MPG* 46, 631-32); on this, see the comments in Synek, *Heilige Frauen* 38ff.

[39] This tendency in the interpretation of Mary Magdalene was continued and developed especially in the New Testament apocrypha. In writings like the Gospel of Mary she was described as an agent of revelation, and she is the leading dialogue partner of Jesus. I will simply refer to the most important literature on this subject here. See especially Anne Jensen, "Auf dem Weg zur Heiligen Jungfrau. Vorformen des Marienkultes in der frühen Kirche," in Elisabeth Gössmann and Dieter R. Bauer, eds., *Maria – für alle Frauen oder über allen Frauen?* (Freiburg, Basel, and Vienna: Herder, 1989) 36–62, at 41ff.; Schmid, "Maria Magdalena in gnostischen Schriften;" Synek, *Heilige Frauen* 28–36; Atwood, *Mary Magdalene* 186ff.

[40] The Greek text can be found in Lipsius and Bonnet, "Πράξεις Παύλου καὶ Θέκλης," in *Acta Apostolorum Apocrypha, post Constantinum Tischendorf, denuo ediderunt Ricardus Adelbertus Lipsius et Maximilianus Bonnet* (Hildesheim: G. Olms, 1959) 235–72; there is an English translation in Edgar Hennecke, *New Testament Apocrypha 2*. Edited by Wilhelm Schneemelcher, English translation edited by Robert McLean Wilson (Philadelphia: Westminster, 1965) 353–64. See also Anne Jensen's German translation in her article, "Thekla. Vergessene Verkündigerin," in Karin Walter, ed., *Zwischen Ohnmacht und Befreiung. Biblische Frauengestalten* (Freiburg, Basel, and Vienna: Herder, 1988) 173–79 and her book, *Thekla, die Apostolin: ein apokrypher Text neu entdeckt, übersetzt und kommentiert* (Freiburg: Herder, 1995).

On this subject see also Carl Schlau, *Die Acten des Paulus und der Thecla und die ältere Thecla-Legende. Ein Beitrag zur christlichen Literaturgeschichte.* Diss. Leipzig, 1877 (Cincinnati, Ohio: Assured Micro-Services, 1983); Harnack, *Expansion* 2:226–28; Zscharnack, *Dienst der Frau* 52–58; Elisabeth Schüssler Fiorenza, *In Memory of Her. A Feminist Theological Reconstruction of Christian Origins* (New York: Crossroad, 1983) 173–75; Ruth Albrecht, *Das Leben der heiligen Makrina auf dem Hintergrund der Thekla-Traditionen. Studien zu den Ursprüngen des weiblichen Mönchtums im 4. Jahrhundert in Kleinasien.* FKDG 38 (Göttingen: Vandenhoeck & Ruprecht, 1986); Jensen, "Thekla," and eadem, *Thekla – die Apostolin. Ein apokrypher Text neu entdeckt, übersetzt und kommentiert.* Frauen – Kultur – Geschichte 3 (Freiburg, Basel, and Vienna: Herder, 1995); eadem, *God's Self-Confident Daughters. Early Christianity and the Liberation of Women.* Translated by O. C. Dean, Jr. (Louisville: Westminster/John Knox, 1996) 79–82; Luise Schottroff, "Frauenwiderstand im frühen Christentum," in Frauenforschungsprojekt zur Geschichte der Theologinnen Göttingen, eds., *Querdenken. Beiträge zur feministisch-befreiungstheologischen Diskussion. FS für Hannelore Erhart zum 65. Geburtstag* (Pfaffenweiler: Centaurus, 1992) 129–59.

[41] Albrecht, *Makrina* 247.

[42] Thus Zscharnack, *Dienst der Frau* 52–53. For the spread of the Thecla traditions in the fourth century in both East and West see Albrecht, *Makrina* 240ff. For their special popularity in Egypt in the fourth century see Carl Schmidt, ed., *Acta Pauli aus der Heidelberger koptischen Papyrushandschrift Nr. 1* (Hildesheim: G. Olms, 1965) 16–17.

[43] Schüssler Fiorenza, *In Memory of Her* 173. Eusebius of Caesarea does not count them among the canonical writings, but distinguishes them from heretical works. Cf. Wilhelm Schneemelcher, "Acts of Paul," *New Testament Apocrypha 2*, 322–90, at 323–24.

[44] See, for example, chs. 38, 41, and 43 of the *Acts of Paul and Thecla.*

[45] The Greek text, with commentary and French translation, can be found in Dagron and Dupré la Tour, *Vie et Miracles de saint Thècle. Texte Grec, Traduction et Commentaire, par Gilbert Dagron avec la collaboration de Marie Dupré la Tour.* SHG 62 (Brussels: Société des bollandistes, 1978). For introductory questions and the content of the document cf. Albrecht, *Makrina* 293–302.

[46] Dagron and Dupré la Tour, *Vie et Miracles de sainte Thècle* 168, 170, 274.

[47] *Egérie, Journal de Voyage (Itinéraire). Introduction, Texte Critique, Traduction, Notes, Index et Cartes par Pierre Maraval. Valerius du Bierzo, Lettre sur La B^se Egérie. Introduction, Texte, et Traduction par Manuel C. Diaz y Diaz.* SC 296 (Paris: Cerf, 1982) 23.

[48] For Nino see especially Albrecht, *Makrina* 194–95, 223, 225, 227; Synek, *Heilige Frauen* 85–161; Jensen, *God's Self-Confident Daughters* 8, 75–78.

[49] Albrecht, *Makrina* 223, following "Die Bekehrung Georgiens. Mokcevay Kartlisay (Verfasser unbekannt)," translated and annotated by Gertrud Pätsch, *Bedi Kartlisa. Révue de Kartvélologie* 23 (1975) 288–337, at 297. For Nino's being called an apostle see also ibid., 323, 335.

[50] M. Tarchnisvili, "Die Legende der heiligen Nino und die Geschichte des georgischen Nationalbewußtseins," *ByZ* 40 (1940) 48–75, at 49.

[51] The text can be found in German translation in "Die Bekehrung Georgiens," 288ff., and in Gertrud Pätsch, ed., *Das Leben Kartlis. Eine Chronik aus Georgien. 300–1200.* Sammlung Dieterich 330 (Leipzig: Dieterich, 1985) 131–200, at 131ff.; see also the English translation by David M. Lang, *Lives and Legends of the Georgian Saints. Selected and Translated from the original texts* (London: Allen & Unwin; New York, Macmillian, 1956) 13–39, at 19ff.

For introductory questions see the text editions, but also especially M. Tarchnišvili's "Legende der heiligen Nino," which discusses the state of research. For these and other traditions about Nino see especially Synek, *Heilige Frauen* 90ff.

[52] For what follows see the 1975 edition by Pätsch, "Die Bekehrung Georgiens," 290–301.

[53] Ibid. 294.

[54] Ibid. 294, 296, 297.

[55] For what follows see Pätsch, "Die Bekehrung Georgiens," 302–37.

[56] Ibid. 302.

[57] For other women as teachers of theology see ch. 4 below.

[58] "Die Bekehrung Georgiens," 306.

[59] Ibid. 318. See on this, at length, Synek, *Heilige Frauen* 98–99.

[60] "Die Bekehrung Georgiens," 308.

[61] Synek, *Heilige Frauen* 110.

[62] "Die Bekehrung Georgiens," 326.

[63] Ibid. 322.

[64] Ibid. 325.

[65] Ibid. 303.

[66] Ibid. 335.

[67] Ibid. 315, 335.

[68] Ibid. 323, 335 ("masterful leader . . . as an apostle of Christ").

[69] Ibid. 318, 321, 335.

[70] Ibid. 313.

[71] On this see also Synek, *Heilige Frauen* 149–54.

[72] Rufinus, Hist. *eccl.* I, 10; cf. also the English translation of this chapter by Lang, *Lives and Legends* 15ff. For a comparative analysis of Rufinus's description and *Socrates,* Hist. eccl. I, 20, Sozomen, Hist. *eccl.* II, 7 (SC 306, 258ff.), and Theodoret, Hist. *eccl.* I, 24 (GCS 44, 74ff.) see Anne Jensen, *God's Self-Confident Daughters* 75–78; it is her thesis that "women apostles were described in such a way [by the early Church historians] that their preaching and teaching activities were no longer visible." Ibid. 78.

[73] "That Christ was [also] God, the Son of the most high God, who brought salvation." Rufinus, Hist. *eccl.* I, 10 (*MPL* 21, 481).

[74] Ibid.

[75] Synek, *Heilige Frauen* 95.

[76] Ibid. 12.

[77] Thus also Synek, *Heilige Frauen* 105.

[78] See at length on this subject Jensen, *God's Self-Confident Daughters* 75–78.

[79] On this, see above.

[80] Synek, *Heilige Frauen* 96.

III. Prophets

A. The Tomb Epigraph of the Prophet Nanas

Asia Minor / Phrygia / Akoluk   IV[1]

BIBLIOGRAPHY:
C. H. E. Haspels, *The Highlands of Phrygia. Sites and Monuments.* 2 vols. (Vol. 1: *The Text*; Vol. 2: *The Plates*). Princeton: Princeton University Press, 1971, 215–16, 338–39 no. 107 (Figs. 630–31, phot. and squeeze).

August Strobel, *Das heilige Land der Montanisten. Eine religionsgeographische Untersuchung.* RVV 37. Berlin and New York: Walter de Gruyter, 1980, 98–101.

προφήτισα
Νανας Ἑρμογένου

εὐχῆς καὶ λιτανίης
προσ‹κ›υνητὸν ἄνακτα
5   ὕμνοις καὶ κολακίης
τὸν ἀθάνατον ἐδυσώπι·
εὐχομένη πανήμερον
παννύχιον θεοῦ φόβον
εἶχεν ἀπ᾽ ἀρχῖς·
10 ἀγγελικὴν ἐπισκοπὴν
καὶ φωνὴν εἶχε μέγιστον
Νανας ηὐλλογημένη
ἧς κημητήρ[ιον - - -]
ΜΑΕΙΤΟ [- - -] σύ-
15 νευνον πολὺ φίλτατον ἄν-
δραν ἦλθε μετ[- - -]
ἐπὶ χθονὶ πο[υλυβοτείρη]
νους ἔργον [- - -]
ἀντεποίησε [- - -]
20 ποθέοντες [- - -]ησ-

63

ατο μέγιστον [- - -]
εἰς ὑπόμνημ[α]²

Lines 1–2: According to Haspels the first two lines are "carved above the main field, in uneven and careless writing, no doubt an addition by another hand."

Line 2: Νανας is a common name for women in Asia Minor.³

Line 3: Eta sigma represents a dative plural of the first declension, in place of -αις.⁴

Line 4: A. M. Woodward, whose advice Haspels sought, conjectures προσκυνητόν instead of προσευνητόν.⁵ The description of God or Christ as ἄναξ occurs with increasing frequency in Christian poetry from the fourth century onward.⁶

Line 5: Compare line 3.

Line 12: The sigma is joined to the eta by a ligature.⁷

Line 16: Haspels reads μετὰ.

Line 17: A. M. Woodward and C. J. Ruijgh, whom Haspels consulted, conjecture πουλυβοτείρη.

Line 20: Haspels reads ἐτιμήσατο.

The prophet Nanas, daughter of Hermogenes. She implored the Lord who is worthy of all reverence, the Immortal One, with prayers and fervent petitions, with songs and hymns of praise, she prayed day and night. She showed fear of the Lord from the beginning, she had visitation(s) of angels and a mighty (?) voice. Nana the highly praised, whose tomb . . .

This tomb epitaph is one of the few remaining tomb inscriptions of Christian prophets in Asia Minor. Unique is the word form προφήτισ<σ>α; there is no example of this form in ancient literature.⁸ The suffix -ισσα is attested from the Hellenistic period onward.⁹ The omission of one sigma was due to the simplification of double consonants in later Greek¹⁰ and indicates that the intended designation was προφήτισσα. We can no longer determine who placed the grave marker. Perhaps it was the mourners (ποθέοντες) mentioned in line 20.¹¹ These could have been believers and followers of Nanas.¹²

The superscription with the title "prophet" has been engraved in the stone by a second hand. The unevenness of the letters suggests that something has been added to the original text of the inscription.¹³ Possible explanations for such a later addition remain hypothetical.

The inscription not only differs in its poetic form from the more numerous prosaic inscriptions in Phrygia, but stands out because of its unusual metrics. C. J. Ruijgh characterizes it as follows: "Most lines are Aeolic-choriambic, but of different types: ll. 3-6 pherecratean, ll. 7-8 choriambic dimeter A, l. 9 adonean, etc. This is comparable with, for example, the metrical structure of the final part of Timotheus' *Persians*. In contemporary Christian poetry, on the other hand, the same verse or stanza is generally used throughout the whole poem (cf. for ex. the hymns of Synesius and Prudentius)."[14] Apart from this unusual form the inscription contains traditional elements as well, including the description of the tomb as κοιμητήριον and a concluding memorial formula. The inscription has no definitively Christian traits; its Christian character can be recognized only from the content and terminology.

The religious topoi mentioned in lines 3-11 characterize Nanas as a prophetically gifted Christian woman:

(a) The manner (εὐχῆς καὶ λιτανίης . . . ὕμνοις καὶ κολακίης . . . ἐδυσώπι) and intensity (εὐχομένη πανήμερον παννύχιον) of her prayer (ll. 3-8).[15]

(b) The reference to visitations of angels (ἀγγελικὴν ἐπισκοπὴν) (l. 10).[16]

(c) The reference to a voice (φωνὴν εἶχε μέγιστον) (l. 11). The interpretation of this line of the tomb epigraph has proved extraordinarily difficult. It is impossible to say whether the voice represents something Nanas heard or whether the reference is to Nanas' own prophetic voice.

In summary, we may say that these elements belong to the traditional categories of prophetic attributes.[17] Nana's designation as a prophet (line 1) is explicable against this background.

The inscription contains no obvious terminology that would indicate a Montanist or Novatianist provenience.[18] Emilie Haspels believes nevertheless that the inscription is "unquestionably heretical."[19] She understands the "appearances of angels" and the "voice" it mentions (ll. 10-11) as ecstatic phenomena and, referring to Tertullian, attributes them to Montanism.[20] It is well known that Tertullian attributes similar phenomena to a Christian woman whom he does not name,[21] and he reports the promise of such phenomena to all chaste Christians as a saying of the Montanist prophet Prisca.[22]

An association of the prophet Nanas with the New Prophecy derived from such parallels proceeds from the premise that after the "Montanist crisis" prophecy in its typical manifestations could be found only in Montanist circles.[23] The progressive disappearance of prophets and prophetic manifestations from Christian literature toward the end of the second century indicates a decline in the importance of Christian prophecy in the communities.[24] Scarcely any traces can be found of "professional prophets," as Adolf von Harnack called them.[25] This observation should not, however, lead to the overhasty conclusion that with the decline of the prophets the prophetic charism also lost all its value in the Christian communities. Visionary and ecstatic gifts were still important.

Cyprian of Carthage (ca. 200/210–258) says of himself that he received "revelations," and he also refers to the "frequent ecstasy of two young prophets *(pueri)* staying with him."[26] Reminiscences of charismatic phenomena are also found in the Church orders of the third to the fifth centuries, especially the *Constitutiones Ecclesiasticae Apostolorum* and the *Testamentum Domini*. It is difficult to say whether these were archaic references, but with all due skepticism we may suppose that they "still corresponded to a factual situation, although it had certainly faded."[27]

In the *Constitutiones Ecclesiasticae Apostolorum,* a document that scholars are increasingly inclined to assign to the first half of the fourth century,[28] we find an association between prayer and revelations similar to that in Nanas' inscription. The description of the duties of the institutionalized widows envisions the following activities for two of the three enrolled widows (χῆραι καθιστανέσθωσαν):

(a) Prayer for all who are being tempted (αἱ δύο προσμένουσαι τῇ προσευχῇ περὶ πάντων τῶν ἐν πείρᾳ).[29]

(b) The reception of revelations when necessary (πρὸς τὰς ἀποκαλύψεις περὶ οὗ ἂν δέῃ) (CEA 21).[30]

In the last of the so-called Church orders, the *Testamentum Domini,* a writing from the fifth century,[31] there is frequent mention of community prophecy (*TD* 1.31, 32; 2.1) and of charismatic phenomena (*TD* 1.23; 1.47).[32] Against such a background it is not surprising that the *Testamentum Domini*'s eucharistic prayer contains the motif of visitations by angels *(angelosque visitatores) (TD* 1.23).[33]

These examples show that the charismatic element was still alive in individual communities into the fifth century, and that it had a place there. Women as vessels of the charismatic gifts were a matter of course in such contexts.

The so-called dialogue of an Orthodox and a Montanist, a writing from the fourth century, also attests the Church's acceptance of women who spoke prophetically not only in Montanist, but also in orthodox circles.[34] Toward the end of the dialogue the question at issue is that of the acknowledgment of the Montanist prophets Maximilla and Priscilla in particular, and of women's prophetic speech in general. The orthodox dialogue partner emphasizes that the Church does acknowledge women's prophesying (ἡμεῖς τὰς προφητείας τῶν γυναικῶν οὐκ ἀποστρεφόμεθα).[35] On the other hand, women's speaking in church (λαλεῖν ἐν ἐκκλησίαις) and their exercise of authority over men (αὐθεντεῖν[36] ἀνδρῶν) (1 Tim 2:12),[37] as well as their writing books in their own name[38] is not allowed. The prohibitions on "speaking" and "exercising authority over men" are New Testament topoi used in a formulaic manner in the dialogue to provide a supporting argument for the prohibition against women's writing books, which cannot be found in any previous literature of the ancient Church. The goal of the argument is to attack this writing of books, which is portrayed as an illegitimate presumption on the part of the Montanists, since the orthodox cannot question their prophetic speaking as such. Accordingly, in what follows he supports the nonacceptance of Maximilla and Priscilla primarily by reference to their activity as writers, as well as because of their conformity to the teachings of Montanus, which shows them to be false prophets (ψευδοπροφήτιδες). It is thus not the fact of their prophetic speech as such that encounters resistance, nor is that fact adequate to demonstrate the illegitimacy of their activity.

On the whole we must agree with Adolf von Harnack that "we . . . are very poorly informed about the continuance of the charisms in the Church [after its official recognition as the Church of the empire]."[39] Literary references to the continuing existence of the prophetic gifts are extremely scarce after the last years of the third century, although we must recall that even in the earliest years of Christianity literary references to prophecy are very difficult to find.[40] However, what is noteworthy in the few references we have is the matter-of-fact way in which they speak of women. This indicates that women's prophetic speaking was recognized by the Church as long as the charismatic element was still important. Against this background it is easy enough to think of Nanas as a prophetically gifted Christian woman in the fourth-century Catholic Church.[41] It remains possible that she belonged to the Montanist movement, but at this period that cannot be established any more certainly than the other alternative: that she was a Catholic Christian.[42]

B. Literary Evidence

Preliminary Note

"Until the end of the second century the prophets, male and female, were regarded in Christianity as a necessary element of the Church in possession of the Holy Spirit. People therefore believed in their presence, and they were in fact there," wrote Adolf von Harnack in 1884 in his study on the *Didache*.[43] He expanded on this insight in a later book: "Nor were even prophetesses awanting; they were to be met with inside the catholic church as well as among the gnostics in particular."[44] This statement has been confirmed by numerous studies.[45]

The question of early Christian women prophets can be appropriately investigated only in the context of the more basic question of early Christian prophecy and its representatives as a whole. "The material the New Testament provides is unfortunately very sparse . . . there are, as it were, only single spotlights that light up the faces of prophecy in earliest Christianity at a few isolated points," wrote Ferdinand Hahn in 1971.[46] Despite increasing interest in and attention to the subject, this observation has not lost its currency; it is equally if not more applicable to the post-New Testament literature. Nevertheless, even in view of the manifold forms of early Christian prophecy,[47] we may feel assured that it was an integral element of early Christianity.[48] Its exercise was not restricted to a group of prophets; "rather, it appears to have been a characteristic of the whole community."[49] Accordingly, prophetic speech occurred even outside the explicit group of the προφῆται[50] among other representatives of the early communities, including the ἀπόστολοι[51] or ἐπίσκοποι,[52] and in community worship as a form of expression by all Christians (1 Corinthians 11–14).[53]

Women Prophets in the New Testament

In the New Testament there are references, especially in Paul's letters, the Acts of the Apostles, and Revelation, to early Christian prophets and early Christian prophecy as a community phenomenon.[54] In what follows we will consider whether in such contexts we also encounter women as representatives of early Christian prophecy.

The oldest and most extensive New Testament witness that thematizes early Christian prophecy and its specific expressions in worship as a community phenomenon is 1 Corinthians 11–14.[55] These chapters give us a glimpse both of Paul's ideas about prophecy[56] and those of the Corinthian community.[57] The mention of women who pray and prophesy during worship (1 Cor 11:5) is an unmistakable indication that women also exercised prophetic functions in the early communities. Paul does not question the prophetic activity of women,[58] but he emphasizes that they should prophesy with their heads covered (1 Cor 11:2-16). Without undertaking a new discussion of Paul's argumentation[59] we can say that women's prayer and prophecy were the normal thing in Corinthian worship assemblies, and that conflicts occurred only over their external form. This finding does not challenge the prohibition on women's speaking in 1 Cor 14:33b-36, since these verses (which in any case are interpolated) speak of λαλεῖν and not of προφητεύειν.[60] Against this background we may posit that there was a distinct group of προφῆται in the Pauline communities,[61] and that women were part of the group (1 Cor 12:28; 14:29, 32).[62]

We also encounter women prophets in the Lukan corpus (Luke 2:36; Acts 21:9) and read of the prophetic work of women (Luke 1:41-45; 1:46-55; Acts 2:17-18 as something promised[63]):[64]

(a) On the day of Jesus' presentation in the Temple (Luke 2:22-40) we hear of the appearance of the προφῆτις Anna (vv. 36-38).[65] It is said of Anna that she praised God (ἀνθομολογέομαι)[66] and spoke (λαλεῖν) of Jesus to all who were looking for the redemption of Jerusalem. The Lukan redaction attributes a "prophetic preaching" to her (Luke 2:38b).[67]

(b) Luke characterizes Elizabeth (Luke 1:41-45) and Mary, the mother of Jesus (Luke 1:46-55), in similar fashion as prophets.[68] Elizabeth "utters a prophetic cry"[69] and Luke places the Magnificat, a text shaped by Old Testament prophecy, on the lips of Mary.[70]

(c) In Acts 21:9 the four daughters of Philip[71] from Caesarea (Judea) are described as prophets.[72] Their activity is described by the verb προφητεύειν,[73] and they are mentioned in the context of prophetic activity (Acts 21:10-14). The reference to the daughters probably comes from Luke's sources.[74] It is not impossible that the daughters were widely known and were mentioned for that reason as well.[75]

The history of reception[76] allows us to conclude that in the early period these women were of great significance. In favor of this is the repeated reference to them by Eusebius. He reports that at Hierapolis Papias learned from Philip's daughters of the raising of a dead person (*Hist. eccl.* 3.39.9). Ulrich Körtner calls this information "trustworthy" because Papias was a contemporary of Philip's daughters and could have heard the story from them directly.[77] It is also possible that Philip and his daughters had in fact moved from Caesarea to Hierapolis.[78] Especially significant in this report by Eusebius is that Philip's daughters appear as the authorities for a tradition; this shows that they were respected in early Christianity. The impression is augmented and strengthened by another reference in Eusebius's work. He quotes from a writing of Miltiades against the New Prophecy (*Hist. eccl.* 5.17.3-4). Miltiades mentions the daughters of Philip as among the prophets of the New Covenant and emphasizes that the Montanist prophets are wrong to cite them as examples. This shows that the daughters of Philip were regarded, in the history of reception, as legitimate prophets of the New Covenant. Even Eusebius raises no objection to them.

In the book of Revelation the fourth of the seven letters to the churches in Asia (Rev 2:1-3, 22; 2:18-29)[79] warns the church in Thyatira against the prophet Jezebel.[80] It is said that she calls herself a prophet (ἡ λέγουσα ἑαυτὴν προφῆτιν) and that she teaches (διδάσκει) the community to practice fornication (πορνεῦσαι) and to eat flesh sacrificed to idols (φαγεῖν εἰδωλόθυτα).[81] These accusations are also found in the letters to the churches in Ephesus and Pergamon in connection with the Nicolaitans (Rev 2:14-15; cf. 2:6) and those who follow the teaching of Balaam (2:14). The concepts of "doctrine" (διδαχή; 2:14, 15, 24) and "teaching" (διδάσκειν; 2:20), words that are avoided in the rest of the book,[82] join these three groups and qualify them as heretics. Similarly, the accusation of immorality and the eating of food sacrificed to idols (Rev 2:14, 15, 20) is part of the polemic against all three groups.[83]

These topoi have frequently invited inferences about the theology and socio-economic background of the opponents thus described.[84] However, the attempt at social-historical location of this polemic against opponents misses its primarily topical character.[85] The accusations of eating flesh sacrificed to idols[86] and of practicing fornication[87] are analogous to the accusations leveled at the followers of Balaam in light of Num 25:1-5,[88] and are meant to characterize them as idolaters. The rhetorical aim of such argumentation is to besmirch the opponents. The accusations leveled in the context of the reference to Jezebel have the same goal. This conclusion is strengthened by the "polemical cover-name"[89] given to the prophet. The name "Jezebel" connects her with the Phoenician princess Jezebel, the wife of Ahab (1 Kings 16:31), who is described as a woman who persecuted the prophets of YHWH (1 Kings 18:4, 14) and supported the prophets of Baal and Asherah (1 Kings 18:19) as well as practicing fornication and magic (2 Kings 9:22).[90] The additional motifs in Revelation's polemic against "Jezebel," including "the motif of seduction in 2:20 and the connection with the powers opposed to God (see 2:24)," are topoi of this kind of polemic against opponents.[91] It is therefore scarcely possible to give any reliable account of Jezebel's teaching.[92]

In spite of all appropriate historical skepticism, our findings make it clear that in the so-called Jezebel we encounter a theologically independent woman who understood herself as a prophet and who had achieved recognition in the church at Thyatira. The topoi of the polemic applied to her are not directed against her as a woman, but simply against her prophecy and teaching.[93]

Women Prophets in the Second and Third Centuries

In the second century both women and men were active as prophets; some were also described *expressis verbis* as prophets.[94] We encounter an established group of prophets in the *Didache* (*Did.* 11–13)[95] and in the *Shepherd of Hermas* (*Herm. mand.* 11).[96] In addition we find reference to the prophetic speech of individuals, such as the prophetic teaching of Theonoe and Myrta in the *Acts of Paul.*[97] Nevertheless the number of προφῆται mentioned by name in early Christian literature is small. We find Ammia and Quadratus,[98] some Montanist[99] and some Gnostic prophets whose names are given.[100] In light of that fact it is especially striking that such a large proportion of those named are women.

In addition to these traditions we find texts that reflect theologically on the gift of prophecy. Justin and Irenaeus of Lyons emphasize in this context that both men and women have received this gift.[101]

Hippolytus of Rome writes a polemic against prophets who, in his opinion, are not real prophets,[102] for example those who are more highly regarded by their followers than the apostles themselves, and whose sayings meet with greater acclaim than the Gospel.[103] However, his polemic raises no challenge in principle to the presence of women among the Christian prophets.

Origen emphasizes "that women could also share in the grace of prophecy because this gift is given not according to the difference of the sexes, but according to the purity of the mind."[104] He in turn does not raise any fundamental objection to women's prophetic speech. At the same time, he does place restrictions on women's prophetic activity in his polemic against Prisca and Maximilla.[105] He rejects the prophetic claims of these women and their appeal to the daughters of Philip, Deborah, Mary, Hulda, and Anna with the observation that these latter did not speak publicly, but only in private.[106]

Especially noteworthy for the second century is the reference to the prophet Ammia of Philadelphia.[107] She is mentioned in one of Eusebius's sources in the context of antimontanist polemic (*Hist. eccl.* V, 16–17).[108] The intent of the source and its reception by Eusebius is to show that the New Prophecy is in fact false prophecy. The writer attempts to show that the prophets of the New Prophecy are wrong in appealing to the prophetic διαδοχή (succession) of the Old and New Covenants.[109] The criterion of distinction is the manner of speaking in the Spirit. The Montanist prophets are accused of prophesying ἐν παρεκστά-σει, and their prophecy is said to begin in voluntary ignorance (ἐξ ἑκουσίου ἀμαθίας) and pass into involuntary frenzy (εἰς ἀκούσιον μανίαν ψυχῆς).[110] The author of the source distances such phenomena from the prophets of the Old and New Covenants. The prophets of the New Covenant he acknowledges are Agabus (Acts 11:28), Judas and Silas (Acts 15:32), the daughters of Philip (Acts 21:9), as well as Ammia of Philadelphia and Quadratus.[111] It is striking that in his argument he mentions women prophets as a matter of course.[112] From the inclusion of Ammia in the prophetic succession of the New Covenant we may surmise that she was an acknowledged prophet in Asia Minor. She probably worked during the first half or middle of the second century.[113]

The literary evidence for prophetic activity becomes sparser everywhere in the third century, but there are still individual references to prophecy in Christian community life and worship. Tertullian and Cyprian provide evidence for Carthage.[114] Tertullian recognized the prophetic speech of women despite his sharp polemic against their kerygmatic and cultic activity even before he turned to Montanism.[115] Cyprian attests to prophetic activity by official leaders of the Church and as a form of expression for charismatic Christians. People who are explicitly called prophets appear only rarely. Heinrich Kraft supposes that "in the third century . . . [it was] the martyrs and confessors who replaced the prophets in upholding the claims of the old pneumatic Christianity" and in the next period this fell primarily to the ascetics.[116] The literature of martyrdom from the third century, with its prophetic features, is an eloquent witness to this development.[117] In this connection it is worth emphasizing the significance of female figures in this form of literature.[118]

The continuing acceptance, here and there, of prophets in the churches of Asia Minor in the third century is attested by a letter of Firmilian, the Metropolitan of Caesarea in Cappadocia.[119] The letter concerns the question of "heretics' baptism." Firmilian vehemently defends the requirement of another baptism of former "heretics." In the course of his argument he asserts that those who confer baptism must also be in possession of the Holy Spirit. This opinion he illustrates with the example of a woman prophet[120] who was supposedly filled not by the Holy Spirit, but by a demon. Firmilian writes that she presented herself as a prophet *(propheten se praeferret)*[121] after the reign of the emperor Alexander (therefore in the 240s),[122] and that she blessed bread and celebrated the Eucharist according to the authorized Church ritual; she also baptized many. According to Firmilian she did this without deviating from the legitimate wording of the baptismal interrogation.[123]

Here, then, we have a woman who for a long time *(per longum tempus)* exercised liturgical and sacramental functions in accordance with the Church's teaching and was honored for it.[124] Firmilian accuses her of sexual immorality and of being possessed by a demon, but he does not support his argument by saying that as a woman she had no right to lay claim to the charism of prophecy and the right to celebrate the sacraments. In chapter 11 he returns to his initial question and summarizes his argument: even a baptism performed according to the Church's norms cannot effect the forgiveness of sins and rebirth if it is done by a demon and not through the Holy Spirit. It would have been easy for Firmilian at this point to condemn the woman because of her sex. The fact that he does not indicates, as does the long prophetic and priestly career of this woman, that women who acted as prophets, liturgists, and sacramentalists were accepted in Christian circles in Cappadocia in the third century.[125]

We may say, therefore, that from the beginnings of Christianity women have acted as prophets (cf. 1 Cor 11:5; Luke 1:41-45, 46-55; 2:36; Acts 21:9; Rev 2:20).[126] The same is true for the subsequent centuries. In the second century Ammia, Prisca, Maximilla, and Philomena, in the third century the prophetic women in Tertullian's writings as well as an Anonyma from Cappadocia, in the fourth century the widows in the *Constitutiones Ecclesiasticae Apostolorum* and Nanas from Phrygia[127] witness to it.

On the whole we can perceive a clear decline in prophetic activity and prophets in Christian literature from the end of the second century onward.[128] This is all the more significant because prophecy was in any case, even in the first century, only visible in a very fragmentary way. It is all the more important, then, that from the very beginning women also appear as prophets, whether the sources call them "orthodox" (e.g., the daughters of Philip,

Ammia, Theonoe, and Myrta) or "heretical" (e.g., Maximilla, Priscilla, Philomena). A tendency to suppress women who were especially active as prophets cannot be derived from the literature of the earliest centuries.[129] This does not exclude the possibility that the criteria by which "true" prophecy was distinguished from "false" and by which the content of teaching was tested were directed just as much against women. In this connection judgments were made that affected both women and men in equal measure. In the polemic against the so-called pseudo-prophets there is no fundamental rejection of women's prophetic speaking. As we have shown, even the antimontanist polemic, confronted with some strong female figures, does not employ any sex-specific topoi to demonstrate that the New Prophecy was a pseudo-prophetic movement.

Notes

[1] C. H. Emilie Haspels, *The Highlands of Phrygia. Sites and Monuments.* 2 vols. (Vol. 1: *The Text*; Vol. 2: *The Plates*) (Princeton: Princeton University Press, 1971) assigns it to the mid-fourth century (p. 216).

[2] Haspels, *Highlands of Phrygia* 338–39: "Akoluk, in the courtyard of a house. Stele of bluish marble, the edges almost entirely crumbled away, the top broken away. Steep pediment, with remains of incised wreath, composed of two branches. Right-hand lower part of main field smoothly worn off, as if the stone had been re-used as a stepping-stone or doorstep. Stele h.0.90 (extant), th.0.16. Main field (filled by inscription lines 3 to 23, with above, row of decoration, diagonals in rectangles), h.046, w. above 0.36, below 0.44. Inscription lines in main field between guide lines, but irregular. Letter h.0.015 to 0.03."

[3] Examples in Ladislav Zgusta, *Kleinasiatische Personennamen* (Prague: Verlag der Tschechoslowakischen Akademie der Wissenschaften, 1964).

[4] Haspels, *Highlands of Phrygia* 339; see also Karl Hauser, *Grammatik der griechischen Inschriften Lykiens* (Basel: Buchdruckerei E. Birkhäuser, 1916) 26.

[5] Haspels, *Highlands of Phrygia* 339.

[6] Cf. G. W. H. Lampe, *A Patristic Greek Lexicon* (Oxford and New York: Clarendon Press, 1969; reprinted 1989) 114.

[7] Haspels, *Highlands of Phrygia* 339, regards this reading as a possible error caused by damage to the stone.

[8] Cf. *Thesaurus Linguae Graece, ab Henrico Stephano constructus.* 9 vols (Graz: Akademische Verlagsanstalt, 1954 [reprint]); H. G. Liddell, Robert Scott, and Henry Stuart Jones, *A Greek-English Lexicon.* With a Supplement by E. A. Barber (Oxford: Clarendon Press, 1968; reprint 1990); Walter Bauer, *A Greek-English Lexicon of the New Testament and Other Early Christian Literature.* Translated and adapted by William F. Arndt and F. Wilbur Gingrich. Revised and augmented by F. Wilbur Gingrich and Frederick W. Danker from Walter Bauer's Fifth Edition, 1958 (Chicago and London: University of Chicago Press, 1979); E. A. Sophocles, *Greek Lexicon of the Roman and Byzantine Periods (145*

B.C.–*1100* A.D.*)* (Hildesheim and New York: G. Olms, 1975; originally published at Boston by Little, Brown, 1870).

⁹ Eduard Schwyzer, *Griechische Grammatik, auf der Grundlage von Karl Brugmanns Griechischer Grammatik*. 3 vols. HAW II/1, vols. 1–3 (2nd ed. Munich: C. H. Beck, 1953) 475 (literature).

¹⁰ On this see Volkmar Schmidt, "τεκνοῦσ(σ)α bei Sophokles und Theophrast und Verwandtes," in H. G. Beck, A. Kambylis, and P. Moraux, eds., *Kyklos. Griechisches und Byzantinisches. Rudolf Keydell zum 90. Geburtstag* (Berlin and New York: Walter de Gruyter, 1978) 38–53, at 50–51 (with additional literature in n. 68).

¹¹ Peter Brown, *The Body and Society. Men, Women and Sexual Renunciation in Early Christianity* (New York: Columbia University Press, 1988) 79 supposes that the husband placed the tomb marker.

¹² Haspels, *Highlands of Phrygia* 216, calls them "disciples or faithful."

¹³ On this see the reproduction of the stone in Haspels, *Highlands of Phrygia*, figures 630–31.

¹⁴ Quoted in Haspels, *Highlands of Phrygia* 339.

¹⁵ For the connection between prayer and prophecy see Gerhard Friedrich, "προφήτης κτλ.," *TDNT* 6:828–61; Gerhard Dautzenberg, *Urchristliche Prophetie. Ihre Erforschung, ihre Voraussetzungen im Judentum und ihre Struktur im ersten Korintherbrief.* BWANT 104 (Stuttgart, Berlin, Cologne, and Mainz: Kohlhammer, 1975) 242 emphasizes the possible, but not necessary connection between prophecy and prayer.

¹⁶ Johannes Lindblom, *Gesichte und Offenbarungen. Vorstellungen von göttlichen Weisungen und übernatürlichen Erscheinungen im ältesten Christentum* (Lund: Gleerup, 1968) 68–77 emphasizes the pervasiveness of the topos of angelic appearances as the medium of divine revelation in the New Testament and points out its traditional character; it is especially important in Jewish apocalyptic. Cf. also Dautzenberg, *Urchristliche Prophetie* 77–80.

¹⁷ Characteristic of prophecy are visionary and auditory experiences: cf. Lindblom, *Gesichte;* Migaku Sato, *Q und Prophetie. Studien zur Gattungs- und Traditionsgeschichte der Quelle Q*. WUNT 29 (Tübingen: Mohr, 1988) 105. On this see also Dautzenberg, *Urchristliche Prophetie* 302.

¹⁸ For the discussion of inscriptions attributed to "schismatic groups," especially the New Prophecy, see W. M. Calder, "Philadelphia and Montanism," *BJRL* 7 (1922/23) 309–54; idem, "The Epigraphy of the Anatolian Heresies," in W. H. Buckler and W. M. Calder, eds., *Anatolian Studies, presented to Sir William Mitchell Ramsay* (Manchester: Manchester University Press; London and New York: Longmans, Green, 1923) 59–91; idem, "Leaves from an Anatolian Notebook," *BJRL* 13 (1929) 254–271; idem, "Early-Christian Epitaphs from Phrygia," *AnSt* 5 (1955) 25–38l; Henri Grégoire, "Epigraphie Chrétienne," *Byz* 1 (1924) 695–716; Wilhelm E. Schepelern, *Der Montanismus und die phrygischen Kulte. Eine religionsgeschichtliche Untersuchung* (Tübingen: Mohr [Siebeck] 1929), esp. 80–82; Elsa Gibson, "Montanist Epitaphs at Usak," *GRBS* 16 (1975) 433–42; eadem, *The "Christians for Christians" Inscriptions of Phrygia. Greek Texts, Translation and Commentary.* HThS 32 (Missoula: Scholars, 1978); W. H. C. Frend, "Montanism: Research and Problems," *RSLR* 20 (1984) 521–37; William Tabbernee, "Remnants of the New Prophecy: Literary and Epigraphical Sources of the Montanist Movement," *StPatr* 21 (1987) 193–201; idem, "Montanist Regional Bishops: New Evidence from Ancient Inscriptions," *Journal of Early Christian Studies* 1 (1993) 249–80.

[19] Haspels, *Highlands of Phrygia* 216.

[20] Ibid.; likewise August Strobel, *Das heilige Land der Montanisten. Eine religions-geographische Untersuchung*. RVV 37 (Berlin and New York: Walter de Gruyter, 1980) 100–101. Brown, *Body and Society* 79, also suggests such an association, but comes to no conclusion.

[21] Tertullian, *De anima* 9,4 (*Quinti Septimi Florentis Tertulliani. De Anima*. Edited with Introduction and Commentary by Jan Hendrik Waszink [Amsterdam: North-Holland Publishing Co., 1947]) 11: *Est hodie soror apud nos revelationum charismata sortita, quas in ecclesia inter dominica sollemnia per ecstasin in spiritu patitur; conversatur cum angelis, aliquando etiam cum domino, et videt et audit sacramenta et quorundam corda dinoscit et medicinas desiderantibus sumit.*

[22] Tertullian, *De exhort. castitatis* 10,5 (SC 319, 106): *uisiones uident, et ponentes faciem deorsum etiam uoces audiunt manifestas, tam salutares quam et occultas.*

[23] One tendency in scholarship attempts even for Christian prophecy in the first century "to dilute or eliminate the visionary components . . . in favor of a pure reception of the word, or to do the same with regard to proclamatory or even leadership roles," according to Dautzenberg, *Urchristliche Prophetie* 224. Heinrich Weinel had written a century ago (*Die Wirkungen des Geistes und der Geister im nachapostolischen Zeitalter bis auf Irenäus* [Freiburg: J.C.B. Mohr, 1899] 94): "It is therefore false for **Bonwetsch**, following the lead of **Cremer** . . . and other theologians of a similar tendency, to adopt the opinion of Anonymous that says of Montanus that he prophesied in a way that offended against the way prophets had spoken in the Church from the time of the apostles, and to repeat Miltiades' saying that 'a (church) prophet could not speak in ecstasy' Euseb. h.e. V 16,7 17,1.2." [Emphasis in original.]

[24] With the exception of the prophetic-apocalyptic writings from the post-New Testament period: cf., for example, the works collected in Edgar Hennecke, *New Testament Apocrypha 2*. Edited by Wilhelm Schneemelcher, English translation edited by Robert McLean Wilson (Philadelphia: Westminster, 1965) section C.

[25] Adolf von Harnack, *Die Lehre der zwölf Apostel nebst Untersuchungen zur ältesten Geschichte der Kirchenverfassung und des Kirchenrechts*. TU II/1, 2 (Leipzig: Hinrichs, 1884; reprint Berlin: Akademie-Verlag, 1991) 123–24. A counter-example is Papyrus Oxyrhynchus I.5. Friedrich, "προφήτης κτλ.," 859 indicates that this document attests the regard for prophets in some circles around the year 300; on this see also Henning Paulsen, "Papyrus Oxyrhynchus I.5 und die ΔΙΑΔΟΧΗ ΤΩΝ ΠΡΟΦΗΤΩΝ," *NTS* 25 (1978/79) 443–53.

[26] Cf. Anne Jensen, *God's Self-Confident Daughters. Early Christianity and the Liberation of Women*. Translated by O. C. Dean, Jr. (Louisville: Westminster/John Knox, 1996) 174; see also her nn. 297–300, with sources and additional literature.

[27] Adolf von Harnack, "Vorläufige Bemerkungen zu dem jüngst syrisch und lateinisch publicirten 'Testamentum domini nostri Jesu Christi,'" (1899) in idem, *Kleine Schriften zur Alten Kirche. Berliner Akademieschriften 1890–1907*. With a Foreword by Jürgen Dummer (Leipzig: Zentralantiquariat der Deutschen Demokratischen Republik, 1980) 385–98, at 391.

[28] Thus Bruno Steimer, *Vertex Traditionis. Die Gattung der altchristlichen Kirchenordnungen*. BZNW 63 (Berlin and New York: Walter de Gruyter, 1992) 65. The first edition was published by J. W. Bickell, *Geschichte des Kirchenrechts* (Gießen, 1843) 1:107–32. In what follows I will cite the Greek text edition by Theodor Schermann, *Die allgemeine*

Kirchenordnung, frühchristliche Liturgien und kirchliche Überlieferung, 1. Teil: Die allgemeine Kirchenordnung des 2. Jahrhunderts. SGKA.E 3,1 (Paderborn: Schöningh, 1914) 12–34, and will follow the division into chapters given there. The Syriac text with an English translation can be found in J. P. Arendzen, "An Entire Syriac Text of the 'Apostolic Church Order,'" *JThS* 3 (1902) 59–80. For further text editions see Paul Bradshaw, "Kirchenordnungen (I. Altkirchliche)," *TRE* 18 (1989) 662–70, at 666–67.

For questions of dating and localization, as well as for literary-critical, form-critical, and tradition-historical problems cf. Adolf von Harnack, *Sources of the Apostolic Canons, with a treatise on the origin of the readership and other lower orders.* Translated by Leonard A. Wheatley, with an Introductory essay on the organisation of the early church and the evolution of the reader by the Rev. John Owen (London: F. Norgate, 1895); Hans Achelis, "Apostolische Kirchenordnung," *RE³* 1 (1896) 730–34; F. X. Funk, "Die Apostolische Kirchenordnung," in idem, *Kirchengeschichtliche Abhandlungen und Untersuchungen II* (Paderborn: Schöningh, 1899) 236–51; Edgar Hennecke, "Zur Apostolischen Kirchenordnung," *ZNW* 20 (1921) 241–48; Bradshaw, "Kirchenordnungen," 666–67; Jeong Ae Han-Rhinow, *Die frühchristlichen Kirchenordnungen und ihr Amtsverständnis als Beitrag zur ökumenischen Diskussion um das Lima-Dokument.* Diss. theol. Munich, 1991, 74ff.; Steimer, *Vertex Traditionis* 60–71.

[29] Here and in what follows I am quoting from Schermann's edition in *Die allgemeine Kirchenordnungen,* here at 29–30.

[30] Harnack, *Sources of the Apostolic Canons* 41 comments: "This order (πρὸς τὰς ἀποκαλύψεις περὶ οὖ ἂν δέῃ) is extremely ancient, and reminds us of a still earlier state of things. In the Διδαχή we read of prophets who speak 'in the spirit,' who order 'in the spirit,' a meal for others, who 'in the spirit' beg for money for the needy, and demand gifts. Of such prophets our Source does not speak, but it has introduced to us in the bishop the mystic; in the presbyters the companion mystics; in the reader the representative of the charismatic teacher. These have shared in the inheritance of the prophets and teachers. Should not the widow also have her share, and should not the revelations which were expected for her be the residuum of those revelations of the prophets who have died out?" Harnack emphasizes that the ἀποκαλύψεις "refer neither to the actual unveiling of women (say at baptism) nor to the 'confidential communications of helpless women' (Bickell), but purely to 'revelations from God!'"—ibid. 20 n. 5.4.

[31] The *Testamentum Domini (TD),* written in Greek, survives only in a Syriac translation from the seventh century. The standard text is the Syriac with Latin translation by Rahmani, *Testamentum Domini nostri Jesu Christi. Nunc primum edidit, latine reddidit et illustravit Ignatius Ephraem II Rahmani* (Hildesheim: G. Olms, 1968; reprint of the 1899 edition); see also the Syriac version of the Synodicon with an English translation by Arthur Vööbus, *The Synodicon in the West Syrian Tradition.* CSCO 367/CSCO.S 161, 1–39; CSCO 368/CSCO.S 162, 27–64 (Louvain: Secrétariat du CorpusSCO, 1975–1976) 27ff. The English translation by James Cooper and Arthur J. MacLean, *The Testament of our Lord. Translated into English from the Syriac, With Introduction and Notes* (Edinburgh: T & T Clark, 1902) is especially useful because of its extensive introduction and the corresponding notes.

The *TD* in its final form is assigned to the fifth century, although that says nothing about the age of the individual traditions it contains. On this see especially Harnack, "Vorläufige Bemerkungen;" Funk, *Das Testament unseres Herrn und die verwandten Schriften.* FChLDG 2/H. 1+2 (Mainz: F. Kirchheim, 1901); Bradshaw, "Kirchenordnungen," 669–70; Steimer, *Vertex Traditionis* 95–105.

There is lack of agreement about the place where the writing originated. Syria, Asia Minor, and Egypt are discussed, but no consensus has been found. On this cf. Cooper and MacLean, *Testament of Our Lord* 42–45, but especially Steimer, *Vertex Traditionis* 101.

[32] This caused scholars around the turn of the last century to regard the *Testamentum Domini* as originally a Montanist Church order, a thesis that evoked no consensus; on this see Cooper and MacLean, *Testament* 15, in the introduction to their English translation incorporating extensive investigations.

[33] *Videntem habemus Patrem luminum cum Filio, angelosque visitatores* (Rahmani, *Testamentum Domini* 39).

[34] The Greek text was edited by Gerhard Ficker, "Dialog zwischen einem Orthodoxen und einem Montanisten: Widerlegung eines Montanisten," *ZKG* 26 (1905) 447–63. It is also printed in Pierre de Labriolle, *Les sources de l'histoire du Montanisme. Texts Grecs, Latine, Syriaque, publiés avec Introduction Critique, Traduction Française, Notes et "Indices," par Pierre de Labriolle.* CF 24 (Fribourg: Librairie de l'Université; Paris: Ernest Leroux, 1913) 93–108 (Greek and French), and in Ronald E. Heine, *The Montanist Oracles and Testimonia.* PatMS 14 (Macon, Ga.: Mercer University Press, 1989) 113–27 (Greek and English). On this see also Roger Gryson, *The Ministry of Women in the Early Church.* Translated by Jean Laporte and Mary Louise Hall (2nd ed. Collegeville: The Liturgical Press, 1980) 75–77; Elisabeth Schüssler Fiorenza, *In Memory of Her. A Feminist Theological Reconstruction of Christian Origins* (New York: Crossroad, 1983) 307–309; Ruth Albrecht, *Das Leben der heiligen Makrina auf dem Hintergrund der Thekla-Traditionen. Studien zu den Ursprüngen des weiblichen Mönchtums im 4. Jahrhundert in Kleinasien.* FKDG 38 (Göttingen: Vandenhoeck & Ruprecht, 1986) 233ff.; Ross S. Kraemer, "Women's Authorship of Jewish and Christian Literature in the Greco-Roman Period," in Amy-Jill Levine, ed., *"Women Like This." New Perspectives on Jewish Women in the Greco-Roman World.* SBL. Early Judaism and its Literature 1 (Atlanta: Scholars, 1991) 221–42, at 238–39; Anne Jensen, *God's Self-Confident Daughters* 171–72.

[35] Here and in what follows I am quoting from de Labriolle's edition, *Sources de l'histoire du Montanisme* 105–106.

[36] For the meaning and incidence of this word see G. W. Knight III, "AΥΘΕΝΤΕΩ in Reference to Women in 1 Timothy 2.12," *NTS* 30 (1984) 143–57; L. E. Wilshire, "The TLG Computer and further reference to AΥΘΕΝΤΕΩ in 1 Timothy 2.12," *NTS* 34 (1988) 120–34.

[37] The author shows a tendency to generalize in interpreting 1 Tim 2:12: διδάσκειν is replaced by the broader λαλεῖν; the singulars ἐπιτρέπω and ἀνήρ are changed to plurals and thus achieve a more comprehensive authority.

[38] Theodoret of Cyrrhus, *Haereticarum fabularum compendium* 3.2 (the text of which is printed in Heine's collection on Montanism [see n. 34 above] at 168ff.) also speaks of prophetic books by Priscilla and Maximilla, which the Montanists are supposed to have prized more than the gospels. From this testimony we may conclude that the Montanist prophets were active in producing literature. For the few surviving logia see de Labriolle, *La Crise Montaniste* (Paris: E. Leroux, 1913) 34–105; Jensen, *God's Self-Confident Daughters* 153–67. For other women in the ancient Church who were active theological writers, and for the surviving writings of early Christian women, see ch. 1 A above.

[39] Harnack, "Vorläufige Bemerkungen," 391.

[40] On this see below.

[41] Whether and, if so, in what manner her prayer, her visions, and her auditions (or her voice) were integrated into the community's eucharistic celebration cannot be determined from the text as we have it.

[42] On the organization of the Montanist communities W. E. Schepelern writes *(Der Montanismus und die phrygischen Kulte* 38–39): "It is therefore certain that at the end of the fourth century the Montanists had a set of officers in which the most important of the spiritual grades in the Great Church were represented, but had at the same time a superstructure consisting of two classes: the pariarchs (or the patriarch) of Pepuza, and οἱ κοινωνοί. We have no reason to doubt the statement of Epiphanius that women could be both ἐπίσκοποι and πρεσβύτεροι, but that can be regarded at most as a testimony to the situation in his own time; at the same time it of course does not exclude the possibility that women also had access to the two special grades of which he does not speak." Nothing more was said of prophets in the fourth century. On this cf. also the logion of Maximilla: "After me there will be no prophet, but the completion." See Ross S. Kraemer, ed., *Maenads, Martyrs, Matrons, Monastics. A Sourcebook on Women's Religions in the Greco-Roman World* (Philadelphia: Fortress, 1998) 230.

For the community constitution among the Montanists see also Johannes Friedrich, "Über die Cenones der Montanisten bei Hieronymus," *SBAW.PPH* 2 (1895) 207–21 (and see Adolf Hilgenfeld's response: Review of J. Friedrich, "Über die Cenones der Montanisten bei Hie-ronymus" [1895], *ZWTh* 38 [1895] 635–38); Adolf Jülicher, "Ein gallisches Bischofs-schreiben des 6. Jahrhunderts als Zeuge für die Verfassung der Montanis-tenkirche," *ZKG* 16 (1896) 664–71; de Labriolle, *La Crise Montaniste* 495ff.; F. E. Vokes, "The Opposition to Montanism from Church and State in the Christian Empire," *StPatr* 4 (1961) 518–26, at 522–23; idem, "Montanism and the Ministry," *StPatr* 9 (1966) 306–15; Joseph A. Fischer, "Die antimontanistischen Synoden des 2./3. Jahrhunderts," *AHC* 6 (1975) 241–73, at 243 (n. 16, with examples); Strobel, *Das heilige Land der Montanisten* 267ff.; Tabbernee, "Remnants of the New Prophecy," 200; idem, "Montanist Regional Bishops;" Gerd Buschmann, "Χριστοῦ κοινωνός (MartPol 6,2), das Martyrium und der ungeklärte κοινω-νός-Titel der Montanisten," *ZNW* 86 (1995) 243–64. For the history of scholarship on Montanism see the review of research by Frend, "Montanism: Research and Problems," *RSLR* 20 (1984) 521–37.

[43] Harnack, *Die Lehre der zwölf Apostel* 123.

[44] Harnack, *The Expansion of Christianity in the First Three Centuries.* 2 vols. Translated and edited by James Moffatt (New York: Putnam, 1904–05) 1:443.

[45] Cf., for example, Leopold Zscharnack, *Der Dienst der Frau in den ersten Jahrhunderten der christlichen Kirche* (Göttingen: Vandenhoeck & Ruprecht, 1902), 59: "The fact that there were women prophets in early Christianity was something even the most energetic opponents of the admission of women to service in the Church, including didactic work, could not deny." Hans Achelis, *Das Christentum in den ersten drei Jahrhunderten.* 2 vols (Leipzig: Quelle & Meyer, 1912) 91–93, summarizes all women's activities in the Church under the heading "women prophets;" see also Reinhold Seeberg, "Über das Reden der Frauen in den apostolischen Gemeinden," in idem, *Gesammelte Aufsätze I. Biblisches und Kirchengeschichtliches. Aus Religion und Geschichte* (Leipzig: A. Deichert, 1906) 123–44; Hans Lietzmann, *Geschichte der Alten Kirche.* 4 vols. (Berlin and Leipzig: Walter de Gruyter, 1932–1944) 1:149–50; Franz J. Leenhardt and Fritz Blanke, *Die Stellung der Frau im Neuen Testament und in der Alten Kirche.* KZF 24 (Zürich, 1949) 14ff.; Blanke, "Die Frau als Wortverkünderin" (1948) 57ff.; Anna Paulsen, *Geschlecht und Person. Das biblische Wort über die Frau* (Hamburg: Wittig, 1960) 153; Johannes Lindblom, *Gesichte und Offenbarungen* 179; Gryson, *The Ministry of Women* 109; Richard P. Hanson, "Amt / Ämter / Amtsver-

ständnis V. Alte Kirche," *TRE* 1 (1978) 533–52, at 545; M. Eugene Boring, *The Continuing Voice of Jesus. Christian Prophecy and the Gospel Tradition* (Louisville: Westminster/John Knox, 1991; original publication 1982 as *Sayings of the Risen Jesus*) writes under the heading "Prophets as Male and Female": "The Spirit that inspires prophecy has always been egalitarian" (p. 120); David Aune, *Prophecy in Early Christianity and the Ancient Mediterranean World* (Grand Rapids: Eerdmans, 1983) 195–98; Elisabeth Schüssler Fiorenza, *In Memory of Her* 294–309; Jensen, *God's Self-Confident Daughters* 173: "Thus the women's question [i.e., regarding prophecy] is not to be seen as the real bone of contention."

[46] Hahn, "Die Sendschreiben der Johannesapokalypse. Ein Beitrag zur Bestimmung prophetischer Redeformen," in Gert Jeremias, Heinz-Wolfgang Kuhn, and Hartmut Stegemann, eds., *Tradition und Glaube. Festgabe K. G. Kuhn* (Göttingen: Vandenhoeck & Ruprecht, 1971) 357–94, at 357. This is evident especially from the state of research on this topic. Cf. Hermann Gunkel, *Die Wirkungen des heiligen Geistes nach der populären Anschauung der apostolischen Zeit und nach der Lehre des Apostels Paulus*. Diss. theol. (Göttingen, 1888); Heinrich Weinel, *Die Wirkungen des Geistes und der Geister im nachapostolischen Zeitalter bis auf Irenäus* (Freiburg: J.C.B. Mohr, 1899); Heinrich Kraft, "Die altkirchliche Prophetie und die Entstehung des Montanismus," *ThZ* 11 (1955) 249–71; Lindblom, *Gesichte und Offenbarungen;* Dautzenberg, *Urchristliche Prophetie;* Boring, *The Continuing Voice of Jesus;* David Aune's comprehensive study, *Prophecy in Early Christianity and the Ancient Mediterranean World,* first appeared in 1983. However, compare the increasing number of individual studies appearing since the 1970s, e.g., the collection by Johannes Panagopoulos, *Prophetic Vocation in the New Testament and Today* (Leiden: Brill, 1977). For further literature see the following notes.

[47] For a fundamental definition and description of both the oral/written and nonliterary forms of early Christian prophecy and their functions see the religious-historical, form-critical, and tradition-critical investigations of Weinel, *Die Wirkungen des Geistes;* Erich Fascher, *ΠΡΟΦΗΤΗΣ. Eine sprach- und religionsgeschichtliche Untersuchung* (Gießen: A. Töpelmann, 1927); Lindblom, *Gesichte und Offenbarungen;* Dautzenberg, *Urchristliche Prophetie;* Ulrich B. Müller, *Prophetie und Predigt im Neuen Testament. Formgeschichtliche Untersuchungen zur urchristlichen Prophetie.* StNT 10 (Gütersloh: Gerd Mohn, 1975); Marie E. Isaacs, *The Concept of Spirit. A Study of Pneuma in Hellenistic Judaism and its Bearing on the New Testament.* HeyM 1 (London: Heythrop College, 1976); Boring, *The Continuing Voice of Jesus;* and especially Aune, *Prophecy in Early Christianity.*

[48] On this see Aune, *Prophecy in Early Christianity* 189ff.

[49] Schüssler Fiorenza, *In Memory of Her* 295. Thus also Aune, *Prophecy in Early Christianity* 200, and similarly Heinrich Kraft, "Vom Ende der urchristlichen Prophetie," in Johannes Panagopoulos, ed., *Prophetic Vocation in the New Testament and Today,* 162–85, at 168: "The existence of prophets who on the basis of their gifts and their emergence could lay special claim to that office did not, however, exclude the fact that all the baptized were called to be prophets, and that each individual could strive for that gift because he [or she] already possessed it in principle." David Hill, "On the Evidence for the Creative Role of Christian Prophets," *NTS* 20 (1973/74) 262–74, at 266–68, points out that not every inspired speech in early Christianity stemmed from prophecy: see idem, "Christian Prophets as Teachers or Instructors in the Church," in Panagopoulos, *Prophetic Vocation* 108–30.

[50] For its appearance in the New Testament and parts of the non-canonical and early Church literature see the detailed summary in Aune, *Prophecy in Early Christianity* 195ff.

For the function of the prophets see Heinrich Greeven, "Propheten, Lehrer, Vorsteher bei Paulus. Zur Frage der 'Ämter' im Urchristentum," *ZNW* 44 (1952/3) 1–43; Hill, "On the Evidence for the Creative Role of Christian Prophets," idem, "Christian Prophets as Teachers;" Boring, *The Continuing Voice of Jesus* 93–122; Aune, *Prophecy in Early Christianity* 201ff.; for other literature on individual writings see below.

   [51] 2 Cor 12:1-4 (Paul speaking of himself).

   [52] Mart. Pol. 16,2 calls Polycarp of Smyrna διδάσκαλος ἀποστολικὸς καὶ προφητικὸς γενόμενος ἐπίσκοπος (an apostolic and prophetic teacher and bishop).

   [53] This does not mean that all Christians would have spoken prophetically in the same way, but at least the possibility was there: cf. Aune, *Prophecy in Early Christianity* 201.

   [54] On this see F. Schnider, "προφήτης, ου, ὁ," *EDNT* 3:183–86

   [55] On this see especially Dautzenberg, *Urchristliche Prophetie;* Margaret Mary Mitchell, *Paul and the Rhetoric of Reconciliation: An Exegetical Investigation of the Language and Composition of 1 Corinthians* (Tübingen: J.C.B. Mohr [Paul Siebeck] 1991; 1st American ed. Louisville: Westminster/John Knox, 1992) 149–75. These chapters are the starting point for a great many studies, e.g., Kraft, "Vom Ende der urchristlichen Prophetie;" Greeven, "Propheten, Lehrer, Vorsteher bei Paulus;" Müller, *Prophetie und Predigt;* Dautzenberg, *Urchristliche Prophetie.*

   [56] Dautzenberg, *Urchristliche Prophetie,* correctly emphasizes that central to Paul's criticism of Corinthian prophecy is not the danger of "false prophecy," as is often supposed from his demand for a διάκρισις πνευμάτων ("discernment of spirits"). This interpretation is suggested by the appearance of this problem in texts primarily from the second century (*Did.* 11,7-12; *Herm. Mand.* IX); in sources from the third and fourth centuries the problem dominates (Eusebius, *Hist eccl.* V, 17; Epiphanius, *Pan.* 48). According to Dautzenberg (ibid. 147) Paul is here primarily "arguing against reckless, individualistic glossolalia (14:1-25) and with undisciplined simultaneous speaking by the prophets or the prophets and pneumatics (14:31-33, 40);" similarly Antoinette C. Wire, "Prophecy and Women. Prophets in Corinth," in James E. Goering, et al., eds., *Gospel Origins and Christian Beginnings, in Honor of James M. Robinson.* Forum Fascicles 1 (Sonoma: Polebridge, 1990) 134–50, at 149, but without Dautzenberg's explicit devaluation of Corinthian prophecy.

   Paul confronts the Corinthian situation with his distinction between two types of prophetic speech: speaking in tongues and mysteries, a speech directed to God (14:2), and speaking to build up, encourage, and console, a speech directed to other human persons (14:3). Since prophecy during worship must be subject to the principle of οἰκοδομή (14:26), speaking ἐν ἀποκαλύψει, ἐν γνώσει, ἐν προφητείᾳ and ἐν διδαχῇ must be given preference over glossolalia. Paul recommends that the latter be used at worship only when an explanation is provided (14:27). As glossolalia is associated with the principle of interpretation, so is prophecy tied to διάκρισις. This argument concludes in vv. 29-33 with a practical direction: let all things be done in order. With these directions Paul assigns a primarily paraenetical function to prophecy during worship; thus also Müller, *Prophetie und Predigt* 38.

   [57] On this see Dautzenberg, *Urchristliche Prophetie* 122ff.; Müller, *Prophetie und Predigt* 23–46; Wire, "Prophecy and Women" 149.

   [58] This is consistent with Paul's missionary cooperation with women (Phil 4:2-3; Romans 16).

   [59] On this see Stefan Lösch, "Christliche Frauen in Corinth (1 Cor. 11,2-16)," *ThQ* 127 (1947) 216–61; Madeleine Boucher, "Some Unexplored Parallels to 1 Cor 11, 11-12 and Gal

3:28: The NT on the Role of Women," *CBQ* 31 (1969) 50–58; Else Kähler, *Die Frau in den paulinischen Briefen: unter besonderer Berücksichtigung des Begriffes der Unterordnung* (Zürich: Gott-helf-Verlag, 1960), 70ff.; Annie Jaubert, "Le Voile des Femmes (I Cor. XI. 2-16)," *NTS* 18 (1971/72) 419–30; Robin Scroggs, "Paul and the Eschatological Woman," *JAAR* 40 (1972) 283–303; idem, "Paul and the Eschatological Woman: Revisited," *JAAR* 42 (1974) 532–37; James B. Hurley, "Did Paul Require Veils or the Silence of Women? A Consideration of 1 Cor 11:2-16 and 1 Cor 14:33b-36," *WThJ* 35 (1972/73) 190–220; Elaine Pagels, "Paul and Women: A Response to Recent Discussion," *JAAR* 42 (1974) 538–49; William O. Walker, "1 Corinthians 11:2-16" (1975); idem, "The 'Theology of Women's Place' and the 'Paulinist' Tradition," *Semeia* 28 (1983) 101–12; Jerome Murphy-O'Connor, "The Non-Pauline Character of 1 Corinthians 11:2-16," *JBL* 95 (1976) 615–21; idem, "Sex and Logic in 1 Corinthians 11:2-16," *CBQ* 42 (1980) 482–500; idem, "Interpolations in 1 Corinthians," *CBQ* 48 (1986) 81–94; John P. Meier, "On the Veiling of Hermeneutics (1 Cor 11:2-16)," *CBQ* 40 (1978) 212–26; Robert Jewett, "The Sexual Liberation of the Apostle Paul," *JAAR* 47 (1979) 55–87; Darrell J. Doughty, "Women and Liberation in the Churches of Paul and the Pauline Tradition," *DGW* 50 (1979) 1–21; Francis X. Cleary, "Women in the New Testament: St. Paul and the Early Pauline Churches," *BTB* 10 (1980) 78–82; Bernadette J. Brooten, "Paul's Views on the Nature of Women and Female Homoeroticism," in Clarissa W. Atkinson, Constance H. Buchanan, and Margaret R. Miles, eds., *Immaculate and Powerful: The Female in Sacred Image and Social Reality* (Boston: Beacon, 1985) 61–87, at 75ff.; Max Küchler, *Schweigen, Schmuck und Schleier. Drei neutestamentliche Vorschriften zur Verdrängung der Frauen auf dem Hintergrund einer frauenfeindlichen Exegese des Alten Testaments im antiken Judentum.* NTOA 1 (Göttingen: Vandenhoeck & Ruprecht, 1986) 73–114, 481–97; Elisabeth Schüssler Fiorenza, *In Memory of Her* 226–36; Dennis R. MacDonald, "Corinthian Veils and Gnostic Androgynes," in Karen L. King, ed., *Images of the Feminine in Gnosticism.* Studies in Antiquity and Christianity 4 (Philadelphia: Fortress, 1988) 276–92, and see Bernadette Brooten's "Response" in the same volume, 293–96; Birgit Bosold, "'Darum soll die Frau einen Schleier tragen . . . .' Überlegungen zu 1. Korinther 11 im Kontext paulinischer Gemeindetheologie und Gemeindeordnung," *Schlangenbrut* 23 (1988) 13–15; Wire, *The Corinthian Women Prophets* 116–34; eadem, "Prophecy and Women;" Troels Engberg-Pedersen, "1 Corinthians 11:16 and the Character of Pauline Exhortation," *JBL* 110 (1991) 679–89; Norbert Baumert, *Woman and Man in Paul: Overcoming a Misunderstanding* (Collegeville: The Liturgical Press, 1996) 182–209; idem, *Antifeminismus bei Paulus? Einzelstudien.* fzb 68 (Würzburg: Echter, 1992) 53–108.

[60] See the summary in Arthur Rowe, "Silence and the Christian Women of Corinth. An Examination of 1 Corinthians 14:33b-36," *CV* 33 (1990) 41–84, a model presentation of the most important aspects of the scholarly discussion of 1 Cor 14:33b-36. But see also Gottfried Fitzer, *"Das Weib schweige in der Gemeinde." Über den unpaulinischen Charakter der mulier-taceat-Verse in 1. Korinther 14.* TEH n.s. 110 (Munich: Kaiser, 1963); Sverre Aalen, "A Rabbinic Formula in I Cor. 14,34," *Studia Evangelica* 87 (1964) 513–25; Hans-Werner Bartsch, *Die Anfänge urchristlicher Rechtsbildungen. Studien zu den Pastoralbriefen.* ThF 34 (Hamburg-Bergstedt: H. Reich, 1965) 68ff.; Hurley, "Did Paul Require Veils or the Silence of Women?"; Dautzenberg, *Urchristliche Prophetie* 257–73; Jewett, "The Sexual Liberation of the Apostle Paul," Cleary, "Women in the New Testament," 81–82; E. Earle Ellis, "The Silenced Wives of Corinth (1 Cor. 14:34-5)," in Eldon Jay Epp and Gordon D. Fee, eds., *New Testament Textual Criticism. Its Significance for Exegesis. Essays in Honour of Bruce M. Metzger* (Oxford: Clarendon Press; New York: Oxford Uni-

versity Press, 1981) 213–20; David W. Odell-Scott, "Let the Women Speak in Church. An Egalitarian Interpretation of 1 Cor 14:33b-36," *BTB* 13 (1983) 90–93; Walker, "The 'Theology of Woman's Place';" Küchler, *Schweigen, Schmuck und Schleier* 54–63; Murphy-O'Connor, "Interpolations," 90–92; Schüssler Fiorenza, *In Memory of Her* 230–33; Winsome Munro, "Women, Text and the Canon: The Strange Case of 1 Corinthians 14:33-35," *BTB* 18 (1988) 26–31 (a report on the tendencies in American exegetical discussion of the passage); Wire, *The Corinthian Women Prophets* 229–32; Baumert, *Woman and Man in Paul* 195–98; idem, *Antifeminismus bei Paulus?* 109–42.

[61] Paul does not mention any of these prophets, male or female, by name.

[62] On this see Helmut Merklein, *Das kirchliche Amt nach dem Epheserbrief.* StANT 33 (Munich: Kösel, 1973).

[63] For the Lukan reception of the Joel tradition cf. Richard F. Zehnle, *Peter's Pentecost Discourse. Tradition and Lukan Reinterpretation in Peter's Speeches of Acts 2 and 3.* SBL.MS 15 (Nashville: Abingdon, 1971) 28–34, 125ff.

[64] For the function of prophets in Acts see Ellis, "The Role of Christian Prophets in Acts," in idem, *Prophecy and Hermeneutic in Early Christianity. New Testament Essays.* WUNT 18 (Tübingen: J.C.B. Mohr, 1978), 129–44; Aune, *Prophecy in Early Christianity* 205.

[65] For what follows see Kurt Niederwimmer, *Askese und Mysterium. Über Ehe, Ehescheidung und Eheverzicht in den Anfängen des christlichen Glaubens.* FRLANT 113 (Göttingen: Vandenhoeck & Ruprecht, 1975) 171; François Bovon, *Das Evangelium nach Lukas (Lk 1,1–9,50).* EKK III/1 (Neukirchen-Vluyn: Neukirchener Verlag, 1989) 134–51; Gerhard Schneider, *Das Evangelium nach Lukas.* ÖTK 3/1–2 (3rd rev. ed. Gütersloh and Würzburg: Gerd Mohn, 1992) 69–73.

[66] For the meaning of the word see Bovon, *Lukas* 149.

[67] Thus also Bovon, *Lukas* 148–50.

[68] Thus also Schüssler Fiorenza, *In Memory of Her* 299.

[69] Bovon, *Lukas* 85.

[70] See the detailed analysis of the text by Bovon, ibid. 87–92. In the history of interpretation this hymn has also been interpreted as Mary's prophetic speech; cf. for example the "Dialogue between an Orthodox Christian and a Montanist."

[71] Philip is known as a former member of the Hellenistic "Seven" (Acts 6:5) and an important missionary in the coastal region (Acts 8:4-40). On Philip see the study by F. Scott Spencer, *The Portrait of Philip in Acts. A Study of Roles and Relations.* JSNT.S 67 (Sheffield: JSOT Press, 1992).

[72] Thus also Ernst Haenchen, *The Acts of the Apostles; A Commentary.* Translated by Bernard Noble and Gerald Shinn, under the supervision of Hugh Anderson, and with the translation revised and brought up to date by Robert McLean Wilson (Philadelphia: Westminster, 1971); Lindblom, *Gesichte und Offenbarungen* 179; Hans Conzelmann, *Acts of the Apostles: A Commentary on the Acts of the Apostles.* Translated by James Limburg, A. Thomas Kraabel, and Donald H. Juel; edited by Eldon Jay Epp with Christopher R. Matthews (Philadelphia: Fortress, 1987) 178; Ellis, "The Role of Christian Prophets," 130; Jürgen Roloff, *Die Apostelgeschichte.* NTD 5 (Göttingen: Vandenhoeck & Ruprecht, 1981) 310; Gerhard Schneider, *Die Apostelgeschichte.* HThK V/1–2 (Freiburg, Basel, and Vienna: Herder, 1982) 304; Ivoni Richter Reimer, *Women in the Acts of the Apostles. A Feminist Liberation Perspective.* Translated by Linda M. Maloney (Minneapolis: Fortress, 1995) 248–49. This interpretation is suggested as well by the history of the text's influence, as I will show.

[73] Schneider, *Apostelgeschichte* 304 n. 26: "In Luke the absolute προφητεύω primarily describes prophetic (i.e., predictive) speech: Luke 1:67; Acts 2:17, 18; 19:6; 21:9."

[74] Thus Haenchen, *Acts* 601; Alfons Weiser, *Die Apostelgeschichte*. ÖTK 5/1 (Gütersloh: Gerd Mohn, 1981, 1985) 591; Rudolf Pesch, *Die Apostelgeschichte*. 2 vols. EKK V/1-2 (Neukirchen-Vluyn: Neukirchener Verlag, 1986) 213; Gerd Lüdemann, *Das frühe Christentum nach den Traditionen der Apostelgeschichte: ein Kommentar* (Göttingen: Vandenhoeck & Ruprecht, 1987) 242. Lüdemann considers it uncertain whether the description of the daughters as virgins was part of the tradition. Their virginity should not be accorded any greater significance (with Niederwimmer, *Askese und Mysterium* 171). Παρθένος means that these women were of marriageable age: thus Joseph A. Fitzmyer, "παρθένος," *EDNT* 3:39–40; Weiser, *Apostelgeschichte* 590; Schneider, *Apostelgeschichte* 304 n. 27; Pesch, *Apostelgeschichte* 213.

Mary Rose D'Angelo, "Women in Luke-Acts: A Redactional View," *JBL* 109 (1990) 441–61, at 453, interprets the fact that the women are not called prophets *expressis verbis* as Luke's attempt to disassociate women from prophecy. If this is correct—although Luke's placing of women in the context of prophetic activity, as shown above (cf. Luke 1:41-55; 2:36-38), and the Lukan reception of Joel (Acts 2:17) speak against it—we would have to suppose that the source called the daughters of Philip "prophets."

[75] Thus Conzelmann, *Acts* 178.

[76] Cf. also Peter Corssen, "Die Töchter des Philippus," *ZNW* 2 (1901) 289–99; Jensen, *God's Self-Confident Daughters* 16–18 (and see her critique of Corssen in n. 65).

[77] Ulrich Körtner, *Papias von Hierapolis. Ein Beitrag zur Geschichte des frühen Christentums.* FRLANT 133 (Göttingen: Vandenhoeck & Ruprecht, 1983) 145. He emphasizes that the appearance of the daughters of Philip does not imply that Papias was acquainted with Acts.

[78] Ibid. 145.

[79] On this see Heinrich Kraft, *Die Offenbarung des Johannes.* HNT 16a (Tübingen: Mohr, 1974) 67ff.; Müller, *Prophetie und Predigt* 66–72; idem, *Die Offenbarung des Johannes.* ÖTK 19 (Gütersloh: Gerd Mohn, 1984) 115ff.; Colin J. Hemer, *The Letters to the Seven Churches of Asia in their Local Setting.* JSNT.S 11 (Sheffield: JSOT, 1986) 106–28. For the form of the letters cf. especially Ferdinand Hahn, "Die Sendschreiben der Johannesapokalypse. Ein Beitrag zur Bestimmung prophetischer Redeformen," in Gert Jeremias, Heinz-Wolfgang Kuhn, and Hartmut Stegemann, eds., *Tradition und Glaube. Festgabe K. G. Kuhn* (Göttingen: Vandenhoeck & Ruprecht, 1971), 357–94; Müller, *Offenbarung* 91–96; Martin Karrer, *Die Johannesoffenbarung als Brief. Studien zu ihrem literarischen, historischen und theologischen Ort.* FRLANT 140 (Göttingen: Vandenhoeck & Ruprecht, 1986).

[80] Cf. Emil Schürer, "Die Prophetin Isabel in Thyatira. Offenb. Joh. 2,20," *Theologische Abhandlungen. FS Carl von Weizsäcker* (Freiburg: J.C.B. Mohr [(Paul Siebeck)], 1892) 37–57; Hugo Odeberg, " Ἰεζάβελ," *TDNT* 3:217–18; Akira Satake, *Die Gemeindeordnung in der Johannesapokalypse.* WMANT 21 (Neukirchen-Vluyn: Neukirchener Verlag, 1966) 65–67; Hemer, *The Letters to the Seven Churches* 117–23 (cf. the critique of Schürer's thesis here); Adela Yarbro Collins, "Women's History and the Book of Revelation," *SBL Seminar Papers* (1987) 80–91; Schüssler Fiorenza, *In Memory of Her* 246; Ingrid Maisch, "Isebel. Autoritätskonflikt – nicht nur in Thyatira," in Karin Walter, ed., *Zwischen Ohnmacht und Befreiung. Biblische Frauengestalten* (Freiburg, Basel, and Vienna: Herder, 1988) 163–72; Horst Goldstein, " Ἰεζάβελ," *EDNT* 2:173.

[81] For prophecy and prophets in Revelation see especially Satake, *Gemeindeordnung* 47–86; David Hill, "Prophecy and Prophets in the Revelation of St John," *NTS* 18 (1971/72) 401–18; Schüssler Fiorenza, "Apokalypsis and Propheteia. The Book of Revelation in the Context of Early Christian Prophecy," in Jan Lambrecht, ed., *L'Apocalypse johannique et l'Apocalyptique dans le Nouveau Testament.* BEThL 53 (Louvain: Leuven University Press, 1980) 105–28; Aune, *Prophecy in Early Christianity* 205ff.

[82] Cf. Karrer, *Johannesoffenbarung als Brief* 195.

[83] The identification of Jezebel with the Nicolaitans is found frequently in the exegetical literature on this passage: e.g., Ernst Lohmeyer, *Die Offenbarung des Johannes.* HNT 16 (Tübingen, J. C. B. Mohr [P. Siebeck] 1926) 28; Kraft, *Offenbarung des Johannes* 74; Maisch, "Isebel," 164; Müller, *Offenbarung des Johannes* 98. Differently Karrer, *Johannesoffenbarung als Brief* 195. He points out that the followers of Balaam are indeed identified with the Nicolaitans (2:14-15), but there are no such indications in the case of Jezebel, and one should avoid identifying her as a Nicolaitan.

[84] See, for example, Müller, *Offenbarung des Johannes* 116ff.; Hemer, *The Letters to the Seven Churches;* Collins, "Women's History and the Book of Revelation," 82–83. For a critique see Karrer, *Johannesoffenbarung als Brief* 201–202.

[85] Hahn, "Die Sendschreiben der Johannesapokalypse," 363, points to the problem: "In this one should not overlook the fact that the statements about the situations in the churches and their danger from false teaching are marked by a perceptible stylization, so that it is not very easy to give an exact description of the special conditions of the individual churches and the particular characteristics of the heresy." On this see especially Karrer, *Johannesoffenbarung als Brief* 196, 200.

[86] Müller, *Offenbarung des Johannes* 97: "Meat sacrificed to idols is either meat eaten at pagan cultic meals or the flesh of animals who have been sacrificed to the gods, the remaining parts of which were subsequently offered for sale."

[87] Lohmeyer, *Offenbarung* 31: "πορνεῦσαι . . . is a common expression in the OT for syncretistic movements. The fact that [these churches] are branded with such hard words is a consequence of the view of the Seer, similar only to what we find in the Fourth Gospel, that there is an unbridgeable gap between the church and the world . . . there is no hint of a fundamental moral liberalism implied by this word." Against Müller, *Offenbarung des Johannes* 97: "Fornication refers to libertinistic sexual behavior." But compare the "two-layered interpretation" in Karrer, *Johannesoffenbarung als Brief* 200.

[88] Cf. Müller, *Offenbarung des Johannes* 97; Karrer, *Johannesoffenbarung als Brief* 196.

[89] Karrer, *Johannesoffenbarung als Brief* 196.

[90] Cf. also 1 Kings 21:5-16, 23-26. On this see Maisch, "Isebel," 164–66. Maisch shows that in the deuteronomistic narrative tradition Jezebel is made the chief villain in the conflict between Ahab and Naboth. She summarizes: "Accordingly, the deuteronomistic historical writing has chosen to characterize Jezebel as a woman led astray to idolatry and apostasy."

[91] Karrer, *Johannesoffenbarung als Brief* 196, with examples and bibliographic references.

[92] Ibid. 198: "Even though, as a consequence, very little can be said about the opponents' 'teaching of Balaam' . . . it remains true that the opponents do connect elements of teaching with Balaam (2:14b) and with the prophet of Thyatira (2:20, 24). The defining characteristic of their prophecy is therefore not prediction of the future—none of the fea-

tures in the letters referring to false teaching indicates any kind of independent significance attributed to the future—but the transmission of knowledge (see esp. 2:24)."

[93] The threat of judgment, Ἰδοὺ βάλλω αὐτὴν εἰς κλίνην (Rev 2:22), when seen as a play on the topos of fornication in the sense that the bed of fornication is replaced by the deathbed (thus Müller, *Offenbarung des Johannes* 119; on this see also Hemer, *The Letters to the Seven Churches* 121) is not sex-specific either. On this see Müller, *Offenbarung des Johannes* 119: "The first part, 'Beware, I am throwing her on a bed,' employs a hebraizing expression modeled on Exod 21:18 (LXX); 1 Macc 1:5; Jdt 8:3."

[94] For what follows see also Aune, *Prophecy in Early Christianity* 291–310; James L. Ash, "The Decline of Ecstatic Prophecy in the Early Church," *TS* 37 (1976) 227–52.

[95] On this see Harnack, *Die Lehre der zwölf Apostel;* Gottfried Schille, "Das Recht der Propheten und der Apostel – gemeinderechtliche Beobachtungen zu Didache Kapitel 11–13," *ThV* 1 (1966) 84–103; Kurt Niederwimmer, *The Didache.* Translated by Linda M. Maloney. Edited by Harold W. Attridge. Hermeneia (Minneapolis: Fortress, 1998) 178–82.

[96] On this see Martin Dibelius, *Der Hirt des Hermas.* HNT Ergänzungsband 4 (Tübingen: J.C.B. Mohr, 1923) 536ff.; J. Reiling, *Hermas and the Christian Prophecy. A Study of the Eleventh Mandate.* NT.S 37 (Leiden: Brill, 1973); Norbert Brox, *Der Hirt des Hermas.* KAV 7 (Göttingen: Vandenhoeck & Ruprecht, 1991) 249ff.

[97] *Acts of Paul, Letter to the Corinthians* 1,8; 9. On this see Schüssler Fiorenza, *In Memory of Her* 300 (with further examples); Jensen, *God's Self-Confident Daughters* 131–33, with commentary on the content of these women's prophecy.

[98] Eusebius, *Hist. eccl.* 5.16.2-3, on which see below.

[99] Maximilla, Priscilla, and Montanus. On the Montanist prophets see Zscharnack, *Dienst der Frau* 179–82; Kraft, "Die altkirchliche Prophetie und die Entstehung des Montanismus," has shown that Montanus was only elevated to the status of prophet at a later time. For the discussion of this thesis see Jensen, *God's Self-Confident Daughters* 153–73. She concludes that *"The real prophetic authority in the 'Montanist' movement lay not with Montanus but with Prisca and Maximilla"* (p. 154; italics in original).

[100] See the summary in Zscharnack, *Dienst der Frau* 156–79. For the prophet and teacher Philomena see ibid., 175–76, but more especially Jensen, "Philumene oder Das Streben nach Vergeistigung," in Karin Walter, ed., *Sanft und rebellisch. Mütter der Christenheit – von Frauen neu entdeckt* (Freiburg, Basel, and Vienna: Herder, 1990) 221–43, and eadem, *God's Self-Confident Daughters* 194–225.

[101] Justin, *Dial.* 88; Irenaeus, *Adv. haer.* 3.11.9. For Irenaeus's interpretation of the spirit see G. Nathanael Bonwetsch, *Die Theologie des Irenäus.* BFChTh 2/9 (Gütersloh: Gerd Mohn, 1925) 65–69.

[102] Hippolytus, *Refutatio* 7.38 (Philomena); 8.19 (Priscilla and Maximilla).

[103] Hippolytus, *Refutatio* 8.19; 10.25.

[104] Hermann Josef Vogt, *Das Kirchenverständnis des Origenes.* BoBKG 4 (Cologne and Vienna: Böhlau, 1974).

[105] Origen, *Fragments on 1 Cor 7.*

[106] See also Origen's commentary on 1 Cor 14:33b-36, published in Ronald E. Heine, ed., *The Montanist Oracles and Testimonia.* PatMS 1 (Macon, Ga.: Mercer University Press, 1989) 98–99.

[107] On Ammia see also Jensen, *God's Self-Confident Daughters* 18–19.

[108] On this see Schepelern, *Der Montanismus und die phrygischen Kulte* 1ff.; Walter Bauer, *Orthodoxy and Heresy in Earliest Christianity*. Translated by a team from the Philadelphia Seminar on Christian Origins, and edited by Robert A. Kraft and Gerhard Krodel (Philadelphia: Fortress, 1971) 132–37, especially 136; Wilhelm Kühnert, "Der antimontanistische Anonymus des Eusebius," *ThZ* 5 (1949) 436–46; Jensen, *God's Self-Confident Daughters* 150–51.

[109] For the motif of the διαδοχὴ τῶν προφητῶν cf. Paulsen, "Papyrus Oxyrynchus I.5 und die ΔΙΑΔΟΧΗ ΤΩΝ ΠΡΟΦΗΤΩΝ." For the notion of success in general see Harnack, *The Constitution and Law of the Church in the First Two Centuries*. Translated by F. L. Pogson; edited by H. D. A. Major (London: Williams & Norgate; New York: G.P. Putnam's Sons, 1910) 121–34; Hans von Campenhausen, *Kirchliches Amt und geistliche Vollmacht in den ersten drei Jahrhunderten*. BHTh 14 (Tübingen: J.C.B. Mohr [Paul Siebeck], 1953; 2nd rev. ed. 1963) 163–94.

[110] Eusebius, *Hist. eccl.* V.17.2. The reproach of ecstatic prophecy is a common topos in antimontanistic polemic; cf. also Epiphanius, *Panarion* 48.

[111] Cf. Eusebius, *Hist. eccl.* III.37.1, where Quadratus is regarded as a prophet in the διαδοχὴ τῶν ἀποστόλων.

[112] Blank, "Die Frau als Wortverkünderin," 59, also emphasizes the nonchalance with which Anonymus refers to women Montanist and Church prophets.

[113] We may draw this conclusion because the Montanist women prophets appealed to her example. Priscilla and Maximilla are thought to have been active in the second half of the second century.

[114] See also above.

[115] Tertullian, *Adv. Marc.* V.8.11; *De anima* 9.4; *De resurr. mort.* 11.2-3.

[116] Kraft, "Die altkirchliche Prophetie und die Entstehung des Montanismus," 257. He continues: "When, with Montanism, the prophets departed from the Church, the martyrs entered into the inheritance of the prophets within the Church; the Holy Spirit now spoke through them, and the charism of the martyrs came into conflict with the official power of the bishops. Then the persecuted and forbidden Church became the state religion. Martyrdom ceased. The authority to instruct the Church in the power of the Holy Spirit was now claimed, in the wake of the prophets and martyrs, by the ascetics, and from then on the episcopal office had to contend with them and to have regard for the demands of their piety." Ibid. 263.

[117] Attempts to associate accounts of the martyrs that contain prophetic and ecstatic features, such as the reports of the martyrs of Lyons (Eusebius, *Hist. eccl.* V.2) with Montanism reveal circular reasoning: the starting point is the assumption that there was no more prophetic speech in the churches after the middle of the second century; consequently sources that nevertheless attest to such speech are regarded as Montanist. W. H. C. Frend, *Martyrdom and Persecution in the Early Church. A Study of a Conflict from the Maccabees to Donatus* (Oxford: Blackwell, 1965) 16 distanced himself from such an assessment of the martyrs of Lyons, against de Labriolle, *La Crise Montaniste* 220ff.; instead of postulating dependency he speaks of parallel religious developments.

[118] On this see especially Jensen, *God's Self-Confident Daughters* 81–124.

[119] Cyprian, *Ep.* 75,9–11 (CSEL 3/2 817–18).

[120] Cyprian, *Ep.* 75,10. Hans Achelis, "Spuren des Urchristentums auf den griechischen Inseln?" *ZNW* 1 (1900) 87–100, at 97 n. 6, interprets her as tending to Montanism.

Friedrich, "Über die Cenones der Montanisten bei Hieronymus," 213; de Labriolle, *La Crise Montaniste* 487–88; and most recently Jensen, *God's Self-Confident Daughters* 182–86 with good reason question a Montanist identification.

[121] Cyprian, *Ep.* 75,10. He says that she fell into ecstasy *(quae in extasin constituta)* and acted as if she were filled with the Spirit *(quasi sancto spiritu plena sic ageret).*

[122] Alexander Severus reigned from 222–235, Maximus Trax from 235–238.

[123] Cyprian, *Ep.* 75,10.

[124] Jensen, *God's Self-Confident Daughters* 184–86, gives good reasons for believing that this account by Firmilian is no invention.

[125] See also, similarly, Seeberg, "Über das Reden der Frauen in den apostolischen Gemeinden," 136.

[126] For women prophets in Q see Luise Schottroff, "Wanderprophetinnen. Eine feministische Analyse der Logienquelle," *EvTh* 51 (1991) 332–34.

[127] The no longer resolvable question whether Nanas the prophet was a Montanist or not is of no importance in this context.

[128] There are many explanations given for the causes of this phenomenon. See Harnack, *Expansion of Christianity* 1:442; Kraft, "Die altkirchliche Prophetie und die Entstehung des Montanismus;" idem, "Vom Ende der urchristlichen Prophetie;" Frederick C. Klawitter, *The New Prophecy in Early Christianity. The Origin, Nature, and Development of Montanism, A.D. 165–220.* Diss. Chicago, 1975 (microfilm); Ash, "The Decline of Ecstatic Prophecy in the Early Church;" Aune, *Prophecy in Early Christianity;* Schüssler Fiorenza, *In Memory of Her* 302–303. Jensen, *God's Self-Confident Daughters* 36–37 speaks, with regard to the early Christian women prophets, of a "silence" of the sources, which she interprets as "suppression." I cannot agree with this thesis, for the reasons given above. The state of the sources is meager not only with regard to women prophets, but for male prophets and early Christian prophecy in general.

[129] Differently Richter Reimer, *Women in Acts* 249: "The struggle against prophetic women reached a climax in the third century . . . ."

IV. Teachers of Theology

A. A Papyrus Letter

Origin unknown   IV

BIBLIOGRAPHY:
Nagel, Marcel. "Lettre chrétienne sur Papyrus (provenant de milieux sectaires du
    IVe siècle?)," *ZPE* 18 (1975) 317–23.
Tibiletti, Giuseppe. *Le lettere private nei papiri greci del III e IV secolo d. C. Tra
    paganesimo e cristianesimo.* Scienze filologiche e letteratura 15 (Milan:
    Vita e pensiero, 1979) 192–93 no. 32.
Horsley, G. H. R. *New Documents Illustrating Early Christianity.* Vol. 1: *A Review
    of the Greek Inscriptions and Papyri published in 1976* (North Ryde,
    N.S.W.: Macquarie Ancient History Association, 1981) 121 no. 79; Vol.
    4: *A Review of the Greek Inscriptions and Papyri published in 1979*
    [1987] 240 no. 122.

. . .
ναι σοι καινη ἐν Ἀλεξανδρεί[ᾳ
ἀδελφὸν κ(ύριό)ν μου Ἰουλ[ι]ανὸν πι[
καὶ ἐὰν θέλετε μ[. .]ον ομου[
μεν ὃ δυνάμεθα καλόν · τὸν . [
5   Κυρίαν τὴν διδάσκαλον · τὸν κ . [
τὸν γράψαντά μοι καὶ ἐπιστολὴν [
κυρ(ίαν) Ξενικὴν, κυρ(ίαν) Ἀρσινόην καὶ π [
ληθείας τὸν σεβασ . ἐλεύθερον κ[
Φιλόξενον καὶ τοὺς σούς · Ὁ κ(ύριο)ς μ[
10 ὁ καλὸς Φοιβάμμων καὶ πᾶσα ἡ ο[ἰκία προσαγορεύου-
σιν ὑμᾶς · Ἡ χάρις τοῦ κ(υρίου) ἡμῶν Ἰη(σοῦ) [Χρ(ιστοῦ)
                    | μετὰ πάντων ὑμῶν.

On the left side of the sheet, vertically alongside the text stands:

12 Κυρ]ίαν τὴν διδάσκ(αλον)

The address is on the verso and consists of two vertical lines on the left side of
the sheet:

13   ἀπόδος τῷ] παναρίστῳ Φιλοξένῳ διδ(ασκάλῳ)

το .... ϱλϱ( )[1]

Line 3:   Nagel considers μ[όν]ον a possible reading.

Line 5:   Κυρία is a personal name (cf. line 12).[2] It is to be distinguished from κ(ύριο)ς (lines 2, 9, and 11) as a designation for Christ and κυρ(ία), abbreviated twice in line 7 as a "courteous form of address in letters."[3]

Line 7:   Ξενική as a personal name is, in contrast to Ξενικός, not otherwise attested.[4]

Line 8:   Nagel adds Ἀ]ληθείας.

Line 10:   καλὸς together with a personal name appears frequently in papyrus letters as a polite expression and form of address.[5]

Lines 10–11: The greeting in the closing formula is traditionally Christian.[6]

Line 13: The form of address is traditional.[7]

. . . newly in Alexandria . . . my lord brother Julianus . . . and if you wish (only?) . . . what we have in the way of good things: the . . . the teacher Kyria: the . . . who also wrote me the letter . . . the lady Xenike, the lady Arsinoe, and . . . the honorable freemen . . . Philoxenos and your own people: the lord . . . the good Phoibammon and the whole household greet you: The grace of our Lord Jesus Christ be with you all.

Left margin: Kyria the teacher.

Address: To the best of all teachers Philoxenos . . .

The geographical origin of the letter is unknown, though the reference to Alexandria in line 1 points to Egypt.[8] The content and purpose of the letter can no longer be determined,[9] because the beginning is lost and the right half of the papyrus has crumbled. The names of three women (lines 5/12; 7) and three men (lines 2; 9; 10/13) are mentioned.[10] This high percentage of women—relative to literary texts—is characteristic of Christian papyrus letters.[11] The additional reference to the teacher Kyria in the vertical writing on the left side of the sheet is the remnant of an additional greeting to her.[12] The only verifiable addressee of the letter is the teacher Philoxenos.[13] The final greetings are clear evidence of the Christian provenience of the letter; they are in the style of New Testament greeting formulae and also contain the *nomen sacrum*. This could indicate that this is not a private letter,[14] but a writing for the purpose of Christian instruction.

The important aspect of this letter is the twofold mention of the teacher (διδάσκαλος) Kyria (lines 5 and 12) and the teacher Philoxenos (line 13). We must ask how these Christian teachers, and especially this Christian woman teacher, can be located in light of the history of the Church in Egypt in the fourth century.

As late as the first third of the third century we have evidence from Origen[15] and Dionysius of Alexandria[16] of an office of Christian teachers in Egypt, parallel to the clergy.[17] In the fourth and fifth centuries these attestations are increasingly sparse because the independent institution of the teaching office was largely subsumed by the clergy from the third century onward.[18] Nevertheless, there are witnesses to the continuance of a group of Christian teachers independent of the clergy in Egypt: Didymus of Alexandria[19] was a lay ascetic and an important Alexandrian teacher of the fourth century; he was in the succession of leaders of the Alexandrian school for catechists.[20] Church orders as late as the fifth century attest to teachers who were responsible for instructing catechumens: these include the *Traditio Apostolica* (*TA* 15, 18, 19, 41)[21] and, following it, the *Constitutiones Apostolorum* (*CA* VIII, 32)[22] and the *Canones Hippolyti* (*Can. Hipp.* 12, 17, 18, 19)[23] as well as the *Testamentum Domini* (*TD* II, 1; 4). The church historian Socrates[24] tells us that in Alexandria in the first half of the fifth century on the stational days the Scriptures were read and interpreted by διδάσκαλοι during the non-eucharistic liturgies of the Word. He emphasizes the antiquity of this custom with a reference to Origen, who taught in the churches on such days.[25] These texts show that in the fourth and fifth centuries there was still a place for Christian teachers who were not members of the clergy, not only as teachers of catechumens, but also as interpreters of Scripture during worship. Against the background of such traditions Kyria and Philoxenos clearly appear as fourth-century Christian teachers.

Having determined that much, we must ask whether women were among these Catholic teachers. On the basis of the idea, nourished by 1 Tim 2:12, that women were not permitted to teach in the Catholic Church, Marcel Nagel assigns this papyrus letter to a heretical milieu. However, there are no indications at all in the fragmentary text of the letter from which one could draw such a conclusion.[26] E. A. Judge, in contrast, attempts to show how it is plausible that Kyria could have been a Catholic teacher in an extraordinary ecclesiastical situation.[27] He refers to a law enacted under Licinius, as reported by Eusebius of Caesarea, whereby the bishops were forbidden to instruct women (καθηγεῖσθαι γυναιξὶ θεοσεβῶν λόγων). Instead, according to Eusebius, Licinius required that only women should instruct women (γυναῖκες δ᾽ αἱρεῖσθαι γυναικῶν διδασκάλους).[28] Apart from the question whether such a law was ever enacted—there are no other sources that report it—it rests on the premise that the authority to teach was entirely restricted to the bishops and that there was no ordinary practice of teaching by women. This opinion is an aspect of Eusebius's literary tendency that is not identical with the complex reality of the ancient Church communities. In the first place it was not only bishops who taught, and in the second place women's teaching was not an interim phase in history, as will be shown.

Besides the sources given above, the *Canones Hippolyti,* originating probably in Alexandria or northern Egypt in the fourth century,[29] are a particularly good witness to (Church) teachers independent of the clergy (*Can. Hipp.* 12, 17, 18, 19). The teachers mentioned there were responsible for the instruction of catechumens. Since *Can. Hipp.* does not acknowledge any prohibition on women's teaching we cannot exclude the possibility that women were also part of the group. This is not contradicted by the fact that the *Canones Hippolyti* forbid the ordination of women (*Can. Hipp.* 9). Since those who taught catechumens did not belong to the clergy they were of course not ordained.

In this connection it is interesting to note the places in Egypt's Christian literature where we encounter traditions that document the teaching activity of women. John Kevin Coyle has pointed out that we can identify the practice of Christian instruction independent of the clergy beyond the third century in "monastic" circles, among others.[30] A glance at Egyptian monasticism confirms this thesis not only for men but also for women.

The sayings of the desert mothers Theodora and Synkletica[31] found in the *Apophthegmata Patrum*[32] are about teaching. Amma Theodora discusses the required characteristics of the διδάσκαλος[33] and Amma Synkletica speaks of the preconditions of διδαχή.[34] The topos of teaching is also constant in the traditions about Synkletike outside the apophthegmatic tradition. In her *Vita* she is described as a teacher in the fullest sense:[35] first, the title of the *Vita* presents her as διδάσκαλος;[36] second, this motif is found throughout the principal section of the *Vita.* Chapters 22 to 103 contain the teaching (τα διδάγματα) of this desert mother. Finally, there are also reflections on her manner of teaching.[37]

This document originated around 400 and belonged to the circle of Athanasius, bishop of Alexandria, but he did not write it.[38] The description of Synkletike as a "true disciple of the blessed Thecla" locates it in the tradition of the missionary teacher Thecla of Asia Minor. That is only one example of the reception and spread of the *Acts of Paul and Thecla* in Egypt in the fourth century.[39]

These traditions of the desert mothers show that women were present and recognized as teachers in ascetic groups, but also in episcopal circles in Egypt. We know that Bishop Synesius of Cyrene had been a pupil of the philosopher Hypatia (370/75–415), the leader of the Neoplatonists in Alexandria.[40] He wrote her seven letters that document his high regard for her.[41] In one of these letters he addresses her as "mother and sister and teacher" (μῆτερ καὶ ἀδελφὴ καὶ διδάσκαλε).[42] Noteworthy, in addition to Synesius' great respect for Hypatia, is the high estimation of her by the church historian Socrates, who wrote:

> There was a woman at Alexandria named Hypatia, daughter of the philosopher Theon, who made such attainments in literature and science, as to far surpass all the philosophers of her own time. Having succeeded to the school of Plato and

Plotinus, she explained the principles of philosophy to her auditors, many of whom came from a distance to receive her instructions. On account of the self-possession and ease of manner, which she acquired in consequence of the cultivation of her mind, she not infrequently appeared in public in presence of the magistrates. Neither did she feel abashed in coming to an assembly of men. For all men on account of her extraordinary dignity and virtue admired her the more. Yet even she fell a victim to the political jealousy which at that time prevailed. . . .[43]

B. Inscriptions

Tomb Epigraph for Magistra Theodora

Italy/Rome/Basilica of St. Agnes, Via Nomentana[44]   382

BIBLIOGRAPHY:
ICUR I 317 (*Supplementum* 1703).
Buecheler, Franz. *Carmina Latina Epigraphica, conlegit, I–II*. Leipzig: Teubner, 1895–1897. *III. Supplementum, curavit Ernestus Lommatsch* (Leipzig: Teubner, 1926) 669.
ILCV I 316 (Vol. 5: *Nuove Correzioni alla Silloge del Diehl Inscriptiones Latinae Christianae Veteres*. Edited by A. Ferrua. SSAC 7 [Vatican City: Pontificio Istituto di archeologia cristiana, 1981]) 12.

Theodora, quae uixit annos XXI, m. VII, / d. XXIII, in pace. est bisomu.*
1   *Amplificam sequitur uitam dum casta Afrodite,*
     Fecit ad astr/a uiam, Christi modo gaudet in aula.
     Restitit haec mundo / semper caelestia quaerens.
     Optima seruatrix legis fideique / magistra
5   *<De>didit egregiam sanctis per secula mentem.*
     Inde p. eximios paradisi / regnat odores,
     Tempore continuo uernant ubi gramina riuis, /
     Expectatque deum superas quo surcat ad auras.
     Hoc posuit corpus tumulo / mortalia linquens
10   *Fundauitque locum coniunx Euac[rius ins]tans.*
dep. die [. . .] / Antonio et Siacrio con[ss.][45]

* *bisomus* = a tomb with space for two graves.[46]
Line 2: Cf. Buecheler, *Carmina Latina* 688, 5: *hic carnis spolium liquit a[d] astra uolans.*
Line 3: Cf. Cicero, *Rep.* 1, 15: *(Panaetius) caelestia vel studiosissime solet quaerere;* Tertullian, *Orat.* 6: *caelestia id est . . . dei nomen, dei voluntatem et dei regnum;* Buecheler, *Carmina Latina* 1424, 9: *tempsisti mundum semper caelestia captans.*

Line 5: Diehl *(ILCV* I 316) emends *dedidit.* Cf. Vergil, *Aeneid* 1, 445: *egregiam . . . per saecula gentem.*

Line 6: De Rossi *(ICUR* I) reads P̄ (Christogram);[47] Buecheler, *Carmina Latina,* reads *p(er).* Cf. Petrus Chrysostomos, *Serm.* 16 f. 214a: *odor paradisi, quid tibi cum foetore?;* Buecheler, *Carmina Latina* 688, 14-15: *paradise, tuas, flagrantia semper gramina et halantes diuinis floribus hortos.*

Line 7: Cf. Vergil, *Eclogues* 10, 29: . . . *nec gramina rivis.*

Line 8: Cf. 2 Pet 3:12 (Vulgate): *expectantes, et properantes in adventum diei Domini, per quem caeli ardentes solventur . . . ;*[48] Buecheler, *Carmina Latina* 279, 18: *superas consurgere in auras.*

Line 9: Cf. Buecheler, *Carmina Latina* 778, 5: *pauperibus donauit opes mortalia linquens.*

While chaste Aphrodite lived a wonderful life,
She prepared for herself a path to the stars,
   and she now lives blissfully in the halls of Christ.
She withstood the course of the world,
   thinking only of heavenly things.
She, the best keeper of the law and the best teacher of the faith,
   devoted her superior spirit through all time to the Holy alone.
Thus she lives now like a queen, in the sweet scents of Paradise,
   where the herbs grow by the streams in an eternal spring,
And she waits for God,
   through whom she desires to be elevated to the uppermost airs.
In this hill she has laid down her body, leaving what is mortal behind,
   and her husband Evacrius has erected her tomb with devotion.

This tomb epigraph was dedicated by Evac[rius] to his wife Theodora (line 10). Its topical form follows that of Latin tomb poetry, which often contained quotations from Latin poetry and biblical texts or allusions to them.[49] This tomb poem, like three-fourths of all *carmina,* refers to eternal life.[50] The acrostic discovered by Franz Buecheler in the tomb epigraph is striking:[51] *Afrodite h(onestissimam) f(eminam).*[52] Aphrodite was probably Theodora's nickname or pet name.

Central to the theme of this book are lines 4 and 5 of the epigraph, where it reads: "She was the best protector of the law and teacher of the faith; throughout her whole life she directed her superior spirit to the saints." Theodora is here described under three aspects:

(a) She was the best protector of the law *(optima servatrix legis).* This formula indicates Theodora's knowledge of the Scriptures. Origen had cultivated the idea of constant meditation on the "delights of the Law."[53] We find the same topos in Jerome, who praised Marcella's meditation on the law, the *"divinarum scripturarum."*[54]

(b) She was a teacher of the faith *(fides magistra)*. This description indicates that she was a theological teacher.

(c) Her designation as teacher of the faith is given further precision by the naming of the audience for her teaching. We read that she directed her superior spirit to the saints *(sanctis),* a reference to the believers in Rome.

All three of these phrases describe Theodora as an active teacher of the faith who devoted all her efforts to the law, the faith, and the saints. A glance at the situation of the Church in Rome during the fourth century illumines this apparently isolated phenomenon of a woman who was a teacher of Christian theology. Jerome's letters, hagiographical literature, and Proba's *Cento* tell us of Roman women who lived their Christian faith very independently in the fourth century, testified to that faith, and taught it as well.

From Jerome we learn of the Christian teacher Marcella († 410),[55] a wealthy aristocrat.[56] When he came to Rome in 382[57] she had already been a widow for decades.[58] Against the will of her mother she had refused to remarry, and she lived entirely according to her own spiritual and religious interests.[59] Her house on the Aventine hill was a gathering place for male and female ascetics, theologians, and clergy.[60] In particular, she gathered around her a group of virgins and widows; she was their teacher.[61] In a number of studies on Christian schools in the first three centuries[62] Gustave Bardy has shown that the "Christian schools in Rome and Alexandria . . . were private institutions begun at the personal initiative of the teacher, and were loose gatherings of teacher and pupils in which pagans, baptismal candidates, and Christians were instructed."[63] The influence of these institutions continued into the fourth and fifth centuries especially in monasticism, as we have already seen.[64] We may suppose that Marcella considered herself part of that school tradition.[65]

Jerome, who had great respect for Marcella, as is evident from his many letters to her,[66] has left us a very revealing assessment of her theological competence. In his necrology he writes of her:

> If, after my departure, there was a difference of opinion about any scriptural text the decision was left to her. And because she was very wise and had the gift that the philosophers call τὸ πρέπον, that is, the ability to decide what is appropriate, she answered when she was asked in such a way that she did not call her opinion her own, but gave it as mine or that of another, so that even when she taught she did so as if she herself was only a learner. For she knew the word of the apostle: "But I do not permit a woman to teach." She did not wish the male sex, sometimes including priests who asked advice about obscure and doubtful passages, to feel any insult."[67]

These words vividly illustrate the discrepancy between Christianity as it was really lived and fidelity to literal exegesis. In fact Marcella was recognized as a teacher *(magistra)* not only by Jerome but by large groups of the clergy; she was called on for advice and accepted as a judge *(iudex)*.[68] "Posing as an exegete,"[69] Jerome felt compelled to bring the facts into harmony with 1 Tim 2:12.[70] He does this through a rhetorical reference to Marcella's knowledge of that particular passage and her respect for such conventions. His clever argument justifies both the action of those seeking advice and Marcella's teaching.[71]

Marcella's own self-understanding and her praxis of life can only be derived indirectly from such argumentation. Jerome also testifies to her engagement in contemporary theological controversies.[72] He mentions, for example, that Marcella had distinguished herself particularly in the battle over Origenism and that she had publicly resisted *(publice restitit)*,[73] which can only mean public verbal participation. All these notes show that Marcella also defended her theological ideas in public whenever she found it necessary.

In scholarship Marcella is generally depicted as Jerome's pupil.[74] That cannot be entirely the case since she had pursued her theological interests for many years before Jerome came to Rome, and was in dialogue with other theologians of her own time.[75] It is more accurate to speak of an intellectual exchange between the two. Clear evidence of this is the great number of surviving letters from Jerome to Marcella,[76] in which at her request he frequently deals with difficult exegetical problems. Her creative participation in such reflections cannot be measured with accuracy because not one of her letters to Jerome has been preserved. But the very fact that Jerome dedicated his commentaries on Daniel and on Galatians to Marcella points to her intellectual participation in those works.[77] In light of his opinion of women's teaching, as described above, Jerome could not have had any inducement to describe her as his own teacher.[78] His praise of her personal competence as a theologian, his letters to her, and her participation in theological controversies in her era compel us, however, to believe that Marcella regarded herself as a theological teacher and was acknowledged as such by others, both women and men.

This image is enhanced by the evidence of other aristocratic Roman women who were theologically active in the fourth century. In Rome in the second half of the fourth century Faltonia Betitia Proba (370)[79] wrote a *Cento,* a recasting of the biblical stories of creation and redemption in Virgilian verse,[80] that some two hundred years later evoked from Isidore of Seville a *laudatio* of its author.[81] Elizabeth Clark writes of the use of this work for teaching: "Proba provides a pedagogic tool for young Christians: we know that her *Cento* was widely used for educational purposes in late antiquity and the Middle Ages."[82]

We also know of Melania the Elder (341/2–410),[83] who was equally well educated,[84] that she, like Marcella, was involved in the theological controversies of her time.[85] In contrast to Marcella, however, she was not opposed to Origenism, and this brought Jerome's wrath upon her. At first he had called her the "second Thecla," but when she did not follow his turn away from Origen he referred to her as a "silly old woman."[86] Melania the Elder[87] was the first in a series of Roman aristocratic women who left Rome and founded monasteries in Palestine.[88] In her footsteps followed Paula (347–404) and her daughter Eustochium,[89] as well as Melania the Younger. While still living in Rome Paula had made her house a *domestica ecclesia*,[90] a form of unspectacular biblical instruction practiced since the first century.[91] Paula and Eustochium founded a monastery for women and men as well as a hostel for pilgrims in Bethlehem.[92]

Melania the Younger (383/5–439),[93] the granddaughter of Melania the Elder, founded monasteries in North Africa and in Jerusalem.[94] It is said of her[95] that she gave regular instruction,[96] teaching both women and men.[97] The virgins in her monastery called her Teacher.[98] Arthur Fischer writes: "she herself lived a life of reading and writing: Scriptural exegesis . . . copying Biblical texts for the use of others, reading in the growing local collections of sermons and tales of heroic holiness, adding daily to her swelling notebooks. Her mastery of both Latin and Greek made each appear to be her native tongue. She was sought avidly as a teacher by the women whom she had inducted . . . ."[99] According to the account of her hagiographer Gerontius, Melania the Younger was a theological teacher of women and men in the fullest sense of the word.[100] This Roman Christian combined an aristocratic origin[101] with a high degree of education,[102] undoubtedly an important precondition for the full development of her religious activities and theological teaching.[103]

In light of the teaching activity of a Marcella, a Melania the Elder, a Melania the Younger, and a Proba, which could be augmented with further examples,[104] Theodora the teacher in the tomb epigraph takes on clearer contours as a woman teacher in Rome. In contrast to Marcella, Melania the Elder, and Melania the Younger, we cannot clearly perceive ascetic tendencies in her case. She was married, like Proba and Melania the Younger, a fact that did not deter those women from pursuing their theological interests and spreading their knowledge. Perhaps Theodora, like Melania the Younger and many other women,[105] opted for a chaste marriage. Line 3 of the tomb epigraph might be a hint of that: *Restitit haec mundo, semper caelestia quaerens.*

Inscription for Theodora the Didaskalos

Macedonia/Beroea   V–VI

BIBLIOGRAPHY:
Orlandos, Anastasios K. "Βεροίας Ἐπιγραφαὶ ἀνέκδοτοι," *AD* 2 (1916) 144–63, 162 no. 31.

Feissel, Denis. *Recueil des inscriptions chrétiennes de Macédoine du IIIe au VIe siècle*. BCH Supplément 8 (Paris: Dépositaire, Diffusion de Boccard, 1983) 64–66, no. 60 (plate XI).

+ ΧΜΓ. Θεῖον δώρημα, ἁγνίας διδάσκαλος,
τὸν μακαρισμὸν Κ(υρίο)υ κτησαμένη,
μήτηρ παρθένων εὐσεβῶν (κ)αθηγεμόν,
λέγω (δ)ὴ Μυγδονίης κ(αὶ) Γρατισήμης,
5   ῥίζης ὁσίης κλάδων ε(ὐγ)ε(ν)εστάτων,
Θεοδώρα τοὔνομ[α], ἀειπάρθενος,
τὸ πν(εῦμ)α παρ[α]{φ}θεμένη τῷ Θ(ε)ῷ κ(αὶ) δεσπότῃ,
τύμβῳ τὸ σῶμα φρουρῖν καταλίψασα·
τὰς ὑπὲρ αὐτῶν ποιεῖτε ἱκεσίας.[106]

Line 1: ΧΜΓ = Χ(ριστὸς) Μ(αρία) γ(εννᾷ)[107] or Χ(ριστὲ) μ(εθ᾽ ἡμῶν) γ(ενοῦ).[108]
Θεῖον δώρημα is a play on the name Theodora.[109]
Line 3: ο rather than ω (καθηγεμών).
Line 4: According to Feissel the Latin name Gratissima underlies Γρατισήμης.[110]
Line 5: ῥιζα / κλάδος is (as a heritage of pagan tomb poetry) a widespread topos in Christian epigraphy.[111]
Lines 6–7: Cf. Luke 23:46.

Christ, born of Mary (?). Divine gift, teacher of chastity, possessing the blessing of the Lord, mother of the pious virgins (and) [their] leader, namely Mygdonia and Gratissima, the most worthy shoots of a pious root, by name Theodora, eternal virgin. Her spirit she offered to God the Ruler and her body she left to the vigilance of the grave: pray for her.

This is one of the few Christian διδάσκαλοι inscriptions from Macedonia. Within that group of inscriptions[112] we find Theodora as one of the few bearers of the title who is clearly verifiable as a Christian teacher.

This tomb poem praises the ἀειπάρθενος Theodora.[113] The concept of the ἀειπάρθενος (line 6) is attested from Eusebius's time onward for persons who vowed to maintain their virginity.[114] The title μήτηρ παρθένων (line 3) indicates that Theodora was the head of a community of women. At the time when this inscription was carved μήτηρ was already a *terminus technicus* for spiritual mothers as the heads of groups of virgins.[115] Theodora's function as a theological teacher is separately emphasized by her title of διδάσκαλος. Ascetic women like Melania the Younger, Syncletica, and (as we will show) Macrina were theological teachers in a broad sense through their function as leaders of groups. In the idea of such ascetic communities life and teaching constituted a unity.[116]

Theodora's spiritual motherhood is metaphorically emphasized in regard to two women, Mygdonia and Gratissima. In the last line of the inscription those who behold the tomb poem are urged to pray not only for the dead woman, but also for her pupils.

It was said of other heads of monasteries, for example Melania the Younger, that they regularly taught. In addition, they were consulted on questions of right belief by women and men who had not vowed themselves to an ascetic life.[117]

The same is true of the monastic leader Macrina,[118] as attested by two writings of her younger brother, Gregory of Nyssa.[119] Shortly after her death (between 380 and 383) he wrote her *Vita,* and later penned his *Dialogus de anima et resurrectione.*[120] Both writings are based on a clear concept: in the *Vita* Macrina is described as a "second Thecla," and in the *Dialogus* she is called a "Christian Socrates." Patricia Wilson-Kastner summarizes the tendency of the *Vita* as follows: "As a second Thecla, Macrina was an exemplary teacher of the Word, respected by men and women, and by lay people and clergy alike."[121] In the *Dialogus,* conceived analogously to Plato's *Phaedrus,* she is given the role of the Socratic teacher of correct theological, philosophical, and scientific knowledge.[122] In both the *Vita* and the *Dialogus* Macrina is "explicitly a teacher of *the Word;* that is, Gregory presents her as an expert in expounding Scripture."[123] This example shows that even for an "outstanding representative of orthodoxy"[124] like Gregory of Nyssa a woman's teaching presented no problem and required no accompanying restrictions. In his literary work he clearly acknowledges Macrina's theological superiority.

Another theologian of Asia Minor, Gregory Nazianzus, also praised women's teaching. However, in his case that praise is—differently from Gregory of Nyssa—accompanied by classical topoi of subordination. On the one hand he emphasizes the theological, pastoral, and ascetic competence and independence of his mother and sister.[125] On the other hand he points to their conformity with the norm of subordination to their own husbands. Striking in this context are his explicit and implicit indications that circumstances touching belief could pose radical challenges to such demands for subordination. This is obvious in statements like: "The first head of the woman is Christ"[126] or "With regard to the faith, however, she was not ashamed to show herself a teacher."[127] Such formulations make it clear which laws, in Gregory's view, were ultimately binding and ought to govern women's behavior.

Theodora's titles, mother of the virgins (μήτηρ παρθένων) and teacher (διδάσκαλος), are found in the traditions of women's monastic life from the third century onward. The spiritual motherhood associated with these concepts appears in connection with Syncletica in Egypt, Melania the Younger in Palestine, and Macrina in Asia Minor—examples that could be extended at will[128]—and it was always associated with instruction.

C. Christian Women Teachers and the New Testament Prohibitions

In the history of early Christianity the community function of teaching or instruction associated with the verb διδάσκω and the noun διδάσκαλος cannot be reduced to a single group of διδάσκαλοι.[129] In the early Church not only the explicit group of teachers, but also and especially the apostles and prophets, the presbyters and widows, the bishops and deacons taught.[130] It would be impossible to overstate the pluralism in the manner and content of their teaching.[131] A precise and universal description of the concrete content that accompanied the teachers' activity cannot be given even for the subsequent centuries; it must be newly determined for every source that testifies to the activity of teachers, as well as those holding Church office who also taught.[132] In his broadly conceived study of Christian teachers Ulrich Neymeyr comes to the conclusion that "the testimonies to the Christian teachers of the second and early third centuries, as well as their self-reporting, confirm the manifold character of the role of Christian teachers in the second century. Despite the meager sources it is evident that in the second century Christian teachers exercised their teaching duties in as many different forms and with as many different self-conceptions as do Christian teachers in the twentieth century." Despite reservations about the possibility of drawing general conclusions, he summarizes: "The teacher was someone who not only conveyed intellectual truths, but also showed the consequences of that truth for practical life and introduced his students to a way of life in accordance with the truth."[133]

In the New Testament no teachers are explicitly identified by name, but Acts offers us a significant tradition about a woman teacher: Prisca, who is said to have been the theological teacher of Apollos[134] (Acts 18:26).[135] Apollos is depicted as a spiritually gifted, educated Alexandrian Jew who was instructed in the way of the Lord. He had come to Ephesus and was teaching accurately (ἀκριβῶς) about Jesus there.[136] We are further told that Prisca and Aquila, after hearing him, showed this same Christian the Way much more accurately (ἀκριβέστερον αὐτῷ ἐξέθεντο τὴν ὁδόν). Luke's intention in this pericope is to depict the integration of a missionary with his own independent style "into the *Una sancta catholica*."[137] For Luke, then, near the beginning of the second century there was no problem in depicting a woman as a Catholic teacher of a Christian man and missionary who was already instructed in the Scriptures and filled by the Holy Spirit. Even in the fourth century John Chrysostom emphasizes in a homily on Romans, without any reservations, that Prisca instructed Apollos. In contrast, he does not mention Aquila at all.

The first restriction of teaching to the appointed officeholders of the Church who were emerging in the second century appears in the Pastoral letters. The restrictive intent is accompanied by a general prohibition on teaching by women. In 1 Tim 2:12 we read: "I permit no woman to teach or to have authority over a man; she is to keep silent."[138] This prohibition is very close in its thought to 1 Cor 14:33b-36.[139] Scholars have often postulated the literary or tradition-historical dependence of 1 Tim 2:12 on the Corinthians text, since the orders in 1 Tim 2:12 make more precise the as yet more open formulation in 1 Cor 14:34:[140] the impersonal ἐπιτρέπεται in 1 Cor 14:34 has become an I-saying of Paul in 1 Tim 2:12. This kind of pseudo-Pauline authorization lends authority to the prohibition. The general and therefore open λαλεῖν has become διδάσκειν. This kind of sharpening corresponds to the intention of the Pastoral letters to withdraw the authority to teach from the community as a whole and restrict it to individual officers. Εἶναι ἐν ἡσυχίᾳ replaces and sharpens ἐν ταῖς ἐκκλησίαις σιγάτωσαν in 1 Cor 14:34 insofar as in 1 Tim 2:12 it is a general statement about women's entire lives.[141]

The prohibition of women's teaching occurs within the first paraenetic section of 1 Timothy (2:1–3:16), which gives instruction for Christians' behavior in the house of God (ἐν οἴκῳ θεοῦ: 3:15).[142] While 1 Tim 2:1-7 contains general advice on Christian prayer, v. 8 continues with concrete prescriptions for how men should pray; this is followed in vv. 9-15 by regulations for women, unequally detailed and extensive as regards "clothing," manner of learning (in subordination), teaching (forbidden), and the obligation and soteriological necessity of bearing children.[143] The thematic shift from the manner of community prayer and that of the men to orders for the basic behavior of women, as well as the unprepared change of number in the transition to v. 11 (singular) and again in v. 15 (plural) indicate that the author was working with traditional material.[144] The regulation of women's "clothing" (vv. 9-10) and the topics of subordination (v. 11) and silence (vv. 11-12) are taken from conservative Greco-Roman ethics and made to serve the author's theological and paraenetic interests.[145]

The prohibition on women's teaching expressed in 1 Tim 2:12 has frequently been associated by scholars with polemic against opponents.[146] It is posited that the opponents found an especially good reception among women. Therefore the command is formulated against some particular, concrete behavior on the part of women. Such attempts to give a concrete location to this polemic against opponents run the risk of losing sight of the fictional character of the anti-heretical polemic and its literary function within 1 Timothy. That polemic serves the various intentions of the author, one of which is the restriction of teaching activity to particular officeholders. Against such a background

"the false teachers with their activities that threaten the Church interest him—
to overstate the case somewhat—as a dark background against which the picture of the office that, on the basis of the Gospel, is responsible for gathering
and leading the community stands out in still sharper contrast."[147] The case is
similar as regards the polemic against women. The reference to opponents'
creeping into houses and being received by women (2 Tim 3:6-7) also serves
such interests. The whole section 2 Tim 3:1-9 is devoted to demonstrating the
corruption of the opponents and is soaked in anti-heretical polemic. The catalogue of vices in vv. 2-4 is one of the longest of its type in the New Testament.[148] Verses 5-6 are shaped by the same intention and serve the purpose of
defamation. The text does not speak of "women," but in a scornful diminutive
of "silly bitches" who are thus morally reviled as well (v. 6b). Such verses are
intended to provide further arguments to undergird the fundamental tendency
of the Pastor's ecclesiology and ethics, shaped according to the norms of conservative Greco-Roman literature on οἰκονομία and implying the firm estab-
lishment of a requirement that women be subordinate. The interpretation of
this kind of polemic in terms of its literary function within the overall plan of
the Pastorals is confirmed by the observation that at another point women are
required to teach, though in a restricted sense according to the prescriptions of
this kind of ethic. The older women (πρεσβύτιδες) are ordered to be teachers
of what is good (καλοδιδασκάλοι)[149] and to instruct the younger women in the
traditional virtues (Titus 2:3-5).[150]

The projected reduction of the religious and social opportunities for
Christian women in the Pastorals is thus owing primarily to the context of this
overarching philosophical and ethical tendency. Even Ceslas Spicq calls them
"anachronistic" in the context of the time of their origin.[151] For Asia Minor in
particular there is a great variety of evidence of women's religious and political activity in the πόλις, in ancient religions, and in Judaism.[152] To regard the
congregational and social situation depicted in the Pastorals as a reflection of
reality is to miss the conception and polemic of their project.[153] We may suppose, with Egbert Schlarb, that at the time when the Pastorals were written
women were active as teachers in the community and at worship, but that according to the theology and ethics of these letters such activity was to have no
future. Schlarb summarizes: "We must therefore presume that at the time the
Pastorals were written a teaching activity on the part of women within the
framework of communal assemblies such as worship gatherings etc. was still
possible and was exercised."[154]

In summary we may say that the prohibition on women's teaching found
in 1 Tim 2:12 is another piece of evidence for the fact of women's teaching in
New Testament times. At the same time 1 Tim 2:12 and 1 Cor 14:33b-36 are

evidence for the existence of animosity in early Christianity against women's active participation in worship and in the Church's teaching. This strand of tradition had a pronounced effect: with the aid of these texts women have repeatedly been silenced or forced to disavow themselves.[155] However, that only marks one line of tradition. Other strands are represented by the epigraphic and literary sources described above, which could be augmented at will. They show that women worked as theological teachers in the first centuries of the Church in a wide variety of ways.

Notes

[1] Nagel, "Lettre chrétienne," 317: "The Greek papyrus 1900 from Strasbourg measures no more than nine centimeters in breadth and eight centimeters in height. The upper part and the right-hand side of the recto are mutilated."

[2] Friedrich Preisigke, *Namenbuch, enthaltend alle griechischen, lateinischen, ägyptischen usw. Menschennamen, soweit sie in griechischen Urkunden (Papyri, Ostraka, Inschriften, Mumienschildern usw.) Ägyptens sich vorfinden* (Heidelberg: by the author, 1922) 188; Daniele Foraboschi, *Onomasticon alterum papyrologicum. Supplemento al Namenbuch di Friedrich Preisigke.* TDSA 16, Serie papirologica 2 (Milan: Istituto editoriale Cisalpino, 1967) 174; *BAGD* 458; Nagel, "Lettre chrétienne"; Tibiletti, *Lettere;* Horsley, *New Documents* 1, 121 and 4, 240.

[3] Adolf Deissmann, *Light from the Ancient East; the New Testament illustrated by recently discovered texts of the Graeco-Roman world.* Translated by Lionel R. M. Strachan (New York: Doran, 1927) 168 n. 5, referring to 2 John 1 and 5. On this see also Tibiletti, *Lettere* 32ff.

[4] Cf. Preisigke, *Namenbuch* 238; Foraboschi, *Onomasticon* 211; Nagel, "Lettre chrétienne," 318.

[5] Nagel, "Lettre chrétienne," 318 (with bibliography); cf. also Mario Naldini, *Il Cristianesimo in Egitto. Lettere private nei papiri dei secoli II–IV.* STP 3 (Florence: Le Monnier, 1968) passim.

[6] For the form of the letter conclusion with final wishes cf. Nagel, "Lettre chrétienne," 318, and Philipp Vielhauer, *Geschichte der urchristlichen Literatur. Einleitung in das Neue Testament, die Apokryphen und die Apostolischen Väter* (Berlin and New York: Walter de Gruyter, 1975) 66.

[7] Cf. ibid. 64.

[8] Nagel, "Lettre chrétienne," also interprets the letter in the context of the history of the Church in Egypt.

[9] So also Nagel, "Lettre chrétienne," 319.

[10] The personal names are not typically Christian: cf. Nagel, "Lettre chrétienne," 319. Ξενική points to a Christian milieu. Georg Kretschmar, "Ein Beitrag zu der Frage nach dem Ursprung frühchristlicher Askese," *ZThK* 61 (1964) 27–67, at 35 n. 20, shows the descriptive ξένος/ξένη for Syrian itinerant ascetics, and Ruth Albrecht, *Das Leben der heiligen Makrina auf dem Hintergrund der Thekla-Traditionen. Studien zu den Ursprüngen des*

weiblichen Mönchtums im 4. Jahrhundert in Kleinasien. FKDG 38 (Göttingen: Vandenhoeck & Ruprecht, 1986) 279, demonstrates the same for those in Asia Minor.

[11] Cf. Naldini, *Il Cristianesimo in Egitto* 45–46.

[12] On this see ibid. 315–16.

[13] We cannot determine whether he is identical with the Philoxenos named in v. 9.

[14] For the specifics of the formula for private letters see Tibiletti, *Il Cristianesimo in Egitto* 28ff.

[15] Cf. the numerous examples in Adolf von Harnack, *Die Lehre der zwölf Apostel nebst Untersuchungen zur ältesten Geschichte der Kirchenverfassung und des Kirchenrechts.* TU II/1, 2 (Leipzig: Hinrichs, 1884; reprint Berlin: Akademie-Verlag, 1991) 143–44; idem, *The Expansion of Christianity in the First Three Centuries.* 2 vols. Translated and edited by James Moffatt (New York: G. P. Putnam's Sons, 1904–05) 1:451–53. On this see also Vogt, *Das Kirchenverständnis des Origenes.* BoBKG 4 (Cologne and Vienna: Böhlau, 1974) 58–70.

[16] Eusebius, *Hist. eccl.* VII, 24, 6 (SC 41, 203). He refers to διδάσκαλοι.

[17] This is emphasized by Harnack, *Lehre der zwölf Apostel* 135; idem, *Expansion* 1:451–53; John K. Coyle, "The Exercise of Teaching in the Postapostolic Church," *EeT* 15 (1984) 23–43, at 38. According to K. H. Rengstorf, "διδάσκω κτλ.," TDNT 2:158–59, independent teachers persisted in Egypt longer than anywhere else.

[18] Thus Harnack, *Lehre der zwölf Apostel* 135–36; idem, *Expansion* 1:454; Wilhelm Bousset, *Jüdisch-Christlicher Schulbetrieb in Alexandria und Rom. Literarische Untersuchungen zu Philo und Clemens von Alexandria, Justin und Irenäus* (Hildesheim and New York: G. Olms, 1975) 319; Rengstorf, "διδάσκω;" Roger Gryson, "The Authority of the Teacher in the Ancient and Medieval Church," *JES* 19 (1982) 176–87; Coyle, "The Exercise of Teaching;" Ulrich Neymeyr, *Die christlichen Lehrer im zweiten Jahrhundert. Ihre Lehrtätigkeit, ihr Selbstverständnis und ihre Geschichte.* SVigChr 4 (Leiden and New York: E. J. Brill, 1989); idem, "Christliche Lehrer im 2. Jahrhundert. Ihre Lehrtätigkeit, ihr Selbstverständnis und ihre Geschichte," *StPatr* 21 (1989) 158–62.

[19] For Didymus of Alexandria see Berthold Altaner and Alfred Stuiber, *Patrologie. Leben, Schriften und Lehre der Kirchenväter.* 9th ed. (Freiburg, Basel, and Vienna: Herder, 1980) 280–81; but especially Bärbel Kramer, "Didymus von Alexandrien," *TRE* 8 (1981) 741–46.

[20] For the school for catechists in Alexandria see Caspar D. G. Müller, "Alexandrien I 3," *TRE* 2 (1978) 248–61.

[21] *TA* 19 says that teachers can be *clericus* or *laicus* (Wilhelm Geerlings, ed., *Traditio Apostolica* = *Apostolische Überlieferung.* FC 1 [Freiburg and New York: Herder, 1991] 143–313 at 252). On this see also Gryson, "The Authority of the Teacher," 178; Coyle, "The Exercise of Teaching," 32.

[22] Here laypersons are also permitted to teach, in accordance with the model text *(TA)*.

[23] Hans Achelis, *Die ältesten Quellen des orientalischen Kirchenrechtes I: Die Canones Hippolyti.* TU VI/H. 4 (Leipzig: J. C. Hinrichs, 1891) 170, identifies the *doctores ecclesiae* with the deacons, without further argument; the text gives no occasion for such an exclusive identification.

[24] Anne Jensen, *God's Self-Confident Daughters. Early Christianity and the Liberation of Women.* Translated by O. C. Dean, Jr. (Louisville: Westminster/John Knox, 1996) 3, characterizes Socrates as "a loyal representative of the mainstream church."

[25] Socrates, *Hist. eccl.* V, 22. On this see also Carl Schmidt, "Zwei altchristliche Gebete," in *Neutestamentliche Studien. Georg Heinrici zu seinem 70. Geburtstag.* UNT 6 (Leipzig: J.C. Hinrichs, 1914) 66–78, at 74ff. He mentions this note of Socrates against the background of a hitherto unpublished prayer text from Egyptian Christianity of the fourth century, which he describes as follows: "It is striking that it has a purely communicative character in that it is the prayer of the whole community and reveals no reference to the priesthood." This prayer text and Socrates, *Hist. eccl.* V, 22 confirm his thesis that "worship life (in the first centuries) was not yet so tightly bound to fixed forms."

[26] Nagel, "Lettre chrétienne." He does not indicate precisely which group he is thinking of. This interpretation is followed by Tibiletti, *Lettere*, and by Ross S. Kraemer, *Her Share of the Blessings. Women's Religions among Pagans, Jews, and Christians in the Greco-Roman World* (New York and Oxford: Oxford University Press, 1992) 188.

[27] Horsley, *New Documents* 1:121, reports Judge's deliberations.

[28] Eusebius, *Vita Const.* I, 53, 1 (GCS Eusebius 1,1,43).

[29] The *Canones Hippolyti (Can. Hipp.)* survive only in an Arabic version, based in turn on a Coptic translation of the original Greek text. The standard version is the edition of the Arabic text, based on twelve manuscripts, by René-Georges Coquin, *Les Canons d'Hippolyte. Edition critique de la version arabe. Introduction et traduction française.* PO 31,2 (Paris: Firmin-Didot, 1966), augmented by a French translation. The Latin translation published by Hans Achelis, *Die ältesten Quellen des orientalischen Kirchenrechtes I: Die Canones Hippolyti.* TU VI/H. 4 (Leipzig: J. C. Hinrichs, 1891) is controversial because of the great number of conjectures in the research; nevertheless Achelis's synopsis of *CanHipp* (Latin), *CEA* (German), and *CA* VIII (Greek) is helpful. See also the German translation of *Can. Hipp.* in Wilhelm Riedel, *Die Kirchenrechtsquellen des Patriarchats Alexandrien, zusammengestellt und zum Teil übersetzt v. Wilhelm Riedel* (Leipzig: A. Deichert, 1900) 193–230.

For questions of dating and location, as well as literary-critical, form-critical, and tradition-critical questions cf. Paul Bradshaw, "Kirchenordnungen (I. Altkirchliche)," *TRE* 18 (1989) 662–70, at 668–69; Bruno Steimer, *Vertex Traditionis. Die Gattung der altchristlichen Kirchenordnungen.* BZNW 63 (Berlin and New York: Walter de Gruyter, 1992).

[30] Coyle, "The Exercise of Teaching," 38, 42.

[31] On these see Benedicta Ward, "Apophthegmata Matrum," *StPatr* 16/2 (1985) 63–66; Joseph M. Soler, "Die geistliche Mutterschaft im frühen Mönchtum als Anfrage an unsere Zeit," *EuA* 63 (1987) 167–83; Jensen, *God's Self-Confident Daughters* 26, 228.

[32] The final shape of the *Apophthegmata Patrum (AP)* stems from the final decades of the fifth century, the first textual models from the second half of the fourth century. The basic material of the *AP* must therefore have originated even earlier. It is not impossible that the Latin text tradition represents older strains of tradition than the Greek. The *apophthegmata* were originally written in Coptic. On this see Heinrich Holze, *Erfahrung und Theologie im frühen Mönchtum. Untersuchungen zu einer Theologie des monastischen Lebens bei den ägyptischen Mönchsvätern Johannes Cassian und Benedikt von Nursia.* FKDG 48 (Göttingen: Vandenhoeck & Ruprecht, 1992) 15–17, with additional literature.

[33] *AP* Theodora 5 (MPG 64, 103). On this see Ruth Albrecht, *Makrina* 222.

[34] *AP* Synkletike 12 (MPG 65, 425).

[35] The text (Pseudo-Athanasius, *Vita et gesta sanctae beataeque magistrae Syncleticae*) is found in MPG 28, 1485–1558; O. B. Bernard, *Vie de Sainte Synclétique. Traduit du grec.* Spiritualité Orientale 9 (Abbaye de Bellefontaine: 1972) 7–79 (French translation with

introduction); Mauro Todde, *Una donna nel deserto. Vita della monaca Sincletica. Traduzione, introduzione e note.* Margaritae: Letture di padri 3 (Milan: 1989) (Italian translation with introduction).

   [36] MPG 28, 1488.

   [37] Ps.-Athan., *Vita et gesta* 56.

   [38] Albrecht, *Makrina* 303.

   [39] Carl Schmidt, ed., *Acta Pauli aus der Heidelberger koptischen Papyrushandschrift Nr. 1* (Hildesheim: G. Olms, 1965) 16–17, speaks of the "extraordinarily wide distribution."

   [40] She was murdered in 415 by monks because she was a friend of the prefect Orestes, who was attempting a reconciliation between Jews and Christians in Alexandria. In the sources on her life, teaching, and death there are no indications that she was not acknowledged because of her sex.

   For the life and work of the philosopher Hypatia see Stephan Wolf, *Hypatia, die Philosophin von Alexandrien. Ihr Leben, Wirken und Lebensende nach den Quellenschriften dargestellt* (Vienna: Hölder, 1879); Wolfgang A. Meyer, *Hypatia von Alexandria. Ein Beitrag zur Geschichte des Neuplatonismus* (Heidelberg: G. Weiss, 1886); J. M. Rist, "Hypatia," *Phoenix* 19 (1965) 214–25; Mary Ellen Waithe, ed., *A History of Women Philosophers.* 4 vols. (Dordrecht, Boston, and Lancaster: M. Nijhoff, 1987, 1991, 1993) 1:169–95; Jane McIntosh Snyder, *The Woman and the Lyre. Women Writers in Classical Greece and Rome* (Carbondale and Edwardsville, Ill.: Southern Illinois University Press, 1989) 113–20; Jensen, *God's Self-Confident Daughters* 52–55; Annemarie Maeger, *Hypatia. Die Dreigestaltige* (Hamburg: Reuter & Klöckner, 1992).

   [41] Synesius, *Ep.* 10, 15, 16, 46, 81, 124, 154 (Anthony Garzya, ed., *Synesii Cyrenensis Epistolas* [Rome: Typis Officinae Polygraphicae, 1979]).

   [42] Synesius, *Ep.* 16 (Garzya, *Epistolas* 36). According to Meyer, *Hypatia von Alexandria* 37, Synesius "remained a friend of Hypatia's to the end of his life!"

   [43] Socrates, *Hist. eccl.* VII, 15, from Jensen, *God's Self-Confident Daughters* 54–55. This is followed by the description of her gruesome murder by Christians. Snyder, *The Woman and the Lyre* 116, comments on Socrates' description in these words: "Ironically, Hypatia's unfortunate end seems to have led Sokrates, as a Christian historian, to regard her as a kind of pagan martyr whose Christian murderers should be condemned for their violent act."

   [44] For the situation and history of the basilica of St. Agnes see F. W. Deichmann, "Die Lage der konstantinischen Basilika der heiligen Agnes an der Via Nomentana" (orig. pub. 1946), in idem, *Rom, Ravenna, Konstantinopel, Naher Osten. Gesammelte Studien zur spätantiken Architektur, Kunst und Geschichte* (Wiesbaden: Steiner, 1982) 283–304; for the excavations see also J. P. Kirsch, "Anzeiger für christliche Archäologie," *RQ* 16 (1902) 76–85, at 78–80.

   [45] *ILCV* I 316. According to Buecheler, *Carmina Latina* 669, the inscription is arranged as an acrostic. *ICUR* I 317: "*Exscripsi in s. Agnetis via Nomentana fragmentum, quod lineolis conclusi, affixum parieti scalarum, quibus ad ecclesiam descenditur; litterae sunt omnino pessimae et attritu consumptae, quarum pars nunc latet.*"

   [46] Cf. Charles Pietri, "Grabinschrift II (lateinisch)," translated by Josef Engemann, *RAC* 12 (1983) 514–90, at 577.

   [47] On this see Naldini, *Il Cristianesimo in Egitto* 23–27.

   [48] For the history of the tradition see Henning Paulsen, *Der Zweite Petrusbrief und der Judasbrief.* KEK XII/2 (Göttingen: Vandenhoeck & Ruprecht, 1992) 169–71.

[49] See the derivations from literary and epigraphic poetry mentioned in the apparatus. A thorough analysis of the history of the traditions and motifs cannot be undertaken within the limits of this study. For the topic of tomb poetry see especially Joachim Gensichen, *De Scripturae Sacrae vestigiis in inscriptionibus latinis christianis* (Greifswald: Julius Abel, 1910) and Richmond A. Lattimore, *Themes in Greek and Latin Epitaphs.* Illinois Studies in Language and Literature 28/1-2 (Urbana: University of Illinois Press, 1942). For epigraphic poetry in general see, besides the text editions mentioned in Chapter 1 C, Carl Maria Kaufmann, *Handbuch der altchristlichen Epigraphik* (Freiburg: Herder, 1917) 327ff.; Charles Pietri, "Grabinschrift II (lateinisch)," at 580ff.

[50] Ibid. 580.

[51] For acrostics, with textual examples, see Henri Leclercq, "Acrostiche," *DACL* I/1 (1924) 356–72; see also Kaufmann, *Handbuch der altchristlichen Epigraphik* 28.

[52] The dedicatory poem of Constantina, the daughter of Constantine and founder of the basilica in the first half of the fourth century, also contains acrostics: *CONSTANTINA DEO.* Cf. the text of the inscription in Deichmann, "Die Lage der konstantinischen Basilika der heiligen Agnes," 285.

[53] On this see Peter Brown, *The Body and Society. Men, Women and Sexual Renunciation in Early Christianity* (New York: Columbia University Press, 1988) 369.

[54] Jerome, *Ep.* 127, 4 (CCSL 56, 148).

[55] For what follows see W. Ensslin, "Marcella," *PRE* XIV (1930) 1436–37; J.N.D. Kelly, *Jerome. His Life, Writings, and Controversies* (New York: Harper & Row, 1975) 91–103. See also Anne Yarbrough, "Christianization in the Fourth Century: The Example of Roman Women," *ChH* 45 (1976) 149–65, at 157–58, and note especially her remarks on the social status of Marcella, Paula, Melania the Elder and Melania the Younger; Rosemary R. Ruether, "Mothers of the Church: Ascetic Women in the Late Patristic Age," in Rosemary R. Ruether and Eleanor McLaughlin, eds., *Women of Spirit. Female Leadership in the Jewish and Christian Tradition* (New York: Simon & Schuster, 1979) 71–98, at 76–78; Ruth Albrecht, *Makrina* 230–31; Anne E. Hickey, *Women of the Roman Aristocracy as Christian Monastics.* SR(AA) 1 (Ann Arbor: UMI Research Press, 1987) 38–40; Rosemarie Nürnberg, "'Non decet neque necessarium est, ut mulieres doceant.' Überlegungen zum altkirchlichen Lehrverbot für Frauen," *JAC* 31 (1988) 57–73, at 71; Karin Sugano, "Marcella von Rom. Ein Lebensbild," in Michael Wissemann, ed., *Roma Renascens. Beiträge zur Spätantike und Rezeptionsgeschichte. FS Ilona Opelt* (Frankfurt, Bern, New York, and Paris: Peter Lang, 1988) 355–70; Brown, *The Body and Society* 366–86; Stefan Rebenich, *Hieronymus und sein Kreis. Prosopographische und sozialgeschichtliche Untersuchungen.* Hist. Einzelschriften 72 (Stuttgart: F. Steiner, 1992) 154ff., 195ff.

[56] On this point see especially Yarbrough, "Christianization in the Fourth Century," and Hickey, *Women of the Roman Aristocracy as Christian Monastics.*

[57] See Jerome, *Ep.* 127, 7, and for the dating J.N.D. Kelly, *Jerome* 92.

[58] Kelly, *Jerome* 92, writes "a quarter of a century."

[59] According to Kelly, ibid., the Egyptian ascetics were among her special interests, awakened by reading Athanasius' *Vita Antonii* and by her contacts with Bishop Peter of Alexandria, who lived in exile in Rome from 373 to 378.

[60] Kelly, *Jerome* 92–93; Brown, *The Body and Society* 367. Later she withdrew with her household to a country house near Rome, while Paula, Eustochium, Paula the Younger,

Melania the Elder, and Melania the Younger devoted themselves to "desert piety" in the East. Yarbrough, "Christianization in the Fourth Century," 157 emphasizes that Marcella's understanding of an ascetic life was more strongly shaped by the Western tradition of a "philosophic life" than by the Eastern tradition of a "flight into the desert."

[61] Jerome, *Ep.* 46, 1 (CCSL 54, 329). This letter, collected with those of Jerome, is actually by Paula and Eustochium; it was written from Palestine to Marcella in Rome. On this see Ruth Albrecht, *Makrina* 57–58.

[62] Cf. Gustave Bardy, "L'église et l'enseignement pendant les trois premiers siècles," *RevScR* 12 (1932) 1–18; idem, "Les écoles romaines au second siècle," *RHE* 28 (1932) 501–32; idem, "Pour l'histoire de l'école d'Alexandrie," *VivPen* 2 (1942) 80–109.

[63] Thus Neymeyr, *Die christlichen Lehrer im zweiten Jahrhundert* 4. He says that Bardy's findings remain undisputed.

[64] Cf. Coyle, "The Exercise of Teaching," 38. Sugano, "Marcella von Rom," 368 n. 36, points to the great significance Marcella had for the beginnings of Western monasticism: "In calling Benedict of Nursia the founder of Western monasticism one ought not to forget Marcella."

[65] For Marcella's teaching activity see also Sugano, "Marcella von Rom," 359ff. Hickey, *Women of the Roman Aristocracy as Christian Monastics* 13, writes of the various types of Christian asceticism in Rome: "This group of ascetic women had one foot in an Egyptian style monasticism in the persons of Melania the Elder, Paula, Eustochium, and Paula the Younger . . . and the other foot in a less rigorous style of monasticism resembling the philosophical *otium* in the persons of Marcella, Asella, Lea, Principia and others . . . ."

[66] E.g., Jerome, *Ep.* 23, 24, 27, 32, 37, 38, 40, 41, 43, 44. Marcella's letters have not been preserved.

[67] Jerome, *Ep.* 127, 7 (CCSL 56, 151), following Ruth Albrecht's translation in *Makrina* 231.

[68] This is supported by a passage from another of Jerome's letters in which he polemicizes against those who learn from women what they are to teach men *(alii discunt—pro pudor!—a feminis, quod viros doceant)* (Jerome, *Ep.* 53, 7; CCSL 54, 453). This polemic and his praise of Marcella cited above show that the praxis in Rome was in fact not in harmony with the prohibitions on teaching in the New Testament. Sugano, "Marcella von Rom," 364 regards Marcella as the leading exegetical authority in Rome.

[69] Brown's accurate description of him in *The Body and Society* 376.

[70] His interpretations of 1 Cor 14:33b-37 (MPL 30, 762) and 1 Tim 2:12 (MPL 30, 878) also show his verbal conformity with the order given there.

[71] For Marcella's teaching activity see, besides Jerome, *Ep.* 127, 7, also *Ep.* 127, 2.3. Letter 59, 1 (CSEL 54, 541) to Marcella begins with the words: *"Magnis nos prouocas questionibus et torpens otio ingenium, dum interrogas, doces."* Sugano, "Marcella von Rom," 365 summarizes: "We must be grateful to Jerome that he . . . has told us about Marcella and placed a monument to this important woman of Christian antiquity, the first publicly active ascetic woman in Rome and the West, the initiator and instructor of a monastic group of women, a theologian who was active in Church politics as well. It is quite possible and even probable that Marcella placed no value in all these designations and titles, for she herself never desired anything more than to dedicate her life to Christ and to serve God with her own talents. Still, that does not absolve us today from the duty to do her the justice that was denied her in her own lifetime and has been denied her in many ways since (if not always as crassly as in Ensslin's article

in *RE* where she is presented as completely dependent on Jerome and is even defined in terms of Jerome as if she had had no life, activity, and significance before him or apart from him), in that her teaching activity has been completely ignored or dismissed as insignificant."

[72] Cf., for example, Jerome, *Ep.* 41–42; 127, 9-10; on this see especially Sugano, "Marcella von Rom," 364–65.

[73] Jerome, *Ep.* 127, 9-10 (CCSL 56, 152).

[74] Thus J.N.D. Kelly, *Jerome* 91; Nürnberg, "'Non decet neque necessarium est,'" 71; Brown, *The Body and Society* 382. For a critique of such an evaluation see especially Sugano, "Marcella von Rom," 365–66.

[75] For example, her group of widows and virgins existed before Jerome came to Rome, and she had contact with Bishop Peter of Alexandria in the 70s. On this see Jerome, *Ep.* 46, 1; 127. Thus also Sugano, "Marcella von Rom," 359 (see especially nn. 26 and 27), 363ff.

[76] See n. 66 above. For letters from Jerome to women see the text edition by F. A. Wright, *Select Letters of St. Jerome, with an English Translation* (London: W. Heinemann, and New York: G. P. Putnam's Sons, 1933; reprinted Cambridge, Mass.: Harvard University Press, and London: W. Heinemann, 1975).

[77] Cf. Jerome, *Comm. in Galat.* "Praefatio" (for which cf. Sugano, "Marcella von Rom," 369 n. 46), and Jerome, *Comm. in Dan.*

[78] For Jerome's ambivalent relationships with women see Elizabeth A. Clark, *Jerome, Chrysostom, and Friends. Essays and Translations.* SWR 2 (New York and Toronto: Edwin Mellen, 1979; 2nd ed. 1982).

[79] For Proba see Patricia Wilson-Kastner et al., eds., *A Lost Tradition. Women Writers of The Early Church* (Washington, D.C.: University Press of America, 1981) 33–44; Elizabeth A. Clark, "Faltonia Betitia Proba and her Virgilian Poem: The Christian Matron as Artist," in eadem, ed., *Ascetic Piety and Women's Faith: Essays on Late Ancient Christianity.* SWR 20 (Lewiston, N.Y., and Queenston, Ontario: Edwin Mellen, 1986) 124–52; Snyder, *The Woman and the Lyre* 136–41; Jensen, *God's Self-Confident Daughters* 53, 272–73 n. 262.

[80] The Latin text of her *Cento,* with English translation, can be found in Elizabeth A. Clark and Diane F. Hatch, eds., *The Golden Bough, the Oaken Cross. The Virgilian Cento of Faltonia Betitia Proba.* AAR.TTS 5 (Chico: Scholars, 1981); see also the English translation by Jeremiah Reedy in Wilson-Kastner, ed., *A Lost Tradition* 45–69.

[81] On this see Jensen, *God's Self-Confident Daughters* 53.

[82] Clark, "Faltonia Betitia Proba and her Virgilian Poem," 129; so also Jensen, *God's Self-Confident Daughters* 53.

[83] For Melania the Elder see especially Paulinus of Nola, *Ep.* 29; Palladius, *Lausiac History* 38, 9; 46; 54; 55; Jerome, *Ep.* 39, 5; as well as the letters of Evagrius Ponticus, *Briefe aus der Wüste, eingeleitet, übersetzt und kommentiert v. Gabriel Bunge.* Sophia 24 (Trier: Paulinus-Verlag, 1986) which are said to have been written to Melania: *Ep.* 1, 8, 31, 32, 35, 37, and 64 (on which see Bunge's commentary at pp. 193ff.). For Melania's exchange of letters with Evagrius Ponticus see Arnold van Lantschoot, "Un opuscule inédit de Fr. C. Conybeare," *Muséon* 77 (1964) 121–35.

For general information on Melania the Elder see Francis X. Murphy, *Rufinus of Aquileia (345–411). His Life and Works.* SMH n.s. 6. (Washington, D.C.: Catholic University of America Press, 1945) 31–58; idem, "Melania the Elder: A Biographical Note," *Tr* 5 (1947) 59–77; Yarbrough, "Christianization in the Fourth Century;" Ruether, "Mothers of the Church," 83–88; Nicole Moine, "Melaniana," *RechAug* 15 (1980) 3–79; Hickey, *Women of the Roman Aristocracy as Christian Monastics* 43–48; Brown, *The Body and Society* 279–82; Arthur L. Fisher, "Women and Gender in Lausiac History," *StMon* 33 (1991) 23–50, at 27ff.

[84] Palladius, *Lausiac History* 55 (see Cuthbert Butler, *The Lausiac History of Palladius. A Critical Discussion together with Notes on Early Egyptian Monachism*. I/II. TaS 6 [Hildesheim: G. Olms, 1967 (reprint of the 1898 Cambridge edition)] 149). "Being very learned and loving literature, she turned night into day perusing every writing of the ancient commentators, including three million (lines) of Origen and two hundred fifty thousand of Gregory, Stephen, Pierius, Basil and other standard writers. Nor did she read them once only and casually, but she laboriously went through each book seven or eight times . . ." The English translation is from Murphy, "Melania the Elder," 71. This image is enhanced by a remark of Paulinus of Nola, *Ep.* 27 (ACW 36:116): "Her hard couch . . . becomes soft as she studies, for her pleasure in reading reduces the hardship of that stiff bed." Quoted from Hickey, *Women of the Roman Aristocracy as Christian Monastics* 47. See also Yarbrough, "Christianization in the Fourth Century," 159; Hickey, *Women of the Roman Aristocracy as Christian Monastics* 46–47; Brown, *The Body and Society* 369.

[85] On this see Palladius, *Lausiac History* 46, 54. This is also emphasized by Yarbrough, "Christianization in the Fourth Century," 159; Moine, "Melaniana," 3; Clark, *The Life of Melania the Younger. Introduction, Translation, and Commentary* by Elizabeth A. Clark. SWR 14 (New York and Toronto: Edwin Mellen, 1984) 141–42.

[86] Rufinus, *Apol. contra Hieronymum* 2, 29 (CCSL 20, 105). On this see J.N.D. Kelly, *Jerome* 99 n. 36; Brown, *The Body and Society* 282. For Jerome's reversal in his estimation of Origen see ibid. 379–85.

[87] Melania the Elder went first to Egypt, where she "remained by the monks in the Nitrian desert from about 373–374," according to Bunge, *Briefe aus der Wüste* 30. In 375 she founded a double monastery on the Mount of Olives in Jerusalem and became its leader. On this see Hugh G. Evelyn White, *The Monasteries of the Wâdi 'N Natrûn. Part II: The History of the Monasteries of Nitria and of Scetis*. Edited by Walter Hauser (New York: Egyptian Expedition Publications of the Metropolitan Museum of Art Egyptian Expedition, 1932; reprint New York: Arno, 1973) 75–76; Brown, *The Body and Society* 280. In 380 Rufinus also came to Jerusalem and helped Melania the Elder in the building up of the monastery.

[88] Thus also Elizabeth Clark, *Melania the Younger* 94: "Melania the Elder's monasteries in Jerusalem marked the beginning of the movement."

[89] See especially Jerome's necrology on Paula: Jerome, *Ep.* 108; Palladius, *Lausiac History* 41. For both women see J.N.D. Kelly, *Jerome* 91–103; Yarbrough, "Christianization in the Fourth Century;" Ruether, "Mothers of the Church," 80–83; Hickey, *Women of the Roman Aristocracy as Christian Monastics* 21–32 (on Paula), 36–37 (on Eustochium); Wolfgang Schuller, *Frauen in der römischen Geschichte* (Konstanz: Universitätsverlag Konstanz, 1992) 108; Nürnberg, "'Non decet neque necessarium est,'" 71–72; Rebenich, *Hieronymus und sein Kreis* 154ff., 193ff.

[90] Cf. Jerome, *Ep.* 30, 14 (CSEL 54, 248).

[91] On this see above.

[92] According to Schuller, *Frauen in der römischen Geschichte* 108; so also Murphy, *Rufinus of Aquileia* 53. From there they sent a letter to their teacher Marcella in Rome:

Jerome, *Ep.* 46; on this see Griet Petersen-Szemerédy, *Zwischen Weltstadt und Wüste: Römische Asketinnen in der Spätantike. Eine Studie zu Motivation und Gestaltung der Askese christlicher Frauen Roms auf dem Hintergrund ihrer Zeit.* FKDG 54 (Göttingen: Vandenhoeck & Ruprecht, 1993) 18–20.

[93] For her person and work see Yarbrough, "Christianization in the Fourth Century;" Ruether, "Mothers of the Church," 88–92; Clark, *Melania the Younger* 83–152; eadem, "Piety, Propaganda, and Politics in the Life of Melania the Younger," *StPatr* 18/2 (1989) 167–83; Ruth Albrecht, *Makrina* 223–24, especially on her teaching; Hickey, *Women of the Roman Aristocracy as Christian Monastics* 43–48; Brown, *The Body and Society* 410; Fisher, "Women and Gender in Lausiac History," 32ff.

[94] Thus Gerontius, *Vita Melaniae* 22, 41, 49. On this see Clark, *Melania the Younger* 94, 111, 115–19.

[95] See *Vie de Sainte Mélanie. Texte Grec, Introduction, Traduction et Notes, par Denys Gorce.* SC 90 (Paris: Cerf, 1962) (Greek and French) and the English translation with introduction and commentary by Clark, *Melania the Younger.* For the leanings and intent of the document see ibid. 141–52, and Clark, "Piety, Propaganda, and Politics."

[96] Gerontius, *Vita Melaniae* 32, 42.

[97] Ibid. 54 (SC 90, 232–34).

[98] Ibid. 64 (SC 90, 256): "ὁδηγὸν ἀγαθὴν καὶ θεόπνευστον διδάσκαλον" (good leader and God-inspired teacher).

[99] Fisher, "Women and Gender in Lausiac History," 34.

[100] Clark, "Claims on the Bones of Saint Stephen: The Partisans of Melania and Eudocia," in eadem, *Ascetic Piety and Women's Faith: Essays on Late Ancient Christianity* 95–123, at 102, writes that "The Greek *Life* reports that Melania talked theology 'from dawn to dusk.'"

[101] On this see especially Hickey's monograph, *Women of the Roman Aristocracy as Christian Monastics.* For Paula, Hickey has shown (p. 48) that she did *not* come from the higher Roman aristocracy as Jerome asserted.

[102] For Melania the Younger see, for example, Gerontius, *Vita Melaniae* 21, 23, 26 (and see Clark, *Melania the Younger* 11–12), 64. Paula and Eustochium's letter to Marcella (Jerome, *Ep.* 46) vividly illustrates their education (see above). But see also Jerome, *Ep.* 108, where he emphasizes among other things that Paula and Eustochium were very successfully learning Hebrew. For Paula's education see also Hickey, *Women of the Roman Aristocracy as Christian Monastics* 30.

[103] For women's opportunities for education see Chapter 1 B above: "Christian Women in their Social Context" at n. 106.

[104] Brown, *The Body and Society* 151–52 gives other examples of women who taught; see also Ruth Albrecht, *Makrina* 221ff.

[105] On this see Yarbrough, "Christianization in the Fourth Century."

[106] Denis Feissel, *Recueil des inscriptions chrétiennes de Macédoine du IIIe au VIe siècle.* BCH Supplément 8 (Paris: Dépositaire, Diffusion de Boccard, 1983) 64: "Collection byzantine de Béroia (n° 413). Autrefois à l'église Hagios Théodôros. Plaque de marbre blanc. Ht. 61; larg. 83; ép. 6; lettres 2,5; interlignes 1,5." [Byzantine collection of Beroea (no. 413). Formerly in the church of St. Theodore. White marble plaque, 61 (cm.) high, 83 broad, 6 deep; letters 2.5 cm. with 1.5 cm. between the lines.]

[107] Ibid. 64, with reservations.

[108] Anastasios K. Orlandos, "Βεροίας Ἐπιγραφαὶ ἀνέκδοτοι," *AD* 2 (1916) 144–63, at 162. For the wide provenance and possible meaning of the abbreviation ΧΜΓ in the late Roman and Byzantine periods see the thorough discussion in Horsley, *New Documents* 2:177–80 (no. 104); see also Kaufmann, *Handbuch der altchristlichen Epigraphik* 74–76; Naldini, *Il Cristianesimo in Egitto* 28–30; S. Kent Brown, "Coptic and Greek Inscriptions from Christian Egypt: A Brief Review," in Birger A. Pearson and James E. Goehring, eds., *The Roots of Egyptian Christianity* (Philadelphia: Fortress, 1986) 26–41.

[109] Cf. Feissel, *Macédoine* 65.

[110] The genitive is a Greek construction; the Latin -*issi*- corresponds to -ιση- with a simplification of the sigma and itacism (η for ι).

[111] Feissel, *Macédoine* 65, with examples. In the literature see Basil of Caesarea, *Ep.* 105, who calls deaconesses "a good root of good shoots" *(Basilius von Caesarea, Briefe. Erster Teil (Nr. 1–94), eingeleitet, übersetzt und erläutert v. Wolf-Dieter Hauschild.* BGrL 32 [Stuttgart: A. Hiersemann, 1990] 2, 30) (. . . ὅτι ἀγαθᾶς ῥίζης ἀγαθὰ βλαστήματά ἐστε . . .) *(Saint Basil. The Letters, with an English Translation,* by Roy J. Deferrari. 4 vols. LCL [Cambridge, Mass.: Harvard University Press, 1950–1961] 2:198).

[112] Cf. Feissel, *Macédoine* no. 123, 2 (with references to other examples); 231, 2.

[113] Feissel, *Macédoine* 64, comments on the metre as follows: "The epigraph contains nine verses divided into eight lines. If the first two are passable iambic trimeters, the following lines depart from strict scansion, but in places (verses 5 and 9) it shows traces of Byzantine dodecasyllables."

[114] Thus G. W. H. Lampe, *A Patristic Greek Lexicon* (Oxford and New York: Clarendon Press, 1969; reprinted 1989), with examples.

[115] See, for example, Gerontius, *Vita Melaniae* 66; Pseudo-Athanasius, *Vita Syncleticae* 101; Lampe, *Lexicon* § 4, gives other examples.

[116] Thus also Neymeyr, *Die christlichen Lehrer im zweiten Jahrhundert* 233.

[117] Gerontius, *Vita Melaniae* 29, 32, 42, 54.

[118] On this see Patricia Wilson-Kastner, "Macrina: Virgin and Teacher," *AUSS* 17 (1979) 105–17; Frits van der Meer, "Makrina. Porträt einer Familie," in Martin Greschat, ed., *Alte Kirche II.* GK 2 (Stuttgart, Berlin, Cologne, and Mainz: Kohlhammer, 1984) 37–47; but especially Ruth Albrecht's monograph, *Makrina* (see n. 10 above); Cornelia Wolfskeel, "Makrina," in Mary Ellen Waithe, ed., *A History of Women Philosophers* (Dordrecht, Boston, and Lancaster: M. Nijhoff, 1987) 1:139–68.

[119] For the significance of Gregory of Nyssa in the history of theology and in Church politics see Heinrich Dörrie, "Gregor III (Gregor von Nyssa)," *RAC* 12 (1983) 863–95; van der Meer, "Makrina" 47, writes: ". . . until his death at the age of sixty he was the first man of the Greek Church."

[120] On this see especially Wilson-Kastner, "Macrina."

[121] Ibid. 109.

[122] Albrecht, *Makrina* 222: ". . . the dialogue 'de anima et resurrectione' has Macrina's teaching activity as its basic theme . . . ." Cf. also ibid. 44–45.

[123] Wilson-Kastner, "Macrina," 110.

[124] Altaner and Stuiber, *Patrologie* 303.

[125] Cf. Gregory Nazianzus, *Or.* 8, 18. In his poem *De vita sua* he calls "his mother Nonna 'μέγας διδάσκαλος'" and portrays her as a leader and director in questions of religious life." Albrecht, *Makrina* 222.

[126] Gregory Nazianzus, *Or.* 8.

[127] Gregory Nazianzus, *Or.* 18 (MPG 35, 993).

[128] Cf. Albrecht, *Makrina* 224–25; Brown, *The Body and Society.*

[129] For teachers in the New Testament and the early Church see Harnack, *Lehre der zwölf Apostel* passim; Floyd V. Filson, "The Christian Teacher in the First Century," *JBL* 60 (1941) 317–28; Heinrich Greeven, "Propheten, Lehrer, Vorsteher bei Paulus. Zur Frage der 'Ämter' im Urchristentum," *ZNW* 44 (1952/3) 1–43; Hermann Stempel, "Der Lehrer in der 'Lehre der zwölf Apostel,'" *VigChr* 34 (1980) 209–17; Gryson, "The Authority of the Teacher;" Alfred F. Zimmermann, *Die urchristlichen Lehrer. Studien zum Tradentenkreis der διδάσκαλοι im frühen Urchristentum.* WUNT II/12 (Tübingen: Mohr, 1984); Coyle, "The Exercise of Teaching;" Heinz Schürmann, "Lehrende in den neutestamentlichen Schriften. Ihre Angewiesenheit auf andere geistliche Gaben und ihre Verwiesenheit an andere geistliche Dienste," in Walter Bauer et al., eds., *Weisheit Gottes – Weisheit der Welt.* Vol. 1: *FS f. Joseph Kardinal Ratzinger* (St. Ottilien: EOS, 1987) 419–40; Neymeyr, *Die christlichen Lehrer im zweiten Jahrhundert;* idem, "Christliche Lehrer im 2. Jahrhundert. Ihre Lehrtätigkeit, ihr Selbstverständnis und ihre Geschichte," *StPatr* 21 (1989) 158–62; Georg Schöllgen, "Wandernde und seßhafte Lehrer in der Didache?" *BN* 52 (1990) 19–26. Cf. also the overview of the material in the New Testament in Hans-Friedrich Weiss, "διδάσκω κτλ.," *EDNT* 1:317–19.

[130] See the corresponding chapters in this book. Similarly Schürmann, "Lehrende in den neutestamentlichen Schriften," 421.

[131] So also Schürmann, ibid. 422: "We must imagine early Christian teaching quite pluralistically: it was done differently in early and later communities, in Palestinian and Hellenistic congregations, in newly-founded communities, those already well established, and those that found themselves again under threat. The 'teaching' was also done with more or less reflection. It could work more with apocalyptic ideas or in the manner of religious Wisdom teaching, with rabbinic methods, Jewish mnemonic techniques, or Hellenistic speculation. Teachers' thinking and imagination could be shaped by Jewish Palestinian, Jewish Hellenistic, Jewish heterodox ideas, or perhaps by popular philosophical Hellenism, Oriental syncretism, or gnosticizing trends." One consequence of this situation was that different Christian groups sometimes accused each other of false teaching.

[132] On this see especially Neymeyr's study, *Die christlichen Lehrer im zweiten Jahrhundert.*

[133] Ibid. 233.

[134] Paul numbers him among the διάκονοι (1 Cor 3:5), συνεργόι θεοῦ (1 Cor 3:9), ἀπόστολοι (1 Cor 4:9), and ἀδελφόι (1 Cor 16:12). On Apollos see E. Earle Ellis, "Paul and his Co-Workers," *NTS* 17 (1970/71) 437–52; Wolf-Henning Ollrog, *Paulus und seine Mitarbeiter. Untersuchungen zu Theorie und Praxis der paulinischen Mission.* WMANT 50 (Neukirchen-Vluyn: Neukirchener Verlag, 1979) 37ff.; Antoinette C. Wire, *The Corinthian Women Prophets. A Reconstruction through Paul's Rhetoric* (Minneapolis: Fortress, 1990) 209–11; John K. Chow, *Patronage and Power. A Study of Social Networks in Corinth.* JSNT.S. 75 (Sheffield: JSOT Press, 1992) 102ff.

[135] On this see, still, Adolf von Harnack, "Über die beiden Rezensionen der Geschichte der Prisca und des Aquila in Act. Apost. 18,1-27," *SPAW* 1900, 48–61.

[136] On this see Jürgen Roloff, *Die Apostelgeschichte.* NTD 5 (Göttingen: Vandenhoeck & Ruprecht, 1981) 279.

¹³⁷ Ernst Käsemann, "Die Johannesjünger in Ephesus" (1952) in idem, *Exegetische Versuche und Besinnungen* (6th ed. Göttingen: Vandenhoeck & Ruprecht, 1970) 1:158–68, at 162. For a critique and a different accent see Michael Wolter, "Apollos und die ephesinischen Johannesjünger (Act 18,24–19,7)," *ZNW* 78 (1987) 49–75. There is good reason to believe that the pericope is Luke's work: see Käsemann, "Johannesjünger;" Hans Conzelmann, *Acts of the Apostles: A Commentary on the Acts of the Apostles*. Translated by James Limburg, A. Thomas Kraabel, and Donald H. Juel; edited by Eldon Jay Epp with Christopher R. Matthews (Philadelphia: Fortress, 1987) 159–60; Ollrog, *Paulus und seine Mitarbeiter* 38ff., and most recently and at length Alfons Weiser, *Die Apostelgeschichte*. ÖTK 5/2 (Gütersloh: Gerd Mohn, 1981, 1985) 505–509. To that extent Apollos's instruction by Prisca and Aquila would not be an event that took place in the way described. Elisabeth Schüssler Fiorenza's suggestion *(In Memory of Her. A Feminist Theological Reconstruction of Christian Origins* [New York: Crossroad, 1983] 179) that Apollos's "Sophia and Spirit theology might have been derived from her catechesis" is thus very hypothetical.

¹³⁸ 1 Tim 2:12: διδάσκειν δὲ γυναικὶ οὐκ ἐπιτρέπω οὐδὲ αὐθεντεῖν ἀνδρός, ἀλλ᾽ εἶναι ἐν ἡσυχίᾳ.

¹³⁹ On this see also ch. 3 B above.

¹⁴⁰ On this see most recently Ulrike Wagener, *Die Ordnung des "Hauses Gottes." Der Ort von Frauen in der Ekklesiologie und Ethik der Pastoralbriefe*. WUNT 65 (Tübingen: Mohr, 1994) 92ff.

¹⁴¹ For a detailed text comparison see Jürgen Roloff, *Der erste Brief an Timotheus*. EKK XV (Neukirchen-Vluyn: Neukirchener Verlag, 1988) 128–30; and Wagener, *Ordnung des "Hauses Gottes"* 92ff.

¹⁴² On this see Roloff, *Der erste Brief an Timotheus* 107. The image of the "house" is the "central ecclesiological metaphor" in the Pastorals; cf. ibid. 213–15; Hermann von Lips, *Glaube – Gemeinde – Amt. Zum Verständnis der Ordination in den Pastoralbriefen*. FRLANT 122 (Göttingen: Vandenhoeck & Ruprecht, 1979) 143ff.; Norbert Brox, *Die Pastoralbriefe. 1 Timotheus, 2 Timotheus, Titus* (5th rev. and expanded ed. Regensburg: Pustet, 1989) 157ff.

¹⁴³ On this see most recently and in detail Wagener, *Ordnung des "Hauses Gottes"* 67ff.; but see also N. J. Hommes, "Taceat mulier in Ecclesia. Een boodschap over Eredienst en vrouwelijk decorum," in *Arcana Relevata, FS Frederik Willem Grosheide*. Kampen: Kok, 1951, 33–43; Hans-Werner Bartsch, *Die Anfänge urchristlicher Rechtsbildungen. Studien zu den Pastoralbriefen*. ThF 34 (Hamburg-Bergstedt: H. Reich, 1965) 60–81; Gottfried Holtz, *Die Pastoralbriefe*. ThHNT 13 (3rd ed. Berlin: Evangelische Verlagsanstalt, 1980) 67–73; Douglas J. Moo, "1 Timothy 2:11-15: Meaning and Significance," *TrinJ* n.s. 1 (1980) 62–83; Philip B. Payne, "Libertarian Women in Ephesus: A Response to Douglas J. Moo's Article, '1 Timothy 2:11-15: Meaning and Significance,'" *TrinJ* n.s. 2 (1981) 169–97; Max Küchler, *Schweigen, Schmuck und Schleier. Drei neutestamentliche Vorschriften zur Verdrängung der Frauen auf dem Hintergrund einer frauenfeindlichen Exegese des Alten Testaments im antiken Judentum*. NTOA 1 (Göttingen: Vandenhoeck & Ruprecht, 1986) 9–53; Alan Padgett, "Wealthy Women at Ephesus. 1 Timothy 2:8-15 in Social Context," *Interp* 41 (1987) 19–31; Roloff, *Der erste Brief an Timotheus* 125–47; Brox, *Pastoralbriefe* 129–30; Paul W. Barnett, "Wives and Women's Ministry (1 Timothy 2:11-15)," *EvQ* 61 (1989) 225–38; Timothy F. Harris, "Why did Paul Mention Eve's Deception? A Critique of P.W. Barnett's Interpretation of 1 Timothy," *EvQ* 62 (1990) 335–52; Gloria N. Redekop, "Let the women learn: 1 Timothy 2:8-15 reconsidered," *SR* 19 (1990) 235–45; Egbert Schlarb, *Die gesunde Lehre. Häresie und*

Wahrheit im Spiegel der Pastoralbriefe. MThSt 28 (Marburg: N.G. Elwert Verlag, 1990) 276–80; Helmut Merkel, *Die Pastoralbriefe.* TNT 9/1 (Göttingen: Vandenhoeck & Ruprecht, 1991) 26ff.; Sharon H. Gritz, *Paul, Women Teachers, and the Mother Goddess at Ephesus. A Study of 1 Timothy 2:9-15 in Light of the Religious and Cultural Milieu of the First Century* (Lanham, Md.: University Press of America, 1991) 123–56.

[144] Thus also Roloff, *Der erste Brief an Timotheus* 126: "All this forces us to suppose that here the author is neither formulating freely nor is able to refer to a closed complex of existing paraenetic material. Instead, he is making use of traditional material of varied provenience and sometimes forces it into the thematic sequence he has conceived."

[145] See extensively on this point Roloff, *Der erste Brief an Timotheus* 126–30. A review of research and discussion of the religious- and philosophical-historical origins of such ethics, which are also found in the New Testament household codes, can be found in Marlis Gielen, *Tradition und Theologie neutestamentlicher Haustafelethik. Ein Beitrag zur Frage einer christlichen Auseinandersetzung mit gesellschaftlichen Normen.* Athenäums Monografien. Theologie 75 (Frankfurt: Hain, 1990) 24ff.; and Wagener, *Ordnung des "Hauses Gottes"* 15ff.

[146] Thus, for example, Brox, *Pastoralbriefe* 132ff.; Schlarb, *Die gesunde Lehre* 276–77.

[147] Roloff, *Der erste Brief an Timotheus* 229.

[148] Brox, *Pastoralbriefe* 254.

[149] The word is "not found elsewhere" (BAGD 400). Lampe, *Lexicon,* and H. G. Liddell, Robert Scott, and Henry Stuart Jones, *A Greek-English Lexicon* (Oxford: Clarendon Press, 1968) do not include it.

[150] For the components of popular "mirrors of virtues" for wives cf. Brox, *Pastoralbriefe* 293–94.

[151] Ceslas Spicq, *Saint Paul. Les Epitres Pastorales* (Paris: J. Gabalda, 1969).

[152] See ch. 1 B above.

[153] Against Lips, *Glaube – Gemeinde – Amt;* Schlarb, *Die gesunde Lehre.*

[154] Ibid. 276–77.

[155] For the history of the influence of these texts see Nürnberg, "'Non decet neque necessarium est.'"

V. Presbyters

A. Epigraphic and Literary Evidence from the East

Inscription for Ammion the Presbytera

Asia Minor / Phrygia / Uçak   III

BIBLIOGRAPHY:

Körte, Alfred. *Inscriptiones Bureschianae.* Wissenschaftliche Beilage zum Vorlesungsverzeichnis der Universität Greifswald. Easter 1902 (Greifswald:
Druck von J. Abel, 1902) 31 n. 55.

Gibson, Elsa. "Montanist Epitaphs at Uçak," *GRBS* 16 (1975) 433–42, at 437–38.

_____. *The "Christians for Christians" Inscriptions of Phrygia. Greek Texts,
Translation and Commentary.* HThS 32 (Missoula: Scholars, 1978)
136.

Drew-Bear, Thomas. "The City of Temenouthyrai in Phrygia," *Chiron* 9 (1979)
275–302, at 301.

Waelkens, Marc. *Die kleinasiatischen Türsteine. Typologische und epigraphische
Untersuchungen der kleinasiatischen Grabreliefs mit Scheintür* (Mainz:
P. von Zabern, 1986) 147–48 no. 367.

Horsley, G. H. R. *New Documents Illustrating Early Christianity.* Vol. 4: *A Review of the Greek Inscriptions and Papyri published in 1979* (North
Ryde, N.S.W.: Macquarie Ancient History Association, 1987) 240.

Διογᾶς ἐβίσκο-
πος Ἀμμίῳ πρεσ-
3   βυτέρᾳ μνήμης
χάριν.[1]

Line 1: Διογᾶς = Διογένης.[2]
         ἐβίσκοπος instead of ἐπίσκοπος is found in other inscriptions from Uçak.[3]
Line 2: Ammion is a woman's name frequently found in Asia Minor.[4]

Bishop Diogas in memory of Ammion the Presbyter.

116

This tombstone is one of a series of the same type from Uçak, made in the first half of the third century.⁵ The first in the series is the tombstone of Bishop Artemidoros:

Δειογᾶς Ἀρτεμιδώρῳ ἐβισκόπῳ
ἐκκ τοῦ κυριακοῦ μνήμης χάριν.⁶

The inscription says that a certain Diogas set up this tombstone for Bishop Artemidoros "with church funds."⁷ Marc Waelkens, using motif- and form-critical criteria, dates the inscription to the first decades of the third century.⁸ The inscription for the πρεσβυτέρα Ammion given above is another in the same series. Diogas probably erected this tombstone for the *presbytera* in his role as bishop. The series concludes with the tombstone of Diogas, the one who dedicated these other two inscriptions. His wife erected the stone for herself while she was still alive, and for him:

Αὐρ. Τατιανὴ ἑαυτῇ ζῶσα καὶ Διογᾷ συνβ[ί]ῳ
ἐπισκόπῳ μνήμης χάριν.⁹

Elsa Gibson and Marc Waelkens assume that the Diogas mentioned in all three inscriptions is the same person. If this is true the episcopate of Diogas can be dated on the basis of this epigraphic evidence to the second quarter of the third century.¹⁰

The only characteristic of Ammion mentioned in the inscription is that she is πρεσβυτέρα. Grammatically this could be the comparative of πρέσβυς and thus describe Ammion either as a woman of advanced age or as the older of two women with the same name. However, the comparative of πρέσβυς can also be interpreted as an official title.¹¹ That is the interpretation given πρεσβυτέρα here by Elsa Gibson and Marc Waelkens; they do not discuss the question of other meanings. However, the ambiguity of the words πρεσβυτέρα and πρεσβύτερος is an element, as we will see, in almost all epigraphical as well as a great many literary examples. We note, however, that frequently the old or elder persons named were at the same time officials of their communities.¹²

Elsa Gibson categorizes this inscription as Montanist solely because of the office assigned to Ammion. She points to Epiphanius, who reports that women were ordained presbyters in Montanist communities *(Pan.* 49, 2).¹³ However, the formula in Ammion's inscription contains no further terms such as πνευματικός that could point to a Montanist provenience and that are regarded in scholarly discussions as characteristic of Montanists.¹⁴

Elsa Gibson's thesis that Ammion was a Montanist presbyter has been accepted by scholars without discussion.¹⁵ This is all the more surprising because August Strobel cast doubt on the Montanist identification of the series of inscriptions to which Ammion's belongs, and Marc Waelkens also reveals certain reservations about such an identification.¹⁶ There are, then, no clear indications that Ammion's inscription should be classified as Montanist. The question whether Ammion was a presbyter among the Montanists or in the Great Church cannot be answered with any certainty.

Epiphanius, in his *Panarion Against Eighty Heresies* (ca. 374–377),[17] mentions Christian groups that install women as bishops and presbyters. In *Pan.* 49 he writes about the Quintillianists, whom he identifies with the Pepuzians, and about the Artotyritans, whom he equates with the Priscillianists. He traces a genetic connection between these groups and the Cataphrygians (Montanists). One aspect of his polemic is that these groups ordain women as bishops and presbyters. He writes: ". . . and they call Moses' sister a prophetess as evidence in favor of the women among them who are ordained members of the clergy (τῶν παρ᾽ αὐτοῖς καθισταμένων γυναικῶν ἐν κλήρῳ). Also, they say, Philip had four daughters who prophesied . . . . They have women bishops, women presbyters, and everything else (ἐπίσκοποί τε παρ᾽ αὐτοῖς γυναῖκες καὶ πρεσβύτεροι γυναῖκες καὶ τὰ ἄλλα), all of which they say is in accord with 'in Christ Jesus there is neither male nor female.' They ordain women among them bishops and presbyters because of Eve (γυναῖκες παρ᾽ αὐτοῖς εἰς ἐπισκοπὴν καὶ πρεσβυτέριον καθίστανται διὰ τὴν Εὔαν) [not hearing] the word of the Lord: 'your desire shall be for your husband, and he shall rule over you' (Gen 3:16). But the apostolic word remains hidden from them: 'I permit no woman to speak or to have authority over a man' (1 Tim 2:12) and again: 'man is not from woman, but woman from man' (1 Cor 11:8) and 'Adam was not deceived, but Eve was first deceived and became a transgressor.'"[18]

From Epiphanius's depiction it appears that within the particular schismatic group he is describing, whose founder, Quintilla, was named earlier, women were ordained as bishops and presbyters. Epiphanius presents, as the group's argument for such ordinations, Exod 15:20; Gal 3:28, and "διὰ τὴν Εὔαν."[19] In the refutation that follows his description he demonstrates that he regards this action as a denial of the inferiority of women to men that is given in creation. He presents this idea by citing one Old Testament passage (Gen 3:16) and three from the New Testament (1 Tim 2:12; 1 Cor 11:8; 1 Tim 2:14) without comment. Apparently he regarded them as fully sufficient. This shows that they were current and common slogans in the discussion of women's ordination.

Epiphanius's view of women as officeholders in the Church is illustrated by his chapter on the Collyridians (*Pan.* 79). Within a description of their eucharistic rites he emphasizes that women have never acted in a priestly role. His arguments are, first, the fact that Jesus was baptized by John and not by Mary, which is said to show that women are not permitted to baptize. He probably derived that argument from the *Didascalia Apostolorum*.[20] Second, he cites a list of apostles and bishops, concluding that women have never been included among them. Third, he says that no priesthood (ἱερατεία) was ever conferred on the daughters of Philip (Acts 21:9) or the prophet Anna (Luke 2:36).

Epiphanius concludes from his discussion that the only official Church office for women is that of deaconess:

> Now [it is evident] that there is an order of deaconesses in the church (δια-κονισσῶν τάγμα ἐστὶν εἰς τὴν ἐκκλησίαν), but not for the purpose of exercising priestly functions or attempting anything of the sort (οὐχὶ εἰς τὸ ἱερατεύειν οὐδέ τι ἐπιχειρεῖν ἐπιτρέπεται); rather it is to protect the modesty of women at the time of baptism or when they are being examined because of some affliction or suffering, and when a woman's body is naked. This is so that she may not be seen by the men engaged in the sacred rites, but by the woman acting as deaconess, who for that occasion is appointed by the priest to look after the woman needing assistance at the time when her body is naked.

References to the divine word (ὁ θεῖος λόγος) follow: it permits women neither to "speak" (1 Cor 14:34) nor to "exercise authority over the man" (1 Tim 2:12).[21] Epiphanius admits that the Church has provided an office for women by establishing the role of deaconess (διακονισσῶν τάγμα). At the same time he makes a great effort to depict the field of deaconesses' activity as narrowly as possible. His description closely follows the regulations for the office of deaconess in the *Didascalia Apostolorum*. There, too, women's participation in baptism is restricted to assisting.[22]

In this chapter against the Collyridians, Epiphanius's particular interest is to show that women are not installed for the purpose of exercising priestly functions such as baptizing and especially the celebration of the Eucharist. Accordingly he summarizes the question of a presbyteral office for women as follows:

> Now it should be observed that church order required only deaconesses (ὅτι ἄχρι διακονισσῶν μόνον τὸ ἐκκλησιαστικὸν ἐπεδεήθη τάγμα); it also included the name "widows" (χήρας τε ὠνόμασε), of whom the older were called "eldresses" (πρεσβύτιδας), but were never assigned the rank of "presbyteresses" (πρεσβυ-τερίδας) or "priestesses" (ἱερίσσας). For that matter, not even the deacons in the church hierarchy were entrusted with celebrating the Eucharist; they only administered the Eucharist once consecrated.[23]

Epiphanius's central purpose is to establish that women had never held the rank of presbyter, i. e., priest, which would have authorized them to celebrate the Eucharist. From the time of the *Traditio Apostolica* it gradually became established in the Great Church that only ordained Church officers were permitted to perform sacramental and liturgical ministries, and ordination was normally conferred only on bishops, presbyters, and deacons.[24] Epiphanius presents the following picture: deaconesses, also called widows, assisted women during liturgical services, for example at baptism. The older deaconesses and widows were called *presbytides* or "eldresses," but according to Epiphanius these *presbytides* had never had the rank of presbyters or priests, as their designation as *presbytides* and the self-understanding of these women appear to have suggested. In his argument Epiphanius attempts to show that women who held different titles (deaconesses, widows, *presbytides*) really exercised the same office, namely that of deaconess—an effort that is not surprising in light of the premise already formulated, that women could not be anything but deaconesses. This picture of a subordinate Church office for women was the result of Epiphanius's concept of creation theology, which determined women's inferiority to men.

Any attempt to derive clear historical facts from Epiphanius's argumentation is scarcely possible in any adequate sense in light of that author's tendency to present women's exercise of Church office in as marginal a fashion as possible. On the other hand, his depiction is all the more informative as regards the conflict over ordination of women in the ancient Church and the arguments put forth in the course of it.

At issue was the question whether women could exercise the offices of bishop and presbyter as well as that of deacon. There apparently were Christian women and men who acknowledged women as bishops and presbyters and who either practiced their ordination to those offices or at least favored it.[24a] If we follow Epiphanius we can say that they appealed to Old Testament traditions like those in Exod 15:20 and to New Testament traditions such as Gal 3:28. Opposed to this group were adamant foes of the admission of women to any office or function in the Church beyond the diaconate. These latter endeavored to demonstrate the inferiority of women by means of an argument grounded in creation theology, appealing, for example, to such scriptural passages as Gen 3:16; 1 Cor 11:8, or 1 Tim 2:12-15. With such "scriptural proofs" the subordination of women within the Church and their subjection to Church officials (and husbands) could be given a foundation and made publicly manifest.

Wilhelm Schneemelcher locates Epiphanius within the fourth-century theological tendency marked by "massive traditionalism." "In those circles dogmatic questions were not theologically thought through, that is, pursued, but instead they were regarded as resolved; a massive traditionalism was normative and harmonized with the equally present biblicism only because exegesis was fundamentally governed by an already-existing dogmatic decision."[25] The accuracy of this evaluation is evident especially from Epiphanius's argument in the texts quoted above (*Pan.* 49 and 79). Epiphanius was a solid opponent of the possibility that women could be clothed with Church offices on an equal basis with men. This premise shaped his argumentation and the choice of scriptural passages he adduced to support his opinion. His view of women's ordination was part and parcel of his general hierarchical conception that cultic activity was to be restricted to the bishops and presbyters, and that all other officeholders, even the deacons, were to be forbidden any participation in the Eucharist beyond mere assistance (*Pan.* 79, 4). Epiphanius was undoubtedly one of the representatives of those circles in the Great Church that sought the centralization of ecclesiastical and priestly authority, and as a consequence attempted to diminish as much as possible the influence of women and the *ordines minores*,[26] but also of deacons and thus, by no means least, of lay people in general.[27]

A further indication of the activity of women presbyters in the Church in Asia Minor in the fourth century is offered by Canon 11 of the Synod of Laodicea. It attests to ordained women presbyters, called *presbytides,* who acted as presidents of their congregations. This canon is a second witness, in addition to Epiphanius, for the existence of such women officeholders on the one hand, and on the other hand for attempts to repress them in the fourth-century Church in Asia Minor. Canon 11 of the Synod of Laodicea orders that so-called *presbytides* or women presiders not be installed in the Church (περὶ τοῦ μὴ δεῖν τὰς λεγομένας πρεσβύτιδας ἤτοι προκαθημένας ἐν ἐκκλησίᾳ καθίστασθαι).[28]

This canon, like the other fifty-nine canons of this synod, survives only in summary form; moreover, there is no exact list of persons present or of signatures, and the date of the synod is unknown.[29] We may suppose that it met between 341 and 381.[30] The introduction of the canon with περὶ τοῦ μὴ δεῖν is formulaic and is found in many of the canons of this synod.

(a) The "so-called *presbytides*" (τὰς λεγομένας πρεσβύτιδας) are mentioned only here in this collection of canons. The addition of λεγομένας shows that the word is used in a technical sense. The reference is not to old women in general,[31] but to women who are called *presbytides* in the sense of a Church office. This understanding of the word is underscored by ἐν ἐκκλησίᾳ καθίστασθαι, which in the canons of this synod refers to the appointment of the higher clergy. We can only conjecture that the office of the *presbytides* is to be understood as analogous to that of the πρεσβύτεροι, but their further description as presiders or presidents makes that a likely interpretation.

(b) The equation of the *presbytides* with the presiders through an emphatic "or" (ἤτοι προκαθημένας) indicates that this group of women had no fixed name, but were designated by at least two. Their description as presiders points more precisely to the women's ecclesiastical function and describes the "so-called *presbytides*" unmistakably in terms of their leadership function within the community. In light of their location—as we must suppose—within the higher clergy we must presume that these women both led the assembly and presided at the Eucharist. The verb προκαθῆσθαι means "preside, stand before, lead" and is found in the letters of Ignatius in connection with the bishop, the presbyters, and the deacons (Ign. *Magn.* 6.1, 2); it is always used in an official and hierarchical sense.[32]

(c) Ἐν ἐκκλησίᾳ καθίστασθαι: Καθίστασθαι is a *terminus technicus* for the installation of clerics.[33] In general the term does not tell whether the installation involves the laying on of hands (χειροτονία) and thus an entry into the higher clergy or whether it may be an installation of clerics in minor orders; these latter received no laying on of hands and had a correspondingly more restricted area of competence.[34] In the canons of the Synod of Laodicea, however, we find καθίστασθαι exclusively to mark installation in an office of the higher clergy (ἱερατεία)[35] (Canons 12, 13, and 57). We may therefore suppose, since installation in an office of the higher clergy was always connected with a laying on of hands, that the *presbytides* also received the imposition of hands and therefore were authorized to serve at the altar.[36]

Canon 44 of the Synod of Laodicea can also be understood in connection with the abolition of the office of the *presbytides*. This canon forbade women to enter the sanctuary (ἐν τῷ θυσιαστηρίῳ εἰσέρχεσθαι).[37] The formulation with the verb εἰσέρχομαι does not make it clear whether this command applied to all women, including those who *bis dato* had served at the altar, or whether it was meant only for laywomen. However, in the context of the restriction of the office of the *presbytides* (in the form of the refusal to grant them Holy Orders) we may suspect that this canon was meant to exclude all women from the space near the altar and to put an end, in principle, to women's serving at the altar.

Ida Raming has very accurately described the overall tendency of the Synod of Laodicea:

> However, since the Synod of Laodicea in its regulations about discipline exhibits a strong ascetic orientation in regard to sexual relations, and since it shows itself concerned about 'more strictness with regard to the hierarchical order,' we can rightly assume that here, and especially in the first factor named, lies the basis for the elimination of women's ecclesiastical office by means of canon 11. So motivated, this in effect anti-feminist action also shows itself especially clearly in Canon 44 of the same Synod, since this canon for the first time presents a general exclusion of women from the chancel area . . . .[38]

In light of the tendency of the synod as Raming outlines it we may suppose that the *presbytides* belonged to the higher clergy, which performed the service at the altar. If the *presbytides* had had only a marginal significance in the Church hierarchy it would scarcely have been necessary to forbid their installation. Instead, here an end was to be set to this general authority of women in Church offices.

The interpretation of the *presbytides* as women presbyters who received the laying on of hands and thus priestly authority is strongly suggested by the Latin history of reception of this canon. Isidore (ca. 360/70–435) and Dionysius Exiguus (497–545) translate καθίστασθαι with a form of *ordinare*.[39] Atto of Vercelli (✝ 960) goes farther in his interpretation of Canon 11 of the Synod of Laodicea, naming the duties of the *presbytides:* "For just as these women who were called priests *(presbyterae)* had assumed the duty of preaching, ordering, and instructing . . . *(hae quae presbyterae dicebantur, praedicandi, iubendi, vel edocendi . . . officium sumpserant),* a practice which today is not at all in use."[40]

Atto of Vercelli did not hesitate to describe the field of the *presbytides'* activity in a way that would have been unspeakable for Epiphanius as far as official activity of women in the Great Church was concerned. According to Epiphanius the *presbytides* were the oldest of the deaconesses. He describes them as the older widows and identifies the latter with deaconesses. It is obvious that such an interpretation was the result of his premises (as described above), but that the real Church in Asia Minor in the fourth century looked very different. Thus also Jean Galot, who has accurately summarized the history of reception of this canon:

> Canon XI of the Council of Laodicea embarrasses the commentators. . . . The uncertainties concern the significance of the terms *presbitidi* and *presidenti* as well as of the verb *stabilire* or *ordinare*. If one should trust the title of the Canon, *It is not allowed to appoint women-priests in the church,* one could understand the *presbitidi* in the sense of "priestesses." But such a definition seems unthinkable in the Catholic Church, and there has been an attempt to identify these *presbitidi* either as higher deaconesses, or as deaconesses, or as elderly women responsible for the overseeing of the women of the church.[41]

We thus find that until some time in the fourth century there were women presbyters, also called *presbytides,* active in the Church in Asia Minor. They were not only to be found in schismatic groups, as Epiphanius tried to show, but also in the Great Church, as attested by Canon 11 of the Synod of Laodicea.[42]

Inscription for Epikto the Presbytis

Greece / Thera   II–IV

BIBLIOGRAPHY:
IG XII/3, 933.
Achelis, Hans. "Spuren des Urchristentums auf den griechischen Inseln?" *ZNW* 1 (1900) 87–100, at 88, 90ff.

Grégoire, Henri. *Recueil des inscriptions grecques chrétiennes d'Asie Mineure 1* (Amsterdam: A. M. Hakkert, 1968; reprint of the Paris edition of 1922) 58 no. 167.

Leclercq, Henri. "Achaie," *DACL* I/1 (1924) 321–40, at 337–38.

_____. "Anges," *DACL* I/2 (1924) 2080–2161, at 2141ff.

Guarducci, Margherita. "Gli 'Angeli' di Tera," in *Mélanges helléniques offerts à Georges Daux* (Paris: E. de Boccard, 1974) 147–57, at 150ff.

Feissel, Denis. "Notes d'Epigraphie Chrétienne (II)," *BCH* 101 (1977) 209–28, at 210–12 (fig. 2).

Horsley, G. H. R. *New Documents Illustrating Early Christianity.* Vol. 1: *A Review of the Greek Inscriptions and Papyri published in 1976* (North Ryde, N.S.W.: Macquarie Ancient History Association, 1981) 121 n. 79.

ἄνγε-
λος
Ἐπι-
κτοῦς
5   πρεσβύ-
τιδος[43]

Angel of the Presbyter Epikto.

This inscription belongs to the group of so-called ἄγγελος inscriptions from the island of Thera in the Cyclades. The group contains about forty-five inscriptions each introduced by the word ἄγγελος.[44] The name of the deceased, in the nominative or genitive, follows.[45]

The fact that the stones in this series contain no obviously Christian characteristics has led to a lively discussion among scholars about their place in the history of religion. The angelology common to all the stones caused Rudolf Weil, in 1877, to assign the stones to Christianity, and most scholars have followed that lead.[46] I will summarize the central issues in the discussion:

(a) The angelology of these inscriptions, epigraphically unique in this form, is usually interpreted as Christian. An inscription from Melos of the third or fourth century offers a Christian parallel for interpreting angels as guardians of tombs: "And because this grave is full I swear to you by the angel who sits before it that no one will dare to bury another in this place. May Jesus Christ aid the one who writes and all his house."[47] However, if the tomb angels named in the angel inscriptions are interpreted not as watchers, but as guardian angels of the dead Christians, there is certainly an abundance of material on that motif in Christian literature.[48]

It is true that the idea of angels is also found in pagan and Jewish contexts.[49] However, against a Jewish attribution of this group of inscriptions is the fact that it contains no Jewish characteristics at all (e.g., menorah, palm branch, ark, scrolls of the Law, or Jewish names).[50] Against a pagan origin is the distinction drawn between the angel and the deceased, for "if we refer . . . ἄγγελος to the condition of the deceased, corresponding to the otherwise common ἥρως, it would conflict with the view of the heroes that never presents the hero and the deceased as two separate concepts."[51] The angel-piety of these inscriptions can be most adequately interpreted as a syncretistic phenomenon, something characteristic of the first centuries of Church history.[52]

(b) A further characteristic of this group of inscriptions is as ambiguous as the angel-piety, and that is the circle appearing on some of the angel inscriptions, whose internal lines could be interpreted as a cross or as four stylized flower petals and thus a pagan rosette.[53] Henri Grégoire interprets the symbol as a local equivalent of the cross, with reference to J. G. C. Anderson, who found this ornament in Christian inscriptions in Phrygia from the third and fourth centuries.[54]

(c) A central argument for the Christian provenance of the angel inscriptions is the titling of Epikto as *presbytis*. Canon 11 of the Synod of Laodicea attests to *presbytides* as Christian officeholders who presided over their congregations. As shown above, these women were presbyters. Thus we should join the majority of interpreters of this inscription in seeing Epikto as the presbyter of the community of Christians on Thera[55] in the second or third century.[56] Hans Achelis summarizes: "If the only office mentioned in Thera is a πρεσβῦτις, she would be the first to whom one would attribute a place at the head of the community."[57]

Label of the Mummy Presb(ytera) Artemidora

Egypt[58]   II / III

BIBLIOGRAPHY:
Baratte, François, and Bernard Boyaval. "Catalogue des étiquettes de momies du Musée du Louvre (C.E.M.L.) – textes grecs," *CRIPEL* 5 (1979) 237–339, at 264 no. 1115.
Horsley, G. H. R. *New Documents Illustrating Early Christianity.* Vol. 4: *A Review of the Greek Inscriptions and Papyri published in 1979* (North Ryde, N.S.W.: Macquarie Ancient History Association, 1987) 240 no. 6.

Ἀρτεμιδώρας
Μικκάλου μη`τ´(ρὸς) Πα-
3   νισκιαίνης πρεσ`β´(υτέρας)
ἐκοιμήθη ἐν κ(υρί)ῳ[59]

(Mummy of) the presbyter Artemidora, the daughter of Mikkalos (and the) mother Paniskiaina. She has fallen asleep in the Lord.

This label from a mummy testifies to the Christian presbyter Artemidora, daughter of Mikkalos and Paniskiaina. The fomula of the label follows the conventions of the Greek labels on mummies from Egypt edited by François Baratte and Bernard Boyaval:[60]

- Name of the deceased
- Line of descent (name of the father, name of the mother preceded by μητρὸς)
- Age
- Place of origin
- Profession or religious title
- Date

Artemidora's label uses an abbreviated formula: name of the deceased, father, mother, religious title, Christian burial formula. The *nomen sacrum* (line 4) shows that this is the only certainly Christian mummy among the 1211 in Baratte and Boyaval's collection.

The abbreviation πρεσ'β' (line 3) is somewhat ambiguous, first as regards the person to whom it refers, and second as to its meaning. First, πρεσ'β' could refer either to the mother[61] or to the daughter. Baratte and Boyaval interpret the abbreviation as a further description of the mother in the sense of "the elder," analogously to the pagan labels they edit.[62] In Christian contexts, however, abbreviations such as πρεσ'β' as a rule refer to the title of presbyter.[63] Hence this abbreviation also can be interpreted as the religious title of the daughter. In accordance with the formula in the labels from mummies contained in this collection, given above, the professional designation or religious title occurs after the naming of the parents, age, and place of origin, and that is where πρεσ'β' appears in Artemidora's label. The final verse of the label, which designates Artemidora as a faithful Christian, underscores the interpretation of her as a Christian presbyter.[64]

In this context we must ask whether Christian women presbyters in the Church in Egypt are attested in literature. One literary witness to an office of women presbyters in the East in the fifth century is the *Testamentum Domini,* which may have originated in Egypt. Women presbyters are twice mentioned explicitly in this document:

(a) They are remembered in the community's prayer (*TD* 1.35) after the bishop, the presbyters, and the deacons, and before the subdeacons, lectors, and deaconesses, in the following words: "For the presbyteresses let us beseech, that the Lord may hear their supplications and keep their hearts perfectly in the grace of the Spirit and help their work *(pro presbyteris [feminis]*[65] *supplicemus, ut Dominus exaudiat earum supplicationes et perfecte in gratia spiritus custodiat ipsarum corda, adjuvetque earundem laborem)."*[66]

(b) In *TD* 2.19 we read: "Let the presbyteresses stay with the bishop till dawn, praying and resting *(Presbyterae maneant apud episcopam usque ad tempus matutinum, orantes et requiescentes)."*[67]

From these references we can see that the women presbyters had a place in the hierarchy between the higher and lower clergy. We may suppose that this placement reflects the conflict over this office, once equal to that of the presbyters, as the similarity of the titles hints. Developments like those reflected in Canon 11 of the Synod of Laodicea led, however, to the result that these women no longer received the laying on of hands and thus lost their placement among the higher clergy. That exclusion was connected with serious forfeitures in the authority of these officeholders. The fact that they are mentioned in the *Testamentum Domini* indicates that in the fifth century they were not yet completely suppressed, and that they still had significance in the congregations. We can discern from the community prayer that their principal task was prayer, but they had other duties that are here summarized as "work" *(labor)* and are not further described.

In summary we may say that epigraphic and literary witnesses from the East attest that women presided over communities as presbyters or *presbytides*. Their official activity was not uncontroversial. In the fourth century the Synod of Laodicea in particular attempted to abolish the office of the *presbytides* and ban women from the altar and vicinity. Alongside these canonical regulations regarding *presbytides* we find Epiphanius's theological interpretation, according to which the *presbytides* had never exercised priestly functions in the Church—an assertion that is not surprising in view of Epiphanius's tendency to subordinate women to men in the Church. Women presbyters in the full sense of the word, that is, women who presided over communities as presbyters and thus had authority both to teach and to exercise sacramental and liturgical functions, existed, according to Epiphanius, only in groups associated with Montanism. If we follow Epiphanius's depiction the presbyter Ammion could only be interpreted as a Montanist presbyter. In light of Canon 11 of the Synod of Laodicea and the *Testamentum Domini*, however, such a polarization of the praxis of the Great Church and that of schismatic groups seems questionable. Epiphanius's portrayal is explained by his effort to free the Catholic tradition from ambivalence and to depict it as being as unilinear and coherent as possible.

However, on the basis of the epigraphic evidence we can suppose that until the fourth century women were active as presbyters in the communities of

Asia Minor, Greece, and Egypt. There is clear evidence of the abolition of that office only in the fourth century. In that light the epigraphically attested presbyters Ammion, Epikto, and Artemidora, whose inscriptions, and in the case of Artemidora the label on her mummy, stem from the period between the second and fourth centuries, are to be interpreted as presiders over their communities. They may not yet have been confronted with the suppression of the women presbyters that began in the fourth century.

B. Epigraphic and Literary Evidence from the West

Inscription for the Presbyter Kale

Sicily / Centuripae   IV–V

BIBLIOGRAPHY:
Manni Piraino, Maria Teresa. *Iscrizioni greche lapidarie del Museo di Palermo.* ΣΙΚΕΛΙΚΑ VI (Palermo: S. F. Flaccovio, 1972) 36–37, no. 13 (Plate VII).
L'Année Epigraphique 1975, no. 454.
Horsley, G. H. R. *New Documents Illustrating Early Christianity.* Vol. 1: *A Review of the Greek Inscriptions and Papyri published in 1976* (North Ryde, N.S.W.: Macquarie Ancient History Association, 1981) 121 n. 79.

ἐνθάδε κῖτε Καλὴ πρε(σ)β(ῦτις)
ζήσ(ασ)α ἔτη ν΄ ἀμέ(μ)πτως.
3   τὸν βίον τελ(ευτᾷ) τῇ πρ(ὸ) ιθ΄ κ(αλα)ν(δῶν)
Ὀκτωβρίων. Christ monogram.[68]

Line 1: Καλὴ is a Greek woman's name.[69]
            πρεβ = πρεσβῦτις[70] or πρεσβυτέρα.

Here lies the presbyter Kale, who lived fifty years without reproach. She ended her life on 14 September.

This inscription attests a woman named Kale who died at the age of fifty. The formula of the inscription is typical for Sicily: introduction with ἐνθάδε κῖτε followed by the name of the deceased, age, and date of death.[71] The epithet ἀμέμπτως applied to the deceased occurs frequently in literature in connection with officeholders.[72] In Greek inscriptions from Sicily the formula ζήσασα ἀμέμπτως is also found regularly for Christians for whom no title of office is given.[73]

The further designation πρεβ for Kale marks her as a πρεσβυτέρα or πρεσβῦτις and thus as a Christian officeholder.[74] Abbreviations of the title of presbyter such as πρεβ are found in Greek inscriptions from the East, as we have shown above, and frequently in Latin inscriptions from the West as well.[75] We cannot determine on the basis of the abbreviation whether Kale was called πρεσβῦτις or πρεσβυτέρα. However, a decision is not really necessary since both words are attested as official titles for women in the fourth century. The reading πρεσβῦτις as meaning "old woman" is excluded for this particular inscription because there is no other instance of that attribute in Sicilian inscriptions.[76] For example, Καλλιτύχη, who died at the age of eighty-eight and for whom it would therefore have been appropriate, is not so described.[77]

A letter of Pope Gelasius I (492–496)[78] may shed some light on this epigraphic witness. In the year 494 he wrote a letter "to all episcopates established in Lucania [modern Basilicata], Bruttium [modern Calabria]—ankle and toe of Italy—and Sicilia [modern Sicily]: 'Nevertheless we have heard to our annoyance that divine affairs have come to such a low state that women are encouraged to officiate at the sacred altars *(feminae sacris altaribus ministrare)*, and to take part in all matters imputed to the offices of the male sex *(cunctaque non nisi virorum famulatui deputata sexum)*, to which they do not belong *(cui non competunt, exhibere).*'"[79]

The command that women should not enter the sanctuary first appears, as we have shown above, in Canon 44 of the Synod of Laodicea, but without further detail, so that it remains open whether women who held Church office were also denied access to the altar. There is none of that ambiguity in Gelasius's letter. He speaks decisively against any service of women at the altar, giving as a reason that such service is reserved to the male sex—a reasoning that is not found in the canons of the Synod of Laodicea. Gelasius's letter to the bishops in southern Italy also shows that there were bishops and congregations there who recognized women as presbyters. The same is indicated by three other inscriptions: those of the presbyter Leta from Bruttium and the presbyter Flavia Vitalia, and the fragment of an inscription for a *sacerdota* from Salona in Dalmatia.

Inscription for Leta the presbitera

Italy / Bruttium / Tropea[80]   IV–V[81]

BIBLIOGRAPHY:

CIL X, no. 8079.

Kaufmann, Carl Maria. *Handbuch der altchristlichen Epigraphik* (Freiburg: Herder, 1917) 256.

ILCV 1, 1192 n.

Leclercq, Henri. "Inscriptions Latines Chrétiennes," *DACL* VII/1 (1926) 694–850, at 768.

Crispo, Anna. "Antichità cristiane della Calabria prebyzantia," *ASCL* 14 (1945) 127–41; 209–10, at 133–34.

Ferrua, Antonio. "Note su tropea paleocristiana," *ASCL* 23 (1954) 9–29, at 11.

Wischmeyer, Wolfgang Karl. *Die archäologischen und literarischen Quellen zur Kirchengeschichte von Apulia et Calabria, Lucania et Bruttii bis zum Jahr 600. Sammlung und Auswertung von Materialien zur Geschichte zweier spätantiker Provinzen.* Dissertation in typescript (Essen, 1972) 91–92.

Otranto, Giorgio. "Note sul sacerdozio femminile nell'antichità in margine a una testimonianza di Gelasio I," *VetChr* 19 (1982) 341–60, at 351–52 (cf. Mary Ann Rossi, "Priesthood, Precedent, and Prejudice. On Recovering the Women Priests of Early Christianity. Containing a translation from the Italian of 'Notes on the Female Priesthood in Antiquity,' by Giorgio Otranto," *JFSR* 7 [1991] 73–94, at 86–87).

```
  B M S  LETA PRESBITERA
  VIXIT ANN • XL M • G̅II • G̅III
  QVEI BENE FECIT MARITVS
  PRECESSIT IN PACE PRIDIE
5 IDVS MAIAS[82]
```

Line 1:　B M S = *b(onae) m(emoriae) s(acrum)*
　　　　　presbitera = presbytera
Line 2:　G̅ = six
Line 3:　*quei = cui.* Ferrua reads *que.*

Sacred in happy memory: The presbyter Leta, who lived forty years, eight months, and nine days, whose husband erected this tombstone. She went forth in peace on the day before the Ides of May (15 May).

This inscription commemorates the presbyter Leta, who died at the age of forty. The wording is characteristic for inscriptions from Tropea: an introduction with the Tropean formula *bonae memoriae sacrum*[83] and the *terminus technicus* for "preparing the grave with love," *bene facere.*[84] The dedicator of the inscription was the husband of the deceased.

Wolfgang Wischmeyer has shown that the oldest Christian inscriptions from Bruttium, Apulia, Calabria, and Lucania stem from the mid-fourth century.[85] The epigraphic material in those regions as a whole is not very large and declines toward the sixth century. Examples attesting to Church organization are especially sparse. For Tropea only one presbyter besides Leta and one deacon are attested. For Tauriana there is epigraphic evidence for one bishop and two deacons, and for Potenza a single ostiary.[86]

Scholars have regularly interpreted Leta as the wife of a presbyter.[87] Reference is made to witnesses from the ancient Church showing that wives of officials bore their husbands' titles. For example, the Council of Tours spoke of the *presbiter cum sua presbiteria aut diaconus cum sua diaconissa aut subdiaconus cum sua subdiaconissa*.[88] However, such witnesses should not lead to the over-hasty conclusion that every reference to a *presbytera, diaconissa,* or *subdiacona* is to the wife of a man holding the corresponding office. That these are wives must be demonstrated from the context.

In the case of the presbyter Leta there is indeed mention of a husband, but he is not said or shown to be an officeholder, and thus should not be interpreted as such without further evidence.[89] Giorgio Otranto has correctly pointed out that the exclusive interpretation of the *presbitera* Leta as wife of a presbyter has been determined primarily by the tradition of Catholic historiography, which excludes the priesthood of women in principle. Against this, Otranto interprets the *presbitera* Leta in light of the letter of Gelasius I as *"una vera e propria presbytera,"* that is, a woman who exercised the office of presbyter in the community at Tropea.[90]

The tomb inscription for Irene, a sixty-five-year-old Christian from the middle of the fifth century, is a further attestation that in Tropea women exercised offices independently of their husbands. Irene is described in her epitaph as a leaseholder *(conductrix):*

B(onae) M(emoriae) S(acrum) FIDELI IN XP(ιστ)O IHES(u)M
HIRENI QUE VIXIT ANNIS LXV M VIII
3   D X CUI BENE FECIT VIR EIUS PRECESSIT FI-
DELIS IN PACE DEPOSITA XVIII KAL. MAIAS
QUE FUIT CONDUCT(rix) M(assae) TRAPEIANAE.[91]

Line 5 says that Irene was *conductrix massae Trapeianae.* Whether the *massa Trapeianae* she rented was state or Church property can no longer be determined with certainty. We may posit, with Anna Crispo, because of the emphasis on *fidelis* (lines 1, 3-4), that she was a leaseholder of Church property.[92] This is also favored by the fact that there is evidence of a Roman Church property in Tropea that was leased by a monastery at the end of the sixth century.[93]

prb Flavia Vitalia

Yugoslavia / Dalmatia / Salona[94]   425

BIBLIOGRAPHY:
Bulic, France. "Iscrizione Inedita. Salona (Solin)," *Bullettino di Archeologia e Storia Dalmata* 21 (1898) 107–11.
Leclercq, Henri. "Inscriptions Latines Chrétiennes," *DACL* VII/1 (1926) 694–850, at 768.

_____. "Presbyter," *DACL* XIV/2 (1948) 1717–1721, at 1721.

Otranto, Giorgio. "Note sul sacerdozio femminile nell'antichità in margine a una testimonianza di Gelasio I," *VetChr* 19 (1982) 341–60, at 353–54 (cf. Mary Ann Rossi, "Priesthood, Precedent, and Prejudice. On Recovering the Women Priests of Early Christianity. Containing a translation from the Italian of 'Notes on the Female Priesthood in Antiquity,' by Giorgio Otranto," *JFSR* 7 [1991] 73–94, at 87–88).

D(ominis) n(ostris) Thaeodosio co(n)s(ule) XI et Valentiniano
viro nobelissimo Caes(are). Ego Thaeodo-
3   sius emi a Fl(avia) Vitalia pr(es)b(ytera) sanc(ta) matrona auri sol(idis) III. Sub d(ie)[95]

Under our Lord Theodosius, consul for the eleventh time, and Valentinian, the noblest man, the emperor. I, Theodosius, have purchased (the tomb) from the *matrona* Flavia Vitalia, the holy presbyter, for three golden *solidi*.

This inscription testifies to a certain Theodosius who purchased a burial place in the cemetery at Salona from the presbyter Flavia Vitalia for three *solidi*. Thanks to the mention of the consular year the inscription can be dated to 425.[96]

Flavia Vitalia is described as a *matrona,* that is, she was a freeborn married woman.[97] As such she exercised the office of presbyter. The abbreviation *prb* is commonly used for the title "presbyter" in Latin inscriptions.[98] In this inscription we see Flavia Vitalia as a presbyter functioning as one who sells burial places. In the fifth century the administration of cemeteries had passed to Church officials, including the presbyters, as a way of counteracting misuse and illegal profiteering.[99] The sale of burial places was, in this situation, a duty belonging to the presbyters.[100] The sale contracts were placed on the tombstones and included the names of the buyer and seller and the sale price, as the above inscription shows. Often witnesses to the contract were also included. This inscription attests that women also worked as presbyters in this matter of burial plot administration.

Inscription for a sacerdota

Yugoslavia / Dalmatia / Salona[101]   V–VI

BIBLIOGRAPHY:
CIL III, 14900.

Bulic, France. "Iscrizioni Inediti. Salona (Solin)," *Bullettino di Archeologia e Storia Dalmata* 21 (1989) 141–48, at 147 n. 2428.

Otranto, Giorgio. "Note sul sacerdozio femminile nell'antichità in margine a una testimonianza di Gelasio I," *VetChr* 19 (1982) 341–60, at 354 (cf. Mary Ann Rossi, "Priesthood, Precedent, and Prejudice. On Recovering the

Women Priests of Early Christianity. Containing a translation from the Italian of 'Notes on the Female Priesthood in Antiquity,' by Giorgio Otranto," *JFSR* 7 [1991] 73–94, at 88).

sace]RDOTAE +

This fragmentary inscription witnesses to another woman who was active in Salona as a presbyter or bishop. Only a small piece of the inscription survives, so that apart from the mere attestation of the word *sacerdota* we have only the cross as further information about the deceased. The latter assures, however, that this fragment comes from the grave of a Christian woman and not from that of a pagan *sacerdota*.[102]

In his investigation of the titles for Christian priests Pierre-Marie Gy has determined that from the second half of the fourth century until the sixth century *sacerdos* was usually applied to bishops, occasionally also to presbyters.[103] We cannot determine with regard to this inscription whether the reference is to the office of bishop or presbyter, since it contains no other information. In light of the fact that the presbyter Flavia Vitalia is attested in Salona this may be the tomb of another woman presbyter. However, the fact that women were active as presbyters in the community at Salona makes it possible that the epigraphically attested *sacerdota* was the bishop of that community.

In summary, we find that women can be shown from epigraphical evidence to have been presbyters and bishops[104] in Sicily, southern Italy, and Yugoslavia from the fourth to the sixth centuries. In the case of one of the presbyters her specific duty is also clear: she worked in the administration of burial places. Beyond the epigraphical evidence we have a letter from Pope Gelasius I from the end of the fifth century attesting that women were sacerdotally active in southern Italy and Sicily. This was apparently accepted by the communities there and encouraged by their bishops—a custom that Gelasius attacks in his letter.

We may therefore assume that the women who are called presbyters were also entrusted with the service of the altar. The small number of remaining epigraphical attestations of women presbyters, however, indicates that women remained a minority in that Church office; this is reinforced by the fact that those who opposed such an office for women, and the women who exercised it, as well as those who encouraged and accepted them in the role, attacked their opponents both in writing and through Church political moves. There are sources from as late as the eighth and ninth centuries that continue to witness to such a struggle against women's liturgical service in the Latin Church.

In a letter from Pope Zachary to Pippin and the Frankish bishops, abbots, and authorities of 5 January 747 the pope writes regarding nuns:

Concerning the nuns, that is, the handmaids of God *(de monachis, id est ancillis Dei):* It is asked concerning them whether they may publicly read the Bible during the celebration of Mass or on the holy Sabbath, sing at Mass or offer an Alleluia or an antiphonal song. This was decided in the book of the decrees of Pope Gelasius, ch. 26: that it is a sin for women to serve at the sacred altars *(feminas sacris altaribus ministrare)* or assume to themselves anything that is assigned to men as their task *(vel aliquid ex his, quae virorum sunt officiis deputata, praesumere).* Nevertheless, as we have learned to our dismay, divine worship has fallen into such disdain that women have presumed to serve at the sacred altars, and that the female sex, to whom it does not belong, perform all the things that are assigned exclusively to men *(feminae sacris altaribus ministrare firmentur cunctaque non nisi virorum famulatui deputata sexum, cui non competit exhibere).*[105]

This letter shows that the conflict over women's service at the altar also existed in monastic contexts. Here, too, women claimed a full sacredotal service. Again and again, Church authorities attempted to forbid them that service—attempts that evidently were not completely successful, as the number of these prohibitory texts shows. Thus we find, for example, a report from his bishops to Emperor Louis the Pious (829) referring not only to nuns, but to women in the congregations in general:

We have attempted in every way possible . . . to prevent women from approaching the altar, as it is forbidden. Since we have learned from a report from reliable persons that in some provinces, contrary to divine law and canonical ordinances women enter the sanctuary, shamelessly take hold of the consecrated vessels, hand the sacerdotal vestments to the priests, and—more monstrous, improper, and inappropriate than all else—give the people the Body and Blood of the Lord and do other things indecent in themselves *(quae ipso dictu turpia sunt exercere),* we have attempted to prevent these things, so that they may not spread. But that women are not allowed to enter the sanctuary is [decreed by] the Council of Chalcedon . . . and in the decrees of Pope Gelasius . . . .[106]

This report underscores the epigraphic evidence: women laid claim to sacerdotal service and were recognized in their offices by bishops and congregations. Apparently it was easier for women to serve as presbyters and bishops in the provinces.

Notes

[1] According to Marc Waelkens, *Die kleinasiatischen Türsteine. Typologische und epigraphische Untersuchungen der kleinasiatischen Grabreliefs mit Scheintür* (Mainz: P. von Zabern, 1986) 147. Ibid. 148: "[discovered] 1895 'in the ruins of the church of Constantinople and Helena' in Uçak. Neither material nor size mentioned. Probably the same type as No. 366 (F or G Uçak 1). 'Small tomb door with spindle, distaff, and small box' . . . Neither

location nor height of the letters is indicated." (For Type F or G Uçak 1 cf. ibid. 144–45). He did not see the inscription himself and for the most part follows the information in Alfred Körte, *Inscriptiones Bureschianae*. Wissenschaftliche Beilage zum Vorlesungsverzeichnis der Universität Greifswald. Easter 1902 (Greifswald: Druck von J. Abel, 1902) 31.

[2] Thus Körte, *Inscriptiones Bureschianae* 31. For further detail see Jeanne and Louis Robert in *BE* (1972) 458; Elsa Gibson, "Montanist Epitaphs at Uçak," *GRBS* 16 (1975) 433–42, at 436; Waelkens, *Türsteine* 147: "Deiogas (Diogas) is a pet name for Diogenes."

[3] Waelkens, *Türsteine* nos. 366 and 375.

[4] See the examples in Ladislav Zgusta, *Kleinasiatische Personennamen* (Prague: Verlag der Tschechoslowakischen Akademie der Wissenschaften, 1964) § 57-20.

[5] On this see Waelkens, *Türsteine* 145 and nos. 366–74.

[6] From Waelkens, *Türsteine* 146–47 no. 366; see also Gibson, "Montanist Epitaphs," 435–36 no. 2 (Plate 4).

[7] On this see Gibson, "Montanist Epitaphs," 436 n. 10. The Church financed burials; in Korykos in Cilicia it owned some tombs: *MAMA* III nos. 772–78 (here: τῆς ἐκκλησίας).

[8] Waelkens, *Türsteine* 147.

[9] From Waelkens, *Türsteine* 150 no. 375; see also Gibson, "Montanist Epitaphs," 436–37 no. 3.

[10] On this see Waelkens, *Türsteine* 145.

[11] On this see, in detail, Günther Bornkamm, "πρέσβυς, πρεσβύτερος, κτλ.," *TDNT* 6:651–83, at 665; and especially the discussion of this topic with regard to Judaism in Bernadette Brooten, *Women Leaders in the Ancient Synagogue. Inscriptional Evidence and Background Issues* (Chico: Scholars, 1982) 41–55.

[12] On this see, with examples, BAGD 699–700, and Bornkamm, "πρέσβυς," 665, 672.

[13] Cf. Gibson, "Montanist Epitaphs," 438, and eadem, *"Christians for Christians"* 136.

[14] On this see William M. Ramsay, *The Cities and Bishoprics of Phrygia. Being an Essay of The Local History of Phrygia from the Earliest Times to the Turkish Conquest.* 2 vols. (Oxford: Clarendon Press, 1895, 1897) 2:490–91, 536–37 n. 393; idem, "Phrygian Orthodox and Heretics 400–800 AD," *Byz* 6 (1931) 1–35; Calder, "Philadelphia and Montanism," *BJRL* 7 (1922/23) 309–54; idem, "Leaves from an Anatolian Notebook," *BJRL* 13 (1929) 254–71; idem, "Early-Christian Epitaphs from Phrygia," *AnSt* 5 (1955) 25–38; Wilhelm E. Schepelern, *Der Montanismus und die phrygischen Kulte. Eine religionsgeschichtliche Untersuchung* (Tübingen: Mohr [Siebeck], 1929) 79ff.; August Strobel, *Das heilige Land der Montanisten. Eine religionsgeographische Untersuchung.* RVV 37 (Berlin and New York: Walter de Gruyter, 1980) 65ff.; Gibson, "Montanist Epitaphs;" eadem, *"Christians for Christians"* (cf. the review by Wolfgang K. Wischmeyer in *JAC* 23 [1980] 166–71); William Tabbernee, "Christian Inscriptions from Phrygia," in G. H. R. Horsley, ed., *New Documents Illustrating Early Christianity* 3 (North Ryde, N.S.W.: Macquarie Ancient History Association, 1983) 128–39.

[15] Strobel, *Land der Montanisten* 103; Waelkens, *Türsteine* 147; Horsley, *New Documents* 4:240; Tabbernee, "Remnants of the New Prophecy: Literary and Epigraphical Sources of the Montanist Movement," *StPatr* 21 (1987) 193–201, at 200.

[16] Strobel, *Land der Montanisten* 102–104; Waelkens, *Türsteine* 145, 147.

[17] See the text edition in three volumes by Karl Holl, *Epiphanius (Ancoratus und Panarion).* GCS 25; 31; 37 (Leipzig: J. C. Hinrichs, 1915–1933); the second edition of volume 2 was edited by Jürgen Dummer (*Epiphanius, II. Panarion haer. 34–64.* GCS 31 [Berlin: Akademie-Verlag, 1980]).

[18] Epiphanius, *Panarion* 49, 2.2-5, 3.2 (GCS 31 [1980] 242ff.). English translation (as far as "because of Eve") from *The Panarion of St. Epiphanius, Bishop of Salamis. Selected Passages.* Translated by Philip R. Amidon (New York and Oxford: Oxford University Press, 1990) 173–74. For Epiphanius's sources for this chapter and the historical value of his description see Richard A. Lipsius, *Zur Quellenkritik des Epiphanios* (Vienna: W. Braumüller, 1865) 230–31.

[19] Epiphanius gives no further clarification of the reference to Eve.

[20] *Didasc.* 14.

[21] Epiphanius, *Pan.* 79, 3, 6; 4, 1. Translation from Amidon, *The Panarion of St. Epiphanius* 353; GCS 37, 478.

[22] *Didasc.* 16.

[23] Epiphanius, *Pan.* 79, 3, 6; 4, 1 (*The Panarion of St. Epiphanius* 353; GCS 37, 478).

[24] On this see Wilhelm Geerlings, ed., *Traditio Apostolica = Apostolische Überlieferung.* FC 1 (Freiburg and New York: Herder, 1991) 143–313, at 160ff. For ordination in early Christianity see Eduard Lohse, *Die Ordination im Spätjudentum und im Neuen Testament* (Göttingen: Vandenhoeck & Ruprecht, 1951); Georg Kretschmar, "Die Ordination im frühen Christentum," *FZPhTh* 22 (1975) 35–69.

[24a] Another explicit documentation of the ordination of a woman as *presbytis,* that is, as a presbyter, is provided by the *Martyrium Matthaei* 28 (Ricardus Adelbert Lipsius and Maximilianus Bonnet, *Acta Apostolorum Apocrypha post Constantinum Tischendorf denuo ediderunt* II, 1 [Darmstadt: Wissenschaftliche Buchgesellschaft, 1959] 217–72, at 259). *Presbytides* as officeholders parallel to presbyters are also attested by the Acts of Philip (probably stemming from fourth-century encratite communities) at I, 9. See the new text edition by Bertrand Bouvier and François Bovon, "Actes de Philippe, I, d'après un manuscrit inédit," in François Bovon, Bertrand Bouvier, and Frederick Amsler, eds., *Acta Philippi: testvs* (Turnhout: Brepols, 1999) 367–94, at 385, and the editors' commentary regarding the *presbytides* at pp. 393–94.

[25] Wilhelm Schneemelcher, "Epiphanius von Salamis," *RAC* 5 (1962) 909–27.

[26] Of enduring value for information on the *ordines minores* is Franz Wieland, *Die genetische Entwicklung der sog. Ordines Minores in den ersten Jahrhunderten.* RQ.S 7 (Rome: Herder, 1897).

[27] For the laity see Adolf M. Ritter, "Laie," *TRE* 20 (1990) 378–85.

[28] Synod of Laodicea, Canon 11 (Friedrich Lauchert, ed., *Die Kanones der wichtigsten altkirchlichen Concilien nebst den apostolischen Kanones.* SQS 12 [Freiburg: J. C. B. Mohr, 1896; reprint Frankfurt: Minerva, 1961] 73). Cf. also the text edition by J. D. Mansi, *Sacrorum conciliorum nova et amplissima collectio.* 53 vols. (Paris: H. Welter, 1901–1927; reprint Graz: Akademische Druck- u. Verlagsanstalt, 1960–1961) 2:563–74 (with text-critical and reception-historical notes).

[29] Eduard Schwartz, "Die Kanonessammlungen der alten Reichskirche" (1936) in idem, *Gesammelte Schriften 4* (Berlin: Walter de Gruyter, 1960) 159–275, at 190.

[30] This time frame can be assumed because in collections of conciliar documents made in the sixth and even in the fifth century the canons of the Synod of Laodicea are placed after those of the Synod of Antioch of 341 and before those of the second General Synod in 381. For discussion of the question of dating see Carl Joseph Hefele, *Conciliengeschichte.* 9 vols.; vols. 8 and 9 edited by J. Hergenröther (Freiburg: Herder, 1855–1890; vols. 1–6, 2nd ed. Freiburg: Herder, 1873–1890) 1:721–25; Edgar Hennecke, "Laodicea, [Synode um 360]," *RE³* 11 (1902) 281. Hans Achelis, "Spuren des Urchristentums auf den griechischen Inseln?"

ZNW 1 (1900) 87–100, at 97, dates the synod to 360; Nicholas Afanasiev, "Presbytides or Female Presidents. Canon 11, Council of Laodicea," in Thomas Hopko, ed., *Women and the Priesthood* (Crestwood, N.Y.: St. Vladimir's Seminary Press, 1983) 61–74, at 61, speaks of the second half of the fourth century. For the complicated tradition-history of canonical collections see Schwartz, "Die Kanonessammlungen der alten Reichskirche," 159–275.

[31] BAGD includes πρεσβῦτις exclusively in the sense of "old(er) woman, elderly lady," with a reference to Titus 2:3. G. W. H. Lampe, *A Patristic Greek Lexicon* (Oxford and New York: Clarendon Press, 1969), in contrast, differentiates between a general and an ecclesiastical usage. Even in the case of the general meaning he cautions: "as used of Christians hard to distinguish from technical sense of a woman possessing eccl. status." He mentions two examples from Eusebius's *History* that illustrate the problem (*Hist. eccl.* 6, 4, 7 and 18).

[32] Examples are collected in Lampe, *Lexicon* 1151.

[33] Cf. ibid. 690, with examples.

[34] For this distinction see especially the canonical developments since the *Traditio Apostolica,* where for the first time a distinction is fixed between the higher and the lower clergy in that only *episkopoi, diakonoi,* and *presbyteroi* receive the laying on of hands and are admitted to service at the altar. On this see Geerlings, *Traditio Apostolica* 160ff.

[35] Synod of Laodicea, Canon 13 (Lauchert, *Die Kanones der wichtigsten altkirchlichen Concilien* 73): καθίστασθαι εἰς ἱερατεῖον.

[36] The laying on of hands (χειροτονία) is mentioned in Canon 5, but without further comment regarding the officeholders who received it.

[37] Synod of Laodicea, Canon 44 (Lauchert, *Die Kanones der wichtigsten altkirchlichen Concilien* 77).

[38] Ida Raming, *The exclusion of women from the priesthood: divine law or sex discrimination? A historical investigation of the juridical and doctrinal foundations of the code of canon law, canon 968, 1.* Translated by Norman R. Adams, with a preface by Arlene and Leonard Swidler (Metuchen, N.J.: Scarecrow Press, 1976) 22.

[39] On this see Hefele, *Conciliengeschichte* 1:733, who gives the exact wording of Isidore's and Dionysius's translations. Isidore translated *in ecclesia tanquam ordinatas constitui non debere,* and Dionysius Exiguus *in ecclesiis ordinari.*

[40] Atto of Vercelli, *Ep.* 8 (MPL 134, 114; Mary Ann Rossi, "Priesthood, Precedent, and Prejudice. On Recovering the Women Priests of Early Christianity. Containing a translation from the Italian of 'Notes on the Female Priesthood in Antiquity,' by Giorgio Otranto," *JFSR* 7 (1991) 73–94, at 90ff. nn. 74, 78-79.

[41] Jean Galot, *La Donna e i ministeri nella Chiesa* (Assisi, 1973) 80, from the English translation by Rossi, "Priesthood, Precedent, and Prejudice," 91.

[42] The context of the canonical collection makes it clear that Canon 11 of the Synod of Laodicea does not refer to women in schismatic groups. The regulations regarding heretics are always explicitly introduced as such (cf. canons 7 and 8).

[43] According to Denis Feissel, "Notes d'Epigraphie Chrétienne (II)," *BCH* 101 (1977) 209–28, at 210 n. 8: "This is no. 2248 in the Musée épigraphique, where we saw the stone (fig. 2). The inscription is engraved on a reused white marble plaque, broken everywhere except on the right. Height: 21 cm.; breadth: 19 cm. at the base and 16 at the top; thickness: 4 cm.; height of the letters: 2 to 2.5 cm." The line breaks follow Henri Grégoire, *Recueil des inscriptions grecques chrétiennes d'Asie Mineure 1* (Amsterdam: A. M. Hakkert, 1968; reprint of the Paris edition of 1922) 58.

[44] Variant readings include ἄνγελος, ἄγγελες, and ἄγγλες. On this see also Margherita Guarducci, "Gli 'Angeli' di Tera," in *Mélanges helléniques offerts à Georges Daux* (Paris: E. de Boccard, 1974) 147–57, at 147.

[45] *IG* XII/3, 455; 933–974; 1636; 1637; Henri Grégoire, *Recueil des inscriptions grecques chrétiennes d'Asie Mineure 1* (Amsterdam: A. M. Hakkert, 1968; reprint of the Paris edition of 1922), nos. 166–97 (see also pp. 56–57).

On this see Rudolf Weil, "Von den griechischen Inseln," *AM* 2 (1877) 59–82, at 77–79; Achelis, "Spuren des Urchristentums," 88ff.; Adolf Deissmann, *Light from the Ancient East; the New Testament illustrated by recently discovered texts of the Graeco-Roman world*. Translated by Lionel R. M. Strachan (London, Hodder & Stoughton, 1910; revised ed. New York: Harper, 1922; repr. Grand Rapids: Baker Book House, 1965, 1978) 280 n. 1; Henri Leclercq, "Anges," *DACL* I/2 (1924) 2080–2161, at 2141ff.; Margherita Guarducci, "Angelos," *SMSR* 15 (1939) 79–89; eadem, "Gli 'Angeli' di Tera;" Antonio Ferrua, "Gli angeli di Tera," *Orientalia christ. periodica* XIII (1947) 149–67; Johann Michl, "Engel I-IX," *RAC* 5 (1962) 53–258, at 55–56; Feissel, "Notes d'Epigraphie Chrétienne (II)," 209–14.

[46] Rudolf Weil, "Von den griechischen Inseln," 78–79; *IG* XII 3 = *Inscriptiones Graecae. Inscriptiones insularum maris Aegaei praeter Delum. Fasc. 3. Inscriptiones Symes, Teutlussae, Teli, Nisyri, Astypalaeae, Anaphes, Therae et Therasiae, Pholegandri, Meli, Cimoli.* Edited by Friedrich Hiller von Gärtringen (Berlin: Akademie der Wissenschaften, 1898. *Supplementum* 1904. Repr. Berlin: Walter de Gruyter, 1939); Achelis, "Spuren des Urchristentums," 88ff.; Grégoire, *Recueil des inscriptions grecques chrétiennes* 57; Leclercq, "Anges," 2141ff.; Lampe, *Lexicon* 1131; Feissel, "Notes d'Epigraphie Chrétienne (II)," 209–14; differently Deissmann, *Light from the Ancient East* 280 n. 1; Adolf von Harnack, *The Expansion of Christianity in the First Three Centuries*. 2 vols. Translated and edited by James Moffatt (New York: G. P. Putnam's Sons, 1904–05) 2:370–71; Guarducci, "Angelos;" eadem, "Gli 'Angeli' di Tera."

[47] *IG* XII/3, 1238. For this inscription for the deacon Agalliasis and those belonging to her see Chapter 7 C below.

[48] On this see Achelis, "Spuren des Urchristentums," 91.

[49] For the breadth and variety of notions of angels in Greco-Roman antiquity see especially Michl, "Engel." For the Jewish and Christian realm see especially Leclercq, "Anges," and Walter Grundmann, Gerhard von Rad, and Gerhard Kittel, "ἄγγελος, κτλ.," *TDNT* 1:74–87.

[50] Cf. Achelis, "Spuren des Urchristentums," 93. For Jewish inscriptions and their characteristics see especially Jean-Baptiste Frey, ed., *Corpus Inscriptionum Iudicarum. Recueil des Inscriptions juives qui vont du IIIᵉ siècle avant Jésus-Christ au VIIᵉ siècle de notre ère.* 2 vols. SSAC 1; 3 (Vatican City: Pontificio istituto di archeologia cristiana, 1936, 1952), as well as the Jewish inscriptions witnessing to women officeholders in Brooten, *Women Leaders*. Cf. her references to the inscriptional evidence for seven Jewish women as elders: *CIJ* 731c, Sophia of Gortyn, elder and head of the synagogue, from Crete in the 4th/5th c.; *CIJ* 692, Rebeka, the elder, from Thrace, 4th/5th c.; three elders from Venosa in Apulia: *CIJ* 581 (= *CIL* IX, 6226), the elder Beronikene, 3rd to 6th c.; *CIJ* 590 (+ *CIL* IX, 6230), the elder Mannine; and *CIJ* 597 (= *CIL* IX, 6209), the elder Faustina. *SEG* 27 (1977) no. 1201 testifies to the elder Mazauzala from Libya, and *CIJ* 400 to the elder Sara Ura from Rome in the 1st to the 3rd c.: ibid. 41–46.

[51] Weil, "Von den griechischen Inseln," 78–79.

[52] On this see ibid. 79. Achelis, "Spuren des Urchristentums," 99–100, writes: "The mixing of religious ideas of Jewish, pagan, and Christian provenience is almost more typical than the primitive Christian offices. That is second-century Christianity."

⁵³ In particular Guarducci, "Gli 'Angeli' di Tera," 149, interprets it as a pagan symbol.

⁵⁴ Grégoire, *Recueil des inscriptions grecques chrétiennes* 57.

⁵⁵ Achelis, "Spuren des Urchristentums," 98. Similarly Gärtringen in *IG* XII/3, 455; Grégoire, *Recueil des inscriptions grecques chrétiennes* 58; Lampe, *Lexicon* 1131 (female presbyter); Feissel, "Notes d'Epigraphie Chrétienne (II)," 212; Horsley, *New Documents* 1:121 n. 79 (probably).

⁵⁶ Achelis, "Spuren des Urchristentums," 90–91 argues, with Gärtringen (*IG* XII/3 455), for a very great age for this group of inscriptions: they date them to the end of the second century but advance the possibility that they may even be from the end of the first century. Grégoire, *Recueil des inscriptions grecques chrétiennes* 57, and Guarducci, "Gli 'Angeli' di Tera," 151, in contrast, will not go back farther than the third century and do not entirely exclude an origin in the fourth century.

⁵⁷ Achelis, "Spuren des Urchristentums," 98.

⁵⁸ The precise origin is unknown; cf. François Baratte and Bernard Boyaval, "Catalogue des étiquettes de momies du Musée du Louvre (C.E.M.L.) – textes grecs," *CRIPEL* 2 (1974) 155–264, at 254.

⁵⁹ Baratte and Boyaval, "Catalogue des étiquettes" 5:264: "Inv. E 10103. 0,055 x 0,13 x 0,01. Ink. Greek. II–IIIᵖ. Rectangular tablet. Hole at the left for hanging. Letters shrink progressively in size. L. 4 written in minuscules. The deceased was a Christian woman."

⁶⁰ For what follows see Baratte and Boyaval, "Catalogue des étiquettes" 2:159ff.

⁶¹ Karen Jo Torjesen, *When Women Were Priests. Women's Leadership in the Early Church and the Scandal of their Subordination in the Rise of Christianity* (San Francisco: HarperSanFrancisco, 1993) 20, interprets it thus, without further explanation.

⁶² Cf., for example, Baratte and Boyaval, "Catalogue des étiquettes" 3, nos. 405, 486, 626.

⁶³ Thus, for example, Πρεσβ, πρεβ, πρβ, πρεσ, πρσ, πρ, πρεσβύ (cf. *MAMA* VII, 155).

⁶⁴ Horsley, *New Documents* 4:240, also considers it much more likely that πρεσ`β´ is to be understood as a title and that Artemidora was a presbyter in the Egyptian Church.

⁶⁵ *Testamentum Domini nostri Jesu Christi. Nunc primum edidit, latine reddidit et illustravit Ignatius Ephraem II Rahmani* (Hildesheim: G. Olms, 1968; reprint of the 1899 edition) 87, indicates in a note that the Syriac word is the translation of the Greek πρεσβύτιδες.

⁶⁶ *TD* 1.35. James Cooper and Arthur John MacLean, eds., *The Testament of our Lord. Translated into English from the Syriac, With Introduction and Notes* (Edinburgh: T & T Clark, 1902) 101; Rahmani, *Testamentum Domini* 86–87.

⁶⁷ *TD* 2.19. Cooper and MacLean, *Testament of our Lord* 134; Rahmani, *Testamentum Domini* 140–41.

⁶⁸ Maria Teresa Manni Piraino, *Iscrizioni greche lapidarie del Museo di Palermo.* ΣΙΚΕΛΙΚΑ VI (Palermo: S. F. Flaccovio, 1972) 36, no. 13. Cf. also the photograph of the inscription (Plate VII): "Marble tablet discovered in October 1877. . . . Height 28 cm., width 56.5 cm., thickness 7.5 cm. Height of letters 3-4.5 cm."

⁶⁹ Cf. Wilhelm Pape and Gustav Eduard Benseler, *Wörterbuch der griechischen Eigennamen.* 2 vols. (3rd ed. Braunschweig: F. Vieweg, 1863–1870; reprint Graz: Akademische Druck- u. Verlagsanstalt, 1959) 1:596, with examples; see also Antonio Ferrua, *Note e Giunte. Alle Iscrizioni Cristiane Antiche della Sicilia.* SSAC 9 (Rome: Tipografia poliglotta vaticana, 1979) 39 no. 130.

⁷⁰ Horsley, *New Documents* 1:121, reads πρεσβῦτις and connects this inscription with that of the πρεσβῦτις Epikto of Thera.

140   *Women Officeholders in Early Christianity*

[71] Cf. *L'Année Epigraphique* 456, 457, 458, 459.

[72] Cf. the examples in Lampe, *Lexicon* 86; for ἄμεμπτος see also ibid., 85. In *1 Clement,* for example, it is used in connection with bishops as well as the offering of sacrifice (*1 Clem.* 44:3, 4, 6).

[73] Cf. Manni Piraino, *Iscrizioni* nos. 26, 109, 141.

[74] Thus also ibid. 37, and Horsley, *New Documents* 1:121; *L'Année Epigraphique* reads πρεσβῦτις and translates without further comment: *"presbyterissa."*

[75] For the Greek abbreviation πρεβ see *MAMA* VII, 155; for the Latin abbreviation *preb* see, for example, *ILCV* 1147A.

[76] Thus also Manni Piraino, *Iscrizioni* 37.

[77] Cf. *L'Année Epigraphique* 1975, no. 456.

[78] For Gelasius I see Walter Ullmann, *Gelasius I. (492–496). Das Papsttum an der Wende der Spätantike zum Mittelalter.* PuP 18 (Stuttgart: A. Hiersemann, 1981); Gert Haendler, "Das Papsttum unter gotischer und byzantinischer Herrschaft," in Martin Greschat, ed., *Das Papsttum I. Von den Anfängen bis zu den Päpsten in Avignon.* GK 11 (Stuttgart: Kohlhammer, 1984) 71–82, at 73–74; Bernard Moreton, "Gelasius I. Bischof von Rom (492–496)," *TRE* 12 (1984) 273–76.

[79] Gelasius I, *Ep.* 14,26 (translation in Rossi, "Priesthood, Precedent, and Prejudice," 80–81; cf. Andreas Thiel, ed., *Epistolae Romanorum Pontificum genuinae et quae ad eos scriptae sunt* [Hildesheim and New York: Olms, 1974; reprint of the Braunsberg ed. of 1867–68] 1:376–77).

[80] Theodor Mommsen, ed., *Corpus Inscriptionum Latinarum,* vol. X. *Inscriptiones Bruttiorum, Lucaniae, Campaniae, Siciliae, Sardiniae Latinae* (Berlin: G. Reimerus, 1883) no. 8079: *Tropeae rep. in turri longa q. d. intus.*

[81] Anna Crispo, "Antichità cristiane della Calabria prebyzantia," *ASCL* 14 (1945) 127–41; 209–10, at 134, agrees with G. B. de Rossi that a dating from the first decades of the fourth century to the middle of the fifth century is possible; Antonio Ferrua, "Note su Tropea paleocristiana," *ASCL* 23 (1954) 9–29, at 25–26, argues on paleographic grounds for the mid-fifth century.

[82] *CIL* X/2, no. 8079.

[83] Cf. *CIL* X 8076, 8077, 8080, 8081; see also Wolfgang Karl Wischmeyer, *Die archäologischen und literarischen Quellen zur Kirchengeschichte von Apulia et Calabria, Lucania et Bruttii bis zum Jahr 600. Sammlung und Auswertung von Materialien zur Geschichte zweier spätantiker Provinzen.* Dissertation in typescript (Essen, 1972) 89.

[84] Thus Carl Maria Kaufmann, *Handbuch der altchristlichen Epigraphik* (Freiburg: Herder, 1917) 131; cf. also Wischmeyer, *Quellen zur Kirchengeschichte* 88–89.

[85] Wischmeyer, *Quellen zur Kirchengeschichte;* for what follows see the new version of the conclusion, 37–40.

[86] Ibid. 91–92, 96, 82–83, 81–82, 84, 74–75.

[87] Kaufmann, *Handbuch der altchristlichen Epigraphik* 256; Henri Leclercq, "Inscriptiones Latines Chrétiennes," *DACL* VII/1 (1926) 694–850, at 768; Crispo, "Antichità cristiane," 134; Ferrua, "Note su Tropea," 11; Wischmeyer, *Quellen zur Kirchengeschichte* 91. Ferrua supposes that Leta was married to Monsis, also attested in Tropea. His inscription reads:

B M S MONSIS PRESBITER
QUI VIXIT ANN L M G̅II D G̅II CUI
BENE FECERUNT FILI PRECESSIT
IN PACE DIE KALD DECEMBRIS.

[88] *Conc. Turon.* Canon 20 (CCSL 148A, 184). For other examples see Giorgio Otranto, "Note sul sacerdozio femminile nell'antichità in margine a una testimonianza di Gelasio I," *VetChr* 19 (1982) 341–60, at 353 n. 47.

[89] Ordinarily the wives of presbyters are made known as such, usually by the word *coniunx*, but not by the title *presbytera*. Cf., for example, *ILCV* 1130: *Gaudentius presb sibi / et coniugi suae Seuerae, castae hac sanc[tissimae] / feminae, qui vixit . . .* ; *ILCV* 1130A: *locus Basili presb. et Felicitati eius / sibi fecerunt; ILCV* 1139A: *. . . pre]sb. titul. Luci[nae . . .] / [. . .] coniugi mihi [. . . ; ILCV* 1154: *Martius Firmissimus presbiter De/cimie Apronianeti co/iugi dulcissime benemer/enti, qui vixit . . .* ; *ILCV* 1163: (a) *Rusticus praesbyter* (b) *amantissimae suae Maxentiae* (c) *. . .* ; *ILCV* 1172: *arca Stephano p͞b͞r et Martanae / iugali eius.*

[90] Otranto, "Sacerdozio femminile," 352, italics in original (Rossi, "Priesthood, Precedent, and Prejudice," 86).

[91] From *CIL* X 8076; cf. also Crispo, "Antichità cristiane," 128ff.; Wischmeyer, *Quellen der Kirchengeschichte* 89–90.

[92] So also Crispo, "Antichità cristiane," 131.

[93] Cf. Wischmeyer, *Quellen der Kirchengeschichte* 90, with evidentiary citations.

[94] France Bulic, "Iscrizione Inedita. (Siculi, Bihaci di Castelnuovo di Traù)," *Bullettino di Archeologia e Storia Dalmata* 37 (1914) 107–11, at 107: "In the basement of the house at No. 153 Cons. giud. Matteo Cipcic-Bragadin at Castelnuovo di Traù there has been preserved, since time immemorial, the lid of a sarcophagus made of limestone. Today it is used as a basin for oil. . . . It is 2.10 m. long, 0.88 m. wide, 0.73 m. tall. The inscribed area, on the front, is 1.31 m. long, 0.30 m. high. The letters are 5-6 cm. high. Some are worn and faint, so that the reading of parts of the third line remains uncertain."

[95] From Otranto, "Sacerdozio femminile," 353.

[96] Cf. Bulic, "Iscrizione Inedita," 110.

[97] On this see the article "Matrona" in *PRE* XIV (1930) 2300–2305.

[98] In the epigraphical evidence a wide variety of abbreviations for "presbyter" survive; besides *prb* (*ILCV* 1125, 1128A, 1152 passim) these include *prbs* (*ILCV* 1156); *presb* (*ILCV* 1128, 1130, 1130A passim); *pbb* (*ILCV* 1133); *pb* (*ILCV* 1136, 1138, 1139B passim); *pbr* (*ILCV* 1155, 1158, 1159 passim); *pr* (*ILCV* 1157); *preb* (*ILCV* 1147A); *prebs* (*ILCV* 1162A); *prbt* (*ILCV* 1165); *prstr* (*ILCV* 1171A).

[99] For the matter of burial places see Pasquale Testini, *Le catacombe e gli antichi cimiteri cristiani in Roma.* RC 2 (Bologna: Cappelli, 1966) 221–26; Jean Guyon, "La vente des tombes à travers l'épigraphie de la Rome chrétienne (IIIe-VIIe siècles): le rôle des fossores, mansionarii, praepositi et prêtres," *MEFRA* 86 (1974) 549–96; Josef Fink and Beatrix Asamer, *Die römischen Katakomben.* AW 9 (Special Number), 1978 (Mainz: Verlag Philipp von Zabern, c1997) 19–24, 57–59.

[100] Ibid. 19.

[101] France Bulic, "Iscrizioni Inedita. Salona (Solin)," *Bullettino di Archeologia e Storia Dalmata* 21 (1989) 141–48, at 147: "On a fragment of the lid of the sarcophagus. The fragment is 0.34 m. high, 0.30 m. long, ca. 0.25 m. thick, with letters 45 mm. high."

[102] See the evidentiary examples in E. A. Andrews, *A Latin Dictionary Founded on Andrews' Edition of Freund's Latin Dictionary.* Revised, enlarged, and in great part rewritten by Charlton T. Lewis, Ph.D., and Charles Short (Oxford: Clarendon Press, 1991, from the 1879 original) 1611.

[103] Pierre-Marie Gy, "Bemerkungen zu den Bezeichnungen des Priestertums in der christlichen Frühzeit," in Jean Guyon, ed., *Das apostolische Amt* (Mainz: 1961) 92–109, at 108; see also 103ff.

[104] In the case of the *sacerdota* it must remain an open question whether she was a bishop or a presbyter, though we should consider that as a rule the word *sacerdos* designated the bishop. For the epigraphical attestation of a woman bishop in Umbria in the fifth century and the witnesses to Bishop Theodora in Rome in the ninth century see Chapter 8 A below.

[105] Letter of Pope Zachary 5 (*Epistola VIII, MPL* 89, 933).

[106] From Haye van der Meer, *Priestertum der Frau? Eine theologiegeschichtliche Untersuchung.* QD 42 (Freiburg, Basel, and Vienna: Herder, 1969) 118.

VI. Enrolled Widows

A. Epigraphic and Literary Evidence from the West

Inscription for the Widow Flavia Arcas

Italy / Rome / Catacomb of Priscilla   II[1]

BIBLIOGRAPHY:

Duchesne, Louis M. O. *Christian Worship. Its Origin and Evolution. A Study of the Latin Liturgy up to the Time of Charlemagne.* Translated by M. L. McClure (5th ed. London: S.P.C.K., 1956. Original: *Origines du culte chrétien,* 1889) 342.

Kaufmann, Carl Maria. *Handbuch der altchristlichen Epigraphik* (Freiburg: Herder, 1917) 293.

Grossi Gondi, Felice. *Trattato di epigrafia cristiana latina e greca del mondo romano occidentale. I. Monumenti Cristiani dei Primi sei Secoli I* (Rome: Università Gregoriana, 1968; reprint of the 1920 edition) 153.

Bopp, Linus. *Das Witwentum als organische Gliedschaft im Gemeinschaftsleben der alten Kirche. Ein geschichtlicher Beitrag zur Grundlegung der Witwenseelsorge in der Gegenwart* (Mannheim, 1950) 125.

Pietri, Charles. "Appendice Prosopographique à la Roma Christiana (311–440)," *MEFRA* 89 (1977) 371–415, at 407.

ICUR IX, 26167.

Carletti, Carlo. *Iscrizioni cristiane inedite del cimitero di Bassilla "ad S. Hermetem."* MPARA 2 (Vatican City: Tipografia Poliglotta Vaticana, 1976) 147.

[Φλαβί]α Ἀρκὰς χήρα ἥτις
[ἔζησε]ν αἴτη πε΄ μητρὶ
3   [γλυκυ]τάτη Φλαβία Θεοφίλα
θυγάτηρ ἐποίησεν.[2]

Line 2: αἴτη = ἔτη.[3]

The widow Flavia Arcas, who lived eighty-five years. Flavia Theophila, her daughter, erected (this epitaph) to the sweetest of mothers.

This is one of the few Christian inscriptions in Rome from the second century. Peter Lampe speaks of an archeological *silentium* finding, in that "with very few exceptions, no Christian inscriptions, sculptures, mosaics or sarcophagi are found in the first two centuries . . . many Christians apparently had little means to afford them."[4]

Louis Duchesne and Carl Kaufmann long ago recognized the inscription for the widow Flavia Arcas as the oldest evidence for an enrolled widow, and thus at the same time as the oldest epigraphical attestation of a member of the Church hierarchy. In favor of Flavia Arcas' "ecclesiastical widowhood" is primarily her title, χήρα, since the designation of women as widows was not customary in inscriptions of the period.[5]

The additional question then arises: what did it mean to be an enrolled widow in Rome in the second century? We may take it from the *Traditio Apostolica*,[6] a Church order from the first third of the third century that is frequently cited to describe conditions at Rome, that widows were enrolled in the Church to pray for the community.[7] In the structure of the *Traditio Apostolica* the widows (*TA* 10) are listed after the bishops (*TA* 2–3), presbyters (*TA* 7), deacons (*TA* 8), and confessors (*TA* 9), who because of their confession have the rank of presbyters.[8]

In terms of Church constitutional history the *Traditio Apostolica* is extraordinarily important because it aims at a hierarchizing of the community that largely succeeded in subsequent centuries, in particular in terms of the separation of clergy and laity. The clergy include bishops, presbyters, and deacons, who are inducted into their offices through a special imposition of hands (χειροτονία).

Widows appear in the *Traditio Apostolica* in a twofold sense: on the one hand as widowed women enrolled by the community for Church duties (*TA* 10), and on the other hand as widows needing community support (*TA* 20, 24, 30). It is said expressly of the enrolled widows in *TA* 10 that hands are not laid on them (οὐ χειροτονεῖν, *non ordinatur*), but that they are chosen *(eligitur ex nomine)* and enrolled (καθίστασθαι, *instituitur*).[9] The only condition for their enrollment is that they have been widows for a long time.

The directions for the widows contain the reason why they are not ordained: the widows are not to receive the imposition of hands *(non imponetur manus super eam)* because they are entrusted with neither sacramental nor liturgical service *(quia non offert oblationem* [προσφορά] *neque habet liturgiam* [λειτουργία]). It is said of them that they are enrolled exclusively for the purpose of prayer *(instituitur propter orationem)*, which at the same time is said to be the duty of the entire community. This ordering must be seen within the horizon of the effort of the *Traditio Apostolica* to restrict sacramental and liturgical service to the clergy (κλῆρος), a tendency in early Christianity that has left its first marks here.

The extensive argument for the exclusion of widows from ordination and the duties at divine worship associated with it indicates that this was not a matter of course. We must suspect that both the refusal of ordination and the restriction of sacramental and liturgical service to bishops, presbyters, and deacons countered a more open praxis. Previously it may be that widows participated in the whole spectrum of community duties, and that they are at this point to be restricted to the service of prayer.[10]

Inscription for Regina, vidua

Italy / Rome / Cemetery of S. Saturninus   IV/V

BIBLIOGRAPHY:

Cabrol, Ferdinand, and Henri Leclercq. *Reliquiae Liturgicae Vetustissimae. Ex SS Patrum Necnon Scriptorum Ecclesiasticorum, Monumentis Selectae.* MELi 1 (Paris, 1900–1902) col. 48 no. 3068.

ILCV I, 1581.

Bopp, Linus. *Das Witwentum als organische Gliedschaft im Gemeinschaftsleben der alten Kirche. Ein geschichtlicher Beitrag zur Grundlegung der Witwenseelsorge in der Gegenwart* (Mannheim, 1950) 125–26.

Pietri, Charles. "Appendice Prosopographique à la Roma Christiana (311–440)," *MEFRA* 89 (1977) 371–415, at 407.

ICUR n.s. IX, 24120.

Carletti, Carlo. *Iscrizioni cristiane di Roma. Testimonianze di vita cristina (secoli III–VII).* BPat 7 (Florence: Nardini: Centro internazionale del libro, 1986) 146–47 no. 136.

Rigine vene merenti filia sua fecit
vene. Rigine matri viduae que se-
3   dit vidua annos LX et eclesa
numqua(m) gravavit, unibyra, que
vixit annos LXXX, mesis V,
6   dies XXVI.[11]

Lines 1–2: *vene = bene* and *fecit vene* is equivalent to *sepulchrum fecit.*[12]
Line 2: Cabrol and Leclercq punctuate: *Bene Regine matri, viduae, ...*
Line 3: *eclesa = ecclesiam*
Line 4: *unibyra = univira*

For the well-deserving Regina her daughter has placed this stone. The mother Regina, the widow, who "sat" as widow for sixty years and was not a burden to the Church, univira, who lived eighty years and five months and twenty-six days.

This inscription attests the widow Regina from Rome, who died at the age of eighty. We may take it from the inscription that Regina was married only once and thus received the honorable title of univira,[13] that she brought at least one daughter into the world, and that she lost her husband when she was twenty. Regina was an enrolled widow, as shown by two formulae in the inscription:

(a) The connection between *vidua* and *sedit* marks Regina as an enrolled widow. This manner of describing officeholders is found in other inscriptions as well. For example, in the inscription for a presbyter:

> hic quiescit Romanus p(res)b(yter),
> qui sedit p(res)b(yter) ann(os) XXVII, m(enses) X.
> 3   dep(ositus) X kal(endas) augus(tas)
> Con(sulatu) Severini v(iri) c(larissimi). i[n pace]![14]

In the case of the widow Regina *sedit* describes Regina's belonging to the *ordo viduarum*.[15]

An inscription from Ferentino, damaged on the left side, testifies to a widow in connection with a basilica as *vidua sedit:*

> [. . . ra]r ˙ i ˙ e x ˙ e ˙ m ˙ ppli
> [. . .] post annu
> [. . .] uidua sedit
> [. . .] basilica a seuis-
> [sima? . . c]urauit, que obita est
> [. . con]iugi.[16]

We may suppose that this enrolled widow exercised her office in the basilica named here, and according to Linus Bopp she had her seat of honor there.[17]

(b) In lines 3-4 it is said of Regina that she was never a burden to the Church *(ecclesiam numquam gravavit)*. This formula is also to be found in other inscriptions for widows at Rome such as the approximately contemporary one for the widow Daphne:[18] *Dafnen uidua, q. coniux[it . . .] / aclesia(m) nih(il) grauauit a[. . .].*[19] These widows were apparently not dependent on contributions from the Church, either because of their own financial security or that of their families. The inscriptions regard this as a mark of distinction.

We may suppose in the case of Regina that she was cared for by her family and therefore did not need to lay claim to the Church support that was her right as a widow. She apparently received care and support from the daughter who placed her grave marker. These evidences show that enrollment as an ecclesiastical widow was not necessarily related to a need for support.

Other Roman inscriptions attesting to widows show by their formulae that the widows in question were enrolled: for example, the *titulus* of Octavia, who was called a *vidua Dei: Oc ˙ ta ˙ ui ˙ ae ˙ M ˙ a ˙ tro ˙ nae ˙ / ui ˙ du ˙ ae ˙ de ˙ i.*[20]

This tomb tablet comes from the late fourth or possibly the fifth century and derives from the church of Saint Sabina on the Aventine.[21]

In other inscriptions we find the motif of a "life in or for God" in connection with women who are more precisely described as widows: thus, for example, the *titulus* of a widow of Rome, framed by palm branches and ivy leaves: *VIDUA · P(ia) FELICISSIMA / IN DEO VIVES.*[22] This motif occurs also in the inscription for Laurentia from Rome and indicates that she was an enrolled widow. Her epigraph, from the fourth century, says:

> HIC DAMASI MATER POSVIT LAVREntia membRA
> QVAE FVIT IN TERRIS CENTVM MINVS . . . aNNOS
> SEXAGINTA DEO VIXIT POsT FOEdera . . .
> PROGENIE QVARTA VIDIT QuAE . . .[23]

Laurentia was the mother of the Damasus who was pope from 366 to 384. The inscription is from the time before his elevation to the papacy,[24] and still shows the ordinary characteristics of monumental inscriptions in the fourth century.[25] The inscription says of Damasus' mother Laurentia, who died at the age of eighty-nine, that she "lived God" *(Deo vixit)* sixty years after her marriage. Such characterizations indicate that these women were enrolled widows.[26]

The inscriptions regarding widows are subject to multiple interpretations. Only in a few cases can we distinguish with certainty between an ecclesiastically enrolled widow and a widow with no association with Church office.[27] Carolyn Osiek accurately calls the widow "one of the most ubiquitous figures in the early church."[28] The epigraphic witnesses confirm her statement. Nevertheless, these inscriptions offer important details regarding the institution of widows in the early Church:

(a) The inscriptions reveal a high degree of respect for widows, something attested by the literary sources as well.[29] The status of widowhood had two main implications. Women's decision for enduring widowhood meant a long-term ascetic life, but also monetary support provided by the Church; the latter, however, was not necessarily accepted by all widows.[30]

(b) The inscriptions show, as does the *Traditio Apostolica,* that some of the widows in the ancient Church were ecclesiastically enrolled. This was expressed in the inscriptions through such phrases as *vidua sedit, vidua Dei, Deo vixit,* or *in Deo vives.*

(c) The inscriptions confirm that not all the enrolled widows were also recipients of Church subvention. This is especially clear in the inscription for the widow Regina, who was an enrolled widow but was not supported by the Church. Thus Regina did not remain a widow in order to achieve security, but in order, as a widow, to undertake certain functions in the Church.

The details of the duties of enrolled widows cannot be determined from the inscriptions. For the Roman community in the first third of the third century the *Traditio Apostolica* tells of no such duties beyond that of prayer. However, such a service should not be underestimated, since intercessory prayer supposes that the widows were well informed by members of the community and consequently must have acted as pastoral workers.[31]

The express direction in *TA* 10 that widows are not to take part in sacramental and liturgical service suggests that widows had duties in that sphere in the first and second centuries. This is favored also by the fact that a restriction of such functions primarily to bishops and presbyters only spread throughout the Church during and after the third century.[32]

B. Literary Evidence from the East

In contrast to the Western Roman Empire, especially Rome, there are almost no epigraphical witnesses to widows in the East.[33] Nevertheless the existence of widows as persons who exercised particular functions in the Church is evident from a rich literary documentation.

As the *Traditio Apostolica* had already shown, a distinction must be drawn between widows who were enrolled for Church service and widows who were recipients of Church assistance. We find them as recipients of aid as early as the New Testament (Acts 6:1; 9:39; 1 Tim 5:3-16). In 1 Tim 5:3-16 there is also evidence of an office of widows[34] that reveals its contours especially in the Church orders of the subsequent centuries.

As we have already noted above, the *Traditio Apostolica* tells of enrolled widows who were not ordained because they were to have no sacramental and liturgical duties. Prayer is named as their particular service. This regulation was taken over by the Church orders dependent on the *Traditio Apostolica* and modified to some extent.

The *Canones Hippolyti,* a document from Alexandria or northern Egypt from the first half of the fourth century whose structure generally follows that of the *Traditio Apostolica,*[35] analogously speaks of enrolled widows (*CanHipp* 9). This document survives only in an Arabic version based in turn on a Coptic translation of the original writing, which was in Greek.[36] Canon 9 reads: "Finally, the widows who are enrolled are not to be ordained—for them there are the precepts of the Apostle . . .—; they are not to be ordained, but you are to pray over them, for ordination is for men. The function . . . of widows is important . . . because of all that falls upon them . . . : frequent prayer, service of the sick, and frequent fasting."[37] The widows are accordingly enrolled. Following *TA* 10, the document expressly emphasizes that they are not ordained, but one is only to pray over them. In its argument for this, namely that ordination is only for men, this canon goes beyond what the *Traditio Apostolica* says. It must be interpreted as a clear denial of an ordained and therefore cultic office for women. Beyond the prayer attested in *TA* this document lists care for the sick as the duty of the enrolled widows, and these duties are given as the reason for the respect accorded them.[38]

The collective *Constitutiones Apostolorum* from late-fourth-century Syria[39] also contains orders for widows in its eighth book, essentially a revision of the *Traditio Apostolica,* which was used as a source. In *CA* 8.25 the document, relying closely on *TA* 10, orders that hands are not to be laid on widows (οὐ χειροτονεῖται); thus they are not ordained. It seems that here, differently from *TA* 10, it was not felt necessary to give a reason why they did not receive the imposition of hands. As precondition for enrollment in the status of widow (κατατασσέσθω εἰς τὸ χηρικόν) the document prescribes that the woman should have lost her husband long previously, have lived chastely and without reproach, and have given the best of care to those in her house.[40] There is no mention of special duties for such widows. It appears from the petitionary prayer that the widows were not numbered among the laity, as they are mentioned separately.[41]

The *Constitutiones Ecclesiasticae Apostolorum (CEA),* a Church order from the fourth century that probably comes from Egypt or Syria,[42] also testify to the office of widows (*CEA* 21). The *CEA* gives directions for the enrollment of three widows (χῆραι καθιστανέσθωσαν). These instructions for the three enrolled widows are found between the instructions for the three διάκονοι (*CEA* 20, 22), which suggests for the final redaction of this document that the activity of the widows was interpreted as close to that of deacons. No cultic functions are listed for widows or deacons. Of the latter it is said particularly that they are to do good works (ἐργάται τῶν καλῶν ἔργων) (*CEA* 22). For two of the enrolled widows the duties mentioned are prayer for those Christians who are under assault. They also have prophetic duties: it is they who are to be the recipients of revelations.[43] The duty of the third widow was, in addition to general works of charity that are not more closely specified, the care of women suffering from diseases. It was also her duty to report as necessary to the presbyters.

In addition to these we note especially the *Testamentum Domini,* a fifth-century Church order from Syria, Asia Minor, or Egypt.[44] It testifies to an influential office of widows (*TD* 1.40-43).[45] It is said of widows in the *TD* that they are elected *(eligitur)* and ordained *(ordinetur)* (*TD* 1.40).[46] Within the hierarchy their place is after the bishop, presbyters, deacons, and confessors (*TD* 1.40-43). This structure follows that in the *Traditio Apostolica,* which was a source for the *TD.* It is therefore all the more noteworthy that the widows in the *TD,* unlike those in the *TA,* are explicitly said to have an ordained office and duties that go far beyond the mere service of prayer.

At divine worship they were seated next to the bishop (*TD* 1.19). *TD* has no idea of banning women from the sanctuary. Widows and deaconesses had their places in the sanctuary behind the curtain *(velum)* during the Lord's Supper, along with the other officeholders (*TD* 1.23). Hence *TD* did not follow any prescriptions like those demanded by the Synod of Laodicea that would have forbidden women to approach the altar.[47] Even a sacramental office for women is attested in *TD*. It is said of the deaconesses that they gave the bread and wine to pregnant women and celebrated communion with them (*TD* 2.20): "Similarly if a woman be pregnant (and) sick, and cannot fast these two days, let her fast that . . . one day . . . , taking on the first (day) bread and water. And if she cannot come, let a deaconess carry the Offering to her *(et si nequit accedere [ad ecclesiam], diaconissa ad ipsam deferat communionem)*."[48]

In general we may say that the widows' field of activity was broad according to *TD*:[49] They were entrusted (a) with the instruction and teaching of women and (b) with testing the deaconesses *(diaconissaque perquirat)*. In addition to these duties of instruction, teaching, and testing, they were commissioned to (c) pray and (d) care for the sick, a duty performed with the help of one or two deacons. In addition, (e) they had duties at baptism, namely anointing the women (*TD* 2.8).

The widows' closeness to the bishop is indicated especially by the order of seating during the eucharistic celebration (*TD* 1.19). This could be a reminiscence of the original close association of the two offices, something that is still visible in the *Didascalia Apostolorum* as well.

The *Didascalia Apostolorum* is a highly revealing source for the existence, and at the same time for attempts to restrict the authority of widows in the early Church in the East.[50] This Church order originated in northern Syria in the first half of the third century, probably around 230.[51] Chapters 14 and 15 treat of widows in general and of the enrollment of widows. From *Didasc.* 14 it appears that widows were enrolled, but not before they had reached the age of fifty: "Appoint . . . as a widow . . . one who is not less than fifty . . . years of age."[52] The lower age limit associated with enrollment of widows has been dropped by ten years from that prescribed in 1 Tim 5:9. As reason for setting such a limit the text mentions the lesser probability of another marriage.

Didascalia 15 contains an extensive paraenesis oriented to traditional topoi of an ethics of office, of the sort we find in germ in 1 Tim 5:3-16.[53] What is striking in this chapter is the extended polemic against supposed bad behavior on the part of the widows. They are accused of lying, embezzlement, and the like. Along with a whole list of minor prohibitions the chapter contains two fundamental and major ones:

(a) The prohibition against teaching: "it is not required nor necessary that women should be teachers, and especially about the name of Christ and about the

redemption of His passion."⁵⁴ The reason given is the calling and sending of the
Twelve by Jesus Christ, with the conclusion that the disciples Mary Magdalene,
Mary the daughter of James, and the other Mary were, on the contrary, not sent.

(b) The prohibition against baptizing: "About this, however, that a woman
should baptize, or that one should be baptized by a woman, we do not counsel,
for it is a transgression of the commandment and a great peril to her who bap-
tizes and to him who is baptized."⁵⁵ The reason here given is that Christ was not
baptized by Mary, his mother, but by John.

Both prohibitions and the reasoning given were received in traditionalist
circles and augmented by further restrictive traditions. Epiphanius, for example, took them over and expanded them.⁵⁶

Hans Achelis draws from this and other prohibitions introduced by the *Didascalia Apostolorum* some implicit conclusions regarding the widows' real
field of activity: they went on mission, spoke about difficult dogmas, traveled
for missionary purposes, baptized, taught, were consulted in questions of faith
and hope, were no less independently active in care for the sick, sought out peni-
tents, fasted with them, and probably forgave their sins after their penance was
completed. "For all these works they received a tangible reward . . . . What we
have here, then, is competition for the episcopal office in all its functions."⁵⁷

The description of the widows as competitors for the episcopal office pro-
moted by the *Didascalia Apostolorum* is a plausible explanation for the exces-
sively harsh polemic against widows it contains. If widows and other women
had not taught, baptized, and worked independently in the community without
consulting the bishop there would have been no reason to issue a prohibition
against their teaching and baptizing.

The tendency of the *Didascalia Apostolorum* is very clear: strengthening
the episcopal office at the expense of the authority of other Church offices. The
picture here presented is that of an episcopal constitution of the first order.
Bruno Steimer summarizes: "As regards the description of the offices, there
can be no doubt that the qualification, leadership, and duties of the bishop are
the center of interest (cc. 4-11); after him the presbyter acts in the role of sta-
tistician, the deacon stands at the side of the bishop as his aide, though his office is more closely defined (c. 16). An extensive treatment of the institution of
widows (cc. 14/15) and a chapter on orphans (c. 17) underscore the relevance
of the constitutional questions."⁵⁸ What Steimer overlooks is the fact that a
woman deacon also stood at the bishop's side.⁵⁹

After the disciplining of the widows, the following duties remain for them
in the *Didascalia Apostolorum:*

(a) Fasting and prayer for donors and for the whole Church. This service of
the widows, which was connected with the reception of gifts and care for them,

was symbolized since Polycarp (*Phil.* 4,3) in the image of the "widow as altar,"[60] a metaphor that, as Carolyn Osiek has shown, serves the interest of a tendency to suppress women in the *Didascalia,* in that widows are forbidden to move about freely, the reason given being that the altar of God does not move.[61]

(b) Despite the explicit prohibition against women's teaching the widows retained a restricted license to teach. They could give theological counsel in questions of righteousness and faith in God: "And when she is asked regarding an affair by anyone, let her not too quickly give an answer, except only about righteousness and about faith in God." They were denied responsibility for all other theological instruction:

> But let her send those who desire to be instructed to the leader . . . . And to those who ask them let them (namely the widows) give answer only . . . about the destruction of idols and about this that there is only one God. It is not right for the widows to teach nor for a layman. About punishment and about the rest . . . and about the kingdom of the name of Christ, and about His dispensation, neither a widow nor a layman ought to speak.[62]

Much the same is true for the deaconesses in the *Didascalia Apostolorum.* They, too, had a restricted license to teach. In spite of the general prohibition on women's teaching they were to instruct and teach the women who were baptized: "teach and educate . . . her in order that the unbreakable seal of baptism shall be (kept) in chastity . . . and holiness."[63]

(c) Widows were, as previously, to visit the sick and lay hands on them.

All the duties listed were, however, conditioned by absolute obedience to the bishop and deacons, which was intended to prevent any independent work on the part of the widows.

In summary we may say that according to the Church orders of the third to fifth centuries widowed women could be enrolled as widows (*Didasc.* 14; *TA* 10; *CanHipp* 9; *CA* 8.25; *CEA* 21) or ordained (*TD* 1.40), and thus became part of the Church hierarchy. The enrolled or ordained widows had a variety of duties: primary were prayer and petition (1 Tim 5:5; *Didasc.* 15; *TA* 10; *CanHipp* 9; *TD* 1.40) as well as theological instruction (*Didasc.* 15; *CA* 3.5; *TD* 1.40). In addition, *TD* mentions the testing of the deaconesses (*TD* 1.40) and the anointing of women at baptism (*TD* 2.8). Beyond this the enrolled widows had duties in the field of care for the sick (*CEA* 21) or visiting the sick (*CanHipp* 9; *TD* 1.40). Finally, their duty to receive offerings is attested by *CEA* 21.

Notes

[1] "The location and paleography place this valuable fragment as early as the second century," according to Carl Maria Kaufmann, *Handbuch der altchristlichen Epigraphik* (Freiburg: Herder, 1917) 293.

[2] Following *ICUR* n.s. IX, 26167: *"Tabulae marmoreae supersunt fragmenta duo,* a cm. 31 x 74,5 x 3,5 b cm. 12,5 x 20,5, litt. altis 4-5." Illus.

[3] Carlo Carletti, *Iscrizioni cristiane inedite del cimitero di Bassilla "ad S. Hermetem."* MPARA 2 (Vatican City: Tipografia Poliglotta Vaticana, 1976) 147.

[4] Peter Lampe, *From Paul to Valentinus. Christians at Rome in the First Two Centuries.* Translated by J. Larrimore Holland and Michael Steinhauser (Minneapolis: Fortress, 2000) 142–43. For the social stratification of the Christians of the city of Rome in the first two centuries see Henneke Gülzow, *Christentum und Sklaverei in den ersten drei Jahrhunderten* (Bonn: R. Habelt, 1969), and idem, "Soziale Gegebenheiten der altkirchlichen Mission," in Heinzgünter Frohnes and Uwe W. Knorr, eds., *Kirchengeschichte als Missionsgeschichte I: Die alte Kirche* (Munich: Kaiser, 1974) 189–226, as well as Lampe, passim.

[5] Thus Louis M. O. Duchesne, *Christian Worship. Its Origin and Evolution. A Study of the Latin Liturgy up to the Time of Charlemagne.* Translated by M. L. McClure (5th ed. London: S.P.C.K., 1956. Original: *Origines du culte chrétien,* 1889) 342; similarly Carl Maria Kaufmann, *Handbuch der altchristlichen Epigraphik* 293. Linus Bopp, *Das Witwentum als organische Gliedschaft im Gemeinschaftsleben der alten Kirche. Ein geschichtlicher Beitrag zur Grundlegung der Witwenseelsorge in der Gegenwart* (Mannheim, 1950) 125 remains undecided whether Flavia Arcas was an "ecclesiastical widow." Duchesne and Kaufmann, basing their theories on the hypothesis that the offices of widow and deaconess were identical, further interpret Flavia Arcas as a deaconess of the Roman community in the second century. However, neither this inscription nor the literary sources of the period give any support to the correctness of their assumption.

[6] The *Traditio Apostolica (TA)* is a Church order of which Bruno Steimer writes in his study on the genre of the ancient Christian Church orders (*Vertex Traditionis. Die Gattung der altchristlichen Kirchenordnungen.* BZNW 63 [Berlin and New York: Walter de Gruyter, 1992]): "For theology, whether in its historical, systematic, or practical discourse, the most important text of this genre is the so-called 'Traditio Apostolica' now being considered. The problems that are concealed behind this title could not, however, be greater for any ancient Christian writing: for the 'writing' exists neither in its original form nor under its original title, and even the name of the author, Hippolytus, is hypothetical . . . . In short: the results of scholarship to date are so speculative that to a degree they scarcely deserve the name."

Even the reconstruction of the text has proved unusually difficult, because the Greek text, except for some isolated fragments, has not survived. In addition to the textual reconstruction, the question of authorship is unresolved. If we suppose the presbyter Hippolytus is the author, the writing should be located at Rome in about 215. But if we doubt Hippolytus's authorship, as Steimer has most recently done (ibid. 35ff.) with very persuasive arguments, the questions of dating and location are also unresolved. Scholars have discussed Alexandria and Syria as places of its origin, as well as Rome: on this see Steimer, *Vertex Traditionis* 28ff., and Jeong Ae Han-Rhinow, *Die frühchristlichen Kirchenordnungen und ihr Amtsverständnis als Beitrag zur ökumenischen Diskussion um das Lima-Dokument* (Diss. theol. Munich, 1991) 51ff.

On the other hand, there is more general consensus about the dating of the document. It is placed in the first third of the third century because the *Traditio Apostolica* served as a source for later Church orders including the *Canones Hippolyti,* the eighth book of the *Constitutiones Apostolorum,* and the *Testamentum Domini.* On this see especially Eduard Schwartz, "Über die pseudapostolischen Kirchenordnungen" (1910) in idem, *Gesammelte Schriften 5* (Berlin: Walter de Gruyter, 1963) 192–273; for the history of research see Steimer, *Vertex Traditionis* 30ff. passim, with bibliography.

   [7] Beyond the enrollment of widows (*TA* 10) the *Traditio Apostolica* also attests certain aspects of the Church's care for widows (*TA* 20, 24, 30). On this see Lampe, *From Paul to Valentinus* 129–30.

   [8] In what follows we will accept the possibility that among the officeholders mentioned in the *TA,* that is, bishops, presbyters, deacons, lectors, subdeacons, and healers, there were also women, since the *TA* contains no tradition of prohibiting women from service like that found, for example, in the more or less contemporary *Didascalia Apostolorum* (*Didasc.* 15).

   [9] *TA* 10 in *La Tradition apostolique de Saint Hippolyte. Essai de Reconstruction, par Bernard Botte.* 5., verb. Aufl. hrsg. v. Albert Gerhards unter Mitarb. v. Sabine Felbecker. LQF 39 (Münster: Aschendorff, 1989) 30.

   [10] It is worth noting that in connection with the exclusion of widows from the clergy there is no argument based on gender. The attempt to restrict the field of the widows' authority should therefore be read in light of the tendency of this document to distribute particular community functions to particular groups, and not primarily as an attempt to suppress a women's office.

   [11] Carlo Carletti, *Iscrizioni cristiane di Roma. Testimonianze di vita cristina (secoli III–VII).* BPat 7 (Florence: Nardini: Centro internazionale del libro, 1986) 146: "Lastra marmorea ora perduta: sulla sinistra è graffita una colomba posata su un ramo" (A marble slab now lost. On the left an engraving of a dove on a palm branch.)

   [12] Ibid.

   [13] The concept of *univira,* also found in the forms *univiria, unibyria, univera,* was applied to women who did not remarry after the death of their husbands or after a divorce. This way of life was highly respected in Roman eyes, and at celebrations and festivals such women received the first places. Thus Bernhard Kötting, *Die Bewertung der Wiederverheiratung (der zweiten Ehe) in der Antike und in der Frühen Kirche.* RhWAS Vorträge G 292 (Opladen: Westdeutscher Verlag, 1988) 19, with examples; see also idem, "'Univira' in Inschriften," in W. den Boer et al., eds., *Romanitas et Christianitas. Studia Iano Henrico Waszink* (Amsterdam: North-Holland, 1973) 195–206, as well as Hermann Funke, "Univira. Ein Beispiel heidnischer Geschichtsapologetik," *JAC* 8/9 (1965/66) 183–88, and Gabriele Heyse, *Mulier non debet abire nuda. Das Erbrecht und die Versorgung der Witwe in Rom.* EHS.R 1541 (Frankfurt: Peter Lang, 1994) 7ff.

   The ideal of a single marriage applied to men as well. The *flamen,* just like the *flaminica,* and the *pontifex maximus* were not permitted to remarry. Cf. Tertullian, *Exhort. cast.* 13; on this see Bernhard Kötting, "Digamus," *RAC* 3 (1957) 1016–24, at 1018–1019.

   [14] From Carletti, *Iscrizioni* 136 no. 126.

   [15] So also Carletti, *Iscrizioni* 147.

   [16] From *ILCV* I, 1738; see also *CIL* X, 5902; Ferdinand Cabrol and Henri Leclercq, *Reliquiae Liturgicae Vetustissimae. Ex SS Patrum Necnon Scriptorum Ecclesiasticorum, Monumentis Selectae.* MELi 1 (Paris, 1900–1902) col. 167 no. 4222.

   [17] Bopp, *Witwentum* 126.

[18] Kaufmann, *Handbuch der altchristlichen Epigraphik* 294, dates it to the late fourth or possibly the fifth century.

[19] From *ILCV* I, 1581 adn.; see also Cabrol and Leclerq, *Reliquiae* col. 169 no. 4237; Kaufmann, *Handbuch der altchristlichen Epigraphik* 294; Felice Grossi Gondi, *Trattato di epigrafia cristiana latina e greca del mondo romano occidentale. I. Monumenti Cristiani dei Primi sei Secoli I* (Rome: Università Gregoriana, 1968; reprint of the 1920 edition) 152; Bopp, *Witwentum* 126; Charles Pietri, "Appendice Prosopographique à la Roma Christiana (311–440)," *MEFRA* 89 (1977) 371–415, at 407; Carletti, *Iscrizioni* 146.

[20] From *ILCV* I, 1735; see also Cabrol and Leclercq, *Reliquiae* col. 78, no. 3417; Kaufmann, *Handbuch der altchristlichen Epigraphik* 293–94; Pietri, "Appendice Prosopographique," 407.

[21] Thus Kaufmann, *Handbuch der altchristlichen Epigraphik* 294.

[22] Cabrol and Leclercq, *Reliquiae* col. 170, no. 4240; *ILCV* I, 1736; Pietri, "Appendice Prosopographique," 407.

[23] Antonio Ferrua, *Epigrammata Damasiana. Recensuit et adnotavit*. SSAC 2 (Rome: Pontificio Istituto di archeologia cristiana, 1942) no. 10, 106; Kaufmann, *Handbuch der altchristlichen Epigraphik* 293. He translates: "Here laid down her bones the mother of Damasus, Laurentia, who lived on earth a hundred years less eleven; sixty years after her first marriage she lived [for] God. After she had seen the fourth generation, she [now] sees the kingdom she longed for." Cf. also Bopp, *Witwentum* 125; Pietri, "Appendice Prosopographique," 407.

[24] As pope, Damasus made a name for himself through his epigraphic works. In his epigrams and those he commissioned "specifically Christian poetry takes its first steps," according to Kaufmann, *Handbuch der altchristlichen Epigraphik* 338; see also 338–65. There is a text edition of Damasus' epigrams: Maximilian Ihm, *Damasi epigrammata; accedunt Pseudodamasiana aliaque ad Damasiana inlustranda idonea* (Leipzig: B. G. Teubner, 1895), and see especially the new edition by Antonio Ferrua, *Epigrammata Damasiana* (n. 23 above).

[25] Kaufmann, *Handbuch der altchristlichen Epigraphik* 359 and 339 n. 2.

[26] Bopp, *Witwentum* 125, also interprets her as a "widow consecrated to God."

[27] For other inscriptions attesting to widows see *ILCV* III, 416, and the excellent collection of all Roman widows known by name between 311 and 440 prepared by Pietri, "Appendice Prosopographique," 407ff.

[28] Carolyn Osiek, "The Widow as Altar: The Rise and Fall of a Symbol," *SecCen* 3 (1983) 159–69, at 159.

[29] For the respect for widowhood in the early Church see Bopp, *Witwentum* 33ff., 186ff.; Bonnie Bowman Thurston, *The Widows: A Women's Ministry in the Early Church* (Minneapolis: Fortress, 1989) passim. For widowhood in antiquity generally see Peter Walcot, "On Widows and their Reputation in Antiquity," *SO* 66 (1991) 5–26.

[30] For the social dimension of widowhood in Rome see Lampe, *From Paul to Valentinus* 129–30. According to the report of Bishop Cornelius of Rome to Fabius of Antioch from the middle of the third century there were 1500 widows and needy who were supported by the church there, together with forty-six presbyters, seven deacons, seven subdeacons, forty-two acolytes, fifty-two exorcists, lectors, and doorkeepers (Eusebius, *Hist. eccl.* VI, 43, 11). For the organization of care for widows in the ancient Church, with further examples, see also Gustav Stählin, "χήρα," *TDNT* 9:440–65, at 460–61.

[31] Ulrike Wagener, *Die Ordnung des "Hauses Gottes." Der Ort von Frauen in der Ekklesiologie und Ethik der Pastoralbriefe*. WUNT 65 (Tübingen: Mohr, 1994) 229 calls

prayer a "position of spiritual leadership." Stählin, "χήρα," with reference to 1 Tim 2:8, also describes prayer and intercession as the supreme service of both women and men (p. 457).

[32] On this see Jochen Martin, *Der priesterliche Dienst III. Die Genese des Amtspriestertums in der frühen Kirche*. QD 48 (Freiburg, Basel, and Vienna: Herder, 1972).

[33] See the indexes to the *Bulletin Epigraphique*.

[34] On this see most recently Wagener, *Ordnung des "Hauses Gottes"* 115ff., but also Johannes Müller-Bardorff, "Zur Exegese von I. Timotheus 5,3-16," in *Gott und die Götter. FS für Erich Fascher* (Berlin: Evang, Verl. Anst., 1958) 113–33; Hans-Werner Bartsch, *Die Anfänge urchristlicher Rechtsbildungen. Studien zu den Pastoralbriefen*. ThF 34 (Hamburg-Bergstedt: H. Reich, 1965) 112ff.; Josef Ernst, "Die Witwenregel des ersten Timotheusbriefes—ein Hinweis auf die biblischen Ursprünge des weiblichen Ordenswesens?" *ThGl* 59 (1969) 434–45; Alexander Sand, "Witwenstand und Ämterstrukturen in den urchristlichen Gemeinden," *BiLe* 12 (1971) 186–97; Jouette Bassler, "The Widows' Tale: A Fresh Look at 1 Tim 5:3-16," *JBL* 103 (1984) 23–41; Thurston, *Widows* 40–55.

[35] The model document has, however, been expanded, rearranged, and paraphrased.

[36] For *CanHipp* see also chs. 6 A and 9 B.

[37] *CanHipp* 9 (following René-Georges Coquin, *Les Canons d'Hippolyte. Edition critique de la version arabe. Introduction et traduction française*. PO 31,2 [Paris: Firmin-Didot, 1966] [95] 363).

[38] As in *TA* the widows are mentioned as recipients of assistance, together with orphans and the poor (*CanHipp* 5). Similarly to *TA* 30, *CanHipp* 35, though with many repetitions, instructs that widows invited to an *agapē* are to leave before sundown.

[39] The *Constitutiones Apostolorum (CA)* represent a compilation and revision essentially of three texts: the *Didascalia Apostolorum (CA* 1–6), the *Didache (CA* 7), and the *Traditio Apostolica (CA* 8). The redactor has revised and expanded all the material. A new edition of the text is offered by Marcel Metzger, *Les Constitutions Apostoliques. Introduction, texte critique, traduction et notes*. 3 vols. SC 320, 329, 336 (Paris: Cerf, 1985–1987).

For questions of date and place, as well as for literary-, form-, tradition-, and redaction-critical aspects see Paul F. Bradshaw, "Kirchenordnungen (I. Altkirchliche)," *TRE* 18 (1989) 662–70, at 663; Marcel Metzger, "Konstitutionen, (Pseud-)Apostolische," *TRE* 19 (1990) 540–44; Steimer, *Vertex Traditionis* 114–33.

[40] *CA* 8.25 (SC 336, 226).

[41] *CA* 8.12, 43 (SC 336, 202). For the widows see also *CA* 3.

[42] On this see also ch. 3 A above.

[43] On this see also ch. 3 A.

[44] On this see also chs. 3 A and 5 A.

[45] On this see especially Roger Gryson, *The Ministry of Women in the Early Church*. Translated by Jean Laporte and Mary Louise Hall (2nd ed. Collegeville: The Liturgical Press, 1980) 64–69.

[46] *Testamentum Domini nostri Jesu Christi. Nunc primum edidit, latine reddidit et illustravit Ignatius Ephraem II Rahmani* (Hildesheim: G. Olms, 1968; reprint of the 1899 edition) 95.

[47] The only exception in *TD* is the menstrual period; during that time they are not to approach the altar: *"Si . . . est menstrua, maneat in templo neque accedet ad altare, non quasi sit polluta, sed propter honorem altaris; et postquam jejunaverit et se laverit, perseveret"* (*TD* 1.42 [Rahmani ed. 101]).

For the menstrual taboo cf. Monika Fander, *Die Stellung der Frau im Markusevan-*

gelium. Unter besonderer Berücksichtigung kultur- und religionsgeschichtlicher Hintergründe. MThA 8 (Altenberge: Oros-Verlag, 1989) 182ff.

[48] *TD* 2.20 (James Cooper and Arthur John MacLean, *The Testament of our Lord. Translated into English from the Syriac, With Introduction and Notes* [Edinburgh: T & T Clark, 1902] 134–35; Rahmani ed. 143).

[49] For what follows see *TD* 1.40 (Rahmani ed. 96ff.).

[50] The *Didascalia Apostolorum (Didasc.)* was originally written in Greek, but "apart from a short fragment of ch. 15 and the revised form in the first six books on the Apostolic Constitutions the original Greek text has been lost. Our knowledge therefore rests essentially on two early translations, one Latin and one Syriac. The Latin version is known only from the Verona palimpsest, which contains about two-fifths of the document. The Syriac version, thus far the sole witness to the complete text, is preserved in part or in whole in a series of manuscripts, the oldest of which stems from the eighth century. The fourth century has been considered the time of the translation, but individual features could point to a somewhat later origin" (Bradshaw, "Kirchenordnungen," 665). Arthur Vööbus has most recently edited the Syriac text and provided an English translation (*The Didascalia Apostolorum in Syriac.* 2 vols. CSCO.S 401/175; 402/176; 407/179; 408/180 [Louvain: Secrétariat du CorpusSCO, 1979]). For the Latin text see F. X. Funk, ed., *Didascalia et Constitutiones Apostolorum.* Vol. 1 (Paderborn: Schöningh, 1905), a synopsis of *Didasc.* and *CA.* There is a German translation by Johannes Flemming in idem and Hans Achelis, eds., *Die ältesten Quellen des orientalischen Kirchenrechts II: Die syrische Didaskalia.* TU 25,2 (Leipzig: J. C. Hinrichs, 1904).

[51] Thus Bradshaw, "Kirchenordnungen," 665. For introductory questions see also Steimer, *Vertex Traditionis* 49–52.

[52] *Didasc.* 14 (CSCO 408/180, 141).

[53] On this see Marlis Gielen, *Tradition und Theologie neutestamentlicher Haustafelethik. Ein Beitrag zur Frage einer christlichen Auseinandersetzung mit gesellschaftlichen Normen.* Athenäums Monografien. Theologie 75 (Frankfurt: Hain, 1990).

[54] *Didasc.* 15 (CSCO 408/180, 145).

[55] *Didasc.* 15 (CSCO 408/180, 151).

[56] On this see ch. 5 A above.

[57] In Achelis and Flemming, eds., *Die ältesten Quellen* 276. This thesis is supported by a statement in *Didasc.:* "For you wish to be wiser and more intelligent . . . not only than the men, but even than the presbyters and the bishops."

[58] Steimer, *Vertex Traditionis* 224 n. 158. The bishop is brought to the center of all theological and community functions and responsibilities to such an extent that Hans von Campenhausen is by no means incorrect when he speaks of "boundless attribution" of authority (*Kirchliches Amt und geistliche Vollmacht in den ersten drei Jahrhunderten.* BHTh 14 [Tübingen: J.C.B. Mohr (Paul Siebeck), 1953; 2nd rev. ed. 1963] 267). For the possible closeness of the ideology of the bishop in the *Didasc.* and in the letters of Ignatius see Allen Brent, "The Relations Between Ignatius and the Didascalia," *SecCen* 8 (1991) 129–56.

[59] Cf. *Didasc.* 16.

[60] Achelis and Flemming, *Die ältesten Quellen* 274, with citation of passages in *Didasc.* For this metaphor in the literature of the early Church see Osiek, "The Widow as Altar."

[61] *Didasc.* 15.

[62] *Didasc.* 15 (CSCO 408/180, 144).

[63] *Didasc.* 16 (CSCO 408/180, 157).

VII. Deacons

In the wake of the recent books by Aimé Georges Martimort[1] and Marie-Josèphe Aubert[2] there is no need to undertake another general discussion of the literary sources for the question of an office of deaconesses in the early Church and at the dawn of the Middle Ages.[3] Instead, this chapter will for the first time undertake a thorough documentation of Greek and Latin inscriptions for women deacons and deaconesses in the Church's first millennium, drawing on selected literary sources for the mutual interpretation of the literature and the inscriptions.[4]

A. Inscriptions from Palestine and Vicinity

Inscription for the diakonos Sophia

Palestine / Jerusalem / Mount of Olives[5]   IV^2

BIBLIOGRAPHY:

Cré, R. P. L. "Epitaphe de la Diaconesse Sophie," *RBI* n.s. 1 (1904) 260–62 (with plate).

Kaufmann, Carl Maria. *Handbuch der altchristlichen Epigraphik* (Freiburg: Herder, 1917) 292.

Alt, Albrecht. *Die griechischen Inschriften der Palaestina tertia westlich der 'Araba* (Berlin and Leipzig: Walter de Gruyter, 1921) no. 17 (with bibliography).

Thomsen, Peter. *Die lateinischen und griechischen Inschriften der Stadt Jerusalem und ihrer nächsten Umgebung* (Leipzig: J. C. Hinrichs, 1922) 85–86, no. 130 (with bibliography).

Guarducci, Margherita. *Epigrafia Greca IV. Epigrafi Sacre Pagane e Cristiane* (Rome: Istituto poligrafico dello Stato, Libreria dello Stato, 1978) 445 (fig. 132).

Meimaris, Yiannis E. *Sacred Names, Saints, Martyrs and Church Officials in the Greek Inscriptions and Papyri pertaining to the Christian Church of Palestine.* ΜΕΛΕΤΗΜΑΤΑ 2 (Athens: National Hellenic Research Foundation, Centre for Greek and Roman Antiquity, 1986) 177 n. 885.

Horsley, G. H. R. *New Documents Illustrating Early Christianity.* Vol. 4: *A Review of the Greek Inscriptions and Papyri published in 1979* (North Ryde, N.S.W.: Macquarie Ancient History Association, 1987) 239, no. 122.

+ ἐνθάδε κῖται ἡ δούλη
καὶ νύμφη τοῦ Χριστοῦ
Σοφία, ἡ διάκονος, ἡ δευ-
τέρα Φοίβη, κοιμηθῖσα
5 ἐν ἰρήνῃ τῇ κα΄ τοῦ Μαρ-
τίου μηνὸς Ἰνδ(ικτιῶνος) ια΄
[...]θίτω κύριος ὁ Θεός
[- - - - - -]ισων πρεσ-
- - - - - - - - - - - -⁶

Line 2: ου at the end of the line with ligature
Line 7: the first half of the line is almost entirely destroyed, so that the year is no longer discernible.⁷

Cross. Here lies the servant and bride of Christ, Sophia, deacon, the second Phoebe, who fell asleep in peace on the twenty-first of the month of March during the eleventh indiction . . . God the Lord . . .

This inscription from Palestine attests a woman named Sophia as a deacon. Datings of the inscription vary from the fourth to the seventh century,⁸ but Margherita Guarducci has made a plausible case for the second half of the fourth century. Albrecht Alt thought he could discern the number 518 in line 7, but in light of the thorough destruction of the stone at the beginning of line 7 we must consider the number of the year to be lost.

The characterization of Sophia in the inscription is remarkable. She is described in the following paired concepts:

(a) δούλη καὶ νύμφη τοῦ Χριστοῦ (lines 1-2). The description of bishops, presbyters, and deacons as δοῦλος or δούλη τοῦ Χριστοῦ is a motif found widely from the third century onward.⁹ Νύμφη τοῦ Χριστοῦ appears in Christian literature from the beginning of the fourth century onward as a description of virgins.¹⁰ Sophia's title, "bride of Christ," is to be interpreted as an indication of her ascetic way of life.

(b) ἡ διάκονος, ἡ δευτέρα Φοίβη (line 3). Sophia's official character as an officer of the Church is indicated not only by her being called a servant of Christ. In line 3 she is unmistakably designated a deacon. The description of a person as "the second . . ." occurs frequently from the fourth century onward in patristic and hagiographic literature.¹¹ Especially favored in that period was the titling of esteemed women theologians and others active in Church politics as "a second Thecla."¹²

G. H. R. Horsley has shown that in non-Christian inscriptions the description "a second Homer" or the like is applied to individuals who gave outstanding service to their city. For Sophia this could mean that her title "the second Phoebe" reflects aspects of Phoebe's activity beyond her work as a deacon (Rom 16:1-2), such as her title of προστάτις. More recently discovered inscriptions have shown that women could also be epigraphically attested as προστάτις,[13] and such a designation witnesses to their economic activity on behalf of political and religious communities.[14] Research in the last decade has shown also with regard to Phoebe that she was not merely a helper in the sense of pastoral assistance, but a businesswoman who gave financial support to the community.[15]

Other women deacons are epigraphically attested in Jerusalem and its neighborhood. From the village of Silvan in the valley of Josaphat we have the inscription of a deaconess (διακονίσ[. . .), badly damaged, dated with some reservation to the seventh century.[16] Peter Thomsen offers a total of six inscriptions from Jerusalem and vicinity that he dates to the fifth-seventh centuries, all of which witness to διάκονοι. Of these six deacons three are male (one δκο and two διακ) and two are female (one διάκονος and one διακονίσ[. . .). One inscription contains only the title (διακ), but the name of the deacon has been destroyed.[17] There is thus a high percentage of epigraphically attested women deacons in the city of Jerusalem and its immediate vicinity.

Inscription for dk Maria

Moab / Mahaiy   643–644

BIBLIOGRAPHY:

Canova, D. Reginetta. *Iscrizioni e monumenti protocristiani del paese di Moab.* SSAC 4 (Vatican City: Pontificio Istituto di archeologia cristiana, 1954) 383, no. 391 (fig. 426).

Meimaris, Yiannis E. *Sacred Names, Saints, Martyrs and Church Officials in the Greek Inscriptions and Papyri pertaining to the Christian Church of Palestine.* ΜΕΛΕΤΗΜΑΤΑ 2 (Athens: National Hellenic Research Foundation, Centre for Greek and Roman Antiquity, 1986) 178, n. 888.

Ἐνθάδε
κ(ε)ῖτ(αι) Μαρία
Οὐάλεντ(ος),
δ(ια)κ(όνισσα), ζήσασ
5   α ἔτ(η) λη΄, τελ
ευτ(ή)σασ(α) τ(οῦ)
ἔτους φλη΄.[18]

Line 3: Οὐάλης, -ητος, -εντος is the Roman name Valens.[19]
Line 7: The year 548 corresponds to 643–644 of our calendar.[20]

Here lies Maria, the daughter of Valens, deacon, who lived thirty-eight years, died in the year 548.

This dated inscription from the seventh century attests the deacon Maria, with her official title abbreviated (δκ). Reginetta Canova augments δ(ια)κ(όνισσα), but διάκονος is equally possible. The inscription tells us that the deacon Maria died at the age of thirty-eight. Accordingly, she is evidence of the fact that in the seventh century young women were still being ordained to the diaconate.

In contrast, Canon 15 of the Council of Chalcedon (451) had set a lower age limit of forty for women deacons: "A deaconess (διακόνισσαν) should not be consecrated (χειροτονεῖσθαι) before her fortieth year of life, and even then only after careful examination. However, if she has received consecration (δεξαμένη τὴν χειροθεσίαν) and already exercised her office for a time (παραμείνασα τῇ λειτουργίᾳ ἑαυτῆς), and if she despises the grace of God by entering into marriage, let her be anathema, together with the one who has married her."[21]

This decision of the council, which is at the same time evidence for the ordination of deaconesses,[22] sets a lower age limit for women deacons. This limit is apparently supposed to guarantee that deaconesses will not marry again after their ordination. The prohibition of marriage connected with ordination was applied by the acts of this council to all ecclesiastical officeholders except for the lectors and cantors.[23] The inscription for the deacon Maria shows, together with other examples,[24] that this lower age limit for women deacons could not be sustained.

There is a laconic sarcophagus inscription from Gadara whose text is engraved in mirror writing: + διακ<ό>νισα Ἑλλαδίς +.[25] An inscription from Nea Sion attests the deacon Nonna: . . . ἡ μα(καρία) Νόννα / ἡ διάκ(ονος) . . . .[26] A wall inscription from Deir el Quilt says: + ἐνθάδε κῖτε / Ἀναστασία διάκ(ονος) . . . .[27]

In summary we can say regarding the epigraphical witnesses for women deacons in Palestine and vicinity that they are as a rule laconic and frequently contain nothing more than the name of the deceased, her title, and a burial formula. Only one of these inscriptions is dated, and thus certainly comes from the seventh century. The undated inscriptions of this region are generally attributed by scholars of epigraphy to the Byzantine era.[28] We may conclude from the inscriptional evidence:

(a) We cannot tell with certainty from the inscriptions what official title was given to women deacons in the region of Palestine, since the title is usually abbreviated (δκ, διακ). Two of the epigraphically attested women deacons are given the full official title: Sophia, from the fourth century, is called διάκονος, and the undatable inscription of Helladis from Gadara is called διακόνισσα. In the case of the διάκονος Sophia it is possible that she was given the title in reference to the διάκονος Phoebe from Rom 16:1-2, but that the more usual title was διακόνισσα.

(b) None of the women named in the inscriptions is connected with a family of her own, an observation that holds also for the male deacons of this region.[29] This points to the probability that the epigraphically attested women deacons of this time and region lived celibate lives, as demanded by Canon 15 of the Council of Chalcedon for all officeholders with the exception of lectors and cantors.[30]

(c) The lower age limit of forty for deaconesses demanded by Canon 15 of the Council of Chalcedon was apparently not maintained in the region of Palestine, as the seventh-century inscription for deacon Maria of Moab shows.

B. Inscriptions from Asia Minor

"Asia Minor, in the fourth century, was the first purely Christian country," wrote Adolf von Harnack.[31] This assertion is supported by, among other things, the multiplicity of surviving Greek Christian inscriptions in Asia Minor.[32] In this section we will document examples of inscriptions attesting women deacons from Cilicia, Cappadocia, Galatia, Phrygia, and Lycaonia, as well as Bithynia and Lycia.

In Cilicia the city of Korykos has preserved inscriptions for women deacons. "In Korykos the city of the living is encircled by a broad band, greater than the former in its breadth, of the city of the dead . . . and the tremendous number of its tomb inscriptions offers a unique insight into the life of the population in the early Byzantine era."[33] The most frequent and characteristic burial form in Korykos was a limestone sarcophagus, with inscriptions usually on the lid, though sometimes on the body of the sarcophagus itself. Another frequent burial form was the chamber tomb.

Pagan, Jewish, and Christian inscriptions appear alongside one another in a colorful mixture in this necropolis. The Christian inscriptions, which are the majority, are signaled by symbols such as crosses or pairs of peacocks. The small altars set in relief on the sides of the caskets point to the pre-Christian period. They are also found on the sarcophagi of Christians, however, since these caskets were used repeatedly for new burials.

The inscriptions are for the most part laconic and contain scarcely anything more than the name of the deceased and her official title, both in the genitive, frequently introduced by σωματοθήκη, λουτρά, θήκη, and other words for the graves.[34]

Inscription for diak Timothea

Asia Minor / Cilicia / Korykos   V–VI[35]

BIBLIOGRAPHY:
MAMA III, 208, no. 744 (plate on p. 207).

Σωματοθήκη
Τιμοθέας διακ(όνου or -ονίσσης)
3   μονῆς ἁ[γί . . .]
[. . .[36]

Grave chamber of the deac(on) Timothea, of the monastery (?) [of Sain . . .

The inscription for this deacon begins, like countless inscriptions from
Korykos, with σωματοθήκη, followed by the name of the deceased in the genitive.[37] Timothea's official title is abbreviated, so it remains uncertain whether
she was called διάκονος or διακόνισσα.

The meaning of μονῆς ἁ[γί . . .] in line 3 can no longer be determined
with certainty because of the damage to the inscription. Μονή can on the one
hand be interpreted metaphorically as "dwelling" or "place of abode," much
like τόπος[38] in the sense of John 14:2,[39] or on the other hand as "monastery."[40]
If the tomb chamber above whose entrance door this inscription was placed belonged to a monastery, then Timothea was probably a monastic deacon.[41] Egeria's travel journal contains literary evidence for a monastic woman deacon in
Isauria. Egeria was a nun from the West who journeyed through the Eastern regions for three years during the fifth century; in her pilgrim journal she reports
that during her travels through Cilicia she encountered her friend, the deaconess *(diaconissa)* Marthana, whom she had previously met in Jerusalem.
Marthana, as *diaconissa,* headed a monastery of virgins *(haec autem monaste-
ria aputactitum seu virginum regebat)* in Isauria, near the place where Thecla
was supposed to have suffered martyrdom.[42] We learn nothing from Egeria's
text about Marthana's activities. She simply reports that prayers were held at
the shrine of Thecla and that the *Acts of Thecla* were read at divine worship.[43]

Other Korykos inscriptions refer to women deacons. A sarcophagus inscription with the conventional formula (the deceased are named, with titles
and other descriptions, in the genitive) attests the deacon Athanasia: [Ἀ]θανα-
σίας διακόνου + κ(αὶ) Μαρίας θρεπτῆς αὐτῆς.[44] The cross shows that both
women were Christians. The inscription tells of the deacon Athanasia, who apparently, as deacon, had adopted an orphan girl named Maria.

Another conventional sarcophagus inscription with an altar in relief witnesses to the deacon Theodora: + Λουτρὰ / Θεοδώρα[ς] erasure / διακόνου.[45]
The altar in relief on the side of the sarcophagus probably comes from the

pre-Christian era[46] and cannot be interpreted as a reference to Theodora's service at the altar. In addition, two laconic inscriptions from sarcophagus lids from Korykos refer to women deacons, the διάκονος Theophila[47] and the δι Charitina. The latter is more precisely described, beyond her name and official title, as a woman of Samaria and the daughter of Epiphanius:

+ Θήκη Χαριτ(ίνης) δι(ακόνου or -ακονίσσης)
Σαμάρισσας
θυγατ(ρὸς) Ἐπιφα-
νίου.[48]

Charitina's official title is abbreviated and could have been either διάκονος or διακόνισσα. In light of the other women deacons attested in Korykos, all of whom had the title διάκονος, we may assume that title for Charitina as well, unless, of course, she brought the title διακόνισσα with her from Samaria.

In summary we may say that as far as Korykos is concerned three of the five epigraphically attested women deacons bore the title διάκονος. The titles of the two other women are abbreviated (διακ, δι). There is no evidence of the use of the word διακόνισσα. In light of the brevity of the inscriptions we can gain very little additional information about these women. It is not impossible, in the case of one deacon, that she was deacon of a monastery. It is striking that only one woman deacon is named along with an adoptive daughter. The others all stand alone. None of these women seems to have founded a family of her own, as indicated similarly by most of the inscriptions for male deacons.[49] These findings are distinctly different from those in central Asia Minor, where there are many witnesses to women deacons who quite frequently appear on the gravestone together with their families.

Inscription for the diakonos Maria

Asia Minor / Cappadocia / Archelais   VI

BIBLIOGRAPHY:
Jacopi, Giulio. *Esplorazioni e studi in Paflagonia e Cappadocia. Relazione sulla seconda Campagna Esplorativa Agosto – Ottobre 1936* (Rome: R. Istituto d'Archeologia e Storia dell'Arte, 1937) 33–36 (figs. 135–36).
Thierry, Nicole. "Un problème de continuité ou de rupture. La Cappadoce entre Rome, Byzance et les Arabes," *CRAI* (1977) 98–145, at 116 no. 2 (fig. 16).
SEG 27 (1977) no. 948 A.
Horsley, G. H. R. *New Documents Illustrating Early Christianity.* Vol. 2: *A Review of the Greek Inscriptions and Papyri published in 1977* (North Ryde, N.S.W.: Macquarie Ancient History Association, 1982) 193–94, no. 109.

Ἐνθάδε κατά-
κιτε ἡ τῆς εὐλαβοῦς κὲ
μακαρίας μνήμης διάκο-
νος Μαρία ἥτις κατὰ τὸ ῥητὸν
5 τοῦ ἀποστόλου ἐτεκνοτρό-
φεσεν, ἐξενοδόχησεν, ἁ-
γίων πόδας ἔνιψε, θλι-
βομένοις τὸ ἄρτον αὐτῆς
διένεμεν. μνήσθητι αὐτῆ(ς)
10 Κύ(ριε), ὅταν ἔρχῃ ἐν τῇ βασιλίᾳ σου.[50]

Lines 1–2: Jacopi reads κατακ(εῖται); Thierry reads κατακ(εῖτε)
Lines 5–8: cf. 1 Tim 5:10
Lines 9–10: cf. Luke 23:42
Line 10: ἔρχῃ is here active.[51]

Here lies the deacon Maria of pious and blessed memory, who according to the words of the apostle raised children, sheltered guests, washed the feet of the saints, and shared her bread with the needy. Remember her, Lord, when she comes into your kingdom.

This inscription is dedicated to the deacon Maria by unknown donors. A significant feature of the text of the inscription is the New Testament citations. Lines five through eight quote 1 Tim 5:10 and indicate, though in stylized fashion, the fields of activity in which Maria worked during her life as a deacon. The inscription closes with a slightly altered version of Luke 23:42.

Lines five through eight review Maria's official activity in an almost literal replication of 1 Tim 5:10, the catalogue of criteria for widows who are to be enrolled (καταλεγέσθω). These are largely motifs borrowed from Hellenistic instructions for professional duties.[52] The quotation is introduced, and thereby authorized, by a reference to the words of the apostle, a common formula in ancient Church literature for quotations from the Corpus Paulinum.[53] Then, following 1 Tim 5:10, the following activities are listed:

(a) The verb τεκνοτροφεῖν (lines 5–6) is a *hapax legomenon* in the New Testament, but the motif of care for children appears throughout the Pastorals as a qualification for those applying for offices in the Church (1 Tim 3:4, 12; Titus 1:6; 2:4). It fits the ecclesiological concept of the Pastorals, which presents the Church structurally as an οἶκος containing all the persons belonging to the household, therefore including children.

G. H. R. Horsley has pointed out that τεκνοτροφεῖν can scarcely be found in inscriptions or documentary papyri before this date. He emphasizes that in the literary tradition both women and men were subjects of the verb; it is not gender-specific to women.[54] It is not simply a matter of the care and training of the children of one's own family.[55]

(b) The verb ξενοδοχεῖν (line 6) is, like τεκνοτροφεῖν, a *hapax* in the New Testament. The motif of hospitality appears in 1 Timothy as a criterion for admission to the episcopal office. The bishop is expected to be φιλόξενος (1 Tim 3:2; Titus 1:8).

The verb has not been found elsewhere in the documentary tradition,[56] but it is very frequent in ancient Church texts. The Cappadocian Gregory Nazianzus speaks in his poem *De vita sua* of sheltering guests—together with feeding the poor and other virtues and religious activities—as an obligation of believers.[57] Hospitality is here not a specific demand connected with Church office, but a value for all the faithful.[58]

(c) The command to wash feet is closely connected in the Pastorals to widows and appears only in the paraenesis for that group (1 Tim 5:10).[59] In the New Testament foot washing is also attested in Luke 7:36-50 and John 13:4-15. Jesus demonstrates his love for his disciples by washing their feet as a sign-action showing their community with him (John 13:1, 8).[60] Luke 7:36-50 tells of a sinful woman who comes into a Pharisee's house and sprinkles Jesus' feet with her tears, dries them with her hair, and anoints them from an alabaster vase (Luke 7:38). In both cases the foot washing is depicted as an act of love (John 13:1; Luke 7:47).

Washing feet[61] was a common custom in antiquity and by no means signified nothing more than the lowliest kind of slave work.[62] Rather it represented "honoring and receiving guests" and "a gesture of love."[63] In the ancient Church it had a variety of meanings.[64] Starting from the Jewish notion of the purifying power of foot washing, the ancient Church taught that such washing had the power to remove sin. In this context foot washing was, from the third century onward, especially in the Western regions, a ritual complementing baptism. In the Eastern Church, on the other hand, there is no trace of such a custom.[65] J. C. Thomas suggests that for the Johannine community and subsequently for the whole ancient Church the religious ritual of foot washing had a sacramental character, that its location was within the Eucharist and that it served to forgive postbaptismal sins.[66] In addition, foot washing had a special significance as a sign of hospitality and was explained by reference to the Lord's action in John 13.

For the deacon Maria washing the feet of the saints certainly represented primarily an act of hospitality; whether sacramental functions were associated with it cannot be determined from the inscription alone.

(d) The formula θλιβομένοις τὸ ἄρτον αὐτῆς διένεμεν (line 8) goes beyond 1 Tim 5:10 in that it makes concrete reference to the aspect of feeding those in need, as Gregory Nazianzus also urges in his poem. The reference to θλιβομένοι recalls charity to the poor above all.

The deacon Maria is one of the few inscriptionally attested women deacons whose field of activity is detailed. According to her inscription she was concerned with raising children, exercised hospitality, and washed the feet of believers. Whether the latter was done as an act of hospitality or, beyond that, as a sacramental act of forgiveness of sins must remain an open question. In addition, she was active in caring for the poor.

A similar field of activity is found in the tomb inscription for a presbyter from Lycaonia: "'The help of widows, orphans, strangers, and poor, [Nestor?, son of Nestor?], presbyter in charge of the sacred expenditure: in remembrance.' (Garland in relief)."[67] Both inscriptions attest that care for widows, orphans, strangers, and the poor was the special duty of those in Church office.[68] The inscription for this presbyter shows that both the presbyters and the deacons were entrusted with such duties, which were financed by the Church.

Inscription for diakonos Basilissa

Asia Minor / Lycaonia / Iconium

BIBLIOGRAPHY:

Cronin, H. S. "First Report of a Journey in Pisidia, Lycaonia, and Pamphylia," *JHS* 22 (1902) 338–76, at 358–60, no. 119.

Ramsay, William M. "The Church of Lycaonia in the Fourth Century," in idem, *Luke the Physician* (London: Hodder and Stoughton, 1980) 329–410, at 394 no. 23.

MAMA VIII, 56, no. 318.

Κοίντος Ἡρακλίου
πρωτοκωμήτης σὺν
τῇ συμβίῳ Ματρώνῃ
καὶ τέκνων Ἀνικήτῳ
5   καὶ Κατίλλῃ οἱ τέσσα-
ρις ἐνθάδε κεῖντε τύμ-
βῳ ἡ δ' ἄλοχος Ἀνικήτου
Βασίλισσα δειάκο-
νος κτίσε τύμβον ἀ-
10   ρεστὸν σὺν παιδὶ
μούνου Νεμετω-
ρίῳ νηπίῳ ὄντι.[69]

Line 2: Cronin: "I have not come across any instance of πρωτοκωμήτης in Asia Minor."[70]

Lines 4 and 11: Cronin: The genitives τέκνων and μούνου after σὺν are a sign of the
    decline in use of the dative.
Line 8:   The female name Βασίλισσα is not uncommon in Asia Minor.[71]

The first man of the village, Quintus, son of Heraclius, with his wife Matrona
and his children Anicetus and Catilla, all four lie in this grave. The wife of Anicetus, the deacon Basilissa, has erected this pleasant tomb together with her
only son Numitorius, who is still an immature child.

This inscription comes from one of the central provinces of Asia Minor,
Lycaonia, which together with Phrygia and Galatia contains an especially rich
heritage of epigraphic material.[72] The deacon Basilissa dedicated this inscription to her deceased husband Anicetus and his family. We may suppose that
Basilissa erected the monument on the occasion of her husband's death. The
youth of her son indicates that Basilissa must still have been a young woman
and that she had lost her husband a short time before.[73] Basilissa may provide
us with evidence of a young, married woman deacon of the Church unless we
presume that she became a deacon only after the death of her husband. In any
case, it is certain that Basilissa was an officeholder in the Church, while her
husband bears no official title.
    Other women are attested in Phrygia as officeholders independently of
their husbands. There is the deacon Strategis from Goslu, who together with
her son Pankratios dedicated a gravestone to her husband Menneas, her sister-
in-law Alexandria, and her son Domnos:

    + Εἰστρατηγὴς δι-
    ακό(νισσα) σὺν τῶ υἱ-
    ῶ μου Πανκρατί-
    ου ἀνεστήσαμεν
5   τῶ ἀνδρί μου Μεν-
    νέο[υ] κὲ τῆ ἀνδραδέλ-
    φη μου Ἀλεξανδρί-
    η κ(ὲ) τῶ υἱοῦ μου Δό-
    μνου μνήμης χάριν.

An arch is depicted above the inscribed tablet, and within the arch is an
ornamental cross in a circle flanked by Ω and A.[74]
    The deacon Aurelia Faustina from Laodicea Combusta placed a grave-
stone for her son, the lector Appas, in the fourth century:[75]

    ἔνθα κατάκιτε Ἀπ[π-
    ας ἀναγνώστης υἱ-

ὸς Φαυστίνου νε-
ώτερος εὐμεγέ-
5 θης ὦ κὲ ἀνήγιρε-
ν τὸ ἡρῷον τοῦτ-
ο ἡ μήτηρ αὐτοῦ
Αὐρηλ. Φαυστῖνα δι-
άκονος μνήμης
10 χ[άρ]ιν.[76]

Aurelia Faustina describes her son Appas as the "younger, well-grown son of Faustinus." The mention of the father, Faustinus, shows that he was not an official of the Church.[77]

In other inscriptions from Asia Minor women deacons are frequently mentioned by their children. The deacon Eugenis from Phrygia dedicated a gravestone together with his son Menneas, to his wife Thecla, his mother, the deaconess Matrona, his sister Leontiane, and his daughters Matrona and Epikthete.[78] The presbyter Alexander from Galatia placed an inscription for his mother, the διακον[ ] Nonna.[79] Another inscription, from Lydia, attests the tomb of the deacon Asterius, his mother the deaconess, his son, and the rest of his household.[80] Other inscriptions from Asia Minor witness to women deacons without their own children or husbands, but frequently with brothers and sisters or other family members.

Inscription for diakonos Paula

Asia Minor / Phrygia / Laodicea Combusta

BIBLIOGRAPHY:
MAMA I 120, no. 226 (photo).

Παῦλα διάκονος πανμάκα-
ρος Χριστῦο + τύμβον Ἑλλα-
δίου κασιγνήτυο φίλοιο
δίματό μ' ἔκτοθι πάτρης
5 ἀρηρότα λαΐνεεσσιν
φύλακα σώματος ἄ[χ]ρι σάλ-
πιξ ἠχήεσσα + ἐκπάγλως ἐ-
γίρουσα βροτοὺς θεσμοῖ-
σι Θεοῖο.[81]

Line 4: μ(ε) refers to τύμβον in line 2.
Lines 6–7: cf. 1 Cor 15:52.

Paula, the most blessed deacon of Christ. [Cross] She built me, the tomb of her dear brother Helladius, outside the fatherland, made of stones as protector of the body until the dreadful sound of the trumpet shall awaken the dead as God has promised.

The deacon Paula dedicated this ambitious tomb epigraph in hexameters, partly with Byzantine pronunciation (according to the length of the vowels),[82] to her brother Helladius, who was not a Church official. In comparison to the other inscriptions from this region[83] it is independent in its form and points to Paula's classical and theological education. The deacon not only composed the text of the inscription in hexameters, but also as a speech by the gravestone itself, a rare but not unknown form of tomb inscription.[84] The freewheeling form is embellished with a New Testament reference (to 1 Cor 15:52).

From the same place, Serai önü, we have another inscription using the ordinary, conventional formula. It, too, attests a woman deacon and her siblings:

+ Φροντῖνος
πρε(σ)β. κὲ Μα-
σα διακ. Αὐρ.
Μαμας υἱὺ
5   Ῥόδωνος πρ-
ε(σ)β. ἀνεστή-
σαμεν τὸν
τίτλον τοῦ-
τον ἑαυτῦς
10 ζῶντες κὲ
φρονοῦντε-
ς μνήμης
χάριν +.[85]

Masa[86] the deacon and her siblings placed their gravestone while they were still living. This custom is often attested, especially in Phrygian inscriptions.[87] An inscription from Lycaonia also witnesses to siblings. Here a pair of siblings placed a memorial stone to their sister, the deaconess Goulasi: Αὐρή. Λούκιος κὲ Αὐρη. / Οὐακα Γουλασι διακο/νίσση ἀδελφῆ γλυ/κυτάτη μνήμης / χάριν.[88]

Inscription for the Deaconess of the Encratites, Elaphia

Asia Minor / Phrygia / Laodicea Combusta / Nevinne(h)   IV

BIBLIOGRAPHY:
    Robinson, David M. "Greek and Latin Inscriptions from Asia Minor," *TAPA* 57
        (1926) 195–237, at 198–99, nos. 2 and 3.

MAMA I, xxv.
MAMA VII 12–13, no. 69 (Plate 5).

(a) Left column

Αὐρ. Ἀντώνιος
Μίρου ἅμα τῇ ἑ-
αὐτοῦ θία Ἐλα-
[φ]ίη διακονίσσῃ
5 [τῆς τῶν Ἐ]γκρατῶν
[θρισκίας] Μεν-
[νέα? κτλ.   ].

(b) Right column

Ἐλαφία διακόνισ-
σα τῆς Ἐνκρατῶν
θρισκίας ἀνέστη-
σα τῷ πρβ. Πέτρω
ἅμα τῷ ἀδελφῷ
αὐτῷ Πολυχρονί-
ῳ μνήμης χάριν. (leaf)[89]

Lines 1b and 3a: The female name Ἐλαφία is attested by another inscription, from
Nevinneh.[90]
Lines 2b and 5a: Ἐνκρατῶν is a variant on Ἐνκρατιτῶν.[91]
Lines 3 and 6a: Itacism: θία for θεία and θρισκίας for θρησκείας.
Line 4b: Robinson reads πρβρ for πρεσβυτέρῳ and considers the form unusual;
Calder, in contrast, reads πρβ with a sign of abbreviation.
Line 6a: Robinson reads ἀνεστήσ]αμεν.
Line 6b: Robinson reads πολυχρονίω (adjectival).

(a) Aurelius Antonius, son of Mirus, together with his aunt Elaphia, deaconess
of the community of the Encratites . . .
(b) I, Elaphia, deaconess of the community of the Encratites, have set [this stone]
in memory of the presbyter Peter, together with the brother Polychronios.

The unique feature of this tablet inscription[92] is that it attests a deaconess
from the schismatic group of the Encratites (διακόνισσα τῶν Ἐνκρατῶν).[93]
The inscription in column (a) of the tablet tomb links Aurelius Antonius with
the deaconess Elaphia. The inscription in column (b) associates this same
Elaphia[94] with the presbyter Peter and the brother Polychronius.

The existence of Encratite communities in Asia Minor is attested in literature
from the fourth century.[95] In the so-called canonical letters of Basil of Caesarea to
Bishop Amphilochius of Iconium from the second half of the fourth century (375)
the Ἐγκρατῖται are mentioned in connection with the discussion of the problem
of heresy and schism and the difficulties in canon law associated with them.[96]

Another witness to Encratites in the fourth century is Epiphanius' *Panarion* (*Pan.* 47,2-7). He writes of them:

They abound even today in Pisidia and in what is called "Burnt Phrygia."[97] . . .
Doubtless this country got the name which it has in the world due to its inhabitants being burnt by the perversion of so great an error. For there are many sects in
the region. They exist as well in parts of Asia, in Isauria, Pamphylia, Cilicia, and

Galatia. This sect was also long ago . . . part of the region of Rome, to say nothing of Antioch in Syria, but not everywhere. . . . They accept primarily the writings called the Acts of Andrew, of John, and of Thomas, certain apocryphal works, and the parts of the Old Testament which they wish. They quite definitely teach that marriage is from the devil. They abhor animal flesh, rejecting it not for the sake of continence or asceticism, but out of fear and for the sake of appearance, lest they be condemned for partaking of animal flesh. They too celebrate the sacraments with water. They never partake of wine, saying that it is of the devil and that those who drink it and use it are lawless folk and sinners.[98]

This polemic description (as usual with Epiphanius) can certainly not be taken as a faithful account of the basic principles of Encratite groups, but it does indicate tendencies that are attested by other sources as well. The first evidences for a group of Encratites from the second century show that, while they were orthodox in their faith in God and Christ, they drank nothing but water, ate a vegetarian diet, and forbade marriage.[99] Their abstention from wine is confirmed by two Encratite tomb inscriptions that warn against wine-drinkers.[100] In the years 381 and 383 the Encratites, together with the Manicheans and other groups, were condemned and banned by a very severe imperial edict.[101]

Inscription for diakonos Eugenia

Asia Minor / Bithynia / Topallar (near Nicomedia)

BIBLIOGRAPHY:
Sahin, Sencer, "Neue Inschriften von der bithynischen Halbinsel," *ZPE* 18 (1975) 27–48, at 46, no. 141.
BE (1976) no. 684.
TAM IV/1, 355.

Περὶ μνήμης Εὐγενίας διακόνου ἀνενεωσάμεθα +
[τ]ὴν καταλιφθῖσαν ἡμῖν πύελον οἱ πτωχοὶ Γηραγαθεως
+[102]

In memory of the deacon Eugenia we, the poor of Geragathis, have restored the coffin we decorated.

The undated inscription for the deacon Eugenia comes from a village near Nicomedia in the province of Bithynia. It says that Eugenia's coffin has been restored by the poor of Geragathis (οἱ πτωχοὶ Γηραγαθέως). It is impossible to determine precisely who these restorers, the poor of Geragathis, were. Γηραγάθις is mentioned in the list of persons in *TAM* IV/1 without further qualification. It is possible that Geragathis was the male or female leader of a house for the poor where Eugenia had once been employed. The poor of the house would then have restored the coffin.[103]

It was from Bithynia[104] that in about 112 C.E. Pliny the Younger wrote the letter to the emperor Trajan that is so important for Christian history (Pliny, *Ep.* X, 96). The letter is significant as a non-Christian witness to the historical questions of persecution of Christians, liturgical worship, and the constitution of the Christian communities in Bithynia at the beginning of the second century.[105] There we read that Pliny had tortured two slave women *(ancillae)* "who are called deacons *(quae ministrae dicebantur)*" to obtain information about Christian beliefs.[106] According to A. N. Sherwin-White, *ministra* should be regarded as a literal translation of διάκονος.[107] The interpretation of the Latin *ministra* as a translation of Greek ἡ διάκονος is confirmed by Ambrosiaster's commentary on Romans.[108] We find a Greek formula parallel to Pliny's Latin in Justin, *Apol.* 1.65, 5: in about 150 he refers to the Church's διάκονοι as οἱ καλούμενοι παρ᾽ ἡμῖν διάκονοι.[109] He describes their duties: they brought the Eucharist in the forms of bread, wine, and water to all those present and also to those absent.[110] The deacons thus clearly exercised sacramental functions. There is no reason to think that this service was not performed by both women and men.[111] Pliny's letter is an early witness to women deacons in northwestern Asia Minor.

We may summarize our findings regarding women deacons in Asia Minor:

(a) As regards the official designation of women deacons, the findings in Asia Minor are varied. They are called both διάκονος and διακόνισσα, insofar as the official titles are not abbreviated.[112] It appears that both titles were used alongside one another as a matter of course.[113]

(b) The fields of the women deacons' activities are not mentioned in the inscriptions. The only exception is that for the deacon Maria for whom are attested, in reference to 1 Tim 5:10, the raising of children, exercise of hospitality, washing the feet of the faithful, and care for the poor.

(c) The family situation of the women clearly illustrated in the inscriptions from Asia Minor proves to have a varied character. Noteworthy in particular are the numerous women deacons who are said to have been mothers and wives. Scarcely any woman deacon appears without her relatives, either her own children or her siblings or parents.

(d) In addition to these women with families there were also monastic women deacons.

(e) A great number of the inscriptions studied were dedicated by women, which underscores the fact that this was a matter of course. The inscription by the deacon Paula reveals her classical and theological education.

(f) The number of surviving inscriptions concerning women deacons in Asia Minor is very extensive.[114] Very early, 1 Tim 3:11 and Pliny, *Ep.* X, 96, 8 attest the presence of women deacons in Asia Minor in the second century. The abundant epigraphic evidence suggests the continuity of an office of women deacons in Asia Minor from the very beginning.

C. Inscriptions from Greece

Inscription for the deacon Agalliasis and those belonging to her

Greece / Cyclades / Melos[115]　　　　　　　　　　　　　　　III/IV

BIBLIOGRAPHY:

CIG IV (= Ernest Curtis and Adolph Kirchhoff, eds., *Corpus Inscriptionum Graecarum*, vol. IV [Hildesheim and New York: G. Olms, 1977; reprint of the Berlin edition of 1877]) 9288.

IG XII/3 (= Friedrich Hiller von Gärtringen, ed., *Inscriptiones Graecae. Inscriptiones insularum maris Aegaei praeter Delum. Fasc. 3. Inscriptiones Symes, Teutlussae, Teli, Nisyri, Astypalaeae, Anaphes, Therae et Therasiae, Pholegandri, Meli, Cimoli* [Berlin: Akademie der Wissenschaften, 1898; *Supplementum* 1904, reprinted Berlin: Walter de Gruyter, 1939]) 1238.

Achelis, Hans. "Spuren des Urchristentums auf den griechischen Inseln?" *ZNW* 1 (1900) 87–100, at 89–90.

Kaufmann, Carl Maria. *Handbuch der altchristlichen Epigraphik* (Freiburg: Herder, 1917) 159.

Grégoire, Henri. *Recueil des inscriptions grecques chrétiennes d'Asie Mineure 1* (Amsterdam: A. M. Hakkert, 1968; reprint of the Paris edition of 1922) 62–63 no. 209.

Guarducci, Margherita. *Epigrafia Greca IV. Epigrafi Sacre Pagane e Cristiane* (Rome: Istituto poligrafico dello Stato, Libreria dello Stato, 1978) 368–70 no. 2.

ἐν Κ(υρί)ῳ
οἱ πρεσβοίτεροι οἱ πάσης μνήμης ἄξιοι Ἀσκλήπις
καὶ Ἐλπίζων κὲ Ἀσκληπι[δο]τ[ο]ς (?) κὲ Ἀγαλίασις
[δ]ιάκονος καὶ Εὐτυχία παρθενεύσασα κὲ Κλαυδιανὴ
5　παρθενεύσασα καὶ Εὐτυχία ἡ τούτων μήτηρ
ἔνθα κεῖντε. καὶ ἐπὶ γέμι τὸ θηκίον τοῦτο,
ἐνορκίζω ὑμᾶς τὸν ὧδε ἐφεστῶτα ἄγγελον
μή τίς ποτε τολμῇ ἐνθάδε τινὰ καταθέσθε.
Ἰησοῦ Χρειστέ, βοήθει τῷ γράψαντι πανοικί.[116]

Line 3: *CIG:* Ἀσκλῆπις [δ]ε[ύ]τε[ρο]ς
　　　　Ἀγαλίασις = Ἀγαλ(λ)ίασις
Line 8: *IG* and Grégoire read τολμή(ση).[117]

The presbyters, worthy in every memory, Asclepis and Elpizon and Asclepiodotos and the deacon Agalliasis and the virgin Eutychia and the virgin Claudiane and Eutychia, their mother, rest here. And because this tomb is full I adjure
you by the angel who sits before it that no one should dare to bury another in
this place. Jesus Christ be the aid of the writer and his whole household.

This inscription belonging to a clergy family of Melos probably derives
from the first half of the fourth century, since none of those from the third century is introduced by the formula EN K(ΥΡΙ)Ω.[118] The introductory formula
and the reference to Jesus Christ in line 9 clearly attest the Christian provenance of the inscription. Hans Achelis long ago pointed to the uniqueness of
this inscription, which lists pagan names like those of the healing god Asclepis
and Asclepiodotos alongside Christian names like Elpizon and Agalliasis.[119]
This finding can be regarded as an indication of the merging of pagan and
Christian heritages. Something similar is true of the reference to the angel who
watches the tomb. Tomb angels are also found in other inscriptions from the
Aegean region, especially the so-called angel inscriptions from Thera.[120]

The inscription witnesses to a mother named Eutychia, her three sons and
three daughters. The sons Asclepis, Elpizon, and Asclepiodotos were presbyters, the daughter Agalliasis a deacon, and the daughters Claudiane and Eutychia lived as virgins and may have received the consecration of virgins.[121]

Inscription for the deacon Agrippiane

Greece / Patras in Achaia   "early Christian" period[122]

BIBLIOGRAPHY:
Petsas, Photios. "ΑΡΧΑΙΟΤΗΤΕΣ ΚΑΙ ΜΝΗΜΕΙΑ ΑΧΑΙΑΣ," *AD* 26 (1971)
    148–85, at 161–63.
Michaud, Jean-Pierre. "Chronique des fouilles et découvertes archéologiques en
    Grèce en 1973," *BCH* 98 (1974) 579–722, at 625 (fig. 116).
BE (1976) no. 288.
Horsley, G. H. R. *New Documents Illustrating Early Christianity.* Vol. 4: *A Re-
    view of the Greek Inscriptions and Papyri published in 1979* (North
    Ryde, N.S.W.: Macquarie Ancient History Association, 1987) 239.

Ἡ θεοφιλεστάτη
διάκονος Ἀγριππια-
3 νὴ ὑπερ εὐχῆς αὐ-
τῆς ἐποίησεν [Petsas: leaf]
τὴν μούσωσιν.[123]

The best beloved of God, the deacon Agrippiane, has laid this mosaic in order to fulfill her vow.

Agrippiane's inscription is a votive incorporated in a mosaic. Votive inscriptions were an increasing phenomenon in the early Byzantine period.[124] They were given by both clerics and lay persons.[125] Origen, for example, explains the vow as a promise to do this or that when one has obtained something from God.[126] The vow could on the one hand combine the two elements of promise and condition, or on the other hand it could be an unconditioned offering to God as an expression of gratitude.

There is also a surviving fourth-century votive inscription from Stobi in Macedonia laid down in the exedra in a mosaic, for the deacon Matrona: (ὑ)περ εὐ[χῆς αὐ]/τῆς Ματ[ρώνα ?] / ἡ εὐλαβ[εστά]/ 4 τη διάκ[ονος] / τὴν ἐξέ[δραν] / ἐψήφω[σεν].[127]

Inscription for the deaconess Athanasia

Greece / Delphi   V

BIBLIOGRAPHY:
Laurent, J. "Delphes chrétien," *BCH* 23 (1899) 206–79, at 272–78.
Guarducci, Margherita. *Epigrafia Greca IV. Epigrafi Sacre Pagane e Cristiane* (Rome: Istituto poligrafico dello Stato, Libreria dello Stato, 1978) 345–47 no. 4 (fig. 99).

```
           +
    [ἡ] εὐλαβε<σ>τάτη
    διακ{ι}όνισσα Ἀθανασία
    ἄμενπτον βίον ζήσασα
    [κ]οσζμίως, κατασταθῖσα
5   δὲ διακόνισα παρὰ τοῦ
    ἁγιωτάτου ἐπισκόπου
           Παντ[α]μιανοῦ,
    ἐποίησεν τὸ μ[ν]ημόριον τοῦτο
    ἔνθ[α τὸ αὐτῆς λί]νψανον κῖτε. εἴ
10  τ[ις δ᾽ ἕτερος τολ]μήσῃ ἀνῦξε τὸ
    μνη[μόριον τοῦ]το, ἔνθα ἡ διακόνισα
    κατε[τέθη, ἐχέτω τ]ὴν μερίδα τοῦ Εἰού-
    δα τοῦ [προδότου] τοῦ δεσπότου ἡ-
    μῶν Ἰη[σοῦ Χριστ]οῦ. οὐδὲν δὲ ἔλατ-
15  τον τῶ[ν κατὰ τοῦτ]ον τὸν κερὸν
```

εύρισκο[μένων κ]ληρικῶν κὲ συνχω-
ρησάντ[ων . . . τεθ]ῆνε τῆς προιρημέ-
νης δ[ιακονίσσης - - - -]υτη μερίδι ὑπὸ
[- - - - - - - - - - - - - τ]οῦ ἁγίου
20 [- - - - - - - - - - - - - - α]ὐτῶν κὲ γε
[- - - - - - - - - - - - -] .. τὴν ἐκλη-
[σίαν - - - - - - - - - - - - κλ]ήρου.[128]

The most pious deaconess Athanasia, who led a blameless life in decorum, was installed as deaconess by the most holy bishop Pantamianos. She has placed this monument. Here lie her mortal remains. If anyone else dares to open this tomb, where the deaconess has been buried, may he suffer the fate of Judas, the betrayer of our Lord Jesus Christ . . .

This inscription attests the deaconess Athanasia from Delphi and is the sole inscription in the present study that mentions the installation (κατα-σταθῖσα) of a deaconess by the bishop. We find notice of installation in none of the other inscriptions here documented. Equally unusual is the length of the inscription and the fact that the deaconess Athanasia erected such a monument to herself. She oriented the text of her inscription to classic epigraphical topoi, as shown especially by the warning formula referring to the fate of Judas.

A brief inscription from Attica attests another Greek woman deacon who was called deaconess: Νεικαγόρη / διακόνισ/σα ἐνθάδε / κεῖμαι.[129]

In summary we can say of inscriptions from Greece referring to women deacons that they are no more unified in their terminology than those from Asia Minor: two women bear the title διάκονος and two are titled δια-κόνισσα. The deacon Agalliasis is mentioned within her family circle. She comes from a clergy family: her three brothers are presbyters and her two sisters may have been consecrated virgins. The other women deacons appear in their inscriptions without relatives. The deacon Agrippiane stands out because she immortalized herself in a mosaic inscription in order to fulfill her vow. Unusual in another sense is the extensive inscription of the deacon Athanasia, who mentions her consecration by Bishop Pantamianos and adds the text of a cursing formula. This inscription is the only one in the present collection that mentions the ordination of a woman as deacon.

D. Inscriptions from Macedonia

Theoprep(e)ia diak

Macedonia / Bonitsa   IV fin.

BIBLIOGRAPHY:

Mastrocostas, E. "Παλαιοχριστιανικαὶ βασιλικαὶ Δρυμοῦ Βονίτσης" (sic). *Athens Annals Arch* 4 (1971) 185–95, at 188–89 (fig. 6).

Popescu, Emilian. "Griechische Inschriften," in Friedhelm Winkelmann and Wolfram Brandes, eds., *Quellen zur Geschichte des frühen Byzanz (4.–9. Jahrhundert). Bestand und Probleme.* BBA 55 (Amsterdam: Gieben, 1990) 81–105, at 95.

+ Ἐνθάδε κεῖτε
ἡ δούλη τοῦ K͞Υ͞
Θεοπρέπια
ἀειπάρθενος καὶ
5   διακ τοῦ X͞Ρ͞Υ͞ ἀσ-
κητικόν, θεόζη-
λον, πάνσεμνόν
τε ἐν Κυρίω Θεῶ
διανήσασα βίον.[130]

Line 2: K͞Υ͞ = K(υρίο)υ
Line 5: X͞Ρ͞Υ͞ = Χρ(ιστο)ῦ
Line 9: διανήσασα = διανύσασα

Here Theoprep(e)ia,[131] the slave of the Lord, eternal virgin and deacon of Christ, who has finished an ascetic, zealous, altogether honorable life in God the Lord.

This inscription is striking in its comprehensiveness. Theoprepeia is shown to be an officeholder in a twofold sense: first by being called the Lord's slave, and second through her designation as deacon. This combination of words is also found in the inscription for Deacon Sophia of Jerusalem.[132]

The inscription places special emphasis on the ascetic way of life of the deacon. Her status as "eternal virgin," that is, as a woman who had vowed long-term virginity and had probably received the consecration of virgins, is underscored by her description as someone who had lived ascetically, zealous for God and altogether honorable. This kind of emphasis on asceticism, zeal for God, and the honorable character of this deacon has been found in none of the other inscriptions for women deacons examined thus far.

diak Posidonia

Macedonia / Philippi   IV–V

BIBLIOGRAPHY:

Heuzey, Léon, and Honoré. Daumet. *Mission archéologique de Macédoine* (Paris, 1876) 95, no. 50.

Jalabert, Louis, and René Mouterde. "Inscriptions Grecques Chrétiennes," *DACL* 7/1 (1926) 623–94, at 652.

Lemerle, Paul. *Philippes et la Macédoine orientale à l'époque chrétienne et byzantine*. Recherches d'Histoire et d'Archéologie (Paris: E. de Boccard, 1945) 92–94.

Feissel, Denis. *Recueil des inscriptions chrétiennes de Macédoine du IIIe au VIe siècle*. BCH Supplément 8 (Paris: Dépositaire, Diffusion de Boccard, 1983) 204–205 no. 241.

+ + +
+ Κοιμ(ητήρια) διαφέρ-
οντα Ποσιδω-
3   νίας διακ(ονίσσης) κ(αὶ) Πα-
νχαρίας ἐλαχ(ίστης)
κανονικῆς. +[133]

Lines 1, 3, 4: There are abbreviation marks over the μ in κοιμ, the κ in διακ, and the χ in ἐλαχ.

The graves belong to the deacon Posidonia and to Panchareia,[134] the least of the canons.

This inscription witnesses to two women officeholders in the Christian community of Philippi in the fourth or early fifth century. They were the deacon Posidonia and the canon Panchareia. The epithet ἐλαχίστη as a self-description, found in another inscription for a lector,[135] suggests that Panchareia wrote the inscription. We cannot determine exactly what is meant by the designation "canon." The literary witnesses for canons in the ancient Church are few.[136] Basil of Caesarea addresses two of his letters to canons. Letter 52 (ca. 370) is to κανονικαὶ and letter 173 (ca. 374) to a κανονική named Theodora. Neither letter gives any further information about the status and field of responsibility of this group. Wolf-Dieter Hauschild interprets κανονική as a woman ascetic, that is, as a virgin or widow subject to the rule of asceticism, a description that became a title in the fourth century and corresponds to the late medieval notion of the "canoness."[137] Their further description as ascetics need not have excluded community functions for these women. It is apparent only from a fragment of Hypatius from the sixth century that canons had responsibility for matters relating to burials.[138] Epigraphically, in addition to this instance from Macedonia, canons are attested in Asia Minor[139] and in Syria.[140]

Agathe diakonos

Macedonia / Philippi   V

BIBLIOGRAPHY:
Bakirtzis, Charalampos. "Exposition des Antiquités Paléochrétiennes au Musée des Philippes," *Athens Annals of Archaeology* 13 (1980) 90–98, at 95.
Abrahamsen, Valerie. "Women at Philippi: The Pagan and Christian Evidence," *JFSR* 3 (1987) 17–30, at 23.

. . . διακόνου Ἀγάθης καὶ
ὑποδέκτου καὶ ὀθωνητου Ἰωάννου . . .[141]

. . . the deacon Agathe and the cashier[142] and linen weaver? John . . .

Another woman deacon in Philippi is attested by this inscription. Her name is Agathe, and she is named together with her husband John, who was a cashier and linen weaver. We join Valerie Abrahamsen in regarding this inscription as evidence that married women were also deacons.[143] Abrahamsen shows, on the basis of the existing literary and epigraphic sources from Philippi, that the community there had developed an independent constitutional profile during the first four centuries. Thus the monarchic episcopate should not be assumed for Philippi before the middle of the fourth century; until that time the dominant institutional form was presbyterial.[144]

Agathokleia diakonos

Macedonia / Edessa   V–VI

BIBLIOGRAPHY:
Mordtmann, J. H. "Inschriften aus Edessa," *AM* 18 (1893) 415–19, at 416–17 no. 3.
Feissel, Denis. *Recueil des inscriptions chrétiennes de Macédoine du IIIe au VIe siècle.* BCH Supplément 8 (Paris: Dépositaire, Diffusion de Boccard, 1983) 40 no. 21 (bibliography).

Μημόριον
Ἀγαθωκλί-
3 ας παρθέν-
νου
καὶ διακώνου.[145]

Monument of Agathokleia,[146] the virgin and deacon.

A significant feature of this inscription from Edessa is the juxtaposition of virginity and the title of deacon. This combination, thus far attested only by the inscription of the deacon Theoprepeia from Bonitsa in Macedonia (see above, p. 78), indicates that Agathokleia was a consecrated virgin before she became a deacon. Another inscription from Edessa shows that virgins and deacons were two distinct groups of women; there could be overlapping between the two groups, but not necessarily.

Theodosia diakonos

Macedonia / Edessa   V–VI

BIBLIOGRAPHY:

Feissel, Denis. *Recueil des inscriptions chrétiennes de Macédoine du IIIe au VIe siècle.* BCH Supplément 8 (Paris: Dépositaire, Diffusion de Boccard, 1983) 39–40 no. 20 (bibliography).

    + + +
Μημόριον Θεο-
δοσίας διακόνου
3   καὶ Ἀσπηλίας
   καὶ Ἀγαθοκλή-
   ας παρθένον.[147]

Line 2: ου in ligature.
Line 5: παρθένον = παρθένων

Monument of the deacon Theodosia and the virgins Aspelia (Aspilia?) and Agathokleia.

This inscription using the common formula (introduction with Μημόριον followed by the names of the deceased and sometimes their titles in the genitive)[148] witnesses to the deacon Theodosia and the virgins Aspilia and Agathokleia. It again shows that the state of virginity was by no means identical with that of a deacon.

It is striking that the women deacons of Macedonia as a rule were called διάκονος. Only one fragmentary inscription from Thasos contains the title διακόνισσα for the fifth/sixth centuries. The name of the deacon in that case has been destroyed, but her title remains: ΔΙΑΚΟΝΙΣ . . . .[149] She was buried in the tomb of a martyr, from which Denis Feissel concludes that she must have been an important woman in the community.[150]

In summary we may say of the Macedonian inscriptions that the term διάκονος dominates. Of the seven documented above,[151] three contain this title, three titles are abbreviated, and one woman is called διακόνισσα. The title διάκονος was thus in use for women as late as the sixth century in this region. As a rule, with the exception of the deacon Agathe, these deacons are not mentioned in the inscriptions in connection with members of their families.[152] Instead, the deacon Posidonia is named together with a canon, and the deacon Theodosia with the virgins Aspilia and Agathokleia. This indicates that there were communities of life apart from the family.

The most striking thing about these inscriptions for deacons from Macedonia is that some have a definite ascetic tendency in that the deacons are also called virgins (Agathokleia) or permanent virgins[153] (Theoprepeia), or are named together with virgins (Theodosia). The joining of the titles of virgin and deacon is not found in inscriptions from other regions. In contrast to this finding we have the deacon Agathe, named in a single inscription with her husband John. Thus women had the choice of exercising their office as unmarried, sometimes in an express condition of virginity, or as married persons.

E. Inscriptions from the West

Inscription for diac Anna

Italy / Rome[154]   VI[155]

BIBLIOGRAPHY:

Kaufmann, Carl Maria. *Handbuch der altchristlichen Epigraphik* (Freiburg: Herder, 1917) 294.

ICUR n.s. II 4788 (G. B. de Rossi, completed and edited by Angelus Silvagni et al., *Inscriptiones christianae urbis Romae septimo saeculo antiquiores.* New series. 11 vols. [Rome: Ex Officina Libraria Doct. Befani, 1922–1985]).

Martimort, Aimé Georges. *Deaconesses: An Historical Study.* Translated by K. D. Whitehead (San Francisco: Ignatius Press, 1985) 202.

DE DONIS D͞I ET BEATI PAVLI APOSTOLI • DOMETIVS DIAC •
ET ARCARIVS S͞C͞A͞E • SED • APOSTOL • ADQVE P͞P • VNA CVM
ANNA DIAC • EIVS GERMANA HOC VOTUM BEATO PAVLO
OPTVLER͞V͞T.[156]

Line 2: SCAE = *sanctae*
         SED = *sedis*
         PP = *papae*

By the gifts of God and the blessed apostle Paul, Dometius, the deacon and manager of the treasury of the holy, apostolic, and papal chair, together with Anna, the deacon, his sister in the body, has presented this vow to the blessed Paul.

This votive inscription attests two Church officials in Rome: the deacon Dometius and his sister, the deacon Anna. Both are designated deacons with the common abbreviation DIAC. Dometius was the deacon and manager of the treasury *(arcarius)* of the papal chair.

The inscription shows that these two siblings had brought a votive offering to the apostle Paul. We cannot tell from the inscription itself what the content was. Vows could be expressed in various forms, sometimes by giving up one's own possessions, by exercising hospitality, or by joining a community, but especially through the vow of chastity.[157] This could be expressed by visible actions such as the endowment of an altar, a crucifix, or the like.

Anna's title of office is abbreviated, so we cannot tell whether she was called *diacona* or *diaconissa*. Both titles are attested in the West cheek by jowl from the fifth century onward.[158]

Inscription for diac Ausonia

Dalmatia / Doclea   VI[159]

BIBLIOGRAPHY:

CIL III 13845 (Mommsen, Theodor, ed. *Corpus Inscriptionum Latinarum*, vol. III. *Inscriptiones Asiae, provinciarum Europae Graecarum, Illyrici Latinae* [Berlin: G. Reimerus, 1873–1902]).

ILCV I 1239 (Diehl, Ernest, ed. *Inscriptiones Latinae Christianae Veteres*. 3 vols. [1925–1931; 2nd ed. Dublin and Zürich: Weidmann, 1961]. Vol. 4: *Supplementum*. Edited by Jacques Moreau and Henri-Irenée Marrou [Zürich: Weidmann, 1967]. Vol. 5: *Nuove Correzioni alla Silloge del Diehl Inscriptiones Latinae Christianae Veteres*. Edited by Antonio Ferrua).

Martimort, Aimé Georges. *Deaconesses: An Historical Study*. Translated by K. D. Whitehead (San Francisco: Ignatius Press, 1985) 202.

+ Ausonia diac <p>ro uoto suo et filiorum suorum fc. +[160]

fc = *fecit*

The deacon Ausonia for her vow and that of her sons [children].

It appears from this inscription that Ausonia was both deacon and mother. The inscription says nothing about a husband. Thus Ausonia was either a widow, and perhaps as such had been ordained a deacon, or else as a married deacon she had made her vow independently of her husband. Canon 17 of the Synod of Orléans of 553 shows that women deacons could be married. The canon forbids the remarriage of ordained women deacons.[161]

Inscription for diaconissa Theodora

Gaul / Ticini in St. Trinitatis   22 July 539[162]

BIBLIOGRAPHY:
CIL V 6467.
Grossi Gondi, Felice. *Trattato di epigrafia cristiana latina e greca del mondo romano occidentale. I. Monumenti Cristiani dei Primi sei Secoli I* (Rome: Università Gregoriana, 1968; reprint of the 1920 edition) 152.
ILCV I 1238.
Martimort, Aimé Georges. *Deaconesses: An Historical Study.* Translated by K. D. Whitehead (San Francisco: Ignatius Press, 1985) 202 n. 22.

+   +   +

hic in pace requiescit b.m.
Theodora diaconissa, quae
uixit in saeculo annos pl. m.
XLVIII. d(eposita) XI kal. Aug. V p.c.
5   Paulini iun. u. c. ind. II
(two Christograms)[163]

Line 1: b.m. = *bonae memoriae*
Line 2: ua in ligature
Line 3: pl.m. = *plus minus*

Here rests in peace, in happy memory, Theodora, the deaconess, who lived 48 years more or less. Buried on 22 July 539.

This dated inscription from the sixth century witnesses to the deaconess Theodora. It follows a traditional formula and contains common terms such as *in pace, requiescit, bonae memoriae,* the age of the deceased *(plus minus),* an exact date, *cruces immissae,* and Christograms. The inscription says of the deceased that she was a deaconess and died at the age of forty-eight.

This inscription shows that women deacons were active in the Church in Gaul in the sixth century. This observation is confirmed by Gallic synods from the end of the fourth to the middle of the sixth centuries that attempted to eliminate the official diaconal activity of women. Canon 2 of the Synod of Nîmes from the year 396 forbids a *ministerium faeminae leviticum.*[164] The office thus described was very probably that of women deacons.[165] Not quite fifty years later the Synod of Orange (441) absolutely forbade the ordination *(omni-modis non ordinandae)* of women deacons *(diaconae)*.[166] In the year 517 the *consecratio* of women deacons *(diaconae)* was forbidden in Canon 21 of the Synod of Epaon,[167] and in 533 the prohibition against ordaining women as deacons *(foeminae diaconalis benedictio)* was repeated in Canon 18 of the Synod of Orléans.[168] These instances show that women were active as deacons in the Church in Gaul and were also ordained. The prohibitions expressed by the synods against the ordination of women deacons and thus against their being made officeholders in the Church apparently were unsuccessful in this period; otherwise they would not have needed repeating.

The Latin inscriptions, though few in number, show, as do the literary witnesses, that women were active as ordained deacons in the Latin Church. The explicit attestation of women deacons begins in the fourth century, which has frequently led scholars to suppose that there were no women deacons in the West in the first three or four centuries.[169] The finding can, however, be interpreted differently: namely as showing that the office of women deacons—in the context of the increasing differentiation and regulation of the Church hierarchy combined with a growing exclusion of women from Church offices—only became a problem in the fourth century. Hence it is only from that time onward that prohibitions of the office are found in the Latin Church, thus making the office of women deacons, which up to that time may well have been a matter of course in the Church, visible for the first time. No unified designation for these women can be derived from the inscriptions or from the literary evidence. Only one of the three inscriptions contains the title *diaconissa* written out; the other two are abbreviated. In the synodical canons the women are as a rule called *diaconae*. It is therefore possible that in previous centuries they bore the title *diacona* and were thus terminologically invisible within the group of *diaconi*. Even apart from such hypotheses, we may regard it as certain that there was an office of women deacons in the Latin Church at least from the fourth century onward.[170]

In light of the sparse epigraphical evidence for women deacons in the West, the wide distribution of those few examples is surprising.[171] Women deacons are found in Gaul, Italy, and Dalmatia.[172]

Notes

[1] Aimé Georges Martimort, *Les Diaconesses. Essai historique*. BEL.S 24 (Rome: C.L.V.-Edizioni liturgiche, 1982). English: *Deaconesses: An Historical Study*. Translated by K. D. Whitehead (San Francisco: Ignatius Press, 1985).

[2] Marie-Josèphe Aubert, *Des Femmes Diacres. Un Nouveau Chemin pour l'Eglise*. Preface by Régine Pernod. PoTh 47 (Paris: Beauchesne, 1987).

[3] See also the older works by Leopold Zscharnack, *Der Dienst der Frau in den ersten Jahrhunderten der christlichen Kirche* (Göttingen: Vandenhoeck & Ruprecht, 1902) 99ff.; Adolf Kalsbach, *Die altkirchliche Einrichtung der Diakonissen bis zu ihrem Erlöschen*. RQ.S 22 (Freiburg, 1926), as well as his summary article in RAC[3] (1957); Roger Gryson, *The Ministry of Women in the Early Church*. Translated by Jean Laporte and Mary Louise Hall (2nd ed. Collegeville: The Liturgical Press, 1980).

[4] For the history of research on the office of deaconess see Dirk Ansorge, "Der Diakonat der Frau. Zum gegenwärtigen Forschungsstand," in Teresa Berger and Albert Gerhards, eds., *Liturgie und Frauenfrage. Ein Beitrag zur Frauenforschung aus liturgiewissenschaftlicher Sicht*. PiLi 7 (St. Ottilien: EOS Verlag, 1990) 31–65, and ch. 1 above, "The 'Office of Deaconess,'" with reference to deacons in the NT.

[5] Differently Albrecht Alt, *Die griechischen Inschriften der Palaestina tertia westlich der ʾAraba* (Berlin and Leipzig: Walter de Gruyter, 1921) 18: "Supposedly found on the Mount of Olives, but probably moved from Bîr es-Sebaʿ."

[6] Following G. H. R. Horsley, *New Documents Illustrating Early Christianity*. Vol. 4: *A Review of the Greek Inscriptions and Papyri published in 1979* (North Ryde, N.S.W.: Macquarie Ancient History Association, 1987) 239. The upper part of a stele (Margherita Guarducci, *Epigrafia Greca IV. Epigrafi Sacre Pagane e Cristiane* [Rome: Istituto poligrafico dello Stato, Libreria dello Stato, 1978] 445). Introduced by a *crux immissa*. Peter Thomsen, *Die lateinischen und griechischen Inschriften der Stadt Jerusalem und ihrer nächsten Umgebung* (Leipzig: J. C. Hinrichs, 1922) 85: "Gravestone, found in 1903 above the tombs of the prophets in the *wakuf* area of the southern peak. Now in the museum in Constantinople. Marble slab broken into five parts. 0,240 x 0,240."

[7] See the photograph in Guarducci, *Epigrafia Greca IV*, fig. 132. Thomsen, *Inschriften der Stadt Jerusalem* 86, had already pointed out that the number of the year has been destroyed.

[8] V (Carl Maria Kaufmann, *Handbuch der altchristlichen Epigraphik* [Freiburg: Herder, 1917]); VI[1] (Alt, *Inschriften*); VI (Thomsen, *Inschriften der Stadt Jerusalem*); VII (Yiannis E. Meimaris, *Sacred Names, Saints, Martyrs and Church Officials in the Greek Inscriptions and Papyri pertaining to the Christian Church of Palestine*. ΜΕΛΕΤΗΜΑΤΑ 2 [Athens: National Hellenic Research Foundation, Centre for Greek and Roman Antiquity, 1986]).

[9] Cf. G. W. H. Lampe, *A Patristic Greek Lexicon* (Oxford and New York: Clarendon Press, 1969; reprinted 1989) 385, with examples.

[10] Ibid. 928 B with examples.

[11] On this see Horsley, *New Documents* 4:240–41, with examples.

[12] One such example was Macrina the Younger: see ch. 4 above.

[13] Other examples are found in Horsley, *New Documents* 4:241ff., and in Joyce Reynolds and Robert Tannenbaum, *Jews and God-Fearers at Aphrodisias: Greek Inscriptions with Commentary.* Cambridge Philological Society, Supp. 23 (Cambridge: Cambridge Philological Society, 1987), which publishes and comments on the inscription from Aphrodisias. There is dispute whether the name of the προστάτις Jael found in this inscription is masculine or feminine. Bernadette Brooten, "The Gender of Ιαηλ in the Jewish Inscription from Aphrodisias," in Harold W. Attridge et al., eds., *Of Scribes and Scrolls: Essays in Honor of John Strugnell* (Lanham, Md.: University Press of America, 1990) 163–73, and eadem, "Iael προστάτης in the Jewish Donative Inscription of Aphrodisias," in Birger A. Pearson, ed., *The Future of Early Christianity. Essays in Honor of Helmut Koester* (Minneapolis: Fortress, 1991) 149–62, has shown that Ιαηλ is a woman's name.

[14] On this see R. A. Kearsley, "Women in Public Life in the Roman East: Iunia Theodora, Claudia Metrodora and Phoibe, Benefactress of Paul," *Ancient Society* (Macquarie University) 15 (1985) 124–37; Horsley, *New Documents* 4:241ff.; Reynolds and Tannenbaum, *Jews and God-Fearers at Aphrodisias;* and by all means see Brooten, "Gender of Ιαηλ," and eadem, "Iael προστάτης," as well as John K. Chow, *Patronage and Power. A Study of Social Networks in Corinth.* JSNT.S. 75 (Sheffield: JSOT Press, 1992).

[15] Thus, for example, Gerd Theissen, "Social Stratification in the Corinthian Community: A Contribution to the Sociology of Early Hellenistic Christianity," in: *The Social Setting of Pauline Christianity: Essays on Corinth.* Edited and translated and with an introduction by John H. Schütz (Philadelphia: Fortress, 1982) 87–89; Wolf-Henning Ollrog, *Paulus und seine Mitarbeiter. Untersuchungen zu Theorie und Praxis der paulinischen Mission.* WMANT 50 (Neukirchen-Vluyn: Neukirchener Verlag, 1979) 100; Gerhard Lohfink, "Weibliche Diakone im Neuen Testament" (1980) in Gerhard Lohfink, Helmut Merklein, and Karlheinz Müller, eds., *Die Frau im Urchristentum.* QD 95 (4th ed. Freiburg, Basel, and Vienna: Herder, 1989) 320–38; Kearsley, "Women in Public Life," 130: "Phoibe did possess an exalted status as benefactor in her own community;" Elisabeth Schüssler Fiorenza, "The 'Quilting' of Women's History: Phoebe of Cenchreae," in Paula M. Cooey, Sharon A. Farmer, and Mary Ellen Ross, eds., *Embodied Love. Sensuality and Relationship as Feminist Values* (San Francisco: Harper & Row, 1987) 35–49; Marlis Gielen, *Tradition und Theologie neutestamentlicher Haustafelethik. Ein Beitrag zur Frage einer christlichen Auseinandersetzung mit gesellschaftlichen Normen.* Athenäums Monografien. Theologie 75 (Frankfurt: Hain, 1990) 96, 98–99.

[16] Thus Thomsen, *Inschriften der Stadt Jerusalem* 79–80, no. 119, with additional bibliography; cf. also the various attempts at reconstruction by J. Germer-Durand, "Epigraphie Chrétienne de Jérusalem," *RB* 1 (1892) 560–88, at 566–67, no. 10, and Meimaris, *Sacred Names* 178 n. 887.

[17] Thomsen, *Inschriften der Stadt Jerusalem* nos. 119, 130, 147, 166, 167, 176.

[18] D. Reginetta Canova, *Iscrizioni e monumenti protocristiani del paese di Moab.* SSAC 4 (Vatican City: Pontificio Istituto di archeologia cristiana, 1954) 383, no. 391: "Funeral stele in stone with incised inscription. Dimensions of the stone 0.55 m. x 0.33 m. by 0.26 m.; height of the letters 30 mm."

[19] Thus Wilhelm Pape and Gustav Eduard Benseler, *Wörterbuch der griechischen Eigennamen.* 2 vols. (3rd ed. Braunschweig: F. Vieweg, 1863–1870; reprint Graz: Akademische Druck- u. Verlagsanstalt, 1959).

[20] Thus Canova, *Iscrizioni e monumenti protocristiani* 383.

[21] Council of Chalcedon, Canon 15. Pierre-Thomas Camelot, *Éphèse et Chalcédoine* (Paris: Editions de l'Orante, 1962). German: *Ephesus und Chalcedon*. Translated by Karl-Heinz Mottausch. GÖK 2 (Mainz: Matthias-Grünewald-Verlag, 1963) 267; Friedrich Lauchert, *Die Kanones der wichtigsten altkirchlichen Concilien nebst den apostolischen Kanones*. SQS 12 (Freiburg: J. C. B. Mohr, 1896; reprint Frankfurt: Minerva, 1961) 93.

[22] The oldest evidence for the ordination of women deacons is Canon 19 of the Council of Nicea (325); cf. the extensive discussion of this canon, with a review of the entire spectrum of research, by Evangelos Theodorou, "Η 'ΧΕΙΡΟΤΟΝΙΑ,' Η 'ΧΕΙΡΟΘΕΣΙΑ' ΤΩΝ ΔΙΑΚΟΝΙΣΣΩΝ," *Theologia* 25 (1954) 430–69, 576–601; 26 (1955) 57–76 (Pages 11ff. in the German translation by Anne Jensen). He discusses the whole mass of source material on the ordination of women deacons and concludes: "From all these witnesses and sources . . . that are investigated in the following chapters with regard to the organic contexts and connections of their content, it appears that the assertion of some investigators that the '*cheirothesia* and installation of the deaconesses in a special ecclesiastical office was already forbidden in the course of the fourth century' . . . is absolutely untenable. They overlook the witnesses to the 'cheirotonia' of deaconesses that extend throughout the entire Byzantine period" (ibid. 17). On this see also ch. 1 above, "The 'Office of Deaconess.'"

[23] Cf. Council of Chalcedon, Canon 14.

[24] Cf., for example, the young widow Olympias, who was ordained deaconess by Nectarius in Constantinople (Sozomen, *Hist. eccl.* VIII, 9).

[25] *SEG* 32 (1983) no. 1504; for this inscription see Michele Piccirillo, *Chiese e Mosaici della Giordania Settentrionale. Disegni di Eugenio Alliata, Cesare Calano, Maurizio Villa.* SBV.CMi 30 (Jerusalem: Franciscan Printing Press, 1981) 31 (plate 19, photo 24), without date; Meimaris, *Sacred Names* 178 n. 891.

[26] Alt, *Inschriften* 23, no. 37.

[27] Meimaris, *Sacred Names* 177 n. 886.

[28] Ibid. 177–78.

[29] For inscriptions of male deacons see Meimaris, *Sacred Names* 165ff., nn. 807–84.

[30] For the marriage of clergy and the history of celibacy in the ancient Church and the early Middle Ages see especially Martin Boelens, *Die Klerikerehe in der Gesetzgebung der Kirche unter besonderer Berücksichtigung der Strafe. Eine rechtsgeschichtliche Untersuchung von den Anfängen der Kirche bis zum Jahre 1139* (Paderborn: Schöningh, 1968); Bernhard Kötting, *Der Zölibat in der Alten Kirche.* Schriften der Gesellschaft zur Förderung der Westfälischen Wilhelms-Universität zu Münster 61 (Münster: Aschendorff, 1970).

[31] Adolf von Harnack, *The Expansion of Christianity in the First Three Centuries.* 2 vols. Translated and edited by James Moffatt (New York: G. P. Putnam's Sons, 1904–05) 2:328.

[32] For Asia Minor as a whole see ibid. 2:326–69; Victor Schultze, *Altchristliche Städte und Landschaften. II. Kleinasien.* 2 vols. (Gütersloh: Gerd Mohn, 1922, 1926); Ulrich Wickert, "Kleinasien," *TRE* 19 (1990) 244–65 (with bibliography). For the edited inscriptions see ch. 1 above.

[33] *MAMA* III (= *Denkmäler aus dem Rauhen Kilikien*. Edited by Josef Keil and Adolf Wilhelm [Manchester: Manchester University Press, 1931]) 120; for what follows see ibid. 120ff. Korykos flourished in the late Roman period and contains more important basilicas

than any other place in Cilicia. On this see Stephen Hill, *The Early Christian Churches of Cilicia*. University of Newcastle upon Tyne, Ph.D. 1984 (11 microfiches), 214.

[34] On this see *MAMA* III, 237.

[35] Lampe, *Lexicon* 353 (II C).

[36] According to *MAMA* III, 208, no. 744: "Above the entrance door to a chamber tomb. Le[tters] 0.05-0.06."

[37] Cf. *MAMA* III, nos. 742, 745, 751.

[38] Cf. *MAMA* III, nos. 69, 217, 347, 489, but always placed first in those inscriptions.

[39] On this see O. Schaefer, "Der Sinn der Rede Jesu von den vielen Wohnungen in seines Vaters Hause und von dem Weg zu ihm (Joh 14, 1-7)," *ZNW* 32 (1933) 210–17.

[40] Lampe, *Lexicon* 880 (4 b).

[41] In other Cilician inscriptions monasteries were called μονηστήριον: cf. *MAMA* III, nos. 101, 102. For monasteries in Cilicia see Hill, *Churches of Cilicia*. See also the inscriptions of the monks: *MAMA* III, nos. 253, 401, 523.

[42] On this and what follows see *Egérie, Journal de Voyage (Itinéraire). Introduction, Texte Critique, Traduction, Notes, Index et Cartes par Pierre Maraval. Valerius du Bierzo, Lettre sur La B^{se} Egérie. Introduction, Texte, et Traduction par Manuel C. Diaz y Diaz*. SC 296 (Paris: Cerf, 1982) 23,2ff. (pp. 226ff.).

[43] For men and women living together in monasteries see Susanna Elm, "Formen des Zusammenlebens männlicher und weiblicher Asketen im östlichen Mittelmeerraum während des vierten Jahrhunderts nach Christus," in Kaspar Elm and Michel Parisse, eds., *Doppelklöster und andere Formen der Symbiose männlicher und weiblicher Religiosen im Mittelalter*. BHSt 18. Ordenstudien VIII (Berlin: Duncker & Humblot, 1992) 13–24; see also the whole of this collected volume.

[44] *MAMA* III, 133, no. 212b; see also the picture on p. 135.

[45] *MAMA* III, 158, no. 395; see also the picture on p. 157.

[46] Thus *MAMA* III, 121 in general concerning these altars in relief.

[47] + Θεοφίλας / διακόνου (*MAMA* III, 161, no. 418; pictured on p. 157).

[48] *MAMA* III, 209, no. 758 (pictured on p. 207). Line 2: Σαμάρισσα instead of Σαμαρῖτις; on this see ibid. Keil and Wilhelm suggest the possibility that Charitina had left the city along with other inhabitants after the overthrow of the rebellion of 529. This hypothesis does make possible an approximate dating of the inscription as not earlier than the sixth century, but there are no other indications to support it.

[49] Cf., in *MAMA* III, nos. 147, 172, 256, 270, 306, 312, as examples. Exceptions are inscriptions that speak of deacons along with their wives or children; cf., for example, *MAMA* III, 299b (a deacon and his wife), 348c (a deacon and his son), 498b (a deacon and his sons).

[50] Horsley, *New Documents* 2:193: "Stele of grey marble; a large cross decorated with ivy tendrils framed within an archway. The text is written beneath the horizontal arms of the cross, on either side of its vertical bar."

[51] Cf. F. T. Gignac, *A Grammar of the Greek Papyri of the Roman and Byzantine Periods*. 2 vols. (Milan: Istituto editoriale cisalpino-La goliardica, 1981) 2:326.

[52] On this see Jürgen Roloff, *Der erste Brief an Timotheus*. EKK XV (Neukirchen-Vluyn: Neukirchener Verlag, 1988) 284.

[53] On this see Horsley, *New Documents* 2:194.

[54] Ibid. In ancient Church literature, surprisingly enough, the verb cannot be found. Cf. Lampe, *Lexicon*.

[55] Thus also Martin Dibelius and Hans Conzelmann, *The Pastoral Epistles*. Translated by Philip Buttolph and Adela Yarbro. Edited by Helmut Koester. Hermeneia (Philadelphia: Fortress, 1972) 75.

[56] Cf. Horsley, *New Documents* 2:194.

[57] Gregory Nazianzus, *Carmina* 2, 1219. For other references cf. Lampe, *Lexicon* 932.

[58] On this see Michaela Puzicha, *Christus peregrinus. Die Fremdenaufnahme (Mt 25,35) als Werk der privaten Wohltätigkeit im Urteil der Alten Kirche*. MBTh 47 (Münster: Aschendorff, 1980) 11ff.

[59] On this see Ulrike Wagener, "Fußwaschung als Frauen-Dienst im frühen Christentum?" *Schlangenbrut* 11/40 (1993) 29–35, and eadem, *Die Ordnung des "Hauses Gottes." Der Ort von Frauen in der Ekklesiologie und Ethik der Pastoralbriefe*. WUNT 65 (Tübingen: Mohr, 1994) 187ff.

[60] For the Johannine foot-washing narrative see Christoph Niemand, *Die Fußwaschungserzählung des Johannesevangeliums. Untersuchungen zu ihrer Entstehung und Überlieferung im Urchristentum*. Studia Anselmiana 114 (Rome: Pontificio Ateneo S. Anselmo, 1993).

[61] On this see Thomas Schäfer, *Die Fußwaschung im monastischen Brauchtum und in der lateinischen Liturgie. Liturgiegeschichtliche Untersuchung*. Texte und Arbeiten I/47 (Beuron: Beuroner Kunstverlag, 1956); Bernhard Kötting, "Fußwaschung," *RAC* 8 (1972) 743–77; Wagener, "Fußwaschung;" Niemand, *Die Fußwaschungserzählung*.

[62] Differently Wagener, "Fußwaschung."

[63] Thus especially Niemand, *Die Fußwaschungserzählung* 177–87, and idem, "Was bedeutet die Fußwaschung: Sklavendienst oder Liebesdienst? Kulturkundliches als Auslegungshilfe für Joh 13,6-8," *Protokolle zur Bibel* 3 (1994) 115–27.

[64] On this see, in detail, Kötting, "Fußwaschung," 761ff.

[65] On this see ibid. 765ff.

[66] John Christopher Thomas, *Footwashing in John 13 and the Johannine Community*. JSNT.S 61 (Sheffield: JSOT Press, 1991).

[67] William M. Ramsay, "The Christian Inscriptions of Lycaonia," *Exp* 12 (1905) 438–59, at 444, who offers no Greek text.

[68] In the *Shepherd of Hermas,* for example, care for widows and orphans appears as a topos of ethical instruction for all the faithful (*Herm. mand.* 8.10; *Herm. sim.* 1.8; 5.3, 7) and primarily as the duty of bishops (*Herm. sim.* 9.27, 2) and deacons (*Herm. sim.* 9.26, 2).

[69] *MAMA* VIII (=*Monuments from Lycaonia, the Pisidio-Phrygian Borderland, Aphrodisias*. Edited by W. M. Calder and J. M. R. Cormack, with contributions from M. H. Ballance and M. R. E. Gough [Manchester: Manchester University Press, 1962]) no. 318: "Zazadin Han. Block with panel. H. 1.14; w. 1.22; letters 0.025 to 0.035."

[70] Cronin ("First Report of a Journey" 359) by contrast refers to literary and inscriptional examples especially from Syria and Egypt.

[71] Examples in ibid. 359.

[72] The epigraphy of these regions of Asia Minor was investigated primarily by William M. Ramsay and William M. Calder. Cf. Ramsay, "Laodicea Combusta and Sinethandos," *AM* 13 (1888) 233–72; idem, "Early Christian Monuments in Phrygia: A Study in the Early History of the Church," *Exp* 8 (1888) 241–67, 401–27; 9 (1889) 141–60, 253–72, 392–400; idem, *The Cities and Bishoprics of Phrygia. Being an Essay of The Local History of Phrygia from the Earliest Times to the Turkish Conquest*. 2 vols. (Oxford: Clarendon Press,

1895, 1897); idem, "Iconium," *Exp* 12 (1905) 193–215, 281–302, 351–69; idem, "The Christian Inscriptions of Lycaonia," *Exp* 12 (1905) 438–59; idem, "The Church of Lycaonia in the Fourth Century," in idem, *Luke the Physician* (London: Hodder and Stoughton, 1980) 329–410; idem, "Phrygian Orthodox and Heretics 400–800 AD," *Byz* 6 (1931) 1–35; Calder, "Philadelphia and Montanism," *BJRL* 7 (1922/23) 309–54; idem, "The Epigraphy of the Anatolian Heresies," in W. H. Buckler and W. M. Calder, eds., *Anatolian Studies, presented to Sir William Mitchell Ramsay* (Manchester: Manchester University Press; London and New York: Longmans, Green, 1923) 59–91; idem, "Leaves from an Anatolian Notebook," *BJRL* 13 (1929) 254–271; idem, "Early-Christian Epitaphs from Phrygia," *AnSt* 5 (1955) 25–38; and the volumes of *MAMA* he edited: *MAMA I: Eastern Phrygia* (Manchester: Manchester University Press, 1928); *MAMA IV: Monuments and Documents from Eastern Asia and Western Galatia*. Edited by W. H. Buckler, W. M. Calder, and W. K. C. Guthrie (Manchester: Manchester University Press, 1933); *MAMA VI: Monuments and Documents from Phrygia and Caria*. Edited by W. H. Buckler and W. M. Calder (Manchester: Manchester University Press, 1939); *MAMA VII: Monuments from Eastern Phrygia* (Manchester: Manchester University Press, 1956); and *MAMA VIII: Monuments from Lycaonia, the Pisidio-Phrygian Borderland, Aphrodisias*. Edited by W. M. Calder and J. M. R. Cormack, with contributions from M. H. Ballance and M. R. E. Gough (Manchester: Manchester University Press, 1962).

[73] Thus also Cronin, "Report of a Journey," 159.

[74] According to *MAMA I* 171, no. 324, with photo. Εἰστρατηγὴς = Στρατηγίς: "The name of the deaconess is Στρατηγίς: the form Ἰστρατηγίς (fem.) occurs in an inscription (324a) of Bulduk in northern Lycaonia (Calder, 1913, 'on a stele with pediment containing a boss. Above the inscription, a defaced male figure and a pruning hook,' Ἰστρατηγὶς Ῥοδαν/ῶ ἀνδρὶ μνήμης / χάριν)" (Calder, *MAMA I* 171).

[75] Ramsay, "Laodicea Combusta," 254–55, no. 65.

[76] According to *MAMA I* 104, no. 194 (photo). (Line 6: Calder: "This block was built into the wall of the heroon mentioned [here]." Line 8: P and Γ instead of H in ligature; the fourth symbol is Λ but the reading Αὐρ. Γλ. makes no sense. Cf. also Ramsay, "Laodicea Combusta," 254–55, no. 65, and idem, "The Church of Lycaonia," 394–95.

[77] On this see Ramsay, "The Church of Lycaonia," 393ff. The deacon Aurelia Leontiane also placed a tombstone, together with her mother, Pribis, and her son, Anenkletos, without any officeholder husband being visible. Since the last line of the inscription has been destroyed we can no longer tell for whom the tomb was intended, whether for the three persons named or for the dead husband, son-in-law, or father: + / Αὐρ. Λεοντιανὴ σὺν τῇ / μ(ητρί) μου Πριβι διάκονος οὔ/σα κὲ τῷ υειῷ μου Ἀνε[ν/κ]λήτου ἀνεστή[σαμεν / . . . (*MAMA I* 172, no. 326 [fig.]).

[78] *MAMA I* 199, no. 383 (photo): + Εὐγένις διά[κων σὺ/ν τῷ υἱῷ μου Μεννέου / ἀνεστήσαμεν τῇ συγ/βίω μου Θέκλης κὲ τ/5 ῇ μητρί μου Ματρώνη / διακονίσσης κὲ τῇ ἀ/δελφῆ μου Λεοντι/ανῆ κὲ τῆς τέκνυς / μοῦ Ματρώνη κὲ Ἐπι/κ]τήτη μνήμης χάριν.

[79] Ἀλέξανδρ/ος πρε(σ)β(ύτερος) τῇ / γλυκυτάτ/η αὐτοῦ μη/ 5 τρὶ Νόννη / διακον[/// / ἀνέσ/τησ[ε]ν μνήμ/ης χάριν. Cf. J. G. C. Anderson, "Exploration in Galatia Cis Halym," *JHS* 19 (1899) 52–134, at 130 no. 155.

[80] *TAM V* no. 643: [+ Ε]ὐγὴ Ἀστερίου τοῦ / [εὐλα]βεστάτου διακόν/[ου .. κ]ὲ τῆς μητρὸς αὐτο/[ῦ Ἐπιφ]ανείας διακονέσης / 5 [.. κὲ το]ῦ υειοῦ αὐτοῦ Ἀστε/[ρίου κ]ὲ παντὸς {τος} τοῦ οἴκ/[ου αὐ]τοῦ. Ἐτελιώθη[. . . On this see Josef Keil and Anton von

Premerstein, *Reisen in Lydien*. 3 vols. DAWW.PH 53/2; 54/2; 57/1 (Vienna: In kommission bei A. Hölder, 1908–1914) 66–67 n. 142; Henri Grégoire, *Recueil des inscriptions grecques chrétiennes d'Asie Mineure 1* (Amsterdam: A. M. Hakkert, 1968; reprint of the Paris edition of 1922) 124 n. 341. Keil/Premerstein and Grégoire read line 1 as: Ε]ὐ[χ]ὴ. In lines 3 and 5 Keil and Premerstein supply the vacancies after διακόνου and διακονέσης with Χρ(ιστοῦ) and date the inscription to the fourth century.

[81] According to *MAMA I* no. 226: "Serai önü, in the wall of the new mosque. Tablet of bluish limestone, H., 0.47; w., 0.74; letters, 0.02 to 0.03. The three upright strokes on the upper border may be part of a cross between two bars."

[82] I am grateful to Volkmar Schmidt for this observation.

[83] On this see *MAMA I* passim.

[84] On this see further examples in H. W. Rose, "The Speaking Stone," *CIR* 37 (1923) 162–63.

[85] *MAMA I* 96, no. 178 (photo), with Latin cross (line 3: κὲ is omitted before Αὐρ.; line 4: υἱὺ = υἱ(οί) stands for τέκνα).

[86] Masa was a common name for women in Asia Minor; cf. the examples in Ladislav Zgusta, *Kleinasiatische Personennamen* (Prague: Verlag der Tschechoslowakischen Akademie der Wissenschaften, 1964) § 875-1; Mamas is a name for a man: cf. ibid. § 850-3.

[87] See, for example, *MAMA I* 177, 182, 185.

[88] *MAMA VIII* 12–13, no. 64. The stone is decorated: "Block with incised tabula ansata. H. 0.87; w. 1.14; th. 0.37; letters 0.025 to 0.03. Above, vine-tendril decoration between quatrefoils or Greek crosses in circles. Outside the upper corners of the panel, set squares with triangular pointers. Below the inscription, two garlands, and between them a Latin cross with oblique appendages and two birds facing each other across the vertical bar." See the photograph in Plate 4. The epithet γλυκυτάτος/η appears frequently in inscriptions from this region: cf. *MAMA VIII* nos. 60, 62, 63. Οὐακα and Γουλασις are female names from Asia Minor: cf. Zgusta, *Personennamen* § 1133-1 and § 233-2.

[89] Thus Calder in *MAMA VII* 13, 12: "Limestone slab with tabula ansata divided into two panels, with a Greek cross on the upper border above either panel, broken on right and below. H. 0.24 (left) to 0.47 (right); w. actual 1.02 (original w. ca. 1.12); th. ca. 0.30; letters, in left panel 0.03 to 0.04; in right panel 0.02 to 0.035."

[90] Cf. ibid., no. 4. David M. Robinson, "Greek and Latin Inscriptions from Asia Minor," *TAPA* 57 (1926) 195–237, sees this as a paraphrase of the Greek Δορκάς.

[91] See ibid. 199, and Calder in *MAMA I*, xxv.

[92] This type of tablet gravestone was common among Encratites in Asia Minor according to Calder, *MAMA I*, xxv, with reference to *MAMA I* no. 175 (with photograph), also published in idem, "The Epigraphy of the Anatolian Heresies," 87 no. 9.

[93] Thus also Robinson, "Inscriptions from Asia Minor," 198–99; *MAMA I*, xxv; *MAMA VII* 12–13. For another Encratite inscription cf. *MAMA VII* no. 96 (and see also Calder, "Two Encratite Tombstones," *ByZ* 30 [1929/30] 645–46, and idem, "Leaves from an Anatolian Notebook," 265).

[94] We should suppose that both inscriptions are about the same woman; so also Robinson, "Inscriptions from Asia Minor," 199. On this see the two almost structurally identical inscriptions on a stone, both of them dedicated by the same man: *MAMA I* no. 175.

⁹⁵ For encratism see Henry Chadwick, "Enkrateia," *RAC* 5 (1962) 343–65, as well as the collective volume edited by Ugo Bianchi, *La tradizione dell' enkrateia. Motivazioni ontologiche e protologiche.* Atti del Colloquio internazionale, Milano, 20–23 aprile 1982 (Rome: Edizioni dell' Ateneo, 1985).

⁹⁶ Basil of Caesarea, *Ep.* 188, 1; 199, 47 (Roy J. Deferrari, ed., *Saint Basil. The Letters, with an English Translation.* 4 vols. LCL [Cambridge, Mass.: Harvard University Press, 1950–1961] 3:16, 130).

⁹⁷ Calder has interpreted "Phrygia Kekaumene" as the region around Laodicea Combusta, which was within the Phrygian territory of the province of Pisidia and in which he was able to locate a great many inscriptions from schismatic groups including those that pointed to an encratite milieu. On this see Calder, "The Epigraphy of the Anatolian Heresies," with examples.

⁹⁸ Epiphanius, *Panarion* 47, I, 2, 3, 5, 6, 7 (*The Panarion of St. Epiphanius, Bishop of Salamis. Selected Passages.* Translated by Philip R. Amidon [New York and Oxford: Oxford University Press, 1990] 168).

⁹⁹ Cf., for example, Irenaeus, *Adv. haer.* I, 28 (tracing their origins to Saturninus and Marcion); Hippolytus, *Philos.* 8, 13.

¹⁰⁰ Cf. Calder, "Two Encratite Tombstones;" *MAMA VII* 19, no. 96.

¹⁰¹ *Cod. Theod.* 16, 5, 7. 11.

¹⁰² From *TAM* IV/1 355. Sencer Sahin, "Neue Inschriften von der bithynischen Halbinsel," *ZPE* 18 (1975) 27–48, at 46: "Marble sarcophagus; it was taken from the ruins of a church in Kirazli near the village of Kabaoglu and brought to the village, where it was used as a collecting trough in the spring house. The dimensions of the remains are: height 0.41 m.; width 3 m.; depth 0.75 m.; height of letters 0.065 m."

¹⁰³ This would be similar to the way in which the deacon in another inscription had restored a coffin at community expense: [τ]ὴν [π]ύελ[ο]ν ταύτην [δ]απά[ν]ῃ [τ]ῆς π[ό]λεως ἀνε[νε]ωσά[μην; cf. *TAM* IV/1 366.

¹⁰⁴ Of the twenty-three Christian inscriptions edited in *TAM* IV, three mention deacons, including this one for the deacon Eugenia, one for a male deacon, and a third inscription in which the name of the deacon (female or male) has not been preserved because of damage to the stone. In addition we find the name of a bishop and the son of a presbyter (*TAM* IV/1 368, 359, 358, 352).

¹⁰⁵ On this see the commentary by A. N. Sherwin-White, *The Letters of Pliny: Historical and Social Commentary* (1966; reissued [with corrections] Oxford: Clarendon Press, 1985) 691ff., with bibliography.

¹⁰⁶ Pliny, *Ep.* X, 96, 8 (see R. C. Kukula, ed., *C. Plini Caecili Secundi. Epistularum Libri Novem, Epistularum ad Traianum Liber Panegyricus* [Leipzig: Teubner, 1912] 317).

¹⁰⁷ Sherwin-White, *The Letters of Pliny* 708.

¹⁰⁸ Ambrosiaster, *Ad Rom.* 16,1 (CSEL 83, 476–77).

¹⁰⁹ Martimort, *Deaconesses* 26, refers to this passage.

¹¹⁰ Justin, *Apol.* 1.65, 5 (Gustav Krüger, *Die Apologien Justins des Märtyrers.* SQS I/1 [4th competely revised ed. Tübingen: Mohr, 1915] 56, 24ff.)

¹¹¹ Women are also mentioned in this connection in 1 Tim 3:11.

¹¹² We find three instances of διάκονος: Paula, Aurelia Leontiane, and Aurelia Faustina; four of διακόνισσα: Elaphia, Nune, Matrona, and Amia; once δι (Charitina); once

διακ (Masa); once διακο (Strategis). Another, but uncertain instance of the use of the title διακόνισσα in Lycaonia is the marble fragment discovered between Lystra and Carsamba Su: [- - -]ουν / [- - - ?κα]ὶ τὴν / [- - δια]κόνισ/[σαν - - -] (*MAMA* VIII 16, no. 91).

[113] The widespread use of the official title διάκονος for women even as late as the sixth century indicates that women must be understood to be included in summary references to διάκονοι.

[114] Another review of the *Bulletin Epigraphique* would permit the material to be expanded at will.

[115] Evangelos Theodorou, "Berühmte Diakonissen der byzantinischen Zeit," in *ΙΣΤΟ-ΡΙΑ ΚΑΙ ΘΕΩΡΙΑ ΤΗΣ ΕΚΚΛΗΣΙΑΣΤΙΚΗΣ ΚΟΙΝΩΝΙΚΗΣ ΔΙΑΚΟΝΙΑΣ* (Athens, 1985) 147–64 (from p. 13 of the German translation by Anne Jensen): In a "monastery that is known even today in Greece as the Christian catacomb of Milos, probably built at the end of the second century and in use until the end of the fifth century."

[116] From Margherita Guarducci, *Epigrafia Greca* IV, 368–69: "Melo, sulla parete di una grotta. Epigrafe con lettere dipinte in rosso su fondo bianco, dentro la sagoma di un cartiglio ansato. Le righe di scrittura sono separate fra loro da tratti orizzontali." (An apple tree on the wall of a cave. Epigraph in red on a white background, behind it an open scroll. The rows of writing are separated by horizontal lines.)

[117] But cf. Gignac, *Grammar* 2:363–64.

[118] Cf. Henri Grégoire, *Recueil des inscriptions grecques chrétiennes d'Asie Mineure 1* (Amsterdam: A. M. Hakkert, 1968; reprint of the Paris edition of 1922) 62. Another example of an inscription from Melos introduced by EN K(ΥΡΙ)Ω is found in *IG* XII/3 1239.

[119] Hans Achelis, "Spuren des Urchristentums auf den griechischen Inseln?" *ZNW* 1 (1900) 87–100, at 90, and Kaufmann, *Handbuch der altchristlichen Epigraphik* 159 interpret Agalliasis as a man's name; Grégoire, *Recueil* 63, and Guarducci, *Epigrafia Greca* IV, 369 correct the interpretation.

[120] See chapter 5 A above.

[121] For virgins in the ancient Church and early Middle Ages see Joseph Wilpert, *Die gottgeweihten Jungfrauen in den ersten Jahrhunderten der Kirche. Nach den patristischen Quellen und den Grabdenkmälern dargestellt* (Freiburg: Herdersche Verlagshandlung, 1892); Hans Achelis, *Virgines subintroductae. Ein Beitrag zu I Kor VII* (Leipzig: J. C. Hinrichs, 1902); Hugo Koch, *Virgines Christi. Die Gelübde der gottgeweihten Jungfrauen in den ersten drei Jahrhunderten.* TU 31/2 (Leipzig: J. C. Hinrichs, 1907) 59–112; Iniga Feusi, *Das Institut der Gottgeweihten Jungfrauen. Sein Fortleben im Mittelalter.* Diss. phil. (Fribourg, 1917); Gabriele Konetzny, "Die Jungfrauenweihe," in Teresa Berger and Albert Gerhards, eds., *Liturgie und Frauenfrage. Ein Beitrag zur Frauenforschung aus liturgiewissenschaftlicher Sicht.* PiLi 7 (St. Ottilien: EOS Verlag, 1990) 475–92; Gisela Muschiol, "'Psallere et legere.' Zur Beteiligung der Nonnen an der Liturgie nach den frühen gallischen 'Regulae ad Virgines,'" in ibid. 77–125.

For virginity in the ancient Church and its emancipatory function for women cf. Rosemary Radford Ruether, "Misogynism and Virginal Feminism in the Fathers of the Church," in eadem, ed., *Religion and Sexism. Images of Women in the Jewish and Christian Traditions* (New York: Simon & Schuster, 1974) 150–83; Jo Ann McNamara, "Sexual Equality and the Cult of Virginity in Early Christian Thought," *FS* 3 (1976) 145–58; Dennis R. MacDonald, "Virgins, Widows, and Paul in Second Century Asia Minor," *SBL Seminar Papers*

1979, 169–84; Ross S. Kraemer, "The Conversion of Women to Ascetic Forms of Christianity," *Signs* 6 (1980) 298–307; Alfred Schindler, "Askese und Mönchtum als Mittel der Emanzipation im antiken Christentum," *Schritte ins Offene* 12 (1982) 7–8; Elizabeth Castelli, "Virginity and its Meaning for Women's Sexuality in Early Christianity," *JFSR* 2 (1986) 61–88; Virginia Burrus, *Chastity as Autonomy. Women in the Stories of the Apocryphal Acts.* SWR 23 (Lewiston, N.Y., and Queenston, Ontario: Edwin Mellen, 1987); Turid Karlsen Seim, "Ascetic Autonomy? New Perspectives on Single Women in the Early Church," *StTh* 43 (1989) 125–40.

[122] Thus Horsley, *New Documents* 4 (1987) 239.

[123] From Jean-Pierre Michaud, "Chronique des fouilles et découvertes archéologiques en Grèce en 1973," *BCH* 98 (1974) 579–722, at 625. See especially the reproduction of the mosaic (fig. 116). Votive inscription incorporated in a mosaic.

[124] Rudolf M. Kloos, *Einführung in die Epigraphik des Mittelalters und der frühen Neuzeit* (Darmstadt: Wissenschaftliche Buchgesellschaft, 1980) 60. On this see Denis Feissel, *Recueil des inscriptions chrétiennes de Macédoine du IIIe au VIe siècle.* BCH Supplément 8 (Paris: Dépositaire, Diffusion de Boccard, 1983) 231, who prints three other mosaic inscriptions from Stobi whose dedicators are named: No. 276: a certain Peristeria has had a mosaic prepared in accordance with a vow (4th c.); No. 279: list of men and women in a mosaic (4th–5th c.); No. 280: list of women's names (4th–5th c.).

[125] Cf. Emilian Popescu, "Griechische Inschriften," in Friedhelm Winkelmann and Wolfram Brandes, eds., *Quellen zur Geschichte des frühen Byzanz (4.–9. Jahrhundert). Bestand und Probleme.* BBA 55 (Amsterdam: Gieben, 1990) 81–105, at 97.

[126] For this and what follows see Karl S. Frank, "Gelübde IV. Katholische Überlieferung und Lehre," *TRE* 12 (1984) 305–309, at 307.

[127] From Feissel, *Macédoine* 231 no. 275 (plate LXII); cf. James Wiseman, *Stobi. A Guide to the Excavations* (Belgrade: Published by the University of Texas at Austin and the National Museum of Titov Veles with a publication grant from the Smithsonian Institution, 1973) 59–61; Horsley, *New Documents* 2:194–95 no. 109 n.

[128] Guarducci, *Epigrafia Greca* IV, 345: "Parte superiore di una stele arrotondata, rotta in tre pezzi combacianti, con una lacuna nel mezzo. Il frammento di destra sembra presentare la fine dell' epigrafe. In alto, al di sopra della medesima, spicina una Croce latina a rilievo, incassata nella pietra." (The upper part of a rounded stele, broken in three pieces that fit together, with a gap in the center. The fragment on the right seems to give the end of the epigraph. Above the center piece a Latin cross appears in relief, deeply set into the stone.)

[129] Horsley, *New Documents* 4:239 n. 1; cf. also *CIG* IV 9318; Charles Bayet, *De titulis Atticae christianis antiquissimis. Commentatio historica et epigraphica* (Paris, 1878) 113–14 no. 105; *IG* III/2 3527.

[130] From E. Mastrocostas, "Παλαιοχριστιανικαὶ βασιλικαὶ Δρυμοῦ Βονίτσης" (sic). *Athens Annals Arch* 4 (1971) 185–95, at 188; cf. also the photograph on p. 189.

[131] On this see Daniele Foraboschi, *Onomasticon alterum papyrologicum. Supplemento al Namenbuch di Friedrich Preisigke.* TDSA 16, Serie papirologica 2 (Milan: Istituto editoriale Cisalpino, 1967).

[132] See above, 158–60.

[133] Feissel, *Macédoine* 204: "Marble stele on a pediment, copied by Heuzey in the 'eastern district of Philippi' and now lost."

¹³⁴ Feminine of Παγχάρης: cf. Friedrich Bechtel, *Die historischen Personennamen des Griechischen bis zur Kaiserzeit* (Halle: M. Niemeyer, 1917).

¹³⁵ Feissel, *Macédoine* no. 225.

¹³⁶ See the instances in Lampe, *Lexicon*.

¹³⁷ Wolf-Dieter Hauschild, ed., *Basilius von Caesarea. Briefe. 2. Teil (Nr. 95–213), eingeleitet, übersetzt und erläutert v. Wolf-Dieter Hauschild.* BGrL 3 (Stuttgart: A. Hiersemann, 1973) 172 n. 194.

For canonesses see K. Heinrich Schäfer, *Die Kanonissenstifter im deutschen Mittelalter. Ihre Entwicklung und innere Einrichtung im Zusammenhang mit dem altchristlichen Sanktimonialentum.* KRA 43, 44 (Stuttgart: F. Enke, 1907), and idem, "Kanonissen und Diakonissen. Ergänzungen und Erläuterungen," *RQ* 24 (1910) II, 49–90; Gertrud Wegener, *Geschichte des Stiftes St. Ursula in Köln.* Veröffentlichungen des Kölnischen Geschichtsvereins e.V. 31 (Cologne: Historisches Archiv, 1971) 9, 107; Petra Heidebrecht and Cordula Nolte, "Leben im Kloster: Nonnen und Kanonissen. Geistliche Lebensformen im frühen Mittelalter," in Ursula A.J. Becher and Jörn Rüsen, eds., *Weiblichkeit in geschichtlicher Perspektive. Fallstudien und Reflexionen zu Grundproblemen der historischen Frauenforschung.* STW 725 (Frankfurt: Suhrkamp, 1988) 79–115; Anna Ulrich, "Die Kanonissen. Ein vergangener und vergessener Stand der Kirche," in Teresa Berger and Albert Gerhards, eds., *Liturgie und Frauenfrage,* 181–94.

¹³⁸ Cf. Lampe, *Lexicon* 701, with the occurrence.

¹³⁹ *MAMA* I no. 375; VII no. 79.

¹⁴⁰ *IGLS* 1130 (a group burial); 9283.

¹⁴¹ Charalampos Bakirtzis, "Exposition des Antiquités Paléochrétiennes au Musée des Philippes," *Athens Annals of Archaeology* 13 (1980) 90–98, at 95.

¹⁴² Peter Pilhofer, *Philippi I: Die erste christliche Gemeinde Europas.* WUNT 87 (Tübingen: Mohr, 1995) 144, also suggests "cashier" here and, with some reservations, defines it as "church custodian."

¹⁴³ Valerie Abrahamsen, "Women at Philippi: The Pagan and Christian Evidence," *JFSR* 3 (1987) 17–30, at 23.

¹⁴⁴ On this see the extended treatment in Abrahamsen, "Women at Philippi," especially p. 28.

¹⁴⁵ Feissel, *Macédoine* 40: "Copied at Hagia Triada, the stone has disappeared. . . . Two birds surrounding a pattee cross inscribed in a circle. Only Mordtmann transcribes a second cross above the first."

¹⁴⁶ Ἀγαθόκλεια was a common name in the imperial period.

¹⁴⁷ According to Feissel, *Macédoine* 40.

¹⁴⁸ Similar is the formula for the deacon Joulios in Feissel, *Macédoine* no. 19.

¹⁴⁹ A. Ἀκακίου + μάρτυρος / B. [---]ανη[..]ις + διακονίσ[σης] / C. (faint traces), according to Feissel, *Macédoine* 214: "Basilica on the agora. Subterranean vault containing three tombs, discovered 21 July 1950 next to the foundations of the north wall of the narthex. At the center is the tomb of the martyr (A); to the north that of a deaconess (B); to the south tomb (C). The inscriptions are painted in black on a brown background on the east side of each tomb. Height of the letters 4 (A); 4.4 (B) and 5 (C)." For this fragment see also *BCH* 75 (1951) 158–60 (no author identified).

¹⁵⁰ Ibid. 214.

¹⁵¹ See also the inscription of the Macedonian deacon Matrona from Stobi, fourth century, mentioned above.

[152] This is true also for the seven male deacons from the fifth and sixth centuries whom Feissel lists in *Macédoine:* Nos. 16, 19, 130B, 133, 139, 255, and 285. Another inscription marks a group tomb for deacons from a single church (no. 138), and in one diavkono~ inscription (no. 218) the name has been destroyed.

[153] See this description also in the inscription for the teacher Theodora from Beroea (fifth-sixth centuries): see ch. 4 B above.

[154] Kaufmann, *Handbuch der altchristlichen Epigraphik* 294, gives no information about the place where this inscription originated. The description of Domitius as *arcarius sanctae sedis apostolicae adque papae* points to Rome.

[155] *ICUR* n.s. II 4788 (G. B. de Rossi, completed and edited by Angelus Silvagni et al., *Inscriptiones christianae urbis Romae septimo saeculo antiquiores.* New series. 11 vols. [Rome: Ex Officina Libraria Doct. Befani, 1922–1985]). Kaufmann, *Handbuch der altchristlichen Epigraphik* 294, considers it considerably more recent than 539.

[156] Kaufmann, *Handbuch der altchristlichen Epigraphik* 294.

[157] Thus Frank, "Gelübde IV," 307.

[158] *Cod. Just.* 1.3.9 *(diaconissa);* Conc. Araus., canon 25 (26) *(diacona).*

[159] Thus Martimort, *Deaconesses* 202. He asserts that there is no doubt that this inscription is from the sixth century, though he gives no reasons. This assumption fits best with his hypothesis that there were no deaconesses in the West before the sixth century.

[160] From *ILCV* 1239. *CIL* III 13845: "Lapis Tiburtinus long. 7 ped. 6. poll., alt. 10 poll., crass. 1 ped. 3 1/2 poll.; Docleae rep. beside the gateway facing the west front of the small church."

[161] Conc. Aurel., canon 17 (CCSL 148A, 101).

[162] Kaufmann, *Handbuch der altchristlichen Epigraphik* 294.

[163] From *ILCV* 1238.

[164] Conc. Nem., canon 2 (CCSL 148, 50).

[165] Lewis and Short (= Andrews, E. A. *A Latin Dictionary Founded on Andrews' Edition of Freund's Latin Dictionary.* Revised, enlarged, and in great part rewritten by Charlton T. Lewis, Ph.D., and Charles Short [Oxford: Clarendon Press, 1991, from the 1879 original]) present a Christian instance of "levites," and define it as "deacon."

[166] Conc. Araus., canon 25 (26) (CCSL 148, 84).

[167] Conc. Epaon., canon 21 (CCSL 148, 29)

[168] Conc. Aurel., canon 18 (CCSL 148A, 101).

[169] See, as representative of these, Martimort, *Deaconesses* 187ff.

[170] For full discussion see ibid.

[171] Felice Grossi Gondi, *Trattato di epigrafia cristiana latina e greca del mondo romano occidentale. I. Monumenti Cristiani dei Primi sei Secoli I* (Rome: Università Gregoriana, 1968; reprint of the 1920 edition) 152 includes one other inscription: Cod. Vatic. 9072, f. 425.

[172] K. Heinrich Schäfer, "Kanonissen und Diakonissen," 64–65, had determined as early as 1910, after a thorough analysis of his sources, that "after all this we may again emphasize that the office of deaconess was also known and was at home at least from the sixth to the eleventh centuries in the West, in Gaul, Italy, and Rome itself; that the consecration of deaconesses was practiced here as well as in the Eastern Church, and not as a mere imitation, but as an indigenous office rooted in previous centuries. . . . In light of these passages it does not appear to me to be possible to dispute the presence of Western deaconesses and

the practice of ordaining them, at least in individual communities in Gaul and Italy, from the fourth century onward."

An extensive evaluation of all the literary sources for women deacons in the Latin Church is found in Martimort, *Deaconesses* 187ff.

VIII. Bishops

A. Inscriptions

Inscription for femina episcopa

Italy / Umbria / Interamna   ca. 500

BIBLIOGRAPHY:

CIL XI 4339 (Bormann, Eugen, ed. *Corpus Inscriptionum Latinarum,* vol. XI. *In-scriptiones Aemiliae, Etruriae, Umbriae Latinae* [Berlin: G. Reimerus, 1888–1926]).

Grossi Gondi, Felice. *Trattato di epigrafia cristiana latina e greca del mondo romano occidentale. I. Monumenti Cristiani dei Primi sei Secoli I* (Rome: Università Gregoriana, 1968; reprint of the 1920 edition) 153.

ILCV 1:1121 and add.; 2:512.

Kalsbach, Adolf. "Diakonisse," *RAC* 3 (1957) 917–28, at 926.

Morris, Joan. *The Lady was a Bishop. The Hidden History of Women with Clerical Ordination and the Jurisdiction of Bishops* (New York and London: Macmillan, 1973) 6.

Irvin, Dorothy. "The Ministry of Women in the Early Church: The Archaeological Evidence," *DDSR* 45 (1980) 76–86, at 81.

+ hunc [titulum nostrum],
si uis, cog[n]o[sce, uia]
tor: hic requie[scit]
uenerabilis fem[ina]
5   episcopa Q[. . .].
depos. in pace V[. . .]
+ Olybrio[1]

Line 6: *depos(ita)*
Line 5: Diehl in *ILCV* 1:1121 reads *qua[e uix. a.*
Line 7: *anno* 491 or 526.[2]

If you will, traveler, recognize this inscription: here rests the venerable Lady
Bishop . . . interred in peace . . .

  This tomb poem stems from Umbria toward the turn from the fifth to the
sixth century. The name of the *episcopa* has been destroyed. In scholarship this
woman has regularly been interpreted as the wife of a bishop,[3] although the
text of the inscription contains no reference at all to a husband.

  The epithet *venerabilis* is found in another *episcopus* inscription from Umbria.[4] As a rule it was applied to clergy but was not reserved to them exclusively.[5]

  This inscription fits within the context of the more or less contemporary
sacerdota inscription and the *presbytera* inscriptions from Dalmatia, southern
Italy, and Sicily. In addition, cultic activity by women is attested for southern
Italy and Sicily by a letter of Gelasius I from 494.[6] Against that background it
is possible to consider that this woman was consecrated a bishop.[7]

  A literary example from the Latin West attests an *episcopia*. This is Canon
14 of the Council of Tours (567), where we read that a bishop (male) who has
no bishop (female) may have no women in his entourage *(Episcopum epis-
cop[i]am non habentem nulla sequatur turba mulierum)*.[8] In this canon the wife
of the bishop is not called simply *coniux,* as, for example, in Canon 13 of the
same council, but *episcop(i)a*. Brian Brennan has linked this finding with Gregory of Tours' (538/39–594) *Historiae,* which contain stories about bishops'
wives.[9] An analysis of Gregory's text, however, shows that while he can offer
extensive accounts of bishops' wives he does not apply the title *episcopa* to
them. He simply calls a bishop's wife *coniux*.[10] There is thus no other instance
in Latin literature of a bishop's wife being titled *episcopa*.[11] We must conclude
from this that as a rule the title *episcopa* was not applied to bishops' wives.

Theodora episcopa

  Two additional inscriptions testify to an *episcopa* who can be proven not
to have been a bishop's wife. This is the *episcopa* Theodora, the mother of
Pope Paschal I. In the *Liber Pontificalis* the father of this pope, Bonosus, is
mentioned without any official title. He was therefore neither a bishop nor
clothed with any other Church office.[12]

  Pope Paschal I (817–824)[13] is known for having engaged in an active
building program during his pontificate. He restored the churches of Santa
Maria in Dominica, Santa Cecilia in Trastevere, and Santa Prassede. On the
eastern flank of the church of Santa Prassede he built the chapel of St. Zeno
and had it decorated with mosaics.[14] This building was erected in the spirit of
the Carolingian Renaissance at the beginning of the ninth century, which
called for a *renovatio* of the Christian art and culture of the fourth century.[15] In

the chapel of St. Zeno there are two inscriptions, one a mosaic and one on a reliquary, attesting the *episcopa* Theodora.

(a) The Mosaic Inscription

Italy / Rome / Santa Prassede / Chapel of St. Zeno   IX[1]

BIBLIOGRAPHY:

Rossi, Giovanni Battista de. *Musaici Cristiani e Saggi dei Pavimenti delle Chiese di Roma anteriori al secolo XV* (Rome: Guglielmo Haass, 1899) 4 (plate XXVII).

Andrieu, Michel. *Les Ordines Romani du Haut Moyen Age.* Vol. 4 (SSL 28) (Louvain: Spicilegium Sacrum Lovaniense Administration, 1956) 145.

Klass, Margo Pautler. *The Chapel of S. Zeno in S. Prassede in Rome.* Ph.D. Bryn Mawr, 1972, 22–23.

Morris, Joan. *The Lady was a Bishop. The Hidden History of Women with Clerical Ordination and the Jurisdiction of Bishops* (New York and London: Macmillan, 1973) 4–6.

Irvin, Dorothy. "The Ministry of Women in the Early Church: The Archaeological Evidence," *DDSR* 45 (1980) 76–86, at 79ff. (plate I).

Asmussen, Marianne Wirenfeldt. "The Chapel of S. Zeno in S. Prassede in Rome," *ARID* 15 (1986) 67–86, at 79 (fig. 4).

Wisskirchen, Rotraut. *Die Mosaiken der Kirche Santa Prassede in Rom.* With color photographs by Franz Schlechter. Zaberns Bildbände zur Archäologie 5 (Mainz: P. von Zabern, 1992) 56–57 (plates 44, 57, 58, 62).

TEPISCOPA
H
E
O
D
O
[R
A][16]

Rotraut Wisskirchen describes the mosaic as follows: "In the lower niche one sees, on the upper part of the lunette, the Lamb on the mountain of Paradise flanked by two stags and two hinds, and on the lower part the bust of *Theodora episcopa,* labeled as such, as well as those of Praxedes, Mary, and Pudentiana."[17] In this mosaic Theodora is depicted with a rectangular halo, ordinarily used to designate living persons of high rank.[18] She is shown on the left next to saints Praxedes and Pudentiana. The woman between these two is

Mary, the mother of Jesus. Above Theodora's head is inscribed "episcopa," and to the left of her portrait is her name, Theodo[ra]; the last two letters of the name are no longer legible.

According to Ursula Nilgen the letters in Theodora's name are smaller than those in the other mosaic inscriptions in the chapel of St. Zeno. On the other hand, there are no traces of restoration in the questionable part of the mosaic.[19] A reliquary tablet, also found in the chapel of St. Zeno, attributes the title *episcopa* to Theodora in the same way, and in addition says that she is the mother of Paschal I. In light of this inscription we may suppose that the chapel of St. Zeno housed the tomb of the *episcopa* Theodora.

(b) The Reliquary Inscription

Italy / Rome / Santa Prassede / Chapel of St. Zeno   IX[20]

BIBLIOGRAPHY:

Duchesne, Louis M. O., ed., *Le Liber Pontificalis. Texte, Introduction et Commentaire.* 2 vols. (Paris: E. de Boccard, 1955) II, 64.

Rossi, Giovanni Battista de. *Musaici Cristiani e Saggi dei Pavimenti delle Chiese di Roma anteriori al secolo XV* (Rome: Guglielmo Haass, 1899) 4 (plate XXVI).

Marucchi, Orazio. *Basiliques et Eglises de Rome* (Paris: Desclée, 1902) 325–26.

Andrieu, Michel. *Les Ordines Romani du Haut Moyen Age.* Vol. 4 (SSL 28) (Louvain: Spicilegium Sacrum Lovaniense Administration, 1956) 145.

Ferrua, Antonio. "Il Catalogo dei Martiri di S. Prassede," *RPARA* 30–31 (1957–1959) 129–40.

Siegwart, Josef. *Die Chorherren- und Chorfrauengemeinschaften in der deutschsprachigen Schweiz vom 6. Jahrhundert bis 1160. Mit einem Überblick über die deutsche Kanonikerreform des 10. und 11. Jh.* SF n.s. 30 (Fribourg: Universitätsverlag, 1962) 51–52.

Klass, Margo Pautler. *The Chapel of S. Zeno in S. Prassede in Rome.* Ph.D. Bryn Mawr, 1972, 166–67.

Morris, Joan. *The Lady was a Bishop. The Hidden History of Women with Clerical Ordination and the Jurisdiction of Bishops* (New York and London: Macmillan, 1973) 5–6.

Nilgen, Ursula. "Die große Reliquieninschrift von Santa Prassede. Eine quellenkritische Untersuchung zur Zeno-Kapelle," *RQ* 69 (1974) 7–29.

Brennan, Brian. "'Episcopae': Bishops' Wives Viewed in Sixth-Century Gaul," *ChH* 54 (1985) 311–23, at 322.

Wisskirchen, Rotraut. *Die Mosaiken der Kirche Santa Prassede in Rom.* With color photographs by Franz Schlechter. Zaberns Bildbände zur Archäologie 5 (Mainz: P. von Zabern, 1992) 57.

Lines 36–41:

....QVOCIRCA ET IN IPSO
INGRESSV BASILICAE MANV DEXTRA VBI VTIQVE
BENIGNISSIMAE SVAE GENETRICIS SCILICET DOM
NAE THEODORAE EPISCOPAE CORPVS QVIESCIT CON
40   DIDIT IAMDICTVS PRAESVL CORPORA VENERABILI
VM HAEC . . .[21]

Therefore the aforenamed Praesul has placed at the very entrance of the basilica, on the right side, where the body of his most gracious mother, the Lady Theodora, the bishop, rests, the following bodies of those worthy of reverence."[22]

    This inscription, containing a total of fifty-six lines, concerns the translation of relics of the saints planned for July 20, 817 (lines 8-9), that is, during the first year of Paschal I's papacy. The first part of the inscription contains the names of a long list of Church officials, popes, bishops, presbyters, and deacons (lines 10-16). There follows another long list of names of martyrs (lines 16-30). The list of martyrs is followed by the names of virgins and widows (lines 31-37). Next comes the text quoted above, concerning the bishop Theodora, which shows that the tomb of this woman was located next to the entrance to the basilica. Then come the names of the presbyter Zeno and other officeholders and martyrs.

    Theodora is more closely described as the most gracious mother of the Praesul named above *(benignissimae suae genetricis . . . iamdictus praesul).* This was Pope Paschal I (lines 2-3). Her description as *domna,* i.e., *domina* Theodora expresses the high regard in which she was held. The placement of the word *episcopa* after this woman's name indicates its titulary character. Theodora therefore had the title *episcopa* as a title of office[23]—a finding that has evoked a great deal of consternation in the reception of this inscription. This is certainly the reason why the official title *episcopa* is frequently omitted in verbal reproductions of the inscription.[24] Rotraut Wisskirchen also characteristically forgets this puzzling title in her translation of vv. 37-41.[25]

    As we have shown above, the title *episcopa* is constantly interpreted by scholars in accordance with Canon 14 of the Council of Tours as an honorific title for bishops' wives. In the case of Theodora, however, that interpretation is certainly inaccurate. Theodora was definitely not the wife of a bishop, as is clear from the mention of Bonosus, the father of Paschal I, in the *Liber Pontificalis.* Bonosus is named without any official title, which proves that he was not a bishop. This finding has led to confusion among scholars. The interpretations have gone in three directions:

(a) Theodora's title of *episcopa* is interpreted as an honorific designation. The title is said to show that, as the mother of a pope, she took the position of a wife at her son's side.[26] The reasons for the granting of such a title of honor could have been Theodora's financial support for the church of Santa Prassede. Her characterization as *benignissima* could be interpreted in the same fashion. *Benigna* not only means "gracious" in the sense of a woman's character, but also "beneficent" as regards her deeds.[27]

(b) Theodora is interpreted as the head of a group of virgins and widows. The listing of virgins and widows in the inscription (lines 31-36) could favor this: NOMINA QVOQVE VIRGINVM SCILICET / ET VIDVARVM. PRAXEDIS PVDENTIANAE / IVLIANAE SIMFEROSAE FELICVLAE MARINAE / CANDIDAE PAVLINAE DARIAE BASILLAE PAV / LINAE MEMMIAE MARTHAE EMERENTIANAE / ZOE ET TIBVRTIADIS. However, the women thus named are not immediately connected to Theodora *episcopa,* which would have been natural if she were their head.

Charles Du Cange suggested that Theodora was an abbess, since he thought that an abbess could also be called *episcopa.*[28] However, against this is the fact that there is neither a literary nor an epigraphical instance of an abbess being titled *episcopa.* The title of abbess was already common in the ninth century, and it could have been included in the inscription if Theodora had been an abbess.[29] Her title of *episcopa* distinguishes her quite clearly from abbesses.

(c) Ursula Nilgen considers the possibility of a later interpolation of the title *episcopa.* Her source-critical investigation has shown that the inscription in its present condition is the result of repeated restorations,[30] as is evident especially from the addition of a second tablet after line 37. Nilgen considers the upper part of the inscription, consisting of the first thirty-seven lines, to be authentic; she assigns it to the time of Paschal I himself. The tablet added just below, probably because of needed restoration, she believes was an expansion from the Quattrocento, imitating both the form of the letters and the wording of the original text, but not to be "regarded literally as an authentic document."[31]

In this connection she considers the possibility of a later interpolation of the title *episcopa,* a title that for her is "incomprehensible." She does not exclude the idea that the title might have been inserted in the Quattrocento as "bowdlerization of an illegible passage in the original."[32] This attempt to eliminate the problem of interpreting the title *episcopa* is not persuasive, primarily because Theodora is called *episcopa* not once, but twice in the chapel of St. Zeno.[33] Besides, the interpolation hypothesis still does not obviate the necessity of interpreting the title.

Nowhere in scholarship does one encounter the suggestion that Theodora might have been a consecrated Roman bishop.[34] Against such an interpretation is the uniqueness of this finding of a bishop in Rome, and especially the fact that for Rome in particular, at the center of the Church's hierarchical structuring in the garments of orthodoxy, a woman bishop is almost unimaginable. Nevertheless, the possibility should not be altogether excluded, especially if we consider the kinds of feuds the bishops and popes of Rome pursued against one another, and the means they employed against each other especially in the ninth century.[35] In other words, there was no more a uniform Catholic Church in Rome than there was in the provinces.

In summary we may say that the meaning of the title *episcopa* in connection with Theodora cannot be determined with absolute certainty. Only one thing is sure: that this woman must have deserved well of the community at the church of Santa Prassede, something that was honored with the title *episcopa* and handed down both in a mosaic and in a reliquary inscription. Her official activity as a bishop in Rome should not be excluded in principle.[36]

B. Women Bishops in the Early Church

The New Testament resources on the office of the ἐπίσκοποι are surprisingly sparse (Phil 1:1; Acts 20:28; 1 Tim 3:2; Titus 1:7) in view of the importance achieved by that office in the Church from the third century onward.[37] In the letters of Paul ἐπίσκοποι are mentioned just once, in a prescript (Phil 1:1), and no information can be drawn from that passage about the service to the community described by the word.[38] Something similar may be said of the reference to ἐπίσκοποι in Acts 20:28.[39] It is only in the deutero-Pauline Pastoral letters that ἐπίσκοποι are more closely defined in the course of a systematization of the ecclesial constitution. Even here their outlines remain extremely vague (1 Tim 3:1-7). What Eduard Lohse has written about the constitution of the New Testament communities is especially applicable to the early Christian episcopal office: "The earliest Christian documents, collected in the canon of the New Testament, contain only sparse information about the external forms of early Christian community life. Both the beginnings of a Church constitution and the development it underwent in the first two generations of early Christianity are shrouded in darkness, dimly illuminated only by a few hints that can be drawn from those sources . . . ."[40] Hans Lietzmann's epigraphical researches have shed some light on the community activities associated with the title ἐπίσκοπος, which are scarcely to be reconstructed at all from the New Testament texts. Lietzmann has shown that in Greco-Roman society ἐπίσκοποι were public officials with a broad variety of functions, but frequently entrusted with administrative duties.[41] In this context it seems probable that the ἐπίσκοποι mentioned in Phil 1:1 are to be understood as the community administrators.[42]

In the framework of this study we must raise the question whether women were also among the Christian ἐπίσκοποι in the New Testament period. No woman is attested with this title in the New Testament, but neither is any man. Thus bishops, female or male, are not identifiable as persons in the New Testament period. Consequently we can only lay out the possible duties of ἐπίσκοποι and discuss whether women were also active in the communities in those ways. As the parallels from Greco-Roman antiquity indicate, the office of the ἐπίσκοποι was primarily administrative in nature.

If we are to discuss the administrative activities required by early Christianity it is appropriate to consider the structure of those early communities, which was primarily shaped by the existence of house churches.[43] These house churches were led by the head of the household. Floyd V. Filson has pointed out that "the house church was the training ground for the Christian leaders who were to build the church after the loss of 'apostolic' guidance, and everything in such a situation favored the emergence of the host as the most prominent and influential member of the group."[44] Leadership of the house churches, with its technical administrative and economic duties, was therefore an early form of the office of ἐπίσκοπος.

The appropriateness of this observation for the context of the Pauline tradition is evident especially from the development around the end of the first and beginning of the second century as revealed in 1 Timothy: The community is described theologically in categories derived from the ethics of the Greco-Roman household codes.[45] The ἐπίσκοπος took on the role of the steward of God's household (Titus 1:7).[46] In the early period these tendencies toward an extraordinarily hierarchical conception of the Church as the household of God as proposed by 1 Timothy are not yet perceptible. For example, the disorders in Corinth that are obvious in 1 Corinthians 11–14 illustrate the fact that there was not yet a fixed system of order involving clearly defined functions and offices.[47]

It is significant in this connection that not only Paul's letters but also later ones such as those of Ignatius from the second century give evidence of women as leaders of house churches. In Paul's time Prisca in particular emerges as the head of such a church (1 Corinthians 16:19). Hans-Josef Klauck has emphasized the significance of Prisca for the early Christian mission in the context of her house church: "She developed her far-reaching influence on the basis of her house church. We have no body of information about any other early Christian house church to compare with this one."[48] House churches led by women are also attested in the following decades: those of Nympha (Col 4:15),[49] Tavia (Ign. *Smyrn.* 13.2),[50] or the widow of Epitropus (Ign. *Pol.* 8.2). In the context of the posited modeling of the episcopacy on the functions of the head of the household it is possible to imagine Prisca and the other women as ἐπίσκοποι.[51]

As already indicated, the organization of the house churches entered into the Pastorals, was modified, and was then applied to the Church as a whole. The *locus classicus* for a New Testament episcopal or supervisory office (ή ἐπίσκοπή) is 1 Tim 3:1-7, the most extensive New Testament statement about this office. It is all the more astonishing that the author does not describe the functions of these officeholders, or of the deacons: "It is certainly striking that he here gives neither a theological basis for the offices of bishop and deacon nor a description of their duties. He restricts himself to listing the qualifications for applicants for these offices, whereby the almost total lack of any spiritual criteria provides a further surprise."[52]

In the paraenesis for bishops (1 Tim 3:1-7) it is apparent that the office of overseer is to be restricted to men. In the list of virtues that should belong to those who aspire to this office the perspective is that of a man: it is proposed that the bishop should be "the husband of one wife" (1 Tim 3:2).[53] Although the restriction of the office to men is not expressly stated, the formulation at least suggests it. Add to this that women who exercise this office are not referred to specifically, as is the case in the following section on διάκονοι (1 Tim 3:11).[54] Within the episcopal paraenesis there are no references to women as exercising such an office. This observation suggests that in the communities addressed by the Pastorals the office of ἐπίσκοπος was no longer to be open to women, an observation that corresponds to the general tendency of the Pastorals, which attempt to effect a drastic reduction in the authority and functions of women within the communities.[55]

In subsequent centuries this tendency in the Pastorals was generally successful, as is evident from the silence of the Greek inscriptions. To date, insofar as the field can be surveyed, no Greek inscription has survived attesting to a woman as ἐπίσκοπος. The development of a monarchic episcopate, which culminated in the third century[56]—that is, in the period when the testimony of Christian inscriptions begins—was certainly a further factor that manifested the expulsion of women from that office.

That need not mean, however, that women did not exercise the duties of presiders, for example as presbyters[57] or enrolled widows, even after the third century in the Church communities of the East. Hans Achelis has demonstrated the probability, as shown above, that in the *Didascalia Apostolorum* the enrolled widows exercised episcopal functions and thus represented competition for the male bishop. This document is at the same time an impressive example of the effort to put down such official authority exercised by women.[58]

In the second century we have literary evidence from Epiphanius of women bishops among the Montanists. His reference shows that the exclusion of women from the episcopal office was not the aim of all Christian groups.[59] In Christian communities in which the Spirit was more important than theological and social norms that denigrated women and attempted to restrict them to domestic activity it was evidently not problematic that women had authority in the Church.

It remains to consider the point that Johannes Neumann has emphasized: "Of the multitude of bishops in the first five centuries we know only relatively few by name. Still smaller is the number of those of whom we know at least some dates. These are for the most part those who were especially prominent in the exercise of their office (as organizers, authors, or confessors)."[60] Thus we should not be too hasty in generalizing the concept of the Pastorals, which aimed at restriction of the authority of women, to the whole of early Church history. We cannot exclude in principle the possibility that the names of women bishops of the early period have simply not been preserved; the same is true for the great majority of the names of men as well.

Martin Leutzsch has suggested that the Grapte mentioned in the second-century *Shepherd of Hermas*[61] might have been a bishop in Rome.[62] In the *Shepherd of Hermas* this woman is responsible for conveying (νουθετήσει) the message of penance to the widows and orphans (*Herm. Vis.* II. 4, 3). Together with her, a certain Clement is also mentioned as a bearer of this message, which is central to the *Shepherd;* he is to send it to the communities at a distance. The matter-of-fact way in which a woman is presented among the group of those responsible for proclaiming the message of penitence shows that women were active in leadership and teaching within the Roman community.[63]

In the first half of the second century a monarchic episcopate in Rome was neither reality nor pretension.[64] At this period the community at Rome was led by presbyters (τῶν πρεσβυτέρων τῶν προϊσταμένων τῆς ἐκκλησίας, *Herm. Vis.* II. 4. 3) from whom, most probably, the ἐπίσκοποι were recruited.[65] As Norbert Brox emphasizes, all that is said in detail of the ἐπίσκοποι is "their persuasive social concern" (*Herm. Sim.* IX. 27, 2).[66] Grapte, like Clement, appears without an official title, so that we can say nothing with certainty about her office in the community. She must have been either a bishop or a deacon because in *Shepherd of Hermas* those two offices are given primary responsibility for care of the widows (*Herm. Sim.* IX. 26, 2; 27, 2).[67] Most commentators interpret Grapte—in line with an androcentric paradigm according to which women are unimaginable as bishops—as deacon of the Roman community.[68] In light of Grapte's prominent mention by name alongside Clement and the presbyters, as well as her assignment to instruct the widows and orphans, however, we should consider the possibility that Grapte was one of the bishops in Rome.[69]

We find that women are not explicitly attested as bishops in early Christian literature. We may take it, as regards the beginnings of the episcopal office, that it was a service of administration and supervision that women exercised in their roles as presiders over house churches. Women such as Prisca and Nympha can be thought of in this sense as ἐπίσκοποι of the early period who in that role performed administrative duties and had responsibility for care of the community. In the first half of the second century 1 Tim 3:1-7 shows that women were to be excluded from this office, a tendency that, judging by the sparse evidence pointing to women bishops, appears to have largely succeeded in the Christian churches.

This conclusion should not, however, obscure the fact that there were Christian groups, such as the Montanists, that did install women as bishops. In addition, on the basis of epigraphical evidence we can posit that women exercised the office of bishop in the Great Church in Rome and in the Roman provinces. The epigraphically attested women bishops are constantly interpreted by scholars as the wives of bishops, in the context of the Catholic paradigm that does not entertain the possibility of female bishops. Nevertheless, the bishop Theodora, with her attestation in the chapel of St. Zeno in the church of Santa Prassede in Rome, was certainly not the wife of a bishop, but the mother of Pope Paschal I. Other Latin inscriptions from Italy and Dalmatia make it probable that women were active there as bishops in the fifth and sixth centuries. This is supported by the epigraphically attested women presbyters of the fourth to sixth centuries in the West, as well as by literary evidence from a later period that attacks, and thereby confirms, the sacerdotal activity of women.[70]

Notes

[1] From *ILCV* 2:1121, p. 512 (in its corrected version). *CIL* XI 4339: "Lapis marmoreus semiesus (. . .) Ex. coemeterio basilicae Valentinianae (. . .)."

[2] *CIL* XI 4339; *ILCV* 1:1121.

[3] Thus *CIL* XI 4339; Felice Grossi Gondi, *Trattato di epigrafia cristiana latina e greca del mondo romano occidentale. I. Monumenti Cristiani dei Primi sei Secoli I* (Rome: Università Gregoriana, 1968; reprint of the 1920 edition) 153; *ILCV* 1:1121; Adolf Kalsbach, "Diakonisse," *RAC* 3 (1957) 917–28, at 926.

[4] *ILCV* 1:1032.

[5] For other inscriptions that apply the epithet *venerabilis* to clergy see *ILCVI* 489 (Rome: . . . v̄v̄. . . . pb̄ro. . .); 973,1 (Rome: praesul . . . venerabilis . . .); 1156 n. (Rome: . . . v. prb. . . .); 1076,1 (Gaul: . . . venerabilis . . . prior p̄r̄b̄r̄ . . .); 1153 (. . . vir venerabilis presbyter . . .); 1174 (between Ragusa and Narona: venera(bilis) . . . p̄r̄b̄.); 1152 n. (Ravenna: viri

vv. presbb.); 1937b (Ravenna: dmn. vrb. . . . arc. episc.); *ILCV* 2:3851 (Capua: . . . b̄b̄. . . . p̄r̄b̄. . . .); 3866 (Rome: . . . benerabilis abbatissa . . .). On this see also Grossi Gondi, *Trattato di epigrafia cristiana* 155.

   [6] See ch. 5 B above.

   [7] So also Joan Morris, *The Lady was a Bishop. The Hidden History of Women with Clerical Ordination and the Jurisdiction of Bishops* (New York and London: Macmillan, 1973) 6, and Dorothy Irvin, "The Ministry of Women in the Early Church: The Archaeological Evidence," *DDSR* 45 (1980) 76–86, at 81 interpret her as "woman bishop" and not as the wife of a bishop.

   [8] Conc. Turon., canon 14 (13) (CCSL 148A, 181).

   [9] Brian Brennan, "'Episcopae': Bishops' Wives Viewed in Sixth-Century Gaul," *ChH* 54 (1985) 311–23.

   [10] Gregory of Tours, *Historiarum libri decem, Zehn Bücher Geschichten, post Brunonem Krusch, auf Grund der Übersetzung W. Griesebrechts neubearb. von Rudolf Buchner.* 2 vols. AQDGMA (Darmstadt: Wissenschaftliche Buchgesellschaft, 1955) II, 17 (in this ed. 1:98,27); IV, 36 (in this ed. 1:246,6); VIII, 39 (in this ed. 2:214,26). For Gregory of Tours' stories and the images of women he thus expresses see Werner Affeldt and Sabine Reiter, "Die Historiae Gregors von Tours als Quelle für die Lebenssituation von Frauen im Frankreich des sechsten Jahrhunderts," in Annette Kuhn, ed., *Frauen in der Geschichte VII. Interdisziplinäre Studien zur Geschichte der Frauen im Frühmittelalter. Methoden – Probleme – Ergebnisse.* Geschichtsdidaktik. Studien Materialien 39 (Düsseldorf: Pädagogischer Verlag Schwann, 1986) 192–208, with additional literature.

   [11] On this see also *Thesaurus Linguae Latinae, editus auctoritate et consilio Academiarum quinque Germanicarum Berolinensis Gottingensis Lipsiensis Monacensis Vindobonensis.* 10 vols. (Leipzig: Teubner, 1900–) 675, 676.

   [12] Louis M. O. Duchesne, ed., *Le Liber Pontificalis. Texte, Introduction et Commentaire.* 2 vols. (Paris: E. de Boccard, 1955) 2:54.

   [13] See especially *Liber Pontificalis* 2:54ff. See also Heinrich Böhmer, "Paschalis I," *RE³* 14 (1904) 716–71; Johannes Fried, "Die Päpste im Karolingerreich von Stephan III. bis Hadrian II.," in Martin Greschat, ed., *Das Papsttum I. Von den Anfängen bis zu den Päpsten in Avignon.* GK 11 (Stuttgart: Kohlhammer, 1984) 115–28, at 122–23.

   [14] Rotraut Wisskirchen, *Das Mosaikprogramm von S. Prassede in Rom. Ikonographie und Ikonologie.* JAC.E 17 (Münster: Aschendorff Verlagsbuchhandlung, 1990) 55. The next note contains bibliography for the chapel of St. Zeno.

   [15] See in detail Margo Pautler Klass, *The Chapel of S. Zeno in S. Prassede in Rome.* Ph.D. Bryn Mawr, 1972; Marianne Wirenfeldt Asmussen, "The Chapel of S. Zeno in S. Prassede in Rome," *ARID* 15 (1986) 67–86; Wisskirchen, *Das Mosaikprogramm von S. Prassede;* eadem, *Die Mosaiken der Kirche Santa Prassede in Rom.* With color photographs by Franz Schlechter. Zaberns Bildbände zur Archäologie 5 (Mainz: P. von Zabern, 1992).

   [16] See the illustrations in ibid., pp. 62, 64: plates 57, 58, and 62.

   [17] Ibid. 56.

   [18] Ursula Nilgen, "Die große Reliquieninschrift von Santa Prassede. Eine quellenkritische Untersuchung zur Zeno-Kapelle," *RQ* 69 (1974) 7–29, at 25 n. 60.

   [19] Ibid., 27 n. 63. However, the author does not entirely exclude the possibility of a restoration before 1877, oriented to the picture on the reliquary.

[20] Nilgen, "Reliquieninschrift," 8–10, discusses the question of dating at length. According to Nilgen the date incorporated in lines 8-9 of the inscription, 20 July 817, does not refer to the execution of the inscription or the completion of the translation, "but, as the text makes clear, only to the first placement of relics beneath the high altar or in the crypt" (ibid. 25).

[21] From Nilgen, "Reliquieninschrift," 29 n. 8: "The tablet, measuring 224 x 89 cm., is composed of two plates, a larger one of white marble above (37 lines) and a smaller of grey-flecked marble ('pavonazzetto') beneath (19 lines). The whole, but especially the central and lower part, contains countless cracks, yet the fragments have been carefully put together, with small missing pieces supplied, using marble or stucco ...." The whole text of the inscription reads:

1   + IN N̄ DN̄I D̄I SALV̄ NR̄I IH̄V XP̄I. TEMPORIBVS SC̄IS
     SIMI AC TER BEATISSIMI ET APOSTOLICI D̄N PASCHALIS
     PAPAE INFRADVCTA SVNT VENERANDA SC̄ORVM COR
     PORA IN HANC SC̄AM ET VENERABILEM BASILICAM
5   BEATAE XP̄I VIRGINIS PRAXEDIS. QVAE PRAEDICTVS
     PONTIFEX DIRVTA EX CYMITERIIS SEV CRYPTIS IACEN
     TIA AVFERENS ET SVB HOC SACROSC̄O ALTARE SVMMA
     CVM DILIGENTIA PROPRIIS MANIBVS CONDIDIT. IN MEN
     SE IVLIO DIE. XX. INDICTIONE DECIMA.
10 NOMINA VERO PONTIFICVM HAEC SVNT. VRBA
     NI STEPHANI ANTHERI MELTIADIS FAVIANI IVLII PON
     TIANI SIRICII LVCII XYSTI FELICIS ANASTASII ET CAELESTINI
     ITEM NOMINA EPISCOPORVM. STRATONICI LEVCII ET
     OPTATI. QVAMQVAM PRESBITERORUM ET LEVITARV̄.
15 NICOMEDIS ARCHIP̄BRI IVSTINI ET CYRINI. CYRIACI DIA
     CONI NEMESII ATQVE IACHEI. ETIAM ET MARTY
     RVM NOMINA ISTA SVNT. ZOTICI HERENEI IACHIN
     THI AMANTII MARI AVDIFAX ABBACV AC SC̄ORVM
     OCTINGENTORVM QVORVM NOMINA SCIT ŌMPS.
20 CASTVLI FELICIS MILITIS GORDIANI EPIMACHI SERVI
     LIANI SVLPICII DIOGENIS BASTI ET ALII LXII. MARCEL
     LIANI MARCI FESTI ET ALII DVO. TERTULLINI FAVSTI BO
     NOSI MAVRI CALVMNIOSI IOHANNIS EXSVPERANTII
     CASTI CVRILLI ET SEPTEM GERMANOS. HONORATI
25 THEODOSII BASILII CRESCENTII LARGI SMARAG
     DI CRESCENTIONIS IASONIS MAVRI YPPOLITI
     PONTIANI CHRYSANTI ET ALII LXVI. SIMVL
     QVE ET ALII MILLE CENTVM VIGINTI QVATTVOR
     QVORUM NOMINA SVNT IN LIBRO VITAE. MAVRI
30 ARTHEMII POLIONIS ET ALII SEXAGINTA DVO MAR
     TYRES. NOMINA QVOQVE VIRGINVM SCILICET
     ET VIDVARVM. PRAXEDIS PVDENTIANAE
     IVLIANAE SIMFEROSAE FELICVLAE MARINAE
     CANDIDAE PAVLINAE DARIAE BASILLAE PAV
35 LINAE MEMMIAE MARTHAE EMERENTIANAE

ZOE ET TIBVRTIADIS. QVOCIRCA ET IN IPSO
INGRESSV BASILICAE MANV DEXTRA VBI VTIQVE
BENIGNISSIMAE SVAE GENETRICIS SCILICET DOM
NAE THEODORAE EPISCOPAE CORPVS QVIESCIT CON
40   DIDIT IAMDICTVS PRAESVL CORPORA VENERABILI
VM HAEC. ZENONIS PRESBITERI ET ALIORVM
DVORVM. PARITERQVE ET IN ORATORIO BEATI
IOHANNIS BAPTISTAE MANV LEVA PRAENOMINA
TAE BASILICAE QVI ET SECRETARIUM ESSE DINOSCI
45   TVR CONDIDIT CORPORA SCILICET. MAVRI ET ALI
ORVM QVADRAGINTA MARTYRVM.
SIMILI MODO ET IN ORATORIO BEATAE X̄P̄Ī VIRGINIS
AGNETIS QVOD SVRSVM IN MONASTERIO SITVM
EST IPSE PASTOR EXIMIVS POSVIT CORPORA PIORVM
50   MARTYRVM VIDELICIT. ALEXANDRI PAPAE
ATQVE EVENTII ET THEODVLI PRESBITERIS.
HOS OMNES D̄Ī ELECTOS FREQVENTIVS DEPRE
CANS QVATENVS PER EORVM VALEAT PRECES
SVAE POST FVNERA CARNIS AD CAELI CONSCEN
55   DERE CVLMEN. AMEN
FIVNT ETIAM INSIMVL OMNES S̄C̄Ī DVO MILIA CCC

[22] From Wisskirchen, *Die Mosaiken der Kirche Santa Prassede* 57, but with the addition of the title "bishop," which she has characteristically forgotten.

[23] For the post-placement of official titles in this inscription see, for example, lines 3, 15–16, and 41.

[24] See Nilgen, "Reliquieninschrift," 20–21, with examples.

[25] See Wisskirchen, *Mosaiken der Kirche Santa Prassede* 57.

[26] Andrieu, *Les Ordines Romani* 4:145 n. 1.

[27] On this see Karl Ernst Georges, *Ausführliches lateinisch-deutsches Handwörterbuch. Aus den Quellen zusammengetragen und mit besonderer Bezugnahme auf Synonymik und Antiquitäten unter Berücksichtigung der besten Hilfsmittel.* 2 vols. (Darmstadt: Wissenschaftliche Buchgesellschaft, 1988; reprint of the 8th ed. [1913], revised and expanded by Heinrich Georges) 814, who first gives the meaning "gracious" as to character; so also Albert Sleumer, *Kirchenlateinisches Wörterbuch.* With the cooperation of Joseph Schmid (Hildesheim, Zürich, and New York: G. Olms, 1990; reprint of the edition at Limburg a. d. Lahn: Gebrüder Steffen, 1926) 157; Edwin Habel and Friedrich Gröbel, eds., *Mittellateinisches Glossar.* With an Introduction by Heinz-Dieter Heimann (2nd ed. Munich, Vienna, and Zürich, 1989 [unrevised reprint]) 36 include *benignus* exclusively as meaning "amiable in character." Lewis and Short (E. A. Andrews, *A Latin Dictionary Founded on Andrews' Edition of Freund's Latin Dictionary.* Revised, enlarged, and in great part rewritten by Charlton T. Lewis, Ph.D., and Charles Short [Oxford: Clarendon Press, 1991, from the 1879 original]) 232, in contrast, write "more freq. of action, *beneficent.*"

[28] Charles D. Du Cange, *Glossarium mediae et infimae latinitatis.* 5 vols. (Graz: Akademische Druck- und Verlagsanstalt, 1954; reprint of the edition of 1883–1887) 2:275–76.

[29] The earliest dated epigraphic example of an abbess is from the basilica of St. Agnes in Rome, from the year 514: + *hic requiescit in pace* + / *Serena abbatissa s(acra) u(irgo), / quae uixit annus pm. LXXXV* / $\overline{dep}$. $\overline{Gll}$ $\overline{id}$. $\overline{Mai}$. *Senatore* / + *uc. cons.* + (so *ILCV* 1650; cf. also Johann Peter Kirsch, "Anzeiger für christliche Archäologie," *RQ* 16 [1902] 76–85, at 80; Carl Maria Kaufmann, *Handbuch der altchristlichen Epigraphik* [Freiburg: Herder, 1917] 290; Henri Leclercq, "Ama," *DACL* I/2 [1924] 1306–1323, at 1313ff. [fig. 307]; Pasquale Testini, *Le catacombe e gli antichi cimitieri cristiani in Roma*. RC 2 [Bologna: Cappelli, 1966] 208 [fig. 85]).

For the office of abbess see especially Leclercq, "Ama," (with numerous epigraphical examples); Hilarius Emonds, "Äbtissin," *RAC* 1 (1950) 126–28; Haye van der Meer, *Priestertum der Frau? Eine theologiegeschichtliche Untersuchung*. QD 42 (Freiburg, Basel, and Vienna: Herder, 1969) 142–58 (treating especially the jurisdictional authority of the abbesses); Morris, *The Lady Was a Bishop;* Elisabeth Gössmann, "Frauen in der Kirche ohne Sitz und Stimme? Oder: Roma locuta – causa non finita sed disputanda," in Norbert Greinacher and Hans Küng, eds., *Katholische Kirche – wohin? Wider den Verrat am Konzil* (Munich: Piper, 1986) 295–306, especially 301–302. There is a collection of a good many lives of abbesses of the sixth to eighth centuries in English translation in Jo Ann McNamara and John E. Halborg, with E. Gordon Whatley, eds. and translators, *Sainted Women of the Dark Ages* (Durham, N.C.: Duke University Press, 1992).

[30] Nilgen, "Reliquieninschrift," 27.

[31] Ibid. 28.

[32] Ibid. 21.

[33] Consequently Nilgen, ibid. 27, must also interpret the mosaic inscription as a possible interpolation.

[34] The only exceptions are Irvin, "Ministry of Women," 79–80, and Karen Jo Torjesen, *When Women Were Priests. Women's Leadership in the Early Church and the Scandal of their Subordination in the Rise of Christianity* (San Francisco: HarperSanFrancisco, 1993) 19; however, they do not develop their statements.

[35] For the struggles surrounding Paschal I see Böhmer, "Paschalis I."

[36] For the more or less contemporary "Pope Joan" see Joan Morris, *Pope John VIII: an English Woman alias Pope Joan* (London: Vrai, 1985); Elisabeth Gössmann, "Die 'Päpstin Johanna.' Zur vor- und nachreformatorischen Rezeption ihrer Gestalt," in Elisabeth Gössmann and Dieter R. Bauer, eds., *Eva: Verführerin oder Gottes Meisterwerk? Philosophie- und theologiegeschichtliche Frauenforschung*. Hohenheimer Protokolle 21 (Stuttgart: Akademie der Diözese Rottenburg-Stuttgart, 1987) 143–66; eadem, "Zur Rezeptionsgeschichte der Gestalt der Päpstin Johanna," in Elisabeth Moltmann-Wendel, ed., *Weiblichkeit in der Theologie. Verdrängung und Wiederkehr* (Gütersloh: Gerd Mohn, 1988) 93–111; and most recently and at length eadem, *Mulier Papa. Der Skandal eines weiblichen Papstes. Zur Rezeptionsgeschichte der Gestalt der Päpstin Johanna*. APTGF 5 (Munich: Iudicium, 1994).

[37] For the episcopal office in the New Testament and in the ancient Church see especially Hermann Wolfgang Beyer and Heinrich Karpp, "Bischof," *RAC* 2 (1954) 394–407; Alfred Adam, "Die Entstehung des Bischofsamtes," *WuD* 5 (1957) 104–29; Ernst Dassmann, "Zur Entstehung des Monepiskopats," *JAC* 17 (1974) 74–90; Josef Hainz, "Die Anfänge des Bischofs- und Diakonenamtes," in idem, ed., *Kirche im Werden. Studien zum Thema Amt und Gemeinde im Neuen Testament* (Munich, Paderborn, and Vienna: Schöningh, 1976) 91–107; Josef Blank and Bogdan Snela, "Priester/Bischof," *NHThG* 3 (1985)

411–41; Eduard Lohse, "Die Entstehung des Bischofsamtes in der frühen Christenheit," *ZNW* 71 (1980) 58–73; Johannes Neumann, "Bischof. I. Das katholische Bischofsamt," *TRE* 6 (1980) 653–82; Raymond E. Brown, "Episkopē and Episkopos: The New Testament Evidence," *TS* 41 (1980) 322–38; Reinhard M. Hübner, "Die Anfänge von Diakonat, Presbyterat und Episkopat in der frühen Kirche," in Albert Rauch and Paul Imhof, eds., *Das Priestertum in der einen Kirche. Diakonat, Presbyterat und Episkopat.* Regensburger Ökumenisches Symposion 1985, *Koinonia IV* (Aschaffenburg: Kaffke, 1987) 45–89.

[38] Philippians 1:1 is the oldest NT occurrence of ἐπίσκοποι. In the prescript to Philippians, contrary to his usual practice, Paul expands the list of addressees (usually just the community itself) to include ἐπίσκοποι καὶ διάκονοι. This instance is puzzling because there is no other mention of ἐπίσκοποι in Paul's letters, nor do we find the absolute usage of διάκονοι elsewhere in Paul's writings. Thus no certain information about the significance and functions of the ἐπίσκοποι can be derived from Paul's letters. The fact of this expanded prescript, unusual for Paul, has led scholars to posit that the bishops and deacons were a later interpolation: cf. most recently Wolfgang Schenk, *Die Philipperbriefe des Paulus. Kommentar* (Stuttgart: Kohlhammer, 1984) 34ff.

[39] On this see Rudolf Schnackenburg, "Episkopos und Hirtenamt. Zu Apg 20,28" (1949) in Theological Faculty of the University of Munich, eds., *Episcopus. Studien über das Bischofsamt. FS f. Michael Kardinal von Faulhaber zum 80. Geburtstag* (Regensburg: Gregorius-Verlag, 1949) 66–88. He suggests that the title ἐπίσκοπος was not so much the designation of an office as the description of an activity, and asserts: "Nowhere does Luke use ἐπίσκοπος as the designation for an early Christian office of presider, so familiar to us" (p. 67). He points out that Acts 1:20 speaks of ἐπισκοπή in connection with the apostolate. Cf. also Hans-Joachim Michel, *Die Abschiedsrede des Paulus an die Kirche Apg 20,17-38. Motivgeschichte und theologische Bedeutung.* StANT 35 (Munich: Kösel, 1973).

[40] Lohse, "Die Entstehung des Bischofsamtes," 60–61.

[41] Hans Lietzmann, "Zur altchristlichen Verfassungsgeschichte," *ZWTh* n.s. 20 (1914) 97–153, at 101ff.; Martin Dibelius, *An die Thessalonicher I, II; an die Philipper.* HNT 11 (3rd rev. ed. Tübingen: Mohr, 1937) 51ff.

[42] In this vein see, for example, Ernst Lohmeyer, *Die Briefe an die Philipper, an die Kolosser und an Philemon.* KEK IX (11th ed. Göttingen: Vandenhoeck & Ruprecht, 1956) 12: "The duties of the apostles, prophets, and teachers are 'charismatic' in nature; those of 'aiding and leading' are technical and practical. The latter must, then, have been entrusted to the episkopoi and deacons: to the latter the function of 'giving aid,' that is, probably here at the end of the letter where thanks are given for the collection the reference is to gathering alms, and to the former the function of administering and distributing them."

[43] On this see Floyd V. Filson, "The Significance of the Early House Church," *JBL* 58 (1939) 105–12; Willy Rordorf, "Die Hausgemeinde der vorkonstantinischen Zeit" (1971) in idem, *Lex orandi, lex credendi. Gesammelte Aufsätze zum 60. Geburtstag.* Paradosis 36 (Fribourg: Universitätsverlag, 1993) 190–237; Hans-Josef Klauck, *Hausgemeinde und Hauskirche im frühen Christentum.* SBS 103 (Stuttgart: Katholisches Bibelwerk, 1981); Werner Vogler, "Die Bedeutung der urchristlichen Hausgemeinden für die Ausbreitung des Evangeliums," *ThLZ* 107 (1982) 785–94; Marlis Gielen, "Zur Interpretation der Formel ἡ κατ᾽ οἶκον ἐκκλησία," *ZNW* 77 (1986) 109–25.

Klauck, in *Hausgemeinde und Hauskirche* 101–102, summarizes his study of the early Christian house churches in these words: "It would be difficult to overestimate the importance of house churches during the early Christian period. The house church was, we may say in summary, the foundational center and cornerstone of the local church, the base for mission, the place of assembly for the Lord's Supper, the space for prayer, the place of catechetical instruction, the crucial instance of Christian brotherhood and sisterhood. The Church of the beginning constituted itself 'house by house.' . . . The distribution of roles within a house church, in part connected to external circumstances (the function of the host, for example, or the higher estimation of the woman of the house) was an essential factor in the development of offices in the Church."

[44] Filson, "Early House Church," 112.

[45] On this see especially Marlis Gielen, *Tradition und Theologie neutestamentlicher Haustafelethik. Ein Beitrag zur Frage einer christlichen Auseinandersetzung mit gesellschaftlichen Normen.* Athenäums Monografien. Theologie 75 (Frankfurt: Hain, 1990), and Ulrike Wagener, *Die Ordnung des "Hauses Gottes." Der Ort von Frauen in der Ekklesiologie und Ethik der Pastoralbriefe.* WUNT 65 (Tübingen: Mohr, 1994) 15ff.

[46] On this see in detail Jürgen Roloff, *Der erste Brief an Timotheus.* EKK XV (Neukirchen-Vluyn: Neukirchener Verlag, 1988) 148ff.

[47] On this see Ernst Käsemann, "Amt und Gemeinde im Neuen Testament" (1960) in idem, *Exegetische Versuche und Besinnungen* (6th ed. Göttingen: Vandenhoeck & Ruprecht, 1970) 1:109–34; Ferdinand Hahn, "Charisma und Amt. Die Diskussion über das kirchliche Amt im Lichte der neutestamentlichen Charismenlehre," *ZThK* 76 (1979) 419–49.

[48] Klauck, *Hausgemeinde und Hauskirche* 26.

[49] On this see, in detail, ibid. 44ff.

[50] Ignatius greets "the household of Tavia." Tavia appears to have been an important woman in the community at Smyrna, as is evident from her being mentioned in this short list of greetings. She was not a widow; otherwise Ignatius would surely have described her as he does, for example, the "widow of Epitropus" (Ign. *Pol.* 8.2). Tavia thus apparently lived in her household community without a husband, and she was the head of the household.

[51] Luise Schottroff, "Die Frauen haben nicht geschwiegen. Über Prophetinnen, Apostelinnen und Bischöfinnen im frühen Christentum," in *". . . das Weib rede in der Gemeinde." Maria Jepsen: Erste lutherische Bischöfin. Dokumente und Stellungnahmen.* GTB 1118 (Gütersloh: Gerd Mohn, 1992) 41–48, at 45, suggests Prisca as a possible bishop against the background of the tradition about her activity in Ephesus (Acts 18:26) and thus in connection with the ἐπίσκοποι of Ephesus, described as shepherds (Acts 20:17-35).

[52] Thus Roloff, *Der erste Brief an Timotheus* 159, accurately summarizes the case.

[53] This formula has caused puzzlement among scholars; on this see ibid. 155–56.

[54] Of course it has been much discussed among scholars whether the women there mentioned are wives of the deacons or are themselves deacons, but we must agree with Jürgen Roloff, who discusses these arguments at length and concludes: "It should be impossible in future to doubt that the 'women' referred to are female deacons and not, for example, the wives of the male deacons mentioned in vv. 8-10, 13" (ibid. 164).

[55] On this see above, ch. 4 C.

[56] Thus Neumann, "Bischof."

[57] On these see ch. 5 A above.

[58] On this see ch. 6 B above.

[59] Epiphanius, *Panarion* 49, 2, 5; on this see, in detail, ch. 5 A above.

[60] Neumann, "Bischof," 659.

[61] The *Shepherd of Hermas* is a document written probably ca. 140 C.E. in Rome. It is frequently cited to describe conditions in Rome. On this see especially Norbert Brox, *Der Hirt des Hermas*. KAV 7 (Göttingen: Vandenhoeck & Ruprecht, 1991) 22ff.

[62] See Martin Leutzsch, *Die Wahrnehmung sozialer Wirklichkeit im "Hirten des Hermas."* FRLANT 150 (Göttingen: Vandenhoeck & Ruprecht, 1989) 161 n. 26.

[63] Brox, *Hirt des Hermas* 108, regards this finding in traditional fashion as a transitional phenomenon: "In *PH* (and then certainly in the Roman Church of his time) women play a striking role, but these are simply 'transitional phenomena'; 'the free customs of the earliest time persisted longer only on the fringes of the Church and among the outsiders.'"

[64] Ibid. 535. On this see especially Peter Lampe, *From Paul to Valentinus. Christians at Rome in the First Two Centuries* (Minneapolis: Fortress, 2000) 396–406.

[65] On this see Brox, *Hirt des Hermas* 533ff.; Lampe, *From Paul to Valentinus* 396–406.

[66] See Brox, *Hirt des Hermas* 534–35.

[67] For the social conflicts among the Roman Christians that can be discerned in *Shepherd of Hermas* see Lampe, *From Paul to Valentinus* 92–101; Leutzsch, *Die Wahrnehmung sozialer Wirklichkeit*.

[68] Thus Lietzmann, "Zur altchristlichen Verfassungsgeschichte," 173; Martin Dibelius, *Der Hirt des Hermas*. HNT Ergänzungsband 4 (Tübingen: J.C.B. Mohr, 1923) 454; Hans von Campenhausen, *Kirchliches Amt und geistliche Vollmacht in den ersten drei Jahrhunderten*. BHTh 14 (Tübingen: J.C.B. Mohr [Paul Siebeck], 1953; 2nd rev. ed. 1963) 103; Leutzsch, *Die Wahrnehmung sozialer Wirklichkeit* 161; Brox, *Hirt des Hermas* 108 remains undecided. Differently Leopold Zscharnack, *Der Dienst der Frau in den ersten Jahrhunderten der christlichen Kirche* (Göttingen: Vandenhoeck & Ruprecht, 1902), who interprets Grapte as a community widow.

[69] Thus also Leutzsch, *Die Wahrnehmung sozialer Wirklichkeit* 161 n. 26.

[70] See the detailed discussion in ch. 5 B above.

IX. Stewards

A. Inscriptions

Inscription for the steward Doxa

Asia Minor / Isauria Nova / Dorla   V[1]

BIBLIOGRAPHY:

Ramsay, A. Margaret. "The Early Christian Art of Isaura Nova," *JHS* 24 (1904) 260–92, at 283 no. 24 (fig. 24).

Ramsay, William M. "The Church of Lycaonia in the Fourth Century," in idem, *Luke the Physician* (London: Hodder and Stoughton, 1908) 392–93 no. 22.

Horsley, G. H. R. *New Documents Illustrating Early Christianity.* Vol. 4: *A Review of the Greek Inscriptions and Papyri published in 1979* (North Ryde, N.S.W.: Macquarie Ancient History Association, 1987) 161 no. 69.

Δόξα οἰκονόμεισσα
ἡ σεμνή.[2]

Line 1: The name Doxa is typically Christian.[3]
For the construction of the feminine with -ισσα see ch. 3 A above.

Doxa, the honorable[4] steward.

This inscription from Lycaonia witnesses to a certain Doxa, who is called "steward" (οἰκονόμεισσα). Those studying this inscription have discussed whether Doxa was a Christian officeholder, that is, a steward, or the wife of a steward.[5] Since the inscription does not mention a husband we must posit that Doxa herself exercised the office of steward.[6]

Margaret and William Ramsay suggest that Doxa was the steward of a monastery, although the inscription offers no clear evidence of that.[7] There is no mention of a monastic community in the text of the inscription. The adjective σεμνή in its definition as "ascetic" could point to a monastic context. However, it also means "holy, sacred," "religious," or "worthy of respect, honorable."[8] The multiple meanings of this epithet thus make it impossible to use it to clarify the inscription. In its meaning of "honorable" it could have applied to Doxa in connection with her office as steward, which she exercised in honorable fashion. The Christian community at Dorla is attested primarily by inscriptions for bishops, and we can easily imagine the steward Doxa in their service.[9]

A Christian steward fits well within the general picture of ancient society. Non-christian inscriptions from Asia Minor also attest to women stewards.[10] The non-Christian office of steward[11] had a variety of expressions: it could be a public political office or a position in a club or association, or it could be exercised on behalf of private persons. It embraced the administration of property and finances in the broadest sense. In the Roman period it underwent a transformation. It was primarily applied "to designate private officials with lesser functions" and the office was exercised almost exclusively by slaves or freedpersons.[12] Inscriptions witness not only to women as stewards employed by others, but also to some who were themselves the employers of such persons.[13]

Within Christianity we can discern the existence of an office of steward[14] in Asia Minor especially beginning in the fourth century. Basil of Caesarea speaks of it as a community office entrusted primarily with the management of goods for the poor.[15] Similarly, we find it also as a monastic office related to administrative duties and care for the poor.[16]

Informative sources for the office of steward are Canons 25 and 26 of the Council of Chalcedon (451). The office is mentioned in connection with the admonition to the metropolitans to consecrate new bishops as quickly as possible for a church that has been deserted. The stewards are to take care of the church's income during the vacancy (can. 25). Beyond this it is ordered, under threat of punishment, that for every church that has a bishop there shall be a steward appointed from the clergy who will administer the goods of the church at the bishop's direction (can. 26).[17] The office of steward was accordingly a clerical office connected with ordination. Carl Maria Kaufmann also emphasizes that "only in exceptional circumstances was it exercised by those who were not priests."[18] The office of steward was therefore, according to the Council of Chalcedon, a clerical office in the Church entrusted with the administration of Church property.[19]

Inscription for the steward Irene

Asia Minor / Borders of Pisidia and Phrygia / Cavundur

BIBLIOGRAPHY:
Sterrett, J. R. Sitlington. *The Wolfe Expedition to Asia Minor.* Papers of the American School of Classical Studies at Athens 3 (Boston: Damrell and Upham, 1888) 216–17 no. 345.

MAMA VIII 70 no. 399 (plate 174). (Calder, W. M., and J. M. R. Cormack, et al., eds., *Monuments from Lycaonia, the Pisidio-Phrygian Borderland, Aphrodisias* [Manchester: Manchester University Press, 1962]).
Spicq, Ceslas. *Saint Paul. Les Epitres Pastorales* (Paris: J. Gabalda, 1969) 408.

Εἰρήνη Λονγιλλιανοῦ καὶ
Σεουήρου οἰκονόμισσα Στά-
3   χυι τῶ ἰδίω ἀνδρὶ σεμνοτάτω
μνείας χάριν.[20]

Line 2: Σεουήρου = Severus.[21]

Irene, the steward of Longillianus and Severus, for Stachus, her own most revered husband, in memorial.

This inscription also witnesses to a woman steward in Asia Minor. Her name, Irene, points to the Christian provenance of the inscription.[22] The text of the inscription does not, of course, describe Irene as steward of the Christian community, but rather as the private steward of two men.

It is possible that these two men were ascetics whom she served. It is said of the monk Evagrius Ponticus that he had a steward to administer the donations he received.[23] It is also reported of the teacher and ascetic Pambo that he had a steward named Origen who, as "presbyter and steward," administered donations to Pambo and distributed them among the brothers and sisters.[24]

Irene dedicated this gravestone to her husband Stachus, who appears without an official title. The inscription is therefore at the same time further evidence that women exercised professions and offices independently of their husbands. Among the persons named in this inscription she is the only one of the four who is described as holding an office. It is worth noting especially as well that Irene indicates her own professional activity on her inscription for her husband without mentioning that of the husband.

B. Stewards in Early Christian Literature

There is no Christian office of steward mentioned in the New Testament. The title οἰκονόμος is found, however, as a description of believers in their dealing with the gospel entrusted to them.[25] Paul uses the concept of stewardship to describe the characteristics of the apostolic office. He calls himself and his coworkers ὑπηρέται Χριστοῦ and οἰκονόμοι μυστηρίων Θεοῦ (1 Cor 4:1-2). This image appears appropriate especially in its theological form; it implies the aspect of commissioning and sending. But it was also significant in its material implications. The office of apostleship was service of the word and of other people. This is especially well illustrated by Paul's striving to gather the collection for Jerusalem, which beyond its theological and church-political dimensions also had an eminently economic meaning.[26] In the letter to Titus the designation οἰκονόμος is restricted to the bishop (Titus 1:7). In accordance with the ecclesiological conception of the Pastorals, which describe the Church in the categories of a "household of God," the bishop is projected as the οἰκονόμος Θεοῦ.[27] Central to the image of the οἰκονόμος Θεοῦ remains, in this context as well, that the mission of the officeholder "is not based on the individual's own power and authority."[28]

Clear indications of the institutionalization of the office of steward emerge from fourth-century sources, as we have shown above. The office of steward is then encountered as a community and monastic office especially in terms of administrative activity.

A further facet of the office of steward is found in the *Canones Hippolyti* (*CanHipp* 25): "The steward, who is responsible for the sick, has the costs paid by the bishop, including the clay vessels, because the sick have need of it: the bishop gives it to the steward."[29] The work of the stewards is here more precisely described as service to the sick. At the same time they are connected to the bishop, who pays for their services. In the *Canones Hippolyti* service to the sick is attested primarily for the widows (*CanHipp* 9). We may therefore presume that women as well as men were stewards in the communities. The fact that the office of steward does not appear as an ordained Church office in the *Canones Hippolyti* underscores the interpretation that both men and women could exercise it, for if the steward's office were portrayed in the *Canones Hippolyti* as an ordained Church office we would have to presume that women did not exercise it, since the *Canones Hippolyti* forbid the ordination of women in principle (*CanHipp* 9).

We can therefore say that women are attested as stewards in both pagan and Christian inscriptions. The Christian Irene was a private steward, and therefore did not exercise her office in service to the Christian community, but possibly in the service of some Christian ascetics. The steward Doxa, on the other hand, was in the service either of a Christian community or a monastery. The latter is less likely because her inscription contains no reference to a monastic community. It is more probable that she was the steward of the community in Dorla, for which bishops are also epigraphically attested, and in whose service she administered the Church property.

Notes

[1] A. Margaret Ramsay, "The Early Christian Art of Isaura Nova," *JHS* 24 (1904) 260–92, at 283. William M. Ramsay, "The Church of Lycaonia in the Fourth Century," in idem, *Luke the Physician* (London: Hodder and Stoughton, 1908) 329–410, at 393, gives a more precise dating: "This epitaph is of the later type which probably began about A.D. 360."

[2] From Ramsay, "The Early Christian Art of Isaura Nova," 283 no. 24. The inscription is decorated with a rosette with six flower petals.

[3] Ibid.

[4] Ramsay, "Church of Lycaonia," 393, translates "revered."

[5] Ramsay, "The Early Christian Art of Isaura Nova," 283; Ramsay, "Church of Lycaonia," 393; E. Hanton, "Lexique explicatif du Recueil des inscriptions grecques chrétiennes d'Asie Mineure," *Byz* 4 (1927/28) 53–136, at 110; G. H. R. Horsley, *New Documents Illustrating Early Christianity. Vol. 4: A Review of the Greek Inscriptions and Papyri published in 1979* (North Ryde, N.S.W.: Macquarie Ancient History Association, 1987) 161.

[6] According to Hanton, "Lexique," 110 she was undoubtedly the wife of a steward.

[7] Ramsay, "The Early Christian Art of Isaura Nova," 283; Ramsay, "Church of Lycaonia," 393.

[8] Cf. G. W. H. Lampe, *A Patristic Greek Lexicon* (Oxford and New York: Clarendon Press, 1969) 1229, with examples.

[9] See Ramsay, "The Early Christian Art of Isaura Nova," 269 n. 3; 272 n. 5.

[10] Cf. the two examples from Bithynia offered by Sencer Sahin, *Katalog der antiken Inschriften des Museums von Iznik (Nikaia) I–II.2.* 4 vols. (Bonn: Habelt, 1979–1987) 239 no. 1466: Eupraxia οἰκονόμισα and Anthousa οἰκονόμισσα. Both these women were private stewards; cf. Peter Landvogt, *Epigraphische Untersuchungen über den OIKONOMOS* (Diss. Strasbourg: Druck von M. Dumont Schauberg, 1908) 16ff. The steward Eupraxia died at the age of twenty-three. That age is not unusual; many inscriptions describe stewards of that age. Cf. Horsley, *New Documents* 4:161. Anthousa calls herself Φοί/βου γυνή, οἰκο/νόμισσα Τειμ/οθέου. This example shows that this woman separated her professional activity from her marriage. Anthousa worked as a steward independently of her husband; so also *IK* 9, 239.

[11] On this see Landvogt, *Epigraphische Untersuchungen über den OIKONOMOS;* Erich Ziebarth, "Oikonomos," *PRE* XVII (1937) 2118–2119; John Reumann, "'Stewards of God' – Pre-Christian Religious Application of Oikonomos in Greek," *JBL* 77 (1958) 339–49.

[12] Landvogt, *Epigraphische Untersuchungen über den OIKONOMOS* 12.

[13] This is also emphasized by Horsley, *New Documents* 4:160–61, with examples. See also the example in Landvogt, *Epigraphische Untersuchungen über den OIKONOMOS* 19.

[14] For Christian stewards see Carl Maria Kaufmann, *Handbuch der altchristlichen Epigraphik* (Freiburg: Herder, 1917) 274ff.; Henri Leclercq, "Econome," *DACL* IV/2 (1921) 1884–1886; Hanton, "Lexique," 109–10; Lampe, *Lexicon* 943–44.

[15] Basil of Caesarea, *Ep.* 150,3; 237,1.

[16] On this see the lengthier treatment by Klaus Koschorke, *Spuren der alten Liebe. Studien zum Kirchenbegriff des Basilius von Caesarea.* Par. 32 (Fribourg: Universitätsverlag, 1991) 216.

[17] For the text see Council of Chalcedon, can. 25, 26 (Friedrich Lauchert, ed., *Die Kanones der wichtigsten altkirchlichen Concilien nebst den apostolischen Kanones*. SQS 12 [Freiburg: J. C. B. Mohr, 1896; reprint Frankfurt: Minerva, 1961] 95–96).

[18] Kaufmann, *Handbuch der altchristlichen Epigraphik* 275, with inscriptional examples.

[19] See the further examples in Lampe, *Lexicon* 944 (n. 3).

[20] From *MAMA VIII* 70 no. 399: "Plain block. H. 0.76; w. (visible) 1.00; letters 0.03."

[21] Wilhelm Pape and Gustav Eduard Benseler, *Wörterbuch der griechischen Eigennamen*. 2 vols. (3rd ed. Braunschweig: F. Vieweg, 1863–1870; reprint Graz: Akademische Druck- u. Verlagsanstalt, 1959) 1374–75.

[22] Ibid. 336 offers a Christian example (CIG 4, 9340).

[23] See Gabriel Bunge, ed., *Briefe aus der Wüste*. Sophia 24 (Trier: Paulinus-Verlag, 1986) 48.

[24] Palladius, *Lausiac History* 10 (see Cuthbert Butler, ed., *The Lausiac History of Palladius. A Critical Discussion together with Notes on Early Egyptian Monachism*. I/II. TaS 6 [Hildesheim: G. Olms, 1967; reprint of the 1898 Cambridge edition] 30, 11; 31, 11).

[25] On this see Otto Michel, "οἶκος κτλ.," *TDNT* 5:119–59, at 150–51; Douglas Webster, "The Primary Stewardship," *ET* 72 (1960/61) 274–76; Wilfred Tooley, "Stewards of God. An Examination of the Terms ΟΙΚΟΝΟΜΟΣ and ΟΙΚΟΝΟΜΙΑ in the New Testament," *SJTH* 19 (1966) 74–86; Hermann von Lips, *Glaube – Gemeinde – Amt. Zum Verständnis der Ordination in den Pastoralbriefen*. FRLANT 122 (Göttingen: Vandenhoeck & Ruprecht, 1979) 147–48; Horst Kuhli, "οἰκονομία κτλ.," *EDNT* 2:498–500.

[26] On this see Dieter Georgi, *Remembering the Poor: The History of Paul's Collection for Jerusalem* (Nashville: Abingdon, 1992).

[27] On this see Lips, *Glaube – Gemeinde – Amt* 143ff., especially 147ff.; Jürgen Roloff, *Der erste Brief an Timotheus*. EKK XV (Neukirchen-Vluyn: Neukirchener Verlag, 1988) 213–17, and ch. 8 B above.

[28] Lips, *Glaube – Gemeinde – Amt* 148.

[29] Following Wilhelm Riedel, ed., *Die Kirchenrechtsquellen des Patriarchats Alexandrien* (Leipzig: A. Deichert, 1900) 193–230, at 216.

X. Source-Oriented Perspectives for a History of Christian Women Officeholders

Articulating the past historically does not mean discovering it "as it really was." It means taking possession of a memory in the way it blazes up at the moment of danger. Historical materialism is concerned to hold fast to an image of the past as it presents itself unexpectedly to the historical subject at the moment of danger. The danger threatens both the existence of the tradition and its recipients. For both it is one and the same danger: that of making oneself a tool of the ruling class. In every epoch the effort must be made to retrieve the tradition anew from the conformity that is about to overpower it. After all, the Messiah comes not only as a redeemer, but also as the one who overcomes the Antichrist. The gift of fanning the sparks of hope in the past dwells only with *that* historian who is saturated with it: even the dead will not be safe from the enemy if he conquers. And that enemy has not ceased to conquer.

Walter Benjamin[1]

To write the history of Christian women is to seek for those women's hidden, forgotten, and suppressed heritage. The history of women in the first centuries of the Church is also a history of a considerable degree of maturity. Its written articulation frequently takes the form of negation, either in the shape of traditions of prohibition or more frequently in passages of Christian literature that have remained unnoticed. The history of Christian women in that literature is above all a history of silencing and restriction. It is difficult to reconstruct within these closed contexts, and its memory has remained largely fragmentary.

This finding has made necessary a way of looking and an instrument that Church history to date, because of its concentration on the literary tradition, has scarcely made use of. The cracks, the broken connections in a history of women, women whose stories only found occasional literary articulation, make an "archaeological" method indispensable.

This "archaeological" method must be applied on the one hand to the literary heritage of the Church that, when "brushed against the grain," yields access to the submerged heritage of women. Even texts that clearly document a repression of women are exceedingly revealing of the existing conflict between the sexes and thus are important for the writing of women's history.

However, the literature of the ancient Church and the early Middle Ages can in no way be reduced to the aspect of women's oppression. It is necessary to make an effort to pay attention and to give additional emphasis to texts that transmit a living tradition about women: hagiographical literature, for example. In this connection there is a need especially for the recovery of women's theological literature, beginning with the first centuries of the Church.

On the other hand, this archaeological work must turn its attention to the material remains of the early Christians: the inscriptions and documentary papyri that witness to individual women and make their voices audible. The fragmentary character of the epigraphical evidence at the same time illustrates the fragmentary and shadowed memory of women.

The Christian inscriptions from the ancient world, from Palestine, Syria, and Asia Minor, the Balkan peninsula and Italy, have preserved that memory. Here lies an overwhelming wealth of material for those who will look at it. A careful contemplation of these material objects illuminates the history of women like a flash of lightning, and yet it remains not quite within our grasp.

In the inscriptions the existence and activity of Christian women through the centuries is recorded at specific points. Women erected gravestones for themselves and others, and on them they recorded themselves as officeholders. Stones were dedicated in turn to the memory of other women, and there they, too, speak to us as officeholders.

It is clear that women were active in the expansion and shaping of the Church in the first centuries: they were apostles, prophets, teachers, presbyters, enrolled widows, deacons, bishops and stewards. They preached the Gospel, they spoke prophetically and in tongues, they went on mission, they prayed, they presided over the Lord's Supper, they broke the bread and gave the cup, they baptized, they taught, they created theology, they were active in care for the poor and the sick, and they were administrators and managers of burial places. In short, to the question whether there were women officeholders in the Church's first centuries our study returns a resounding answer: yes!

Notes

[1] Walter Benjamin, "Über den Begriff der Geschichte VI," in idem, *Gesammelte Schriften,* edited by Rolf Tiedemann and Hermann Schweppenhäuser, with the assistance of Theodor W. Adorno and Gershom Scholem. 7 vols. in 15 (Frankfurt: Surhkamp, 1972–1989) I/2:695.

Abbreviations

Most of the abbreviations are those given by Siegfried M. Schwertner in *TRE* (2nd rev. and expanded ed. Berlin and New York: Walter de Gruyter, 1994). Those most frequently used, plus a few additional abbreviations, are as follows:

AD	Ἀρχαιολογικὸν Δελτίον
AE	*L'Année Epigraphique*
AM	Mitteilungen des deutschen archäologischen Instituts. Athenische Abteilung
AP	Apophthegmata Patrum
BCH	*Bulletin de correspondance hellénique*
BE	*Bulletin Epigraphique*
CA	*Constitutiones Apostolorum*
CanHipp	*Canones Hippolyti*
CEA	*Constitutiones Ecclesiasticae Apostolorum*
CIG	*Corpus inscriptionum Graecarum*
CIJ	*Corpus inscriptionum Judaicarum*
CIL	*Corpus inscriptionum Latinarum*
CRIPEL	Cahiers de Recherches de l'Institut de Papyrologie et d'Egyptologie de Lille
Didasc.	*Didascalia Apostolorum*
Exp.	*Expositor*
Herm.	*Shepherd of Hermas*
ICUR	*Inscriptiones christianae urbis Romae*
ICURns	*Inscriptiones christianae urbis Romae. New series*

IG	*Inscriptiones Graecae*
IGLS	*Inscriptions grecques et latines de la Syrie*
ILCV	*Inscriptiones Latinae Christianae Veteres*
MAMA	*Monumenta Asiae Minoris Antiqua*
PLRE	*Prosopography of the Later Roman Empire*
SEG	*Supplementum Epigraphicum Graecum*
TA	*Traditio Apostolica*
TAM	*Tituli Asiae Minoris*
TAPA	*Transactions and Proceedings of the American Philological Association*
TD	*Testamentum Domini*

Bibliography

A. Reference Works

1. Introductions and Bibliographies for Epigraphy and Papyrology

Almar, Knud Paasch. *Inscriptiones Latinae. Eine illustrierte Einführung in die lateinische Epigraphik.* OUCS 14. Odense: Odense University Press, 1990.

Bérard, François, et al. *Guide de l'Epigraphiste. Bibliographie choisie des épigraphies antiques et médiévales.* Bibliothèque de l'Ecole normale supérieure, Guides et Inventaires Bibliographiques II. Paris: Presses de l'Ecole normale supérieure, 1986.

Bernard, Etienne. "Le Corpus des inscriptions grecques de l'Egypte," *ZPE* 26 (1977) 95–117.

Besevliev, Ladislav. "Probleme der byzantinischen Epigraphik," in Johannes Irmscher and Kurt Treu, eds., *Das Korpus der Griechischen Christlichen Schriftsteller. Historie, Gegenwart, Zukunft. Eine Aufsatzsammlung.* TU 120. Berlin: Akademie Verlag, 1977, 179–82.

Clauss, Manfred. "Ausgewählte Bibliographie zur lateinischen Epigraphik der römischen Kaiserzeit (1.–3. Jh.)," *ANRW* II/1 (1974) 796–855.

Grossi Gondi, Felice. *Trattato di epigrafia cristiana latina e greca del mondo romano occidentale. I. Monumenti Cristiani dei Primi sei Secoli I.* Rome: Università Gregoriana, 1968. (Reprint of the 1920 edition.)

Hondius, Jacobus Johannes Ewoud. *Saxa loquuntur. Inleiding tot de Grieksche Epigraphiek.* Leiden: A.W. Sijthoff, 1938.

Horst, Pieter Willem van der. *Ancient Jewish Epitaphs. An Introductory Survey of a Millennium of Jewish Funerary Epigraphy (300 BCE–700 CE).* Contributions to Biblical Exegesis and Theology 2. Kampen: Kok Pharos, 1991.

Jalabert, Louis, and René Mouterde. "Inscriptions Grecques Chrétiennes," *DACL* 7/1 (1926) 623–94.

Kaufmann, Carl Maria. *Handbuch der altchristlichen Epigraphik.* Freiburg: Herder, 1917.

Kloos, Rudolf M. *Einführung in die Epigraphik des Mittelalters und der frühen Neuzeit.* Darmstadt: Wissenschaftliche Buchgesellschaft, 1980.

Larfeld, Wilhelm. *Handbuch der griechischen Epigraphik.* 2 vols. Leipzig: O. R. Reisland, 1898–1907.

Leclercq, Henri. "Inscriptions Latines Chrétiennes," *DACL* VII/1 (1926) 694–850.

Marucchi, Orazio. *Christian Epigraphy. An Elementary Treatise with a Collection of Ancient Christian Inscriptions Mainly of Roman Origin.* Translated by J. Armine Willis. Chicago: Ares Publishers, 1974. (Original: *Epigrafia cristiana.* Milan: U. Hoepli, 1910).

Meyer, Ernst. *Einführung in die lateinische Epigraphik.* 2nd ed. Darmstadt: Wissenschaftliche Buchgesellschaft, 1983.

Mihaescu, Haralambie. "Lateinische Inschriften," in Friedhelm Winkelmann and Wolfram Brandes, eds., *Quellen zur Geschichte des frühen Byzanz (4.–9. Jahrhundert). Bestand und Probleme.* BBA 55. Amsterdam: Gieben, 1990, 106–19.

Mitteis, Ludwig, and Ulrich Wilcken. *Grundzüge und Chrestomathie der Papyruskunde.* 2 vols. Hildesheim: G. Olms, 1963. (Reprint of the B. Teubner edition of 1912).

Oates, John F., et al. *Checklist of Editions of Greek and Latin Papyri, Ostraca and Tablets.* 4th ed. Atlanta: Scholars, 1993.

Pfohl, Gerhard. "Grabinschrift I (griechische)," *RAC* 12 (1983) 467–514.

Pietri, Charles. "Grabinschrift II (lateinisch)," translated by Josef Engemann, *RAC* 12 (1983) 514–90.

Popescu, Emilian. "Griechische Inschriften," in Winkelmann and Brandes, eds., *Quellen zur Geschichte des frühen Byzanz,* 81–105.

Rengen, Wilfried van. "L'épigraphie grecque et latine de Syrie. Bilan d'un quart de siècle de recherches épigraphiques," *ANRW* II, 8 (1977) 31–53.

Robert, Louis. *Die Epigraphik der klassischen Welt.* (Translated by Helmut Engelmann from "L'histoire et ses méthodes," *Encyclopédie de la Pléiade.* Paris: Gallimard, 1961, 453–97). Bonn: R. Habelt, 1970.

Testini, Pasquale. *Archeologia cristiana; nozioni generali della origini alla fine del sec. VI.* Rome: Desclée, 1958; 2nd ed. with analytic index and bibliographic appendix Bari: Edipuglia, 1980.

Treu, Kurt. "Byzantinische Papyri," in Winkelmann and Brandes, eds., *Quellen zur Geschichte des frühen Byzanz,* 120–33.

Woodhead, A. Geoffrey. *The Study of Greek Inscriptions.* Cambridge: Cambridge University Press, 1959.

2. Greek and Latin Dictionaries

Bauer, Walter. *Griechisch-deutsches Wörterbuch zu den Schriften des Neuen Testaments und der übrigen frühchristlichen Literatur.* 6th fully revised edition prepared by Kurt Aland and Barbara Aland. Berlin and New York: Walter de Gruyter, 1988. English: *A Greek-English Lexicon of the New Testament and Other Early Christian Literature.* Translated and adapted by William F. Arndt and F. Wilbur Gingrich. Revised and augmented by F. Wilbur Gingrich and Frederick W. Danker from Walter Bauer's Fifth Edition, 1958. Chicago and London: University of Chicago Press, 1979.

Du Cange, Charles D. *Glossarium mediae et infimae latinitatis.* 5 vols. Graz: Akademische Druck- und Verlagsanstalt, 1954. (Reprint of the edition of 1883–1887).

Georges, Karl Ernst. *Ausführliches lateinisch-deutsches Handwörterbuch. Aus den Quellen zusammengetragen und mit besonderer Bezugnahme auf Synonymik und Antiquitäten unter Berücksichtigung der besten Hilfsmittel.* 2 vols. Darmstadt: Wissenschaftliche Buchgesellschaft, 1988. (Reprint of the 8th ed. [1913], revised and expanded by Heinrich Georges).

Habel, Edwin, and Friedrich Gröbel, eds. *Mittellateinisches Glossar.* With an Introduction by Heinz-Dieter Heimann. 2nd ed. Munich, Vienna, and Zürich: Schöningh, 1989 (unrevised reprint).

Lampe, Geoffrey William Hugo, ed. *A Patristic Greek Lexicon.* Oxford and New York: Clarendon Press, 1969 (reprinted 1989).

Lewis, Charlton T., and Charles Short. *A Latin Dictionary: founded on Andrews' ed. of Freund's Latin Dictionary.* Revised, enlarged, and in large part rewritten. Oxford: Clarendon Press, 1987.

Liddell, Henry George, Robert Scott, and Henry Stuart Jones. *A Greek-English Lexicon.* With a Supplement by E. A. Barber. Oxford: Clarendon Press, 1968 (reprint 1990).

Niermeyer, Jan Frederik. *Mediae latinitatis lexicon minus. Lexique latin médiéval-Français/Anglais. A Medieval Latin-French/English Dictionary, perficiendum curavit C. van de Kieft.* 2 vols. Leiden: Brill, [1954]–1976.

Preisigke, Friedrich. *Wörterbuch der griechischen Papyrusurkunden mit Einschluß der griechischen Inschriften, Aufschriften, Ostraka, Mumienschilder usw. aus Ägypten.* Edited and published by Emil Kiessling. 3 vols. Berlin: by his heirs, 1925–1931. Supplement 1, edited under the direction of the publisher by Winfried Rübsam. Amsterdam: A.M. Hakkert, 1969.

Sleumer, Albert. *Kirchenlateinisches Wörterbuch.* With the cooperation of Joseph Schmid. Hildesheim, Zürich, and New York: G. Olms, 1990. (Reprint of the edition at Limburg a. d. Lahn: Gebrüder Steffen, 1926).

Sophocles, Evangelinus A. *Greek Lexicon of the Roman and Byzantine Periods (145 B.C.–1100 A.D.).* Hildesheim and New York: G. Olms, 1975. (Originally published at Boston by Little, Brown, 1870.)

Thesaurus Linguae Graecae, ab Henrico Stephano constructus. 9 vols. Graz: Akademische Verlagsanstalt, 1954 (reprint).

Thesaurus Linguae Latinae, editus auctoritate et consilio academiarum quinque Germanicarum: Berolinensis, Gottingensis, Lipsiensis, Monacensis, Vindobonensis. 10 vols. to date. Leipzig: Teubner, 1900– .

3. Grammars

Blass, Friedrich, and Albert Debrunner. *Grammatik des neutestamentlichen Griechisch.* Edited by Friedrich Rehkopf. 15th rev. ed. Göttingen: Vandenhoeck & Ruprecht, 1979.

Bornemann, Eduard. *Griechische Grammatik*. With the cooperation of Ernst Risch. 2nd ed. Frankfurt, Berlin, and Munich: 1978.

Gignac, Francis Thomas. *A Grammar of the Greek Papyri of the Roman and Byzantine Periods*. 2 vols. Milan: Istituto editoriale cisalpino-La goliardica, 1981.

Hauser, Karl. *Grammatik der griechischen Inschriften Lykiens*. Basel: Buchdruckerei E. Birkhäuser, 1916.

Kühner, Raphael, and Carl Stegmann. *Ausführliche Grammatik der lateinischen Sprache*. 2 vols. 3rd ed. revised by Andreas Thierfelder. Hannover: Hahnsche Buchhandlung, 1955.

Radermacher, Ludwig. *Neutestamentliche Grammatik. Das Griechisch des Neuen Testaments im Zusammenhang mit der Volkssprache*. HNT 1. 2nd ed. Tübingen: J. C. B. Mohr [Paul Siebeck], 1925.

Schwyzer, Eduard. *Griechische Grammatik, auf der Grundlage von Karl Brugmanns Griechischer Grammatik*. 3 vols. HAW II/1, vols. 1–3. 2nd ed. Munich: C. H. Beck, 1953.

4. Books of Names

Bechtel, Friedrich. *Die historischen Personennamen des Griechischen bis zur Kaiserzeit*. Halle: M. Niemeyer, 1917.

Foraboschi, Daniele. *Onomasticon alterum papyrologicum. Supplemento al Namenbuch di Friedrich Preisigke*. TDSA 16, Serie papirologica 2. Milan: Istituto editoriale Cisalpino, 1967.

Fraser, Peter Marshall, and Elaine Matthews. *A Lexicon of Greek Personal Names. I: The Aegean Islands, Cyprus, Cyrenaica*. Oxford: Clarendon Press, 1987.

Kajanto, Iiro. *The Latin Cognomina*. Commentationes Humanarum Litterarum 36/2. Helsinki: Societas Scientiarum Fennica, 1965.

_____. *Onomastic Studies in the Early Christian Inscriptions of Rome and Carthage*. Acta Instituti Romani Finlandiae 2/1. Helsinki: IRF, 1963.

Pape, Wilhelm, and Gustav Eduard Benseler. *Wörterbuch der griechischen Eigennamen*. 2 vols. 3rd ed. Braunschweig: F. Vieweg, 1863–1870. Reprint Graz: Akademische Druck- u. Verlagsanstalt, 1959.

Preisigke, Friedrich. *Namenbuch, enthaltend alle griechischen, lateinischen, ägyptischen usw. Menschennamen, soweit sie in griechischen Urkunden (Papyri, Ostraka, Inschriften, Mumienschildern usw.) Ägyptens sich vorfinden*. Heidelberg: by the author, 1922.

Prosopography of the Later Roman Empire. I: A.D. *260–395*, edited by Arnold H. Jones, John R. Martindale, and J. Morris. *II:* A.D. *395–527*, edited by J. R. Martindale. Cambridge: Cambridge University Press, 1975, 1980.

Solin, Heikki. *Die Griechischen Personennamen in Rom. Ein Namenbuch*. 3 vols. Corpus inscriptionum Latinarum. Auctarium Berlin and New York: Walter de Gruyter, 1982.

Wuthnow, Heinz. *Die semitischen Menschennamen in griechischen Inschriften und Papyri des Vorderen Orients*. Leipzig: Dietrich, 1930.

Zgusta, Ladislav. *Kleinasiatische Personennamen.* Prague: Verlag der Tsche-choslowakischen Akademie der Wissenschaften, 1964.

_____. *Neue Beiträge zur kleinasiatischen Anthroponymie.* Prague: Academia, 1970.

5. Thematic Bibliographies

Arthur, Marylin B. "Review Essay: Classics," *Signs* 2 (1976) 382–403.

Berger, Teresa. "Women and Worship: A Bibliography," *StLi* 19 (1989) 96–110.

Bibliographia Patristica. Internationale Patristische Bibliographie. Edited by Wilhelm Schneemelcher, et al. Berlin: Walter de Gruyter, 1956– .

Bibliographie zur Feministischen Theologie, Stand 1988. Reprinted from *Schritte ins Offene,* collected by Ursula Vock and Ursula Riedi in cooperation with Ina Prae-torius. Zürich: 1988.

Crouzel, Henri. *Bibliographie critique d'Origène.* IP 8. *Supplement I.* IP 8A. Den Haag: Steenbrugge, 1971, 1982.

Ganghofer, Odile. *The Woman in the Church/La Femme dans l'Eglise. International bibliography 1973–June 1975 indexed by computer/Bibliographie interna-tionale 1973–juin 1975 établie par ordinateur.* RIC Supplement 21. Strasbourg: Cerdic Publications, 1975.

Gardiner, Anne Marie. "A Selected Bibliography of Women and Priesthood (1965–1975)," in eadem, ed., *Women and Catholic Priesthood. An Expanded Vi-sion.* Proceedings of the Detroit Ordination Conference. New York: Paulist, 1976, 199–208.

Goodwater, Leanna. *Women in Antiquity. An Annotated Bibliography.* Metuchen, N. J.: Scarecrow Press, 1976.

Kendall, Patricia A. *Women and the Priesthood: A Selected and Annotated Bibliogra-phy.* [Philadelphia]: Committee to Promote the Cause of and to Plan for the Or-dination of Women to the Priesthood, The Episcopal Diocese of Pennsylvania, 1976.

Kraemer, Ross S. "Women in the Religions of the Greco-Roman World," *RSR* 9 (1983) 127–39.

Lindboe, Inger Marie. *Women in the New Testament. A Select Bibliography.* University of Oslo, Faculty of Theology, Bibliography Series 1. Oslo: University of Oslo, 1990.

Millwood, Dorothea, and Iris J. Benesch, eds. *Bibliography on Feminist Theology 1980–1986.* Geneva: Lutheran World Federation, Department of Studies, Women in Church and Society, 1986.

Pomeroy, Sarah B. "Selected Bibliography on Women in Classical Antiquity," in John Peradotto and J. P. Sullivan, eds., *Women in the Ancient World.* Albany: SUNY Press, 1984, 315–72.

Sieben, Hermann Josef. *Exegesis Patrum. Saggio bibliografico sull' esegesi biblica dei Padri della Chiesa.* SuPa 2. Rome: Istituto patristico Augustinianum, 1983.

_____. *Kirchenväterhomilien zum Neuen Testament. Ein Repertorium der Textaus-gaben und Übersetzungen.* IP 22. The Hague: Nijhoff; Steenbrugge [Belgium]: In Abbatia S. Petri, 1991.

B. Primary Sources

1. Inscriptions and Documentary Papyri

Agnello, Santi Luigi. *Silloge di Iscrizioni Paleocristiane della Sicilia*. Rome: "L'Erma" di Bretschneider, 1953.

_____. "Scoperte e studi di Epigrafia cristiana in Sicilia," *Atti del VI congresso internazionale di archeologia cristiana* (Ravenna 23–30 Sept. 1962 [*Studi di antichità cristiana* 26] Vatican City: Pont. Inst. di Archeologia Cristiana, 1965) 215–22.

Aigrain, René. *Manuel d'Epigraphie chrétienne*. 2 vols. Paris: Bloud, 1912–1913.

Alt, Albrecht. *Die griechischen Inschriften der Palaestina tertia westlich der 'Araba*. Berlin and Leipzig: Walter de Gruyter, 1921.

Anderson, John George Clark. "A Summer in Phrygia," *JHS* 18 (1898) 81–128.

_____. "Exploration in Galatia Cis Halym," *JHS* 19 (1899) 52–134.

_____, Franz Cumont, and Henri Grégoire. *Studia Pontica III, Fasc. 1: Recueil des inscriptions grecques et latines du Pont et de l'Arménie*. Brussels: Lamertin, 1910.

Bandy, Anastasius C. *The Greek Christian Inscriptions of Crete*. Athens: Christian Archaeological Society, 1970.

Bakirtzis, Charalampos. "Exposition des Antiquités Paléochrétiennes au Musée des Philippes," *Athens Annals of Archaeology* 13 (1980) 90–98.

Baratte, François, and Bernard Boyaval. "Catalogue des étiquettes de momies du Musée du Louvre (C.E.M.L.) – textes grecs," 4 parts: *CRIPEL* 2 (1974) 155–264; 3 (1975) 151–261; 4 (1976) 173–254; 5 (1979) 237–339.

Bayet, Charles. *De titulis Atticae christianis antiquissimis. Commentatio historica et epigraphica*. Paris: Thorin, 1878.

Bees, Nikos A. *Corpus der griechisch christlichen Inschriften von Hellas. Inschriften von Peloponnes, 1. Isthmos – Korinthos*. Chicago: Ares, 1978.

Besevliev, Veselin, ed., *Spätgriechische und spätlateinische Inschriften aus Bulgarien*. BBA 30. Berlin: Akademie-Verlag, 1964.

Blant, Edmond le. *Inscriptions Chrétiennes de la Gaule antérieures au VIIIe siècle*. 2 vols. Paris: l'Imprimerie impériale, 1856–1865.

_____. *L'Epigraphie chrétienne en Gaule et dans l'Afrique Romaine*. Paris: Leroux, 1890.

_____. *Nouveau Recueil des Inscriptions chrétiennes de la Gaule antérieures au VIIIe siècle*. Paris: Imprimerie nationale, 1892.

_____. *Paléographie des Inscriptions latines du IIIe siècle à la fin du VIIe*. Paris: E. Leroux, 1898.

Buecheler, Franz. *Carmina Latina Epigraphica, conlegit, I–II*. Leipzig: Teubner, 1895–1897. *III. Supplementum, curavit Ernestus Lommatsch*. Leipzig: Teubner, 1926.

Bulic, France. "Iscrizioni Inedite. Salona (Solin)," *Bullettino di Archeologia e Storia Dalmata* 21 (1989) 141–48.

_____. "Iscrizione Inedita. (Siculi, Bihaci di Castelnuovo di Traù)," *Bullettino di Archeologia e Storia Dalmata* 37 (1914) 107–11.

Bulletin Epigraphique, de Jeanne et Louis Robert, in *REG* 1938ff. (reprinted in 10 vols., Paris: Les belles lettres, 1972–1982). *Index I: Les mots grecs.* Paris: Les belles lettres, 1972. *II: Les publications.* Paris: Les belles lettres, 1974. *III: Les mots français.* Paris: Institut Fernand Courby, 1975. Jean Marcillet-Jaubert and Anne-Marie Verilhac, eds., *Index du Bulletin Epigraphique 1966–1973. Mots grecs, Publications, Mots français.* Paris: Les belles lettres, 1979. Jean Marcillet-Jaubert and Anne-Marie Verilhac, eds., *Index du Bulletin Epigraphique 1974–1977.* Paris: Les belles lettres, 1983.

Cabrol, Fernando, and Henri Leclercq. *Reliquiae liturgicae vetustissimae: ex es Patrum necnon Scriptorum Ecclesiasticorum.* MELi 1. Paris: Firmin-Didot 1900–1902.

Calder, William M. "Philadelphia and Montanism," *BJRL* 7 (1922/23) 309–54.

_____. "The Epigraphy of the Anatolian Heresies," in William H. Buckler and William M. Calder, eds., *Anatolian Studies, presented to Sir William Mitchell Ramsay.* Manchester: Manchester University Press; London and New York: Longmans, Green, 1923, 59–91.

_____. "Leaves from an Anatolian Notebook," *BJRL* 13 (1929) 254–271.

_____. "Two Encratite Tombstones," *ByZ* 30 (1929/30) 645–46.

_____. "Early-Christian Epitaphs from Phrygia," *AnSt* 5 (1955) 25–38.

Canova, D. Reginetta. *Iscrizioni e monumenti protocristiani del paese di Moab.* SSAC 4. Vatican City: Pontificio Istituto di archeologia cristiana, 1954.

Carletti, Carlo. *Iscrizioni cristiane inedite del cimitero di Bassilla "ad S. Hermetem."* MPARA 2. Vatican City: Tipografia Poliglotta Vaticana, 1976.

_____. *Iscrizioni cristiane di Roma. Testimonianze di vita cristina (secoli III–VII).* BPat 7. Florence: Nardini: Centro internazionale del libro, 1986.

Cavassini, Maria Teresa. "Lettere cristiane nei papiri greci d'Egitto," *Aeg* 34 (1954) 266–82.

CIG IV = Corpus Inscriptionum Graecarum, vol. IV, edited by Ernest Curtis and Adolph Kirchhoff. Hildesheim and New York: G. Olms, 1977. (Reprint of the Berlin edition of 1877.)

CIJ = Corpus Inscriptionum Iudicarum. Recueil des Inscriptions juives qui vont du IIIe siècle avant Jésus-Christ au VIIe siècle de notre ère, edited by Jean-Baptiste Frey. 2 vols. SSAC 1; 3. Vatican City: Pontificio istituto di archeologia cristiana, 1936, 1952.

CIL III = Corpus Inscriptionum Latinarum, vol. III. *Inscriptiones Asiae, provinciarum Europae Graecarum, Illyrici Latinae,* edited by Theodor Mommsen. Berlin: G. Reimerus, 1873–1902.

CIL V = Corpus Inscriptionum Latinarum, vol. V. *Inscriptiones Galliae Cisalpinae Latinae,* edited by Theodor Mommsen. Berlin: G. Reimerus, 1872–1877.

CIL X = Corpus Inscriptionum Latinarum, vol. X. *Inscriptiones Bruttiorum, Lucaniae, Campaniae, Siciliae, Sardiniae Latinae,* edited by Theodor Mommsen. Berlin: G. Reimerus, 1883.

CIL XI = Corpus Inscriptionum Latinarum, vol. XI. *Inscriptiones Aemiliae, Etruriae, Umbriae Latinae*, edited by Eugen Bormann. Berlin: G. Reimerus, 1888–1926.

Cré, R. P. L. "Epitaphe de la Diaconesse Sophie," *RBI* n.s. 1 (1904) 260–62.

Creaghan, John S., and Antony Erich Raubitschek, "Early Christian Epitaphs from Athens," *Hesp* 16 (1947) 1–54.

Crispo, Anna. "Antichità cristiane della Calabria prebyzantia," *ASCL* 14 (1945) 127–41; 209–10.

Cronin, Harry S. "First Report of a Journey in Pisidia, Lycaonia, and Pamphylia," *JHS* 22 (1902) 338–76.

Cumont, Franz. "Les inscriptions chrétiennes de l'Asie Mineure," *MAH* 15 (1895) 245–99.

Dagron, Gilbert, and Denis Feissel. *Inscriptions de Cilicie*. TMCB. Collège de France, Monographies 4. Paris: De Boccard, 1987.

Drew-Bear, Thomas. "The City of Temenouthyrai in Phrygia," *Chiron* 9 (1979) 275–302.

Duval, Noel, "Les recherches d'épigraphie chrétienne en Afrique du Nord (1962–1972)," *MEFRA* 85 (1973) 335–44.

Fabretti, Raffaello. *Inscriptionum antiquarum, quo in aedibus paternis asservantur explicatio et additamentum una cum aliquot emendationibus Gruterianis*. Rome: 1702. In fol.

Feissel, Denis. "Notes d'Epigraphie Chrétienne (II)," *BCH* 101 (1977) 209–28.

_____. *Recueil des inscriptions chrétiennes de Macédoine du IIIe au VIe siècle*. BCH Supplément 8. Paris: Dépositaire, Diffusion de Boccard, 1983.

Ferrua, Antonio. *Epigrammata Damasiana. Recensuit et adnotavit*. SSAC 2. Rome: Pontificio Istituto di archeologia cristiana, 1942.

_____. "Gli angeli di Tera," *Orientalia christ. periodica* XIII (1947) 149–67.

_____. "Note su Tropea paleocristiana," *ASCL* 23 (1954) 9–29.

_____. "Il Catalogo dei Martiri di S. Prassede," *RPARA* 30–31 (1957–1959) 129–40.

_____. "I 'Carmina epigraphica' del Bücheler e la silloge del Diehl. Una concordanza," *VetChr* 112 (1975) 111–20.

_____. *Corona di osservazioni alle iscrizioni cristine di Roma incertae originis*. MPARA 3. Vatican City: Tipografia poliglotta vaticana, 1979.

_____. *Note e Giunte. Alle Iscrizioni Cristiane Antiche della Sicilia*. SSAC 9. Rome: Tipografia poliglotta vaticana, 1979.

Fitzgerald, G. M. *A Sixth Century Monastery at Beth-Shan (Scythopolis)*. PPSP 4. Philadelphia: Published for the University Museum by the University of Pennsylvania Press, 1939.

Germer-Durand, J. "Epigraphie Chrétienne de Jérusalem," *RB* 1 (1892) 560–88.

Ghedini, Giuseppe. *Lettere cristiane dai papiri greci del III e IV secolo*. Suppl. ad Aegyptus Ser. div. – Sez. gr.-rom. 3. Milan: Soc. Ed. 'Vita e Pensiero,' 1923.

Gibson, Elsa. "Montanist Epitaphs at Uşak," *GRBS* 16 (1975) 433–42.

_____. *The "Christians for Christians" Inscriptions of Phrygia. Greek Texts, Translation and Commentary*. HThS 32. Missoula: Scholars, 1978.

Grégoire, Henri. *Recueil des inscriptions grecques chrétiennes d'Asie Mineure 1.* Amsterdam: A. M. Hakkert, 1968. (Reprint of the Paris edition of 1922.)

_____. "Epigraphie Chrétienne," *Byz* 1 (1924) 695–716.

_____. "Du nouveau sur la hiérarchie de la secte Montaniste," *Byz* 2 (1925) 329–37.

Guarducci, Margherita. "Angelos," *SMSR* 15 (1939) 79–89.

_____. "Gli 'Angeli' di Tera," in *Mélanges helléniques offerts à Georges Daux.* Paris: E. de Boccard, 1974, 147–57.

_____. *Epigrafia Greca IV. Epigrafi Sacre Pagane e Cristiane.* Rome: Istituto poligrafico dello Stato, Libreria dello Stato, 1978.

Hanton, E. "Lexique explicatif du Recueil des inscriptions grecques chrétiennes d'Asie Mineure," *Byz* 4 (1927/28) 53–136.

Haspels, C. H. Emilie. *The Highlands of Phrygia. Sites and Monuments.* 2 vols. (Vol. 1: *The Text*; Vol. 2: *The Plates*). Princeton: Princeton University Press, 1971.

Heuzey, Léon, and Honoré Daumet. *Mission archéologique de Macédoine.* Paris: Firmin-Didot, 1876.

Horbury, William, and David Noy. *Jewish Inscriptions of Graeco-Roman Egypt. With an index of the Jewish inscriptions of Egypt and Cyrenaica.* Cambridge and New York: Cambridge University Press, 1992.

Horsley, G. H. R. *New Documents Illustrating Early Christianity.* 5 vols. (Vol. 1: *A Review of the Greek Inscriptions and Papyri published in 1976* [1981]; Vol. 2: *A Review of the Greek Inscriptions and Papyri published in 1977* [1982]; Vol. 3: *A Review of the Greek Inscriptions and Papyri published in 1978* [1983]; Vol. 4: *A Review of the Greek Inscriptions and Papyri published in 1979* [1987]; Vol. 5: *Linguistic Essays, with Cumulative Indexes to vols. 1–5 newly prepared by S. P. Swinn* [1989]). North Ryde, N.S.W.: Macquarie Ancient History Association, 1981–1989.

ICUR = Inscriptiones christianae urbis Romae septimo saeculo antiquiores, edited by Ioannes Baptista de Rossi. 3 vols. Rome: Ex Officina Libraria Pontificia, 1857–1915. *Supplementum,* fasc. 1, edited by Joseph Gatti. Rome: Ex Officina Cuggiani, 1915.

ICURns = Inscriptiones christianae urbis Romae septimo saeculo antiquiores. New series, begun by Ioannes Baptista de Rossi, completed and edited by Angelus Silvagni et al. 11 vols. Vatican City: Pont. Inst. Archaeologiae Christianae, 1922–1985.

IG XII 3 = Inscriptiones Graecae. Inscriptiones insularum maris Aegaei praeter Delum. Fasc. 3. Inscriptiones Symes, Teutlussae, Teli, Nisyri, Astypalaeae, Anaphes, Therae et Therasiae, Pholegandri, Meli, Cimoli. Edited by Friedrich Hiller von Gärtringen. Berlin: Akademie der Wissenschaften, 1898. *Supplementum* 1904. Repr. Berlin: Walter de Gruyter, 1939.

IGLS = Inscriptions grecques et latines de la Syrie. Edited by Louis Jalabert, René Mouterde, and J.-P. Rey-Coquais. Paris: P. Geuthner, 1929–1982.

Ihm, Maximilian. *Damasi epigrammata; accedunt Pseudodamasiana aliaque ad Damasiana inlustranda idonea.* Edited and with notes by Maximilian Ihm. Anthologiae latinae supplementa 1. Leipzig: B. G. Teubner, 1895.

IK 9–10,3 = *Katalog der antiken Inschriften des Museums von Iznik (Nikaia) I–II.2.* Edited by Sencer Sahin. 4 vols. Bonn: Habelt, 1979–1987.

IK 23/1 = *Die Inschriften von Smyrna, Teil I: Grabschriften, postume Ehrungen, Grabepigramme.* Edited by Georg Petzl. Bonn: Habelt, 1982.

ILCV = Inscriptiones Latinae Christianae Veteres. Edited by Ernest Diehl. 3 vols. (1925–1931). 2nd ed. Dublin and Zürich: Weidmann, 1961. Vol. 4: *Supplementum.* Edited by Jacques Moreau and Henri-Irénée Marrou. Zürich: Weidmann, 1967. Vol. 5: *Nuove Correzioni alla Silloge del Diehl, Inscriptiones Latinae Christianae Veteres.* Edited by Antonio Ferrua. SSAC 7. Vatican City: Pontificio Istituto di archeologia cristiana, 1981.

Jacopi, Giulio. *Esplorazioni e studi in Paflagonia e Cappadocia. Relazione sulla seconda Campagna Esplorativa Agosto – Ottobre 1936.* Rome: R. Istituto d'Archeologia e Storia dell'Arte, 1937.

Keil, Josef, and Anton von Premerstein. *Reisen in Lydien.* 3 vols. DAWW.PH 53/2; 54/2; 57/1. Vienna: In Kommission bei A. Hölder, 1908–1914.

Kubinska, Jadwiga. *Inscriptions grecques chrétiennes. Faras IV.* Warsaw: PWN 1974.

Körte, Alfred, ed. *Inscriptiones Bureschianae.* Wissenschaftliche Beilage zum Vorlesungsverzeichnis der Universität Greifswald. Easter 1902. Greifswald: Druck von J. Abel, 1902.

Laurent, J. "Delphes chrétien," *BCH* 23 (1899) 206–79.

Lefebvre, M. Gustave. *Recueil des inscriptions grecques-chrétiennes d'Egypte.* Le Caire: Impr. de l'Institut français d'archéologie orientale, 1907.

Lemerle, Paul. *Philippes et la Macédoine orientale à l'époque chrétienne et byzantine.* Recherches d'Histoire et d'Archéologie. Paris: E. de Boccard, 1945.

Llewelyn, S. R. *New Documents Illustrating Early Christianity.* Vol. 6: *A Review of the Greek Inscriptions and Papyri published in 1980–81;* Vol. 7: *A Review of the Greek Inscriptions and Papyri published in 1982–83,* with the collaboration of R. A. Kearsley. North Ryde, N.S.W.: Macquarie University: 1992, 1994.

Marinucci, Alfredo. "Ostia. Iscrizioni cristiane inedite o parzialmente edite," *RivAC* 67 (1991) 75–113.

MAMA I = Eastern Phrygia. Edited by William M. Calder. Manchester: Manchester University Press, 1928.

MAMA II = Meriamlik und Korykos, zwei christliche Ruinenstätten des Rauhen Kilikiens. Photos by Ernst Herzfeld with an accompanying text by S. Guyer. Manchester: Manchester University Press, 1930.

MAMA III = Denkmäler aus dem Rauhen Kilikien. Edited by Josef Keil and Adolf Wilhelm. Manchester: Manchester University Press, 1931.

MAMA IV = Monuments and Documents from Eastern Asia and Western Galatia. Edited by William H. Buckler, William M. Calder, and William K. C. Guthrie. Manchester: Manchester University Press, 1933.

MAMA V = Monuments from Dorylaeum and Nacolea. Edited by Christopher W. Cox and Archibald Cameron. Manchester: Manchester University Press, 1937.

MAMA VI = Monuments and Documents from Phrygia and Caria. Edited by William H. Buckler and William M. Calder. Manchester: Manchester University Press, 1939.

MAMA VII = Monuments from Eastern Phrygia. Edited by William M. Calder. Manchester: Manchester University Press, 1956.

MAMA VIII = Monuments from Lycaonia, the Pisidio-Phrygian Borderland, Aphrodisias. Edited by William M. Calder and James M. R. Cormack, with contributions from M. H. Ballance and M. R. E. Gough. Manchester: Manchester University Press, 1962.

Manni Piraino, Maria Teresa. *Iscrizioni greche lapidarie del Museo di Palermo*. ΣΙΚΕΛΙΚΑ VI. Palermo: S. F. Flaccovio, 1972.

Mastrocostas, E. "Παλαιοχριστιανικαὶ βασιλικαὶ Δρυμοῦ Βονίτσης" (sic). *Athens Annals Arch* 4 (1971) 185–95.

Meimaris, Yiannis E. *Sacred Names, Saints, Martyrs and Church Officials in the Greek Inscriptions and Papyri pertaining to the Christian Church of Palestine*. ΜΕΛΕΤΗΜΑΤΑ 2. Athens: National Hellenic Research Foundation, Centre for Greek and Roman Antiquity, 1986.

Mentzu-Meimare, Konstantina. "'Η παρουσία της γυναίκας στὶς 'Ελληνικές επιγραφές, από τόν Δ' μέχρι τόν Γ' μ.Χ. αιωνα" (sic). *JÖB* 32/2 (1982) 433–43.

Michaud, Jean-Pierre. "Chronique des fouilles et découvertes archéologiques en Grèce en 1973," *BCH* 98 (1974) 579–722.

Mihailov, Georgi. "Epigraphica," *Bulletin de l'Institut d'Archéologie* 25 (1962) 205–16.

Mordtmann, Johannes H. "Inschriften aus Edessa," *AM* 18 (1893) 415–19.

Mussies, Gerard. "Christelijke Inscripties in Palestina," in Roelof van den Broek et al., eds., *Kerk en kerken in Romeins-Byzantijns Palestina. Archeologie en geschiedenis*. Palestina Antiqua deel 6. Kampen: Kok, 1988, 186–211.

Nagel, Marcel. "Lettre chrétienne sur Papyrus (provenant de milieux sectaires du IVe siècle?)," *ZPE* 18 (1975) 317–23.

Naldini, Mario. *Il Cristianesimo in Egitto. Lettere private nei papiri dei secoli II–IV*. STP 3. Florence: Le Monnier, 1968.

Negev, Avraham. *The Greek Inscriptions from the Negev*. SBF.CMi 25. Jerusalem: Franciscan Printing Press, 1981.

Nilgen, Ursula. "Die große Reliquieninschrift von Santa Prassede. Eine quellenkritische Untersuchung zur Zeno-Kapelle," *RQ* 69 (1974) 7–29.

Orlandos, Anastasios K. "Βεροίας 'Επιγραφαὶ ἀνέκδοτοι," *AD* 2 (1916) 144–63.

Orsi, Paolo. "Gli scavi a S. Giovanni di Siracusa," *RQ* 10 (1896) 1–59.

Petsas, Photios "ΑΡΧΑΙΟΤΗΤΕΣ ΚΑΙ ΜΝΗΜΕΙΑ ΑΧΑΙΑΣ," *AD* 26 (1971) 148–85.

Piccirillo, Michele. *Chiese e Mosaici della Giordania Settentrionale. Disegni di Eugenio Alliata, Cesare Calano, Maurizio Villa*. SBV.CMi 30. Jerusalem: Franciscan Printing Press, 1981.

Pietri, Charles. "Appendice Prosopographique à la Roma Christiana (311–440)," *MEFRA* 89 (1977) 371–415.

Ramsay, A. Margaret. "The Early Christian Art of Isaura Nova," *JHS* 24 (1904) 260–92.

Ramsay, William M. "Laodicea Combusta and Sinethandos," *AM* 13 (1888) 233–72.

_____. "Early Christian Monuments in Phrygia: A Study in the Early History of the Church," *Exp* 8 (1888) 241–67, 401–27; 9 (1889) 141–60, 253–72, 392–400.

_____. *The Cities and Bishoprics of Phrygia. Being an Essay of The Local History of Phrygia from the Earliest Times to the Turkish Conquest.* 2 vols. Oxford: Clarendon Press, 1895, 1897.

_____. "The Worship of the Virgin Mary at Ephesus," *Exp* 12 (1905) 81–98.

_____. "Iconium," *Exp* 12 (1905) 193–215, 281–302, 351–69.

_____. "The Christian Inscriptions of Lycaonia," *Exp* 12 (1905) 438–59.

_____. "The Church of Lycaonia in the Fourth Century," in idem, *Luke the Physician.* London: Hodder and Stoughton, 1908, 329–410.

_____. "Phrygian Orthodox and Heretics 400–800 AD," *Byz* 6 (1931) 1–35.

Rengen, Wilfried van. "L'épigraphie grecque et latine de Syrie. Bilan d'un quart de siècle de recherches épigraphiques," *ANRW* II/8 (1977) 31–53.

Reynolds, Joyce, and Robert Tannenbaum. *Jews and God-Fearers at Aphrodisias: Greek Inscriptions with Commentary.* Cambridge Philological Society, Supp. 23. Cambridge: Cambridge Philological Society, 1987.

Robinson, David M. "Greek and Latin Inscriptions from Asia Minor," *TAPA* 57 (1926) 195–237.

Rose, H. W. "The Speaking Stone," *CIR* 37 (1923) 162–63.

Rossi, Giovanni Battista de. *Bulletino di archeologia cristiana.* Rome: Tipi del Salviucci, 1863–1894.

_____. *Musaici Cristiani e Saggi dei Pavimenti delle Chiese di Roma anteriori al secolo XV.* Rome: Guglielmo Haass, 1899.

_____. *Inscriptiones christianae urbis Romae septimo saeculo antiquiores.* Completed and edited by Angelus Silvagni et al. New series. 11 vols. Rome: Ex Officina Libraria Doct. Befani, 1922–1985.

Sahin, Sencer, "Neue Inschriften von der bithynischen Halbinsel," *ZPE* 18 (1975) 27–48.

Sterrett, J. R. Sitlington. *The Wolfe Expedition to Asia Minor.* Papers of the American School of Classical Studies at Athens 3. Boston: Damrell and Upham, 1888.

Strazzula, Vincentius. *Mvsevm Epigraphicvm seu Inscriptionvm Christianarvm, quae in Siracusanis catacumbis repertae sunt. Corpusculum.* Documenti alla Storia di Sicilia III/3. Panormi, 1897.

Syria-Princeton III A = Syria. Publications of the Princeton University Archaeological Expeditions to Syria in 1904–5 and 1909, Division III. Greek and Latin Inscriptions. A. Southern Syria. Edited by Enno Littmann, David Magie, and Duane Reed Stuart. Leiden: E. J. Brill, 1904–1921.

Syria-Princeton III B = Publications of the Princeton University Archaeological Expeditions to Syria in 1904–5 and 1909, Division III. Greek and Latin Inscriptions. B. Northern Syria. Edited by William K. Prentice. Leiden: E. J. Brill, 1908–1922.

Tabbernee, William. "Christian Inscriptions from Phrygia," in G. H. R. Horsley, ed., *New Documents Illustrating Early Christianity* 3. North Ryde, N.S.W.: Macquarie Ancient History Association, 1983, 128–39.

TAM IV = Tituli Bithyniae linguis Graeca et Latina conscripti. 1. Paeninsula Bithynica praeter Chalcedonem. Nicomedia et ager Nicomedensis cum septentrionali meridianoque litore sinus Astaceni et cum lacu Sumonensi. Edited by Friedrich Karl Dörner, with the assistance of Maria-Barbara von Stritzky. Vienna: In Kommission bei R. M. Rohrer, 1978.

TAM V = Tituli Lydiae linguis Graeca et Latina conscripti. 1. Regio septentrionalis ad orientem vergens. Edited by Peter Herrmann. Vienna: In Kommission bei R. M. Rohrer, 1981.

Thierry, Nicole. "Un problème de continuité ou de rupture. La Cappadoce entre Rome, Byzance et les Arabes," *CRAI* (1977) 98–145.

Thomsen, Peter. *Die lateinischen und griechischen Inschriften der Stadt Jerusalem und ihrer nächsten Umgebung.* Leipzig: J. C. Hinrichs, 1922.

Tibiletti, Giuseppe. *Le lettere private nei papiri greci del III e IV secolo d. C. Tra paganesimo e cristianesimo.* Scienze filologiche e letteratura 15. Milan: Vita e pensiero, 1979.

Waelkens, Marc. *Die kleinasiatischen Türsteine. Typologische und epigraphische Untersuchungen der kleinasiatischen Grabreliefs mit Scheintür.* Mainz: P. von Zabern, 1986.

Weil, Rudolf. "Von den griechischen Inseln," *AM* 2 (1877) 59–82.

Welles, Charles Bradford. "The Inscriptions of Gerasa," in Carl H. Kraeling, ed., *Gerasa. City of the Decapolis.* New Haven: American Schools of Oriental Research, 1938, 355–616.

Wessel, Carolus. *Inscriptiones graecae christianae veteres occidentis. Curaverunt Antonio Ferrua et Carolus Carletti.* Bari: Edipuglia, 1988.

Wischmeyer, Wolfgang Karl. *Die archäologischen und literarischen Quellen zur Kirchengeschichte von Apulia et Calabria, Lucania et Bruttii bis zum Jahr 600. Sammlung und Auswertung von Materialien zur Geschichte zweier spätantiker Provinzen.* Dissertation in typescript. Essen, 1972.

_____. "Review of Gibson, *The 'Christians for Christians' Inscriptions*," *JAC* 23 (1980) 166–71.

_____, ed. *Griechische und lateinische Inschriften zur Sozialgeschichte der Alten Kirche.* TKTG 28. Gütersloh: Gerd Mohn, 1982.

Wiseman, James, and Djordje Mano-Zissi. "Excavations at Stobi, 1971," *AJA* 76 (1972) 407–24.

_____. *Stobi. A Guide to the Excavations.* Belgrade: Published by the University of Texas at Austin and the National Museum of Titov Veles with a publication grant from the Smithsonian Institution, 1973.

Zilliacus, Henrik. *Sylloge inscriptionum christianarum veterum musei Vaticani.* 2 vols. AIRF 1/1–2. Helsinki: Instituti Romani Finlandiae, 1963.

2. Literary Sources

Acts of Paul and Thecla

"Πράξεις Παύλου καὶ Θέκλης," in *Acta Apostolorum Apocrypha 1, post Constantinum Tischendorf, denuo ediderunt Ricardus Adelbertus Lipsius et Maximilianus Bonnet.* Hildesheim: G. Olms, 1959, 235–72.

Acts of the Martyrs

Ausgewählte Märtyrerakten. Neubearbeitung der Knopfschen Ausgabe von Gustav Krüger, 4. Aufl., mit einem Nachtrag von Gerhard Ruhbach. SQS n.s. 3. Tübingen: J.C.B. Mohr [Paul Siebeck],1965.

Ambrosiaster

Das Corpus Paulinum des Ambrosiaster, hrsg. v. Heinrich Josef Vogels. BBB 13. Bonn: P. Hanstein, 1957.

Ambrosiastri qui dicitur commentarius in Epistulas Paulinas, recensuit Henricus Iosephus Vogels. 3 vols. CSEL 81/I–III. Vienna: Hoelder-Pichler-Tempsky, 1966–1969.

Anthologies:

A Lost Tradition. Women Writers of The Early Church. Edited by Patricia Wilson-Kastner, et al. Washington, D.C.: University Press of America, 1981.

Dichterinnen des Altertums und des frühen Mittelalters. Zweisprachige Textausgabe. Eingeleitet, übersetzt und mit bibliographischem Anhang versehen von Helene Homeyer. Paderborn, Munich, Vienna, and Zürich: F. Schöningh, 1979.

Maenads, Martyrs, Matrons, Monastics. A Sourcebook on Women's Religions in the Greco-Roman World. Edited by Ross S. Kraemer. Philadelphia: Fortress, 1988.

Monumenta de viduis diaconissis virginibusque tractantia. Collegit notis et prolegomenis instruxit Josephine Mayer. FlorPatr 42. Bonn: P. Hanstein, 1938.

Pauluskommentare aus der griechischen Kirche, aus Katenenhandschriften gesammelt v. Karl Staab. NTA 15. Münster: Aschendorff, 1933.

Sainted Women of the Dark Ages. Edited and translated by Jo Ann McNamara and John E. Halborg, with E. Gordon Whatley. Durham, N.C.: Duke University Press, 1992.

Women's Life in Greece and Rome. A Source Book in Translation. Edited by Mary R. Lefkowitz and Maureen B. Fant. London: Duckworth, and Baltimore: Johns Hopkins University Press, 1982; 2nd ed. 1985.

Apophthegmata Patrum, in *MPG* 65, 71–440.

Weisung der Väter. Apophthegmata Patrum, auch Gerontikon oder Alphabeticum genannt, hrsg. v. Bonifaz Miller. Sophia 6. Freiburg: Lambertus, 1965.

Apostolic Fathers

Die Apostolischen Väter, eingeleitet, herausgegeben, übertragen und erläutert von Joseph A. Fischer. SUC 1. Munich: Kösel, 1956; 9th revised ed. Darmstadt: Wissenschaftliche Buchgesellschaft, 1986.

Die Apostolischen Väter. Griechisch-deutsche Parallelausgabe auf der Grundlage der Ausgaben von Franx Xaver Funk, Karl Bihlmeyer, und Molly Whitaker, mit Übersetzungen von Martin Dibelius und Dietrich-Alex Koch, neu übersetzt und hrsg. v. Andreas Lindemann und Henning Paulsen. Tübingen: J.C.B. Mohr [Paul Siebeck], 1992.

Basil of Caesarea

Saint Basil. The Letters, with an English Translation, by Roy J. Deferrari. 4 vols. LCL. Cambridge, Mass.: Harvard University Press, 1950–1961.

Basilius von Caesarea. Briefe. 2. Teil (Nr. 95–213), eingeleitet, übersetzt und erläutert v. Wolf-Dieter Hauschild. BGrL 3. Stuttgart: A. Hiersemann, 1973.

Basilius von Caesarea, Briefe. Erster Teil (Nr. 1–94), eingeleitet, übersetzt und erläutert v. Wolf-Dieter Hauschild. BGrL 32. Stuttgart: A. Hiersemann, 1990.

Canons of Hippolytus

Die ältesten Quellen des orientalischen Kirchenrechtes I: Die Canones Hippolyti, hrsg. v. Hans Achelis. TU VI/H. 4. Leipzig: J. C. Hinrichs, 1891.

Die Kirchenrechtsquellen des Patriarchats Alexandrien, zusammengestellt und zum Teil übersetzt v. Wilhelm Riedel. Leipzig: A. Deichert, 1900, 193–230.

Les Canons d'Hippolyte. Edition critique de la version arabe. Introduction et traduction française, par René-Georges Coquin. PO 31,2. Paris: Firmin-Didot, 1966.

Clement of Alexandria

Clemens Alexandrinus, Dritter Band: Stromata Buch VII und VIII – Excerpta ex Theodoto – Eclogae Propheticae – Quis dives salvetur – Fragmente, hrsg. v. Otto Stählin. GCS 17/III. Leipzig: J. C. Hinrichs, 1909.

Des Clemens von Alexandreia Mahnrede an die Heiden. Der Erzieher, Buch I, aus dem Griechischen übersetzt v. Otto Stählin. BKV II/7. Munich: J. Kösel & F. Pustet, 1934.

Des Clemens von Alexandreia Mahnrede an die Heiden. Der Erzieher, Buch II–III. Welcher Reiche wird gerettet werden? aus dem Griechischen übersetzt v. Otto Stählin. BKV II/VIII. Munich: J. Kösel & F. Pustet, 1934.

Clemens Alexandrinus. Vierter Band: Register, hrsg. v. Otto Stählin. GCS 39/IV. Leipzig: J. C. Hinrichs, 1936.

Clemens Alexandrinus. Erster Band: Protrepticus und Paedagogus, hrsg. v. Otto Stählin. 3., durchges. Aufl. von Ursula Treu. GCS 12/I. Berlin: Akademie-Verlag, 1972.

Conciliar Acts:

Conciliengeschichte. Nach den Quellen bearbeitet v. Carl Joseph Hefele. 9 vols. (vols. 8 and 9 edited by J. Hergenröther). Freiburg: Herder, 1855–1890. Vols. 1–6, 2nd ed. Freiburg: Herder, 1873–1890.

Sacrorum conciliorum nova et amplissima collectio, cuius Joannes Dominicus Mansi. 53 vols. Paris: H. Welter, 1901–1927; reprint Graz: Akademische Druck- u. Verlagsanstalt, 1960–1961.

Die Kanones der wichtigsten altkirchlichen Concilien nebst den apostolischen Kanones, hrsg. v. Friedrich Lauchert. SQS 12. Freiburg: J. C. B. Mohr, 1896; reprint Frankfurt: Minerva, 1961.

Concilia Galliae. A. 314 – A. 506, cura et studio Charles Munier. CCSL 148. Turnhout: Brepols, 1963.

Concilia Galliae. A. 511 – A. 695, cura et studio Charles de Clercq. CCSL 148A. Turnhout: Brepols, 1963.

Concilia Africae. A. 345 – A. 525, cura et studio Charles Munier. CCSL 149. Turnhout: Brepols, 1974.

Constitutiones Apostolorum

Didascalia et Constitutiones Apostolorum, ed. Franciscus Xaverius Funk. Vol. I. Paderborn: F. Schöningh, 1905.

Les Constitutions Apostoliques. Introduction, texte critique, traduction et notes par Marcel Metzger. 3 vols. SC 320; 329; 336. Paris: Cerf, 1985–1987.

Constitutionis Ecclesiasticae Apostolorum
  Geschichte des Kirchenrechts I, by Johann Wilhelm Bickell. Gießen: Heyer, 1843, 107–32.
  "An Entire Syriac Text of the 'Apostolic Church Order,'" by J. P. Arendzen, *JThS* 3 (1902) 59–80.
  Die allgemeine Kirchenordnung, frühchristliche Liturgien und kirchliche Über-lieferung, 1. Teil: Die allgemeine Kirchenordnung des 2. Jahrhunderts, hrsg. v. Theodor Schermann. SGKA.E 3,1. Paderborn: Schöningh, 1914, 12–34.
Conversion of Georgia: see Ninotraditions
Corpus Iuris Civilis
  Corpus Iuris Civilis, ed. Paul Krüger, Theodor Mommsen, Rufus Schoell, and Wilhelm Kroll. 3 vols. Berlin: Weidmann, 1877–1892.
Corpus Iuris Canonici
  Codex des Kanonischen Rechtes, Lateinisch-deutsche Ausgabe mit Sachverzeichnis, hrsg. im Auftr. d. Dt. und d. Berliner Bischofskonferenz u.a. 2nd rev. and expanded ed. Kevelaer: Butzon & Bercker, 1984.
Cyprian
  S. Thasci Caecili Cypriani. Opera omnia, recensuit et commentario critico instruxit Wilhelm Hartel. 3 vols. CSEL 3/1–3. Vienna: apud C. Geroldi filium, 1868–1871.
Dialogue Between an Orthodox and a Montanist
  "Dialog zwischen einem Orthodoxen und einem Montanisten: Widerlegung eines Montanisten," hrsg. v. Gerhard Ficker. *ZKG* 26 (1905) 447–63.
Didache
  Didache = Zwölf-Apostel-Lehre, übersetzt und eingeleitet v. Georg Schöllgen. FC 1. Freiburg et al.: Herder, 1991, 25–139.
Didascalia Apostolorum
  Die ältesten Quellen des orientalischen Kirchenrechts II: Die syrische Didaskalia, übers. und erkl. v. Hans Achelis und Johannes Flemming. TU 25,2. Leipzig: J. C. Hinrichs, 1904.
  Didascalia et Constitutiones Apostolorum, hrsg. v. Franciscus Xaverius Funk. Vol. 1. Paderborn: Schöningh, 1905.
  The Didascalia Apostolorum in Syriac. Edited by Arthur Vööbus. 2 vols. CSCO.S 401/175; 402/176; 407/179; 408/180. Louvain: Secrétariat du CorpusSCO, 1979.
Egeria
  Egérie, Journal de Voyage (Itinéraire). Introduction, Texte Critique, Traduction, Notes, Index et Cartes par Pierre Maraval. Valerius du Bierzo, Lettre sur La B^{se} Egérie. Introduction, Texte, et Traduction par Manuel C. Diaz y Diaz. SC 296. Paris: Cerf, 1982.
Epiphanius of Salamis
  Epiphanius (Ancoratus und Panarion), hrsg. v. Karl Holl. 3 vols. GCS 25; 31; 37. Leipzig: J. C. Hinrichs, 1915–1933.
  Epiphanius, II. Panarion haer. 34–64. 2., bearbeitete Aufl. hrsg. v. Jürgen Dummer. GCS 31. Berlin: Akademie-Verlag, 1980.

The Panarion of Epiphanius of Salamis. Book I (Sects. 1–46). Translated by Frank Williams. NHS 35. Leiden and New York: E. J. Brill, 1987.

The Panarion of St. Epiphanius, Bishop of Salamis. Selected Passages. Translated by Philip R. Amidon. New York and Oxford: Oxford University Press, 1990.

Eusebius of Caesarea

Eusèbe de Césarée, Histoire Ecclésiastique. Livres I–X et les Martyrs en Palestine, Texte grec, Traduction et Notes. Introduction par Gustave Bardy; Index par Pierre Perichon. 4 vols. SC 31; 41; 55; 73. Paris: Cerf, 1952–1960.

Über das Leben des Kaisers Konstantin, Eusebius Werke I/1, hrsg. v. Friedhelm Winkelmann. GCS Eus. 1,1. Berlin: Akademie-Verlag, 1975.

Evagrius Ponticus

Briefe aus der Wüste, eingeleitet, übersetzt und kommentiert v. Gabriel Bunge. Sophia 24. Trier: Paulinus-Verlag, 1986.

Faltonia Betitia Proba

The Golden Bough, the Oaken Cross. The Virgilian Cento of Faltonia Betitia Proba. Edited by Elizabeth A. Clark and Diane F. Hatch. AAR.TTS 5. Chico: Scholars, 1981.

A Lost Tradition. Women Writers of The Early Church. Edited by Patricia Wilson-Kastner. Washington, D.C.: University Press of America, 1981, 33–69.

Gelasius I

Epistolae Romanorum Pontificum genuinae et quae ad eos scriptae sunt. Tomus I: A S. Hilaro usque ad Pelagium II, recensuit et edidit Andreas Thiel. Hildesheim and New York: Olms, 1974 (reprint of the Braunsberg ed. of 1867–68) 287–613.

Gerontius

The Life of Melania the Younger. Introduction, Translation, and Commentary by Elizabeth A. Clark. SWR 14. New York and Toronto: Edwin Mellen, 1984.

Vie de Sainte Mélanie. Texte Grec, Introduction, Traduction et Notes, par Denys Gorce. SC 90. Paris: Cerf, 1962.

Gregory Nazianzus

Gregor von Nazianz. De vita sua. Einleitung, Text, Übersetzung, Kommentar, herausgegeben, eingeleitet, und erklärt von Christoph Jungck. Heidelberg: C. Winter, 1974.

Grégoire de Nazianze, Discours 32–37. Introduction, Texte Critique, et Notes par Claudio Moreschini, Traduction par Paul Gallay. SC 318. Paris: Cerf, 1985.

Gregory of Nyssa, in *MPG* 46, 627–51

Grégoire de Nysse, Vie de Sainte Macrine. Introduction, Texte Critique, Traduction, Notes et Index, par Pierre Maraval. SC 178. Paris: Cerf, 1971.

Gregory of Tours

Historiarum libri decem, Zehn Bücher Geschichten, post Brunonem Krusch, auf Grund der Übersetzung W. Griesebrechts neubearb. von Rudolf Buchner. 2 vols. AQDGMA 1. Darmstadt: Wissenschaftliche Buchgesellschaft, 1955.

Hippolytus of Rome

Hippolytus. Refutatio Omnium Haeresium. Edited by Miroslav Marcovich. PTSt 25. Berlin and New York: Walter de Gruyter, 1986.

Exegetische und homiletische Schriften, Hippolytus Werke I, hrsg. v. G. Nathanael
  Bonwetsch and Hans Achelis. GCS 1. Leipzig: J. C. Hinrichs, 1897, 341–74.
Irenaeus of Lyons
  *Irénée de Lyon, Contre les Hérésies, Livre III. Texte Latin, Fragments Grecs, Intro-
  duction, Traduction et Notes de François Sagnard.* SC. Paris: Cerf, 1952.
  *Irénée de Lyon, Contre les Hérésies, Livre III. Edition critique par Adelin Rousseau
  et Louis Doutrelau, I: Introduction, Notes Justificatives, Tables; II: Texte et Tra-
  duction.* SC 210; 211. Paris: Cerf, 1974.
Jerome
  Commentarii in Epistolas Sancti Pauli, In Epistolam ad Romanos. MPL 30,
  645–718.
  Commentarii in Epistolas Sancti Pauli, In primam Epistolam ad Corinthos. MPL 30,
  717–72.
  Commentarii in Epistolas Sancti Pauli, In primam Epistolam ad Timotheum. MPL
  30, 875–88.
  Sancti Eusebii Hieronymi Epistulae, recensuit Isidore Hilberg. 3 vols. CSEL 54–56.
  Vienna: Verl. der Österreichischen Akademie der Wissenschaften, 1910–1918.
  Select Letters of St. Jerome, with an English Translation by Frederick A. Wright. LCL
  262. London: W. Heinemann, and New York: G. P. Putnam's Sons, 1933. Reprinted
  Cambridge, Mass.: Harvard University Press, and London: W. Heinemann, 1975.
  *Commentariorum in Danielem Libri III <IV>, S. Hieronymi Presbyteri Opera. Pars
  I: Opera Exegetica* 5. CCSL 75A. Turnhout: Brepols, 1964.
John Chrysostom
  Commentarius in Epistolam ad Romanos. MPG 60, 391–682.
  *Jean Chrysostome, Lettre d'exil. A Olympias et à tous les Fidèles (Quod nemo lae-
  ditur). Introduction, Texte Critique, Traduction et Notes par Anne-Marie Malin-
  grey.* SC 103. Paris: Cerf, 1964.
Justin Martyr
  Die Apologien Justins des Märtyrers, hrsg. v. Gustav Krüger. SQS I/1. 4th com-
  pletely revised ed. Tübingen: J.C.B. Mohr, 1915.
Liber Pontificalis
  *Le Liber Pontificalis. Texte, Introduction et Commentaire, par Louis Marie Olivier
  Duchesne.* 2 vols. Paris: Thorin et al., 1955. Vol. 3: *Additions et Corrections d.
  Mgr. L. Duchesne.* Published by Cyril Vogel. Paris: E. de Boccard, 1955–1957.
Liturgikon
  "Messbuch" der byzantinischen Kirche, hrsg. v. Neophytos Edelby. Reckling-
  hausen: A. Bongers, 1967.
Melania the Elder
  "Un opuscule inédit de Fr. C. Conybeare," by Arnold van Lantschoot. *Muséon* 77
  (1964) 121–35.
Montanism
  *Les sources de l'histoire du Montanisme. Texts Grecs, Latine, Syriaque, publiés avec
  Introduction Critique, Traduction Française, Notes et "Indices," par Pierre de
  Labriolle.* CF 24. Fribourg: Librairie de l'Université; Paris: Ernest Leroux, 1913.

The Montanist Oracles and Testimonia. Edited by Ronald E. Heine. PatMS 14. Macon, Ga.: Mercer University Press, 1989.

Ninotraditions

Lives and Legends of the Georgian Saints. Selected and Translated from the original texts, by David Marshall Lang. London: Allen & Unwin; New York, Macmillan, 1956, 13–39.

"Die Bekehrung Georgiens. Mokcevay Kartlisay (Verfasser unbekannt)," translated and annotated by Gertrud Pätsch, *Bedi Kartlisa. Révue de Kartvélologie* 23 (1975) 288–337.

Das Leben Kartlis. Eine Chronik aus Georgien. 300–1200, hrsg. v. Gertrud Pätsch. Sammlung Dieterich 330. Leipzig: Dieterich, 1985, 131–200.

Origen

"Origen on 1 Corinthians," edited by Claude Jenkins. *JThS* 9 (1908) 231–47, 353–72, 500–14; 10 (1909) 29–51.

Origène. Commentaire sur Saint Jean. Livres I–XX. Texte Grec, Introduction, Traduction et Notes par Cécile Blanc. 4 vols. SC 120; 157; 222; 290. Paris: Cerf, 1966–1982.

Origenis commentariorum in epistulam S. Pauli ad Romanos libri decem. MPG 14, 831–1292.

Origenes. Commentarii in epistulam ad Romanos: Liber Primus, Liber Secundus / Römerbriefkommentar: Erstes und zweites Buch, übersetzt und eingeleitet von Theresia Heither. FC 2/1. Freiburg and New York: Herder, 1990.

"The commentary of Origen on the Epistle to the Romans," edited by A. Ramsbotham. *JThS* 13 (1912) 209–24, 357–68; 14 (1913) 10–22.

"Neue Fragmente aus dem Kommentar des Origenes zum Römerbrief," by Karl Staab. *BZ* 18 (1929) 72–82.

Palladius

The Lausiac History of Palladius. A Critical Discussion together with Notes on Early Egyptian Monachism, by Cuthbert Butler. I/II. TaS 6. Hildesheim: G. Olms, 1967 (reprint of the 1898 Cambridge edition).

Pliny the Younger

C. Plini Caecili Secundi. Epistularum Libri Novem, Epistularum ad Traianum Liber Panegyricus, recensuit Richard C. Kukula. Leipzig: Teubner, 1912.

Pseudo-Athanasius

Vita et gesta sanctae beataeque magistrae Syncleticae. MPG 28, 1485–1558.

Vie de Sainte Synclétique. Traduit du grec, par Odile Bénédicte Bernard. Spiritualité Orientale 9. Begrolles-en-Mauge: Abbaye de Bellefontaine, 1972, 7–79.

"Pseudo-Athanasius. The Life and Activity of the Holy and Blessed Teacher Syncletica," by Elizabeth Castelli in Vincent L. Wimbush, ed., *Ascetic Behavior in Greco-Roman Antiquity.* Minneapolis: Fortress, 1990, 265–311.

Una donna nel deserto. Vita della monaca Sincletica. Traduzione, introduzione e note, par Mauro Todde. Margaritae: Letture di padri 3. Milan: CENS, 1989.

Rufinus

Historia Ecclesiastica. Libri Duo. MPL 21, 465–540.

Tyrannius Rufinus, Historia Monachorum sive de Vita Sanctorum Patrum, hrsg. v. Eva Schulz-Flügel. PTS 34. Berlin and New York: Walter de Gruyter, 1990.

Shepherd of Hermas
Die Apostolischen Väter I. Der Hirt des Hermas, edited by Molly Whittaker. GCS I. Berlin: Akademie-Verlag, 1956.

Socrates Scholasticus
Historia Ecclesiastica. MPG 67, 33–842.

Sophronius of Jerusalem
Vita S. Mariae Aegyptiacae, MPG 87/3, 3687–3726.

Sozomen
Kirchengeschichte, hrsg. v. Joseph Bidez. Eingeleitet, zum Druck besorgt und mit Registern versehen von Günther Christian Hansen. GCS 50. Berlin: Akademie-Verlag, 1960.

Sozomène. Histoire ecclésiastique. Livres I–II. Texte Grec de l'Edition J. Bidez, Introduction par Bernard Grillet et Guy Sabbah, Traduction par André-Jean Festugière, Annotation par Guy Sabbah. SC 306. Paris: Cerf, 1983.

Synesius of Cyrene
Synesii Cyrenensis Epistolas, recensuit Antonius Garzya. Rome: Typis Officinae Polygraphicae, 1979.

Synodicon
The Synodicon in the West Syrian Tradition. Translated by Arthur Vööbus. CSCO 367/CSCO.S 161, 1–39; CSCO 368/CSCO.S 162, 27–64. Louvain: Secrétariat du CorpusSCO, 1975–1976.

Tertullian
Quinti Septimi Florentis Tertulliani. De Anima. Edited with Introduction and Commentary by Jan Hendrik Waszink. Amsterdam: North-Holland Publishing Co., 1947.

Tertullien, Traité du Baptême. Texte, Introduction et Notes de R. François Refoulé, Traduction en collaboration avec M. Drouzy. SC 35. Paris: Cerf, 1952.

Tertullien, Traité de la prescription contre les Hérétiques. Introduction, Texte Critique, et Notes de R. François Refoulé, Traduction de Pierre de Labriolle. SC 46. Paris: Cerf, 1957.

Tertullien, La Toilette des Femmes (De cultu feminarum). Introduction, Texte Critique, Traduction et Commentaire de Marie Turcan. SC 173. Paris: Cerf, 1971.

Tertullian. De virginibus velandis. Übersetzung, Einleitung, Kommentar. Ein Beitrag zur altkirchlichen Frauenfrage, by Christoph Stücklin. EHS.T 26. Frankfurt: Peter Lang, 1974, 11–73.

Tertullien, Exhortation à la Chasteté. Introduction, Texte Critique et Commentaire par Claudio Moreschini, Traduction par Jean-Claude Fredouille. SC 319. Paris: Cerf, 1985.

Tertullien, A son Epouse. Introduction, Texte Critique, Traduction et Notes de Charles Munier. SC 273. Paris: Cerf, 1980.

Tertullien, Le Mariage Unique (de monogamia). Introduction, Texte Critique, Traduction et Commentaire de Paul Mattei. SC 343. Paris: Cerf, 1988.

Testamentum Domini

Testamentum Domini nostri Jesu Christi. Nunc primum edidit, latine reddidit et illustravit Ignatius Ephraem II Rahmani. Hildesheim: G. Olms, 1968 (reprint of the 1899 edition).

The Testament of our Lord. Translated into English from the Syriac, With Introduction and Notes, by James Cooper and Arthur John MacLean. Edinburgh: T & T Clark, 1902.

Traditio Apostolica

Der aethiopische Text der Kirchenordnung des Hippolyt. Nach 8 Handschriften hrsg. u. übers. v. Hugo Duensing. AAWG.PH III/32. Göttingen: Vandenhoeck & Ruprecht, 1946.

Ἀποστολικὴ Παράδοσις, *The Treatise on the Apostolic Tradition of St Hippolytus of Rome, Bishop and Martyr.* Edited by Gregory Dix, reissued with corrections, preface, and bibliography by Henry Chadwick. London: Published for the Church Historical Society by S.P.C.K., 1968.

Hippolyte de Rome. La Tradition Apostolique d'après les Anciennes Versions. Introduction, Traduction, et Notes par Bernard Botte. SC 11bis. 2nd ed. Paris: Cerf, 1984.

La Tradition apostolique de Saint Hippolyte. Essai de Reconstruction, par Bernard Botte. 5., verb. Aufl. hrsg. v. Albert Gerhards unter Mitarb. v. Sabine Felbecker. LQF 39. Münster: Aschendorff, 1989.

Traditio Apostolica = Apostolische Überlieferung, hrsg. v. Wilhelm Geerlings. FC 1. Freiburg and New York: Herder, 1991, 143–313.

Theodoret of Cyrrhus

Theodoret Kirchengeschichte, hrsg. v. Léon Parmentier. GCS 44. Leipzig: J. C. Hinrichs, 1911. 2nd ed. by Felix Scheidweiler. Berlin: Akademie-Verlag, 1954.

Beati Theodoreti Episcopi Cyrensis Interpretatio Epistolae ad Romanos. MPG 82, 43–226.

Theophylact of Bulgaria

Theophylacti archiepiscopi Bulgariae enarratio in Evangelium Joannis. MPG 123, 1127–1348.

Vergil

P. Vergili Maronis, Opera. Apparatu critico in artius contracto, iterum recensuit Otto Ribbeck. I–IV. Hildesheim: G. Olms, 1966. (Reprint of the 1894–95 edition.)

Vita Melaniae: see Gerontius

Vita of Nino: see Ninotraditions

Vita S. Mariae Aegyptiacae: see Sophronius of Jerusalem

Vita Syncleticae: see Pseudo-Athanasius

Vita Theclae

Vie et Miracles de saint Thècle. Texte Grec, Traduction et Commentaire, par Gilbert Dagron avec la collaboration de Marie Dupré la Tour. SHG 62. Brussels: Société des bollandistes, 1978.

C. Secondary Literature

Aalen, Sverre. "A Rabbinic Formula in I Cor. 14,34," *Studia Evangelica* 87 (1964) 513–25.

Abrahamsen, Valerie. "Women at Philippi: The Pagan and Christian Evidence," *JFSR* 3 (1987) 17–30.

Achelis, Hans. "Apostolische Kirchenordnung," *RE³* 1 (1896) 730–34.

_____. "Apostolische Konstitutionen und Kanones," *RE³* 1 (1896) 734–41.

_____. "Diakonissen, altkirchliche," *RE³* 4 (1898) 616–20.

_____. "Spuren des Urchristentums auf den griechischen Inseln?" *ZNW* 1 (1900) 87–100.

_____. *Virgines subintroductae. Ein Beitrag zu I Kor VII.* Leipzig: J. C. Hinrichs, 1902.

_____. *Das Christentum in den ersten drei Jahrhunderten.* 2 vols. Leipzig: Quelle & Meyer, 1912.

_____. "Presbyter," *RE³* 16 (1905) 5–9.

Adam, Alfred. "Die Entstehung des Bischofsamtes," *WuD* 5 (1957) 104–29.

Afanasiev, Nicholas. "Presbytides or Female Presidents. Canon 11, Council of Laodicea," in Thomas Hopko, ed., *Women and the Priesthood.* Crestwood, N.Y.: St. Vladimir's Seminary Press, 1983, 61–74.

Affeldt, Werner, and Sabine Reiter. "Die Historiae Gregors von Tours als Quelle für die Lebenssituation von Frauen im Frankreich des sechsten Jahrhunderts," in Annette Kuhn, ed., *Frauen in der Geschichte VII. Interdisziplinäre Studien zur Geschichte der Frauen im Frühmittelalter. Methoden – Probleme – Ergebnisse.* Geschichtsdidaktik. Studien Materialien 39. Düsseldorf: Pädagogischer Verlag Schwann, 1986, 192–208.

Albrecht, Ruth. "Asketinnen im 4. und 5. Jahrhundert in Kleinasien," *JÖB* 32/2 (1982) 517–24.

_____. "'Der Natur nach bin ich eine Frau.' Asketinnen in der frühen Kirche," *Schlangenbrut* 3 (1983) 6–11.

_____. "Die Frau in der Frühzeit der Kirche," in Volker Hochgrebe and Michaela Pilters, eds., *Geteilter Schmerz der Unterdrückung. Frauenbefreiung im Urchristentum.* Stuttgart: Kreuz, 1984, 41–52.

_____. *Das Leben der heiligen Makrina auf dem Hintergrund der Thekla-Traditionen. Studien zu den Ursprüngen des weiblichen Mönchtums im 4. Jahrhundert in Kleinasien.* FKDG 38. Göttingen: Vandenhoeck & Ruprecht, 1986.

_____. "Wir gedenken der Frauen, der bekannten wie der namenlosen. Feministische Kirchengeschichtsschreibung," in Christine Schaumberger and Monika Maasen, eds., *Handbuch Feministische Theologie.* Münster: Morgana, 1986, 3rd ed. 1989, 312–22.

_____. "Apostolin/Jüngerin," *WFT* (1991) 24–28.

_____. "Prophetin II. Neues Testament," *WFT* (1991) 332–35.

Alföldy, Geza. *Flamines provinciae hispaniae citerioris.* Anejos de Archivo Español de Arqueologia VI. Madrid: Consejo Superior de Investigaciones Científicas, Instituto Español de Arqueología, 1973.

Alic, Margaret. *Hypatia's Heritage: A History of Women in Science from Antiquity through the Nineteenth Century.* Boston: Beacon, 1986.

Allworthy, Thomas Bateson. *Women in the Apostolic Church. A Critical Study of the Evidence in the New Testament for the Prominence of Women in Early Christianity.* Cambridge: W. Heffer & Sons, 1917.

Altaner, Berthold, and Alfred Stuiber. *Patrologie. Leben, Schriften und Lehre der Kirchenväter.* 9th ed. Freiburg, Basel, and Vienna: Herder, 1980.

Andrieu, Michel. *Les Ordines Romani du Haut Moyen Age.* 5 vols. SSL 11; 23; 24; 28; 19. Louvain: Spicilegium Sacrum Lovaniense Administration, 1931–1965.

Ansorge, Dirk. "Der Diakonat der Frau. Zum gegenwärtigen Forschungsstand," in Teresa Berger and Albert Gerhards, eds., *Liturgie und Frauenfrage. Ein Beitrag zur Frauenforschung aus liturgiewissenschaftlicher Sicht.* PiLi 7. St. Ottilien: EOS Verlag, 1990, 31–65.

Arat, Kristin. "Die Weihe der Diakonin in der armenisch-apostolischen Kirche," in idem, 67–76.

Arzt, Peter. "Iunia oder Iunias? Zum textkritischen Hintergrund von Röm 16,7," in Friedrich V. Reiterer and Petrus Eder, eds., *Liebe zum Wort. Beiträge zur klassischen und biblischen Philologie, P. Ludger Bernhard zum 80. Geburtstag.* Salzburg: Müller, 1993, 83–102.

Ash, James L. "The Decline of Ecstatic Prophecy in the Early Church," *TS* 37 (1976) 227–52.

Asmussen, Marianne Wirenfeldt. "The Chapel of S. Zeno in S. Prassede in Rome," *ARID* 15 (1986) 67–86.

Atkinson, P. C. "The Montanist Interpretation of Joel 2:28.29 (LXX 3:1,2)," *Studia Evangelica* 7 (1982) 11–15.

Atwood, Richard. *Mary Magdalene in the New Testament Gospels and Early Tradition.* EHS.T 457. Bern et al.: Peter Lang, 1993.

Aubert, Marie-Josèphe. *Des Femmes Diacres. Un Nouveau Chemin pour l'Eglise.* Preface by Régine Pernoud. PoTh 47. Paris: Beauchesne, 1987.

Aune, David E. *Prophecy in Early Christianity and the Ancient Mediterranean World.* Grand Rapids: Eerdmans, 1983.

Baker, Tony. "Men, Women and the Presbyterate: Does Scripture Speak Clearly?" *Churchman* 104 (1990) 43–50.

Balsdon, John P.V.D. *Roman Women: Their History and Habits.* London: Bodley Head, 1962; 5th ed. 1977.

Bangerter, Otto. *Frauen im Aufbruch. Die Geschichte einer Frauenbewegung in der Alten Kirche. Ein Beitrag zur Frauenfrage.* Neukirchen-Vluyn: Neukirchener Verlag, 1971.

Bardy, Gustave. "L'église et l'enseignement pendant les trois premiers siècles," *RevScR* 12 (1932) 1–18.

_____. "Les écoles romaines au second siècle," *RHE* 28 (1932) 501–32.

_____. "Pour l'histoire de l'école d'Alexandrie," *VivPen* 2 (1942) 80–109.

Barnett, Paul W. "Wives and Women's Ministry (1 Timothy 2:11-15)," *EvQ* 61 (1989) 225–38.

Barrois, Georges. "Women and the Priestly Office According to the Scriptures," in Thomas Hopko, ed., *Women and the Priesthood*. Crestwood, N.Y.: St. Vladimir's Seminary Press, 1983, 39–60.

Barthes, Roland. *Literatur oder Geschichte*. Translated from French by Helmut Scheffel. edition suhrkamp 303. Frankfurt: Suhrkamp 1969.

Bartsch, Hans-Werner. *Die Anfänge urchristlicher Rechtsbildungen. Studien zu den Pastoralbriefen*. ThF 34. Hamburg-Bergstedt: H. Reich, 1965.

Bassler, Jouette M. "The Widows' Tale: A Fresh Look at 1 Tim 5:3-16," *JBL* 103 (1984) 23–41.

Bauer, Walter. *Rechtgläubigkeit und Ketzerei im ältesten Christentum*. BHTh 10. 2nd. rev. ed. with an appendix, ed. Georg Strecker. Tübingen: J.C.B. Mohr [Paul Siebeck], 1964. English: *Orthodoxy and Heresy in Earliest Christianity*. Translated by a team from the Philadelphia Seminar on Christian Origins, and edited by Robert A. Kraft and Gerhard Krodel. Philadelphia: Fortress, 1971.

Baumert, Norbert. *Frau und Mann bei Paulus. Überwindung eines Mißverständnisses*. Würzburg: Echter, 1992. English: *Woman and Man in Paul: Overcoming a Misunderstanding*. Translated by Patrick Madigan and Linda M. Maloney. Collegeville: The Liturgical Press, 1996.

_____. *Antifeminismus bei Paulus? Einzelstudien*. fzb 68. Würzburg: Echter, 1992.

Beauvoir, Simone de. *Le Deuxième Sexe*. Paris: Gallimard, 1949. English: *The Second Sex*. Translated and edited by H. M. Parshley. 1st American ed. New York: Knopf, 1953.

Behr-Sigel, Elisabeth. "Ordination von Frauen? Ein Versuch des Bedenkens einer aktuellen Frage im Lichte der lebendigen Tradition der orthodoxen Kirche," in Elisabeth Gössmann and Dietmar Bader, eds., *Warum keine Ordination der Frau? Unterschiedliche Einstellungen in den christlichen Kirchen*. Munich: Schnell & Steiner, 1987, 50–72.

_____. *Le ministère de la femme dans l'eglise*. Paris: Cerf, 1987. English: *The Ministry of Women in the Church*. Translated by Steven Bigham. Redondo Beach, Cal.: Oakwood, 1991.

Beinert, Wolfgang, ed. *Frauenbefreiung und Kirche. Darstellung – Analyse – Dokumentation. Mit Beiträgen von Wolfgang Beinert, Herlinde Pissarek-Hudelist, Rudolf Zwank*. Regensburg: Pustet, 1987.

Benjamin, Walter. *Gesammelte Schriften*, edited by Rolf Tiedemann and Hermann Schweppenhäuser, with the assistance of Theodor W. Adorno and Gershom Scholem. 7 vols. in 15. Frankfurt: Suhrkamp, 1972–1989.

Bengtson, Hermann. *Einführung in die Alte Geschichte*. 7th rev. and expanded ed. Munich: Beck, 1975. English: *Introduction to Ancient History*. Translated from the 6th ed. by R. I. Frank and Frank D. Gilliard. Berkeley: University of California Press, 1970.

Bernet-Strahm, Silvia. "'Die Sieger schreiben die Geschichte – auf ihre Weise' (E. Pagels)," *Fama* 3 (1986) 9–10.

Bertini, Ferrucio, ed. *Medioevo al femminile*. Rome: Laterza, 1989. German: *Heloise und ihre Schwestern. Acht Frauenporträts aus dem Mittelalter*. Translated by Ernst Voltmer. Munich: Beck, 1991.

Beyer, Hermann Wolfgang. "διακονέω, κτλ.," *TDNT* 2:81–93.

Beyer, Hermann Wolfgang, and Heinrich Karpp. "Bischof," *RAC* 2 (1954) 394–407.

Beyerhaus, Peter. "Eine geistliche Katastrophe. Für manche konservative Theologen ist das Bischofsamt vakant," in *". . . das Weib rede in der Gemeinde." Maria Jepsen: Erste lutherische Bischöfin. Dokumente und Stellungnahmen*. GTB 1118. Gütersloh: Gerd Mohn, 1992, 86–88.

Bianchi, Ugo. *La tradizione dell' enkrateia. Motivazioni ontologiche e protologiche*. Atti del Colloquio internazionale, Milano, 20–23 aprile 1982. Rome: Edizioni dell'Ateneo, 1985.

Bienert, Wolfgang A. "Das Apostelbild in der altchristlichen Überlieferung," in Wilhelm Schneemelcher, ed., *Neutestamentliche Apokryphen in deutscher Übersetzung II*. 5th ed. Tübingen: J.C.B. Mohr [Paul Siebeck], 1989, 6–28. Cf. Walter Bauer and Manfred Hornschuh, "The Picture of the Apostle in Early Christian Tradition," in Edgar Hennecke, *New Testament Apocrypha 2*. Edited by Wilhelm Schneemelcher, English translation edited by Robert McLean Wilson. Philadelphia: Westminster, 1965, 35–87.

Blank, Josef, and Bogdan Snela. "Priester/Bischof," *NHThG* 3 (1985) 411–41.

Blum, Georg Günter. "Das Amt der Frau im Neuen Testament," *NT* 7 (1964/65) 142–61.

_____. "Apostel /Apostolat/ Apostolizität II. Alte Kirche," *TRE* 3 (1978) 445–66.

Bock, Gisela. "Historisches Fragen nach Frauen. Historische Frauenforschung: Fragestellungen und Perspektiven," in Karin Hausen, ed., *Frauen suchen ihre Geschichte. Historische Studien zum 19. und 20. Jahrhundert*. Beck'sche Schwarze Reihe 276. Munich: Beck, 1983, 22–60.

_____. "Der Platz der Frau in der Geschichte," in Herta Nagl-Docekal and Franz Wimmer, eds., *Neue Ansätze in der Geschichtswissenschaft*. Conceptus-Studien 1. Vienna: VWGO, 1984, 108–27.

_____. "Patriarchat. Vom Nutzen und Nachteil eines Konzepts für Frauengeschichte und -politik," *Journal für Geschichte* 5 (1986) 12–21, 58.

_____. "Geschichte, Frauengeschichte, Geschlechtergeschichte," *GeGe* 14 (1988) 364–91.

Boelens, Martin. *Die Klerikerehe in der Gesetzgebung der Kirche unter besonderer Berücksichtigung der Strafe. Eine rechtsgeschichtliche Untersuchung von den Anfängen der Kirche bis zum Jahre 1139*. Paderborn: Schöningh, 1968.

Böhmer, Heinrich. "Paschalis I," *RE³* 14 (1904) 716–71.

Bolkestein, Hendrik. *Wohltätigkeit und Armenpflege im vorchristlichen Altertum. Ein Beitrag zum Problem "Moral und Gesellschaft."* Alternate title: *Charity and poor welfare in pre-Christian antiquity: a contribution to the problem "Ethics and Society."* Utrecht: A. Oosthoek, 1939; New York: Arno, 1979.

Bonwetsch, G. Nathanael. *Die Schriften Tertullians nach der Zeit ihrer Abfassung.* Bonn: A. Marcus, 1878.

_____. *Die Geschichte des Montanismus.* Erlangen: Verlag von Andreas Deichert, 1881.

_____. "Epiphanius," *RE³* 5 (1898) 417–21.

_____. "Märtyrer und Bekenner," *RE³* 12 (1903) 48–52.

_____. *Die Theologie des Irenäus.* BFChTh 2/9. Gütersloh: Gerd Mohn, 1925.

Bopp, Linus. *Das Witwentum als organische Gliedschaft im Gemeinschaftsleben der alten Kirche. Ein geschichtlicher Beitrag zur Grundlegung der Witwenseelsorge in der Gegenwart.* Mannheim: Wohlgemuth, 1950.

Boring, M. Eugene. *The Continuing Voice of Jesus. Christian Prophecy and the Gospel Tradition.* Louisville: Westminster/John Knox, 1991. (Original title: *Sayings of the Risen Jesus.* Cambridge and New York: Cambridge University Press, 1982.)

Børresen, Kari Elisabeth. *Subordination et équivalence. Nature et rôle de la femme d'après Augustin et Thomas d'Aquin.* Oslo: Universitetsforlaget, 1968. English: *Subordination and Equivalence. The Nature and Role of Woman in Augustine and Thomas Aquinas.* Translated by Charles H. Talbot. Washington, D.C.: University Press of America, 1981.

_____. "Die anthropologischen Grundlagen der Beziehung zwischen Mann und Frau in der klassischen Theologie," *Conc(GB)* 12 (1976) 10–17.

_____. "Männlich-Weiblich: eine Theologiekritik," *US* 35 (1980) 325–34.

_____. "Women's Studies of the Christian Tradition," *Contemporary philosophy* 6 (1990) 901–1001.

_____. "The Ordination of Women: To Nurture Tradition by Continuing Inculturation," *StTh* 46 (1992) 3–13.

Bornkamm, Günther. "πρέσβυς, πρεσβύτερος, κτλ.," *TDNT* 6:651–83.

Bosold, Birgit. "'Darum soll die Frau einen Schleier tragen . . . .' Überlegungen zu 1. Korinther 11 im Kontext paulinischer Gemeindetheologie und Gemeindeordnung," *Schlangenbrut* 23 (1988) 13–15.

Bousset, Wilhelm. *Jüdisch-Christlicher Schulbetrieb in Alexandria und Rom. Literarische Untersuchungen zu Philo und Clemens von Alexandria, Justin und Irenäus.* Hildesheim and New York: G. Olms, 1975. (Reprint of the Göttingen edition of 1915.)

Bovon, François. *Das Evangelium nach Lukas (Lk 1,1–9,50).* EKK III/1. Neukirchen-Vluyn: Neukirchener Verlag, 1989.

Bowman, Ann L. "Women in Ministry: An Exegetical Study of 1 Timothy 2:11-15," *BS* 149 (1992) 193–213.

Brackmann, Albert. "Liber pontificalis," *RE³* 11 (1902) 439–46.

Bradshaw, Paul F. "Kirchenordnungen (I. Altkirchliche)," *TRE* 18 (1989) 662–70.

Braunstein, Otto. *Die politische Wirksamkeit der griechischen Frau. Eine Nachwirkung griechischen Mutterrechtes.* Leipzig: Druck von A. Hoffmann, in Kommission bei G. Fock, 1911.

Brennan, Brian. "'Episcopae': Bishops' Wives Viewed in Sixth-Century Gaul," *ChH* 54 (1985) 311–23.

Brent, Allen. "The Relations Between Ignatius and the Didascalia," *SecCen* 8 (1991) 129–56.

Brock, Sebastian P., and Susan Ashbrook Harvey, eds. *Holy Women of the Syrian Orient*. The Transformation of the Classical Heritage 13. Berkeley, Los Angeles, and London: University of California Press, 1987.

Brockhaus, Ulrich. *Charisma und Amt. Die paulinische Charismenlehre auf dem Hintergrund der frühchristlichen Gemeindefunktionen.* Wuppertal: Theologischer Verlag Brockhaus, 1972.

Brooten, Bernadette J. "Junia . . . Outstanding among the Apostles," in Leonard Swidler and Arlene Swidler, eds., *Women Priests: A Catholic Commentary on the Vatican Declaration.* New York: Paulist, 1977, 141–44.

_____. "Feminist Perspectives on New Testament Exegesis," *Concilium* (Oct. 1980) 55–61.

_____. *Women Leaders in the Ancient Synagogue. Inscriptional Evidence and Background Issues.* BJSt 36. Chico: Scholars, 1982.

_____. "Jüdinnen zur Zeit Jesu. Ein Plädoyer für Differenzierung," in Bernadette J. Brooten and Norbert Greinacher, eds., *Frauen in der Männerkirche.* Munich: Kaiser, 1982, 141–48.

_____. "Konnten Frauen im alten Judentum die Scheidung betreiben? Überlegungen zu Mk 10,11-12 und 1 Kor 7,10-11," *EvTh* 42 (1982) 65–80.

_____. "Zur Debatte über das Scheidungsrecht der jüdischen Frau," *EvTh* 43 (1983) 466–78.

_____. "Early Christian Women and their Cultural Context: Issues of Method in Historical Reconstruction," in Adela Yarbro Collins, ed., *Feminist Perspectives on Biblical Scholarship.* Chico: Scholars, 1985, 65–91.

_____. "Paul's Views on the Nature of Women and Female Homoeroticism," in Clarissa W. Atkinson, Constance H. Buchanan, and Margaret R. Miles, eds., *Immaculate and Powerful: The Female in Sacred Image and Social Reality.* Boston: Beacon, 1985, 61–87.

_____. "Jewish Women's History in the Roman Period: A Task for Christian Theology," *HThR* 79 (1986) 22–30.

_____. "Response to 'Corinthian Veils and Gnostic Androgynes' by Dennis R. MacDonald," in Karen L. King, ed., *Images of the Feminine in Gnosticism.* Studies in Antiquity and Christianity 4. Philadelphia: Fortress, 1988.

_____. "The Gender of Ιαηλ in the Jewish Inscription from Aphrodisias," in Harold W. Attridge et al., eds., *Of Scribes and Scrolls: Essays in Honor of John Strugnell.* Lanham, Md.: University Press of America, 1990, 163–73.

_____. "Iael προστάτης in the Jewish Donative Inscription of Aphrodisias," in Birger A. Pearson, ed., *The Future of Early Christianity. Essays in Honor of Helmut Koester.* Minneapolis: Fortress, 1991, 149–62.

Brosch, Joseph. *Charismen und Ämter in der Urkirche.* Bonn: P. Hanstein, 1951.

Brown, Peter. *The Body and Society. Men, Women and Sexual Renunciation in Early Christianity.* New York: Columbia University Press, 1988.

Brown, Raymond E. "Episkopē and Episkopos: The New Testament Evidence," *TS* 41 (1980) 322–38.

Brown, Schuyler. "Apostleship in the New Testament as an Historical and Theological Problem," *NTS* 30 (1984) 474–80.

Brown, S. Kent. "Coptic and Greek Inscriptions from Christian Egypt: A Brief Review," in Birger A. Pearson and James E. Goehring, eds., *The Roots of Egyptian Christianity*. Philadelphia: Fortress, 1986, 26–41.

Brox, Norbert. "Kirchenordnungen," *SM* 2 (1968) 1222–1226.

_____. "Häresie," *RAC* 13 (1986) 248–97.

_____. *Die Pastoralbriefe. 1 Timotheus, 2 Timotheus, Titus.* 5th rev. and expanded ed. Regensburg: Pustet, 1989.

_____. *Der Hirt des Hermas.* KAV 7. Göttingen: Vandenhoeck & Ruprecht, 1991.

Bühner, Jan-Adolf. "ἀποστέλλω," *EDNT* 1:141–42.

_____. "ἀπόστολος, ου, ὁ," *EDNT* 1:142–46.

Burrus, Virginia. "Chastity as Autonomy. Women in the Stories of the Apocryphal Acts," *Semeia* 38 (1986) 101–17.

_____. *Chastity as Autonomy. Women in the Stories of the Apocryphal Acts.* SWR 23. Lewiston, N.Y., and Queenston, Ontario: Edwin Mellen, 1987.

_____. "The Heretical Woman as Symbol in Alexander, Athanasius, Epiphanius, and Jerome," *HThR* 84 (1991) 229–48.

Buschmann, Gerd. "Χριστοῦ κοινωνός (MartPol 6,2), das Martyrium und der ungeklärte κοινωνος-Titel der Montanisten," *ZNW* 86 (1995) 243–64.

Camelot, Pierre-Thomas. *Éphèse et Chalcédoine.* Paris: Editions de l'Orante, 1962. German: *Ephesus und Chalcedon.* Translated by Karl-Heinz Mottausch. GÖK 2. Mainz: Matthias-Grünewald-Verlag, 1963.

Campbell, Gerard J. "St. Jerome's Attitude toward Marriage and Women," *AEcR* 143 (1960) 310–20, 384–94.

Campenhausen, Hans von. "Der urchristliche Apostelbegriff," *StTh* 1 (1947/48) 96–130.

_____. *Kirchliches Amt und geistliche Vollmacht in den ersten drei Jahrhunderten.* BHTh 14. Tübingen: J.C.B. Mohr [Paul Siebeck], 1953; 2nd rev. ed. 1963.

Cancik-Lindemaier, Hildegard. "Kultische Priviligierung und gesellschaftliche Realität. Ein Beitrag zur Sozialgeschichte der virgines vestae," *Saec* 41 (1990) 1–16.

Castelli, Elizabeth. "Virginity and its Meaning for Women's Sexuality in Early Christianity," *JFSR* 2 (1986) 61–88.

_____. "Interpretations of Power in 1 Corinthians," *Semeia* 54 (1992) 197–222.

Cervin, Richard S. "A Note Regarding the Name 'Junia(s)' in Romans 16.7," *NTS* 40 (1994) 464–70.

Chadwick, Henry. "Enkrateia," *RAC* 5 (1962) 343–65.

Cherian, Kunnel Kurien. *Paul's Understanding of Diakonia as Proclamation according to 2 Corinthians 2:14–7:4.* Th.D. thesis, Lutheran School of Theology at Chicago, 1986. Microfiche.

Chesnut, Glenn F. *The First Christian Histories. Eusebius, Socrates, Sozomen, Theodoret, and Evagrius.* ThH 46. Paris: Beauchesne, 1977.

Chow, John K. *Patronage and Power. A Study of Social Networks in Corinth.* JSNT.S. 75. Sheffield: JSOT Press, 1992.

Chrysos, Evangelos. "Konzilsakten," in Friedhelm Winkelmann and Wolfram Brandes, eds., *Quellen zur Geschichte des frühen Byzanz (4.-9. Jahrhundert). Bestand und Probleme.* BBA 55. Amsterdam: Gieben, 1990, 149–55.

Clark, Elizabeth A. "John Chrysostom and the Subintroductae," *ChH* 46 (1977) 171–85; reprinted in eadem, *Ascetic Piety and Women's Faith: Essays on Late Ancient Christianity.* SWR 20. Lewiston, N.Y., and Queenston, Ontario: Edwin Mellen, 1986, 265–90.

_____. *Jerome, Chrysostom, and Friends. Essays and Translations.* SWR 2. New York and Toronto: Edwin Mellen, 1979; 2nd ed. 1982.

_____. "Ascetic Renunciation and Feminine Advancement: A Paradox of Late Ancient Christianity," *ATR* 63 (1981) 240–57.

_____. "Jesus as Hero in the Vergilian Cento of Faltonia Betitia Proba" (with Diane F. Hatch, orig. 1981), in Elizabeth A. Clark, *Ascetic Piety and Women's Faith: Essays on Late Ancient Christianity* (1986) 153–71.

_____. "Faltonia Betitia Proba and her Virgilian Poem: The Christian Matron as Artist" (orig. 1982), in ibid. 124–52.

_____. "Devil's Gateway and Bride of Christ" (orig. 1982), in ibid. 23–60.

_____. "Claims on the Bones of Saint Stephen: The Partisans of Melania and Eudocia" (orig. 1982), in ibid. 95–123.

_____. "Introduction to John Chrysostom, On Virginity; Against Remarriage" (orig. 1983), in ibid. 229–64.

_____. "Piety, Propaganda, and Politics in the Life of Melania the Younger," *StPatr* 18/2 (1989) 167–83.

_____. "Authority and Humility: A Conflict of Values in Fourth-Century Female Monasticism" (orig. 1985), in eadem, *Ascetic Piety and Women's Faith: Essays in Late Ancient Christianity* (1986) 209–28.

_____. "Theory and Practice in Late Ancient Asceticism: Jerome, Chrysostom, and Augustine," *JFSR* 5 (1989) 25–46.

_____. "Early Christian Women: Sources and Interpretation," in Lynda L. Coon, Katherine J. Haldane, and Elisabeth W. Sommer, eds., *That Gentle Strength: Historical Perspectives on Women in Christianity.* Charlottesville: University Press of Virginia, 1990, 19–35.

Cleary, Francis X. "Women in the New Testament: St. Paul and the Early Pauline Churches," *BTB* 10 (1980) 78–82.

Cole, Susan Guettel. "Could Greek Women Read and Write?" in Helene P. Foley, ed., *Reflections on Women in Antiquity.* New York: Gordon and Breach Science Publishers, 1981 (2nd ed. 1984), 219–45.

Collins, Adela Yarbro. "Women's History and the Book of Revelation," *SBL Seminar Papers* (1987) 80–91.

Collins, John N. *Diakonia. Re-interpreting the Ancient Sources.* New York and Oxford: Oxford University Press, 1990.

_____. "The Mediatorial Aspect of Paul's Role as Diakonos," *ABR* 40 (1992) 34–44.

Colson, Jean. *Les Fonctions Ecclésiales: aux deux premiers siècles.* Paris: Desclée de Brouwer, 1956.

Conway, Martin. "Frauen im Priestertum. Die kurzfristigen Konsequenzen der Entscheidung der Kirche von England für die Frauenordination," *MdKI* 45 (1994) 3–6.

Conzelmann, Hans. *Die Apostelgeschichte.* HNT 7. 2nd rev. ed. Tübingen: J.C.B. Mohr [Paul Siebeck], 1972. English: *Acts of the Apostles: A Commentary on the Acts of the Apostles.* Translated by James Limburg, A. Thomas Kraabel, and Donald H. Juel; edited by Eldon Jay Epp with Christopher R. Matthews. Philadelphia: Fortress, 1987.

Coon, Lynda L., Katherine J. Haldane, and Elisabeth W. Sommer. "Introduction," in eaedem, eds., *That Gentle Strength: Historical Perspectives on Women in Christianity.* Charlottesville: University Press of Virginia, 1990, 1–18.

Corssen, Peter. "Die Töchter des Philippus," *ZNW* 2 (1901) 289–99.

Cox, James J. C. "Prolegomena to a Study of the Dominical logoi as Cited in the Didascalia Apostolorum," *AUSS* 13 (1975) 23–29.

Coyle, John Kevin. "The Fathers on Women's Ordination," *EeT* 9 (1978) 51–101; also published in David M. Scholer, ed., *Women in Early Christianity.* Studies in Early Christianity 14. New York: Garland, 1993, 117–67.

_____. "The Exercise of Teaching in the Postapostolic Church," *EeT* 15 (1984) 23–43.

D'Angelo, Mary Rose. "Women Partners in the New Testament," *JFSR* 6 (1990) 65–86.

_____. "Women in Luke-Acts: A Redactional View," *JBL* 109 (1990) 441–61.

Danielou, Jean. *The Ministry of Women in the Early Church.* Translated by Glyn Simon. London: Faith Press; New York: Morehouse-Barlow, 1961. (Originally published in *La Maison Dieu* 61, 1960).

". . . das Weib rede in der Gemeinde." Maria Jepsen: Erste lutherische Bischöfin. Dokumente und Stellungnahmen.* GTB 1118. Gütersloh: Gerd Mohn, 1992.

Dassmann, Ernst. "Zur Entstehung des Monepiskopats," *JAC* 17 (1974) 74–90.

_____. *Ämter und Dienste in den frühchristlichen Gemeinden.* Hereditas 8. Bonn: Borengässer, 1994.

Dautzenberg, Gerhard. *Urchristliche Prophetie. Ihre Erforschung, ihre Voraussetzungen im Judentum und ihre Struktur im ersten Korintherbrief.* BWANT 104. Stuttgart, Berlin, Cologne, and Mainz: Kohlhammer, 1975.

_____. "Zur Stellung der Frauen in den paulinischen Gemeinden," in Gerhard Dautzenberg, Helmut Merklein, and Karlheinz Müller, eds., *Die Frau im Urchristentum.* QD 95. Freiburg, Basel, and Vienna: Herder, 1983, 182–224.

Davies, John G. "Deacons, Deaconesses and the Minor Orders in the Patristic Period," *JEH* 14 (1963) 1–15; also published in Everett Ferguson, ed., *Church, Ministry, and Organization in the Early Church Era.* Studies in Early Christianity 13. New York: Garland, 1993, 237–51.

Davies, Stevan L. *The Revolt of the Widows. The Social World of the Apocryphal Acts.* Carbondale: Southern Illinois University Press; London: Feffer and Simons, 1980.

_____. "Women, Tertullian and the Acts of Paul," *Semeia* 38 (1986) 139–43.

Deichmann, Friedrich Wilhelm. "Die Lage der konstantinischen Basilika der heiligen Agnes an der Via Nomentana" (orig. pub. 1946), in idem, *Rom, Ravenna, Konstantinopel, Naher Osten. Gesammelte Studien zur spätantiken Architektur, Kunst und Geschichte.* Wiesbaden: Steiner, 1982, 283–304.

Deissmann, Adolf. *Licht vom Osten. Das Neue Testament und die neuentdeckten Texte der hellenistisch-römischen Welt.* Original publication 1908. 4th rev. ed. Tübingen: J.C.B. Mohr [Paul Siebeck], 1923. English: *Light from the Ancient East; the New Testament illustrated by recently discovered texts of the Graeco-Roman world.* Translated by Lionel R. M. Strachan. New York: Doran, 1927.

Demers, Patricia. *Women as Interpreters of the Bible.* New York and Mahwah, N.J.: Paulist, 1992.

Deuel, Leo. "Pearls from Rubbish Heaps: Grenfell and Hunt," in idem, *Testaments of Time. The Search for Lost Manuscripts and Records.* New York: Knopf; London: Secker & Warburg, 1966, 132–49.

Dibelius, Martin. *Der Hirt des Hermas.* HNT Ergänzungsband 4. Tübingen: J.C.B. Mohr [Paul Siebeck], 1923.

_____. *An die Galater.* HNT 13. 3rd ed. revised by Hans Conzelmann. Tübingen: J.C.B. Mohr [Paul Siebeck], 1932.

_____. *An die Thessalonicher I, II; an die Philipper.* HNT 11. 3rd rev. ed. Tübingen: J.C.B. Mohr [Paul Siebeck], 1937.

_____. *Die Pastoralbriefe.* HNT 13. 3rd ed. revised by Hans Conzelmann. Tübingen: J.C.B. Mohr [Paul Siebeck], 1955. English: *The Pastoral Epistles.* Translated by Philip Buttolph and Adela Yarbro. Edited by Helmut Koester. Hermeneia. Philadelphia: Fortress, 1972.

Dobson, Elizabeth Spalding. "Pliny the Younger's Depiction of Women," *CIB* 58 (1982) 81–85.

Dölger, Franz Joseph. "Beiträge zur Geschichte des Kreuzzeichens, I–III," *JAC* 1 (1958) 5–19; 2 (1959) 15–29; 3 (1960) 5–16.

Donaldson, James. *Woman; Her Position and Influence in Ancient Greece and Rome, and among Early Christians.* New York and London: Longmans, Green, 1907; reprint New York: Gordon, 1973.

Donfried, Karl P. "Ministry: Rethinking the Term Diakonia," *CTQ* 56 (1992) 1–15.

Dörrie, Heinrich. "Gregor III (Gregor von Nyssa)," *RAC* 12 (1983) 863–95.

Doughty, Darrell J. "Women and Liberation in the Churches of Paul and the Pauline Tradition," *DGW* 50 (1979) 1–21.

Dronke, Peter. *Women Writers of the Middle Ages. A Critical Study of Texts from Perpetua (✝ 203) to Marguerite Porete (✝ 1310).* Cambridge and New York: Cambridge University Press, 1984.

Duchesne, Louis M. O. *Christian Worship. Its Origin and Evolution. A Study of the Latin Liturgy up to the Time of Charlemagne.* Translated by M. L. McClure. 5th ed. London: S.P.C.K., 1956. (Original: *Origines du culte chrétien,* 1889).

Dummer, Jürgen. "Griechische Hagiographie," in Winkelmann and Brandes, eds., *Quellen zur Geschichte des frühen Byzanz,* 284–96.

Egger, Wilhelm. *Galaterbrief, Philipperbrief, Philemonbrief.* NEB 9/11/15. Würzburg: Echter, 1985.

Eichenauer, Monika. *Untersuchungen zur Arbeitswelt der Frau in der römischen Antike.* EHS.G. 360. Frankfurt and New York: Peter Lang, 1988.

Eingartner, Johannes. *Isis und ihre Dienerinnen in der Kunst der römischen Kaiserzeit.* Mn.S 115. Leiden and New York: E. J. Brill, 1991.

Ellis, E. Earle. "Paul and his Co-Workers," *NTS* 17 (1970/71) 437–52.

_____. "'Spiritual' Gifts in the Pauline Community," *NTS* 20 (1974) 128–44.

_____. "The Role of Christian Prophets in Acts," in idem, *Prophecy and Hermeneutic in Early Christianity. New Testament Essays.* WUNT 18. Tübingen: J.C.B. Mohr [Paul Siebeck], 1978, 129–44.

_____. "The Silenced Wives of Corinth (1 Cor. 14:34-5)," in Eldon Jay Epp and Gordon D. Fee, eds., *New Testament Textual Criticism. Its Significance for Exegesis. Essays in Honour of Bruce M. Metzger.* Oxford: Clarendon Press; New York: Oxford University Press, 1981, 213–20.

Elm, Susanna K. *The Organization and Institutions of Female Asceticism in Fourth Century Cappadocia and Egypt.* Diss.Phil. Oxford (1986). Microfiche.

_____. *Virgins of God: The Making of Asceticism in Late Antiquity.* Oxford and New York: Oxford University Press, 1994.

_____. "Formen des Zusammenlebens männlicher und weiblicher Asketen im östlichen Mittelmeerraum während des vierten Jahrhunderts nach Christus," in Kaspar Elm and Michel Parisse, eds., *Doppelklöster und andere Formen der Symbiose männlicher und weiblicher Religiosen im Mittelalter.* BHSt 18. Ordenstudien VIII. Berlin: Duncker & Humblot, 1992, 13–24.

Elshtain, Jean Bethke. *Public Man, Private Woman. Women in Social and Political Thought.* Princeton, N.J.: Princeton University Press, 1981.

Emmett, Alanna. "Female Ascetics in the Greek Papyri," *JÖB* 32 (1982) 507–15.

Emonds, Hilarius. "Äbtissin," *RAC* 1 (1950) 126–28.

Engberg-Pedersen, Troels. "1 Corinthians 11:16 and the Character of Pauline Exhortation," *JBL* 110 (1991) 679–89.

Eno, Robert B. "Authority and Conflict in the Early Church," *EeT* 7 (1976) 41–60.

Ensslin, Wilhelm. "Marcella," *PRE* XIV, 2 (1930) 1436–37.

Ernst, Josef. "Die Witwenregel des ersten Timotheusbriefes—ein Hinweis auf die biblischen Ursprünge des weiblichen Ordenswesens?" *ThGl* 59 (1969) 434–45.

Evelyn White, Hugh G. *The Monasteries of the Wâdi ʾN Natrûn. Part II: The History of the Monasteries of Nitria and of Scetis.* Edited by Walter Hauser. New York: Egyptian Expedition Publications of the Metropolitan Museum of Art Egyptian Expedition, 1932; reprint New York: Arno, 1973.

Fabrega, Valentin. "War Junia(s), der hervorragende Apostel (Röm 16,7), eine Frau?" *JAC* 27/28 (1984/85) 47–64.

Fander, Monika. "'Und ihnen kamen diese Worte vor wie leeres Geschwätz, und sie glaubten ihnen nicht' (Lk 24,11). Feministische Bibellektüre des neuen Testaments. Eine Reflexion," in Christine Schaumberger and Monika Maassen, eds., *Handbuch Feministische Theologie,* 299–311.

_____. "Das Frauenbild im Neuen Testament. Methoden der Feministischen Bibellektüre," *Schlangenbrut* 23 (1988) 10–12.

_____. *Die Stellung der Frau im Markusevangelium. Unter besonderer Berücksichtigung kultur- und religionsgeschichtlicher Hintergründe.* MThA 8. Altenberge: Oros-Verlag, 1989.

_____. "Frauen in der Nachfolge Jesu. Die Rolle der Frau im Markusevangelium," *EvTh* 52 (1992) 413–32.

_____. "Frauen im Urchristentum am Beispiel Palästinas," *JBTh* 7 (1992) 165–85.

Fangauer, Georg. *Stilles Frauenheldentum oder Frauenapostolat in den ersten drei Jahrhunderten des Christentums.* Münster: Aschendorff, 1922.

Farge, Arlette. "Method and Effects of Women's History," in Michelle Perrot, ed., *Writing Women's History,* translated by Felicia Pheasant; from an original idea by Alain Paire. Oxford, UK; Cambridge, Mass.: Blackwell, 1992, 10–24. (Original: "Pratique et effets de l'histoire des femmes," in *Une histoire des femmes est-elle possible?* sous la direction de Michelle Perrot et à l'initiative d'Alain Paire. Paris: Rivages, 1984) 18–35.

Farmer, Sharon. "Persuasive Voices: Clerical Images of Medieval Wives," *Spec* 61 (1986) 517–43.

Fascher, Erich. *ΠΡΟΦΗΤΗΣ. Eine sprach- und religionsgeschichtliche Untersuchung.* Gießen: A. Töpelmann, 1927.

Ferguson, Everett. "Τόπος in 1 Timothy 2:8," *RestQ* 33 (1991) 65–73.

Ferrari, G. "La diaconesse nella Traditione Orientale," *OrCr(P)* 14 (1974) 28–50.

Feusi, Iniga. *Das Institut der Gottgeweihten Jungfrauen. Sein Fortleben im Mittelalter.* Diss.phil. Fribourg: 1917.

Field-Bibb, Jacqueline. "'By any other name': The Issue of Inclusive Language," *MCM* 31/2 (1989) 5–9.

_____. *Women towards Priesthood. Ministerial Politics and Feminist Praxis.* Cambridge and New York: Cambridge University Press, 1991.

_____. "From Deaconess to Bishop: The Vicissitudes of Women's Ministry in the Protestant Episcopal Church in the USA," *HeyJ* 33 (1992) 61–78.

Fietze, Katharina. "Interdisziplinäre Aspekte von historischer und philosophischer Frauenforschung," *Die Philosophin* 4 (1993) 33–39.

Filson, Floyd V. "The Significance of the Early House Church," *JBL* 58 (1939) 105–12.

_____. "The Christian Teacher in the First Century," *JBL* 60 (1941) 317–28.

Fink, Josef, and Beatrix Asamer. *Die römischen Katakomben.* AW 9 (Special Number), 1978. Mainz: Verlag Philipp von Zabern, 1997.

Fischer, Joseph A. "Die antimontanistischen Synoden des 2./3. Jahrhunderts," *AHC* 6 (1975) 241–73.

Fisher, Arthur L. "Women and Gender in Lausiac History," *StMon* 33 (1991) 23–50.

Fitzer, Gottfried. *"Das Weib schweige in der Gemeinde." Über den unpaulinischen Charakter der mulier-taceat-Verse in 1. Korinther 14.* TEH n.s. 110. Munich: Kaiser, 1963.

Fitzgerald, Kyriaki Karidoyanes. "The Characteristics and Nature of the Order of the Deaconess," in Thomas Hopko, ed., *Women and the Priesthood,* 75–95.

Fitzmyer, Joseph A. "παρθένος, ου, ἡ (ὁ)," *EDNT* 3:39–40.

Flender, Helmut. "Lehren und Verkündigung in den synoptischen Evangelien," *EvTh* 25 (1965) 701–14.

Forschungsprojekt zur Geschichte der Theologinnen Göttingen, eds. *Querdenken. Beiträge zur feministisch-befreiungstheologischen Diskussion. FS für Hannelore Erhart zum 65. Geburtstag.* Pfaffenweiler: Centaurus, 1992.

Frank, Karl Suso. "Gelübde IV. Katholische Überlieferung und Lehre," *TRE* 12 (1984) 305–309.

Freeman, G. "Montanism and the pagan cults of Phrygia," *DomSt* 3 (1950) 297–316.

Frend, William H. C. *Martyrdom and Persecution in the Early Church. A Study of a Conflict from the Maccabees to Donatus.* Oxford: Blackwell, 1965.

_____. "Montanism: Research and Problems," *RSLR* 20 (1984) 521–37.

Frevert, Ute. *Frauen-Geschichte. Zwischen Bürgerlicher Verbesserung und Neuer Weiblichkeit.* Neue Historische Bibliothek, edition suhrkamp n.s. 284. Frankfurt: Suhrkamp, 1986.

_____. "Bewegung und Disziplin in der Frauengeschichte. Ein Forschungsbericht," *GeGe* 14 (1988) 240–62.

Fried, Johannes. "Die Päpste im Karolingerreich von Stephan III. bis Hadrian II.," in Martin Greschat, ed., *Das Papsttum I. Von den Anfängen bis zu den Päpsten in Avignon.* GK 11. Stuttgart: Kohlhammer, 1984, 115–28.

Friedländer, Ludwig. *Darstellungen aus der Sittengeschichte Roms in der Zeit von Augustus bis zum Ausgang der Antonine.* 4 vols. 10th ed. Leipzig: Hirzel, 1921–23. English: *Roman Life and Manners under the Early Empire.* Translated by Leonard A. Magnus. New York: Arno, 1979.

Friedrich, Gerhard. "προφήτης κτλ.," *TDNT* 6:828–61.

Friedrich, Johannes. "Über die Cenones der Montanisten bei Hieronymus," *SBAW.PPH* 2 (1895) 207–21.

Frohnhofen, Herbert. "Die Stellung der Frau im frühen Christentum," *StZ* 203 (1985) 844–52.

_____. "Weibliche Diakone in der frühen Kirche," *StZ* 204 (1986) 269–78. (See idem, "Women Deacons in the Early Church," *ThD* 34 [1987] 149–53.)

Funk, Franz Xaver. *Die Apostolischen Konstitutionen. Eine litterar-historische Untersuchung.* Frankfurt: Minerva, 1970. (Reprint of the Rottenburg edition of 1891.)

_____. "Die Apostolische Kirchenordnung," in idem, *Kirchengeschichtliche Abhandlungen und Untersuchungen II.* Paderborn: Schöningh, 1899, 236–51.

_____. *Das Testament unseres Herrn und die verwandten Schriften.* FChLDG 2/H. 1+2. Mainz: F. Kirchheim, 1901.

Funke, Hermann. "Univira. Ein Beispiel heidnischer Geschichtsapologetik," *JAC* 8/9 (1965/66) 183–88.

Galot, Jean. *La Donna e i ministeri nella Chiesa.* Assisi, 1973.

Gardner, Jane F. *Women in Roman Law and Society.* London: Croom Helm; Bloomington: Indiana University Press, 1986.

Geldbach, Erich. "Frauenordination: Dienst an der Ökumene?" *MdKI* 43 (1992) 103–107.

Gensichen, Joachim. *De Scripturae Sacrae vestigiis in inscriptionibus latinis christia-nis.* Diss. phil. Greifswald: Julius Abel, 1910.

Georgi, Dieter. *Die Gegner des Paulus im 2. Korintherbrief. Studien zur religiösen Pro-paganda in der Spätantike.* WMANT 11. Neukirchen-Vluyn: Neukirchener Ver-lag, 1964. English: *The Opponents of Paul in Second Corinthians: A Study of Religious Propaganda in Late Antiquity.* Philadelphia: Fortress, 1986.

_____. *Die Geschichte der Kollekte des Paulus für Jerusalem.* ThF 38. Hamburg-Berg-stedt: Reich, 1965. English: *Remembering the Poor: The History of Paul's Col-lection for Jerusalem.* Nashville: Abingdon, 1992.

Gerberding, Keith A. "Women Who Toil in Ministry, Even as Paul," *CThMi* 18 (1991) 285–91.

Gielen, Marlis. "Zur Interpretation der Formel ἡ κατ᾽ οἶκον ἐκκλησία," *ZNW* 77 (1986) 109–25.

_____. *Tradition und Theologie neutestamentlicher Haustafelethik. Ein Beitrag zur Frage einer christlichen Auseinandersetzung mit gesellschaftlichen Normen.* Athenäums Monografien. Theologie 75. Frankfurt: Hain, 1990.

Gilbert, George H. "Women in Public Worship in the Churches of Paul," *BW* 2 (1893) 38–47.

Gillmann, Franz. "Weibliche Kleriker nach dem Urteil der Frühscholastik," *AKathKR* 93 (1913) 239–53.

Gnilka, Joachim. *Der Philipperbrief.* HThK X/3. 4th ed. Freiburg, Basel, and Vienna: Herder, 1987.

Goehring, James E. "Libertine or Liberated: Women in the So-called Libertine Gnostic Communities," in Karen L. King, ed., *Images of the Feminine in Gnosticism.* Studies in Antiquity and Christianity 4. Philadelphia: Fortress, 1988, 329–44.

Goehring, James E., and Robert F. Boughner. "Egyptian Monasticism (Selected Pa-pyri)," in Vincent L. Wimbush, ed., *Ascetic Behavior in Greco-Roman Antiquity.* Minneapolis: Fortress, 1990, 456–63.

Goldstein, Horst. " Ἰεζάβελ," *EDNT* 2:173.

Goltz, Eduard von der. *Der Dienst der Frau in der christlichen Kirche. Geschichtlicher Überblick mit einer Sammlung von Urkunden.* 2 parts. 2nd. revised ed. Potsdam: Stiftungsverlag, 1914.

Gössmann, Elisabeth. *Die Frau und ihr Auftrag. Die Liebe zum Vergänglichen.* Freiburg, et al.: Herder, 1961.

_____. "Frauen in der Kirche ohne Sitz und Stimme? Oder: Roma locuta – causa non finita sed disputanda," in Norbert Greinacher and Hans Küng, eds., *Katholische Kirche – wohin? Wider den Verrat am Konzil.* Munich: Piper, 1986, 295–306.

_____. "Äußerungen zum Frauenpriestertum in der christlichen Tradition," in Elisa-beth Gössmann and Dietmar Bader, eds., *Warum keine Ordination der Frau? Unterschiedliche Einstellungen in den christlichen Kirchen.* Munich: Schnell & Steiner, 1987, 9–25.

_____. "Philosophie- und theologiegeschichtliche Frauenforschung. Eine Einführung," in Elisabeth Gössmann and Dieter R. Bauer, eds., *Eva: Verführerin oder Gottes Meisterwerk? Philosophie- und theologiegeschichtliche Frauenforschung.*

Hohenheimer Protokolle 21. Stuttgart: Akademie der Diözese Rottenburg-Stuttgart, 1987, 19–35.

_____. *Wie könnte Frauenforschung im Rahmen der Katholischen Kirche aussehen?* EichHR 57. Munich: Minerva-Publ., 1987.

_____. "Die 'Päpstin Johanna.' Zur vor- und nachreformatorischen Rezeption ihrer Gestalt," in Gössmann and Bauer, eds., *Eva: Verführerin oder Gottes Meisterwerk?* 143–66.

_____. "Zur Rezeptionsgeschichte der Gestalt der Päpstin Johanna," in Elisabeth Moltmann-Wendel, ed., *Weiblichkeit in der Theologie. Verdrängung und Wiederkehr.* Gütersloh: Gerd Mohn, 1988, 93–111.

_____. "Maria Magdalena als Typus der Kirche. Zur Aktualität mittelalterlicher Reflexionen," in Dietmar Bader, ed., *Maria Magdalena – Zu einem Bild der Frau in der christlichen Verkündigung.* Schriftenreihe der Katholischen Akademie der Erzdiözese Freiburg. Munich and Zürich: Schnell and Steiner, 1990, 51–71.

_____. "The Construction of Women's Difference in the Christian Theological Tradition," *Concilium* (Dec. 1991) 50–59.

_____. "Geschichte – Philosophiegeschichte – feministische Theorie," *Die Philosophin* 4 (1993) 40–47.

_____. *Mulier Papa. Der Skandal eines weiblichen Papstes. Zur Rezeptionsgeschichte der Gestalt der Päpstin Johanna.* APTGF 5. Munich: Iudicium, 1994.

Gottlieb, Elfriede. *Die Frau in der frühchristlichen Gemeinde.* Quellenhefte zum Frauenleben in der Geschichte 5. Berlin: Herbig, 1927.

Grant, Robert M. *Eusebius as Church Historian.* Oxford: Clarendon Press, 1980.

_____. "Theological Education at Alexandria," in Birger A. Pearson and James E. Goehring, eds., *The Roots of Egyptian Christianity.* Philadelphia: Fortress, 1986, 178–89.

Grasmück, Ernst Ludwig. "Vom Presbyter zum Priester. Etappen der Entwicklung des neuzeitlichen katholischen Priesterbildes," in Paul Hoffmann, ed., *Priesterkirche.* TzZ 3. Düsseldorf: Patmos, 1987, 96–131.

Greeven, Heinrich. "Propheten, Lehrer, Vorsteher bei Paulus. Zur Frage der 'Ämter' im Urchristentum," *ZNW* 44 (1952/3) 1–43.

Gritz, Sharon Hodgin. *Paul, Women Teachers, and the Mother Goddess at Ephesus. A Study of 1 Timothy 2:9-15 in Light of the Religious and Cultural Milieu of the First Century.* Diss. theol. Lanham, Md.: University Press of America, 1991.

Gryson, Roger. *Le Ministère des Femmes dans l'Eglise Ancienne.* Gembloux: Duclot 1972. English: *The Ministry of Women in the Early Church.* Translated by Jean Laporte and Mary Louise Hall. 2nd ed. Collegeville: The Liturgical Press, 1980.

_____. "The Authority of the Teacher in the Ancient and Medieval Church," *JES* 19 (1982) 176–87.

Gülzow, Henneke. *Christentum und Sklaverei in den ersten drei Jahrhunderten.* Bonn: R. Habelt, 1969.

_____. "Soziale Gegebenheiten der altkirchlichen Mission," in Heinzgünter Frohnes and Uwe W. Knorr, eds., *Kirchengeschichte als Missionsgeschichte I: Die alte Kirche.* Munich: Kaiser, 1974, 189–226.

Gunkel, Hermann. *Die Wirkungen des heiligen Geistes nach der populären Anschauung der apostolischen Zeit und nach der Lehre des Apostels Paulus.* Diss. theol. Göttingen: 1888.

Günther, Rosmarie. *Frauenarbeit – Frauenbindung. Untersuchungen zu unfreien und freigelassenen Frauen in den stadtrömischen Inschriften.* Veröffentlichungen des Historischen Instituts der Universität Mannheim 9. Munich: W. Fink, 1987.

Gustafsson, Berndt. "Eusebius' Principles in handling his sources found in his Church History Books I–VIII," *StPatr* 4/2 (1961) 429–41.

Guyon, Jean. "La vente des tombes à travers l'épigraphie de la Rome chrétienne (IIIe-VIIe siècles): le rôle des fossores, mansionarii, praepositi et prêtres," *MEFRA* 86 (1974) 549–96.

Gy, Pierre-Marie. "Bemerkungen zu den Bezeichnungen des Priestertums in der christlichen Frühzeit," in Jean Guyot, ed., *Das apostolische Amt.* Mainz: Matthias-Grünewald, 1961, 92–109.

_____. "Ancient Ordination Prayers," in Everett Ferguson, ed., *Church, Ministry, and Organization in the Early Church Era,* 122–45.

Häberlin, Susanna, Rachel Schmid, and Eva Lia Wyss. *Übung macht die Meisterin. Ratschläge für einen nichtsexistischen Sprachgebrauch.* Munich: Verlag Frauenoffensive, 1992.

Haenchen, Ernst. *Die Apostelgeschichte.* KEK III. 12th ed. Göttingen: Vandenhoeck & Ruprecht, 1959. English: *The Acts of the Apostles; A Commentary.* Translated by Bernard Noble and Gerald Shinn, under the supervision of Hugh Anderson, and with the translation revised and brought up to date by R. McLean Wilson. Philadelphia: Westminster, 1971.

Haendler, Gert. "Das Papsttum unter gotischer und byzantinischer Herrschaft," in Martin Greschat, ed., *Das Papsttum I,* 71–82.

Hahn, Ferdinand. "Die Sendschreiben der Johannesapokalypse. Ein Beitrag zur Bestimmung prophetischer Redeformen," in Gert Jeremias, Heinz-Wolfgang Kuhn, and Hartmut Stegemann, eds., *Tradition und Glaube. Festgabe K. G. Kuhn.* Göttingen: Vandenhoeck & Ruprecht, 1971, 357–94.

_____. "Neuorientierung in der Erforschung des frühen Christentums?" *EvTh* 33 (1973) 537–44.

_____. "Der Apostolat im Urchristentum. Seine Eigenart und seine Voraussetzungen," *KuD* 20 (1974) 54–77.

_____. "Charisma und Amt. Die Diskussion über das kirchliche Amt im Lichte der neutestamentlichen Charismenlehre," *ZThK* 76 (1979) 419–49.

Hainz, Josef. *Ekklesia. Strukturen paulinischer Gemeinde-Theologie und Gemeinde-Ordnung.* BU 9. Regensburg: Pustet, 1972.

_____. "Die Anfänge des Bischofs- und Diakonenamtes," in idem, ed., *Kirche im Werden. Studien zum Thema Amt und Gemeinde im Neuen Testament.* Munich, Paderborn, and Vienna: Schöningh, 1976, 91–107.

_____. "Amt und Amtsvermittlung bei Paulus," in idem, 109–22.

Han-Rhinow, Jeong Ae. *Die frühchristlichen Kirchenordnungen und ihr Amtsverständnis als Beitrag zur ökumenischen Diskussion um das Lima-Dokument.* Diss. theol. Munich, 1991.

Hansel, Hans. *Die Maria-Magdalena-Legende. Eine Quellenuntersuchung.* Diss. phil. Greifswald, 1937.

Hanson, Richard P. "Amt / Ämter / Amtsverständnis V. Alte Kirche," *TRE* 1 (1978) 533–52.

Harnack, Adolf von. *Die Lehre der zwölf Apostel nebst Untersuchungen zur ältesten Geschichte der Kirchenverfassung und des Kirchenrechts.* TU II/1, 2. Leipzig: Hinrichs, 1884; reprint Berlin: Akademie-Verlag, 1991.

_____. *Die Quellen der sogenannten Apostolischen Kirchenordnung nebst einer Untersuchung über den Ursprung des Lectorats und der anderen niederen Weihen.* Leipzig: Hinrichs, 1886. English: *Sources of the Apostolic Canons, with a treatise on the origin of the readership and other lower orders.* Translated by Leonard A. Wheatley, with an Introductory essay on the organisation of the early church and the evolution of the reader by the Rev. John Owen. London: F. Norgate, 1895.

_____. *Die Apostellehre und die jüdischen beiden Wege.* 2nd rev. and expanded ed. Leipzig: Hinrichs, 1896.

_____. "Vorläufige Bemerkungen zu dem jüngst syrisch und lateinisch publicirten 'Testamentum domini nostri Jesu Christi,'" (1899) in idem, *Kleine Schriften zur Alten Kirche. Berliner Akademieschriften 1890–1907*. With a Foreword by Jürgen Dummer. Leipzig: Zentralantiquariat der Deutschen Demokratischen Republik, 1980, 385–98.

_____. "Über die beiden Rezensionen der Geschichte der Prisca und des Aquila in Act. Apost. 18, 1-27," *SPAW* 1900, 48–61 (reprinted in idem, *Kleine Schriften* 399–410).

_____. "Probabilia über die Adresse und den Verfasser des Hebräerbriefs," *ZNW* 1 (1900) 16–41.

_____. *Die Mission und Ausbreitung des Christentums in den ersten drei Jahrhunderten.* 2 vols. Leipzig: Hinrichs, 1902; 4th revised and expanded ed. 1924. English: *The Expansion of Christianity in the First Three Centuries.* 2 vols. Translated and edited by James Moffatt. New York: G. P. Putnam's Sons, 1904–05 (numerous reprints).

_____. *Entstehung und Entwicklung der Kirchenverfassung und des Kirchenrechts in den zwei ersten Jahrhunderten. Urchristentum und Katholizismus.* Darmstadt: Wissenschaftliche Buchgesellschaft, 1990 (reprint of the Leipzig ed. of 1910). English: *The Constitution and Law of the Church in the First Two Centuries.* Translated by F. L. Pogson; edited by H. D. A. Major. London: Williams & Norgate; New York: G.P. Putnam's Sons, 1910.

_____. "Κόπος (Κοπιᾶν, Οἱ Κοπιῶντες) im frühchristlichen Sprachgebrauch," *ZNW* 27 (1928) 1–10.

Harris, Timothy F. "Why did Paul Mention Eve's Deception? A Critique of P.W. Barnett's Interpretation of 1 Timothy," *EvQ* 62 (1990) 335–52.

Harvey, Susan Ashbrook. "Women in Early Syrian Christianity," in Averil Cameron and Amélie Kuhrt, eds., *Images of Women in Antiquity.* Detroit: Wayne State University Press, 1983, 288–98.

Hasdenteufel-Röding, Maria. *Studien zur Gründung von Frauenklöstern im frühen Mittelalter. Ein Beitrag zum religiösen Ideal der Frau und seiner monastischen Umsetzung.* Diss. phil. Freiburg, 1991.

Hatch, Edwin. *The Organization of the Early Christian Churches: eight lectures delivered before the University of Oxford, in the year 1880, on the foundation of the late Rev. John Bampton.* 2nd revised ed. London: Rivingtons, 1882.

Hauck, Albert. "Synoden," *RE³* (1907) 262–77.

Hauke, Manfred. *Die Problematik um das Frauenpriestertum vor dem Hintergrund der Schöpfungs- und Erlösungsordnung.* KKTS 46. Paderborn: Verlag Bonifatius-Druckerei, 1982. English: *Women in the Priesthood? A Systematic Analysis in the Light of the Order of Creation and Redemption.* Translated by David Kipp. San Francisco: Ignatius Press, 1988.

Hauschildt, H. "ΠΡΕΣΒΥΤΕΡΟΙ in Ägypten im I–III Jahrhundert n. Chr.," *ZNW* 4 (1903) 235–42.

Hausen, Karin. "Einleitung," in eadem, ed., *Frauen suchen ihre Geschichte. Historische Studien zum 19. und 20. Jahrhundert.* Beck'sche Schwarze Reihe 276. Munich: C. H. Beck, 1983, 7–20.

Hausen, Karin, and Helga Nowotny, eds. *Wie männlich ist die Wissenschaft?* STW 590. Frankfurt: Suhrkamp, 1986; 3rd ed. 1990.

Heidebrecht, Petra, and Cordula Nolte. "Leben im Kloster: Nonnen und Kanonissen. Geistliche Lebensformen im frühen Mittelalter," in Ursula A. J. Becher and Jörn Rüsen, eds., *Weiblichkeit in geschichtlicher Perspektive. Fallstudien und Reflexionen zu Grundproblemen der historischen Frauenforschung.* STW 725. Frankfurt: Suhrkamp, 1988, 79–115.

Heiler, Friedrich. "Wertung und Wirksamkeit der Frau in der christlichen Kirche," in Willy Falkenhahn, ed., *Veritati. Eine Sammlung geistesgeschichtlicher, philosophischer und theologischer Abhandlungen.* FS Johannes Hessen. Munich: E. Reinhardt, 1949, 116–40.

_____. *Die Frau in den Religionen der Menschheit.* TBT 33. Berlin and New York: Walter de Gruyter, 1977.

Heine, Susanne. *Frauen der frühen Christenheit. Zur historischen Kritik einer feministischen Theologie.* Göttingen: Vandenhoeck & Ruprecht, 1986. English: *Women and Early Christianity: A Reappraisal.* Translated by John Bowden. 1st U.S. ed. Minneapolis: Augsburg, 1988.

_____. "Eine Person von Rang und Namen. Historische Konturen der Magdalenerin," in Dietrich-Alex Koch, Gerhard Sellin, and Andreas Lindemann, eds., *Jesu Rede von Gott und ihre Nachgeschichte im frühen Christentum. Beiträge zur Verkündigung Jesu und zum Kerygma der Kirche.* FS für Willi Marxsen. Gütersloh: Gerd Mohn, 1988, 179–94.

Heinzelmann, Gertrud. *Die geheiligte Diskriminierung. Beiträge zum kirchlichen Feminismus.* Bonstetten: Interfeminas, 1986.

_____, ed. *Wir schweigen nicht länger! Frauen äussern sich zum II. Vatikanischen Konzil // We Won't Keep Silence Any Longer! Women Speak Out to Vatican Council II.* Zürich: Interfeminas, 1964.

Hemer, Colin J. "Towards a new Moulton and Milligan," *NT* 24 (1982) 97–123.

———. *The Letters to the Seven Churches of Asia in their Local Setting*. JSNT.S 11. Sheffield: JSOT, 1986.

Hengel, Martin. "Maria Magdalena und die Frauen als Zeugen," in Otto Betz, Martin Hengel, and Peter Schmidt, eds., *Abraham unser Vater. Juden und Christen im Gespräch über die Bibel. FS für Otto Michel zum 60. Geburtstag*. Leiden: E. J. Brill, 1963, 243–56.

———. "Die Ursprünge der christlichen Mission," *NTS* 18 (1971/72) 15–38.

———. *Zur urchristlichen Geschichtsschreibung*. Stuttgart: Calwer, 1979. English: *Acts and the History of Earliest Christianity*. Translated by John Bowden. Philadelphia: Fortress, 1980.

Hennecke, Edgar. "Laodicea, [Synode um 360]," *RE³* 11 (1902) 281.

———. "Zur Apostolischen Kirchenordnung," *ZNW* 20 (1921) 241–48.

Hering, Rainer. "Frauen auf der Kanzel? Die Auseinandersetzung um Frauenordination und Gleichberechtigung der Theologinnen in der Hamburger Landeskirche. Von der Pfarramtshelferin zur ersten evangelisch-lutherischen Bischöfin der Welt," *ZVHaG* 79 (1993) 163–209.

Herzog, Rudolf. "Zwei griechische Gedichte des 4. Jahrhunderts aus St. Maximin in Trier," *TrZ* 13 (1938) 79–120.

Hesberg-Tonn, Bärbel von. *Coniunx Carissima. Untersuchungen zum Normcharakter im Erscheinungsbild der römischen Frau*. Stuttgart: Historisches Institut der Universität Stuttgart, 1983.

Heschel, Susannah. *On Being a Jewish Feminist. A Reader*. New York: Schocken, 1983.

———. "From the Bible to Nazism: German Feminists on the Jewish Origins of Patriarchy," *Tel Aviver Jahrbuch für Deutsche Geschichte* 21 (1992) 319–33.

Heyse, Gabriele. *Mulier non debet abire nuda. Das Erbrecht und die Versorgung der Witwe in Rom*. EHS.R 1541. Frankfurt: Peter Lang, 1994.

Hickey, Anne Ewing. *Women of the Roman Aristocracy as Christian Monastics*. SR(AA) 1. Ann Arbor: UMI Research Press, 1987.

Hilgenfeld, Adolf. Review of J. Friedrich, "Über die Cenones der Montanisten bei Hieronymus" (1895), *ZWTh* 38 (1895) 635–38.

———. *Die Ketzergeschichte des Urchristentums*. Darmstadt: Wissenschaftliche Buchgesellschaft, 1966. (Reprint of the Leipzig ed. of 1884.)

Hilkert, Mary Catherine. "'Women Preaching the Gospel,'" *ThD* 33 (1986) 423–40.

Hill, David. "Prophecy and Prophets in the Revelation of St John," *NTS* 18 (1971/72) 401–18.

———. "On the Evidence for the Creative Role of Christian Prophets," *NTS* 20 (1973/74) 262–74.

———. "Christian Prophets as Teachers or Instructors in the Church," in Johannes Panagopoulos, ed., *Prophetic Vocation in the New Testament and Today*. Leiden: Brill, 1977, 108–30.

———. *New Testament Prophecy*. Atlanta: John Knox, 1979.

Hill, Stephen. *The Early Christian Churches of Cilicia*. University of Newcastle upon Tyne, Ph.D. 1984 (11 microfiches).

_____. *The Early Byzantine Churches of Cilicia and Isauria.* Birmingham Byzantine and Ottoman monographs 1. Aldershot [England]; Brookfield, Vt.: Variorum, 1996.

Hoffmann, Paul. "Priestertum und Amt im Neuen Testament. Eine Bestandsaufnahme," in idem, ed., *Priesterkirche,* 12–61.

Holl, Karl. "Der Kirchenbegriff des Paulus in seinem Verhältnis zu dem der Urgemeinde" (1921) in idem, *Gesammelte Aufsätze zur Kirchengeschichte. II. Der Osten.* Tübingen: J.C.B. Mohr [Paul Siebeck], 1928, 44–67.

Holtz, Gottfried. *Die Pastoralbriefe.* ThHNT 13. 3rd ed. Berlin: Evangelische Verlagsanstalt, 1980.

Holze, Heinrich. *Erfahrung und Theologie im frühen Mönchtum. Untersuchungen zu einer Theologie des monastischen Lebens bei den ägyptischen Mönchsvätern Johannes Cassian und Benedikt von Nursia.* FKDG 48. Göttingen: Vandenhoeck & Ruprecht, 1992.

Holzmeister, Urban. "Die Magdalenenfrage in der kirchlichen Überlieferung," *ZKTh* 46 (1922) 402–22; 556–84.

Hommes, Nicolaas J. "Taceat mulier in Ecclesia. Een boodschap over Eredienst en vrouwelijk decorum," in *Arcana Relevata, FS Frederik Willem Grosheide.* Kampen: Kok, 1951, 33–43.

Hopko, Thomas, ed. *Women and the Priesthood.* Crestwood, N.Y.: St. Vladimir's Seminary Press, 1983.

_____. "Women and the Priesthood: Reflections on the Debate," in idem, ed., *Women and the Priesthood* (1983) 169–90.

_____. "Galatians 3:28: On Orthodox Interpretation," *SVTQ* 35 (1991) 169–86.

Hoppin, Ruth. *Priscilla. Author of the Epistle to the Hebrews, and Other Essays.* New York: Exposition, 1969.

Horsley, G.H.R. "The Inscriptions of Ephesos and the New Testament," *NT* 34 (1992) 105–68.

Horst, Pieter W. van der. "Juden und Christen in Aphrodisias im Licht ihrer Beziehungen in anderen Städten Kleinasiens," in Jacobus van Amersfoort and Johannes van Oort, eds., *Juden und Christen in der Antike.* Kampen: Kok, 1990, 125–43.

_____. "Das Neue Testament und die jüdischen Grabinschriften aus hellenistisch-römischer Zeit," *BZ* 36 (1992) 161–78.

Howe, E. Margaret. *Women & Church Leadership.* Grand Rapids: Zondervan, 1982.

Hübner, Reinhard M. "Die Anfänge von Diakonat, Presbyterat und Episkopat in der frühen Kirche," in Albert Rauch and Paul Imhof, eds., *Das Priestertum in der einen Kirche. Diakonat, Presbyterat und Episkopat.* Regensburger Ökumenisches Symposion 1985, *Koinonia* IV. Aschaffenburg: Kaffke, 1987, 45–89.

Hünermann, Peter. "Conclusions Regarding the Female Diaconate," *TS* 36 (1975) 325–33.

Hugenberger, Gordon P. "Women in Church Office: Hermeneutics or Exegesis? A Survey of Approaches to 1 Tim 2:8-15," *JETS* 35 (1992) 341–60.

Hummerich-Diezun, Waltraud, "'Unbeschreiblich weiblich.' Zum Subjekt feministischer Theologie," in Forschungsprojekt zur Geschichte der Theologinnen Göttingen, eds., *Querdenken,* 103–28.

Hurley, James B. "Did Paul Require Veils or the Silence of Women? A Consideration of 1 Cor 11:2-16 and 1 Cor 14:33b-36," *WThJ* 35 (1972/73) 190–220.

Ide, Arthur Frederick. *Women in Early Christianity and Christian Society.* Mesquite, Tex.: Ide House, 1980.

_____. *Women in Ancient Greece.* Mesquite, Tex.: Ide House, 1980.

_____. *Woman as Priest, Bishop and Laity in the Early Catholic Church to 440 A.D. With a translation and critical commentary on Romans 16 and other relevant Scripture and patrological writings on women in the early Christian Church.* Mesquite, Tex.: Ide House, 1984.

_____. *God's Girls. Ordination of Women in the Early Christian & Gnostic Churches.* Garland, Tex.: Tangelwüld, 1986.

Irigaray, Luce. *Ce sexe qui n'en est pas un.* Paris: Editions de Minuit, 1977. English: *This Sex Which Is Not One.* Translated by Catherine Porter with Carolyn Burke. Ithaca, N.Y.: Cornell University Press, 1985.

_____. "How Do We Become Civil Women?" in eadem, *Le Temps de la différence: Pour une révolution pacifique.* Paris: Librairie Générale Française, 1989. English: *Thinking the Difference: for a peaceful revolution.* Translated by Karin Montin. New York: Routledge, 1994, 37–64.

Irvin, Dorothy. "The Ministry of Women in the Early Church: The Archaeological Evidence," *DDSR* 45 (1980) 76–86.

Isaacs, Marie E. *The Concept of Spirit. A Study of Pneuma in Hellenistic Judaism and its Bearing on the New Testament.* HeyM 1. London: Heythrop College, 1976.

Janowsky, J. Christine. "Umstrittene Pfarrerin. Zu einer unvollendeten Reformation der Kirche," in Martin Greiffenhagen, ed., *Das evangelische Pfarrhaus. Eine Kultur- und Sozialgeschichte.* Stuttgart: Kreuz, 1984; 2nd ed. 1991, 83–107.

Jaubert, Annie. "Le Voile des Femmes (I Cor. XI. 2-16)," *NTS* 18 (1971/72) 419–30.

Jensen, Anne. "Thekla. Vergessene Verkündigerin," in Karin Walter, ed., *Zwischen Ohnmacht und Befreiung. Biblische Frauengestalten.* Freiburg, Basel, and Vienna: Herder, 1988, 173–79.

_____. "Auf dem Weg zur Heiligen Jungfrau. Vorformen des Marienkultes in der frühen Kirche," in Elisabeth Gössmann and Dieter R. Bauer, eds., *Maria – für alle Frauen oder über allen Frauen?* Freiburg, Basel, and Vienna: Herder, 1989, 36–62.

_____. "Philumene oder Das Streben nach Vergeistigung," in Karin Walter, ed., *Sanft und rebellisch. Mütter der Christenheit – von Frauen neu entdeckt.* Freiburg, Basel, and Vienna: Herder, 1990, 221–43.

_____. "Maria von Magdala – Traditionen der frühen Christenheit," in Dietmar Bader, ed., *Maria Magdalena – Zu einem Bild der Frau in der christlichen Verkündigung.* Schriftenreihe der Katholischen Akademie der Erzdiözese Freiburg. Munich and Zürich: Schnell and Steiner, 1990, 33–50.

_____. "Die ersten Christinnen der Spätantike," in Veronika Straub, ed., *Auch wir sind die Kirche. Frauen in der Kirche zwischen Tradition und Aufbruch.* Munich: J. Pfeiffer, 1991, 35–58.

_____. "Diakonin," *WFT* 1991, 58–60.

_____. *Gottes selbstbewußte Töchter. Frauenemanzipation im frühen Christentum?* Freiburg, Basel, and Vienna: Herder, 1992. English: *God's Self-Confident Daughters. Early Christianity and the Liberation of Women.* Translated by O. C. Dean, Jr. Louisville: Westminster/John Knox, 1996.

_____. *Thekla – die Apostolin. Ein apokrypher Text neu entdeckt, übersetzt und kommentiert.* Frauen – Kultur – Geschichte 3. Freiburg, Basel, and Vienna: Herder, 1995.

Jeremias, Joachim. *Die Briefe an Timothus und Titus.* NTD 9. Göttingen: Vandenhoeck & Ruprecht, 1975, 1–77.

Jervell, Jacob. "Die Töchter Abrahams. Die Frau in der Apostelgeschichte," in Jarmo Kiilunen, Vilho Riekkinen, and Heikki Räisänen, eds., *Glaube und Gerechtigkeit. In Memoriam Rafael Gyllenberg.* Helsinki: Suomen Eksegeettisen Seura, 1983, 77–93.

Jewett, Paul K. *The Ordination of Women. An Essay on the Office of Christian Ministry.* Grand Rapids: Eerdmans, 1980.

Jewett, Robert. "The Sexual Liberation of the Apostle Paul," *JAAR* 47 (1979) 55–87.

_____. "Paul, Phoebe, and the Spanish Mission," in Jacob Neusner, ed., *The Social World of Formative Christianity and Judaism, in Tribute to Howard Clark Kee.* Philadelphia: Fortress, 1988, 142–61.

Jordan, Hermann. *Das Frauenideal des Neuen Testaments und der ältesten Christenheit.* Leipzig: A. Deichert'sche Verlagsbuchhandlung Nachf. (G. Böhme), 1909.

Jülicher, Adolf. "Ein gallisches Bischofsschreiben des 6. Jahrhunderts als Zeuge für die Verfassung der Montanistenkirche," *ZKG* 16 (1896) 664–71.

Judge, Edwin A., and S. R. Pickering. "Papyrus Documentation of Church and Community in Egypt to the Mid-Fourth Century," *JAC* 20 (1977) 47–71.

_____. "The Earliest Use of Monachos for 'monk' (P.Coll.Youtie 77)," *JAC* 20 (1977) 72–89.

Kähler, Else. *Die Frau in den paulinischen Briefen: unter besonderer Berücksichtigung des Begriffes der Unterordnung.* Zürich: Gotthelf-Verlag, 1960.

Käsemann, Ernst. "Die Johannesjünger in Ephesus" (1952) in idem, *Exegetische Versuche und Besinnungen.* 6th ed. Göttingen: Vandenhoeck & Ruprecht, 1970, 1:158–68.

_____. "Amt und Gemeinde im Neuen Testament" (1960) in idem, *Exegetische Versuche und Besinnungen* 1:109–34.

Kalsbach, Adolf. "Die Diakonissenweihe im Kan. 19 des Konzils von Nicäa," *RQ* 32 (1924) 166–69.

_____. *Die altkirchliche Einrichtung der Diakonissen bis zu ihrem Erlöschen.* RQ.S 22. Freiburg: Herder, 1926.

_____. "Diakonie," *RAC* 3 (1957) 909–17.

_____. "Diakonisse," *RAC* 3 (1957) 917–28.

Kampen, Natalie. *Image and Status: Roman Working Women in Ostia.* Berlin: Mann, 1981.

Karrer, Martin. *Die Johannesoffenbarung als Brief. Studien zu ihrem literarischen, historischen und theologischen Ort.* FRLANT 140. Göttingen: Vandenhoeck & Ruprecht, 1986.

_____. "Das urchristliche Ältestenamt," *NT* 32 (1990) 152–88.

_____. "Apostel, Apostolat," *EKL³* 1:221–23.

Kattenbusch, Ferdinand. "Der Märtyrertitel," *ZNW* 4 (1903) 111–27.

Kearsley, R. A. "Women in Public Life in the Roman East: Iunia Theodora, Claudia Metrodora and Phoibe, Benefactress of Paul," *Ancient Society* (Macquarie University) 15 (1985) 124–37.

Kee, Howard Clark. "Changing Modes of Leadership in the New Testament Period," *SocComp* 39 (1992) 241–54.

_____. "The Changing Role of Women in the Early Christian World," *ThTo* 49 (1992) 225–38.

Kelly, Joan. "The Social Relation of the Sexes. Methodological Implications of Women's History" (1976) in eadem, *Women, History & Theory. The Essays of Joan Kelly*. Chicago: University of Chicago Press, 1984, 1–18.

_____. "The Doubled Vision of Feminist Theory" (1979) in ibid. 51–64.

Kelly, John Norman Davidson. *Jerome. His Life, Writings, and Controversies*. New York: Harper & Row, 1975.

Kertelge, Karl. *Gemeinde und Amt im Neuen Testament*. BiH 10. Munich: Kösel, 1972.

_____, ed. *Das Kirchliche Amt im Neuen Testament*. WdF 439. Darmstadt: Wissenschaftliche Buchgesellschaft, 1977.

Ketter, Peter. *Die Magdalenenfrage*. Trier: Paulinus-Dr., 1929.

Kirsch, Johann Peter. *Die römischen Titelkirchen im Altertum*. SGKA 9/1, 2. Paderborn: Schöningh, 1918.

_____. "Anzeiger für christliche Archäologie," *RQ* 16 (1902) 76–85.

Klass, Margo Pautler. *The Chapel of S. Zeno in S. Prassede in Rome*. Ph.D. Bryn Mawr, 1972.

Klauck, Hans-Josef. *Hausgemeinde und Hauskirche im frühen Christentum*. SBS 103. Stuttgart: Katholisches Bibelwerk, 1981.

Klawitter, Frederick C. *The New Prophecy in Early Christianity. The Origin, Nature, and Development of Montanism*, A.D. 165–220. Diss. Chicago, 1975 (microfilm).

_____. "The Role of Martyrdom and Persecution in Developing the Priestly Authority of Women in Early Christianity: A Case Study of Montanism," *ChH* 49 (1980) 251–61 (reprinted in David M. Scholer, ed., *Women in Early Christianity*, 105–15).

Klein, Günter. *Die zwölf Apostel. Ursprung und Gehalt einer Idee*. FRLANT 77. Göttingen: Vandenhoeck & Ruprecht, 1961.

Klingenberg, Georg. "Grabrecht (Grabmulta, Grabschändung)," *RAC* 12 (1983) 590–637.

Knight, George W. III. "ΑΥΘΕΝΤΕΩ in Reference to Women in 1 Timothy 2.12," *NTS* 30 (1984) 143–57.

Knott, Betty I. "The Christian 'Special Language' in the Inscriptions," *VigChr* 10 (1956) 65–79.

Koch, Hugo. *Virgines Christi. Die Gelübde der gottgeweihten Jungfrauen in den ersten drei Jahrhunderten*. TU 31/2. Leipzig: J. C. Hinrichs, 1907, 59–112.

Koester, Helmut, and James M. Robinson. *Trajectories through Early Christianity*. Philadelphia: Fortress, 1971.

Konetzny, Gabriele. "Die Jungfrauenweihe," in Teresa Berger and Albert Gerhards, eds., *Liturgie und Frauenfrage*, 475–92.

Kornemann, Ernst. *Grosse Frauen des Altertums. Im Rahmen zweitausendjährigen Weltgeschehens*. Sammlung Dietrich 86. Wiesbaden: Dietrich, 1952.

Körtner, Ulrich H.J. *Papias von Hierapolis. Ein Beitrag zur Geschichte des frühen Christentums*. FRLANT 133. Göttingen: Vandenhoeck & Ruprecht, 1983.

Koschorke, Klaus. "Eine neugefundene gnostische Gemeindeordnung. Zum Thema Geist und Amt im frühen Christentum," *ZThK* 76 (1977) 30–60.

———. *Spuren der alten Liebe. Studien zum Kirchenbegriff des Basilius von Caesarea*. Par. 32. Fribourg: Universitätsverlag, 1991.

Kötting, Bernhard. "Digamus," *RAC* 3 (1957) 1016–24.

———. *Der Zölibat in der Alten Kirche*. Schriften der Gesellschaft zur Förderung der Westfälischen Wilhelms-Universität zu Münster 61. Münster: Aschendorff, 1970.

———. "Fußwaschung," *RAC* 8 (1972) 743–77.

———. "'Univira' in Inschriften," in W. den Boer et al., eds., *Romanitas et Christianitas. Studia Iano Henrico Waszink*. Amsterdam: North-Holland, 1973, 195–206.

———. "Die Stellung des Konfessors in der Alten Kirche," *JAC* 19 (1976) 7–23.

———. *Die Bewertung der Wiederverheiratung (der zweiten Ehe) in der Antike und in der Frühen Kirche*. RhWAS Vorträge G 292. Opladen: Westdeutscher Verlag, 1988.

Kraabel, Alf Thomas. *Judaism in Western Asia Minor under the Roman Empire, with a Preliminary Study of the Jewish Community at Sardis, Lydia*. Diss. Cambridge, Mass.: Harvard University Library Microreproduction, 1968.

Kraemer, Ross S. *Ecstatics and Ascetics: Studies in the Functions of Religious Activities for Women in the Greco-Roman World*. Diss. Princeton 1976. Ann Arbor: University Microfilms, 1978.

———. "The Conversion of Women to Ascetic Forms of Christianity," *Signs* 6 (1980) 298–307 (also published in David M. Scholer, ed., *Women in Early Christianity*, 152–261).

———. "A New Inscription from Malta and the Question of Women Elders in the Diaspora Jewish Communities," *HThR* 78 (1985) 431–38.

———. "Non-Literary Evidence for Jewish Women in Rome and Egypt," in M. B. Skinner, ed., *Rescuing Creusa: New Methodological Approaches to Women in Antiquity*. Special number of the periodical *Helios*, n.s. 13/2 (1986) 85–101.

———. "Hellenistic Jewish Women: The Epigraphical Evidence," *SBL Seminar Papers* (1986) 183–200.

———. "On the Meaning of the Term 'Jew' in Greco-Roman Inscriptions," *HThR* 82 (1989) 35–53.

———. "Monastic Jewish Women in Greco-Roman Egypt: Philo Judaeus on the Therapeutrides," *Signs* 14 (1989) 342–70.

———. "Women's Authorship of Jewish and Christian Literature in the Greco-Roman Period," in Amy-Jill Levine, ed., *"Women Like This." New Perspectives on Jewish Women in the Greco-Roman World*. SBL. Early Judaism and its Literature 1. Atlanta: Scholars, 1991, 221–42.

_____. *Her Share of the Blessings. Women's Religions among Pagans, Jews, and Christians in the Greco-Roman World*. New York and Oxford: Oxford University Press, 1992.

Kraft, Heinrich. "Die altkirchliche Prophetie und die Entstehung des Montanismus," *ThZ* 11 (1955) 249–71.

_____. *Die Offenbarung des Johannes*. HNT 16a. Tübingen: J.C.B. Mohr [Paul Siebeck], 1974.

_____. "Die Anfänge des geistlichen Amtes," *ThLZ* 100 (1975) 81–98.

_____. "Vom Ende der urchristlichen Prophetie," in Johannes Panagopoulos, ed., *Prophetic Vocation in the New Testament and Today*, 162–85.

_____. "Die Lyoner Märtyrer und der Montanismus," in *Pietas. FS Bernhard Kötting*. JAC.E 8 (1980) 250–66.

_____. *Die Entstehung des Christentums*. Darmstadt: Wissenschaftliche Buchgesellschaft, 1981.

_____. "χήρα, ας, ἡ," *EDNT* 3:465–66.

Kramer, Bärbel. "Didymus von Alexandrien," *TRE* 8 (1981) 741–46.

Kretschmar, Georg. "Ein Beitrag zu der Frage nach dem Ursprung frühchristlicher Askese," *ZThK* 61 (1964) 27–67.

_____. "Die Ordination im frühen Christentum," *FZPhTh* 22 (1975) 35–69.

Kretschmer, Paul. "Die griechische Benennung des Bruders," *Glotta* 2 (1910) 201–13.

Küchler, Max. *Schweigen, Schmuck und Schleier. Drei neutestamentliche Vorschriften zur Verdrängung der Frauen auf dem Hintergrund einer frauenfeindlichen Exegese des Alten Testaments im antiken Judentum*. NTOA 1. Göttingen: Vandenhoeck & Ruprecht, 1986.

Kuhli, Horst. "οἰκονομία κτλ.," *EDNT* 2:498–500.

Kühnert, Wilhelm. "Der antimontanistische Anonymus des Eusebius," *ThZ* 5 (1949) 436–46.

Kunze, Konrad. *Studien zur Legende der heiligen Maria Aegyptiaca im deutschen Sprachgebiet*. PStQ 49. Berlin: E. Schmidt, 1969.

Labriolle, Pierre de. *La Crise Montaniste*. Paris: E. Leroux, 1913.

Lampe, Peter. "Iunia/Iunias: Sklavenherrschaft im Kreise der vorpaulinischen Apostel (Röm 16,7)," *ZNW* 76 (1985) 132–34.

_____. *Die stadtrömischen Christen in den ersten beiden Jahrhunderten*. WUNT II/18. 2nd ed. Tübingen: J.C.B. Mohr [Paul Siebeck], 1989. English: *From Paul to Valentinus. Christians at Rome in the First Two Centuries*. Translated by J. Larrimore Holland and Michael Steinhauser. Minneapolis: Fortress, 2000.

Landvogt, Peter. *Epigraphische Untersuchungen über den OIKONOMOS*. Diss. Strasbourg: Druck von M. Dumont Schauberg, 1908.

Lang, Judith. *Ministers of Grace. Women in the Early Church*. Middlegreen, Slough: St. Paul's Publications, 1989.

LaPorte, Jean. *The Role of Women in Early Christianity*. SWR 7. New York and Toronto: Edwin Mellen, 1982.

Lattimore, Richmond A. *Themes in Greek and Latin Epitaphs*. Illinois Studies in Language and Literature 28/1-2. Urbana: University of Illinois Press, 1942.

Leclercq, Henri. "Diacre," *DACL* IV/1 (1920) 738–46.

_____. "Econome," *DACL* IV/2 (1921) 1884–1886.

_____. "Evêque," *DACL* V/1 (1922) 938–49.

_____. "Achaie," *DACL* I/1 (1924) 321–40.

_____. "Acrostiche," *DACL* I/1 (1924) 356–72.

_____. "Ama," *DACL* I/2 (1924) 1306–1323.

_____. "Anges," *DACL* I/2 (1924) 2080–2161.

_____. "Marcella," *DACL* X/2 (1932) 1760–1762.

_____. "Presbyter," *DACL* XIV/2 (1948) 1717–1721.

Leder, Paul August. *Die Diakonen der Bischöfe und Presbyter und ihre urchristlichen Vorläufer.* KRA 23, 24. Amsterdam: P. Schippers, 1963. (Reprint of the Stuttgart ed. of 1905.)

Leenhardt, Franz J., and Fritz Blanke. *Die Stellung der Frau im Neuen Testament und in der Alten Kirche.* KZF 24. Zürich: Zwingli, 1949.

Lefkowitz, Mary R. "Did Ancient Women Write Novels?" in Amy-Jill Levine, ed., *"Women Like This,"* 199–219.

Legrand, Hervé. "Die Frage der Frauenordination aus der Sicht katholischer Theologie. 'Inter Insigniores' nach zehn Jahren," in Elisabeth Gössmann and Dietmar Bader, eds., *Warum keine Ordination der Frau?* 89–111.

_____. "Traditio Perpetua Servata? The Non-Ordination of Women: Tradition or Simply Historical Fact?" *OiC* 29 (1993) 1–23.

Leipoldt, Johannes. *Die Frau in der antiken Welt und im Urchristentum.* Leipzig: Koehler & Amelang, 1954.

Leisch-Kiesl, Monika. *Eva als Andere: eine exemplarische Untersuchung zu Frühchristentum und Mittelalter.* Cologne, Weimar, and Vienna: Bohlau, 1992.

Lemaire, André. "Pastoral Epistles: Redaction and Theology," *BTB* 2 (1972) 25–42.

_____. "The Ministries in the New Testament. Recent Research," *BTB* 3 (1973) 133–66.

Leutzsch, Martin. *Die Wahrnehmung sozialer Wirklichkeit im "Hirten des Hermas."* FRLANT 150. Göttingen: Vandenhoeck & Ruprecht, 1989.

Levine, Amy-Jill, ed. *"Women Like This." New Perspectives on Jewish Women in the Greco-Roman World.* SBL. Early Judaism and its Literature I. Atlanta: Scholars, 1991.

Libreria delle donne di Milano. *Das Patriarchat ist zuende. Es ist passiert—nicht aus Zufall.* Translated from the Italian original, *Il patriarcato è finito. E' accaduto non per caso,* by Traudel Sattler. Rüsselsheim: Göttert, 1996.

Lies, Lothar. "Zur Exegese des Origenes," *ThRv* 88 (1992) 89–96.

Lietzmann, Hans. "Zur altchristlichen Verfassungsgeschichte," *ZWTh* n.s. 20 (1914) 97–153 (reprinted in idem, *Kleine Schriften I.* TU 67. Berlin: Akademie-Verlag, 1958, 141–85).

_____. *An die Korinther I/II.* HNT 9. 3rd ed. Tübingen: J.C.B. Mohr [Paul Siebeck], 1931.

_____. *Geschichte der Alten Kirche.* 4 vols. Berlin and Leipzig: Walter de Gruyter, 1932–1944.

Lightfoot, Joseph B. *Saint Paul's Epistle to the Galatians.* 9th ed. London: Macmillan, 1887.

Lindblom, Johannes. *Gesichte und Offenbarungen. Vorstellungen von göttlichen Weisungen und übernatürlichen Erscheinungen im ältesten Christentum.* Lund: Gleerup, 1968.

Lindboe, Inger Marie. "Recent Literature: Development and Perspectives in New Testament Research on Women," *StTh* 43 (1989) 153–63.

Lindemann, Andreas. *Die Clemensbriefe.* HNT 17. Tübingen: J.C.B. Mohr [Paul Siebeck], 1992.

Lindgren, Uta. "Wege der historischen Frauenforschung," *HJ* 109 (1989) 211–19.

Linss, Wilhelm C. "Ministry in the New Testament: 'In the Beginning . . . ,'" *CThMi* 17 (1990) 6–14.

Linton, Olof. *Das Problem der Urkirche in der neueren Forschung. Eine kritische Darstellung.* Diss. theol. Uppsala: Almqvist & Wiksells, 1932.

Lips, Hermann von. *Glaube – Gemeinde – Amt. Zum Verständnis der Ordination in den Pastoralbriefen.* FRLANT 122. Göttingen: Vandenhoeck & Ruprecht, 1979.

Lipsius, Richard Adelbert. *Zur Quellenkritik des Epiphanios.* Vienna: W. Braumüller, 1865.

_____. *Die Quellen der aeltesten Ketzergeschichte.* Leipzig: J. A. Barth, 1875.

Loening, Edgar. *Die Gemeindeverfassung des Urchristenthums. Eine kirchenrechtliche Untersuchung.* Aalen: Scientia Verlag, 1966. (Reprint of the Halle ed. of 1888.)

Lohfink, Gerhard. "Weibliche Diakone im Neuen Testament" (1980) in Gerhard Lohfink, Helmut Merklein, and Karlheinz Müller, eds., *Die Frau im Urchristentum.* QD 95. 4th ed. Freiburg, Basel, and Vienna: Herder, 1989, 320–38.

Lohmeyer, Ernst. *Die Briefe an die Philipper, an die Kolosser und an Philemon.* KEK IX. 11th ed. Göttingen: Vandenhoeck & Ruprecht, 1956. Beiheft by Werner Schmauch, Göttingen: Vandenhoeck & Ruprecht, 1964.

_____. *Die Offenbarung des Johannes.* HNT 16. Tübingen, J.C.B. Mohr [P. Siebeck], 1926.

Lohse, Eduard. *Die Ordination im Spätjudentum und im Neuen Testament.* Göttingen: Vandenhoeck & Ruprecht, 1951.

_____. "Die Entstehung des Bischofsamtes in der frühen Christenheit," *ZNW* 71 (1980) 58–73.

Loofs, Friedrich. "Die urchristliche Gemeindeverfassung mit spezieller Beziehung auf Loening und Harnack," *ThStKr* 63 (1890) 619–58.

Lösch, Stefan. "Christliche Frauen in Corinth (1 Cor. 11,2-16)," *ThQ* 127 (1947) 216–61.

Luck, Georg. "Die Dichterinnen der griechischen Anthologie" (1954) in Gerhard Pfohl, ed., *Das Epigramm. Zur Geschichte einer inschriftlichen und literarischen Gattung.* Darmstadt: Wissenschaftliche Buchgesellschaft, 1969, 85–109.

Ludolphy, Ingetraut. "Frau. V. Alte Kirche und Mittelalter," *TRE* 11 (1983) 436–41.

Lüdemann, Gerd. *Das frühe Christentum nach den Traditionen der Apostelgeschichte: ein Kommentar.* Göttingen: Vandenhoeck & Ruprecht, 1987.

Ludwig, August. "Weibliche Kleriker in der altchristlichen und frühmittelalterlichen Kirche," *Theologisch-praktische Quartalschrift* 20 (1910) 548–57, 609–17; 21 (1911) 141–49.

Lührmann, Dieter. "Erwägungen zur Geschichte des Urchristentums," *EvTh* 32 (1972) 452–67.

MacDonald, Dennis Ronald. "Virgins, Widows, and Paul in Second Century Asia Minor," *SBL Seminar Papers* 1979, 169–84.

_____. *The Legend and the Apostle. The Battle for Paul in Story and Canon*. Philadelphia: Westminster, 1983.

_____. "The Role of Women in the Production of the Apocryphal Acts of Apostles," *IliffRev* 40/4 (1984) 21–38.

_____. "Corinthian Veils and Gnostic Androgynes," in Karen L. King, ed., *Images of the Feminine in Gnosticism*. Studies in Antiquity and Christianity 4. Philadelphia: Fortress, 1988, 276–92.

MacMullen, Ramsay. "Women in Public in the Roman Empire," *Hist* 29 (1980) 208–18.

Maeger, Annemarie. *Hypatia. Die Dreigestaltige*. Hamburg: Reuter & Klöckner, 1992.

Maisch, Ingrid. "Isebel. Autoritätskonflikt – nicht nur in Thyatira," in Karin Walter, ed., *Zwischen Ohnmacht und Befreiung,* 163–72.

Malinowski, Francis X. "The Brave Women of Philippi," *BTB* 15 (1985) 60–64.

Marcovich, Miroslav. "Hippolyt von Rom," *TRE* 15 (1986) 381–87.

Marrou, Henri-Irénée. *Histoire de l' éducation dans l'antiquité*. 3rd ed. Paris: Editions du Seuil, 1955.

Martimort, Aimé Georges. *Les Diaconesses. Essai historique*. BEL.S 24. Rome: C.L.V.-Edizioni liturgiche, 1982. English: *Deaconesses: An Historical Study.* Translated by K. D. Whitehead. San Francisco: Ignatius Press, 1985.

Martin, Jochen. *Der priesterliche Dienst III. Die Genese des Amtspriestertums in der frühen Kirche*. QD 48. Freiburg, Basel, and Vienna: Herder, 1972.

Marucchi, Orazio. *Basiliques et Eglises de Rome*. Paris: Desclée, 1902.

Massey, Lesly F. *Women and the New Testament. An Analysis of Scripture in Light of New Testament Era Culture*. Jefferson, N.C.: McFarland & Co., 1989.

Maurer, Wilhelm. "Von Ursprung und Wesen kirchlichen Rechts," review of Hans Freiherr von Campenhausen, *Kirchliches Amt und geistliche Vollmacht in den ersten drei Jahrhunderten* (Tübingen: J.C.B. Mohr [Paul Siebeck], 1953), *ZevKR* 5 (1956) 1–32.

Mayer, Günter. *Die jüdische Frau in der hellenistisch-römischen Antike*. Stuttgart, Berlin, Cologne, and Mainz: Kohlhammer, 1987.

McKenna, Mary Lawrence. *Women of the Church. Role and Renewal*. New York: P. J. Kenedy, 1967.

McNamara, Jo Ann. "Sexual Equality and the Cult of Virginity in Early Christian Thought," *Feminist Studies* 3 (1976) 145–58.

_____. "Wives and Widows in Early Christian Thought," *International Journal of Women's Studies* 2 (1979) 575–92.

_____. *A New Song: Celibate Women in the First Three Christian Centuries*. New York: Institute for Research in History; Haworth Press, 1983.

Meeks, Wayne A. *The First Urban Christians. The Social World of the Apostle Paul*. New Haven: Yale University Press, 1983.

Meer, Frits van der. "Makrina. Porträt einer Familie," in Martin Greschat, ed., *Alte Kirche II*. GK 2. Stuttgart, Berlin, Cologne, and Mainz: Kohlhammer, 1984, 37–47.

Meer, Haye van der. *Priestertum der Frau? Eine theologiegeschichtliche Unter-suchung.* QD 42. Freiburg, Basel, and Vienna: Herder, 1969. English: *Women Priests in the Catholic Church? A theological-historical investigation.* Trans-lated and with a foreword and afterword by Arlene and Leonard Swidler. Fore-word by Cynthia C. Wedel. Philadelphia: Temple University Press, 1973.

Meier, John P. "On the Veiling of Hermeneutics (1 Cor 11:2-16)," *CBQ* 40 (1978) 212–26.

Merkel, Helmut. *Die Pastoralbriefe.* TNT 9/1. Göttingen: Vandenhoeck & Ruprecht, 1991.

Merklein, Helmut. *Das kirchliche Amt nach dem Epheserbrief.* StANT 33. Munich: Kösel, 1973.

Metzger, Marcel. "Konstitutionen, (Pseud-)Apostolische," *TRE* 19 (1990) 540–44.

Meyer, Charles R. "Ordained Women in the Early Church," *ChiSt* 4 (1965) 285–308.

Meyer, Wolfgang Alexander. *Hypatia von Alexandria. Ein Beitrag zur Geschichte des Neuplatonismus.* Heidelberg: G. Weiss, 1886.

Meyer-Wilmes, Hedwig. *Rebellion auf der Grenze. Ortsbestimmung feministischer Theologie.* Freiburg: Herder, 1990.

Michaelis, Wilhelm. *Das Ältestenamt der christlichen Gemeinde im Lichte der Heili-gen Schrift.* Bern: Haller, 1953.

Michel, Hans-Joachim. *Die Abschiedsrede des Paulus an die Kirche Apg 20,17-38. Motivgeschichte und theologische Bedeutung.* StANT 35. Munich: Kösel, 1973.

Michel, Otto. "οἶκος κτλ.," *TDNT* 5:119–59.

_____. *Der Brief an die Römer.* KEK IV. 12th rev. and expanded ed. Göttingen: Van-denhoeck & Ruprecht, 1963.

Michl, Johann. "Engel I-IX," *RAC* 5 (1962) 53–258.

Mitchell, Margaret Mary. *Paul and the Rhetoric of Reconciliation: An Exegetical In-vestigation of the Language and Composition of 1 Corinthians.* Hermeneutische Untersuchungen zur Theologie 28. Tübingen: J.C.B. Mohr [Paul Siebeck] 1991; 1st American ed. Louisville: Westminster/John Knox, 1992.

Mitchell, Stephen. "The Life of Saint Theodotus of Ancyra," *AnSt* 32 (1982) 93–113.

Mohler, S. L. "Feminism in the Corpus Inscriptionum Latinarum," *ClW* 25 (1932) 113–17.

Moine, Nicole. "Melaniana," *RechAug* 15 (1980) 3–79.

Moltmann-Wendel, Elisabeth. *Ein eigener Mensch werden. Frauen um Jesus.* Güters-loh: Gerd Mohn, 1980. English: *The Women Around Jesus.* Translated by John Bowden. New York: Crossroad, 1982.

_____. "Maria Magdalena II. In der Tradition," *WFT* (1991) 277–79.

Montgomery, Hugo. "Women and Status in the Greco-Roman World," *StTh* 43 (1989) 115–24.

Moo, Douglas J. "1 Timothy 2:11-15: Meaning and Significance," *TrinJ* n.s. 1 (1980) 62–83.

Moreton, Bernard. "Gelasius I. Bischof von Rom (492–496)," *TRE* 12 (1984) 273–76.

Morris, Joan. *The Lady was a Bishop. The Hidden History of Women with Clerical Or-dination and the Jurisdiction of Bishops.* New York and London: Macmillan,

1973 (= *Against Nature and God. The History of Women with Clerical Ordination and the Jurisdiction of Bishops.* London and Oxford: Mowbrays, 1973).

_____. *Pope John VIII: an English Woman alias Pope Joan.* London: Vrai, 1985.

Mott, Stephen Charles. "The Power of Giving and Receiving: Reciprocity in Hellenistic Benevolence," in Gerald F. Hawthorne, ed., *Current Issues in Biblical and Patristic Interpretation.* Grand Rapids: Eerdmans, 1975, 60–72.

Moutsoulas, E. "Der Begriff 'Häresie' bei Epiphanius von Salamis," *StPatr* 7 (1966) 362–71.

Mühlsteiger, Johannes. "Zum Verfassungsrecht der Frühkirche," *ZKTh* 99 (1977) 129–55, 257–85.

Müller, Caspar D. G. "Alexandrien I 3," *TRE* 2 (1978) 248–61.

Müller, Karl. *Beiträge zur Geschichte der Verfassung der alten Kirche.* APAW.PH 3. Berlin: Verlag der Akademie der Wissenschaften in Kommission bei der Vereinigung wissenschaftlicher Verleger Walter de Gruyter u. Co., 1922.

Müller, Karlheinz. "Die Haustafel des Kolosserbriefes und das antike Frauenthema. Ein kritischer Rückschau auf alte Ergebnisse," in Gerhard Lohfink, Helmut Merklein, and Karlheinz Müller, eds., *Die Frau im Urchristentum,* 263–319.

Müller, Ulrich B. *Prophetie und Predigt im Neuen Testament. Formgeschichtliche Untersuchungen zur urchristlichen Prophetie.* StNT 10. Gütersloh: Gerd Mohn, 1975.

_____. *Die Offenbarung des Johannes.* ÖTK 19. Gütersloh: Gerd Mohn, 1984.

Müller-Bardorff, Johannes. "Zur Exegese von I. Timotheus 5,3-16," in *Gott und die Götter. FS für Erich Fascher.* Berlin: Evang. Verl. Anst., 1958, 113–33.

Munro, Winsome. "Women, Text and the Canon: The Strange Case of 1 Corinthians 14:33-35," *BTB* 18 (1988) 26–31.

Murphy, Francis X. *Rufinus of Aquileia (345–411). His Life and Works.* SMH n.s. 6. Washington, D.C.: Catholic University of America Press, 1945.

_____. "Melania the Elder: A Biographical Note," *Tr* 5 (1947) 59–77.

Murphy-O'Connor, Jerome. "The Non-Pauline Character of 1 Corinthians 11:2-16," *JBL* 95 (1976) 615–21.

_____. "Sex and Logic in 1 Corinthians 11:2-16," *CBQ* 42 (1980) 482–500.

_____. "Interpolations in 1 Corinthians," *CBQ* 48 (1986) 81–94.

Muschiol, Gisela. "'Psallere et legere.' Zur Beteiligung der Nonnen an der Liturgie nach den frühen gallischen 'Regulae ad Virgines,'" in Teresa Berger and Albert Gerhards, eds., *Liturgie und Frauenfrage,* 77–125.

Nagl-Docekal, Herta. "Frauengeschichte als Perspektive und Teilbereich der Geschichtswissenschaft. Bemerkungen zum Referat 'Der Platz der Frauen in der Geschichte' von Gisela Bock," in Herta Nagl-Docekal and Franz Wimmer, eds., *Neue Ansätze in der Geschichtswissenschaft,* 128–32.

_____. "Feministische Geschichtswissenschaft – ein unverzichtbares Projekt," *L'Homme* 1 (1990) 7–18.

_____. "Für eine geschlechtergeschichtliche Perspektivierung der Historiographieforschung," in Wolfgang Küttler, Jörn Rüsen, and Ernst Schulin, eds., *Geschichtsdiskurs.* Vol. 1: *Grundlagen und Methoden der Historiographiegeschichte.* Frankfurt: Fischer Taschenbuch Verlag, 1993, 233–56.

Neumann, Johannes. "Bischof. I. Das katholische Bischofsamt," *TRE* 6 (1980) 653–82.

Newton, Judith. "History as Usual? Feminism and the 'New Historicism,'" *Cultural Critique* 9 (1988) 87–121.

Neymeyr, Ulrich. *Die christlichen Lehrer im zweiten Jahrhundert. Ihre Lehrtätigkeit, ihr Selbstverständnis und ihre Geschichte.* SVigChr 4. Diss. theol. Leiden and New York: E. J. Brill, 1989.

_____. "Christliche Lehrer im 2. Jahrhundert. Ihre Lehrtätigkeit, ihr Selbstverständnis und ihre Geschichte," *StPatr* 21 (1989) 158–62.

Niederwimmer, Kurt. *Askese und Mysterium. Über Ehe, Ehescheidung und Ehe-verzicht in den Anfängen des christlichen Glaubens.* FRLANT 113. Göttingen: Vandenhoeck & Ruprecht, 1975.

_____. *Die Didache.* KAV 1. Göttingen: Vandenhoeck & Ruprecht, 1989. English: *The Didache.* Translated by Linda M. Maloney. Edited by Harold W. Attridge. Hermeneia. Minneapolis: Fortress, 1998.

Niemand, Christoph. *Die Fußwaschungserzählung des Johannesevangeliums. Untersuchungen zu ihrer Entstehung und Überlieferung im Urchristentum.* Studia Anselmiana 114. Rome: Pontificio Ateneo S. Anselmo, 1993.

_____. "Was bedeutet die Fußwaschung: Sklavendienst oder Liebesdienst? Kulturkundliches als Auslegungshilfe für Joh 13,6-8," *Protokolle zur Bibel* 3 (1994) 115–27.

Nürnberg, Rosemarie. "'Non decet neque necessarium est, ut mulieres doceant.' Überlegungen zum altkirchlichen Lehrverbot für Frauen," *JAC* 31 (1988) 57–73.

Odeberg, Hugo. " Ἰεζάβελ," *TDNT* 3:217–18.

Odell-Scott, David W. "Let the Women Speak in Church. An Egalitarian Interpretation of 1 Cor 14:33b-36," *BTB* 13 (1983) 90–93.

Oepke, Albrecht. "Der Dienst der Frau in der urchristlichen Gemeinde," *NAMZ* 16 (1939) 39–53, 81–86.

Ogilvie, Marilyn Bailey. *Women in Science. Antiquity through the Nineteenth Century. A Biographical Dictionary with Annotated Bibliography.* Cambridge, Mass., and London: M.I.T. Press, 1986; 2nd ed. 1988.

Ohler, Annemarie. *Frauengestalten der Bibel.* 2nd ed. Würzburg: Echter, 1987.

Ohme, Heinz. "Die orthodoxe Kirche und die Ordination von Frauen – Zur Konferenz von Rhodos vom 30. Oktober bis 7. November 1988," *ÖR* 42 (1993) 52–65.

Ollrog, Wolf-Henning. *Paulus und seine Mitarbeiter. Untersuchungen zu Theorie und Praxis der paulinischen Mission.* WMANT 50. Neukirchen-Vluyn: Neukirchener Verlag, 1979.

Opitz, Claudia. "Der 'andere Blick' der Frauen in die Geschichte – Überlegungen zu Analyse- und Darstellungsmethoden feministischer Geschichtsforschung," in *beiträge zur feministischen theorie und praxis. Frauenforschung oder feministische Forschung?* 7/11, 2. Cologne: Eigenverlag des Vereins Beiträge zur Feministischen Theorie und Praxis (corrected ed. 1984) 61–70.

Orioli, Giorgio. "Il Testo dell'Ordinazione delle Diaconesse nella Chiesa di Antiochia dei Siri," *Apoll.* 62 (1989) 633–40.

Osiek, Carolyn. "The Church Fathers and the Ministry of Women," in Leonard Swidler and Arlene Swidler, eds., *Women Priests*, 75–80.

_____. "The Ministry and Ordination of Women according to the Early Church Fathers," in Carroll Stuhlmueller, ed., *Women and Priesthood: Future Directions.* Collegeville: The Liturgical Press, 1978, 59–68.

_____. "The Widow as Altar: The Rise and Fall of a Symbol," *SecCen* 3 (1983) 159–69.

_____. "The Feminist and the Bible: Hermeneutical Alternatives," in Adela Yarbro Collins, ed., *Feminist Perspectives on Biblical Scholarship*, 93–105.

_____. "Christian Prophecy: Once upon a Time?" *CThMi* 17 (1990) 291–97.

Otranto, Giorgio. "Note sul sacerdozio femminile nell'antichità in margine a una testimonianza di Gelasio I," *VetChr* 19 (1982) 341–60.

Oeyen, Christian. "Frauenordination: Was sagt die Tradition wirklich?" *IKZ* 17 (1985) 97–118.

Padgett, Alan. "Wealthy Women at Ephesus. 1 Timothy 2:8-15 in Social Context," *Interp* 41 (1987) 19–31.

Pagels, Elaine H. "Paul and Women: A Response to Recent Discussion" *JAAR* 42 (1974) 538–49.

Parvey, Constance F. "The Theology and Leadership of Women in the New Testament," in Rosemary Radford Ruether, ed., *Religion and Sexism. Images of Women in the Jewish and Christian Traditions.* New York: Simon & Schuster, 1974, 117–49.

_____, ed. *The Ordination of Women in Ecumenical Perspective: Workbook for the Church's Future.* Faith and Order Paper 105. Geneva: World Council of Churches, 1980.

Paulsen, Anna. *Das biblische Wort über die Frau.* Hamburg: Wittig, 1960.

Paulsen, Henning. *Studien zur Theologie des Ignatius von Antiochien.* FKDG 29. Göttingen: Vandenhoeck & Ruprecht, 1978.

_____. "Papyrus Oxyrhynchus I.5 und die ΔΙΑΔΟΧΗ ΤΩΝ ΠΡΟΦΗΤΩΝ," in idem, *Zur Literatur und Geschichte des frühen Christentums*, ed. Ute E. Eisen. WUNT 99. Tübingen: Mohr Siebeck, 1997, 162–72.

_____. "Zur Wissenschaft vom Urchristentum und der alten Kirche – ein methodischer Versuch," in idem, *Zur Literatur und Geschichte* 365–95.

_____. "Einheit und Freiheit der Söhne Gottes – Gal 3 26-29," in idem, *Zur Literatur und Geschichte* 21–42.

_____. *Die Briefe des Ignatius von Antiochia und der Brief des Polykarp von Smyrna.* HNT 18/II. 2nd rev. ed. of the interpretation by Walter Bauer. Tübingen: J.C.B. Mohr [Paul Siebeck], 1985.

_____. "Auslegungsgeschichte und Geschichte des Urchristentums: die Überprüfung eines Paradigmas" (1989) in idem, *Zur Literatur und Geschichte* 412–25.

_____. *Der Zweite Petrusbrief und der Judasbrief.* KEK XII/2. Göttingen: Vandenhoeck & Ruprecht, 1992.

Payne, Philip B. "Libertarian Women in Ephesus: A Response to Douglas J. Moo's Article, '1 Timothy 2:11-15: Meaning and Significance,'" *TrinJ* n.s. 2 (1981) 169–97.

Perrot, Michelle. "Women, Power, and History," in eadem, ed., *Writing Women's History*, translated by Felicia Pheasant; from an original idea by Alain Paire. Oxford, UK;

Cambridge, Mass.: Blackwell, 1992, 160–174. Original: "Les femmes, le pouvoir, l'histoire," in *Une histoire des femmes est-elle possible?* Paris: Rivages, 1984, 205–22.

Pesch, Rudolf. *Römerbrief.* NEB 6. Würzburg: Echter, 1983.

_____. *Die Apostelgeschichte.* 2 vols. EKK V/1-2. Neukirchen-Vluyn: Neukirchener Verlag, 1986.

Petersen-Szemerédy, Griet. *Zwischen Weltstadt und Wüste: Römische Asketinnen in der Spätantike. Eine Studie zu Motivation und Gestaltung der Askese christlicher Frauen Roms auf dem Hintergrund ihrer Zeit.* FKDG 54. Göttingen: Vandenhoeck & Ruprecht, 1993.

Peterson, Erik. *ΕΙΣ ΘΕΟΣ. Epigraphische, formgeschichtliche und religionsgeschichtliche Untersuchungen.* Göttingen: Vandenhoeck & Ruprecht, 1926.

Pilhofer, Peter. *Philippi I: Die erste christliche Gemeinde Europas.* WUNT 87. Tübingen: J.C.B. Mohr [Paul Siebeck], 1995.

Pietri, Charles. *Roma Christiana. Recherches sur l'Eglise de Rome, son organisation, sa politique, son idéologie de Miltiade à Sixte III (311–440).* 2 vols. Bibliothèque des Ecoles françaises d'Athènes et de Rome. Rome: Ecole française de Rome, 1976.

Plaskow, Judith. "Blaming the Jews for the Birth of Patriarchy," in Evelyn Tornton Beck, ed., *Nice Jewish Girls. A Lesbian Anthology.* Trumansburg, N.Y.: The Crossing Press, 1982, 250–54.

_____. "Feministischer Antijudaismus und der christliche Gott," translated by Jutta Flatters, *KuI* 5 (1990) 9–25.

_____. *Standing Again at Sinai. Judaism from a Feminist Perspective.* San Francisco: Harper & Row, 1990.

Poland, Franz. *Geschichte des griechischen Vereinswesens.* Leipzig: Zentral-Antiquariat der Deutschen Demokratischen Republik, 1967. (Reprint of the 1909 Teubner edition.)

Pomeroy, Sarah B. *Goddesses, Whores, Wives, and Slaves. Women in Classical Antiquity.* New York: Schocken, 1975; 9th ed. 1985.

_____. "Women in Roman Egypt. A preliminary study based on papyri," in Helene P. Foley, ed., *Reflections on Women in Antiquity,* 303–22.

_____. *Women in Hellenistic Egypt. From Alexander to Cleopatra.* New York: Schocken, 1984.

Portefaix, Lilian. *Sisters Rejoice. Paul's Letter to the Philippians and Luke-Acts as Seen by First-Century Philippian Women.* CB.NT 20. Uppsala: Almqvist & Wiksell, 1988.

_____. "Women and Mission in the New Testament: Some Remarks on the Perspective of Audience. A Research Report," *StTh* 43 (1989) 141–52.

Porter, Stanley E. "What does it Mean to be 'Saved by Childbirth' (1 Timothy 2.15)?" *JSNT* 49 (1993) 87–102.

Procopé, John. "Erbauungsliteratur I. Alte Kirche," *TRE* 10 (1982) 28–43.

Puhle, Hans-Jürgen. "Frauengeschichte und Gesellschaftsgeschichte. Kommentar zum Beitrag von Gisela Bock," in Herta Nagl-Docekal and Franz Wimmer, eds., *Neue Ansätze in der Geschichtswissenschaft,* 133–36.

Pusch, Luise F., ed. *Feminismus: Inspektion der Herrenkultur. Ein Handbuch.* edition suhrkamp n.s. 192. Frankfurt: Suhrkamp, 1983.

_____. *Das Deutsche als Männersprache. Aufsätze und Glossen zur feministischen Linguistik.* edition suhrkamp n.s. 217. Frankfurt: Suhrkamp, 1984.

_____. *Alle Menschen werden Schwestern. Feministische Sprachkritik.* edition suhrkamp n.s. 565. Frankfurt: Suhrkamp, 1990.

Puzicha, Michaela. *Christus peregrinus. Die Fremdenaufnahme (Mt 25,35) als Werk der privaten Wohltätigkeit im Urteil der Alten Kirche.* MBTh 47. Münster: Aschendorff, 1980.

Quesnell, Quentin. "The Women at Luke's Supper," in Richard J. Cassidy and Philip Scharper, eds., *Political Issues in Luke-Acts.* Maryknoll, N.Y.: Orbis, 1983, 59–79.

Rahner, Karl. "Priestertum der Frau?" *StZ* 102 (1977) 291–301 (= "Women and the Priesthood," in idem, *Concern for the Church.* Theological Investigations XX. Translated by Edward Quinn. New York: Crossroad, 1981, 35–47).

Raming, Ida. *Der Ausschluß der Frau vom priesterlichen Amt. Gottgewollte Tradition oder Diskriminierung? Eine rechtshistorisch-dogmatische Untersuchung der Grundlagen von Kanon 968 § 1 des Codex Iuris Canonici.* Cologne: Böhlau, 1973. English: *The exclusion of women from the priesthood: divine law or sex discrimination? A historical investigation of the juridical and doctrinal foundations of the code of canon law, canon 968, 1.* Translated by Norman R. Adams, with a preface by Arlene and Leonard Swidler. Metuchen, N.J.: Scarecrow Press, 1976.

_____. "Frauenordination. Fortschritt auf dem Weg zur Befreiung der Frau in der katholischen Kirche," *Schlangenbrut* 22 (1988) 10–14.

_____. *Frauenbewegung und Kirche. Bilanz eines 25jährigen Kampfes für die Gleichberechtigung und Befreiung der Frau seit dem 2. Vatikanischen Konzil.* Weinheim: Deutscher Studien, 1989.

_____. "Priestertum der Frau," *WFT* (1991) 328–30.

Rebenich, Stefan. *Hieronymus und sein Kreis. Prosopographische und sozialgeschichtliche Untersuchungen.* Hist. Einzelschriften 72. Stuttgart: F. Steiner, 1992.

Redekop, Gloria Neufeld. "Let the women learn: 1 Timothy 2:8-15 reconsidered," *SR* 19 (1990) 235–45.

Reichert, Eckhard. *Die Canones der Synode von Elvira. Einleitung und Kommentar.* Hamburg: 1990.

Reichle, Erika. "Frauenordination," in Claudia Pinl et al., eds., *Frauen auf neuen Wegen. Studien und Problemberichte zur Situation der Frauen in Gesellschaft und Kirche.* Kennzeichen 3. Gelnhausen and Berlin: Burckhardthaus-Verlag; Stein/Mfr.: Laetare-Verlag, 1978, 103–80.

Reiling, Jannes. *Hermas and the Christian Prophecy. A Study of the Eleventh Mandate.* NT.S 37. Leiden: Brill, 1973.

Rengstorf, Karl Heinrich. "ἀπόστολος, κτλ.," *TDNT* 1:407–47.

_____. "διδάσκω κτλ.," *TDNT* 2:135–65.

Reumann, John. "'Stewards of God' – Pre-Christian Religious Application of Oikonomos in Greek," *JBL* 77 (1958) 339–49.

Revel, Jacques. "Masculine and Feminine: the Historiographical Use of Sexual Roles," in Michelle Perrot, ed., *Writing Women's History,* 90–105.

Reville, Jean. "Le rôle des veuves dans les communautés chrétiennes primitives," *BEHE.R* 1 (1889) 231–51.

Richter Reimer, Ivoni. *Frauen in der Apostelgeschichte des Lukas. Eine feministisch-theologische Exegese.* Gütersloh: Gerd Mohn, 1992. English: *Women in the Acts of the Apostles. A Feminist Liberation Perspective.* Translated by Linda M. Maloney. Minneapolis: Fortress, 1995.

Ringeling, Hermann. "Frau. IV. Neues Testament," *TRE* 11 (1983) 431–36.

Rist, John M. "Hypatia," *Phoenix* 19 (1965) 214–25.

Ritter, Adolf Martin. "Laie," *TRE* 20 (1990) 378–85.

Röckelein, Hedwig. "Historische Frauenforschung. Ein Literaturbericht zur Geschichte des Mittelalters," *HZ* 255/2 (1992) 377–409.

Rohde, Joachim. *Urchristliche und frühkatholische Ämter. Eine Untersuchung zur frühchristlichen Amtsentwicklung im Neuen Testament und bei den apostolischen Vätern.* ThA 33. Berlin: Evangelische Verlagsanstalt, 1976.

_____. "ἐπισκέπτομαι, ἐπισκοπέω," *EDNT* 2:33–34.

_____. "ἐπισκοπή, ης, ἡ," *EDNT* 2:35.

_____. "ἐπίσκοπος, ου, ὁ," *EDNT* 2:35–36.

_____. "πρεσβυτέριον, ου, τό," *EDNT* 3:148.

_____. "πρεσβύτερος, 3," *EDNT* 3:148–49.

Rohde-Dachser, Christa. *Expedition in den dunklen Kontinent. Weiblichkeit im Diskurs der Psychoanalyse.* 2nd ed. Berlin and Heidelberg: Springer, 1992.

Roloff, Jürgen. *Apostolat – Verkündigung – Kirche. Ursprung, Inhalt und Funktion des kirchlichen Apostelamtes nach Paulus, Lukas und den Pastoralbriefen.* Gütersloh: Gerd Mohn, 1965.

_____. *Die Apostelgeschichte.* NTD 5. Göttingen: Vandenhoeck & Ruprecht, 1981.

_____. "Amt / Ämter / Amtsverständnis. IV. Neues Testament," *TRE* 2 (1978) 509–33.

_____. "Apostel / Apostolat / Apostolizität. I. Neues Testament," *TRE* 3 (1978) 430–45.

_____. "Das Amt und die Ämter," *ThBeitr* 15 (1984) 201–18.

_____. "Die Apostolizität der Kirche und das kirchliche Amt nach dem Zeugnis der Heiligen Schrift" (1984) in idem, *Exegetische Verantwortung in der Kirche. Aufsätze,* edited by Martin Karrer. Göttingen: Vandenhoeck & Ruprecht, 1990, 363–79.

_____. *Der erste Brief an Timotheus.* EKK XV. Neukirchen-Vluyn: Neukirchener Verlag, 1988.

Romaniuk, Kazimierz. "Was Phoebe in Romans 16,1 a Deaconess?" *ZNW* 81 (1990) 132–34.

Rordorf, Willy. "Die Hausgemeinde der vorkonstantinischen Zeit" (1971) in idem, *Lex orandi, lex credendi. Gesammelte Aufsätze zum 60. Geburtstag.* Paradosis 36. Fribourg: Universitätsverlag, 1993, 190–237.

Rossi, Mary Ann. "Priesthood, Precedent, and Prejudice. On Recovering the Women Priests of Early Christianity. Containing a translation from the Italian of 'Notes on the Female Priesthood in Antiquity,' by Giorgio Otranto," *JFSR* 7 (1991) 73–94.

Rowe, Arthur. "Silence and the Christian Women of Corinth. An Examination of 1 Corinthians 14:33b-36," *CV* 33 (1990) 41–84.

Rubenson, Samuel. "Evagrios Pontikos und die Theologie der Wüste," in Hanns Christof Brennecke, Ernst Ludwig Grasmück, and Christoph Markschies, eds., *Logos. FS Luise Abramowski.* BZNW 67. Berlin and New York: Walter de Gruyter, 1993, 384–401.

Ruether, Rosemary Radford. "Misogynism and Virginal Feminism in the Fathers of the Church," in eadem, ed., *Religion and Sexism,* 150–83. (Reprinted in David M. Scholer, ed., *Women in Early Christianity,* 262–95.)

_____. "Frau und kirchliches Amt in historischer und gesellschaftlicher Hinsicht," *Conc(GB)* 12 (1976) 17–23.

_____. "Mothers of the Church: Ascetic Women in the Late Patristic Age," in Rosemary R. Ruether and Eleanor McLaughlin, eds., *Women of Spirit. Female Leadership in the Jewish and Christian Tradition.* New York: Simon & Schuster, 1979, 71–98.

_____. "Spirit and Matter, Public and Private: The Challenge of Feminism to Traditional Dualisms," in Paula M. Cooey, Sharon A. Farmer, and Mary Ellen Ross, eds., *Embodied Love. Sensuality and Relationship as Feminist Values.* San Francisco: Harper & Row, 1987, 65–76.

_____, and Eleanor McLaughlin, "Women's Leadership in the Jewish and Christian Traditions: Continuity and Change," in Ruether and McLaughlin, eds., *Women of Spirit,* 15–28.

Russell, Letty M., ed. *The Liberating Word. A Guide to Nonsexist Interpretation of the Bible.* Philadelphia: Westminster, 1976.

Sand, Alexander. "Witwenstand und Ämterstrukturen in den urchristlichen Gemeinden," *BiLe* 12 (1971) 186–97.

Sasse, Christoph. *Die Constitutio Antoniniana. Eine Untersuchung über den Umfang der Bürgerrechtsverleihung auf Grund des Papyrus Giss. 40 I.* Wiesbaden: O. Harrassowitz, 1958.

Satake, Akira. *Die Gemeindeordnung in der Johannesapokalypse.* WMANT 21. Neukirchen-Vluyn: Neukirchener Verlag, 1966.

Sato, Migaku. *Q und Prophetie. Studien zur Gattungs- und Traditionsgeschichte der Quelle Q.* WUNT 29. Tübingen: J.C.B. Mohr [Paul Siebeck], 1988.

Saxer, Victor. "Les Saintes Marie Madeleine et Marie de Béthanie dans la tradition liturgique et homilétique orientale," *RevScR* 32 (1958) 1–37.

_____. "Maria Maddalena," *BSS* 8 (1966) 1078–1104.

Schäfer, Klaus. *Gemeinde als "Bruderschaft." Ein Beitrag zum Kirchenverständnis des Paulus.* EHS.T 333. Frankfurt: Peter Lang, 1989.

Schäfer, K. Heinrich. *Die Kanonissenstifter im deutschen Mittelalter. Ihre Entwicklung und innere Einrichtung im Zusammenhang mit dem altchristlichen Sanktimonialentum.* KRA 43, 44. Stuttgart: F. Enke, 1907.

_____. "Kanonissen und Diakonissen. Ergänzungen und Erläuterungen," *RQ* 24 (1910) II, 49–90.

Schäfer, Theodor. *Die weibliche Diakonie in ihrem ganzen Umfang dargestellt. Vorträge.* 3 vols. *I: Die Geschichte der weiblichen Diakonie. Vorträge.* Stuttgart: Verlag von D. Gundert, 1887–94.

Schäfer, Thomas. *Die Fußwaschung im monastischen Brauchtum und in der lateinischen Liturgie. Liturgiegeschichtliche Untersuchung.* Texte und Arbeiten I/47. Beuron: Beuroner Kunstverlag, 1956.

Scharffenorth, Gerta, and Erika Reickle. "Frau. VII. Neuzeit," *TRE* 11 (1983) 443–67.

_____, and Heidi Lauterer-Pirner. "Frauen in der Geschichte als Problem männlicher Geschichtsdarstellung. Zwei Beispiele verdrängter Geschichte," *ThPr* 22 (1987) 176–89.

Schaumberger, Christine, ed. *Weil wir nicht vergessen wollen . . . zu einer Feministischen Theologie im deutschen Kontext.* AnFragen 1. Diskussionen Feministischer Theologie. Münster: Morgana, 1987.

Schelkle, Karl Hermann. *Der Geist und die Braut. Frauen in der Bibel.* Düsseldorf: Patmos, 1977. English: *The Spirit and the Bride: Woman in the Bible.* Translated by Matthew J. O'Connell. Collegeville: The Liturgical Press, 1979.

Schenk, Wolfgang. *Die Philipperbriefe des Paulus. Kommentar.* Stuttgart: Kohlhammer, 1984.

Schepelern, Wilhelm Ernst. *Der Montanismus und die phrygischen Kulte. Eine religionsgeschichtliche Untersuchung.* Tübingen: J.C.B. Mohr [Paul Siebeck], 1929.

Schiessl, Johanna. "Priestertum der Frau," *StZ* 211 (1993) 115–22.

Schille, Gottfried. "Das Recht der Propheten und der Apostel – gemeinderechtliche Beobachtungen zu Didache Kapitel 11–13," *ThV* 1 (1966) 84–103.

_____. *Die urchristliche Kollegialmission.* AThANT 48. Zürich: Zwingli Verlag, 1967.

Schillebeeckx, Edward. *Ministry: Leadership in the Community of Jesus Christ.* Translated by John Bowden. New York: Crossroad, 1981.

Schindler, Alfred. "Askese und Mönchtum als Mittel der Emanzipation im antiken Christentum," *Schritte ins Offene* 12 (1982) 7–8.

Schlau, Carl. *Die Acten des Paulus und der Thecla und die ältere Thecla-Legende. Ein Beitrag zur christlichen Literaturgeschichte.* Diss. Leipzig, 1877. Cincinnati, Ohio: Assured Micro-Services, 1983.

Schlarb, Egbert. *Die gesunde Lehre. Häresie und Wahrheit im Spiegel der Pastoralbriefe.* MThSt 28. Marburg: N.G. Elwert Verlag, 1990.

Schlier, Heinrich. *Der Brief an die Galater.* KEK 7. 11th rev. ed. Göttingen: Vandenhoeck & Ruprecht, 1951.

Schmid, Renate. "Maria Magdalena in gnostischen Schriften." Material-Edition 29. Staatsexamensarbeit, Munich 1990.

Schmidt, Carl, ed. *Acta Pauli aus der Heidelberger koptischen Papyrushandschrift Nr. 1.* Hildesheim: G. Olms, 1965.

_____. "Zwei altchristliche Gebete," in *Neutestamentliche Studien. Georg Heinrici zu seinem 70. Geburtstag.* UNT 6. Leipzig: J.C. Hinrichs, 1914, 66–78 (charts 2 and 3).

Schmidt, Volkmar. "τεκνοῦσ(σ)α bei Sophokles und Theophrast und Verwandtes," in H. G. Beck, A. Kambylis, and P. Moraux, eds., *Kyklos. Griechisches und Byzantinisches. Rudolf Keydell zum 90. Geburtstag.* Berlin and New York: Walter de Gruyter, 1978, 38–53.

Schmitt-Pantel, Pauline. "The Difference Between the Sexes: History, Anthropology and the Greek City," in Michelle Perrot, ed., *Writing Women's History* 70–89. (Original: "La différence des sexes, histoire, anthropologie, et cité grecque," in *Une histoire des femmes est-elle possible?* Paris: Rivages, 1984, 97–119).

Schmithals, Walter. *Das kirchliche Apostelamt. Eine historische Untersuchung.* FRLANT 79. Göttingen: Vandenhoeck & Ruprecht, 1961.

Schnackenburg, Rudolf. "Episkopos und Hirtenamt. Zu Apg 20,28" (1949) in Theological Faculty of the University of Munich, eds., *Episcopus. Studien über das Bischofsamt. FS f. Michael Kardinal von Faulhaber zum 80. Geburtstag.* Regensburg: Gregorius-Verlag, 1949, 66–88.

Schneemelcher, Wilhelm. "Epiphanius von Salamis," *RAC* 5 (1962) 909–27.

_____, and Knut Schäferdiek. "Apostelgeschichten des 2. und 3. Jahrhunderts. Einleitung," in idem, ed., *Neutestamentliche Apokryphen in deutscher Übersetzung II.* 5th ed. Tübingen: J.C.B. Mohr [Paul Siebeck], 1989, 71–93. English: "Introduction" to ch. XIII, "Second and Third Century Acts of Apostles," in Edgar Hennecke, *New Testament Apocrypha 2.* Edited by Wilhelm Schneemelcher, English translation edited by Robert McLean Wilson. Philadelphia: Westminster, 1965, 167–88.

_____. "Paulusakten," in idem, ed., *Neutestamentliche Apokryphen in deutscher Übersetzung II,* 193–241. English: "Acts of Paul," *New Testament Apocrypha 2,* 322–90.

Schneider, Gerhard. *Die Apostelgeschichte.* HThK V/1–2. Freiburg, Basel, and Vienna: Herder, 1982.

_____. *Das Evangelium nach Lukas.* ÖTK 3/1–2. 3rd rev. ed. Gütersloh and Würzburg: Gerd Mohn, 1992.

Schnider, Franz. "προφητεία, ας, ἡ," *EDNT* 3:183.

_____. "προφήτης, ου, ὁ," *EDNT* 3:183–86.

Schoedel, William R. *The Letters of Ignatius of Antioch. A Commentary on the Letters of Ignatius of Antioch.* Edited by Helmut Koester. Hermeneia. Philadelphia: Fortress, 1985.

Schöllgen, Georg. "Wandernde und seßhafte Lehrer in der Didache?" *BN* 52 (1990) 19–26.

Schottroff, Luise. "Frauen in der Nachfolge Jesu in neutestamentlicher Zeit," in Willy Schottroff and Wolfgang Stegemann, eds., *Traditionen der Befreiung. Sozialgeschichtliche Bibelauslegungen.* Vol. 2: *Frauen in der Bibel.* Munich: Kaiser, 1980, 91–133. English: "Women as Disciples of Jesus in New Testament Times," in Luise Schottroff, *Let the Oppressed Go Free. Feminist Perspectives on the New Testament.* Translated by Annemarie S. Kidder. Louisville: Westminster/John Knox, 1992, 80–130.

_____. "Maria Magdalena und die Frauen am Grab," *EvTh* 42 (1982) 3–25. English: "Mary Magdalene and the Women at Jesus' Tomb," in eadem, *Let the Oppressed Go Free,* 168–203.

_____. "Wie berechtigt ist die feministische Kritik an Paulus? Paulus und die Frauen in den ersten christlichen Gemeinden im Römischen Reich," in Friedrich-Wilhelm Marquardt, Dieter Schellong, and Michael Weinrich, eds., *Einwürfe. Zur Bibel Lek-*

türe und Interesse. Munich: Kaiser, 1985, 2:94–111. English: "How Justified is the Feminist Critique of Paul?" in Luise Schottroff, *Let the Oppressed Go Free*, 35–59.

_____. "'Anführerinnen der Gläubigkeit' oder 'einige andächtige Weiber.' Frauengruppen als Trägerinnen jüdischer und christlicher Religion im ersten Jahrhundert n. Chr.," in Christine Schaumberger, ed., *Weil wir nicht vergessen wollen*, 73–87. English: "'Leaders of the Faith' or 'Just Some Pious Womenfolk?'" in Luise Schottroff, *Let the Oppressed Go Free*, 60–79.

_____. "Lydia. Eine neue Qualität der Macht," in Karin Walter, ed., *Zwischen Ohnmacht und Befreiung*, 148–54. English: "Lydia: A New Quality of Power," in Luise Schottroff, *Let the Oppressed Go Free*, 131–37.

_____. "Die mutigen Frauen aus Galiläa und der Auferstehungsglaube," *Diak.* 20 (1989) 221–26.

_____. "BotschafterInnen an Christi Statt," in Frithard Scholz and Horst Dickel, eds., *Vernünftiger Gottesdienst. Kirche nach der Barmer Theologischen Erklärung. FS zum 60. Geburtstag von Hans-Gernot Jung.* Göttingen: Vandenhoeck & Ruprecht, 1990, 271–92.

_____. "Dienerinnen der Heiligen. Der Diakonat der Frauen im Neuen Testament," in Gerhard K. Schäfer and Theodor Strohm, eds., *Diakonie – biblische Grundlagen und Orientierungen. Ein Arbeitsbuch.* VDWI 2. Heidelberg: Heidelberger Verlagsanstalt, 1990, 222–42.

_____. "Wanderprophetinnen. Eine feministische Analyse der Logienquelle," *EvTh* 51 (1991) 332–34.

_____. "Maria Magdalena I. Neues Testament," *WFT* (1991) 275–77.

_____. "Die Frauen haben nicht geschwiegen. Über Prophetinnen, Apostelinnen und Bischöfinnen im frühen Christentum," in *". . . das Weib rede in der Gemeinde." Maria Jepsen: Erste lutherische Bischöfin,* 41–48.

_____. "Frauenwiderstand im frühen Christentum," in Frauenforschungsprojekt zur Geschichte der Theologinnen Göttingen, eds., *Querdenken,* 129–59.

_____. *Lydias ungeduldige Schwestern. Feministische Sozialgeschichte des frühen Christentums.* Gütersloh: Gerd Mohn, 1994. English: *Lydia's Impatient Sisters.* Translated by Barbara Rumscheid and Martin Rumscheid. Louisville: Westminster/John Knox, 1995.

_____, and Willy Schottroff. "Hanna und Maria," in Luise Schottroff and Johannes Thiele, eds., *Gotteslehrerinnen. Dorothee Sölle zum 60. Geburtstag.* Stuttgart: Kreuz, 1989, 23–45.

Schrenk, Gottlob. "ἱερεύς κτλ.," *TDNT* 3:257–83.

Schuller, Wolfgang. *Frauen in der griechischen Geschichte.* Konstanzer Bibliothek 3. Konstanz: Universitätsverlag Konstanz, 1985.

_____. *Frauen in der römischen Geschichte.* Konstanz: Universitätsverlag Konstanz, 1992.

Schultze, Victor. *Altchristliche Städte und Landschaften. II. Kleinasien.* 2 vols. Gütersloh: Gerd Mohn, 1922, 1926.

Schüngel-Straumann, Helen. "Die Frau: (nur) Abglanz des Mannes? Zur Wirkungsgeschichte biblischer Texte im Hinblick auf das christliche Frauenbild," in Dieter R. Bauer and Elisabeth Gössmann, eds., *Eva – Verführerin oder Gottes Meister-werk? Philosophie- und theologiegeschichtliche Frauenforschung.* Hohenheimer Protokolle 21. Stuttgart: Akademie der Diözese Rottenburg-Stuttgart, 1987, 37–71.

_____. "Maria von Magdala – Apostolin und erste Verkünderin der Osterbotschaft," in Dietmar Bader, ed., *Maria Magdalena – Zu einem Bild der Frau in der christlichen Verkündigung.* Schriftenreihe der katholischen Akademie der Erzdiözese Freiburg. Munich and Zürich: Schnell and Steiner, 1990, 9–32.

Schürer, Emil. *Die Gemeindeverfassung der Juden in Rom in der Kaiserzeit. Nach den Inschriften dargestellt.* Leipzig: Hinrichs, 1879.

_____. "Die Prophetin Isabel in Thyatira. Offenb. Joh. 2,20," *Theologische Abhand-lungen. FS Carl von Weizsäcker.* Freiburg: J.C.B. Mohr [Paul Siebeck], 1892, 37–57.

Schürmann, Heinz. "Lehrende in den neutestamentlichen Schriften. Ihre Angewiesen-heit auf andere geistliche Gaben und ihre Verwiesenheit an andere geistliche Dienste," in Walter Bauer et al., eds., *Weisheit Gottes – Weisheit der Welt.* Vol. 1: *FS f. Joseph Kardinal Ratzinger.* St. Ottilien: EOS, 1987, 419–40.

Schüssler Fiorenza, Elisabeth. "Women Apostles: The Testament of Scripture," in Anne Marie Gardiner, ed., *Women and Catholic Priesthood,* 94–102.

_____. "The Twelve," in Leonard Swidler and Arlene Swidler, eds., *Women Priests,* 114–22.

_____. "The Apostleship of Women in Early Christianity," in ibid., 135–40.

_____. "Women in the Pre-Pauline and Pauline Churches," *USQR* 33 (1978) 153–66.

_____. "Word, Spirit and Power: Women in Early Christian Communities," in Rose-mary Ruether and Eleanor McLaughlin, eds., *Women of Spirit,* 29–70.

_____. "The Study of Women in Early Christianity: Some Methodological Considera-tions," in J. T. Ryan, ed., *Critical History and Biblical Faith: New Testament Per-spectives.* Villanova, Pa.: College Theology Society: *Horizons,* 1979, 30–58.

_____. "Der Beitrag der Frau zur urchristlichen Bewegung. Kritische Überlegungen zur Rekonstruktion urchristlicher Geschichte," in Willy Schottroff and Wolfgang Stegemann, eds., *Traditionen der Befreiung,* 2:60–90.

_____. "The Biblical Roots for the Discipleship of Equals," *DDSR* 45 (1980) 87–97.

_____. "Apokalypsis and Propheteia. The Book of Revelation in the Context of Early Christian Prophecy," in Jan Lambrecht, ed., *L'Apocalypse johannique et l'Apo-calyptique dans le Nouveau Testament.* BEThL 53. Louvain: Leuven University Press, 1980, 105–28.

_____. *In Memory of Her. A Feminist Theological Reconstruction of Christian Origins.* New York: Crossroad, 1983.

_____. *Bread Not Stone. The Challenge of Feminist Biblical Interpretation.* Boston: Beacon, 1984.

_____. "Emanzipation aus der Bibel. Gegen ein patriarchalisches Christentum," *EK* 16 (1983) 195–98.

_____. "Remembering the Past in Creating the Future: Historical-Critical Scholarship and Feminist Biblical Interpretation," in Adela Yarbro Collins, ed., *Feminist Per-spectives on Biblical Scholarship,* 43–63.

_____. "Breaking the Silence—Becoming Visible," *Concilium* (Dec. 1985) 3–16.

_____. "The 'Quilting' of Women's History: Phoebe of Cenchreae," in Paula M. Cooey, Sharon A. Farmer, and Mary Ellen Ross, eds., *Embodied Love*, 35–49.

_____. "Die Anfänge von Kirche, Amt und Priestertum in feministisch-theologischer Sicht," in Paul Hoffmann, ed., *Priesterkirche*, 62–95.

_____. "'Waiting at Table': A Critical Feminist Reflection on Diakonia," *Concilium* (Aug. 1988) 84–94.

_____. "Text as Reality – Reality as Text: The Problem of a Feminist Historical and Social Reconstruction Based on Texts," *StTh* 43 (1989) 19–34.

_____. "Commitment and Critical Inquiry," *HThR* 82 (1989) 1–11.

Schütz, Jakob. *Der Diakonat im Neuen Testament*. Dissertation in typescript. Mainz, 1952.

Schwartz, Eduard. "Über die pseudapostolischen Kirchenordnungen" (1910) in idem, *Gesammelte Schriften 5*. Berlin: Walter de Gruyter, 1963, 192–273.

_____. "Die Kanonessammlungen der alten Reichskirche" (1936) in idem, *Gesammelte Schriften 4*. Berlin: Walter de Gruyter, 1960, 159–275.

Schweizer, Eduard. *Gemeinde und Gemeindeordnung im Neuen Testament*. AThANT 35. Zürich: Zwingli Verlag, 1959. English: *Church Order in the New Testament*. Translated by Frank Clarke. Naperville, Ill.: A.R. Allenson, 1961.

Scopello, Madeleine. "Jewish and Greek Heroines in the Nag Hammadi Library," in Karen L. King, ed., *Images of the Feminine in Gnosticism*. Studies in Antiquity and Christianity 4. Philadelphia: Fortress, 1988, 71–90.

Scott, Joan Wallach. *Gender and the Politics of History*. New York: Columbia University Press, 1988.

Scroggs, Robin. "Paul and the Eschatological Woman," *JAAR* 40 (1972) 283–303.

_____. "Paul and the Eschatological Woman: Revisited," *JAAR* 42 (1974) 532–37.

Seagraves, Richard. *Pascentes cum Disciplina. A Lexical Study of Clergy in the Cyprianic Correspondence*. Par. 37. Fribourg: Editions universitaires, 1993.

Seeberg, Reinhold. "Über das Reden der Frauen in den apostolischen Gemeinden," in idem, *Gesammelte Aufsätze I. Biblisches und Kirchengeschichtliches. Aus Religion und Geschichte 1*. Leipzig: A. Deichert, 1906, 123–44.

Seim, Turid Karlsen. "Ascetic Autonomy? New Perspectives on Single Women in the Early Church," *StTh* 43 (1989) 125–40.

Selb, Walter. *Orientalisches Kirchenrecht II. Die Geschichte des Kirchenrechts der Westsyrer (von den Anfängen bis zur Mongolenzeit)*. Veröffentlichungen der Kommission für antike Rechtsgeschichte 6. DÖAW.PH 543. Vienna: Verlag der Österreichischen Akademie der Wissenschaften, 1989.

Sherwin-White, Adrian N. *The Letters of Pliny: Historical and Social Commentary* (1966), reissued (with corrections) Oxford: Clarendon Press, 1985.

Siegele-Wenschkewitz, Leonore, ed. *Verdrängte Vergangenheit, die uns bedrängt. Feministische Theologie in der Verantwortung für die Geschichte*. Munich: Kaiser, 1988.

Siegwart, Josef. *Die Chorherren- und Chorfrauengemeinschaften in der deutschsprachigen Schweiz vom 6. Jahrhundert bis 1160. Mit einem Überblick über die deutsche Kanonikerreform des 10. und 11. Jh.* SF n.s. 30. Fribourg: Universitätsverlag, 1962.

Slenczka, Richard. "Die Ordination von Frauen zum Amt der Kirche," in *". . . das Weib rede in der Gemeinde." Maria Jepsen: Erste lutherische Bischöfin,* 57–71.

Snyder, Jane McIntosh. *The Woman and the Lyre. Women Writers in Classical Greece and Rome.* Carbondale and Edwardsville, Ill.: Southern Illinois University Press, 1989.

Söder, Rosa. *Die apokryphen Apostelgeschichten und die romanhafte Literatur der Antike.* Stuttgart, Berlin, Cologne, and Mainz: Kohlhammer, 1969.

Soler, Joseph M. "Die geistliche Mutterschaft im frühen Mönchtum als Anfrage an unsere Zeit," *EuA* 63 (1987) 167–83.

Specht, Edith. *Schön zu sein und gut zu sein. Mädchenbildung und Frauensozialisation im antiken Griechenland.* Reihe Frauenforschung 9. Vienna: Wiener Frauenverlag, 1989.

Spencer, Aida Besançon. *Beyond the Curse. Women Called to Ministry.* Nashville: Thomas Nelson, 1985.

Spencer, F. Scott. *The Portrait of Philip in Acts. A Study of Roles and Relations.* JSNT.S 67. Sheffield: JSOT Press, 1992.

Spicq, Ceslas. *Saint Paul. Les Epitres Pastorales.* Paris: J. Gabalda, 1969.

Stählin, Gustav. "χήρα," *TDNT* 9:440–65.

_____. "Das Bild der Witwe. Ein Beitrag zur Bildersprache der Bibel und zum Phänomen der Personifikation in der Antike," *JAC* 17 (1974) 5–20.

Steichele, Hanneliese. "Geist und Amt als kirchenbildende Elemente in der Apostelgeschichte," in Josef Hainz, ed., *Kirche im Werden. Studien zum Thema Amt und Gemeinde im Neuen Testament.* Munich, Paderborn, and Vienna: Schöningh, 1976, 185–203.

_____. "Priska. Ein verdrängter Fall," in Karin Walter, ed., *Zwischen Ohnmacht und Befreiung,* 155–62.

Steimer, Bruno. *Vertex Traditionis. Die Gattung der altchristlichen Kirchenordnungen.* BZNW 63. Berlin and New York: Walter de Gruyter, 1992.

Steinmann, Jean. *Saint Jérôme.* Paris: Cerf, 1958. English: *Saint Jerome and His Times.* Translated by Ronald Matthews. Notre Dame, Ind.: Fides, 1959.

Steinwenter, Artur. "Corpus iuris," *RAC* 3 (1957) 453–63.

Stempel, Hermann. "Der Lehrer in der 'Lehre der zwölf Apostel,'" *VigChr* 34 (1980) 209–17.

Stiefel, Jennifer H. "Women Deacons in 1 Timothy: A Linguistic and Literary Look at 'Women likewise . . .' (1 Tim 3.11)," *NTS* 41 (1995) 442–57.

Stuhlmueller, Carroll, ed. *Women and Priesthood: Future Directions. A Call to Dialogue from the Faculty of The Catholic Theological Union at Chicago.* Collegeville: The Liturgical Press, 1978.

Stöcker, Lydia. *Die Frau in der alten Kirche.* Tübingen: J.C.B. Mohr [Paul Siebeck], 1907.

Strobel, August. *Das heilige Land der Montanisten. Eine religionsgeographische Untersuchung.* RVV 37. Berlin and New York: Walter de Gruyter, 1980.

Sugano, Karin. "Marcella von Rom. Ein Lebensbild," in Michael Wissemann, ed., *Roma Renascens. Beiträge zur Spätantike und Rezeptionsgeschichte. FS Ilona Opelt*. Frankfurt, Bern, New York, and Paris: Peter Lang, 1988, 355–70.

Synek, Eva Maria. *Heilige Frauen der frühen Christenheit: zu den Frauenbildern in hagiographischen Texten des christlichen Ostens*. Würzburg: Augustinus-Verlag, 1994. (Citations in text are from the unpublished manuscript.)

Tabbernee, William. "Remnants of the New Prophecy: Literary and Epigraphical Sources of the Montanist Movement," *StPatr* 21 (1987) 193–201.

_____. "Montanist Regional Bishops: New Evidence from Ancient Inscriptions," *Journal of Early Christian Studies* 1 (1993) 249–80.

Tarasar, Constance J. "Women in the Mission of the Church – Theological and Historical Reflections," *IRM* 81 (1992) 189–200.

Tarchnišvili, Michael. "Die Legende der heiligen Nino und die Geschichte des georgischen Nationalbewußtseins," *ByZ* 40 (1940) 48–75.

Tavard, George H. *Women in Christian Tradition*. Notre Dame, Ind.: University of Notre Dame Press, 1973.

Testini, Pasquale. *Le catacombe e gli antichi cimiteri cristiani in Roma*. RC 2. Bologna: Cappelli, 1966.

Tetlow, Elisabeth M. *Women and Ministry in the New Testament*. New York: Paulist, 1980.

Theissen, Gerd. "Social Stratification in the Corinthian Community: A Contribution to the Sociology of Early Hellenistic Christianity," in idem, *The Social Setting of Pauline Christianity: Essays on Corinth*. Edited and translated and with an introduction by John H. Schütz. Philadelphia: Fortress, 1982, 69–119.

Theodorou, Evangelos. "Η 'ΧΕΙΡΟΤΟΝΙΑ,' Η 'ΧΕΙΡΟΘΕΣΙΑ' ΤΩΝ ΔΙΑΚΟΝΙΣΣΩΝ," *Theologia* 25 (1954) 430–69, 576–601; 26 (1955) 57–76. (References in the text are to the German translation by Anne Jensen, approved by the author, in the library of the Institute for Ecumenical Research at the University of Tübingen.)

_____. "Das Diakonissenamt in der griechisch-orthodoxen Kirche," in World Council of Churches, *Die Diakonisse. Ein Dienst der Frau in der heutigen Welt*. English: *The Deaconess; a Service of Women in the World of Today*. (Report of the consultation in Presinge, 1965, and short studies.) Geneva: World Council of Churches, 1966.

_____. "Das Amt der Diakoninnen in der kirchlichen Tradition. Ein orthodoxer Beitrag zum Problem der Frauenordination." Translation from Greek, with notes, by Theodor Nikolaou. *US* 33 (1973) 162–72.

_____. "Berühmte Diakonissen der byzantinischen Zeit," in *ΙΣΤΟΡΙΑ ΚΑΙ ΘΕΩΡΙΑ ΤΗΣ ΕΚΚΛΗΣΙΑΣΤΙΚΗΣ ΚΟΙΝΩΝΙΚΗΣ ΔΙΑΚΟΝΙΑΣ*. (Athens, 1985), 147–64.

_____. "Die Tradition der orthodoxen Kirche in bezug auf die Frauenordination," in Elisabeth Gössmann and Dietmar Bader, eds., *Warum keine Ordination der Frau?* 26–49.

Thoma, Clemens. "Amt / Ämter / Amtsverständnis III. Judentum," *TRE* 1 (1978) 504–509.

Thomas, John Christopher. *Footwashing in John 13 and the Johannine Community.* JSNT.S 61. Sheffield: JSOT Press, 1991.

Thomas, W. Derek. "The Place of Women in the Church of Philippi," *ET* 83 (1971/2) 117–20.

Thraede, Klaus. "Frau," *RAC* 8 (1972) 197–269.

———. "Ärger mit der Freiheit. Die Bedeutung von Frauen in Theorie und Praxis der alten Kirche," in Gerta Scharffenorth and Klaus Thraede, eds., *"Freunde in Christus werden . . . ." Die Beziehung von Mann und Frau als Frage an Theologie und Kirche.* Kennzeichen 1. Gelnhausen and Berlin: Burckhardthaus Verlag, 1977, 31–178.

———. "Zum historischen Hintergrund der 'Haustafeln' des NT," in *Pietas. FS Bernhard Kötting.* JAC.E 8. Münster: Aschendorff, 1980, 359–68.

———. "Zwischen Eva und Maria: das Bild der Frau bei Ambrosius und Augustin auf dem Hintergrund der Zeit," in Werner Affeldt, ed., *Frauen in Spätantike und Frühmittelalter. Lebensbedingung – Lebensnormen – Lebensformen. Beiträge zu einer internationalen Tagung am Fachbereich Geschichtswissenschaften der Freien Universität Berlin 18. bis 21. Februar 1987.* Sigmaringen: J. Thorbecke, 1990, 129–39.

Thüsing, Wilhelm. "Dienstfunktion und Vollmacht kirchlicher Ämter nach dem Neuen Testament," *BiLe* 14 (1973) 77–88.

Thurston, Bonnie Bowman. *The Widows. A Women's Ministry in the Early Church.* Minneapolis: Fortress, 1989.

Tielsch, Elfriede Walesca. "Die Philosophin. Geschichte und Ungeschichte ihres Berufsstandes seit der Antike," in Halina Bendkowski and Brigitte Weisshaupt, eds., *Was Philosophinnen denken. Eine Dokumentation.* Zürich: Ammann, 1983, 309–28.

Tooley, Wilfred. "Stewards of God. An Examination of the Terms ΟΙΚΟΝΟΜΟΣ and OIKONOMIA in the New Testament," *SJTH* 19 (1966) 74–86.

Torjesen, Karen Jo. "In praise of noble women: Gender and Honor in Ascetic Texts," *Semeia* 56–58 (1992) 41–64.

———. *When Women Were Priests. Women's Leadership in the Early Church and the Scandal of their Subordination in the Rise of Christianity.* San Francisco: HarperSanFrancisco, 1993.

———. "Reconstruction of Women's Early History," in Elisabeth Schüssler Fiorenza, ed., *Searching the Scriptures I: A Feminist Introduction.* New York: Crossroad, 1993, 290–310.

Trebilco, Paul R. *Jewish Communities in Asia Minor.* MSSNTS 69. New York: Cambridge University Press, 1991.

Treggiari, Susan. "Jobs for Women," *American Journal of Ancient History* 1 (1976) 76–104.

Trevett, Christine. "Prophecy and Anti-Episcopal Activity: a Third Error Combatted by Ignatius?" *JEH* 34 (1983) 1–18.

———. "Ignatius and the Monstrous Regiment of Women," *StPatr* 21 (1989) 202–14.

Trömel-Plötz, Senta. *Frauensprache. Sprache der Veränderung.* Frankfurt: Fischer Taschenbuch Verlag, 1982.

_____. "Feminismus und Linguistik," in Luise F. Pusch, ed., *Feminismus. Inspektion der Herrenkultur,* 33–51.

_____. *Vatersprache – Mutterland. Beobachtungen zu Sprache und Politik.* 2nd rev. ed. Munich: Frauenoffensive, 1993.

_____, ed. *Gewalt durch Sprache. Die Vergewaltigung von Frauen in Gesprächen.* Frankfurt: Fischer Taschenbuch Verlag, 1984.

Tuilier, André. "Didache," *TRE* 8 (1981) 731–36.

Turcan, Marie. "Saint Jérôme et les femmes," *BAGB,* 4th ser. (1968) 159–272.

Uhlhorn, Gerhard. *Die christliche Liebesthätigkeit.* 2nd rev. ed. Stuttgart: D. Gundert, 1895.

Ullmann, Walter. *Gelasius I. (492–496). Das Papsttum an der Wende der Spätantike zum Mittelalter.* PuP 18. Stuttgart: A. Hiersemann, 1981.

Ulrich, Anna. "Die Kanonissen. Ein vergangener und vergessener Stand der Kirche," in Teresa Berger and Albert Gerhards, eds., *Liturgie und Frauenfrage,* 181–94.

Vagaggini, Cipriano. "L'ordinazione delle diaconesse nella tradizione greca e bizantina," *OrChrP* 40 (1974) 145–89.

Via, E. Jane. "Women, the Discipleship of Service, and the Early Christian Ritual Meal in the Gospel of Luke," *St. Luke's Journal of Theology* 29 (1985) 37–60.

Vielhauer, Philipp. *Geschichte der urchristlichen Literatur. Einleitung in das Neue Testament, die Apokryphen und die Apostolischen Väter.* Berlin and New York: Walter de Gruyter, 1975.

_____., and Georg Strecker. "Einleitung (Apokalypsen und Verwandtes)" in Wilhelm Schneemelcher, ed., *Neutestamentliche Apokryphen in deutscher Übersetzung II* 491–547. English: "Introduction" to section 2, "Apocalypses and Related Subjects," in Edgar Hennecke, *New Testament Apocrypha 2,* 581–607.

Vogels, Heinrich Josef. *Untersuchungen zum Text paulinischer Briefe bei Rufin und Ambrosiaster.* BBB 9. Bonn: P. Hanstein, 1955.

Vogler, Werner. "Die Bedeutung der urchristlichen Hausgemeinden für die Ausbreitung des Evangeliums," *ThLZ* 107 (1982) 785–94.

Vogt, Hermann Josef. *Das Kirchenverständnis des Origenes.* BoBKG 4. Cologne and Vienna: Böhlau, 1974.

_____. "Die Witwe als Bild der Seele in der Exegese des Origenes," *ThQ* 165 (1985) 105–18.

Voigt, Heinrich Gisbert. *Eine verschollene Urkunde des antimontanistischen Kampfes. Die Berichte des Epiphanius über die Kataphrygier und Quintillianer.* Leipzig: Fr. Richter, 1891.

Vokes, Frederick E. "The Opposition to Montanism from Church and State in the Christian Empire," *StPatr* 4 (1961) 518–26.

_____. "Montanism and the Ministry," *StPatr* 9 (1966) 306–15.

Wagener, Ulrike. "Fußwaschung als Frauen-Dienst im frühen Christentum?" *Schlangenbrut* 11/40 (1993) 29–35.

_____. *Die Ordnung des "Hauses Gottes." Der Ort von Frauen in der Ekklesiologie und Ethik der Pastoralbriefe*. WUNT 65. Tübingen: J.C.B. Mohr [Paul Siebeck], 1994.

Wagner, Beate. *Zwischen Mythos und Realität. Die Frau in der frühgriechischen Gesellschaft*. Frankfurt: Haag & Herchen, 1982.

Waithe, Mary Ellen, ed. *A History of Women Philosophers*. 4 vols. Dordrecht, Boston, and Lancaster: M. Nijhoff, 1987, 1991, 1993.

Walcot, Peter. "On Widows and their Reputation in Antiquity," *SO* 66 (1991) 5–26.

Walker, William O. "The 'Theology of Women's Place' and the 'Paulinist' Tradition," *Semeia* 28 (1983) 101–12.

Ward, Benedicta. "Apophthegmata Matrum," *StPatr* 16/2 (1985) 63–66.

Webster, Douglas. "The Primary Stewardship," *ET* 72 (1960/61) 274–76.

Wegener, Gertrud. *Geschichte des Stiftes St. Ursula in Köln*. Veröffentlichungen des Kölnischen Geschichtsvereins e.V. 31. Cologne: Historisches Archiv, 1971.

Weigel, Sigrid. *Topographien der Geschlechter. Kulturgeschichtliche Studien zur Literatur*. re 514. Reinbek bei Hamburg: Rowohlt Taschenbuch Verlag, 1990.

Weinel, Heinrich. *Die Wirkungen des Geistes und der Geister im nachapostolischen Zeitalter bis auf Irenäus*. Freiburg: J.C.B. Mohr [Paul Siebeck], 1899.

Weiser, Alfons. *Die Apostelgeschichte*. ÖTK 5/1, 2. Gütersloh: Gerd Mohn, 1981, 1985.

_____. "Die Rolle der Frau in der urchristlichen Mission," in Gerhard Dautzenberg, Helmut Merklein, and Karlheinz Müller, eds., *Die Frau im Urchristentum*. QD 95. Freiburg, Basel, and Vienna: Herder, 1983, 158–81.

_____. "διακονέω κτλ.," *EDNT* 1:302–304.

Weiss, Hans-Friedrich. "διδάσκω κτλ.," *EDNT* 1:317–19.

_____. "διδαχή, ῆς, ἡ," *EDNT* 1:319–20.

Weisshaupt, Brigitte. "Dissidenz als Aufklärung. Elemente feministischer Wissenschaftskritik," in Manon Andreas-Grisebach and Brigitte Weisshaupt, eds., *Was Philosophinnen denken II*. Zürich: Ammann, 1986, 9–19.

_____. "Spuren jenseits des Selben. Identität und Differenz," in Psychoanalytisches Seminar Zürich, eds., *Bei Lichte betrachtet wird es finster. Frauensichten*. Frankfurt: Athenäum, 1987, 105–19.

Wemple, Suzanne Fonay. *Women in Frankish Society. Marriage and the Cloister 500 to 900*. Philadelphia: University of Pennsylvania Press, 1981.

Whelan, Caroline F. "Amica Pauli: The Role of Phoebe in the Early Church," *JSNT* 49 (1993) 67–85.

Wickert, Ulrich. "Kleinasien," *TRE* 19 (1990) 244–65.

Wickham, Lionel R. "Chalkedon, ökumenische Synode (451)," *TRE* 7 (1981) 668–75.

Wiechert, Friedrich. "Die Geschichte der Diakonissenweihe," *EHK* 21 (1939) 57–79.

Wieland, Franz, *Die genetische Entwicklung der sog. Ordines Minores in den ersten Jahrhunderten*. RQ.S 7. Rome: Herder, 1897.

Wieland, Irmgard. "Wie verstand die alte Kirche bis zur Mitte des 3. Jahrhunderts die Worte des Paulus über die Frau im Leben der Gemeinde?" Master's thesis, Tübingen: J.C.B. Mohr [Paul Siebeck], 1989.

Wikenhauser, Alfred. "Apostel," *RAC* 1 (1950) 553–55.

Wilckens, Ulrich. *Der Brief an die Römer.* 3 vols. EKK VI/1–3. 2nd rev. ed. Neukirchen-Vluyn: Neukirchener Verlag, 1987–1989.

Wilpert, Joseph. *Die gottgeweihten Jungfrauen in den ersten Jahrhunderten der Kirche. Nach den patristischen Quellen und den Grabdenkmälern dargestellt.* Freiburg: Herdersche Verlagshandlung, 1892.

Wilshire, Leland Edward. "The TLG Computer and further reference to ΑΥΘΕΝΤΕΩ in 1 Timothy 2.12," *NTS* 34 (1988) 120–34.

_____. "1 Timothy 2:12 Revisited: A Reply to Paul W. Barnett and Timothy J. Harris," *EvQ* 65 (1993) 43–55.

Wilson-Kastner, Patricia. "Macrina: Virgin and Teacher," *AUSS* 17 (1979) 105–17.

Wipszycka, Ewa. *Les ressources et les activités économiques des églises en Egypte du IVᵉ au VIIIᵉ siècle (Papy. Brux. 10).* Brussels: Fondation Égyptologique Reine Élisabeth, 1972.

_____. "Remarques sur les Lettres Privées Chrétiennes des IIᵉ-IVᵉ Siècles (A Propos d'un Livre de M. Naldini)," *JJP* 18 (1974) 203–21.

Wire, Antoinette Clark. "The Social Functions of Women's Asceticism in the Roman East," in Karen L. King, ed., *Images of the Feminine in Gnosticism,* 308–23.

_____. *The Corinthian Women Prophets. A Reconstruction through Paul's Rhetoric.* Minneapolis: Fortress, 1990.

_____. "Prophecy and Women. Prophets in Corinth," in James F. Goering et al., eds., *Gospel Origins and Christian Beginnings, in Honor of James M. Robinson.* Forum Fascicles 1. Sonoma: Polebridge, 1990, 134–50.

Wischmeyer, Wolfgang Karl. "M. Iulius Eugenius. Eine Fallstudie zum Thema 'Christen und Gesellschaft im 3. und 4. Jahrhundert,'" *ZNW* 81 (1990) 225–46.

_____. *Von Golgatha zum Ponte Molle. Studien zur Sozialgeschichte der Kirche im dritten Jahrhundert.* FKDG 49. Göttingen: Vandenhoeck & Ruprecht, 1992.

Wisskirchen, Rotraut. *Das Mosaikprogramm von S. Prassede in Rom. Ikonographie und Ikonologie.* JAC.E 17. Münster: Aschendorff Verlagsbuchhandlung, 1990.

_____. *Die Mosaiken der Kirche Santa Prassede in Rom.* With color photographs by Franz Schlechter. Zaberns Bildbände zur Archäologie 5. Mainz: P. von Zabern, 1992.

Witherington, Ben III. *Women in the Earliest Churches.* MSSNTS 59. New York: Cambridge University Press, 1989.

Wolf, Stephan. *Hypatia, die Philosophin von Alexandrien. Ihr Leben, Wirken und Lebensende nach den Quellenschriften dargestellt.* Vienna: Hölder, 1879.

Wolfskeel, Cornelia. "Makrina," in Mary Ellen Waithe, ed., *A History of Women Philosophers.* Dordrecht, Boston, and Lancaster: M. Nijhoff, 1987, 1:139–68.

Wolter, Michael. "Apollos und die ephesinischen Johannesjünger (Act 18,24–19,7)," *ZNW* 78 (1987) 49–75.

Wunder, Heide. "Historische Frauenforschung – Ein neuer Zugang zur Gesellschaftsgeschichte," in Werner Affeldt, ed., *Frauen in Spätantike und Frühmittelalter,* 31–41.

Wyss, Bernhard. "Gregor II (Gregor von Nazianz)," *RAC* 12 (1983) 793–863.

Yarbrough, Anne. "Christianization in the Fourth Century: The Example of Roman Women," *ChH* 45 (1976) 149–65.

Young, Frances M. "Did Epiphanius know what he meant by Heresy?" *StPatr* 17/1 (1982) 199–205.

_____. "John Chrysostom on First and Second Corinthians," *StPatr* 18/1 (1985) 349–52.

Ysebaert, Joseph. "The deaconesses in the Western Church of late Antiquity and their origin," in Gerhardus J.M. Bartelink, A. Hilhorst, and C.H. Kneepkens, eds., *Eulogia: mélanges offerts à Antoon A.R. Bastiaensen à l'occasion de son soixante-cinquième anniversaire.* Instrumenta patristica 24. Steenbrugge: in Abbatia S. Petri; The Hague: Nijhoff, 1991, 421–36.

_____. *Die Amtsterminologie im Neuen Testament und in der Alten Kirche. Eine lexikographische Untersuchung.* Breda: Eureia, 1994.

Zahn, Theodor. *Ignatius von Antiochien.* Gotha: Perthes, 1873.

Zappella, Marco. "A proposita di febe ΠΡΟΣΤΑΤΙΣ (Rom 16,2)," *RivBib* 37 (1989) 167–71.

Zehnle, Richard F. *Peter's Pentecost Discourse. Tradition and Lukan Reinterpretation in Peter's Speeches of Acts 2 and 3.* SBL.MS 15. Nashville: Abingdon, 1971.

Zernov, Militza. "Women's Ministry in the Church," *ECR* 7 (1975) 34–39.

Ziebarth, Erich. "Oikonomos," *PRE* XVII, 2 (1937) 2118–2119.

Zimmermann, Alfred F. *Die urchristlichen Lehrer. Studien zum Tradentenkreis der διδάσκαλοι im frühen Urchristentum.* WUNT II/12. Tübingen: J.C.B. Mohr [Paul Siebeck], 1984.

Zimmermann, Heinrich. "Die Wahl der Sieben (Apg 6,1-6). Ihre Bedeutung für die Wahrung der Einheit in der Kirche," in Wilhelm Corsten, Augustinus Frotz, and Peter Linden, eds., *Die Kirche und ihre Ämter und Stände. FG Joseph Kardinal Frings.* Cologne: J. P. Bachem, 1960, 364–78.

Zollitsch, Robert. *Amt und Funktion des Priesters. Eine Untersuchung zum Ursprung und zur Gestalt des Presbyterats in den ersten zwei Jahrhunderten.* FThSt 96. Freiburg, Basel, and Vienna: Herder, 1974.

Zscharnack, Leopold. *Der Dienst der Frau in den ersten Jahrhunderten der christlichen Kirche.* Göttingen: Vandenhoeck & Ruprecht, 1902.

Zunhammer, Nicole P. "Feministische Hermeneutik," in Christine Schaumberger and Monika Maassen, eds., *Handbuch Feministische Theologie,* 256–84.

Index of Women's Names from Antiquity and the Middle Ages

Index of Epigraphical and Papyrus Sources

II. Papyri, Labels

Index of Ancient Literature

II. Other Sources from Antiquity

Index of Modern Authors

Rossi, Giovanni Baptista de, 43, 94, 140, 182, 197, 201–202
Rossi, Mary Ann, 32, 130, 132–33, 137, 140–41
Rowe, Arthur, 81
Ruether, Rosemary Radford, 33, 107, 109–111, 194
Ruijgh, C. J., 64
Rüsen, Jörn, 23, 196
Russell, Letty M., 26

Sahin, Sencer, 172, 193, 221
Sand, Alexander, 35, 156
Satake, Akira, 83–84
Sato, Migaku, 74
Saxer, Victor, 59
Schaefer, O., 189
Schäfer, Gerhard K., 33, 35
Schäfer, K. Heinrich, 12, 27, 33–34, 196–97
Schäfer, Theodor, 34
Schäfer, Thomas, 190
Scharffenorth, Gerta, 36
Schaumberger, Christine, 21–22, 38
Schelkle, Karl Hermann, 28
Schenk, Wolfgang, 214
Schepelern, Wilhelm E., 74, 78, 86, 135
Schermann, Theodor, 75–76
Schiessl, Johanna, 31
Schille, Gottfried, 58, 85
Schillebeeckx, Edward, 29
Schindler, Alfred, 195
Schlarb, Egbert, 102, 114–115
Schlau, Carl, 60
Schmid, Joseph, 212
Schmid, Rachel, 26
Schmid, Renate, 59–60
Schmidt, Carl, 60, 105–106
Schmidt, Peter, 58
Schmidt, Volkmar, 74, 192
Schmithals, Walter, 57–58
Schmitt Pantel, Pauline, 24, 26, 36
Schnackenburg, Rudolf, 214
Schneemelcher, Wilhelm, 60, 75, 120, 136

Schneider, Gerhard, 82–83
Schnider, F., 80
Scholem, Gershom, 224
Scholer, David M., 30
Schöllgen, Georg, 113
Scholz, Frithard, 33
Schottroff, Luise, 11, 22, 28, 32–35, 39, 58–60, 87, 215
Schottroff, Willy, 33
Schulin, Ernst, 23
Schuller, Wolfgang, 36, 110
Schultze, Victor, 42, 188
Schüngel-Straumann, Helen, 59
Schürer, Emil, 83
Schürmann, Heinz, 113
Schüssler Fiorenza, Elisabeth, 11, 21, 26–28, 33–34, 46, 55, 57, 60, 77, 79, 81–85, 87, 114, 187
Schütz, John H., 187
Schwartz, Eduard, 136, 154
Schweizer, Eduard, 29, 74
Schweppenhäuser, Hermann, 224
Scopello, Madeleine, 25
Scott, Robert, 73, 115
Scroggs, Robin, 81
Seeberg, Reinhold, 78, 87
Seim, Turid Karlsen, 195
Sellin, Gerhard, 59
Sherwin-White, A. N., 173, 193
Short, Charles, 141, 197, 212
Siegele-Wenschkewitz, Leonore, 38
Siegwart, Josef, 202
Silvagni, Angelus, 43, 182, 197
Skinner, M. B., 38
Sleumer, Albert, 212
Snela, Bogdan, 213
Snyder, Jane McIntosh, 37, 106, 109
Soler, Joseph M., 105
Sommer, Elisabeth W., 22, 36
Sophocles, E. A., 73
Specht, Edith, 38
Spencer, F. Scott, 82
Spicq, Ceslas, 102, 115, 219
Staab, Karl, 56

Stählin, Gustav, 155–56
Staudt, Rose, 37
Stegemann, Hartmut, 79, 83
Stegemann, Wolfgang, 33
Steimer, Bruno, 46, 75–77, 105, 151, 153–54, 156–57
Stempel, Hermann, 113
Sterrett, J. R. Sitlington, 218
Stiefel, Jennifer H., 35
Stöcker, Lydia, 28
Straub, Veronika, 25
Strazzula, Vincentius, 44
Strobel, August, 63, 74, 78, 117, 135
Strohm, Theodor, 33, 35
Stuart, Duane Reed, 42
Stuhlmueller, Carroll, 30–31
Stuiber, Alfred, 104, 112
Sugano, Karin, 107–109
Swidler, Arlene, 25, 28, 30–31, 33, 55, 57, 137
Swidler, Leonard, 25, 28, 30–31, 33, 55, 57, 137
Synek, Eva Maria, 54–55, 59–62

Tabbernee, William, 74, 78, 135
Tannenbaum, Robert, 187
Tarchnisvili, M., 61
Testini, Pasquale, 40, 141
Tetlow, Elisabeth M., 28, 36
Theissen, Gerd, 187
Theodorou, Evangelos, 14, 34–35, 188, 194
Thiel, Andreas, 140
Thierry, Nicole, 164
Thomas, John Christopher, 166, 190
Thomsen, Peter, 42, 158, 160, 186–87
Thraede, Klaus, 36
Thurston, Bonnie Bowman, 35, 155–56
Tibiletti, Giuseppe, 45, 89, 103–105
Tiedemann, Rolf, 224
Tielsch, Elfriede W., 37
Todde, Mauro, 106
Tooley, Wilfred, 222
Torjesen, Karen Jo, 23, 46, 139, 213

Trebilco, Paul R., 37, 39
Treggiari, Susan, 16, 36
Treu, Kurt, 40, 45
Trömel-Plötz, Senta, 26

Ullmann, Walter, 140
Ulrich, Anna, 196

Vagaggini, Cipriano, 35
Verilhac, Anne-Marie, 41
Vielhauer, Philipp, 103
Vogels, Heinrich Josef, 56
Vogler, Werner, 214
Vogt, Hermann Josef, 85, 104
Vokes, F. E., 78
Vööbus, Arthur, 76, 157

Waelkens, Marc, 41, 116–117, 134–35
Wagener, Ulrike, 35, 114–115, 155–56, 190, 215
Waithe, Mary Ellen, 37, 106, 112
Walcot, Peter, 155
Walker, William O., 81–82
Walter, Karin, 25, 60, 83, 85
Ward, Benedicta, 105
Waszink, Jan Hendrik, 75
Webster, Douglas, 222
Wedel, Cynthia C., 30
Wegener, Gertrud, 196
Weigel, Sigrid, 24
Weil, Rudolf, 124, 138
Weinel, Heinrich, 75, 79
Weiser, Alfons, 33, 35, 83, 114
Weiss, Hans-Friedrich, 113
Weisshaupt, Brigitte, 37
Welles, Charles B., 43
Wessel, Carolus, 43
Whatley, E. Gordon, 213
Wickert, Ulrich, 188
Wiechert, Friedrich, 35
Wieland, Franz, 136
Wikenhauser, Alfred, 57
Wilcken, Ulrich, 45
Wilckens, Ulrich, 55
Wilhelm, Adolf, 188–89

Wilpert, Joseph, 194
Wilshire, L. E., 77
Wilson, Robert McLean, 60, 75
Wilson-Kastner, Patricia, 25, 99, 109, 112
Wimmer, Franz, 23
Winkelmann, Friedhelm, 40, 44–45,
    178, 195
Wipszycka, Ewa, 45
Wire, Antoinette C., 80–82, 113
Wischmeyer, Wolfgang Karl, 33, 39–40,
    44, 130, 135, 140–41
Wiseman, James, 195
Wissemann, Michael, 107
Wisskirchen, Rotraut, 201–203, 210,
    212
Witherington, Ben, III, 28, 33, 36
Wolf, Stephan, 106
Wolfskeel, Cornelia, 112
Wolter, Michael, 114
Woodhead, A. G., 40, 44

Woodward, A. M., 64
Wörrle, Michael, 37
Wright, F. A., 109
Wunder, Heide, 23
Wuthnow, Heinz, 43
Wyss, Eva Lia, 26

Yarbrough, Anne, 107, 109–111
Ysebaert, Joseph, 34

Zahn, Theodor, 13, 34
Zehnle, Richard F., 82
Zgusta, Ladislav, 42, 73, 135, 192
Ziebarth, Erich, 221
Zimmermann, Alfred F., 113
Zollitsch, Robert, 31
Zscharnack, Leopold, 13, 27, 30, 33–35,
    46, 55, 60, 78, 85, 186, 216
Zunhammer, Nicole, 21
Zwank, Rudolf, 57